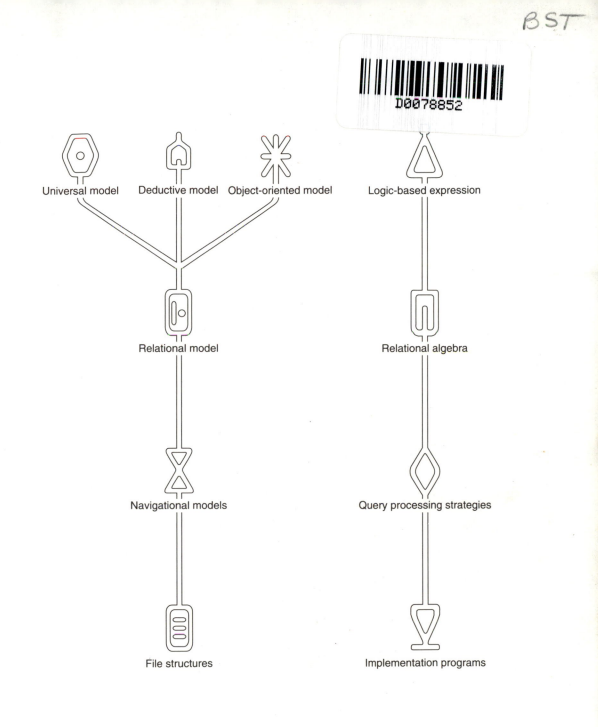

Universal model

Deductive model

Object-oriented model

Relational model

Navigational models

File structures

Data abstraction hierarchy

Logic-based expression

Relational algebra

Query processing strategies

Implementation programs

Algorithmic maps

The Science of Database Management

The Science of Database Management

Paul Helman
University of New Mexico

Burr Ridge, Illinois
Boston, Massachusetts
Sydney, Australia

This symbol indicates that the paper in this book is made of recycled paper. Its fiber content exceeds the recommended minimum of 50% waste paper fibers as specified by the EPA.

Senior sponsoring editor:	Tom Tucker
Editorial assistant:	Damian Comito
Marketing manager:	Robb Linsky
Project editor:	Ethel Shiell
Cover designer:	Paul Uhl
Production manager:	Bob Lange
Art coordinator:	Heather Burbridge
Art studio:	Electronic Publishing Services
Compositor:	Interactive Composition Corporation
Typeface:	10/12 Times Roman
Printer:	R. R. Donnelley & Sons Company

Library of Congress Cataloging-in-Publication Data

Helman, Paul.

The science of database management / Paul Helman.

p. cm.

Includes bibliographical references and index.

ISBN 0-256-13438-3 ISBN 0-256-15881-9 (International ed.)

1. Data base management. I. Title.

QA76.9.D3H474 1994

005.75′6—dc20 93–2681

Printed in the United States of America

1 2 3 4 5 6 7 8 9 0 DOC 0 9 8 7 6 5 4 3

For my Stephanie,
our Zachary,
and his four grandparents.

PREFACE

Database management is a broad subject, encompassing such areas as data structures, file structures, data abstraction, the theory of formal specifications, optimization, operating systems, semantic modeling, and formal logic. This book demonstrates how these diverse areas converge to form database theory and how database theory is put into practice by database management systems.

We approach database management from the perspective of data abstraction, a perspective that gives unity to this broad subject. The **relational data model (RDM)** is introduced as an abstract data type (ADT) that embodies the requirements of a practical database management system, and the solution techniques at the core of database management are developed as we attempt to design and implement the RDM.

INTENDED AUDIENCE

The intended audience for the book is an upper division undergraduate, or first-year graduate, course in a rigorous computer science curriculum. A computer science department might offer such a course under any one of several titles, including

Introduction to Database Management
Introduction to Database Systems
Introduction to Database Theory
File Structures and Database Systems
Information Storage and Retrieval

The book includes material that is central to the theory and practice of database management, most of which can be reasonably covered in a single semester. In addition, material is included which can serve as a foundation for a more advanced course, presenting overviews of research areas such as query optimization, leading-edge data models (e.g., the object-oriented, universal relation, and deductive database models), and advanced topics from relational design theory. A student who masters the book's material will be well prepared for conducting research and development in the database field.

OVERVIEW OF THE ORGANIZATION

One of the main features of the book is that it treats database management from the perspective of data abstraction. Data abstraction serves as a vehicle for unifying many of the classic topics of database management. From the perspective of data abstraction, the material of database management is naturally continuous with that of the prerequisite computer science and mathematics courses.

The two particular ADTs on which the book focuses are the **search table** and the **relational data model.** The search table is perhaps the most intuitive and important of all ADTs. The search table operations—add data to a search table, remove data from a search table, and ask questions about the data in a search table—are the essence of database management. The RDM is an ADT composed of a collection of search tables, and the study of this ADT fleshes out many of the most important techniques and theories of relational databases.

The book is organized into four parts:

Part One: Definition of the Relational Data Model Abstract Data Type

Part Two: Design of the Relational Data Model Abstract Data Type

Part Three: Implementations of the Relational Data Model Abstract Data Type — The Structures

Part Four: Implementations of the Relational Data Model Abstract Data Type — The Algorithms

We now present an overview of each part. Following the overview, we summarize the dependencies of chapters so that the instructor can tailor the book to his or her own course.

PART ONE: DEFINITION OF THE RELATIONAL DATA MODEL ABSTRACT DATA TYPE

Chapters 1, 2, and 3 deal primarily with the definitions of the search table and RDM. Chapter 1 presents an overview of database management problems and asks what types of operations should define an ADT that addresses these problems. As a first approximation of a solution, the chapter informally introduces relational algebra and a simple, SQL-like language.

Chapter 2 more formally defines relational algebra. The perspective is that the relational operators are the operators that define the RDM. In addition, the chapter peeks behind the "wall" separating an ADT's definition from its implementation by considering internal memory implementations for the RDM. This allows us to review several of the key internal memory data structures (and to demonstrate continuity with this familiar material) and also to preview external implementations and the problem of query optimization.

Chapter 3 introduces the less procedural predicate-calculus–based languages. The perspective here is that a higher level ADT is defined on top of relational algebra and that query optimization algorithms are required to map from the higher level of abstraction to the lower.

The chapter contains an extensive review of predicate calculus and a tutorial development of tuple calculus. This is essential material that is often missing from the students' prior training. In addition to the abstract predicate calculus, the chapter studies the American National Standards Institute's (ANSI) SQL, and extensions in power to the basic languages, such as recursion, aggregate operators, and host-language interfaces. Chapter 13 studies these extensions to the relational model in more depth.

PART TWO: DESIGN OF THE RELATIONAL DATA MODEL ABSTRACT DATA TYPE

Chapters 4, 5, and 6 address design issues, focusing on how best to define the logical schema of an RDM. Chapter 4 begins the study by formally defining the entity/relation (E/R) model, which is used informally in the first three chapters. The chapter considers the problem of mapping to an RDM schema an application's informational requirements represented initially within the E/R model. This treatment of the design process not only develops principles for obtaining a sound RDM schema from an E/R diagram but also highlights some of the shortcomings of the RDM, most notably the model's lack of support for a strong notion of object identity. This discovery leads us to consider the object-oriented data model as an enhancement to the RDM.

Building on the design principles developed intuitively in Chapter 4, Chapters 5 and 6 focus on the normalization process. Chapter 5 introduces the theories of data dependency and normalization. In particular, we develop here the formalism of functional dependencies, the basic normal forms, the notion of a lossless join decomposition, and a simple normalization algorithm.

Chapter 6 considers more advanced logical design issues, including functional dependency–preserving decompositions, the problems associated with view updating, multivalued dependencies, and higher normal forms. The chapter also presents the main algorithmic results of elementary normalization theory. These include methods for computing and representing logical closures of sets of functional dependencies, algorithms for testing for lossless and functional dependency–preserving decompositions, and a closer look at the third normal form synthesis algorithm first presented in Chapter 5. For many introductory database courses, the instructor will wish only to summarize, or omit completely, several of this chapter's sections. On the other hand, the chapter contains sufficient material for a course that emphasizes formal aspects of logical design and can also serve as foundational material for a more advanced database theory course that studies the research literature.

PART THREE: IMPLEMENTATIONS OF THE RELATIONAL DATA MODEL ABSTRACT DATA TYPE—THE STRUCTURES

The book's third part turns to the problem of implementing the RDM in external storage. Chapter 7 begins the coverage by presenting a simple model of external storage. The model characterizes aspects of external storage that are most relevant to external implementations of the RDM, including block addressability, the cost of block accesses, the pseudorandom nature of a disk, the organization of blocks into files, and operating system considerations (e.g., how an operating system manages and allocates blocks to a file and the consequences of paging). The model of external storage is illustrated with an external sorting algorithm; we develop a two-way merge sort and then consider the problem of selecting the optimal *k* for a *k*-way merge sort.

Chapter 8 considers the problem of implementing a single search table in external memory. The problem considered in Chapter 2 of implementing a single search table in internal memory led to a review of several fundamental data structures; in Chapter 8, we see how to modify these data structures so that they become appropriate file structures for supporting the search table operations. The chapter presents not only a collection of specific techniques but develops basic principles of file structures. These principles provide a coherent relationship between file structure characteristics and the efficiency with which structures support various types of search table and RDM operations, such as exact-math selections, range selections, sorted traversals, joins, and updates.

We study three of the most important file structures, indexed sequential access mechanisms, B-trees, and hashed structures. We consider several variations of the basic B-tree file structure, including B-trees with ordered and nonordered data files and B-trees with and without sequence sets in the leaves. We demonstrate how the selection of a B-tree variant depends on the anticipated processing (e.g., types of selections, traversals, and joins) as well as on the computing environment's characteristics (e.g., how many B-tree nodes can be held simultaneously in internal memory). While B-trees are the most useful general-purpose file structure, hashed structures are important also, especially as a special-purpose structure. In particular, hashing provides the fastest support of exact-match retrievals and update operations. Dynamic hashing schemes are especially useful because, like B-trees, a dynamic hashing scheme can adapt gracefully to changes in the size of the data file. We present in some detail the elegant extendible hashing scheme of Fagin et al. (1979).

The structures presented in Chapter 8 for storing a search table's data in external memory are the primitives from which we build RDM implementations. Hence, we are ready in Chapter 9 to consider the problem of designing an RDM's physical schema. Physical schema design includes the problems of mapping implementation-level tables to files and of choosing structures for these files. We also consider the question of how attributes should be aggregated into implementation-level tables. In this context, we discuss how logical design—as embodied by the theory of normalization—often conflicts with concerns for efficiency. Since normalization's elimination of redundancy usually is an overriding design consideration, we are led to seek structures that mitigate the degradation in efficiency that is often a consequence of normalizing decompositions. We introduce a heterogeneous file structure that hierarchically nests the tuples of tables that must be joined often as one means of mitigating this penalty. The chapter concludes with a large design problem that invites the reader to go from a specification of an application's informational and processing requirements to logical and physical RDM schemata.

PART FOUR: IMPLEMENTATIONS OF THE RELATIONAL DATA MODEL ABSTRACT DATA TYPE—THE ALGORITHMS

Chapter 10 begins our study of algorithmic issues for RDM implementations by considering the problem of transaction management. The transaction manager is a component of an RDM implementation responsible for ensuring that database transactions execute correctly. One concern of the transaction manager is that the database retain its integrity in the face of concurrently executing programs and program and system failures. A second concern of the transaction manager is that transactions share resources in a manner that ensures every transaction completes in a timely fashion and, in particular, that the phenomena known as deadlock, livelock, and starvation are avoided. The solution techniques we consider include locking, protocols, scheduling policies, timestamping, logging, and recovery. The chapter looks also at two other issues that impact on database integrity: integrity constraint enforcement and database security.

The book's final three chapters consider query optimization. It is not expected that a single semester introductory database course will cover all the query optimization material; rather, the instructor can select a subset of this material for emphasis, leaving the remaining material for a more advanced course and independent research. For example, the instructor, without loss of continuity, can pick and choose from among the many join algorithms presented in Chapter 11. Further, most of Chapter 13's material on leading-edge data models can be covered after only a brief introductory summary of the query optimization material contained in the preceding two chapters.

Chapter 11 studies the primitives of the query optimization problem: implementation-level algorithms for the relational operators. We consider algorithms for both the select and join operators, with the focus on the latter. We present an extensive and methodical study of a good number of join algorithms, including simple loop joins, merge join variants, and algorithms that build and utilize specialized structures. This coverage is a precursor to our coverage in Chapter 12 of the query optimization search problem since the reader will come to appreciate the many factors that must be considered when choosing an algorithm for processing a particular join. The query optimization problem is previewed again when we consider the selection of a join tree for an expression containing multiple joins. We make final preparations for studying the query optimization problem by considering the problem of cost evaluation.

Chapter 12 considers the process of query optimization, a topic to which entire books and research careers are devoted. We adopt a transformation-based perspective, a perspective that (a) allows us to present general principles of query optimization rather than a collection of seemingly disjoint algorithms; (b) is highly compatible with our data abstraction theme, as it views the optimizer as mapping a high-level query through a sequence of abstraction levels until a processing algorithm is obtained; and (c) has found favor as a solution to the problem of query optimization for extensible data models, such as those considered in Chapter 13. In the context of this transformation-based view of query optimization, we present several specific query optimization techniques, including algebraic transformation rules and dynamic programming search algorithms.

The book concludes with a chapter on "leading-edge" data models: the universal relation model, the deductive database model, the object-oriented database model, and the distributed database model. These data models are at the center of a great deal of active research, and the chapter serves as a survey for advanced study. We view these models as an abstraction level above the relational model and indicate how implementations for these models can be built over the relational model. We also consider new problems that are consequences of the new models, for example, recursive query processing in the deductive database model and extensible query optimization in the object-oriented model. Rather than focusing on specific versions of the leading-edge models, we emphasize the new concepts that these models support and the problems that these concepts address. For example, when we revisit the object-oriented model (introduced initially in Chapter 4), we focus on how the architecture of a relational query optimizer must be modified to support the extensibility inherent in this data model.

The following figure summarizes the dependencies of the chapters. We would expect a first database course, either at the upper division undergraduate, or graduate, level, to begin with Chapters 1, 2, and 3. Following this foundational material, the instructor can choose how much logical design and data modeling (Chapters 4, 5, and 6 and parts of 13) and how much implementation (Chapters 7 through 12 and parts of 13) to cover. A second database course, presumably at the graduate level, could use various combinations of Chapters 6 and 10 through 13 as a springboard to the literature.

Each chapter concludes with a summary and annotated bibliography and a full set of exercises. The exercises range from simple problems to research projects; the more challenging exercises are marked with asterisks.

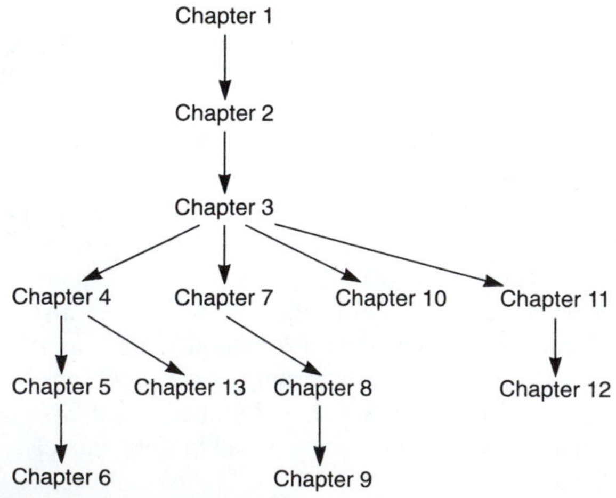

ACKNOWLEDGMENTS

The book reflects a perspective that was formed over the past decade while teaching and conducting research in database management. It therefore goes without saying that the work of a large number of researchers has influenced my perspective and, hence, the book's contents. In addition to the specific literature citations that appear in the text, I am delighted to acknowledge in particular two friends and colleagues who have had a great effect on the thinking reflected in this book—Robert Veroff of the University of New Mexico and Arnon Rosenthal of MITRE Corporation.

Bob Veroff and I wrote **Walls and Mirrors,** a sophomore level computer science text. It was in the course of this writing that I developed an appreciation for the importance of data abstraction. Bob and I also collaborated on research in deductive database design theory, and Chapter 6's perspective of update maps and Chapter 13's introduction to deductive databases are influenced greatly by our joint work.

Arnie Rosenthal has conducted extensive research in physical database design, query optimization, and the theory of combinatorial optimization. I have been fortunate to have collaborated with Arnie on several research papers, beginning with my thesis work at the University of Michigan in the late 1970s. Much of the material in Chapter 12 and much of Chapter 13's material on extensible query optimization and generalized transitive closures have roots in Arnie's research.

I wish to extend my warmest thanks also to my editor, Tom Casson. I began writing this book in the mid-1980s, a time of upheaval in the publishing world. The numerous mergers and buyouts of my publishers resulted in a somewhat rocky road for me and this book. Tom, however, was a much appreciated constant through much of this turmoil. His faith in me and support for this project had much to do with its success, from initiation to completion.

Paul Helman

CONTENTS IN BRIEF

CONTENTS

*Section may be omitted without loss of continuity.

The Science of Database Management

PART ONE

Definition of the Relational Data Model Abstract Data Type

CHAPTER *1*

Introduction

Database management systems are the software realizations of a vast amount of foundational research. This research comes from areas as diverse as data structures, file structures, data abstraction, the theory of formal specifications, optimization, operating systems, semantic modeling, and formal logic. The primary goals of this book are to demonstrate how these diverse areas converge to form database theory, and to demonstrate how database theory is put into practice by database management systems.

What are the functions that a database system must perform that necessitate such an immense theoretical foundation? Broadly stated, a database system has the task of managing data. More specifically, a database system must support **queries** and **updates** against a collection of interrelated information. On the surface, this may seem like a fairly straightforward task, requiring little more than the application of some fundamental data structuring techniques. What makes the task far more difficult than it at first may appear are the contexts and the environments in which information must be maintained. The users of a database system typically desire a very powerful and flexible interface to the information. The amount of information that must be maintained is typically so massive that it must be stored in external memory devices rather than in the internal memory of a computer. Several users may access the same information, often simultaneously, leading to concerns that the information remain valid and be protected from unauthorized access. It may even be that a single collection of information is stored across several different computer systems and that these computer systems reside in geographically distant sites. In the face of all these requirements, extremely severe constraints are often imposed on response times for user requests and on the amount of storage that the information may occupy. In view of such application environments, one can begin to appreciate why the database management problem is so enormously difficult.•

In this chapter, we introduce several of the issues central to database management. In Section 1.1, we consider the many ways that users can interact with a database. In Sections 1.2 and 1.3, we review the principles of data abstraction and demonstrate how these principles apply to the database management problem. These sections also introduce two abstract data types—the search table and the relational data model—that are central to much of the material in this book. Section 1.4 considers alternative data models, namely, the network, hierarchical, and universal models. The chapter concludes by surveying several important characteristics of potential application environments, such as the quantity of data that must be maintained, the types of processing tasks that are anticipated, and whether concurrent access by many users to the database must be supported. Characteristics such as these determine the solution techniques that are required for a successful implementation.

1.1 INTERACTING WITH A DATABASE

We begin with the basics. Suppose that we must support the following three types of operations against a given collection of information:

- Insert: Insert into the collection a new piece of information.
- Retrieve: Retrieve from the collection all information that matches a user-supplied description.
- Delete: Delete from the collection all information that matches a user-supplied description.

We intentionally have been vague with regard to the form of these operations precisely because the first issue we wish to consider is the diversity of forms that these operations can take. We choose to also ignore for the moment, how—and even where (e.g., in internal memory or on disk, at a single physical site or at several physical sites)—this information is stored. This decision is mandated by the fact that the material presented in this and the following sections is independent of such issues.

Perhaps the most familiar incarnation of the three abstract operations Insert, Retrieve, and Delete is in the form of **record-processing** operations. For example, let us suppose that we maintain a database for a large department store. Consider the EMPLOYEE record type illustrated in Figure 1.1. This record

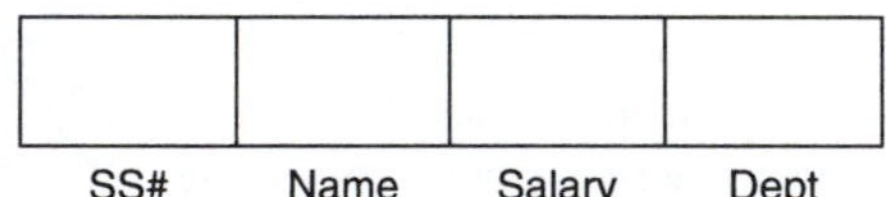

Figure 1.1 EMPLOYEE record type

type contains four fields: SS#, Name, Salary, and Dept. Suppose our application requires that we maintain a collection of **instances** of this record type, one for each employee who works in our department store. The required operations are defined as follows:

- Insert(EMPLOYEE, R): Insert into the collection of EMPLOYEE records the record R, which specifies a value for each of the four fields.
- Retrieve(EMPLOYEE, R, X, Fail): Retrieve into R the record from the collection of EMPLOYEE records with SS#$=X$. It is assumed that at most one record in the collection has SS#$=X$. If there is no such record, Fail is returned TRUE; otherwise, Fail is returned FALSE. Since the Retrieve operation is based on a social security number, the SS# field of the EMPLOYEE record type is called the **search key** for the record type.

- Retrieve_Arbitrary(EMPLOYEE, *R*, Fail): Retrieve into *R* some arbitrary record from the collection of EMPLOYEE records. Note that the operation does not specify which record in the collection is returned. If there are no records in the collection, Fail is returned TRUE; otherwise, Fail is returned FALSE.
- Retrieve_Another(EMPLOYEE, *R*, Fail): Retrieve into *R* a record from the collection of EMPLOYEE records. It is assumed that a successful call to either Retrieve or Retrieve_Arbitrary precedes the first call to Retrieve_Another. Retrieve_Another does not specify which record in the collection is returned, but a sequence of calls beginning with Retrieve (or Retrieve_Arbitrary) followed by *N* calls to Retrieve_Another (*N* is the number of records in the collection) will return each record in the collection exactly once and will return Fail=TRUE on the *N*th call. Subsequent calls to Retrieve_Another will also fail, until a call is made to Retrieve or Retrieve_Arbitrary, at which time the process begins anew. Examples later in this chapter will illustrate how the three Retrieve operations can be utilized to perform a large number of information processing tasks.
- Delete(EMPLOYEE, *X*): Delete from the collection the record with SS#=*X*.

It is typical for operations such as those just described to be embedded in a program written in a host programming language such as C, FORTRAN, COBOL, or Pascal. (For purposes of illustration, we shall use Pascal-like pseudocode.) For example, the request "Print the salary of the person with SS#=*X*" can be answered with the following program:

```
Retrieve(EMPLOYEE, R, X, Fail)
if (not Fail)
  PRINT(R.Salary)
else
  PRINT(There is no record with SS#=X)
endif
```

Similarly, the request "Print the salaries of the people in the toys department" can be answered with this program:

```
Retrieve_Arbitrary(EMPLOYEE, R, Fail)
while (not Fail)
  if (R.Dept = "Toys")
    PRINT(R.Salary)
  endif
  Retrieve_Another(EMPLOYEE, R, Fail)
end while
```

Many primitive database management systems provide interfaces based on record processing operations such as the ones we have defined. One of the problems with such interfaces is that, as our examples illustrate, they force the users to write programs to satisfy even the simplest requests for information. Although the preceding programs are not very complex (as programs go), we must keep in mind that many of the potential interrogators of a database will not know how to program at all! Further, the typical database application requires us to maintain far more complex collections of information than a simple collection of records, and the users of such a database typically must satisfy far more complex requests for information than those illustrated in our examples. Satisfying these requests by means of an interface based on record-processing operations would require rather complex programs. For such applications, interfaces based on record-processing operations are not acceptable.

Modern applications require interfaces to information that are far more powerful and user friendly than a collection of record-processing operations that must be embedded in host language programs. In contrast to such interfaces, a modern database system would allow its users to satisfy the request "Print the salaries of the people in the toys department" with an expression looking something like

```
SELECT EMPLOYEE.Salary
  WHERE EMPLOYEE.Dept = "Toys"
```

This **SELECT query** retrieves the Salary field of the EMPLOYEE records whose Dept field contains the value Toys. More precisely, the *WHERE condition* EMPLOYEE.Dept = "Toys" specifies a logical condition that each EMPLOYEE record whose salary is returned must satisfy, namely that the EMPLOYEE record must have the value Toys in its Dept field. We shall see additional examples of queries described by logical conditions in the discussion that follows and, in Chapter 3, shall formalize the concept. Interfaces that support queries based on logical conditions are extremely attractive since they allow their users to specify, without constructing programs, a great majority of the most common requests for information.

Further motivations for SELECT-like interfaces are found when one considers collections of information more complex than the simple collection of EMPLOYEE records. Suppose, for example, that in addition to maintaining EMPLOYEE records, we maintain DEPARTMENT records such as illustrated in Figure 1.2. A DEPARTMENT record type contains fields Dept, Manager, Location, and D_Desc.

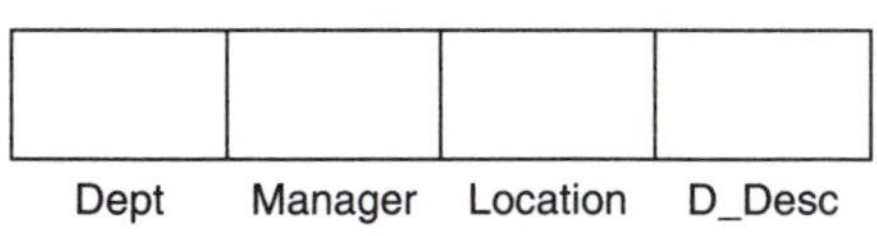

Figure 1.2 DEPARTMENT record type

We can easily conceive of requests for information against this collection of records analogous to the requests considered against the EMPLOYEE records. Of greater significance, however, is that the simultaneous presence of the two collections of records makes possible an entirely new class of requests: requests based on *relationships* between the two collections of records. Note, for example, that a department name appears in both record types, making meaningful requests for information such as the following:

- Retrieve the location at which the employee with SS#=*X* works.
- Retrieve the salary of the manager of the toys department.
- Retrieve the names of all employees who work in a department located on floor 10C.

If a database system were capable of retrieving data only by means of the Retrieve, Retrieve_Arbitrary, and Retrieve_Another operations against isolated collections of records (and thus did not support a relationship between records in the two collections), requests such as these would be nontrivial to satisfy. For example, assuming that the Dept field is the search key of the DEPARTMENT record type, the last of these requests would require a program such as

```
Retrieve_Arbitrary(EMPLOYEE, R, Fail)
while (not Fail)
  Retrieve(DEPARTMENT, S, R.Dept, Fail)
  if ( (not Fail) and (S.Location = "10C") )
    PRINT(R.Name)
  endif
  Retrieve_Another(EMPLOYEE, R, Fail)
end while
```

High-level SELECT queries, on the other hand, easily satisfy such requests for information. For example, the query

```
SELECT EMPLOYEE.Name
  WHERE (EMPLOYEE.Dept = DEPARTMENT.Dept)
    AND (DEPARTMENT.Location = "10C")
```

retrieves the Name field of each EMPLOYEE record whose Dept field matches the Dept field of at least one DEPARTMENT record whose Location field has value 10C. From the user's perspective, the database system neatly supports the necessary relationship between EMPLOYEE records and DEPARTMENT records.

The complexity of the previous request stems from the fact that it requires information about distinct, though *related,* real-world **entities,** that is, the EMPLOYEE entity (which represents information maintained about the department store's employees) and the DEPARTMENT entity (which represents information maintained about the department store's departments). Given that the presence of two entities leads to complex types of queries, imagine an application in which we must maintain information about a large number of entities. The **entity/relation diagram** (**E/R diagram**) is a convenient means of depicting such situations (see Figure 1.3). The boxes represent **entities** (real-world objects that typically are realized in a database by a record type), the tags represent **attributes** (i.e., the information we store about the entity—typically realized by record fields), and the arcs represent **relationships** be-

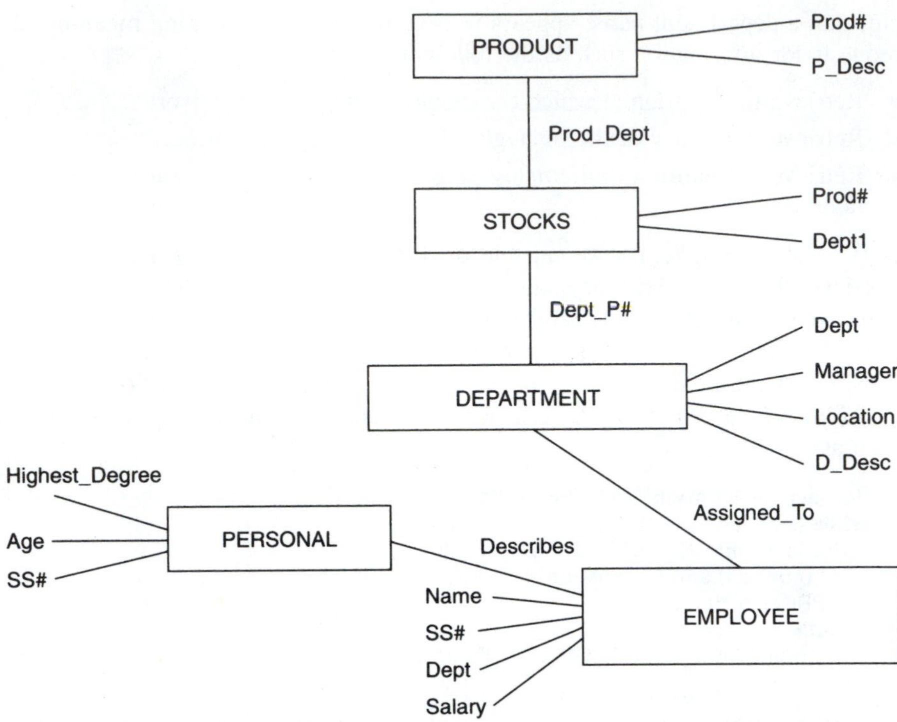

Figure 1.3 E/R diagram for department store database

tween entities. E/R diagrams will be defined more fully in Chapter 4 and used throughout the book.

The E/R diagram is an example of a **data model.** A data model is defined by a collection of primitives that are used to represent a collection of information and the operations on the information that are to be supported. For example, the primitives of the E/R diagram data model include entities, attributes, and arcs. The arcs between entities indicate that the operation "follow a relationship between the entities" is to be supported. A **schema** based on a particular data model is an *instance* of the data model that specifies specific occurrences of the data model's primitives that correspond to the information of a specific application. For example, a schema based on the E/R data model is a collection of specific entity types and arcs such as those shown in Figure 1.3.

E/R diagrams often are employed as a tool for designing database implementations. Typically, the user community employs an E/R diagram to describe to a database designer the informational requirements of an application, and the database designer then must determine the best way to implement the information described in the E/R diagram. For example, the most basic issue is how to implement an E/R diagram's entities. The most straightforward method is to implement each entity as a record type with fields corresponding to the entity's attributes. Typically, the instances of each record type are stored in a single file that is structured using the techniques to be considered later in the book. Chapters 4 and 9 contain detailed discussions of how E/R diagrams are mapped into database implementations.

An implementation issue of immediate concern for us is how to support relationships between entities. This issue has two important aspects: What file structure and algorithmic techniques are employed to support the relationships, and how does an interface provide the user with the ability to interrogate the database based on these relationships? For the time being, we concentrate on the interface aspect of the problem. Consider, for example, the request "Find the highest degree obtained by each employee who works in a department located on floor 10C." An interface based on Retrieve commands would require a complex program such as the following:

```
Retrieve_Arbitrary(EMPLOYEE, R1, Fail1)
while (not Fail1)
  Retrieve(DEPARTMENT, R2, R1.Dept, Fail2)
  if ( (not Fail2) and (R2.Location = "10C") )
    Retrieve(PERSONAL, R3, R1.SS#, Fail3)
    if (not Fail3)
      PRINT(R3.Highest_Degree)
    endif
  endif
  { Get another EMPLOYEE record }
  Retrieve_Another(EMPLOYEE, R1, Fail1)
end while
```

(As an exercise, consider alternative methods for performing this query. For example, start at the DEPARTMENT record. What search keys are necessary for this method to be maximally efficient? With these search keys present, is the method more efficient than the one just presented? What knowledge must the user have to make this judgment?)

In contrast, a relatively simple SELECT query satisfies the request as

```
SELECT PERSONAL.Highest_Degree
  WHERE (PERSONAL.SS# = EMPLOYEE.SS#)
     AND (EMPLOYEE.Dept = DEPARTMENT.Dept)
     AND (DEPARTMENT.Location = "10C")
```

This example draws a sharp contrast between the quality of the two interfaces. It is apparent that a SELECT-based interface makes information accessible to a far larger class of users than does the Retrieve-based interface. If one attempted to identify why the SELECT interface is so convenient, the theme that the interface is *high level* would doubtlessly emerge. There are several senses in which the SELECT interface is higher level than the Retrieve interface, including the following:

1. SELECT interfaces can answer most queries with a *single, self-contained* expression, while Retrieve-based commands must be embedded in the control structures of a host programming language. An interface that does not require

its users to program is, for obvious reasons, very desirable. Interfaces that support self-contained queries often are referred to as **query languages,** highlighting the fact that interaction with an "external" host programming language is not necessary for most tasks.

2. Not only is a SELECT query self-contained, it is *nonprocedural*. That is, a SELECT query states a logical condition, and all data satisfying that condition are retrieved. Contrast this with the Retrieve-based interface where every detail of a retrieval algorithm must be specified by the user. Not only does a nonprocedural query language simplify the user's task, it also gives the database system the opportunity to determine the most efficient strategy for processing a query, for example, allowing the database system to determine in what sequence records should be retrieved and inspected. This is a significant benefit since modern database systems often construct better processing strategies than could even the moderately sophisticated user.

A high-level, nonprocedural query language is thus crucial to the success of a database system. This fact leads us to one of the central problems addressed in this book: *Given that a computer is a bit-manipulating, procedural machine, how do we provide high-level, nonprocedural interfaces to the data stored in its memory?* The theory of **data abstraction** provides us with a solid foundation on which to build solutions to this problem. In the following sections, we review the principles of data abstraction, demonstrate how data abstraction applies to the problem of database management, and define two abstract data types that are at the core of our approach.

1.2 DATA ABSTRACTION AND THE PROBLEM OF DATABASE MANAGEMENT

The term *data abstraction* refers to the practice of defining a collection of information in terms of its functionality, without regard to its implementation. This task typically is accomplished by rigorously defining a set of operators that allows one to interface with a collection of information. Such a set of operators specifies an **abstract data type** or **ADT.** A simple example of an ADT is a **stack.** A stack can be specified by the following five operators:

- Create(S): Initialize S to be an empty stack.
- Push(S, X): Add to stack S data item X.
- Pop(S): Remove from stack S the data item that was added most recently.
- Top(S): Return the data item (without altering S) that was added most recently.
- Empty(S): Indicate whether the stack is empty.

A stack can be conceptualized by a diagram such as shown in Figure 1.4. The diagram depicts a stack as a linear structure with a distinguished end, called the top, and indicates that only the item at the top is immediately acces-

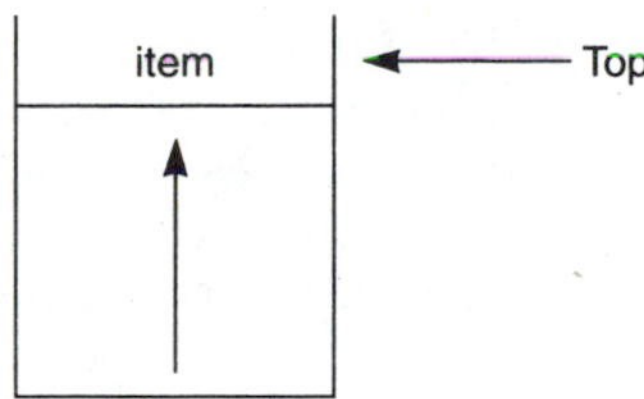

Figure 1.4 Stack

sible. Further, items can be added to and removed from only the top. Observe that these characteristics of a stack are consequences of the definitions of the ADTs operators; the diagram is merely a *representation* of the ADT—it helps us to visualize what operations are permissible and the effects of these operations. In this sense, the figure is a data model for the ADT stack—a conceptualization of what operations can be performed on the data "stored in" a stack. We emphasize that in no sense is the figure to be construed as depicting how the stack's data actually is stored in the computer's memory.

The use of ADTs in the construction of large programs is an accepted software engineering practice. ADTs serve to restrict the interaction between the portions of a program responsible for *managing* the data (e.g., the data structures and their associated routines) and the portions of the program that *utilize* the data. For example, the following program segment uses the stack operators to print in reverse order a string read from input:

```
Create(S)
while (not end of input)
  read(ch)
  Push(S,ch)
end while
while (not Empty(S)) do
  ch ← Top(S)
  PRINT(ch)
  Pop(S)
end while
```

Observe that while this program segment utilizes the stack operators, it in no way depends on how those operators are implemented. As a result, a change in the stack's implementation would not necessitate a change in the portions of the program that utilize the stack operators. Another way to say this is that data abstraction fosters **data independence,** a decoupling of the definition of an ADT's operators from the implementation of the ADT. Consequently, from the user's perspective, there is a decoupling of the ADT's data model from the implementation of the ADT.

We have on several occasions used the term *implementation*. Although the reader probably has some idea of what is meant by this term in general, it is important to gain a precise understanding of the concept of implementation as it applies to ADTs in particular. It is common to view one ADT, such as a stack, as being implemented in terms of a second, more primitive ADT, such as an array. The implementing ADT is more primitive than the original ADT in that it is closer to a realization in available algorithms and data structures. To be a valid implementation, the second ADT must provide the functionality specified by the original ADT. That is, for each operator *op* of the first ADT, the second ADT must have an operator, or sequence of operators, that is guaranteed to have the same behavior as *op*.

For example, an array is commonly used to implement a stack. This implementation is depicted in Figure 1.5.[1] Although we do not usually think of an

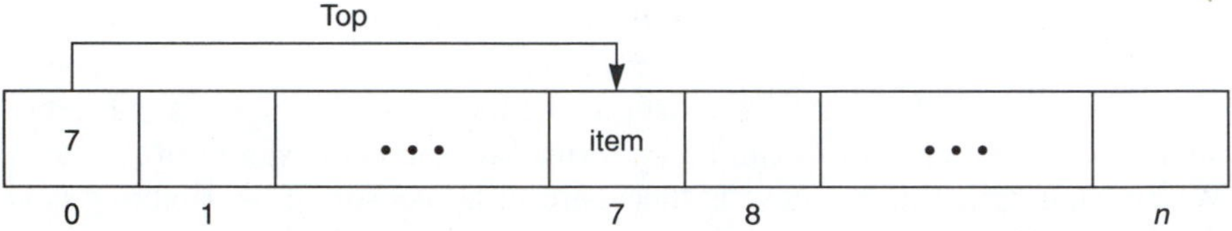

Figure 1.5 Stack implemented as array; $A[0]$ points to top

array as an ADT, it in fact can be viewed as a primitive ADT that is supported directly by almost all high-level programming languages. The operators of the ADT array include:

- Create(A, n) (realized as a declaration): Create a new array $A[0..n]$.
- Store(A, i, v) (written $A[i] \leftarrow v$): Associate with "position i" of array A the value v. Any value previously associated is lost.
- Retrieve(A, i) (written $A[i]$): Return the value that has been associated with "position i" of array A.

The stack operators can be implemented as follows in terms of the array operators:

```
Create(S)
  { Assume array S[0..n] has been created }
  S[0] ← 0
end Create

Push(S, X)
  if (S[0] = n)
    PRINT('STACK FULL')
  else
    S[0] ← S[0] + 1
    S[S[0] ] ← X
  endif
end Push
```

[1] Better style would be a record containing a TOP field and the body of array A. However, we do not wish to blur the main point with an extra level of abstraction.

```
Empty(S)
  { Returns a Boolean value }
  return(S[0] = 0 )
end Empty
Top(S)
  { Returns a stack item }
  if (Empty(S) )
    PRINT('STACK Empty')
  else
    return(S[ S[0] ])
  endif
end Top
Pop(S)
  if (Empty(S) )
    PRINT('STACK Empty')
  else
    S[0] ← S[0] − 1
  endif
end Pop
```

Figure 1.6 depicts the implementation as *mappings between ADTs at different levels of abstraction*. The mappings are algorithms, such as the preceding five algorithms, that realize the higher level ADT's operators as sequences of operators of the lower level ADT. It is important to observe that the correctness of the high-level ADT's implementation does not depend on how the lower level ADT happens to be implemented. For example, regardless of how a particular compiler or assembler happens to implement an array, as long as the array implementation is correct, so too will be the stack implementation. If the array implementation should change (but remain correct), the stack implementation will remain correct also. This is another instance of the data independence fostered by data abstraction.

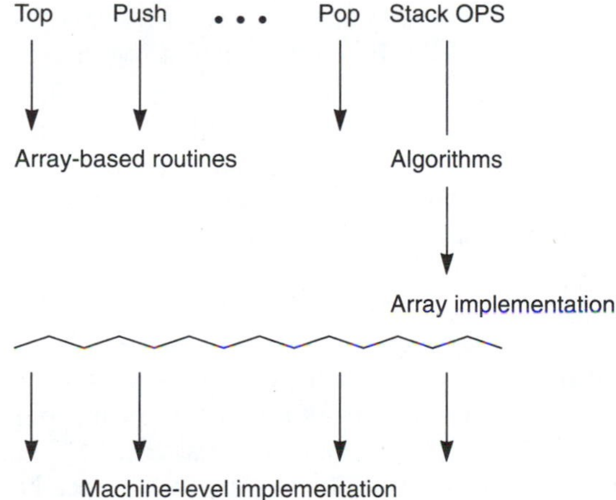

Figure 1.6 Mapping from stack ADT to array ADT

In general, the implementation of an ADT may involve several levels of abstraction with each level of abstraction utilizing more primitive ADTs than the previous level. Just how many levels of abstraction are present in an implementation depends on the original ADT, what primitives are supported directly in our environment (e.g., our programming language and operating system primitives and our library of available algorithms and data and file structures), and how big a jump we choose to make between levels of abstraction. Eventually, however, we reach an implementation based entirely on primitives (e.g., records, arrays, linked lists, search trees, hashed files) that are supported directly in our environment.

For example, consider the proposed stack implementation depicted in Figure 1.6. The implementation typically would be considered completely specified since virtually every programming language supports directly the ADT array. However, it will be instructive to consider for a moment an assembly language–level environment. In this environment, an array is itself an ADT that must be implemented by the programmer in terms of more primitive operators. The Create(A,n) operator is realized by associating with A $n+1$ contiguous bytes of memory. (This assumes, of course, that each array element requires one byte of storage.) The Store and Retrieve operators are implemented by mapping array position i into a memory location and operating on the byte in question. From this perspective, our stack implementation has three levels of abstraction: the ADT stack, the ADT array, and machine-level operations.

In most contexts, software engineers don't consider ADT implementations at levels of abstraction as low as the assembly language level because compilers and assemblers perform the mappings to these levels and below for them. However, if the focus of study were compilers, we certainly would consider such mappings. The focus of study in this book, of course, is the problem of database management and database management systems (DBMSs). A DBMS plays a role that parallels that of a compiler, mapping queries stated in terms of a high-level interface ADT into sequences of operators at the file-processing level (e.g., operators that resemble our Retrieve operators). Therefore, to rigorously study the problem of database management, we must rigorously study the mappings performed by the DBMS.

Let us then begin to focus on our primary interest in data abstraction—its value as a tool for addressing the database management problem. At the close of the previous section, we posed the question of how to provide a high-level, nonprocedural interface to data stored in a low-level, procedural computer. The data abstraction approach, with its mappings between levels of abstraction, provides the foundation for a solution.

A database interface will be specified as an ADT, that is, as a collection of rigorously defined operators with which users construct their queries. The interface will be implemented by means of a sequence of mappings between levels of abstraction. For example, a nonprocedural SELECT-based query language will be implemented in terms of a slightly more procedural ADT, which in turn is implemented in terms of a highly procedural Retrieve-based ADT, which (after several more intermediate levels of implementation) is implemented in terms of any one of several possible file and data structure schemes.

The data independence inherent in the data abstraction approach insulates the users of a database from the lower levels of abstraction. To interact with the database, a user need be aware only of the "interface ADT" that the typical user conceptualizes in terms of some convenient data model. In database terminology, an instance of the user's data model specific to a given application is called the **logical schema.** For example, if the user's data model is an E/R diagram, a logical schema might be the instance of the E/R diagram shown in Figure 1.3. A description of the implementation at the lowest levels of abstraction (e.g., the level of file structures and algorithms that operate on file structures) is referred to as the **physical schema.** A major component of a DBMS is a collection of algorithms that perform mappings between the logical and physical schemas. For example, nonprocedural SELECT-like queries composed against the logical schema are mapped by the DBMS through several levels of abstraction until a processing algorithm is obtained. This processing algorithm is built from low-level, procedural operations stated with respect to the physical schema. The data abstraction approach not only gives the users a high-level interface but also insulates the users' queries from changes in the implementation. Changes in implementation are "absorbed" by the DBMS's mappings and thus are invisible to the database's users and have no effect on the correctness of their queries.

1.3 TWO ADTS FOR DATABASE MANAGEMENT

Now that we have motivated the data abstraction approach in principle, we must investigate what specific ADTs are most appropriate for the database management problem.

Recall the two desirable characteristics of a database interface discussed at the end of Section 1.1: The interface should provide a query language that can answer most queries with a single, self-contained expression, and this expression should be nonprocedural. A SELECT-based query language scores well on both of these criteria. However, for the time being, we shall concentrate on another type of query language that, although theoretically equivalent to a form of the SELECT-based query language, requires expressions that appear somewhat more procedural than SELECT expressions. This query language is based on an ADT we call the **relational data model (RDM).** The RDM provides a collection of high-level operators, called **relational operators,** from which users construct their queries. The relational operators are sufficiently high level that any single, self-contained SELECT expression can be stated as a single, self-contained expression over the relational operators. (We shall refer to an expression over the relational operators as a **relational expression.**)

To illustrate the RDM, we introduce at an intuitive level two relational operators, σ (Select) and Π (Project). For now we can think of these operators as applying to an entity type of an E/R diagram and as having the following meanings:

Select: The expression $\sigma_{cond}(ENT)$ "returns" as its value the subset of instances of entity *ENT* which satisfy the condition described by *cond*.

Project: The expression $\Pi_{<Att\_list>}(ENT)$ "returns" as its value all instances of entity *ENT*, but for each instance includes only those attributes appearing in *Att_list*.

These operators soon will be defined in a more formal setting. For now, however, we consider the relational expression

$$\Pi_{<SS\#>}(\sigma_{Sal>20000}\ EMPLOYEE)$$

as an example of a query constructed from these operators.

This relational expression has the following meaning: "Retrieve the SS# of those employees who earn more than $20,000." Notice that while this is a self-contained expression (it does not require the control structures of a programming language), it appears to be somewhat more procedural than a SELECT query since a sequence of actions seems to be implied by the query's construction. For example, the expression $\Pi_{<SS\#>}(\sigma_{Sal>20000}\,EMPLOYEE)$ seems to imply the following sequence of actions:

Action 1: Apply the Select operator to the EMPLOYEE entity, selecting those employees with a salary greater than $20,000.

Action 2: Apply the Project operator to the result of the application of Select, projecting (keeping) only the SS# attribute.

It is reasonable to ask why, if an RDM interface is more procedural than a SELECT-like interface, we are going to spend most of our time studying the RDM ADT. There are several motivations:

1. Nonprocedural queries can be mapped relatively easily to relational expressions. Thus, even when a system does supply the user with a nonprocedural query language, most of the interesting implementation issues arise *after* a nonprocedural query is mapped to a relational expression. For this reason, we shall generally describe query-processing algorithms as operating on relational expressions (which perhaps result from the translation of SELECT-like queries).

2. While it is true that the RDM requires the user to compose operators in a procedural manner, most query-processing algorithms are rather insensitive to the particulars of the composition. That is, at least in principle, a query-processing algorithm will take a relational expression and determine the best processing strategy for evaluating that expression. In this sense, the query-processing algorithm actually does treat the relational expression as nothing more than a logical condition that specifies what data is required. Since the query processor is free to find the best processing strategy for retrieving this

data, one major fault of a procedural interface—that it places on the user the burden of specifying a good processing strategy—is not really a fault in the context of the RDM. We shall consider the **query optimization** problem—the problem of construction of a good processing strategy for a user query—at many junctures throughout the book.

3. We are interested in the data and file structures used to store data, and relational operators are an appropriate level of abstraction at which to analyze file structures. That is, we often shall analyze a data or file structure by asking how well it supports the relational operators.

It therefore is appropriate for us to concentrate our attention on the RDM ADT and its relational operators.

The preceding observations are reflected in the architecture of many modern DBMSs. The interface supplied to the user is typically SELECT-like. This highest level ADT is implemented in terms of the RDM ADT and its relational operators. The RDM is then implemented in terms of query-processing and file-structure algorithms. A user's query thus might pass though the following sequence of processing steps:

SELECT-like query → relational expression → processing algorithm

At each step, the DBMS maps a query stated in terms of one ADT into a query that is stated in terms of the ADT at the next lower level of abstraction.

The Search Table and the RDM

The previous section informally introduced, in the setting of E/R diagrams, the operators σ and Π. We now begin to formalize the definitions of these operators and to introduce a third relational operator, the **Join** operator. Before we do this, however, we introduce the data model that typically is used to conceptualize the RDM.

The RDM interface is typically conceptualized by a data model consisting of a collection of **tables.** A table is really not very different from an entity in our E/R diagram. The columns of a table correspond to the attributes of an entity, and, in fact, the identifiers that label the columns of a table are called attributes (see Figure 1.7). Instances of the entity correspond to rows in the table, and these rows usually are referred to as **tuples.**

A significant difference between a collection of tables and an E/R diagram is that the explicit representation in an E/R diagram of interentity relationships has no direct analogue in the collection of tables. This does not indicate a shortcoming in the RDM but, much to the contrary, reflects the *flexibility* of the RDM. An important premise of the RDM is that many relationships between tables are possible and that users should have the ability to define relationships dynamically, as their need arises. For example, we see in the E/R diagram of Figure 1.3 that there is a relationship Assigned_To between entities EMPLOYEE and DEPARTMENT. This relationship facilitates a request such as

EMPLOYEE

SS#	Name	Salary	Department	
0001	Jones	25000	Toys	
9999	Smith	30000	Books	← tuple
⋮	⋮	⋮	⋮	

DEPARTMENT

Dept	Manager	Location	D_Desc
Toys	0111	10C	← tuple
⋮	⋮	⋮	

Figure 1.7 Example of a collection of table instances

"Retrieve the SS# of the manager of the employee with SS#=999999999" since the data model would support an operation that, given an employee, allows the direct retrieval of the department to which that employee is assigned. But suppose a user needs to satisfy the request "Retrieve the age of the manager of the toys department." This request is based on a perceived relationship Describes_Manager between entities PERSONAL and DEPARTMENT. Since this relationship is not supported by the E/R diagram, the request is more difficult to satisfy. (See Exercise 1.2.) One of the great virtues of the RDM is that it includes operators (e.g., the Join operator that will be defined shortly) that give the user the ability to construct queries based on relationships that may not have been identified in advance.[2]

In light of this flexibility of the RDM, its conceptualization should include either all potentially meaningful arcs between entities or no arcs at all, implicitly indicating that all such arcs are supported. The latter convention is typically adopted. Of course, a single user who is concerned with only a specific subset of the possible relationships might well conceptualize the RDM in terms of an E/R diagram with the relevant relationships explicitly represented. Such **user schemas** are derived from the global data model that is typically an arcless collection of tables.

The Search Table Operators

We now define more formally the relational operators Select and Project, each of which operates on a single table.

[2] We point out that SELECT-based query languages are also typically conceptualized as operating on a collection of tables. The virtue of the RDM interface that it can define dynamically relationships is equally true of the SELECT interface.

Select: The Select operator σ_E is applied to a table T and evaluates to the table $\sigma_E(T)$ consisting of those tuples satisfying the logical expression E. E can be any logical expression qualifying the values of one or more attributes of table T [e.g., E is ((Dept="Toys") *and* (Salary > 20,000))]. The Select operator can be thought of as returning a horizontal subset of its operand. Notice how this operator generalizes the Retrieve(EMPLOYEE, R, X, Fail) operation from Section 1.1 by allowing qualifications to be based on arbitrary logical combinations of attribute values. (See Figure 1.8.)

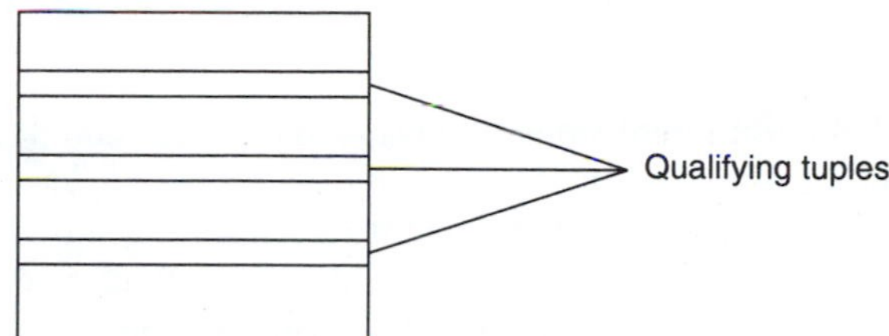

Figure 1.8 Horizontal subset

Project: The Project operator Π_L is applied to a table T and evaluates to the table $\Pi_L(T)$ consisting of all the tuples in the table T, but including in each tuple only those attributes appearing in list L (e.g., L is <SS#, Name>). The Project operator can be thought of as returning a vertical subset of its operand (see Figure 1.9).

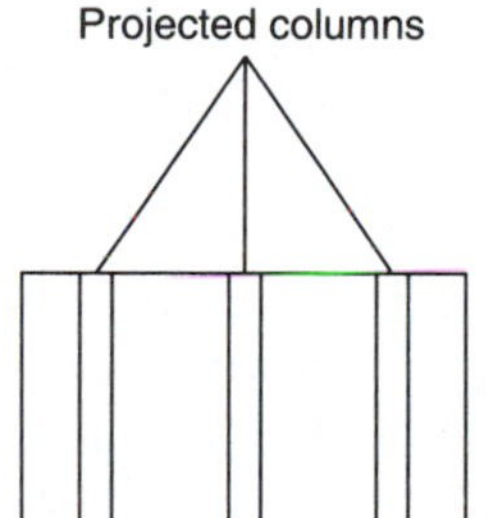

Figure 1.9 Vertical subset

Note Well: As is standard for ADT operators, these relational operators are used to form expressions that take on values (which in this case are tables) and do not alter their arguments. For example, the relational expression $\Pi_{<Name>}$ ($\sigma_{Dept=\text{"Toys"}}$ (*EMPLOYEE*)) evaluates to a table containing the names of the employees from the toys department. Also, we shall assume the existence of a print operator PRINT that can be applied to any table-valued expression [e.g., PRINT(T), PRINT($\sigma_E(T)$)].

The set of operators {Select, Project} (plus operators that allow tables to be created and tuples to be added and deleted) form an important ADT called the **search table.** Although the search table lacks the crucial Join operator of the RDM (see following), it is nevertheless an important ADT. The search table is important both because it is a very powerful and useful ADT in its own right and because in many respects it is the foundation of the RDM. To illustrate the power of the search table, we again consider the request "Print the salaries of people in the toys department." Recall that a complex program was required to satisfy this request in terms of the Retrieve-based interface. In contrast, the request easily is satisfied in terms of the Project and Select operators:

$$PRINT(\Pi_{<Salary>}(\sigma_{Dept=\text{"Toys"}}EMPLOYEE))$$

The Relational Data Model

The reader at this point might wonder why, if the search table is such a powerful ADT, there is a need to introduce the more complex RDM. To justify the introduction of the RDM, we must demonstrate that the search table, despite its power, is not completely adequate for our purposes. The inadequacies of the search table as a general-purpose database interface become apparent when we consider an application involving many real-world entities. When confronted with such an application, a natural first approach is to define many search tables, one for each entity. For example, we might model as an individual search table each of the five entities EMPLOYEE, DEPARTMENT, PRODUCT, STOCKS, and PERSONAL. (An alternative approach is to define a single, large search table that contains all the information of the entities. This approach is explored within Section 1.4.)

The problem with the approach of having several, independent search tables is that each search table is isolated from the others in the sense that there are no operators that span tables—both the Select and Project operators are unary, taking as operand a single table. Consequently, the scheme offers no direct support for the relationships that exist between tables, and thus queries based on such relationships can be difficult to satisfy. As an illustration of the problem, consider the request for a list of employees who work in a department located on floor 10C. Satisfying this request in terms of the tables described earlier and the unary Select and Project operators requires a program of the following form:

```
{ Create a temporary table consisting of the subset of DEPARTMENT
  tuples whose Location attribute has value 10C. }
TEMP ← σ_{Location="10C"} DEPARTMENT
for (each tuple t in TEMP)
  D ← t.Dept
  PRINT(Π_{<Name,SS#>}(σ_{Dept=D} EMPLOYEE))
end for
```

Observe that this task requires us to assume the existence of a mechanism that allows the **for** loop to iterate through the tuples in table TEMP. Since we shall be moving away from this type of solution, for the time being we shall not concern ourselves with how such a mechanism might be integrated with the search table ADT.

In general, the of lack of intertable operators prevents the user from being able to satisfy with self-contained expressions many common requests for information. Instead, the user often must satisfy a seemingly simple retrieval request by embedding within the control structures of a host programming language the unary search table operators Select and Project. The result is an interface only marginally superior to the Retrieve-based interface that we have already rejected as inadequate.

Before remedying this situation with the introduction of the RDM ADT, we observe that the isolated search table approach and the resulting need for host-language implementations of queries is not only an inconvenience for the user, but can also impact negatively on efficiency. The negative impact on efficiency results because the isolated search table approach limits the choice of implementation schemes and processing algorithms. Since each search table is a separate, autonomous ADT, each must be implemented with its own autonomous structure. In particular, there is no opportunity for connecting the implementing structures of a group of tables in an attempt to speed requests that involve several tables simultaneously.

To illustrate this last point, consider a scheme in which each tuple in the DEPARTMENT table somehow "points to" the tuples in the EMPLOYEE table that correspond to the employees who work in that department. This could be accomplished, for example, by supplying each tuple of the DEPARTMENT table with a list of the memory addresses at which corresponding EMPLOYEE tuples reside. The benefit of this scheme is that it allows rapid retrieval of the employees who work in a given department, once the department tuple in question has been retrieved. Such an implementation is impossible under the search table scheme since the tables are distinct ADTs and thus must be implemented in isolation of one another. (The principles of data abstraction mandate that implementation information for the EMPLOYEE table—the physical location of a tuple for example—must not be utilized outside the boundary of the implementation.) Observe also that, even if we agreed to consider the two tables as being part of a common ADT and thus permitted the implementation of the two tables to interact, the Select and Project operators could not exploit the pointer information. Once a DEPARTMENT tuple is retrieved, a selection against the EMPLOYEE table cannot utilize the address information contained in the tuple since Select is defined in terms of only attribute values. We conclude that to enable the type of scheme described here, it is necessary that the tables be part of a *single ADT* and that this ADT include operators in addition to Select and Project.

It is now apparent that the basic search table model must be extended to handle better an application that requires multiple tables. Rather than modeling our information in terms of many isolated search tables, it will be far better to introduce a new ADT that conveniently supports intertable relationships. The RDM is such an ADT. The RDM consists of one or more components, each of which greatly resembles a single search table. Because the tables are part of a common ADT, it is possible to define operators that span tables, thus greatly simplifying the specification of retrieval tasks based on intertable relationships. Further, the RDM allows us to address the efficiency concerns raised previously.

The operators that define the RDM ADT, like the search table operators, are referred to as relational operators. A full complement of relational operators is defined formally in Chapter 2. Presently, we consider three of the RDM's operators, Select (σ), Project (Π), and Equi-join ($\bowtie$). We already have introduced Select and Project in the context of the search table ADT, and these unary operators operate on a single component (i.e., table) of the RDM in the same manner in which they operate on a search table. The Equi-join operator is new and operates as follows on a pair of tables:

Equi-Join: The Equi-join operator $\bowtie$ spans a pair of the tables in the RDM. The expression $T_1 \underset{A1=A2}{\bowtie} T_2$ evaluates to the table consisting of tuples formed by concatenating tuples from tables T_1 and T_2. The tuple $t_1 \cdot t_2$ is in the table $T_1 \underset{A1=A2}{\bowtie} T_2$ if and only if t_1 is in T_1, t_2 is in T_2, and the value in attribute A_1 of t_1 is equal to the value in attribute A_2 of t_2.

For example, suppose that T_1 and T_2 are the following table instances:

T_1:

A	B	C	D
a	b	c	d
x	y	z	w
v	b	c	d
v	y	z	w

T_2:

E	F	G
a	f	g
v	f	g
v	n	q
m	f	g

The value of the expression $T_1 \underset{A=E}{\bowtie} T_2$ is the table instance

A	B	C	D	E	F	G
a	b	c	d	a	f	g
v	b	c	d	v	f	g
v	b	c	d	v	n	q
v	y	z	w	v	n	q
v	y	z	w	v	f	g

The Equi-join operator conveniently supports queries based on intertable relationships, for example, (EMPLOYEE $\underset{Dept=Dept}{\bowtie}$ DEPARTMENT) returns each EMPLOYEE tuple "joined with" the tuple for that employee's department.

To demonstrate the power of the relational operators, consider again the query "Find the highest degree obtained by each employee who works in a department located on floor 10C." This query can be answered elegantly in terms of the relational operators:

$$\Pi_{<Highest\_Degree>}(((PERSONAL \underset{SS\#=SS\#}{\bowtie} EMPLOYEE) \underset{Dept=Dept}{\bowtie} (\sigma_{Location=\text{"10C"}}\ DEPARTMENT)))$$

It is important to emphasize that the RDM ADT is fundamentally different from a collection of single search table ADTs. The focal point of the difference between the two ADTs is the fact that, while a collection of single search tables is a collection of disjoint ADTs, an RDM is a *single* ADT that integrates many components. The ability to define an ADT operator, such as Equi-join, that spans tables is one *consequence* of the fact that the tables belong to a single ADT. Another consequence of this fact is that implementations of the RDM ADT are not restricted to disjoint structures that implement each table in isolation (as is the case for a collection of single search table ADTs). When appropriate, two or more components of the RDM ADT can be implemented with a common structure or with related structures. Such implementations often have a very positive effect on efficiency.

The RDM ADT is at the heart of relational database systems. The typical relational database system allows its users to interface with a collection of tables by means of a query language whose syntax resembles that of the SELECT queries presented earlier. Most relational database systems implement a SELECT-like query language by means of a sequence of maps resembling the sequence described earlier in this section.

SELECT-like query
↓
Relational operators (operate on an RDM ADT)
↓
Implementation-level operators (operate on the implementation of the RDM)

The first map translates a SELECT-like query into an expression composed of the relational operators. For example, the query

```
SELECT EMPLOYEE.Name
  WHERE EMPLOYEE.Dept = DEPARTMENT.Dept
     AND DEPARTMENT.Manager = 888888888
```

might be translated into the expression

$$\Pi_{<Name>}(\text{EMPLOYEE} \underset{Dept=Dept}{\bowtie} \sigma_{Manager=888888888}(\text{DEPARTMENT}))$$

Next, the relational expression is mapped by the DBMS into implementation-level operators. Depending on the ADT's implementation, these operations may operate on internal data structures (e.g., an array or linked list), or, more typically, they operate on external file structures. In either case, these implementation-level operators may be embedded within some control structures, forming an implementation program.

We note that often there are many possible translations, both from a SELECT query to a relational expression and from a relational expression to a program containing implementation-level operators. It is often the case that two equally correct translations (i.e., both translations will retrieve the required data) have drastically different efficiencies when executed. The best translation often depends on how the RDM is implemented and even on characteristics of the operating system and hardware devices. A **query optimizer** is an extremely sophisticated collection of algorithms that has the responsibility of translating a SELECT-like query into an optimal, or near optimal, implementation program. Needless to say, a good query optimizer is crucial to the success of any system that is based on the RDM ADT (e.g., a relational DBMS). We shall encounter the query optimization problem in many contexts throughout the book and, in Chapters 11, 12, and 13, we shall study extensively query optimization algorithms.

1.4 ALTERNATIVE DATA MODELS

It should come as no surprise that the RDM is not the only data model that has been proposed for addressing the database management problem. Historically, the **network** and **hierarchical** data models have been the bases of many commercial DBMSs. In addition, current research considers data models that extend the RDM in attempts to obtain models that are even more powerful and user friendly than the RDM. These experimental data models include the **universal relational model,** the **deductive database model,** and several **object-oriented models.** In this section, we introduce briefly the network, hierarchical, and universal data models. Chapter 4 introduces the object-oriented model, while Chapter 13 considers in more detail the object-oriented and universal models and also considers the deductive model.

As we discuss the data models, the reader would do well to focus on their unity rather than on their diversity. Data abstraction allows us to view these data models as points along a continuum of abstraction levels, with mappings between the levels relating the points (see Figure 1.10). From this perspective, we see clearly that a primary difference between the models is where the brunt of the burden lies for constructing implementation-level programs for satisfying user queries. The higher level models place most of this burden on the database system's query-processing algorithms that perform the mappings from a nonprocedural user query to implementation-level programs. In contrast, the lower level models, such as the network and hierarchical models, place much of this burden on the user by requiring him or her to specify fairly detailed processing algorithms in order to interact with the database.

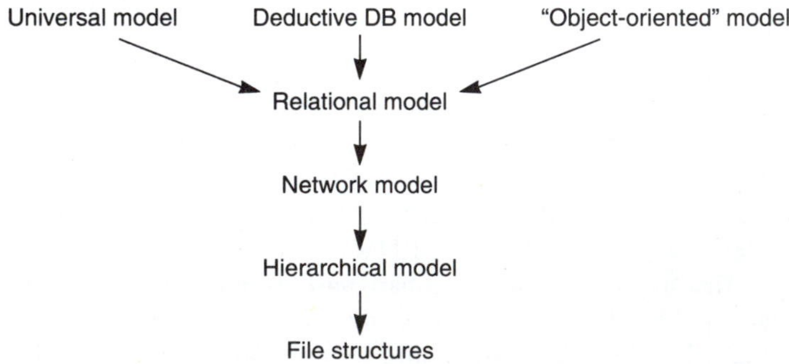

Figure 1.10 Data models as points on an abstract continuum

The maps from a high-level model to implementation-level programs often pass through processing stages that very much resemble user interactions with the lower level models. For example, a user query stated in terms of the universal relation model might first be mapped into a query against the RDM. This query might then be mapped into a program resembling a user-specified interaction with the network or hierarchical model. Finally, this program would be mapped into an implementation-level program, containing file- and operating system–level operations. No matter which of the data models the user query is originally stated against, the ultimate result of a database system's mappings will be quite similar. Consequently, a good number of the techniques and issues studied in the context of any one of the data models apply to many of the other data models as well.

The Network and Hierarchical Models

From the mid-1960s, when DBMSs first began to appear, to the late 1970s, when relational database systems began to win widespread acceptance, a vast majority of commercial DBMSs were based on either the network or hierarchical data model. These models are quite similar to one another, both presenting the user with a graphlike view of the data very much resembling E/R diagrams. Network and hierarchical systems provide collections of commands that allow the user to navigate the relationships of the graph—users interact with the database by embedding these navigational commands in programs written in a standard high-level programming language.

Consider, for example, the following abstract versions of three basic navigational commands:

- Find_Match(E, rec, val, Fail): Retrieve into *rec* the instance of the entity type E with value *val* in its search key attribute. If there is no such record, Fail is returned TRUE; otherwise, Fail is returned FALSE.
- Find_Related(E1, rel_name, rec, Fail): *rel_name* is a relationship between entity type $E1$ and another entity type, call it $E2$. It is assumed that some instance $e2$ of entity type $E2$ has previously been retrieved. Find_Related will return into *rec* an instance of entity type $E1$ that is related to $e2$ by means of relationship *rel_name*. If there is no such record, Fail is returned TRUE; otherwise, Fail is returned FALSE.
- Find_Next_Related(E1, rel_name, rec, Fail): *rel_name* is a relationship between entity type $E1$ and another entity type, call it $E2$. It is assumed that some instance $e1$ of entity type $E1$ has previously been retrieved by means of the Find_Related command (and that this instance $e1$ is related to instance $e2$ of entity type $E2$ by means of relationship *rel_name*). Each call to Find_Next_Related will return into *rec* an instance of entity type $E1$ that is related to $e2$ by means of relationship *rel_name*. When all instances of entity $E1$ that are related to $e2$ by means of *rel_name* have been returned, Fail is returned TRUE.

To illustrate the use of these commands, we construct a program to satisfy the request "List the product number of each product stocked by the toys department." The program can be thought of as navigating through the E/R "network" diagram of Figure 1.3.

```
Find_Match(DEPARTMENT, R, "Toys", Fail1)
if (not Fail1)
   Find_Related(STOCKS, Dept_P#, S, Fail2)
   while (not Fail2)
      PRINT(S.Prod#)
      Find_Next_Related(STOCKS, Dept_P#, S, Fail2)
   end while
endif
```

This interface does improve somewhat on that supported by the basic Retrieve commands introduced earlier. Observe, for example, that the Find_Related and Find_Next_Related commands explicitly support the relationships identified in the E/R diagram, making requests such as the foregoing easier to satisfy than if we had available only the basic Retrieve commands introduced in Section 1.1. Nevertheless, the interface still is rather procedural, forcing the user to specify a detailed algorithm for processing a query. It was once felt by advocates of network and hierarchical systems that this high degree of proceduralness actually was advantageous in comparison to the less procedural query languages of the relational model. The argument of these advocates was based on the belief that a sophisticated programmer could devise a more efficient algorithm for satisfying many queries than could a query optimizer. Today, however, most researchers agree that the best query optimizers are competitive with the best programmers and that the trend is toward even better query optimizers. Further, current software engineering principles certainly imply that the simplicity of nonprocedural interfaces is preferable to procedural interfaces, even if the latter allow for somewhat more efficient implementations of some queries.

Universal Relation Model

Recall the two desirable characteristics of a database interface that were discussed at the end of Section 1.1: The interface should provide a query language that is both self-contained and nonprocedural. While the interfaces provided by most network and hierarchical systems are neither self-contained nor nonprocedural, interfaces provided by relational systems generally are self-contained and reasonably nonprocedural. We observe, however, that "nonproceduralness" is a relative concept, and there is a continuum of possibilities. Even the relatively nonprocedural SELECT queries we have been studying do not lie at the extreme end of the continuum. While it is true that SELECT queries require the user to specify little more than a logical description of the desired information, this description does necessarily include a specification of the tables with which the desired information is associated. For example, in composing the query

```
SELECT EMPLOYEE.Salary
  WHERE EMPLOYEE.Dept=DEPARTMENT.Dept
    AND DEPARTMENT.Manager=888888888
```

the user is specifying that the attributes Salary and Dept are part of the EMPLOYEE table and that the attributes Dept and Manager are part of the DEPARTMENT table.

This observation leads us to ask whether interfaces even higher level and less procedural than the SELECT interface are possible. For example, is it possible to define an ADT that can be conceptualized as a single table? Consider table *U* in Figure 1.11.

U(Name, SS#, Dept, Salary, Highest_Degree, Age, Manager, Location, D_Desc, Prod#, P_Desc)

Figure 1.11 Collapse tables into single table *U*

We have formed table *U* by collapsing tables EMPLOYEE, DEPARTMENT, PRODUCT, STOCKS, and PERSONAL based on the relationships in the E/R diagram of Figure 1.3. In other words, the table *U* that is presented to the user is the join

$$EMPLOYEE \underset{SS\#=SS\#}{\bowtie} PERSONAL \underset{Dept=Dept}{\bowtie} DEPARTMENT \underset{Dept=Dept}{\bowtie} STOCKS \underset{Prod\#=Prod\#}{\bowtie} PRODUCT$$

An interface such as table *U* might be desirable since it frees the user from having to keep track of how the attributes are divided among various tables (attributes in SELECT queries no longer have to be *qualified* by table names) and from having to use the join operator. For example, the interface allows the user to pose the previous query simply as

```
SELECT Salary
  WHERE Manager=888888888
```

The single table interface that we have been describing is known as the universal relation model. It is important to note that the universal relation model is intended *only as an interface*. Observe that table *U* is plagued by a large amount of redundancy. For example, the same combination of <Dept, Manager, Location, D_Desc> values is repeated many times in table *U*. If we attempted to implement table *U* directly as a single file with a one-to-one correspondence between tuples and records, this redundancy would result in much wasted storage, as well as many other serious problems that we shall study later in the context of normalization theory.

Fortunately, the data abstraction approach allows us to implement the single table *U* of the universal relation interface in terms of an RDM ADT consisting of several tables. For example, in Figure 1.12 we see two levels of implemen-

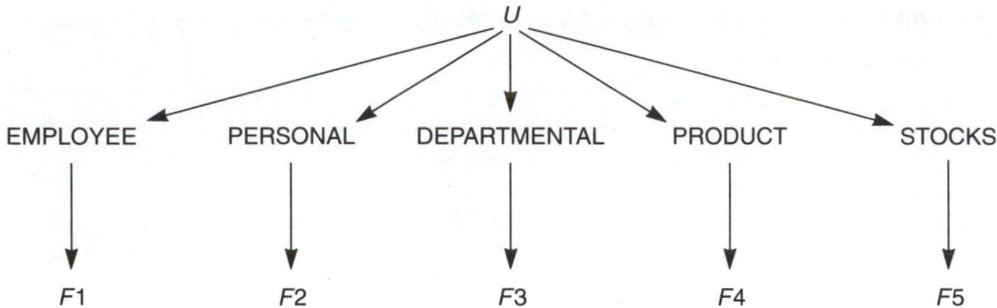

Figure 1.12 Implementation of table *U*

tation. At the first level, table *U* is implemented in terms of an RDM containing tables EMPLOYEE, DEPARTMENT, PRODUCT, STOCKS, and PERSONAL. At the second level, each of these tables is implemented as a file of records. The implementation contains mappings between the levels so that a user query against *U* is translated first into a query against the five tables and then into an implementation-level program against the files. The benefit of this extra level of implementation is that it frees the user from having to qualify attributes with table names and from having to use the Join operator, yet it avoids the redundancy problems that would arise if table *U* were stored directly.

The universal relation model is viewed by researchers as an ideal and is the subject of much current investigation. Unfortunately, there are many theoretical limitations to the approach of representing information as a single table, making it unlikely that the universal relation model could ever serve as a general-purpose interface.

As a simple example of a limitation of the universal relation model, consider the request "Retrieve the salary of the manager of the toys department." A naive user presented with table *U* would very likely attempt to satisfy this request with the query

```
SELECT Salary
  WHERE Dept = "Toys"
```

Observe that this query is not what the user desires since it results in the salaries of all the employees who work in the toys department. While it is true that the user could construct a query such as

```
SELECT Salary
  WHERE Dept = "Toys"
     AND SS# = Manager
```

that satisfies this request correctly, it is apparent that the user requires intimate knowledge of the relationships and joins that were used to form table *U* in the first place. Even more serious shortcomings are seen when we attempt to update table *U*. (See Exercise 1.10.) In Chapter 13 we shall discuss further the universal relation model.

1.5 CHARACTERISTICS AND CONSEQUENCES OF APPLICATION ENVIRONMENTS

Now that we have introduced the ADT RDM, we survey several important factors that determine how, for a given application, the ADT should be implemented. Additionally, we describe some special problems that arise as consequences of the most common of these application environments.

We begin by introducing a two-dimensional scheme for classifying an information management problem in terms of the information's basic characteristics as illustrated in Figure 1.13. The first dimension specifies whether a single search table suffices to model the information or whether an RDM with multiple search table components is required. The former case can be considered an RDM with a single table component. The second dimension specifies whether the ADT is to reside in the internal memory of the computer or on an external memory device such as a direct access disk.

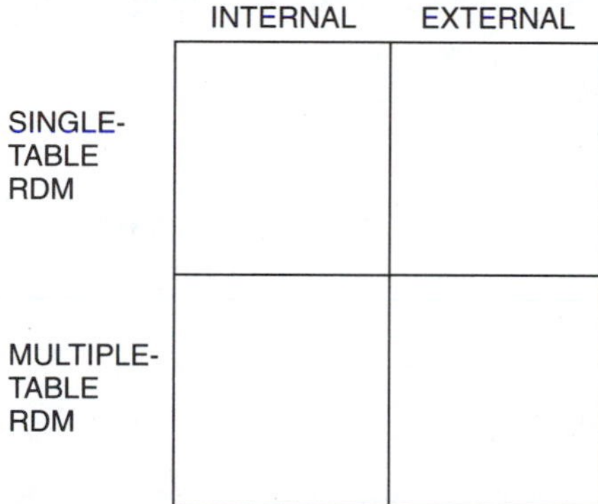

Figure 1.13 Primary dimensions

The requirements of the application of interest determine in which of these quadrants we find ourselves. Whether the information for a particular application should be modeled as a single search table or as an RDM with multiple search tables is based primarily on the characteristics of the information itself, including the expected usage of the information. In most applications of interest, an RDM with multiple search tables will be appropriate. Whether the RDM is to be stored internally or externally is determined primarily by the quantity of the information to be maintained and by the memory constraints of the computer system. When possible, it is generally desirable to store the ADT internally since this would allow the ADT operations to be far more time efficient than if the data were stored externally. Unfortunately, for most applications of interest, there is far more information than can be stored in the internal memory of a computer, forcing us to manage information residing on external storage devices. Further, many applications require the data to be persistent (i.e., to exist independently of the execution of a program) and to be accessible by several users simultaneously. Currently, these two characteristics are supported best by external memory. The multiple-table RDM/external quadrant therefore defines the environment of most interest to us—we shall refer to this environment as the **database environment.**

In whichever of the four quadrants of Figure 1.13 we find ourselves, time- and space-efficient implementations are often crucial to the success of an application. As is true of most ADTs, the RDM has many alternative implementations, and we must analytically weigh the trade-offs inherent in the alternatives. These trade-offs include issues of time versus space efficiency and the relative quality of support for the different ADT operations. The significance of these trade-offs is greatest in the context of the database environment, both because of the complexity of multiple-table operations and because the characteristics of external memory devices amplify the inefficiencies of an implementation.

A successful external implementation of the RDM ADT generally requires highly sophisticated techniques. Often, these techniques are generalizations of simpler, internal memory implementation techniques. In Chapter 2, we shall review several important internal memory data structures and demonstrate how they are modified to provide internal memory implementations for the search table and RDM ADTs. Beginning in Chapter 7, we consider external implementations.

We shall consider now characteristics of the information management problem that divide each of the four quadrants of Figure 1.13 and further influence implementation decisions.

Usage Characteristics

Once we have placed our information management problem in one of the four quadrants from Figure 1.13, we further characterize the problem in terms of the anticipated usage of the information. Any one of the four quadrants can be subdivided, at the grossest level, into **static** versus **dynamic** information management problems. The information to be managed is static if, once initially supplied, it will not change. Thus, a static information management problem requires us to support only retrieve operations such as Select, Project, and, in the case of the multiple-table quadrants, intertable operations such as Join. A dynamic information management problem, on the other hand, requires us to support update operations (e.g., Insert and Delete operations) as well as the retrieval operations.

The static versus dynamic characterization provides only a gross subdivision of information management problems. This subdivision is hardly an adequate characterization of the anticipated usage of information since it is rare to encounter a problem in which the information is completely static. More commonly, we encounter information management problems that are best characterized by the **relative frequencies** of retrieval and update operations. What's more, the anticipated **usage patterns** of an information management problem should be characterized in as much detail as possible. Usage patterns should include not only the relative frequencies of retrievals and updates but also a specification of *how* the information is expected to be requested and updated. For example, how often is an Equi-join to be performed between specific pairs of tables; how often are Selects based on given attributes to be performed; how many tuples are to be inserted into a table per time unit? Also important is an indication of which tasks are to be performed interactively and which are to be performed in batch mode (in which case, time efficiency is less critical). Such usage patterns significantly affect both the way in which the information is modeled with an RDM (e.g., how the information is organized into tables) and how the RDM is implemented (e.g., the choice of file and data structures). These considerations are of the utmost importance to the success of an application.

Single- versus Multiple-User Environment

A common characteristic of the database environment is that more than one user or program interacts with the information. Multiple-user environments lead to special considerations, including the following:

1. *Concurrency control:* Typically, we wish to allow many users to access a database simultaneously. When this is the case, care must be taken to coordinate access to the database, or else serious problems can arise. As an example of the types of problems that can arise from uncoordinated access to a database, consider the following scenario based on an airline reservation system. Ticket agents 1 and 2 process customer requests by accessing and updating the same database:

Agent 1: Agent 1 begins processing a request for one seat on flight 888. The reservation system accesses the database and displays the following tuple:

Flight	Seats_Remaining
888	1

The customer ponders whether or not to reserve the seat.

Agent 2: While agent 1's customer is deciding whether to make the reservation, agent 2 processes a request of another customer for one seat on flight 888. Since agent 1 has not yet sold the remaining seat, the reservation system displays to agent 2 the same tuple:

Flight	Seats_Remaining
888	1

Agent 2's customer immediately reserves the seat. The reservation system implements this transaction by decrementing the value of the Seats_Remaining attribute of the tuple retrieved by agent 2 and replacing in the database flight 888's tuple with the new tuple:

Flight	Seats_Remaining
888	0

Agent 1: At this point, agent 1's information that a seat remains on flight 888 is inaccurate, but agent 1 has no way of knowing this—agent 1 is still working from the previously retrieved tuple:

Flight	Seats_Remaining
888	1

Unfortunately, agent 1's customer decides to reserve the "remaining" seat. The reservation system implements this transaction by decrementing the value of the Seats_Remaining attribute of the tuple that had been retrieved for agent 1 (which we are assuming is unaffected by agent 2's update of the database) and replacing in the database flight 888's tuple with the tuple:

Flight	Seats_Remaining
888	0

Flight 888 is now oversold!

There are many variations on the problem illustrated by this scenario.

Systems that allow concurrent access to a database must employ techniques to safeguard against the type of problem illustrated in the preceding scenario. One common approach to coordinating concurrent access is to "lock" a portion of the database when that portion is being accessed. This strategy leads to questions about selectivity. How strong should a lock be? For example, if one user is only going to read some data, should all other users be prevented from reading the same data? Another question is, How selective should a lock be? In the airline reservation system, once agent 1 initiated his transaction, should we have locked the entire database, the table containing the flight information, the tuple for flight 888, or only the Seats_Remaining attribute of that tuple? A fine locking strategy (e.g., lock only the Seats_Remaining attribute) supports a high level of concurrent accesses but is difficult to implement. We shall study concurrency control techniques in Chapter 10.

2. *Failure recovery:* Failure recovery refers to the techniques a system employs to recover from the premature termination of a transaction. Such a premature termination might be caused by hardware or software failure or even by one of the techniques a system employs to control concurrent access to the database. The recovery from such premature termination must ensure that the database is in a state consistent with reality. For example, returning to our airline reservation scenario, suppose that after agent 2's customer decides to purchase a ticket on flight 888, the customer inquires about flight 222, and suppose that the reservation system treats as a single transaction the customer's inquiries regarding flights 888 and 222. If the system crashes before the customer makes a decision on flight 222, the reservation the customer thinks she made on flight 888 might not have been entered into the database.

Although failure recovery is necessary even in single-user environments, in multiple-user environments failure recovery and concurrency control techniques must be carefully coordinated. The integrated techniques for failure recovery and concurrency control, referred to as **transaction management,** are studied in Chapter 10.

3. *Semantic integrity:* In the previous examples, the content of the database became inconsistent with reality. This occurred because two users updated the database with an unfortunate sequence of operations or because of a system failure. However, the users were not to blame, even in the example illustrating the problems associated with concurrent database access; each user's action, by itself, was perfectly valid. A second way a database can become inconsistent with reality is by a user operation that *by itself* is not semantically valid. For example, suppose our university maintains a table FACULTY(Professor, Dept, Salary, Student). Note that if a professor has 30 students, the table FACULTY will contain 30 tuples for that professor. In addition to much wasted storage, this table has a good chance of becoming inconsistent. Consider, for example, an attempt to perform the update "Give a 10 percent raise to all professors who teach student Smith." A user could well attempt to perform this update by searching the FACULTY table for tuples with Smith in their Student attribute and increasing the Salary attribute of all such tuples. The problem, of course, is that the same professor will now be listed in different tuples as having different salaries.

The problem we have just seen was caused by a semantically unsound user operation to the FACULTY table. However, the user who performed the update is only partially to blame. The table itself is poorly designed and prone to such problems. In a multiple-user environment, we cannot expect all our users to be familiar with the semantics of each table in the database. Rather, we should take care to design our tables to minimize the likelihood of such semantic errors. In addition, some database systems provide the capability for us to make an assertion such as "If a pair of tuples in the FACULTY table agree on the Professor attribute then they must agree on the Salary attribute." Such a system would enforce this constraint by disallowing the update considered previously. In Chapters 5 and 6, we shall consider further approaches to maintaining the semantic integrity of a database.

4. *Security:* We may wish to allow each user of a database to be able to access only specified portions of the data. Perhaps only some users should be able to update a certain portion of the database, and perhaps only some other users should be able to even read another portion of the database. As with concurrency, there is an issue of how finely we should define "security locks." For example, should we control access at the table, tuple, or attribute level? Other security issues arise as well. For example, in some applications, we must prevent users from posing a sequence of queries, each one of which does not violate our security constraints, but when taken together give the user information that should not be made available. Another type of security issue involves the secu-

rity limitations of the operating system. Security issues are considered in Chapter 10.

5. *Views:* A user view (also called a subschema) defines a subset of the database with which a user can interact. Different users can have different views; the idea is to present each user with the data in a way that reflects how he or she needs to interact with the database. Views can be used to partially address the issues of semantic integrity and security discussed earlier. A view might be defined to include a subset of a table (restricting either the attributes or the tuples, or both, that a user can access), or it might even combine two or more tables to make certain queries easier to state (e.g., by removing the user's need to join two tables). A view is a "logical" entity only—a view does not reflect how the data actually is stored—and implementation software is responsible for deriving from the stored data a user view. While views are an extremely useful mechanism, their presence leads to many very interesting theoretical questions and limitations. We study these issues in Chapters 6 and 13.

Centralized versus Distributed Environment

The information management problem in a multiple-user database environment sometimes includes the characteristic that the data is to reside at more than one physical site. These physical sites may be different computers contained within a single room, or they may be computers spread around the world. There are several motivations for distributing a database, including the following:

1. *Maximizing locality:* If an organization has branches in several cities around the world, it may be advantageous to store the data accessed most often by a local branch in that branch's computer. This is an attractive alternative to storing the organization's entire database in one central site and forcing the local branches to access the required data via data communication links.
2. *Maximizing distributed processing:* If the processing an organization must perform on its database can be partitioned into well-defined and independent tasks, performance may benefit from distributing these tasks, and the data required for the tasks, across several computers. This would allow, for example, several tasks to be performed simultaneously and the computing environment of each computer to be tailored to its specific set of tasks.
3. *Maximizing security:* By storing different portions of the database on different computers, we can restrict a user's access to certain portions of the database by restricting his or her access to certain computers.
4. *Maximizing reliability:* The data and algorithms required for certain crucial tasks can be replicated at several different computers. In this manner, the crucial tasks can be performed provided at least one of these computers is operational.

Information management applications in which the data is to be distributed lead to the following additional implementation considerations:

1. *Topology design:* How should the computer network be structured? How many sites should be in the system? What type of computer should be at each site? How should the sites be linked together?
2. *Partition of the database:* Given a topology, how should portions of the database be allocated to the sites? Should a copy of the entire database reside at each site? If not, how do we decide which portion of the database to store at each site?
3. *Distributed query processing:* The data distribution should be transparent to the user. That is, the user should be able to pose a query as if the data were stored in a single database, and the query processing algorithms should determine how best to retrieve the data from remote sites when necessary. Thus query processing in a distributed database environment is far more complex than in a centralized environment. Further increasing the complexity of distributed query processing are the additional concurrency control and failure recovery techniques that it requires.

Some of the problems associated with distributed query processing will be considered in Chapter 13.

SUMMARY AND ANNOTATED BIBLIOGRAPHY

In this chapter, we have attempted to introduce the central issues of database management. At its core, the problem of database management requires that an interface be provided to the user allowing him or her to interrogate and modify a complex collection of information. Thus, the initial question to consider is, What form does this interface take? Historically, the first interfaces supplied by DBMSs were procedural and were based on the network and hierarchical data models outlined in Section 1.4. The reader is referred to Bradley (1983), Date (1982), Martin (1976), and Sibley (1976) for detailed coverage of these models. Sibley includes a description of the original American National Standards Institute (ANSI) Committee on Data Systems Languages (CODYSL) network database model.

In this chapter, we have argued that the record-oriented interfaces often associated with the network and hierarchical models are inappropriate for many information processing tasks. The two main faults of these interfaces are (1) they are not self-contained, forcing users to write programs to interrogate and modify the database, and (2) they are procedural, forcing these user programs to specify intricate details of the strategy to be employed in performing the tasks. The relational data model, first proposed by Childs (1968) and Codd (1970), is a basis for interfaces that, to a large extent, overcome these problems. Newer interfaces, such as the universal model, object-oriented models, and the deductive database model, provide important extensions to the relational model, resulting in greater expressive power and increased ease of use. These models are discussed in Chapter 13.

Our treatment of the relational data model is grounded in data abstraction. Data abstraction is a standard tool of software engineers and theoreticians alike, allowing a data type to be defined by its operations, independent of its implementation. The reader is referred to Aho, Hopcroft, and Ullman (1983); Helman and Veroff (1986); Lewis and Denenberg (1991); and Guttag (1977) for general discussions of data abstraction. The separation of information's usage from its implementation is referred to by the database community as data independence. Data abstraction applied to the database management problem led us to introduce the abstract data types search table and relational data model. There are two standard, equivalent formalisms for defining these ADTs: the relational algebra, which we shall study in Chapter 2, and predicate calculus–based languages, which we shall study in Chapter 3.

Techniques for implementing the relational data model are central to the study of database management. In this introductory chapter, we have attempted to expose the reader to several problems, including data storage, query optimization, semantic design, concurrency control, and failure recovery. Each of these is a major topic to be studied in later chapters.

EXERCISES

1. In Section 1.1, we presented a program for finding the highest degree obtained by each employee who works in a department located on floor 10C. Write an alternative program for performing the same task but whose outer loop retrieves DEPARTMENT records rather than EMPLOYEE records. Under what conditions will the alternative program be more efficient than the original? Could the alternative strategy be made even more attractive with different choices of search keys?
2. Referring to the E/R diagram of Figure 1.3, write Retrieve-based programs, SELECT-based queries, and relational algebra expressions to satisfy each of the following tasks:
   - *a.* Retrieve the manager of employee Smith.
   - *b.* What is the salary of the manager of the toys department?
   - *c.* What is the age of the manager of the toys department?
   - **d.* Which programmers have salaries higher than that of their manager? Why can't this query be expressed in the SELECT-based language as we have defined it in this chapter?

The E/R diagram of Figure 1.14 and the following queries are the basis of Questions 3–9.

- *a.* Which sports does student Jane Doe play?
- *b.* Which professors does student John Smith take courses from?

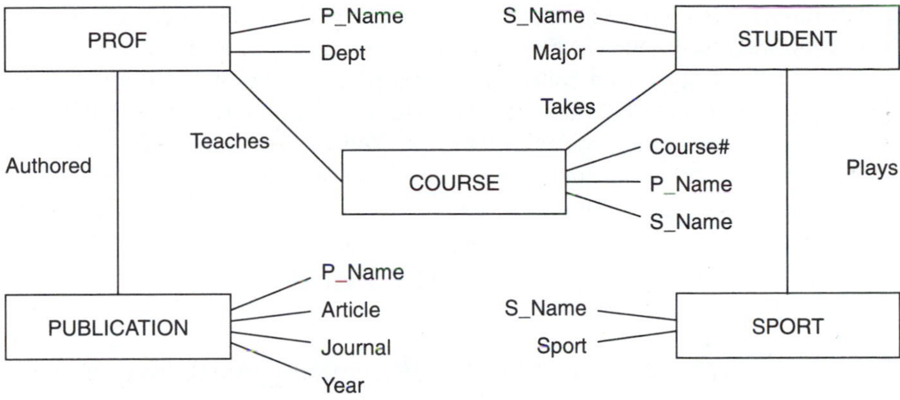

Figure 1.14 University E/R diagram

c. Which students do professors in the Computer Science Department teach?

d. Which soccer players do professors in the Computer Science Department teach?

e. Which soccer players do professors in the Math Department who had one or more publications in 1980 teach?

3. For each of the preceding queries, write a program using the basic Retrieve commands from Section 1.1. In many cases, there are several different reasonable algorithms. What information must be available to the programmer to allow him or her to make a good choice?
4. Answer question 3 in terms of the navigational commands of Section 1.4.
5. Describe how the information of the above E/R diagram can be represented by an RDM.
6. Write SELECT-based and relational algebra expressions against the RDM of question 5 to satisfy each of the preceding tasks.
7. A query optimizer must map high-level queries to implementation-level programs consisting of commands for retrieving data from implementation structures. Describe at an abstract level an algorithm for mapping to implementation-level programs high-level queries such as those of question 6. What factors affect the best choice of implementation-level program?
8. Suppose we are in an environment in which navigational commands such as those of Section 1.4 are supported against an E/R diagram data model. What types of update operators (e.g., insertion and deletion operators) are necessary in the face of the relationships on which the navigational commands are based?

9. Suppose that we wish to store in internal memory the information represented by the above E/R diagram. We might consider implementing each entity type as a collection of records, with pointers linking together the records to form complex structures. Describe a scheme that efficiently supports operations such as Retrieve by search key value, Find_Related, and Find_Next_Related, as well as the Update operations you proposed in question 8.
10. One of the limitations of the universal relation model is its ability to support certain updates. For example, referring to table *U* of Section 1.4,
    a. Suppose a user wishes to insert a new Prod# and its description (P_Desc) but without specifying departments which stock the product. How could this task be stated against *U*?
    b. Suppose a user wishes to delete information about a department. How could this task be stated against *U*? What are the various interpretations your statement could have as operations against the tables EMPLOYEE, PERSONAL, DEPARTMENT, STOCKS, and PRODUCTS. Could some of these operations against the tables EMPLOYEE, PERSONAL, DEPARTMENT, STOCKS, and PRODUCTS have unintended effects on the value of *U* presented to the user?
11. Propose a "locking scheme" that would prevent the ill effects of the airline reservation scenario of Section 1.5. Keep in mind that your scheme must attempt to minimize delays imposed on the customers attempting to make reservations.

CHAPTER 2

Search Table and Relational Data Model Fundamentals

In this chapter, we formalize and expand on several of the concepts previewed in Chapter 1. We saw in Chapter 1 that the single search table abstract data type (ADT) is not a completely adequate representation of the information necessary for many applications and, as a solution, we introduced the relational data model (RDM) ADT. Despite its limitations, the single search table ADT is central to the study of database management because, in many respects, it is the foundation of the RDM ADT. It is therefore appropriate to take a closer look at the search table ADT, defining the ADT more rigorously and presenting several internal memory implementations. After laying the ADT search table foundation, we return to the RDM ADT and consider some basic issues involving its definition and implementation. More advanced issues regarding the design and implementation of the RDM ADT are studied in the chapters that follow.•

2.1 A SUMMARY OF MATHEMATICAL NOTATION AND TERMINOLOGY

In this section, we briefly summarize some mathematical notation and terminology used in this and the following chapters.

Sets

- Set **union** is denoted $\cup$. $S \cup T$ is the set $\{x \mid x \in S \text{ or } x \in T\}$.
- Set **intersection** is denoted $\cap$. $S \cap T$ is the set $\{x \mid x \in S \text{ and } x \in T\}$.
- Set **difference** is denoted $-$. $S - T$ is the set $\{x \mid x \in S \text{ and } x \notin T\}$.
- The **Cartesian product** of the sets S and T is denoted $S \times T$ and is the set of ordered pairs $\{(s,t) \mid s \in S \text{ and } t \in T\}$.

Example

Let S and T be the following sets:

$$S = \{a,b,c,d\}$$
$$T = \{c,d,e\}$$

We have that

$S \cup T = \{a,b,c,d,e\}$

$S \cap T = \{c,d\}$

$S - T = \{a,b\}$

$T - S = \{e\}$

$T \times S = \{(a,c),(a,d),(a,e),(b,c),(b,d),(b,e),(c,c),(c,d),(c,e),(d,c),(d,d),(d,e)\}$

Functions

- If f is a function and x is a member of the domain of f, we shall use both $f(x)$ and $f[x]$ to denote the value of f when applied to x. If $L = <x_1, \cdots, x_k>$ is a list of elements from the domain of f, $f[L]$ denotes the list of values $<f(x_1), \cdots, f(x_k)>$.
- The **image** of f is the set $\{y \mid y = f(x)$ for some x in the domain of $f\}$.
- A function f is **injective** if $f(x) = f(x')$ implies that $x = x'$.
- g is the **inverse** of f if $g(f(x)) = x$ for all x in the domain of f and if $f(g(y)) = y$ for all y in the image of f. Observe that a function can have an inverse only if it is injective.
- If f is a function with domain D and $S \subseteq D$, the **restriction** of f to S is a function f' with domain S, such that $f'(x) = f(x)$ for all $x \in S$.

Example

Let f and h be functions with domain equal to the set of all integers and defined by

$$f(x) = 2x$$
$$h(x) = x^2$$

The image of f is the set of even integers, and the image of h is the set of integers that are perfect squares. If L is the list $L=<-2,-1,0,1,2>$ of integers,

$$f[L] = <-4,-2,0,2,4>$$
$$h[L] = <4,1,0,1,4>$$

Function f is injective since $f(x) = f(y) = z$ implies that both x and y are equal to $\frac{z}{2}$; the function $g(x) = \frac{x}{2}$ is the inverse of f. In contrast, function h is not injective since, for example, $h(2) = h(-2) = 4$, and, hence, h has no inverse. However, the restriction h' of h to the set of positive integers is injective with inverse $q(x) = +sqr\_root(x)$.

Special Symbols Used in Definitions

- The symbol :: is read *is defined as*.
- The symbol <string> means that "string" is to be defined further.
- $(x)^*$ means zero or more occurrences of x.
- $(x)^+$ means one or more occurrences of x.

Example

```
IDENTIFIER :: <letter>(<letdig>)*
```

where letter is an upper- or lowercase letter and where letdig is an upper- or lowercase letter or a digit.

This defines IDENTIFIER to be a sequence of characters beginning with an upper- or lowercase letter, followed by zero or more letters or digits.

2.2 SINGLE SEARCH TABLE DEFINITIONS

We adopt a semiformal definition of the ADT search table; while the definition is sufficient for our purposes, it is not a completely rigorous definition in the sense of formal specification theory. A rigorous definition typically is given in the form of a system of axioms, such as the axioms suggested in Exercise 2.17.

The operators of interest are applied to search tables. A search table T consists of a **table scheme,** which is invariant over the life of the table and, at any point in time, a set of tuples **consistent with** the scheme. Such a set of tuples is called the current **value** or **instance** of table T. More precisely,

Definition 2.1 A **table scheme** consists of a table name and an attribute list, defined as follows:

```
Table_Scheme :: T(<attribute_list>)
```

where T is the name of the table and attribute_list specifies the "form" of the table. We say that <attribute_list> is the scheme of T, although, technically, T together with <attribute_list> is a table scheme.

```
Attribute_List :: (att_name=domain_name)+
```

where att_name is the name of an attribute and domain_name is a standard, predefined set of values such as integer, real, or string. Each domain is assumed to be scalar valued, thus disallowing such domains as vectors of integers. (In Chapter 5, we shall motivate this restriction, which is known as First Normal Form.) Dom(T, att_name) is used to denote the domain associated with att_name in table T's scheme. We assume additionally that any att_name appears at most once in Attribute_List.

The following are examples of table schemes.

EMPLOYEE(SS#=integer, Name=string, Salary=real, Dept=string)
PERSONAL(SS#=integer, Age=integer, Highest_Degree=string)
DEPARTMENT(Dept=string, Manager=integer, Location=string,
D_Desc=string)
PRODUCT(Prod#=integer, P_Desc=string)
STOCKS(Prod#=integer, Dept=string)

A **tuple** can be viewed as a vector of values. Tuple t is **consistent with** scheme T(<attribute_list>) if the value of the ith coordinate of t is a member Dom(T, att_i). While these definitions of "tuple" and "consistent with" will usually be sufficient for our purposes, it will sometimes be necessary to have a more formal definition.

Definition 2.2 A **tuple** t is **consistent with** scheme T(<attribute_list>) if t is a function

$$t: \{A \mid A \text{ is an att\_name in } T\text{'s scheme}\} \rightarrow \bigcup_{\{A \mid A \text{ is an att\_name in } T\text{'s scheme}\}} \text{Dom}(T, A)$$

such that $t[A] \in \text{Dom}(T, A)$ for each att_name A in the scheme. A set of tuples S is **consistent** with table scheme T(<attribute_list>) if each tuple in S is consistent with T(<attribute_list>).

For example, each of the following tuples is consistent with the table scheme EMPLOYEE(SS#=integer, Name=string, Salary=real, Dept=string).

t_1[SS#]=123456789; t_1[Name]=Smith; t_1[Salary]=20000; t_1[Dept]=Toys
t_2[SS#]=123456888; t_2[Name]=Jones; t_2[Salary]=40000; t_2[Dept]=Books

The collection of tuples that is the current instance of a table scheme typically is written in tabular form shown in Figure 2.1.

EMPLOYEE

	SS#	Name	Salary	Dept
(t_1)	123456789	Smith	20000	Toys
(t_2)	123456788	Jones	40000	Books

Figure 2.1 Tabular representation

The definition of the ADT search table provides the following seven operators.

Definition of the ADT Search Table Operators

1. Create(T, <att_list>)

   This operator creates a search table with scheme T(<att_list>) and initializes the value of search table T to the empty set of tuples. If T had previously been created, the association between T and its previous scheme is broken, and the current instance of that scheme is lost.

Example

Create(EMPLOYEE, <SS#=integer, Name=string, Salary=real, Dept=string>) creates the search table EMPLOYEE(SS#=integer, Name=string, Salary=real, Dept=string) and initializes it to the empty set of tuples.

The following definitions assume that search table *T* with scheme *TS* has been created.

2. $\sigma_E\,(T)$ (Select)

   E is a well-formed Boolean expression consisting of operands that are constants or attributes from *T*'s scheme, comparison operators (e.g., =, <, >), and logical connectives (*and*, *or*, and *not*). The expression $\sigma_E\,(T)$ evaluates to a table containing the tuples from *T* satisfying *E*. More formally, let *t* be a tuple consistent with *T*'s scheme (recall *t* is a function). Then *E*(*t*) denotes the expression resulting from replacing with the constant value *t*[*A*] each attribute A appearing in *E*. The expression

   $$\sigma_E\,(T)$$

   evaluates to a table whose current instance is the set of tuples

   $$\{t \in T \mid E(t) \textit{ evaluates to true}\}$$

   This table **inherits** table *T*'s scheme; that is, the resulting table has the same scheme as *T*.

Example

The expression $\sigma_{(Salary\,>\,20000)\text{ and }(Dept=\text{“}Toys\text{”})}EMPLOYEE$ evaluates to the table with the same scheme as EMPLOYEE and contains those tuples in the EMPLOYEE table with Salary > 20,000 and Dept = Toys.

---

3. $\Pi_L(T)$ (Project)

   L is list of distinct attributes appearing in *T*'s scheme. The expression $\Pi_L\,(T)$ evaluates to a table containing all the tuples in *T*, but each tuple in the resulting table contains values for only the attributes in L. More formally, the expression evaluates to the table whose current instance is the set of tuples

$$\{ t' \mid t' \text{ is a restriction to L of some function } t \in T\}$$

The resulting table R inherits the table scheme consisting of the attributes in L, such that for each such attribute att_name, Dom(R, att_name) = Dom(T, att_name).

Example

The expression $\Pi_{<SS\#,\ Name>}$ *EMPLOYEE* evaluates to the table with scheme (SS#=string, Name=string) and whose tuples are the tuples of table EMPLOYEE restricted to these two attributes.

The operators σ and Π are referred to as **relational operators.** In addition to Create and the two relational operators, we define four **update operators:**

4. $\leftarrow$ (Assignment)

   The $\leftarrow$ operator is used to *assign* to a search table a new value. More formally, assignment is written as

   $$T \leftarrow E$$

   where E represents a set of tuples. Often, E will be an expression over one or more tables and the relational operators. (Such an expression is called a **relational expression**.) If T is a table that previously has been created, the value of E must be a set of tuples that is consistent with the scheme of T. If T does not exist, E must be a relational expression. In this case, table T is created and given the scheme inherited by the relational expression E.

5. Add(T, t)

   t is a tuple consistent with the scheme of T. The operation assigns to table T a new value:

   $$T \leftarrow \{t' \mid t' \in T \text{ or } t' = t\}$$

   The scheme for table T is unchanged by the Add operator. Observe that since the value of table T is a *set* of tuples, the operation Add(T, t) has no effect when t is a member of the current instance of T.

6. Delete(T, E)

   E is a Boolean expression as in the definition of the Select operator.

The operation assigns to table T a new value:

$$T \leftarrow T - \{t \mid t \in T \text{ and } E(t) \text{ is true}\}$$

The scheme for table T is unchanged by the Delete operator.

7. Modify(T, E, val_list)

   In many applications, it is desirable to include in the definition of the search table a Modify operator that can change the values of specified tuples in the search table. Although this task could be accomplished by a sequence of Select, Delete, and Add operations (see Exercise 2.12), this method could be awkward for the user as well as inefficient (i.e., it could well be far more efficient to implement the modification of tuples directly rather than by simulating the Modify operation by finding the tuples, deleting the tuples, and finally inserting appropriately modified versions of the tuples.) We therefore add to the search table the operator Modify(T, E, val_list), where E is a Boolean expression and val_list supplies new values for a subset of the attributes in T's scheme. The effect of the operator is to change the value of the attributes as specified in val_list of the tuples in table T that satisfy the expression E. The scheme for table T is unchanged by the Modify operator.

Important Observation The value of a search table is always a *set* of tuples. This implies that a search table never contains duplicate tuples and that there is no order associated with a search table's tuples. The fact that a search table's tuples are necessarily unordered is sometimes an inconvenience since, for many applications, it would be desirable to be presented with data sorted on some attribute. Nevertheless, we shall assume that tuples are presented to the user in an arbitrarily ordered manner. However, when discussing an implementation structure for a search table or RDM, we often shall consider how well the structure supports sorted retrievals. The motivations for this analysis include the facts that such retrievals usually are an option supported by commercial database systems and that such retrievals often are performed as part of the implementation of other relational operators (e.g., the Join operator).

To summarize, the definition of the ADT search table includes the Create operator, the two relational operators σ and Π, and the four update operators $\leftarrow$, Add, Delete, and Modify.

Search Table Operators

Scheme operator: Create

Relational Operators: σ, Π

Update Operators: $\leftarrow$, Add, Delete, Modify

2.3 INTERNAL IMPLEMENTATIONS FOR THE ADT SEARCH TABLE

In this section, we shall peek at some basic implementations of the ADT search table. Although the first half of the book focuses on definitional issues that, for the most part, are independent of implementation issues, this peek at the lower levels of abstraction should provide the reader with some useful perspective.

Recall from Chapter 1 that the implementation of a high-level ADT can be viewed as a sequence of maps to successively lower level ADTs. The implementation is complete when we reach ADTs that are supported directly by our environment. Often, it is appropriate to view the lowest level "implementation objects" as data and file structures rather than as ADTs. Such a perspective allows us to focus on the development and analysis of implementation techniques for the search table and RDM. Consequently, in our presentation, we shall map the search table and RDM operators directly into algorithms that operate on concrete data and file structures (see Figure 2.2).

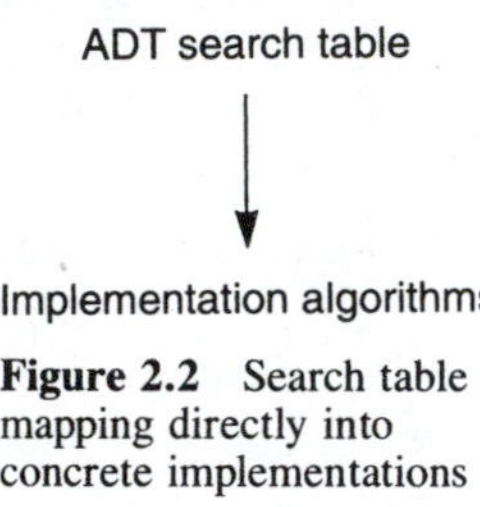

Figure 2.2 Search table mapping directly into concrete implementations

This perspective allows us to conveniently study the efficiency of various implementation methods while preserving data independence. Because database users access the data only by means of the search table and RDM ADTs, any change in implementation methods will be invisible to the user—except, of course, for a difference in the response time of the operations.

In this section, we consider internal memory implementations for the ADT

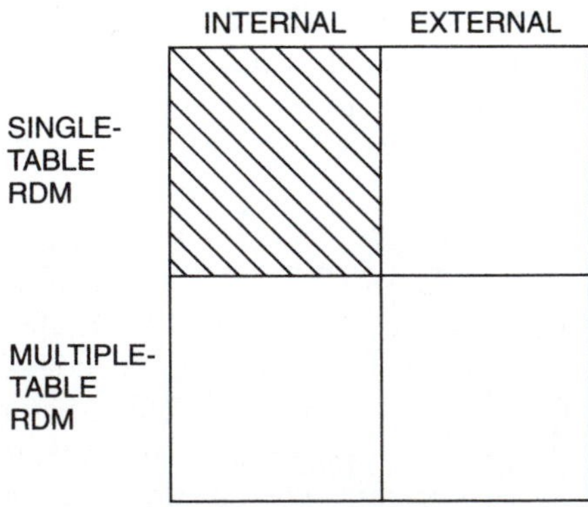

Figure 2.3 Internal/single quadrant

search table (see Figure 2.3). These implementations are built on such elementary data structures as arrays, linked lists, search trees, and hashing schemes. We briefly review the most relevant data structures and then demonstrate how they can be adapted to provide efficient support for the search table operators. The material in this section is important not only because many applications can be addressed successfully with a search table (or with several isolated search tables) implemented in internal memory but also because the structures and techniques presented here are the foundations of the most common implementations, both internal and external, for the RDM ADT. Additionally, current hardware trends are toward reduced cost for internal memory. This will stimulate the development and use of main memory database machines, computers in which a large portion of the database is stored in internal memory. Good internal search table and RDM implementations will be necessary if such machines are to be utilized to their full advantage.

Review of Basic Internal Memory Implementation Structures

Although we shall be dealing most often with search tables and RDM ADTs so large that they must be stored externally, there certainly are applications for which they can be stored internally. An internal implementation is almost always desirable (though not always possible because of the limited availability of main memory) because the time required to perform operations on data is, in general, far less when the data reside in the internal memory of a computer than when the data reside externally.

In this section, we present a very brief review of the data structures that serve as the primitives for the most important internal memory implementations. These data structures are classified as linear structures, search trees, and hashing schemes. Since these structures are all standard topics for an elementary data structures course, we present only a brief summary of how the structures work and a brief analysis of their efficiencies. The reader is referred to any one of the the large number of data structure texts for further background [e.g., Aho, Hopcroft, and Ullman (1983), Helman and Veroff (1986), Horowitz and Sahni (1976), Knuth (1973), Lewis and Denenberg (1991), and Riengold and Hanson (1983)].

Criteria for the Preliminary Analysis

Before considering the basic data structures, we observe that each of them, in its standard form, is appropriate only for a restricted version of the ADT search table. Recall that the search table's Select, Delete, and Modify operators permit values to be specified for any logical combination of table attributes. The standard form of each of these data structures, however, organizes the data with respect to a *single, predefined attribute*, called the **search key.** For example, we might implement the search table EMPLOYEE(SS#=integer, Name=string, Salary=real, Dept=string) with an array of records sorted on the SS# attribute. While the selection

$$\sigma_{SS\#=123456789}\, EMPLOYEE$$

can be performed efficiently with a binary search of the array, a selection such as

$$\sigma_{Salary=50000}\, EMPLOYEE$$

requires a scan of the entire array.

Thus, the basic data structures summarized in the following subsections are appropriate for implementing only restricted versions of the search table operators Select, Delete, and Modify. Specifically, for the moment, we restrict attention to how well an implementation supports the following operations:

- Select, restricted to a single, predefined search key
- Project
- Insert
- Delete, restricted to a single, predefined search key
- Modify, restricted to a single, predefined search key

Following the summary of the basic data structures, we introduce the techniques necessary for building from them efficient implementations for the (unrestricted) search table ADT.

Observe that even when restricted to a single search key, the logical expression for each of the operators Insert, Delete, and Modify may qualify more than one tuple. For example, consider the expressions:

1. $\sigma_{Salary=200000}\, EMPLOYEE$
2. $\sigma_{((Salary \geq 20000) AND (Salary \leq 50000))}\, EMPLOYEE$
3. $\sigma_{(((Salary=200000) OR (Salary=400000)) OR (Salary=100000))}\, EMPLOYEE$

As the first expression illustrates, a search key in general need not uniquely identify a tuple. Consequently, even a Selection with a single equality qualification (called an **exact match** qualification) may return more than one tuple. The second and third expressions clearly may return more than one tuple since each admits more than one salary value. The second expression, however, differs in a significant way from the third expression—the salaries that the second expression qualifies are guaranteed to be *logically consecutive*. A qualification with this property is called a **range** qualification. (Note that an exact match qualification is a special case of a range qualification.) Range qualifications are significant both because they are common and because some implementations handle such qualifications far more efficiently than do other implementations. Therefore, an implementation's ability to efficiently support range qualifications often is a major consideration.

When considering a search table or RDM implementation, we in general analyze the efficiencies of the Select, Delete, and Modify operations as *a function of both the total number N of tuples in the table and of the number K of tuples qualified by the operation*. Further, our analysis considers explicitly only range qualifications (which include exact matches as a special case). This is a reasonable approach because most operations containing other types of qualifications (e.g., expression 3) often are processed in one of two ways:

1. Scan the entire data structure for qualifying attribute values. This method requires O(N) time.
2. Break the qualification into multiple expressions, each of which contains a range qualification. For example, the expression $\sigma_{(((Salary=200000) OR (Salary=400000)) OR (Salary=100000))}$ *EMPLOYEE* might be processed as $\sigma_{Salary=200000}$ *EMPLOYEE* followed by $\sigma_{Salary=400000}$ *EMPLOYEE* followed by $\sigma_{Salary=1000000}$ *EMPLOYEE*. The time required for this method is derivable from the time required for each of the expressions containing range qualifications.

Although a good query optimizer might find a better processing strategy than this for some expressions, for the moment we simply assume that one of these methods is used. This allows us to obtain, from our analysis of range qualifications, an upper bound on the efficiency with which an implementation supports any given Select, Delete, or Modify operation.

A final criterion for evaluating search table implementations, and one that is very much related to how well a data structure supports range qualifications, is whether a data structure supports **ordered-stream retrievals.** An ordered-stream retrieval returns qualifying tuples ordered by some criterion. For our purposes, we assume that this criterion is *sorted on the search key value*. Although the search table operators never specify an ordering of the resulting table's tuples (they cannot because tables are unordered sets of tuples), ordered-stream retrievals often are useful in practice. The obvious motivation for ordered-stream retrievals is to enable output to be presented to the user in some convenient format. A less obvious motivation for ordered-stream retrievals is that they are required to support some important query processing algorithms to be considered later.

We now are ready to summarize the three basic classes of internal data structures.

Linear Structures: The most basic class of data structures stores a collection of records in a linear fashion. This class of structures includes arrays and linked lists. With either the array or linked-list implementation, there is the option of storing the records sorted on the search key. If the records are not sorted, each of the operators (except Insert) always requires a scan of the entire data structure, and ordered-stream retrievals are not supported. Storing the records sorted, on the other hand, allows both the array and linked-list implementation to support ordered-stream retrievals. Further, storing the records sorted is particularly beneficial in the context of the array implementation since this allows a binary search to locate in O(log N) time one of the records that satisfies the qualification of a Select, Delete, or Modify operation, and all other qualifying records are guaranteed to be in contiguous array locations. As Fig-

	unsortarray	sortarray	unsortlink	sortlink
Select	N	$\log N+K$	N	N
Project	N	N	N	N
Insert	1	N	1	N
Delete	N	N	N	N
Modify	N	$\log N+K$	N	N
Ordered-stream retrieval	No	Yes	No	Yes

Figure 2.4 Approximate worst-case behavior; N = # records; K = # qualifying

ure 2.4 indicates, however, none of the four linear implementations supports both the Insert and Delete operators in less than O(N) time. [The sorted array requires O(N) time on Insert and Delete because records must be shifted once a binary search has established the location for the insertion or deletion.]

The linked-list implementation does have one potential advantage over the array implementation that is not apparent from Figure 2.4. This concerns space efficiency. In many contexts (e.g., when programming in most high-level programming languages), the size of an array must be declared in advance and remain fixed. Consequently, an array often must be declared to be of a "worst-case" maximum size, potentially leading to much wasted space. In contrast, the storage for a linked-list implementation can be allocated dynamically, thus allowing the amount of memory devoted to the implementation to grow and shrink as required, at the cost of only one or two bytes per pointer.

Search Trees: Search trees are a class of structures designed to provide logarithmic time (in N, when K is fixed) support for the operators Select, Insert, Delete, and Modify. Figure 2.5 shows a search table implemented as the most basic type of search tree, a binary search tree. Given a search key value, the first record with that search key can be located in time proportional to the height h of the tree. The next $K - 1$ logically consecutive search keys can be

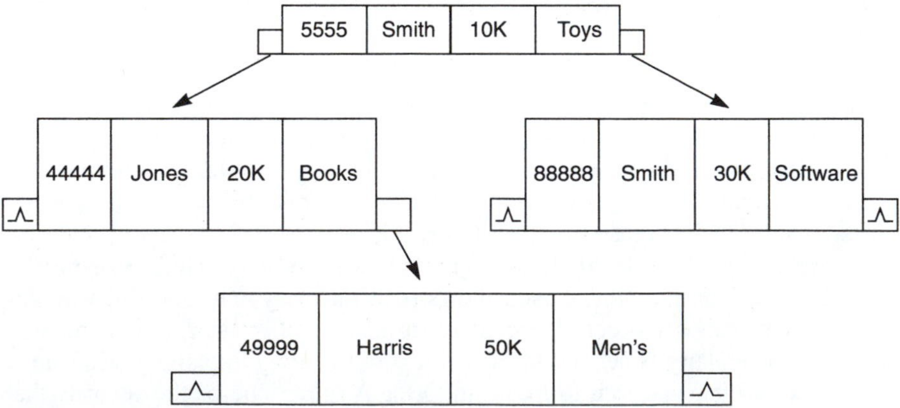

Figure 2.5 Binary search tree table implementation

located in O(K) time—these are contained in the records that follow in the in-order traversal of the tree the first matching record found. Hence, the Select and Modify operations can be performed in O(h+K) time. Insert (a single record) can be implemented in O(h) time and Delete (k records) can be implemented in O($k*h$) time.

The height h of a binary search tree can range between approximately $\log_2 N$ and N. It can be shown that if insertions and deletions occur in a random and uniform pattern, the expected height of the tree is O(log$N$). However, because the worst-case performance of O(N) is unacceptable for many applications, variations of the binary search tree in which the height is guaranteed to be O(log$N$) often are employed. Perhaps the two best known variants are the AVL tree and the 2–3 tree. Figure 2.6 shows a search table implemented as a 2–3 tree. The reader should review 2–3 trees [see, e.g., Aho, Hopcroft, and Ullman (1983) and Helman and Veroff (1986)] if he or she is not comfortable with them, as this data structure is the basis for an important file structure known as the B-tree. Figure 2.7 summarizes the behavior of a 2–3 tree implementation.

Search trees typically are implemented using dynamically allocated storage, giving them the same benefits as those attributed to linear linked lists.

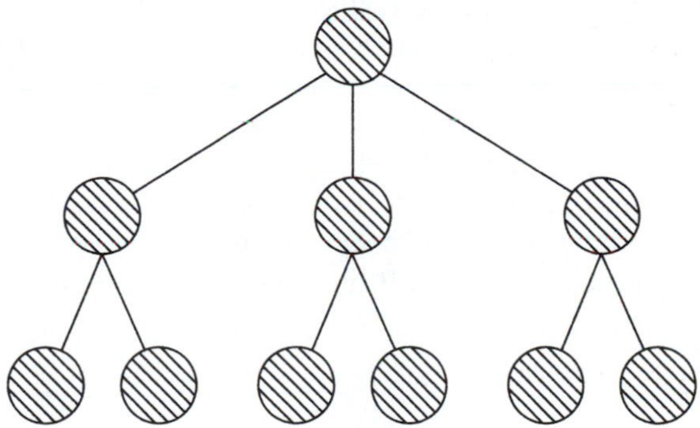

Figure 2.6 2–3 tree table implementation

	2–3 search tree
Select	log$N$+K
Project	N
Insert	log$N$
Delete	$K\cdot$log$N$
Modify	log$N$+K
Ordered-stream retrieval	Yes

Figure 2.7 Approximate worst-case behavior; N = # records; K = # qualifying

Hashing Schemes: Hashing schemes are a class of structures that, at their best, provide constant time (when the number K of qualifying tuples is fixed) support for the operators Select, Insert, Delete, and Modify. Figure 2.8 illustrates the basic idea behind a hashing scheme. A hash function maps a search key into a single array location. The hash function is used to determine both where to insert a new tuple and where to search for a tuple with a specified search key value. Ideally, the time to Select, Insert, Delete, or Modify a single tuple depends only on the time to compute the hash function, and this typically requires only a few simple operations (e.g., a division).

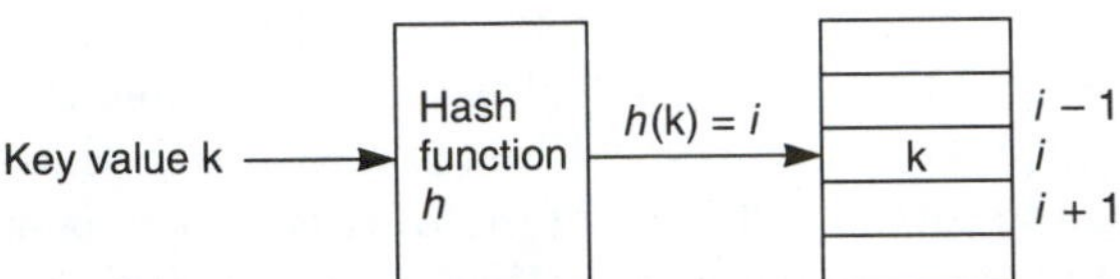

Figure 2.8 Address calculator

A major problem with hashing schemes is **collisions.** A collision occurs when more than one tuple hashes to the same array location. There are two sources of collisions. One source of collisions is that two tuples with the same search key will always hash to the same location. A second source of collisions is **synonyms,** different search keys that hash to the same location. (Observe, e.g., that if social security numbers are search keys, unless we are willing to have 10^9 array locations, there will be synonyms.) In general, both types of collisions are unavoidable, leading to two important issues: how to choose a hash function that minimizes the number of collisions and how to resolve collisions when they do occur. Figure 2.9 illustrates two common collision resolution methods.

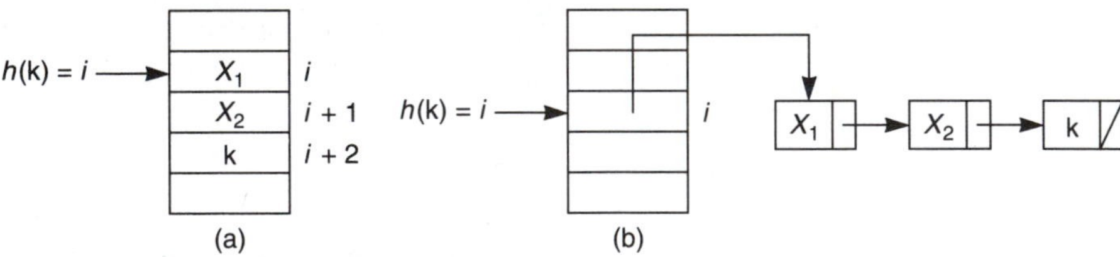

Figure 2.9 Open addressing and chaining

Open addressing refers to a class of collision resolution methods in which a tuple is placed in an alternative array location when the array location into which the tuple hashes is occupied. For example, under one open addressing scheme, if a tuple hashes into array location i, but location i is occupied, we place the tuple in the first unoccupied location "following" i ($i + 1$, or $i + 2$, and so forth, wrapping around to position 0 if necessary). Operations Select,

Delete, and Modify reproduce this sequence of "probes" when searching for a particular search key value.

Chaining is a second class of collision resolution methods. In chaining, all tuples that hash into the same array location are placed in an auxiliary data structure (such as the linked list shown in Figure 2.9b) that is hung off the array location. An immediately evident advantage of chaining over open addressing is that, like the other linked data structures we have considered, chaining can utilize dynamic storage. Further, chaining is easily adapted to the environment of external storage. Consequently, in the following discussions of hashing schemes, we shall assume that chaining is used to resolve collisions.

Hashing provides outstanding time efficiency for most search table operations, as long as the maximum length of any chain is kept small. This implies that the number B of array locations, or **buckets,** should be close to the number N of tuples expected in the search table. Observe, however, that it is not sufficient that the average chain length N/B be small. We additionally desire the chains to be of approximately the same length, implying that no chain is much larger than average. To accomplish this, a **uniform** hash function is employed. A hash function is uniform (with respect to the set of possible search key values and a probability distribution for selecting a value) if, for any bucket i, a randomly selected search key value (selected in accordance with the probability distribution) hashes into bucket i with probability $1/B$. The problem of constructing uniform hash functions is well studied and many good functions are known [see, e.g., Knuth (1973)]. Unfortunately, uniform hash functions generally "randomize" search keys in the sense that consecutive search key values do not necessarily map into the same, or even nearby, buckets. Consequently, hashing schemes in general are incompatible with efficient processing of search table operations that qualify several consecutive search keys and with ordered-stream retrievals.

The table in Figure 2.10 summarizes the efficiency of the search table operations, assuming that each chain has length N/B. It must be noted that no matter how good our choice of a hash function might seem, the actual data might not be as expected. In the extreme case, it is possible that all tuples hash to the same bucket. In this case, all operations (except Insert) are $O(N)$. We note,

Operation	Efficiency
Select, single qualifying value	N/B
Select, K qualifying values	$M*(N/B)$ (tuples spread in $M \leq \min\{K,B\}$ buckets)
Project	N
Insert	1
Delete, single qualifying value	N/B
Delete, K qualifying values	$M*(N/B)$ (tuples spread in $M \leq \min\{K,B\}$ buckets)
Modify, single qualifying value	N/B
Modify, K qualifying values	$M*(N/B)$ (tuples spread in $M \leq \min\{K,B\}$ buckets)
Ordered-stream retrieval	No

Figure 2.10 Hash efficiency, assuming each chain has length N/B

however, that worst-case performance can be improved by hanging a search tree off each bucket rather than a linear linked list.

Implementing the ADT Search Table

The primary limitation of search table implementations of the data structures presented in the previous section is that each organizes its data with respect to a single, predefined search key. Since the search table ADT includes a Select operator that is extremely flexible, modifications to the data structures must be made to obtain ADT implementations that provide acceptable performance. In this section, we consider implementations that support rapid selection based on the value of a single, *arbitrary* attribute; that is, the attribute is *not* identified in advance as a search key. The following section considers implementations that support rapid selections based on logical combinations of the values of several attributes.

To support rapid selection based on the value of an arbitrary attribute, it would seem that an implementation must provide many different organizations of the data simultaneously. In so doing, however, the implementation must not inflict unreasonably large costs on other aspects of the application. Note that this second requirement rules out the most obvious way to satisfy the first requirement: maintaining many copies of the same data, with each copy structured to support selections based on a different attribute (e.g., one tree organized by Salary and another tree organized by Dept). Thus, for example, to satisfy the query

$$\sigma_{Salary=40000}\ EMPLOYEE$$

we would search the tree organized by Salary. To satisfy the query

$$\sigma_{Dept=\text{"Toys"}}\ EMPLOYEE$$

we would search the tree organized by Dept. (Question: How would we satisfy a query, such as

$$\sigma_{(\text{Salary}=40000) and (Location=\text{"Toys"})}\ EMPLOYEE$$

that is based on a logical combination of attribute values?)

The problem with the implementation just described is that maintaining multiple copies of the same data can have some very negative consequences. Specifically,

- *Extra storage:* The amount of memory required is obviously increased greatly over the basic (single copy) data structure. This is especially damaging for an internal memory implementation since internal memory generally is limited and expensive.
- *Update overhead:* Consider an operation that updates the search table (i.e., Add, Delete, or Modify a tuple). The corresponding data structure operations must be performed against *each* of the structures used in the

implementation. For example, to delete a tuple t, each copy of the corresponding data record must be located and deleted. This greatly degrades the efficiency of such operations.

- *Increased danger of the database losing its integrity:* A correct implementation of the search table's update operators must reflect changes in all copies of the data. For example, suppose that the redundant data implementation is used. If the tuple for employee Smith is modified to give Smith a 10 percent raise, the algorithms that implement the ADT Modify operation must modify all copies of the data records appropriately. Although this process is slow, a correct implementation of the Modify operator ensures that all copies of Smith's data record remain consistent. However, in general there is no way to ensure that some "super user" will not bypass the ADT operators and update Smith's salary directly. (We are not concerned here with the problem of unauthorized access—to focus on the integrity problem, assume the super user has the authority to update salaries.) For example, this super user might simply "scan" (e.g., with a record-processing type program) *one* of the files that contains a copy of the table's data records. When the record for Smith is encountered, the super user simply modifies the salary field. At this point, the database has lost its integrity because the multiple copies of Smith's tuple are not consistent. A general rule of thumb in information management is that *maintaining redundant data begs for trouble*. In Chapter 5 we shall begin to study this issue from a formal perspective.

These consequences of redundant data are quite damaging in the contexts of most applications, and, thus, the search table implementation based on redundant data usually is not acceptable.

Indexing

Fortunately, a general technique is available that yields virtually the same benefits as the redundant data scheme with respect to flexible selections yet keeps additional costs at a more acceptable level. The general technique is called **indexing.** Indexing is a conceptually simple technique that allows multiple organizations of data to be maintained without requiring the data to be duplicated. The central idea behind indexing is to store the data in one structure while maintaining one or more **indices** into the structure containing the data.

Let us begin by supposing that we store the tuples of a search table as an unstructured **heap** of records. (In database terminology, heap refers to a collection of records with no organization; the term should not be confused with the common implementation of the same name for the ADT priority queue.) To efficiently support the search table operations, we construct indices into the heap. For example, each of the data structures described in the previous section can be turned into an index into the heap of data records by storing in the data structure *pointers to the data records rather than the data records themselves*.

The type of index that we shall describe here is called a **dense index.** A dense index contains one **index record** for each data record. Typically, the index record corresponding to data record R is a pair (*Att_val*, *dataptr*), where *Att_val* is record R's value for the search table attribute (e.g., Name) on which the index is maintained, and *dataptr* is a pointer to R. The records that comprise a dense index are organized into a structure that supports efficient searching and updating. For example, a simple structure might store the index records sorted in an array. A more complex structure might organize the index as a search tree, storing one or more index record in each tree node. Figure 2.11 shows a 2–3 tree node for an index on the Name attribute, and Figure 2.12 shows the entire index structure.

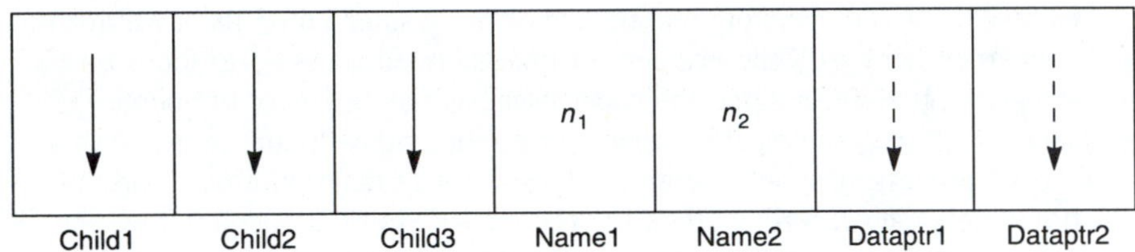

Figure 2.11 2–3 tree node containing two index records

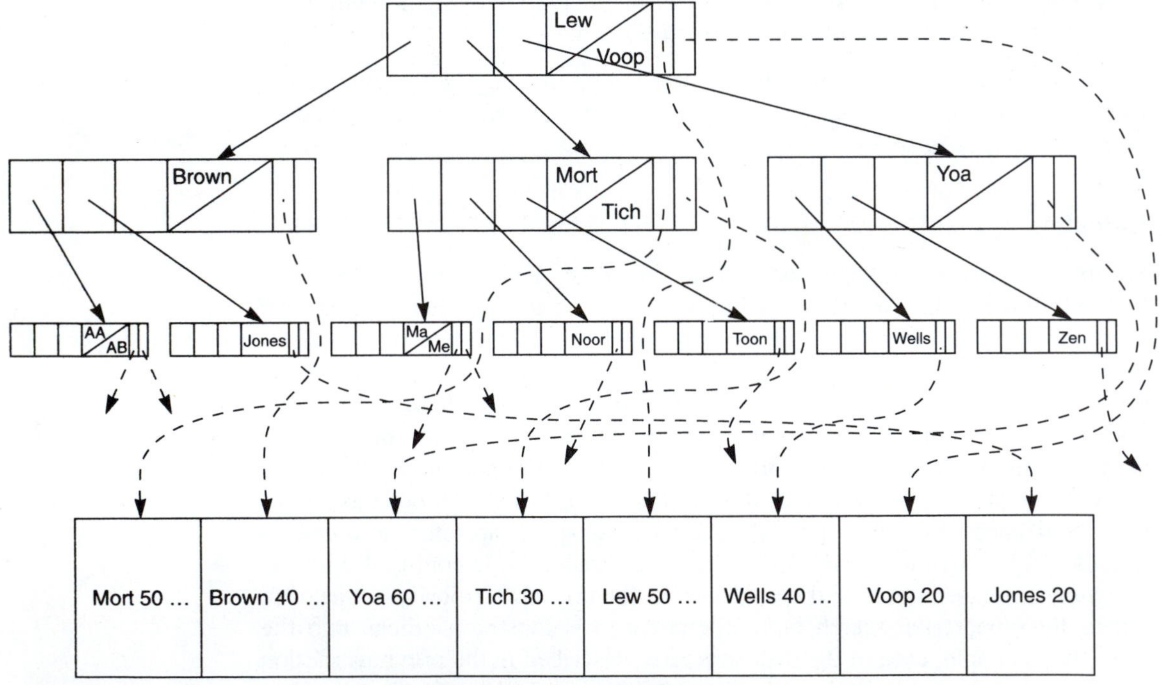

Figure 2.12 An index on Name structured as a 2–3 tree

We can build as many indices into a *single* heap of data records as we wish. For example, we can build an index (call it *index_A*) for each attribute *A* in the search table. Note that, since an index record in general is far smaller than a data record, the amount of storage required by this indexing implementation typically is dramatically less than the storage required by the redundant data record implementation. Further, the search table operations are supported with either virtually equal, or significantly better, efficiency under the indexing implementation.

Consider first the Select operator. When the indexing implementation is used, a selection of the form

$\sigma_{A=V}$ *EMPLOYEE*

is processed by searching *index_A* for the index record(s) that match value *V* (using the standard Retrieve algorithm for the index's data structure) and then following the pointer of each of the matching index records to the corresponding data record. Note that this process requires only one additional step for each matching tuple (following each index record's pointer) over what would be required if the search table were implemented using the redundant data record scheme.

The task of modifying the values of an existing tuple is accomplished far more efficiently under the indexing implementation than under the redundant data record implementation. To change the value of attribute *A* of a given tuple, we need only (1) locate the corresponding data record, (2) modify the value of attribute *A* in the data record, and (3) update *index_A*. Recall that under the redundant data record implementation, *every* copy of the data record has to be located and modified.

Unfortunately, insertions and deletions are no more efficient under the indexing implementation than under the redundant data record implementation. The following describes the required processing under the indexing implementation:

```
Insert (tuple t)
  create a data record for the new tuple and initialize its fields
  add the new data record to the heap
  add an index record for each indexed attribute A—the
    index record contains the value of attribute A in the new
    data record and a pointer to the new data record
Delete (A=v)
  use index on A to locate the data records with attribute A=v
  remove the data records from the heap
  remove the corresponding index records from each index
```

For most applications, indexing schemes are far superior to the redundant data scheme. Nevertheless, each index we build incurs the overhead of additional storage and added time for insertions and deletions. We thus are led to the **index selection problem:** Given a search table scheme $T(A_1, A_2, \ldots, A_N)$, how do we decide which attributes to index? An important **secondary in-**

dex design problem is: Once it is decided to index attribute A, how should we structure *index_A* (e.g., as a hashed index or a 2–3 tree)?

These design problems involve classic time and space trade-offs. The more indices we build, the more storage is required, and the slower Insert and Delete operations will be. On the other hand, the more indices we build, the more kinds of selections will we be able to support efficiently. Further, with regard to the secondary index design problem, a hashed index supports exact-match queries very well, while a 2–3 tree should be used if range queries are present. Clearly, before we can solve these index design problems, we must have a description of the expected usage patterns for our application (e.g., the percentage of insertions and deletions, the percentage of selections based on each attribute, the relative costs in our application environment of time and space). Unfortunately, precise information of this type often is not available, and even when it is available, the index selection problem is extremely difficult (in fact, NP-hard). In Chapter 9, in the context of external memory implementations, we shall return to the index selection problem.

Additional Implementation Considerations

To this point, we have considered search table implementations with respect to only a subset of the ADT's operators. We have considered the operators Insert, Delete, Modify, and Select based on one attribute value at a time. This leaves the more general Select operator (based on a logical combination of attribute values) and the Project operator. In addition, we must consider expressions such as $\sigma_{Dept\,=\,\text{``Toys''}}(\Pi_{<SS\#,Dept>}\,EMPLOYEE)$, which contain more than one relational operator.

Project: Most of the interesting implementation issues regarding the support of the Project operator arise in the context of external storage implementations. In the context of internal implementations, support for the Project operator generally adds little to our previous discussions. Projection requires merely that we retrieve the data records corresponding to the tuples of the search table and then extract the fields specified in the projection. If projection is composed with selection in the same query, there is an issue of in what order to perform the operations. We discuss this problem briefly under the Query Optimization Issues heading at the conclusion of this section.

Multiple Attribute Selection: The most important form of multiple-attribute selection is called a **partial-match retrieval.** Here, we have a conjunction of attribute qualifications of the form

$$\sigma_{((A_1 op_1 V_1) AND \cdots AND (A_k op_k V_k))} T$$

where each op_i is a logical comparison operator (e.g., $=$, $<$, $>$). The need to support partial match retrievals leads to two issues:

1. How to choose which fields to index.
2. How best to utilize existing indices when processing the query.

The first issue is a generalization of the index selection problem raised in the previous section. The second question illustrates the interaction between implementation structures and the problem of query optimization. We shall consider the latter issue in a moment.

Before introducing query optimization issues, we note that there are approaches to the partial-match retrieval problem that differ from what we describe here. These approaches utilize structures specifically designed for partial-match retrievals. While such structures are ideal for partial-match retrievals (especially when many attribute values are specified), in general they are not as good for simple selections (and the Join queries we shall study in Section 2.4) as the basic single-attribute indices we have been discussing. In Chapter 9, in the context of external memory, we consider the problem of designing RDM implementations that efficiently support partial-match retrievals.

Query Optimization Issues: Let us suppose that we have chosen the implementation structures for our search table ADT, inserted into the table an initial set of tuples, and that we now are ready to process queries against the table. As noted in Chapter 1, there generally are many different ways to process a single query against the given implementation structures. **Query optimization** is the problem of choosing, for any given query (or update operation), the best processing strategy, and the **query optimizer** is the component of the search table or RDM implementation that addresses the query optimization problem. In terms of our perspective of ADT implementations as maps between levels of abstraction, the query optimizer has the task not only of mapping a relational expression into a correct sequence of low-level operations, but, when more than one correct sequence exists, of choosing the most efficient (or at least a very good) sequence.

As a very simple example of the query optimization problem, suppose that we have implemented the search table EMPLOYEE(SS#, Name, Salary, Dept) as a heap of data records (one record for each tuple in the table) with indices on attributes SS#, Salary, and Dept. Assume each index is structured as a 2–3 tree.

Consider first the query

$$\sigma_{(Name = \text{"Smith"}) AND (Dept = \text{"Toys"})} EMPLOYEE$$

At a high level, there are at least two plausible strategies for answering this query:

1. Find all employee records with Name = "Smith", and from these records, select the records with Dept = "Toys".
2. Find all employee records with Dept = "Toys", and from these records, select the records with Name = "Smith".

Because attribute Dept is indexed while attribute Name is not, strategy 2 is clearly superior. This strategy can be refined into the following algorithm:

```
Use index_Dept to retrieve into Temp all data records
  with Employee.Dept = "Toys"
Result ← ∅
for (each record R in Temp)
  if (R.Name = "Smith")
    Result ← Result ∪ {R}
  endif
end for
```

This algorithm can actually be improved a bit by performing the Name selection on record R at the time R is retrieved:

```
Result ← ∅
for (each index record in index_Dept with attribute value "Toys")
  Retrieve the corresponding data record R
  if (R.Name = "Smith")
    Result ← Result ∪ {R}
  endif
end for
```

This version of the algorithm improves on the first version in that it does not require temporary storage for all records with (Dept = "Toys"), and it does not require a second pass to select the records from Temp with (Name = "Smith").

As a second example of query optimization in processing partial match retrievals, consider the query

$$\sigma_{(Dept\ =\ \text{"Toys"})AND(Salary<25000)}\ EMPLOYEE$$

Since there is an index on each of the attributes Dept and Salary, there are several viable processing strategies, including,

```
Result ← ∅
for (each index record in index_Dept with attribute value "Toys")
  Retrieve the corresponding data record R
  if (R.Salary < 25000)
    Result ← Result ∪ {R}
  endif
end for
```

and

```
Result ← ∅
for (each index record in index_Salary with attribute value < 25000)
  Retrieve the corresponding data record R
  if (R.Dept = "Toys")
    Result ← Result ∪ {R}
  endif
end for
```

Which of these two strategies is better depends on which index will "filter" more records. That is, the **for** loop should iterate through the index that has the smaller number of records matching the specified value(s). A good query optimizer must have available to it information that allows such a decision to be made.

A second class of query optimization problem involves processing queries that contain more than one operator. Consider, for example, the query

$$\sigma_{Dept=\text{"Toys"}}(\Pi_{<SS\#,Dept>}\ EMPLOYEE)$$

It is easy to see that this query is equivalent to (in the sense that it evaluates to the same set of tuples) the query

$$\Pi_{<SS\#,Dept>}(\sigma_{Dept\ =\ \text{"Toys"}}\ EMPLOYEE)$$

This suggests two alternative processing strategies:

1. Form the projection of the EMPLOYEE table, placing the result in Temp. Select from Temp those tuples with (Dept = "Toys").
2. Select from the EMPLOYEE table those tuples with (Dept = "Toys"), placing the result in Temp. Form the projection of the tuples in Temp.

Strategy 2 is far superior because only it can use *index_Dept* to avoid retrieving all the EMPLOYEE records. (Observe that strategy 1 must not only retrieve all EMPLOYEE records to form the projection, but the selection from the Temp table must be performed by inspecting every tuple in Temp since *index_Dept* does not "point into" Temp and thus Temp is not indexed.)

There is a third strategy that is superior to either of the preceding two strategies. This strategy applies both operators in a single pass:

```
Result ← ∅
for (each index record in index_Dept with attribute value = "Toys")
  Retrieve the corresponding data record R
  Result ← Result ∪ {<R.SS#, R.Dept>}
end for
```

This is analogous to the single-pass strategy developed for the partial-match retrieval, but it introduces a significant new issue: *The query optimizer should be free to process a relational expression as a unit, rather than being restricted to applying the operators in sequence.* For example, if the optimizer could perform only a Select followed by a Project (or vice versa) and not interweave the required processing, the most efficient solution would not be available. In general, a query optimizer has more options than simply processing one relational operator after another; it may process a query using algorithms designed to implement certain combinations of the operators.[1] Consequently, a good implementation of the ADT search table or RDM requires more than efficient support of each individual ADT operator.

---

[1] This somewhat extends the traditional notion of an ADT implementation.

Even in the context of these simple examples, we see that a sophisticated query optimizer is a critical component of a good search table implementation. The query optimizer must be sensitive to what indices are present and have a means of estimating the number of tuples that match a given attribute value. In addition, the last example illustrates that a query optimizer must be more than "the sum of strategies for processing each relational operator." At the end of this chapter, in the context of the RDM ADT, we shall again consider query optimization issues, and query optimization will be an important topic when, later in the book, we study external implementations for the RDM ADT.

2.4 THE RELATIONAL DATA MODEL

The definition of the RDM ADT is built on the definition of the search table ADT developed in Section 2.2. The RDM $\mathcal{R}$ consists of a **relational scheme** and an **instance** of the relational scheme, where

Relational Scheme :: $\mathcal{R}$((<table_scheme>)*)

That is, a relational scheme is a list of zero or more table schemes. An instance of the relational scheme $\mathcal{R}$ is a collection of table scheme instances, one for each table scheme in $\mathcal{R}$'s list.

The definition of the ADT RDM provides 11 operators: σ, Π, $\leftarrow$, Add, Delete, and Modify defined previously for the search table, plus five new operators.

Definition of the ADT Relational Data Model Operators

1. Add_Scheme($\mathcal{R}$, *TS*)

   The Add_Scheme operator is analogous to the ADT search table's Create operator. If $\mathcal{R}$ is a relation scheme that does not yet exist, Add_Scheme($\mathcal{R}$,*TS*) creates the relation scheme $\mathcal{R}(TS)$ and initializes $\mathcal{R}(TS)$ to the instance that consists of the empty instance of table scheme *TS*. If relation scheme $\mathcal{R}$ $(TS_1, \ldots, TS_k)$ already exists, the effect of the operation Add_Scheme($\mathcal{R}$, *TS*) is to expand $\mathcal{R}$'s relation scheme to $\mathcal{R}$ $(TS_1, \ldots, TS_k, TS)$ and to initialize the current instance of the new relation scheme to the previous instance of the relation scheme plus the empty instance of table scheme *TS*. If *TS* is already part of the relation scheme $\mathcal{R}(TS)$, then Add_Scheme($\mathcal{R}$, *TS*) is a no-op.

2. Purge_Scheme($\mathcal{R}$,*TS*)

   A second operator on relation schemes is Purge_Scheme($\mathcal{R}$, TS_i). If $\mathcal{R}$ $(TS_1, \ldots, TS_i, \ldots, TS_k)$ is a relation scheme, then Purge_Scheme($\mathcal{R}$, TS_i) results in the relation scheme $\mathcal{R}$ $(TS_1, \ldots, TS_{i-1}, TS_{i+1}, \ldots, TS_k)$ and initializes the current instance of the new relation scheme to the previous instance of the relation scheme $\mathcal{R}$ minus the instance of table scheme TS_i that was part of the instance of relation scheme $\mathcal{R}$. The operation

Purge_Scheme($\mathcal{R}$, *TS*) is a no-op if table scheme *TS* is not part of the relation scheme $\mathcal{R}$ or if $\mathcal{R}$ does not exist.

The Relational Operators

The following five operators are referred to as **relational operators.** Their definitions assume the existence of a relational scheme $\mathcal{R}$ that contains the table schemes *T*(<att_list>) and *S*(<att_list>).

3–4. σ and Π (Select and Project)

These operators apply to any single table in the relational scheme, and their definitions are identical to the definitions given for the corresponding search table operators.

5. $T \cup S$ (Union)

T and *S* are tables from relational scheme $\mathcal{R}$, such that the schemes of *T* and *S* are over the same list of attribute names, though the domains of corresponding attributes may differ between the schemes. The expression evaluates to the table whose current instance is the set of tuples that is the union of the current instances of *T* and *S*. The resulting table inherits the scheme of the operand tables, where the domains of corresponding attributes are unioned together if they differ between the two operand table schemes.

6. $T - S$ (Difference)

T and *S* are tables from relational scheme $\mathcal{R}$, such that the schemes of *T* and *S* are over the same list of attribute names, though the domains of corresponding attributes may differ between the schemes. The expression evaluates to the table whose current instance is the set of tuples that is the difference of the current instances of *T* and *S*. The resulting table inherits the scheme of the operand tables, where the domains of corresponding attributes are unioned together if they differ between the two operand table schemes.

7. $T \times S$ (Cartesian product)

The Cartesian product operator resembles the Equi-join operator introduced in Chapter 1 but is a more primitive operator. The Cartesian product $T \times S$ is the table containing tuples $t \cdot s$ such that $t \in T$ and $s \in S$. For example, suppose that the values of tables *T* and *S* are

T

A	B	C
a	b	c
d	e	f
g	h	i

S

D	E
w	x
y	z

Then the value of the expression $T \times S$ is the table

A	*B*	*C*	*D*	*E*
a	*b*	*c*	*w*	*x*
a	*b*	*c*	*y*	*z*
d	*e*	*f*	*w*	*x*
d	*e*	*f*	*y*	*z*
g	*h*	*i*	*w*	*x*
g	*h*	*i*	*y*	*z*

More formally, the set of tuples that is the current instance of the resulting table is defined as follows: Let $A_1, \ldots, A_n$ be the attributes in T's scheme and $A_{n+1}, \ldots, A_m$ be the attributes in S's scheme. For each $1 \leq i \leq m$ let D_i denote the domain of A_i. Then, the resulting set of tuples is

$$\{ r \mid r: \bigcup_{i=1}^{m} \{A_i\} \rightarrow \bigcup_{i=1}^{m} D_i$$
$$\exists\, t \in T, s \in S$$
$$r[A_i] = t[A_i] \text{ if } 1 \leq i \leq n$$
$$r[A_i] = s[A_i] \text{ if } n + 1 \leq i \leq m \}$$

The resulting table inherits the table scheme with attribute list $<A_1 = D_1, \ldots, A_n = D_n, A_{n+1} = D_{n+1}, \ldots, A_m = D_m>$. If an attribute from table T and an attribute from table S have a common name, in the result of the Cartesian product, these attribute names are prefixed with either "T." or "S." to indicate from which table the attribute came, for example, $T.A_i$ or $S.A_i$. Alternatively, it sometimes is convenient to use $A_i(1)$ and $A_i(2)$ to indicate from which operand table an occurrence of attribute A_i is derived.

Note that the Cartesian product operator differs from the Equi-join operator in that the result of a Cartesian product is the concatenation of all tuple pairs, *without restriction to matching attribute values*. The Equi-join $T \underset{A=B}{\bowtie} S$ can be written as a composition of the Select and Cartesian product operators: $\sigma_{A=B}(T \times S)$. Because Equi-join models an important and frequent task, we retain the symbol as shorthand for the preceding composition of Select and Cartesian product, though we do not include Equi-join as a primitive operator. Note that since a query optimizer may process the query $\sigma_{A=B}(T \times S)$ in ways different from a Cartesian product followed by a selection (see the discussions at the end of Section 2.3 and Section 2.5), we do not sacrifice anything in the way of efficiency by not including Equi-join as a primitive operator in the definition of the RDM ADT.

In addition to the ADD_Scheme and Purge_Scheme operators and the five relational operators, the RDM retains from the search table definition the four update operators ←, Add, Delete, and Modify. Hence, the following summarizes the 11 primitive operators of the RDM:

RDM Operators
Scheme operators: Add_Scheme, Purge_Scheme
Relational operators: σ, Π, $\cup$, $-$, $\times$
Update operators: $\leftarrow$, Add, Delete, Modify

We make one final comment regarding the definition of the RDM. From our previous discussions, the reader may have the impression that the RDM derives its name from the fact that intertable relationships are so conveniently supported. In truth, the term derives from the more traditional definition of the RDM that is based on the mathematical notion of a relation:

Given a collection of sets $S_1, \ldots, S_n$, the **Cartesian product** of the S_i (not to be confused with the Cartesian product operator) is the set of n-ary vectors

$$S_1 \times \cdots S_n = \{<v_1 \ldots v_n> | v_i \in S_i\}$$

A **relation** over the sets $S_1, \cdots, S_n$ is any subset of the Cartesian product $S_1 \times \ldots \times S_n$.

The mathematical notion of a relation thus corresponds closely to our definition of an instance of a search table.

Properties of the RDM Operators

When one studies a set of operators there are, in general, two important questions to consider: Is the set of operators **independent,** and is the set **complete**? A set S of operators is independent if removing any one of the operators *op* from the set would diminish the set's power, that is, if there exists an expression involving the operators in S whose value is not attained by any expression involving the operators in $S - \{op\}$. (Equivalently, a set S is *not* independent if it contains an operator *op* that is **redundant** in the sense that *op* can be expressed in terms of the operators in $S - \{op\}$.) There are many motivations for defining an ADT in terms of an independent set of operators: An attempt to define the RDM with a system of axioms (see exercise 2.17) will convince the reader of the undesirability of having to rigorously specify more operators than is necessary. In fact, it can be established that the set of relational operators $\{\sigma, \Pi, \cup, -, \times\}$ is an independent set.

A set of operators is complete if it is capable of expressing "everything." Obviously, completeness must be measured with respect to some benchmark! Typically, a query language that is a form of the first-order predicate calculus is the benchmark against which database operators are measured. (SELECT queries from Chapter 1 are a restricted form of the first-order calculus language.) We shall say that a set of operators is complete if it is capable of expressing everything that is expressible in the first-order predicate calculus query language. In Chapter 3, we formally define a predicate calculus query language and argue that it and our set of five relational operators have equivalent expressive power.

Additional Operators

We introduce three additional operators that are shorthand for common tasks that would otherwise require complex relational expressions.

The Natural Join Operator: Consider the following pair of table instances:

INVENTORY

Manuf	Model	Price	Quantity
IBM	360	1 mil	3
IBM	XT	5K	100
DEC	11/780	100k	20
DEC	II	20K	30

DESCRIPTION

Manuf	Model	Desc
IBM	360	Big
IBM	XT	Nice
DEC	11/780	Reliable
DEC	II	Wonderful

A very natural request is to build a single table containing all the information about each item contained in the two tables. This request can be satisfied using the Cartesian product operator, as in the following relational expression:

$$\Pi_{<Manuf, Model, Price, Quantity, Desc>}(\sigma_{INVENTORY.Model = DESCRIPTION.Model \wedge INVENTORY.Manuf = DESCRIPTION.Manuf})$$
$$(INVENTORY \times DESCRIPTION))$$

When applied to the instances of these tables, the relational expression evaluates to the table:

Manuf	Model	Price	Quantity	Desc
IBM	360	1 mil	3	Big
IBM	XT	5K	100	Nice
DEC	11/780	100k	20	Reliable
DEC	II	20K	30	Wonderful

Observe that this task requires a generalized type of Equi-join—matching values of all attributes with the same name—followed by a projection to eliminate the redundant attributes from the resulting table. This task is so natural that we introduce the **natural join** operator, denoted $\bowtie$, to carry it out. Thus, the preceding task can be written as

INVENTORY $\bowtie$ DESCRIPTION

The Θ-Join Operator: The Θ-join generalizes Equi-join in a somewhat different manner than does the natural join. To illustrate the Θ-join operator, suppose that we have the following pair of table instances:

PRICES

Prod#	Price
001	255
006	350
999	10,000

CUSTOMERS

Acct#	Cash_Available
634	500
564	275
777	20,000

and we desire a listing of customer accounts along with the products each can afford to purchase. This request can be satisfied using the Cartesian product operator, as in the following relational expression:

$$\Pi_{<Acct\#, Prod\#>} (\sigma_{Cash\_Available \geq Price} (CUSTOMERS \times PRICES))$$

The Θ-join operator (denoted generically as $\underset{\Theta}{\bowtie}$) combines a simple selection criterion with the Cartesian product operator and allows the preceding query to be written as follows:

$$\Pi_{<Acct\#, Prod\#>} (CUSTOMERS \underset{Cash\_Available \geq Price}{\bowtie} PRICES)$$

In general, Θ can be any one of the standard logical comparators (i.e., $=$, $<$, $>$, $\leq$, $\geq$, $\neq$). Note that the Equi-join operator is the special case of the Θ-join when Θ is equality.

The Divide Operator: Consider the following table instances:

TEACHES

Prof	Course
Smith	CS101
Smith	CS102
Smith	CS103
Jones	CS101
Jones	CS103
Freed	CS101

OFFERINGS

Course	Description
CS101	Programming
CS102	Analysis of algorithms
CS103	AI

Suppose we wish to answer the following query: "List the names of the professors who teach *every* course listed in OFFERINGS." Assuming the table instances shown, the result of this query would consist of the single professor Smith.

This query is difficult to express in terms of the relational operators, but the following expression does the trick:

$$(\Pi_{<Prof>} \mathit{TEACHES}) - (\Pi_{<Prof>}((\Pi_{<Prof>} \mathit{TEACHES} \times \Pi_{<Course>} \mathit{OFFERINGS}) - \mathit{TEACHES}))$$

Observe that the inner difference results in a table consisting of all $<Prof,Course>$ tuples such that *Prof* does not teach *Course*, where *Course* appears in OFFERINGS. Hence, the outer difference results in the professors who teach every course listed in OFFERINGS.

The Divide operator ($\div$) is introduced to simplify the statement of queries such as this. Let T be a table with the n attributes $A_1, \cdots, A_{(n-m)}, A_{(n-m+1)}, \cdots, A_n$ and let S be a table with m attributes $B_1, \cdots, B_m$ $(n > m)$. The expression $T \div S$ evaluates to a table with the $n - m$ attributes $A_1, \cdots, A_{n-m}$, such that t is a tuple in $T \div S$ if and only if for *every* tuple $s \in S$ there exists a tuple v over the attributes $\{A_{(n-m+1)}, \cdots, A_n\}$, where $v[A_{(n-m)+j}] = s[B_j]$ $(1 \leq j \leq m)$, and where $t \cdot v$ is a tuple in T.

This request illustrates the utility of the Divide operator; it can be expressed simply as $\mathit{TEACHES} \div (\Pi_{<Course>} \mathit{OFFERINGS})$.

2.5 BASIC INTERNAL IMPLEMENTATION ISSUES FOR THE RDM ADT

Once again we take a peek at the lower levels of abstraction and consider some basic implementation issues for the RDM ADT. As is the case for the search table, our study of internal implementations for the RDM previews, in a simple form, the techniques used in external storage implementations.

Many of the issues and techniques introduced in the context of search table implementations apply to the RDM as well. Especially important are the indexing schemes we developed to support the flexible Select operator common to both ADTs. The new issues that arise in the implementation of the RDM ADT primarily concern the support of the binary operators Join, Union, and Difference. In this section, we concentrate on the basic issues that arise when supporting the Join operator. In Chapter 11, we shall study Join implementations in far greater depth, while the exercises consider implementations of the Union and Difference operators.

We shall consider here only Equi-joins of the form

$$R \underset{A=B}{\bowtie} S$$

This is by far the most common multiple-table operation, and its internal implementations are the building blocks for implementations of the other multiple-table operations, both internal and external.

There is a close relationship between the structures used to implement the RDM and the processing algorithms the query optimizer can select to perform a join. The following discussion is organized around the several possible implementations of tables R and S, the components of the RDM involved in the join in question. For each of several possible organizations, we describe and analyze an algorithm that could be used to perform the join.

1. *Neither Join attribute is indexed:* If there is not an index on either attribute A of table R or attribute B of table S (and the data records are stored in a random heap), the join can be slow. In this case, the basic join algorithm has the following form:

```
Result ← ∅
for (each tuple r in table R)
  for (each tuple s in table S)
    if (r.A = s.B)
      Result ← Result ∪ {r·s}
    endif
  end for
end for
```

   This **unindexed loop join** requires $O(|R| * |S|)$ time, where $|R|$ and $|S|$ denote the number of tuples in the current instances of tables R and S, respectively.

2. *A Join attribute is indexed:* If there is an index on either attribute A of table R or attribute B of table S, the join can be performed significantly more efficiently than in the preceding case. Here, the Join algorithm has the following form (assume the index is on attribute B of table S):

```
Result ← ∅
for (each tuple r in table R)
  Use index_B to retrieve each tuple s with s.B = r.A
    for (each tuple s retrieved)
      Result ← Result ∪ {r·s}
    end for
end for
```

   The time required for this algorithm depends on the efficiency of retrievals via *index_B* and on the number of tuples in the resulting join. Assume that the time to retrieve via *index_B* k tuples with the same value in attribute B is $\log(|S|) + k$ [and the time to determine that no tuple in table S has attribute value V is $\log(|S|)$]. Then, since the outer **for** loop is executed $|R|$ times and a total of $|R \underset{A=B}{\bowtie} S|$ tuples are retrieved via *index_B*, the total time for this **indexed loop join** is $O(|R| * \log(|S|) + |R \underset{A=B}{\bowtie} S|)$. Note that when joining two tables, each of which has an index on the Join attribute, the table with fewer tuples should play the role of R in the preceding algorithm.

3. *Each Join attribute is indexed with a dense ordered index:* An index structure (e.g., a 2–3 tree) is an **ordered index** on an attribute if it sup-

ports efficient retrieval of tuples ordered by that attribute. If both Join attributes have an ordered index, the join can be performed by a linear "merge" of the indices:

```
Result ← ∅
ARec ← first record from index_A
BRec ← first record from index_B
r_Set ← ∅
s_Set ← ∅
while (more index records in both index files)
  if (ARec.A < BRec.B)
    advance through index_A until a new value is encountered
    { ARec is the first record with the new value }
  elseif (ARec.A > BRec.B)
    advance through index_B until a new value is encountered
    { BRec is the first record with the new value }
  else { attribute values match—common value is V }
    { use index_A and index_B to get data records with value V }
    while (ARec.A = V)
      add to r_Set data record pointed to by ARec
      ARec ← next record in index_A
    end while
    while (BRec.B = V)
      add to s_Set data record pointed to by BRec
      BRec ← next record in index_B
    end while
    { form Cartesian product of r_Set and s_Set adding to Result }
    Result ← RESULT U r_Set X s_Set
  endif
  r_Set ← ∅
  s_Set ← ∅
end while
```

The algorithm is linear in that we start at the beginning of each index and visit each index record only once in an ordered traversal. This technique assumes that for each attribute value V, we have sufficient temporary memory to store the sets *r_Set* and *s_Set* of matching tuples. Once the sets *r_Set* and *s_Set* have been constructed, the Cartesian product can be computed in time $O(|r\_Set| * |s\_Set|)$. Since the sum over all matching attribute values V of the sizes of these products is $|R \underset{A=B}{\bowtie} S|$, the total time for this **merge join** is $O(|R| + |S| + |R \underset{A=B}{\bowtie} S|)$.

The three implementations described thus far do not exploit the fact that tables R and S are components of a single RDM ADT. That is, the implementations we have considered store each table as an isolated collection of data records. Although each of these tables may be indexed on the Join attribute to speed the Join, each such index is part of the *isolated implementation of one of the tables*. We now consider an implementation that exploits the fact that the tables R and S are components of a single ADT and builds a structure that *con-*

nects the tables. This connecting structure allows the Join to be performed more efficiently than is possible under the implementations considered previously.

Suppose tables R and S are initially implemented using one of the techniques described in Section 2.3, without regard to efficient support for the Join. Conceptually, we add a new intermediate table RJS "connecting" R and S. For each tuple $r \cdot s$ that appears in the Join $R \underset{A=B}{\bowtie} S$, we store in table RJS a tuple containing the value $V = R.A = S.B$, along with pointers to tuples $r \in R$ and $s \in S$. Table RJS is then implemented as any other table (e.g., it may be indexed on attribute V) but is invisible to the users and is used only by query-processing algorithms when performing the Join. The Join $R \underset{A=B}{\bowtie} S$ is performed by traversing RJS, following each pair of pointers to $r \in R$ and $s \in S$ and adding tuple $r \cdot s$ to the result of the Join. The time required to perform the join with this scheme is $O(|R \underset{A=B}{\bowtie} S|)$.

The drawbacks of the scheme of course are the additional space required for the table RJS and the additional time required to perform operations that update tables R and S. (Note that to perform an update to table R or S, we must compute the update's effect on the Join and update table RJS accordingly.) Whether or not an intermediate join table is appropriate depends on the expected frequency of the Join as compared with that of update operations, memory constraints, and the expected sizes of tables R and S as compared with the expected size of the Join of these tables (which can be anywhere between 0 and $|R|*|S|$ tuples). Note that when the size of the Join is relatively small, not only is the additional space and update overhead incurred by the join table small, but the increased efficiency in performing the Join afforded by the join table is large. For example, the advantage of an $O(|R \underset{A=B}{\bowtie} S|)$ time join over the $O(|R + |S| + |R \underset{A=B}{\bowtie} S|)$ time required for a merge join grows as $|R \underset{A=B}{\bowtie} S|$ shrinks in comparison to $|R|$ and $|S|$.

We have barely scratched the surface of the issues surrounding the implementation of the Join operator. In the context of external memory implementations of the RDM, we shall further consider methods for supporting Joins between tables. Many of the external methods are similar to those we have introduced here. Other methods adopt new strategies in an attempt to reduce the inefficiencies created by the characteristics of external storage devices.

In the context of query optimization (Chapters 11 and 12), we shall study a second issue related to the processing of Join operations. This issue concerns the processing of a query that contains several Join operators and possibly several other relational operators as well [e.g., the query $\sigma_{A=V}(R \underset{A=B}{\bowtie} (S \underset{C=D}{\bowtie} T))$]. As we shall see, the order in which we apply the operators can have a dramatic effect on efficiency (see exercise 2.14). The optimal order for performing the operators depends on factors such as how the tables involved are implemented, the sizes of the tables, and the sizes of the intermediate results. The solution of this type of optimization problem is one of the major tasks confronting the implementors of an RDM.

SUMMARY AND ANNOTATED BIBLIOGRAPHY

In this chapter, we defined the ADT search table and RDM in terms of relational operators (as well as operators that modify schemes and table instances). The relational operators are based on Codd's original definitions [see Codd (1970)]. While these definitions are of sufficient rigor for our purpose, an important problem for theoreticians and software engineers is to define ADTs in a manner that supports formal analyses. For example, proofs of correctness of a software system (e.g., a DBMS) that utilizes ADTs require a completely formal definition of the operators. A system of axioms is the most common mechanism for formally defining an ADT. The exercises briefly consider this approach; for more details, the reader is referred to Aho, Hopcroft, and Ullman (1983); Goguen, Thatcher, and Wagner (1977); Guttag (1977); Lewis and Denenberg (1991); and Moret (1983).

The RDM is at the heart of relational DBMSs. This chapter previewed issues critical to the successful implementation of a relational DBMS by introducing implementation issues for internal memory storage structures. While a relational DBMS is traditionally implemented on external memory devices such as disks, the internal memory techniques presented here are important as they foreshadow many of the most important external memory techniques. Further motivating our interest in internal memory techniques is the fact that main memory database machines, in which large portions of the database are stored internally, define an increasingly important implementation environment. Of the data structures presented here, 2–3 trees and hashed structures will be the most important for our study of external memory implementations, which begins in Chapter 7. The reader is referred to Aho, Hopcroft, and Ullman (1983); Helman and Veroff (1986); Horowitz and Sahni (1976); Knuth (1973); Lewis and Denenberg (1991); and Riengold and Hanson (1983), for a discussion of these internal data structures. Knuth in particular presents an extensive study of the selection of hash functions to reduce collisions and of collision resolution methods.

This chapter previewed also the query optimization problem. Just as internal storage structures foreshadow external storage structures, the query optimization problem for an internal implementation environment foreshadows the problem of query optimization in an external implementation environment. The most important query optimization issues previewed in this chapter include choosing between alternative algorithms for implementing a relational operator and selecting the order in which to apply the operators that appear in a relational expression. The satisfactory solution to both problems requires that the query optimizer consider such factors as table sizes, the distribution data values, and the existence of auxiliary structures such as indices. We study in ernest query optimization beginning in Chapter 11.

EXERCISES

1. Demonstrate that a function can have an inverse only if it is injective.
2. Consider the following two table instances:

R

A	B	C
a	x	y
a	z	w
b	x	k
b	m	j
c	x	y
f	g	h

S

D	E
x	y
z	w

Give the *exact* table instance that will result from each of the following queries:

a. $\Pi_{<A>}(R \underset{B \neq D}{\bowtie} S)$
b. $\Pi_{<A>}(R) - \Pi_{<A>}(R \underset{B=D}{\bowtie} S)$
c. $\Pi_{<A>}(R) - \Pi_{<A>}(R \div S)$
d. $\Pi_{<A>}(R) - \Pi_{<A>}(R \times S)$

3. Consider the following two table instances:

R

A	B	C	D
a	1	2	x
a	2	2	x
b	1	2	x
b	1	3	x
b	2	2	x
c	5	2	x

S

B	C	D	E
1	2	x	p
1	3	x	q
2	2	x	r

Give the *exact* table instance that will result from each of the following queries:

a. $R \bowtie S$
b. $R \div \Pi_{<B,C,D>}(S)$
c. $R \div \Pi_{<B>}(S)$
d. $R \underset{B \neq B}{\bowtie} S$

4. Consider the following two table instances:

R

A	B	C
a_1	b_1	c_1
a_1	b_2	c_2
a_2	b_1	c_1

S

B	C
b_1	c_1
b_2	c_2

Give the *exact* table instance that will result from each of the following queries:

a. $R \div S$
b. $R \div (\sigma_{B \neq b_2} S)$
c. $(R \times S) - \sigma_{R.C=S.C}(R \underset{(B=B)}{\bowtie} S)$

5. Consider the following table schemes of an RDM:

   EMPLOYEE(SS#, Name, Salary, Dept)
   PERSONAL(SS#, Age, Highest_Degree)
   DEPARTMENT(Dept, Manager, Location, D_Desc)

   Assume that the semantics of these schemes are as discussed throughout the chapter. Express each of the following in relational algebra:

   a. Retrieve the SS# and name of all employees of the toys department who earn between $20,000 and $40,000.

   b. Retrieve the SS# and name of all employees whose highest degree is a BA and who earn between $20,000 and $40,000.

   c. Retrieve the SS# and name of all employees whose manager is Smith and who earn between $20,000 and $40,000.

   d. Retrieve the SS# and name of all employees whose highest degree is a BA, whose manager is Smith, and who earn between $20,000 and $40,000.

6. Consider the following table schemes of an RDM:

   EMPLOYEE(Name, Dept, Salary)
   DEPARTMENT(Dept, Manager)

   Assume that managers are also employees, that every department has exactly one manager, that every manager manages exactly one department, and that no two employees have the same name. Express each of the following in relational algebra:

   a. Retrieve nonmanagers who earn more than at least one manager.

   b. Retrieve nonmanagers who earn more than all managers.

   c. Retrieve nonmanagers who earn more than their own manager.

7. Consider the following table schemes of an RDM:

   PATIENT(Name, Disease, Treatment)
   DOCTOR(Name, Specialty)

   Assume that Names uniquely identify both patients and doctors and that some doctors may also be patients. Assume that diseases and specialties are the same kinds of things (e.g., Flu might be both a disease and a specialty). A doctor may have more than one specialty, a patient may have more than one disease, and each disease a patient has may be treated in more than one way. Express each of the following in relational algebra:

   a. Retrieve the names of doctors who have a disease that is one of their specialties.

   b. Retrieve the names of doctors who have all the diseases that are their specialties.

   c. Retrieve the diseases for which there is only one treatment.

d. Retrieve the names of the patients P with some disease (call it D) such that if any other patient P' is receiving some treatment T for D, then P also is receiving T for D. That is, we want those patients with some disease who are receiving all known treatments for that disease.

8. Consider the following table schemes of an RDM:

    SHIP(S_Name, Captain)
    CREW(C_Name, Planet, S_Name)
    GROWS(Planet, Flower)
    ALLERGIES(C_Name, Flower)

    Express each of the following in relational algebra:

    a. Get the names of crewmembers allergic to no flowers that grow on their home planet.

    b. Get the names of crewmembers allergic to all flowers that grow on their home planet.

    c. Get the names of crewmembers allergic only to flowers that grow on their home planet (and possibly grow elsewhere).

    d. Get the names of crewmembers allergic to all the flowers that do not grow on their home planet.

    e. Get the names of crewmembers allergic to exactly the same flowers their captains are allergic to.

9. Let $R(A,B,C)$ and $S(A,B,C)$ be table schemes. Prove or disprove: For all instances of R and S

    $$\Pi_{<A>}(R-S) = \Pi_{<A>}(R)-\Pi_{<A>}(S)$$

10. Let $R(A_1, \ldots, A_i, A_{i+1}, \ldots, A_k)$ be any table scheme. Consider, for any i, $1 \leq i < k$, the algebraic expression

    $$((\Pi_{<A_1,A_2,\ldots,A_i>}(R) \underset{A_i T A_{i+1}}{\bowtie} \Pi_{<A_{i+1},\ldots,A_k>}(R)) \cap R)$$

    Write an equivalent algebraic expression that contains a single relational algebra operator.

11. As we have discussed, the index selection problem requires that we select both the attributes of a table that are to be indexed and the structure for each index we choose to maintain. In some situations, it might be appropriate to maintain more than one index on the same attribute. Describe a situation that would mandate maintaining both a hashed index and a 2–3 tree index on a single attribute. What penalties are incurred when multiple indexes are maintained?

12. We included in our definitions of the search table and RDM the operation Modify(T, E, val_list). Demonstrate that this operation can be expressed as a sequence of Select, Delete, and Add operations, provided that a facility exists for iterating through the set of tuples returned by a

Select operation. What are the potential disadvantages of expressing Modify in such a manner?

13. Let $T_1(A,B,C)$ and $T_2(A,B,C)$ be two tables of an RDM, each of which is implemented in an internal array.
    a. Describe and analyze algorithms for performing $T_1 - T_2$ and $T_1 \cup T_2$ under the assumption that no index structures exist on these tables.
    b. What index structures would make these operations more efficient? Describe and analyze algorithms that exploit such index structures.
    c. Can either of these operations be aided if the arrays are stored sorted? Justify your answer.

14. Consider the relational expression $((R \bowtie (S) \bowtie T))$. Because the Natural Join operator is associative, each of the following strategies computes the required result:
    i. Compute $R \bowtie S$ and Join the result with T. This strategy corresponds to the associatiion $((R \bowtie (S) \bowtie T))$.
    ii. Compute $S \bowtie T$ and Join the result with R. This strategy corresponds to the associatiion $((R \bowtie (S) \bowtie T))$.
    a. Analyze how the existence of indices on various combinations of the tables affects the best choice of an association.
    b. Analyze how the sizes of the current instances of the tables and the size of the table resulting from the first Join affect the best choice of an association.
    c. Based on your analyses in parts *a* and *b*, propose general rules of thumb for determining which association a query optimizer should select.

15. Consider the table schemes and queries of exercise 5. Suppose that each of EMPLOYEE, PERSONAL, and DEPARTMENT is stored in an internal array. Suppose further that 2–3 tree indices are maintained on EMPLOYEE.SS#, EMPLOYEE.Salary, and PERSONAL.SS#, while hashed indices are maintained on EMPLOYEE.Dept, PERSONAL. Highest_Degree, DEPARTMENT.Dept, and Department.Manager.
    a. Construct for each query of exercise 5 at least two reasonable processing algorithms.
    b. What information (e.g., table sizes, distribution of data values) would you need to know to select between the processing algorithms?
    c. Postulate information of the type identified in part *b* and analyze the algorithms of part *a* with respect to these postulates.

16. Let $R(A,B)$ and $S(C)$ be two tables stored in internal arrays R and S. Assume that each tuple in R corresponds to a record with fields A and B and that each tuple in S corresponds to a record with field C. Assume further that the records in S are stored sorted on field C and that the

records in R are stored sorted on field A, such that records with equal values on field A are further sorted on field B. Describe an efficient algorithm for implementing the operation $R \div S$. Analyze the efficiency of your algorithm.

*17. Typically, when we wish to rigorously define an ADT, we construct a system of axioms. For example, the following system defines the ADT stack:

Empty(Create(S)) = TRUE
Empty(Push(S,X)) = FALSE
Top(Create(S)) = ERROR
Top(Push(S,X)) = X
Pop(Create(S)) = ERROR
Pop(Push(S,X)) = S

a. Construct a system of axioms that defines the ADT search table.

b. Construct a system of axioms that defines the ADT RDM.

CHAPTER 3

Nonprocedural Query Languages

In Chapter 1, we introduced the nonprocedural SELECT-based query language, and in Chapter 2, we studied the somewhat more procedural relational operators. In this chapter, we develop the mathematical foundations of nonprocedural languages and explore the relationship between nonprocedural languages and the relational algebra. Additionally, we study SQL, the most prevalent commercial query language.•

As Figure 3.1 illustrates, we can view the processing required by nonprocedural languages in terms of two major steps: mapping nonprocedural queries into more procedural relational expressions and mapping these relational expressions into file- and data structure–level operations. A good query optimizer must construct maps that not only are correct, but that are efficient as well. In this chapter, we explore some issues of query optimization, especially those pertaining to the mapping from a nonprocedural query to a relational expression. Later chapters consider how to map from relational expressions to efficient processing strategies at the file structure level.

Nonprocedural language
↓
Relational algebra (RDM operators)
↓
Data/file structures and algorithms

Figure 3.1 Query processing map

3.1 MATHEMATICAL DEVELOPMENT OF NONPROCEDURAL QUERY LANGUAGES

Nonprocedural query languages are based on formal mathematical logic. The basic query language with which we will work—**tuple calculus**—is based on **first-order predicate calculus.** It is not possible in this book to present a complete review of the predicate calculus. For such a review, the reader is referred to Bridge (1977), and Chang and Lee (1979). Here we present a summary of those aspects of predicate calculus that bear most directly on the tuple calculus.

First-order predicate calculus is a language for making statements of fact. Every legal expression in the predicate calculus is a statement of fact that **evaluates** to either **true** or **false.** The fundamental concepts are best illustrated by an example. Consider the following predicate calculus expression:

$$(\forall x)(\exists y)(PERSON\ (x) \Rightarrow (PERSON(y) \wedge LOVES(y,x)))$$

This expression contains all the components that make up predicate calculus expressions in general:

1. *Variables:* x and y are variables. Shortly, we will formalize the kinds of values that these variables take on, but for now, suppose that each variable can take on any value in *the entire universe;* e.g., x can take on the value of my dog Max, my computer, the planet Uranus, or my friend Bob.
2. *Predicates:* PERSON and LOVES are predicates. A predicate often takes variables as arguments and, intuitively speaking, makes an assertion about the values of its arguments. For example, PERSON(x) can be interpreted as making the assertion that the value of x is a person, and LOVES(y,x) can be interpreted as making the assertion that the value of y loves the value of x. A predicate, along with its arguments, is called an **atom** [e.g., LOVES(y,x) in our sample predicate calculus expression is an atom]. An atom, like the predicate calculus expression that contains it, evaluates to either true or false based on the validity of its assertion.
3. *Logical connectives:* The symbols $\Rightarrow$ and $\wedge$ are logical connectives that have the standard meaning of logical implication and logical conjunction, respectively. Other logical connectives include $\vee$ (or) and $\neg$ (not). Every logical connective in a predicate calculus expression is a Boolean-valued function over one or more Boolean-valued arguments. For example, in our sample predicate calculus expression, $\wedge$ is a Boolean-valued function with the Boolean-valued expressions PERSON(y) and LOVES(y,x) as its arguments.
4. *Quantifiers:* $\forall$ (the **universal quantifier**) and $\exists$ (the **existential quantifier**) are quantifiers. Each quantifier takes one variable as argument (the quantifier is said to **range** over this variable) and specifies "how sweeping" the predicate calculus expression is with respect to this variable. For example, $\forall x$ is read "for all x" and specifies that the statement holds for all values x can have. In contrast, $\exists\, y$ is read "There exists at least one y" and specifies that the statement holds for at least one value that y can have. As we soon shall see, the choice and placement of quantifiers is critical to the meaning of an expression.

Putting together these four components, we can attach to our sample predicate calculus expression the following meaning:

> For all x, there exists at least one y such that x is a person implies that y is a person and y loves x.

Several subtle points arise from this English translation:

1. While the "natural" meaning of PERSON(x), PERSON(y), and LOVES(y,x) may be that x and y are persons and that y loves x, predicates are merely symbols. It was an arbitrary decision to attach the

meanings we did to these predicates. For example, a less natural, though equally valid, translation of the predicate calculus expression is

> For all x, there exists at least one y such that x is a dog implies that y is a dog and y speaks to x in French.

Given that these translations are equally valid, how can we evaluate to true or false a predicate calculus expression? The answer is that we can do so only in the context of an **interpretation.** As we shortly shall see, one effect of specifying an interpretation for a predicate calculus expression is to associate with predicate symbols "semantic meaning." We shall return to interpretations later.

2. The appearance in a predicate calculus expression of the logical implication connective (⇒) is for many people a source of confusion. As was mentioned earlier, a logical connective is a Boolean-valued function of Boolean arguments. Logical implication is a function of two arguments, and, for convenience, we review here the truth table that defines this function:

arg1	**arg2**	**arg1 ⇒ arg2**
T	*T*	*T*
T	*F*	*F*
F	*T*	*T*
F	*F*	*T*

With this in mind, consider the following subexpression of our predicate calculus expression:

$(PERSON(x) \Rightarrow (PERSON(y) \wedge LOVES(y,x)))$

Note, for example, that (assuming for the moment the natural meaning of the predicates)

a. If y is a person and y loves x then the subexpression evaluates to true *regardless of whether x is a person.*

b. If x is not a person, the subexpression evaluates to true *regardless of whether y is a person and regardless of whether y loves x.*

3. The choice and placement of the quantifiers is critical to the meaning of the predicate calculus expression. Our sample expression contains the construction $(\forall x)(\exists y)$. The meaning given by this construction to the expression

$(\forall x)(\exists y)(PERSON(x) \Rightarrow (PERSON(y) \wedge LOVES(y,x)))$

is that the expression evaluates to true if and only if for any x in our universe, we can find at least one y in our universe such that the subexpression

$$(PERSON(x) \Rightarrow (PERSON(y) \wedge LOVES(y,x)))$$

evaluates to true. To illustrate, we consider some steps that might be performed in the course of evaluating the expression. In the following, we again attach to the predicates their "natural" meaning and assume that the variables can take on any values in the universe.

a. We first consider the subexpression when x has John Doe as its value. We must find a value for y (from our universe of values) that causes the subexpression to evaluate to true. We find in our universe the value Jane Doe. It turns out that not only is Jane Doe a person but that Jane loves her husband John. Hence, the right side $(PERSON(y) \wedge LOVES(y,x)))$ of the implication

$$(PERSON(x) \Rightarrow (PERSON(y) \wedge LOVES(y,x)))$$

evaluates to true for these values of x and y, and thus, we have demonstrated that when x has the value of John Doe, we can find at least one y for which the subexpression

$$(PERSON(x) \Rightarrow (PERSON(y) \wedge LOVES(y,x)))$$

evaluates to true.

b. We now consider the subexpression when x has Bill Smith as its value. Unfortunately, Jane Doe does not love Bill Smith, and, since Bill Smith is a person, the subexpression

$$(PERSON(x) \Rightarrow (PERSON(y) \wedge LOVES(y,x)))$$

evaluates to false for these values of x and y. However, this does not mean that the expression

$$(\forall x)(\exists y)(PERSON(x) \Rightarrow (PERSON(y) \wedge LOVES(y,x)))$$

evaluates to false. The placement as $(\forall x)(\exists y)$ of the quantifiers specifies that we can choose a different y for each x under consideration. Since Mary Smith loves Bill Smith, when x has the value of Bill Smith we can choose for y the value of Mary Smith and the expression

$$(PERSON(x) \Rightarrow (PERSON(y) \wedge \mathrm{LOVES}(y,x)))$$

will evaluate to true.

c. We now consider the subexpression when x has the rock on my desk as its value. It turns out that we cannot find in the universe of values a value that loves this rock. Does this mean that the expression

$$(\forall x)(\exists y)(PERSON(x) \Rightarrow (PERSON(y) \wedge LOVES(y,x)))$$

evaluates to false? No, because for this value of x the left side of the subexpression

$$(PERSON(x) \Rightarrow (PERSON(y) \wedge LOVES(y,x)))$$

evaluates to false, and thus the subexpression is true regardless of what value we choose for *y*. In a sense, the structure of the subexpression gives us a free ride when the *x* under consideration is not a person—in this case, the subexpression will *evaluate to true for any value of y*.

d. At what point do we conclude that we have considered enough values for *x* and that we are able to decide on the value of the expression? Clearly, if we consider a value for *x* (from our universe) for which we can't find a *y* such that the subexpression

   (PERSON(x)⇒(PERSON(y)∧LOVES(y,x)))

   evaluates to true, we can stop and conclude that the expression

   (∀x)(∃y)(PERSON(x)⇒(PERSON(y)∧LOVES(y,x)))

   evaluates to false. However, before we can conclude that the expression evaluates to true, we would have to demonstrate that for every *x* in our universe we can find in our universe a value for *y* for which the expression evaluates to true. If our universe is infinite, we certainly can't demonstrate this by continuing on a case-by-case basis. Often, when dealing with an infinite universe, we exhibit an algorithm that, given any *x* value, constructs the required *y* value. In the database contexts with which we shall deal, however, the universe of possible values for our quantified variables will always be finite.

Before moving on to the important topic of interpretations, we reinforce some of the previous points by considering the effect on meaning of several different modifications in the construction of our sample tuple calculus expression.

1. *(∃y)(∀x)(PERSON(x)⇒(PERSON(y)∧LOVES(y,x)))*

   The English translation of this expression is

   > There exists at least one *y* such that for all *x*, *x* is a person implies that *y* is a person and *y* loves *x*.

   This meaning differs from that of the original expression in that the new expression evaluates to true if and only if there is a *single* value for *y* that causes the subexpression

   (PERSON(x)⇒(PERSON(y)∧LOVES(y,x)))

   to evaluate to true for *all values of x*. Hence, it is not sufficient to find for each *x* a person *y* that loves *x*; rather, there needs to be a single person *y* that loves all persons *x*. This change in meaning is a direct result of the reversal of the quantifiers.

2. *(∀x)(∃y)(((PERSON(x)∧PERSON(y))∧LOVES(y,x)))*

An expression such as this often is constructed in a failed attempt to convey the meaning of our original expression. The English translation of this expression is

> For all x, there exists at least one y such that x is a person and y is a person and y loves x.

The expression evaluates to true if and only if for any x in our universe, we can find at least one y in our universe such that the subexpression

$$((PERSON(x) \wedge PERSON(y)) \wedge LOVES(y,x))$$

evaluates to true. Note that, if in our universe there is a value for x that is not a person, there will be no value for y such that the subexpression evaluates to true for this nonperson x. This is the case because for such a value of x, PERSON(x) is false, which implies immediately that the entire conjunction $((PERSON(x) \wedge PERSON(y)) \wedge LOVES(y,x))$ evaluates to false.

3. $(\forall x)(\exists y)((PERSON(x) \wedge PERSON(y)) \Rightarrow LOVES(y,x))$

   This expression illustrates an effect of logical implication. The English translation of this expression is

   > For all x, there exists at least one y such that x is a person and y is a person implies that y loves x.

   The expression evaluates to true if and only if for any x in our universe, we can find at least one y in our universe such that the subexpression

   $$((PERSON(x) \wedge PERSON(y)) \Rightarrow LOVES(y,x))$$

   evaluates to true. Note that, if in our universe there is a value for y such that y is not a person, this value will cause the subexpression to evaluate to true regardless of the value of x. This is the case because for such a y value, the left side $((PERSON(x) \wedge PERSON(y))$ of the implication is false, which means that the entire subexpression evaluates to true.

Interpretations

When we say that a tuple calculus expression evaluates to true or false, what we mean is that in the context of some **interpretation,** the expression evaluates to true or false. For our purposes, it suffices to define as follows **an interpretation for a predicate calculus expression.**

Definition 3.1 If E is a predicate calculus expression, an interpretation I for E consists of

1. A specification of a nonempty domain D for the variables that appear in E, that is, a specification of the values that the variables can assume.

2. A specification of the *relation* that each predicate represents. Recall that a k-ary relation on domains $D_1, D_2, \ldots, D_k$ simply is a subset of the Cartesian product $D_1 \times D_2 \times, \ldots, \times D_k$. If P is a predicate over k arguments, the interpretation must associate with P a k-ary relation.[1] Each k-ary relation in our interpretations will be a subset of D^k.

To illustrate, let us specify an interpretation for our sample predicate calculus expression

$$(\forall x)(\exists y)(PERSON(x) \Rightarrow (PERSON(y) \wedge LOVES(y,x)))$$

1. The domain will be the set of all living creatures on the planet Earth.
2. The unary relation PERSON will contain all x in our domain that are people. The binary relation LOVES will contain all (y,x) such that x and y are each in the domain and y loves x.

When evaluating a predicate calculus expression in the context of an interpretation, a predicate $P(x_1, \ldots, x_k)$ evaluates to true for the specific values $<x_1 = v_1, \ldots, x_k = v_k>$ (each v_i comes from the domain D) if and only if the tuple $(v_1, \ldots, v_k)$ is a member of the relation the interpretation associates with the predicate P. Hence, at least when domains (and consequently relations) are finite, any expression can be evaluated by inspection in the context of a given interpretation.

The predicate calculus is a topic that, by itself, could be studied for years. A thorough study of the predicate calculus would have far more to say about interpretations, how to handle infinite domains and relations, notions of valid and satisfiable expressions, and inference mechanisms. Since these topics do not arise in our study of query languages, we do no more than refer the interested reader to Bridge (1977), and Chang and Lee (1979).

Tuple Calculus

To begin, we view the predicate calculus as a primitive query language. Expressions are defined as before, but our interest is restricted to a single interpretation. This interpretation is determined by the current values of the tables in the RDM we are querying.

For example, consider again the tuple calculus expression

$$(\forall x)(\exists y)(PERSON(x) \Rightarrow (PERSON(y) \wedge LOVES(y,x)))$$

Suppose the RDM scheme for the database being queried contains the table schemes PERSON(Name = string), LOVES(Name1 = string, Name2 = string). Because computer representations of data types such as integer, string, and real are finite, we assume from this point that all domains are finite. Suppose that the current values of these tables are

[1] Here we use the term *relation* in the mathematical sense, as it was defined in Section 2.4.

PERSON	LOVES	
Name	Name1	Name2
Jane Doe	John Doe	Jane Doe
John Doe	Jane Doe	John Doe
Mary Smith	Bill Smith	Mary Smith
Bill Smith	Mary Smith	Bill Smith

The interpretation we consider for our expressions makes the natural association between predicate names and tables,[2] and the domain is the set of all values appearing in the current instance of the database (which we assume to be nonempty), across all tables. Thus, given the preceeding table instances, the domain is D = {John Doe, Jane Doe, Mary Smith, Bill Smith}. We shall refer to this natural interpretation as the **database interpretation.**

We evaluate a predicate calculus expression against the database interpretation just as we would against any finite interpretation. As such, an expression will always evaluate to either true or false. Obviously, such a query language is of limited use! For example, we could pose the query "Does John Doe love Mary Doe?" but we could not pose the query "Whom does John Doe love?"

We wish to modify the predicate calculus so that it becomes a viable query language. In particular, we wish to modify the predicate calculus so that an expression *evaluates to a table instance rather than to a Boolean value*. The modification of the predicate calculus we shall develop is known as **tuple calculus.**

To begin, let us return to our department store application and consider some sample queries. We assume the following RDM scheme:

```
EMPLOYEE(SS#=integer, Name=string, Salary=real, Dept=string)
PERSONAL(SS#=integer, Age=integer, Highest_Degree=string)
DEPARTMENT(Dept=string, Manager=integer, Location=string, D_Desc=string)
PRODUCT(Prod#=integer, P_Desc=string)
STOCKS(Prod#=integer, Dept=string)
```

Consider the query "Retrieve all the information associated with each employee who works in the toys department." In relational algebra, this query is stated as

$$\sigma_{Dept=\text{"Toys"}} EMPLOYEE$$

In tuple calculus, this query is stated as

$$\{t \mid (EMPLOYEE(t) \wedge t[Dept] = \text{"Toys"})\}$$

This tuple calculus expression somewhat resembles a predicate calculus expres-

---

[2] Observe that the predicate names in the query need not match the relation names in the RDM since an interpretation allows us to make arbitrary associations, provided that the arities match. For simplicity, however, in what follows we shall assume that predicates are restricted to table names and that queries are evaluated in the context of the interpretation that associates in the natural manner predicate names to tables.

sion. The most notable difference between a tuple and a predicate calculus expression is that in the former, as the preceeding example suggests, the expression evaluates to a *set*, while in the latter, the expression evaluates to a Boolean value. More particularly, a tuple calculus expression evaluates to a *set of tuples*, each of which (in general) has the same arity. In other words, a tuple calculus expression evaluates to a table instance.

Let us consider intuitively the meaning attached to the foregoing tuple calculus expression. The expression evaluates to

the set of all tuples t such that t is in the relation EMPLOYEE and t[Dept] = "Toys"

A tuple calculus expression specifies a *logical condition* that each tuple in the result set must satisfy and that every tuple over the domain that satisfies this condition is in the result set. A tuple calculus expression is highly nonprocedural in the sense that the expression in no way specifies how tuples that satisfy its condition are to be found, specifying only the conditions that tuples must satisfy. When, in the following, we consider more complex queries, the nonprocedural nature of tuple calculus expressions as compared with relational algebra expressions will become more apparent.

We are now ready to formally define the syntax and semantics of tuple calculus expressions. Recall that the interpretation I of interest is the current instance of the database and that the domain D of I is the set of all values appearing in the current instance.

Definition 3.2 A **well-formed formula** is a formula Ψ of one of the following forms:

1. Ψ is one of the following **atoms:**
   a. $T(s)$, where T is a table name and s is a **tuple variable,** a variable that ranges over tuples. This atom makes the assertion that s is a tuple in the current instance of table T.
   b. A comparison of the form $(s[A]\ \Theta\ t[B])$, $(s[A]\ \Theta\ c)$, $(c\ \Theta\ s[A])$, or $(c\ \Theta\ c')$, where s and t are tuple variables, A and B are attribute names, c and c' are constants, and Θ is a logical comparison operator such as $=$, $\neq$, $>$, etc. This atom makes the obvious assertion about the values being compared. By convention, if A is not in the domain of function s (i.e., A is not one of the attributes from function s), then any comparison containing $s[A]$ evaluates to false.

   Each variable appearing in an atom is said to be **free** since in the atom the variable is not bound to a quantifier.
2. If Ψ is a formula, so too are $(\exists s)(\Psi)$ and $(\forall s)(\Psi)$. If s is free in formula Ψ, it is bound to the outer quantifier in the formulas $(\exists s)(\Psi)$ and $(\forall s)(\Psi)$; otherwise, s remains bound in $(\exists s)(\Psi)$ and $(\forall s)(\Psi)$ as it is in Ψ. The meaning of these quantifiers was illustrated previously.

3. If Ψ and Ψ' are formulas, then so too are $(\Psi \wedge \Psi')$, $(\Psi \vee \Psi')$, $(\Psi \Rightarrow \Psi')$, and $(\neg\Psi)$. The logical connectives combine the truth values of their operands in the obvious way and do not alter the bindings of tuple variables appearing in the operands.

Definition 3.3 A **tuple calculus expression** is an expression

$$E = \{t\colon [A_1, A_2, \ldots, A_k] \mid \Psi\}$$

where $A_1, A_2, \ldots, A_k$ are attribute names, each of which appears in RDM scheme $\mathcal{R}$, and Ψ is a well-formed formula whose only free variable is t. If the same attribute name must appear more than once in the attribute list $[A_1, A_2, \ldots, A_k]$, the occurrences of the attribute are numbered [e.g., Dept(1) and Dept(2)] and the numbered occurrences can be referenced in Ψ. The value of expression E is the set of functions (tuples) $\bar{t}$ mapping elements of $\{A_1, A_2, \ldots, A_k\}$ into values from D, such that Ψ evaluates to true in the context of the database interpretation when function $\bar{t}$ replaces in Ψ all occurrences of variable t. When the attribute names from which t maps are implied by Ψ [e.g., Ψ implies the condition $T(t)$, where T is a table name], the attribute list $[A_1, A_2, \ldots, A_k]$ may be omitted. Note that, whether the attribute list is present explicitly or implicitly only, the value of a tuple calculus expression is a set of tuples consistent with a *single* table scheme.

For consistency with our definition of the relational algebra, we add to the preceding definition the following restriction: Expression Ψ must be constructed so that for each A_i appearing in the attribute list $[A_1, A_2, \ldots, A_k]$ and for each tuple t that qualifies for inclusion in the result set, $t[A_i] = s[A_i]$, where s is a tuple in some table instance whose scheme includes attribute A_i. Similarly, a numbered occurrence $A_i(j)$ appearing in the attribute list must be restricted in an analogous manner. This structural condition on Ψ is satisfied if, for example, Ψ implies $T(t)$, where table scheme T includes attribute A_i, or if Ψ implies $(t[A_i] = s[A_i])$, where Ψ restricts s to a table whose scheme contains attribute A_i.

We make the following two observations:

1. The value of any tuple calculus expression is finite since tuples map from a fixed (and finite-length) attribute list into the finite domain D. The property that all expressions are finite valued is known as **safety.**
2. An expression such as $\{t\colon [SS\#, Name, Salary, Dept] \mid \neg\, EMPLOYEE(t)\}$ is not syntactically legal since a qualifying tuple t may map an attribute $A \in \{SS\#, Name, Salary, Dept\}$ to a value v for which there is no tuple s in any table instance with $s[A] = v$. Many treatments of tuple calculus permit such an expression, but in that case, equivalence with the relational algebra (see Theorem 3.1) requires that the relational operators $\cup$ and $-$ apply to operand tables even when their lists of attribute names differ. While there are advantages and disadvantages to the two

approaches, our more restrictive definitions might be regarded as a bit more natural and appear to be closer to what most existing database systems support.

How powerful is the tuple calculus query language? The following definition and theorem establishes that the tuple calculus and the relational algebra have exactly the same expressive power.

Definition 3.4 Let each of E_1 and E_2 be either a tuple calculus or relational algebra expression over the RDM scheme $\mathcal{R}$ and the same set of constant symbols. E_1 and E_2 are **equivalent** with respect to $\mathcal{R}$ if for all instances I of $\mathcal{R}$ we have that $E_1(I) = E_2(I)$; that is, the expressions evaluate to the same table instance for all instances I of $\mathcal{R}$.

Theorem 3.1 Let $\mathcal{R}$ be any RDM scheme. Then,

1. For every relational algebra expression E_A over $\mathcal{R}$, there exists a tuple calculus expression E_C over $\mathcal{R}$ equivalent to E_A with respect to $\mathcal{R}$.
2. For every tuple calculus expression E_C over $\mathcal{R}$, there exists a relational algebra expression E_A over $\mathcal{R}$ equivalent to E_C with respect to $\mathcal{R}$.

We shall not present a formal proof of this theorem. Rather, in this section, we shall indicate how a relational algebra expression can be translated into a tuple calculus expression, and in the following section, we shall consider translation in the other direction.

We begin by demonstrating informally that each relational operator can be expressed as a tuple calculus expression.

Select: The example that precedes Theorem 3.1 demonstrates how to express in the tuple calculus a relational algebra expression containing a simple selection. An expression containing a more complex selection is handled in a similar manner. For example, the relational algebra expression

$$\sigma_{(Name=\text{"Smith"}) \wedge (Salary>20000) \wedge (Dept=\text{"Toys"})}\ EMPLOYEE$$

is expressed in the tuple calculus as

$$\{t \mid (EMPLOYEE(t) \wedge (t[Name]=\text{"Smith"}) \wedge (t[Salary]>20000) \wedge (t[Dept] = \text{"Toys"}))\}$$

Project: Consider the query

"Retrieve the name of each employee in EMPLOYEE"

In relational algebra, this query is stated as

$$\Pi_{<Name>}\ EMPLOYEE$$

To state this seemingly simple query in tuple calculus, we must introduce a second tuple calculus variable. To see why this is so, consider the following partial attempts at a tuple calculus solution:

1. $\{t \mid EMPLOYEE(t) \ldots$
2. $\{t\text{: } [Name] \mid EMPLOYEE(t) \ldots$

The first attempt is doomed to failure because, no matter how the partial expression is completed, each tuple in the answer set will have arity 3, and thus no completion of the partial expression can evaluate to the required projection. The second attempt is doomed to failure because there are no tuples of arity 1 in EMPLOYEE, and hence, no matter how the partial expression is completed, it will evaluate to the empty set of tuples.

To resolve the dilemma, we must introduce a second tuple variable and write

$$\{t\text{: } [Name] \mid (\exists s)(EMPLOYEE(s) \land (t[Name]=s[Name]))\}$$

This expression is analyzed semantically as follows:

1. The component t: [*Name*] of the expression specifies that each tuple in the answer set has arity 1 and, in particular, is a function that maps the attribute Name into a value from our universe. Observe that the previous expression for selection did not require such a specification because the tuple variable t was restricted by a component of the form *TABLENAME*(t), which had the effect of fixing t's structure.
2. The subexpression $(\exists s)(EMPLOYEE(s) \land (t[Name]=s[Name]))$ states the logical condition that qualifying tuples t (whose form is already restricted as described in item 1) must satisfy. That is, the answer set consists of exactly those tuples t: [*Name*] that satisfy the subexpression, which states that there exists at least one tuple s such that s is in the current instance of the EMPLOYEE table and such that tuples s and t map the Name attribute to the same value.

It is instructive to consider the tuple calculus expression

$$\{t\text{: } [Name] \mid (\exists s)(EMPLOYEE(s) \land (t[Name]=s[Name]))\}$$

from the slightly more procedural perspective that it induces a test for a tuple t's membership in the answer set. Consider any tuple of arity 1 that maps Name into the universe of values. Consider, for example, the tuple $t[Name] = Smith$ of arity 1. Tuple t qualifies for inclusion in the answer set if and only if we can find a tuple s such that s is in the current instance of EMPLOYEE and such that s and t agree on the Name attribute. If the current instance of EMPLOYEE is

EMPLOYEE

Name	SS#	Salary	Dept
Harris	999999999	20K	Books
Trent	888888888	25K	Software
Smith	123456789	30K	Toys

we see that $t[Name] = Smith$ qualifies for inclusion in the answer set since the third tuple listed in EMPLOYEE is the required s. On the other hand, the tuple $t'[Name] = Jones$ does not qualify for inclusion in the answer set since we can not find in the current instance of EMPLOYEE the required tuple s. While this more procedural perspective of the tuple calculus expression may be useful in gaining an understanding of the expression's meaning, it must be emphasized that it is more proper to treat a tuple calculus expression as a purely *logical description* of an answer set of tuples and *not* as an algorithm for testing tuples for inclusion in the answer set.

It also is instructive to note why each component of the preceding tuple calculus expression is necessary. Consider the following modifications to the expression

$$\{t\text{: }[Name] \mid (\exists s)(EMPLOYEE(s) \wedge (t[Name]=s[Name]))\}$$

1. Omit the attribute list from t: $[Name]$, resulting in the expression

   $$\{t \mid (\exists s)(EMPLOYEE(s) \wedge (t[Name]=s[Name]))\}$$

   This expression is not syntactically legal since the attribute list of tuple t is not implied by the remainder of the expression. Hence, the set would include tuples over different schemes and arities.
2. Omit the term $EMPLOYEE(s)$, resulting in the expression

   $$\{t\text{: }[Name] \mid (\exists s)(t[Name]=s[Name])\}$$

   This expression is not syntactically legal since it violates the restriction that, for qualifying tuple t, $t[Name]$ be equal to the Name attribute of a tuple in some table instance.
3. Omit the term $t[Name] = s[Name]$, resulting in the expression

   $$\{t\text{: }[Name] \mid (\exists s)(EMPLOYEE(s))\}$$

   This expression is not syntactically legal for the same reason given in item 2.

Union: To illustrate the translation of the union operator, we temporarily add the following table scheme to the RDM scheme:

EMPLOYEE2(Name, SS#, Salary, Dept)

Consider the query "Retrieve all the information about employees who are in either table EMPLOYEE or table EMPLOYEE2." In relational algebra, this query is answered as $EMPLOYEE \cup EMPLOYEE2$. In tuple calculus, the query is answered as

$$\{t \mid (EMPLOYEE(t) \vee EMPLOYEE2(t))\}$$

Difference: Consider the query "Retrieve all the information about employees who are in table EMPLOYEE but who are *not* also in table EMPLOYEE2." In relational algebra, this query is answered as

EMPLOYEE − *EMPLOYEE*2. In tuple calculus, the query is answered as

$$\{t \mid (EMPLOYEE(t) \wedge \neg EMPLOYEE2(t))\}$$

Cartesian Product: Consider the relational algebra expression *EMPLOYEE* × *DEPARTMENT*. Observe that the tuples in the answer set have arity 8 and hence come from neither the EMPLOYEE nor DEPARTMENT table. Thus, as was required in the translation of the Project operator, we must introduce additional tuple calculus variables. In the case of the Cartesian product operator, we observe that each tuple in the answer set is a concatenation of a pair of tuples coming from the operand tables. Consequently, the tuple calculus expression requires the introduction of two additional tuple variables:

$$\begin{aligned}&\{t\text{: } [Name, SS\#, Salary, Dept(1), Dept(2), Location, Manager, D\_Desc] \mid \\ &(\exists e)(\exists d)(EMPLOYEE(e) \wedge DEPARTMENT(d)) \\ &\wedge ((t[Name]=e[Name]) \wedge (t[SS\#]=e[SS\#]) \wedge (t[Salary]=e[Salary]) \\ &\wedge (t[Location]=d[Location]) \wedge (t[Dept(1)]=e[Dept]) \\ &\wedge (t[Dept(2)]=d[Dept]) \wedge (t[Manager]=d[Manager]))\}\end{aligned}$$

Thus, we have indicated how each of the five relational algebra operators can be expressed in terms of tuple calculus. A formal proof of part 1 of Theorem 3.1 would require not only that we generalize the preceding examples to apply to arbitrary relations (and arbitrary combinations of attributes and values for Select and Project) but also that we demonstrate that any relational algebra expression containing *zero or more* operators can be translated into tuple calculus. That is, a relational algebra expression, in general, is a composition of zero or more relational operators, and we must demonstrate that such an expression can be expressed in tuple calculus. The following high-level recursive algorithm describes a method for translating an arbitrary relational algebra expression into an equivalent tuple calculus expression:

```
Alg_To_Calc(E_A)
{ E_A is a syntactically correct relational algebra expression
  over RDM scheme ℛ. }
  case: (E_A contains 0 relational operators)
    begin
      { E_A is L(t). Let the scheme of L be L(A_1, . . . ,A_k) }
      return( {t: [A_1, . . . ,A_k] | L(t)} )
    end
  case: (E_A is Π_<A_1,...,A_k> E)
    begin
      exp := Alg_To_Calc(E)
      { exp is of the form {s: [B_1, . . . ,B_m] | Ψ} {B_1, . . . ,B_m} ⊇ {A_1, . . . , A_k} }
      return( {t: [A_1, . . . , A_k] | (∃s)(Ψ ∧ (t[A_1]=s[A_1] ∧ · · · ∧ t[A_k]=s[A_k]))})
    end
  case: (E_A is σ_F E)
   { F is a Boolean formula. Let t⊙F denote the Boolean formula
     obtained by replacing in F all occurrences of A_i with t[A_i]. }
```

begin
exp: = Alg_To_Calc(E)
{ exp is of the form $\{t: [A_1, \ldots, A_k] \mid \Psi\}$ }
return($\{t: [A_1, \ldots, A_k] \mid (\Psi \wedge t \odot F)\}$)
end

case: (E_A is $E_1 \cup E_2$)
{ E_1 and E_2 evaluate to tables over the same scheme; let $(A_1, \ldots, A_k)$ be the attribute list of this scheme. }
begin
exp$_1$: = Alg_To_Calc(E_1)
{ exp$_1$ is of the form $\{t: [A_1, \ldots, A_k] \mid \Psi_1\}$ }
exp$_2$: = Alg_To_Calc(E_2)
{ exp$_2$ is of the form $\{t: [A_1, \ldots, A_k] \mid \Psi_2\}$ }
return($\{t: [A_1, \ldots, A_k] \mid (\Psi_1 \vee \Psi_2)\}$)
end

case: (E_A is $E_1 - E_2$)
{ E_1 and E_2 evaluate to tables over the same scheme; let $(A_1, \ldots, A_k)$ be the attribute list of this scheme. }
begin
exp$_1$:= Alg_To_Calc(E_1)
{ exp$_1$ is of the form $\{t: [A_1, \ldots, A_k] \mid \Psi_1\}$ }
exp$_2$:= Alg_To_Calc(E_2)
{ exp$_2$ is of the form $\{t: [A_1, \ldots, A_k] \mid \Psi_2\}$ }
return($\{t: [A_1, \ldots, A_k] \mid (\Psi_1 \wedge (\neg \Psi_2))\}$)
end

case: (E_A is $E_1 \times E_2$)
begin
exp$_1$:= Alg_To_Calc(E_1)
{ exp$_1$ is of the form $\{s: [A_1, \ldots, A_k] \mid \Psi_1\}$ }
exp$_2$:= Alg_To_Calc(E_2)
{ exp$_2$ is of the form $\{u: [B_1, \ldots, B_m] \mid \Psi_2\}$ }
return($\{t: [A_1, \ldots, A_k, B_1, \ldots, B_m] \mid (\exists s)(\exists u)((\Psi_1 \wedge \Psi_2)$
$\wedge ((t[A_1]=s[A_1]) \wedge \cdots \wedge (t[A_k]=s[A_k]) \wedge (t[B_1]=u[B_1]) \wedge \cdots$
$\wedge (t[B_m]=u[B_m]))))\}$)
end
end {Alg_To_Calc}

Although correct, this algorithm is somewhat naive in that the tuple calculus expression it produces for a given relational algebra expression is not necessarily the most concise translation possible. For example, the resulting expression will often contain more tuple variables and terms than is necessary. The algorithm, however, suffices to demonstrate that a translation from a relational algebra expression to a tuple calculus expression always exists.

Inspection of the preceding algorithm reveals an important fact: The universal quantifier ∀ is never required to express a relational algebra expression in tuple calculus. This should come as no surprise, however, since, in predicate calculus, any expression containing the quantifier ∀ can be translated into an equivalent expression containing only the existential quantifier ∃. For example,

$(\forall x)(PERSON(x) \Rightarrow (MALE(x) \vee FEMALE(x)))$

is equivalent to

$$\neg(\ (\exists x)\ \neg(PERSON(x) \Rightarrow (MALE(x) \vee FEMALE(x))\ )\ )$$

which is equivalent to

$$\neg(\ (\exists x)(\ PERSON(x) \wedge \neg MALE(x) \wedge \neg FEMALE(x)\ )\ )$$

Observe that these expressions contain negated existential quantifiers. In general, every predicate calculus expression containing the universal quantifier is equivalent to some expression containing a negated existential quantifier. Observe further that, in the recursive translation algorithm, the relational operator $-$ is the only operator that introduces negation. In particular, the translation algorithm introduces negation exactly when it is invoked (either initially or recursively) on an expression of the form $\Psi_1 - \Psi_2$. Hence, the Difference operator corresponds closely to universal quantification. (Also, recall the discussion in Section 2.4 of the Divide operator.)

For example, if we apply the algorithm to the relational algebra expression

$$\Pi_{<Name>}(EMPLOYEE) - \Pi_{<Name>}(EMPLOYEE2)$$

we obtain the tuple calculus expression

$$\{t: [Name] \mid (\exists e)(EMPLOYEE(e) \wedge (t[Name]=e[Name])) \\ \wedge \neg((\exists e')(EMPLOYEE2(e') \wedge (t[Name]=e'[Name])))\}$$

We can apply to this tuple calculus expression the laws of predicate calculus to obtain the equivalent expression

$$\{t: [Name] \mid (\exists e)(EMPLOYEE(e) \wedge (t[Name]=e[Name])) \\ \wedge (\forall e')(\neg EMPLOYEE2(e') \vee (t[Name] \neq e'[Name]))\}$$

and then the equivalent expression

$$\{t: [Name] \mid (\exists e)(\forall e')(EMPLOYEE(e) \wedge (t[Name]=e[Name]) \\ \wedge (EMPLOYEE2(e') \Rightarrow (t[Name] \neq e'[Name])))\}$$

To summarize, we have presented an algorithm for translating an arbitrary relational algebra expression into a tuple calculus expression. However, given an English query that we wish to pose against an instance of an RDM scheme, it is a very unnatural process to first state the query as a relational algebra expression and then translate this expression into tuple calculus. After all, tuple calculus (or its realizations in the form of commercial languages) is purported to be more convenient for the user than the relational algebra! Hence, it is beneficial to spend a bit more time building intuition on how to state English queries directly in tuple calculus.

1. Consider the query "Retrieve the name of each employee along with the employee's manager." In relational algebra, this is stated as

   $$\Pi_{<Name, Manager>}(EMPLOYEE \underset{Dept=Dept}{\bowtie} DEPARTMENT)$$

   In tuple calculus, this is stated as

$$\{t: [Name, Manager] \mid (\exists e)(\exists d)(EMPLOYEE(e) \wedge DEPARTMENT(d)) \wedge ((t[Name]=e[Name]) \wedge (t[Manager]=d[Manager])) \wedge (e[Dept]=d[Dept])\}$$

The reader should compare this tuple calculus expression with the one that results from applying the recursive translation algorithm to the preceding relational algebra expression.

2. Consider the query "Retrieve the departments that do *not* stock the product with Prod# 555." (Assume that each department stocks at least one product.) In relational algebra, this is stated as

$$(\Pi_{<Dept>}(STOCKS) - \Pi_{<Dept>}(\sigma_{Prod\#=555}\, STOCKS))$$

We could obtain a tuple calculus expression by applying the translation algorithm to this relational algebra expression. (The reader is encouraged to perform this translation and to compare its result with the expression we construct later.) However, we instead construct a tuple calculus expression directly. First consider the tuple calculus expression

$$\{t: [Dept] \mid (\exists s)(Stocks(s) \wedge t[Dept]=s[Dept] \wedge s[Prod\#]\neq 555)\}$$

This expression is not correct since it will return each department that stocks at least one product different from 555, even if the department also stocks product 555. That is, this expression is equivalent to the relational algebra expression

$$\Pi_{<Dept>}(\sigma_{Prod\#\neq 555}\, STOCKS)$$

A correct tuple calculus expression for the query is

$$\{t: [Dept] \mid (\exists s)\neg((\exists s')STOCKS(s) \wedge t[Dept]=s[Dept] \wedge STOCKS(s') \wedge (s'[Dept]=s[Dept]) \wedge (s'[Prod\#]=555))\}$$

Equivalently, we can express the query as follows using the universal quantifier:

$$\{t: [Dept] \mid (\exists s)(\forall s')STOCKS(s) \wedge (t[Dept]=s[Dept]) \wedge (STOCKS(s') \wedge (s'[Dept]=s[Dept]) \Rightarrow (s'[Prod\#]\neq 555))\}$$

The placement of the terms on the left side of the implication is crucial. If, for example, we were to write

$$\{t: [Dept] \mid (\exists s)(\forall s')STOCKS(s) \wedge STOCK(s') \wedge (t[Dept]=s[Dept]) \wedge (s'[Dept]=s[Dept] \Rightarrow s'[Prod\#]\neq 555)\}$$

the answer set, in general, would be empty because the expression makes the assertion that all tuples s' (over our domain of values) are in the current instance of the relation STOCKS.

Observe also that each of the expressions

$$\{t: [Dept] \mid (\exists s)(\forall s')STOCKS(s) \wedge (t[Dept]=s[Dept]) \wedge (STOCKS(s') \Rightarrow (s'[Prod\#]\neq 555))\}$$

and

$$\{t\colon [Dept] \mid (\exists s)\neg((\exists s')STOCKS(s) \land (t[Dept]=s[Dept]) \land STOCKS(s') \land (s'[Prod\#]=555))\}$$

makes the assertion that no tuple in the relation STOCKS has a Prod# of 555 and hence is an incorrect translation.

3. Now consider the query "Retrieve each department that stocks *all* the products in the current instance of table PRODUCTS." This query can be stated as follows in terms of the Divide operator (defined in Section 2.4):

$$\Pi_{<Dept>}(STOCKS \div (\Pi_{<Prod\#>} PRODUCTS))$$

(The reader is encouraged to state this query in terms of the five primitive relational algebra operators and then to use the general translation algorithm to obtain a tuple calculus expression.) A tuple calculus expression for this query is as follows:

$$\{t\colon [Dept] \mid (\forall p)(\exists s)(STOCKS(s) \land (t[Dept]=s[Dept]) \land (PRODUCT(p) \Rightarrow (s[Prod\#]=p[Prod\#])))\}$$

Pitfalls such as those discussed in the previous example are often encountered when attempting to state a query such as the one under current consideration in tuple calculus. In addition, consider the preceding expression with the quantifiers reversed:

$$\{t\colon [Dept] \mid (\exists s)(\forall p)(STOCKS(s) \land (t[Dept]=s[Dept]) \land (PRODUCT(p) \Rightarrow (s[Prod\#]=p[Prod\#])))\}$$

Provided that the current instance of table PRODUCT contains at least two distinct product numbers, this expression will evaluate to the empty set of tuples. Why?

Select Queries

In Chapter 1, we informally introduced a SELECT-based query language. This language actually is a simplified and restricted version of SQL, today's most important commercial query language. In Section 3.3, we shall consider SQL, but before doing so, it will be instructive to consider by means of example how a simple SELECT query corresponds to a tuple calculus expression.

Consider the SELECT query:

```
SELECT EMPLOYEE.Name, EMPLOYEE.Salary
  WHERE DEPARTMENT.Manager = 888888888
    AND DEPARTMENT.Dept = EMPLOYEE.Dept
```

The meaning of this SELECT query is "Retrieve the names and salaries of all employees who work in a department managed by the employee with SS# 888888888." The translation to the tuple calculus of this query is

$\{t\colon [Name, Salary] \mid (\exists e)(\exists d)$
$(EMPLOYEE(e) \wedge DEPARTMENT(d)$
$\wedge (t[Name]=e[Name]) \wedge (t[Salary]=e[Salary])$
$\wedge (e[Dept]=d[Dept]) \wedge (d[Manager]=888888888))\}$

An important observation is that the resulting tuple calculus expression contains only positive (i.e., not negated) existentially quantified tuple variables. In fact, we have been assuming implicitly that every SELECT query translates to a tuple calculus expression containing only positive existentially qualified tuple variables. Consequently, the simple SELECT query language we have been using is not as powerful as tuple calculus and hence not as powerful as relational algebra. In Section 3.3, we shall consider how the commercial language SQL extends our simple SELECT language to obtain a language with the power of relational algebra and tuple calculus.

3.2 AN OVERVIEW OF QUERY OPTIMIZATION

In the previous section, we demonstrated how to translate any relational algebra expression to the tuple calculus, hence informally establishing part 1 of Theorem 3.1. To establish part 2 of Theorem 3.1, we could demonstrate how to translate any tuple calculus expression to the relational algebra. This translation, however, is more complex than the algebra-to-calculus translation. Rather than presenting the details of such a translation algorithm, we shall consider in this section and in Chapters 11 and 12 this translation as it arises as an aspect of query optimization.

As previously indicated, there are several levels of abstraction inherent in implementations of a nonprocedural interface to the RDM. A sequence of maps, reflected in the architecture of many commercial database systems, has the form shown in Figure 3.2. Each of the maps shown in Figure 3.2 must

Tuple calculus stated against RDM $\mathcal{R}$
↓
Relational algebra stated against RDM $\mathcal{R}$
↓
File and data structure operations stated against implementation structures of $\mathcal{R}$

Figure 3.2 Query processing map

have the property that it preserves equivalence. That is, if E_C is the tuple calculus expression stated by the user, then the result of the first map must be a relational algebra expression E_A equivalent to E_C. The second map, when applied to E_A, must result in a processing strategy at the file- and data structure–level that, when executed against the current instance of $\mathcal{R}$, produces as output the table instance that is the value of the expression E_A.

This description specifies what is necessary for a *correct* translation. A query optimizer, however, must do far more than produce correct translations—it must produce *efficient translations*. That is, even if we had algorithms for translating from tuple calculus to relational algebra and from relation algebra to processing strategies, we would not necessarily have a satisfactory RDM implementation. At issue is the fact that each of the maps shown in Figure 3.2 is one-to-many: Given any tuple calculus expression, there are *many* equivalent relational algebra expressions to which we can map, and given any relational algebra expression, there are *many* implementation level strategies to which we can map.

As a consequence of the one-to-many nature of the maps shown in Figure 3.2, there are several opportunities for optimization:

1. Even before mapping a given tuple calculus expression E_C into a relational algebra expression, there are transformations we can perform on E_C to obtain an equivalent, but (for one reason or another) more desirable, tuple calculus expression.
2. Much effort can be spent determining the relational algebra expression E_A to which the tuple calculus expression resulting from step 1 should be mapped. We shall always map to an expression equivalent to the tuple calculus expression, but the expression we choose can have a significant impact on the steps that follow.
3. We can transform the relational algebra expression resulting from step 2 into an equivalent, but possibly more desirable, relational algebra expression. Recall that in Section 2.5 we indicated, in the context of an internal RDM implementation, the potential benefits of rearranging a relational expression.
4. There are many ways to map the relational expression resulting from step 3 into a processing strategy.
5. The processing strategy resulting from step 4 can be transformed into an equivalent, but potentially more efficient, processing strategy.
6. A strategy can even be dynamic in that future actions can depend on partial results. That is, certain aspects of the optimization can be performed during execution.

There are two fundamental considerations that determine the quality of a query optimizer. The first consideration contributing to the quality of an optimization is *the cost of executing the strategy that the optimization produces*. Note that, in theory, we can put all the optimization effort into steps 5 and 6 and completely bypass the intermediate relational algebra steps. However, saying that there is no need for the intermediate steps ignores the second fundamental consideration of query optimization: The task of query optimization is extremely difficult and generally must be performed in real time. Hence, a second consideration contributing to the quality of an optimization is *the amount of time required to produce the strategy*. Experience with the design of optimizers typically leads to an organization of the optimization that, at least abstractly, resembles the process we have described. It should be emphasized once again, however, that the term *query optimization*—no matter how well the query optimizer is designed—is a misnomer since, in general, good but suboptimal strategies are produced. This is an unavoidable consequence of the fact that even small subproblems of the overall query optimization problem are NP-hard, and hence the problem of producing exact optimizations is intractable.

We delay our detailed treatment of query optimization until Chapter 11. While the six optimization steps outlined here suffice as a high-level description of the query optimization process, as we shall see later, there is often much interaction between the steps, and often there are additional steps. Nevertheless, it is useful from the point of view of instruction and modularization of the query optimizer to view the optimization as having subproblems such as those described. When we do study query optimization in earnest in Chapters 11 and 12, we shall present a more detailed and accurate description of the optimization process.

3.3 SQL: THE ANSI STANDARD QUERY LANGUAGE

We consider in this section today's most important commercial query language, SQL. SQL has been adopted as the ANSI standard query language and is supported by such systems as INGRES, ORACLE, SYBASE, and IBM's DB2. Rather than focusing on the syntactic details of SQL, we primarily consider how SQL embodies the concepts and power of tuple calculus and relational algebra.

SQL's primary query construct is the SELECT statement. SQL's SELECT statement has syntax and semantics quite similar to that of our simple SELECT queries. To illustrate, consider again the SELECT query

```
SELECT EMPLOYEE.Name, EMPLOYEE.Salary
  WHERE DEPARTMENT.Manager = 888888888
     AND DEPARTMENT.Dept = EMPLOYEE.Dept
```

The same query in SQL is

```
SELECT EMP.Name, EMP.Salary
   FROM EMPLOYEE EMP, DEPARTMENT DPT
  WHERE DPT.Manager = 888888888
     AND DPT.Dept = EMP.Dept
```

Semantically, the queries are identical, each being equivalent to the tuple calculus expression:

$$\{t\colon [Name,Salary] \mid (\exists e)(\exists d)\ EMPLOYEE(e) \land DEPARTMENT(d) \land t[Name]=e[Name] \land t[Salary]=e[Salary] \land e[Dept]=d[Dept] \land d[Dept]=888888888\ \}$$

The only syntactic difference between our SELECT query and the SQL query is that the latter contains a FROM clause whose function is to declare tuple variables that, like tuple variables in tuple calculus expressions, range over tuples of table instances. The FROM clause

```
FROM EMPLOYEE EMP, DEPARTMENT DPT
```

declares tuple variable EMP to range over table EMPLOYEE [analogous to the tuple calculus assertion EMPLOYEE(EMP)] and the tuple variable DPT to range over the table DEPARTMENT [analogous to the tuple calculus assertion DEPARTMENT(DPT)].

We note that if a table name appears in a FROM clause by itself, without a tuple variable, the effect is to declare a tuple variable with name equal to the table name and ranging over that table. For example, the FROM clause

```
FROM EMPLOYEE, EMPLOYEE EMP, DEPARTMENT DPT
```

in addition to declaring tuple variables EMP and DPT, declares EMPLOYEE to be a tuple variable ranging over table EMPLOYEE. Using this feature, the previous query can be written as

```
SELECT EMPLOYEE.Name, EMPLOYEE.Salary
   FROM EMPLOYEE, DEPARTMENT
  WHERE DEPARTMENT.Manager = 888888888
     AND DEPARTMENT.Dept = EMPLOYEE.Dept
```

However, a table name cannot be used as a tuple variable unless the table name appears in the from clause; hence

```
SELECT EMPLOYEE.Name, EMPLOYEE.Salary
  WHERE DEPARTMENT.Manager = 888888888
     AND DEPARTMENT.Dept = EMPLOYEE.Dept
```

is not legal in standard SQL.

At first, the declaration of tuple variables may seem inconsequential. However, a facility for explicitly declaring tuple variables is quite desirable. Consider, for example, the query "Retrieve the name of each employee who works in the same department that Smith works in." This query can be expressed in the tuple calculus as follows:

$$\{t: [Name] \mid (\exists e)(\exists f) \\ (EMPLOYEE(e) \wedge (EMPLOYEE(f)) \\ \wedge f[Name]="Smith" \wedge e[Dept]=f[Dept] \\ \wedge t[Name]=e[Name]\}$$

This query can be expressed in SQL as follows:

```
SELECT E1.Name
   FROM EMPLOYEE E1, EMPLOYEE E2
  WHERE E2.Name = "Smith"
     AND E2.Dept = E1.Dept
```

The reader should convince himself or herself that this query cannot be stated without two distinct tuple variables ranging simultaneously over the table EMPLOYEE.

The preceding examples serve to introduce informally SQL's SELECT statement. An important observation to make is that, as we saw at the conclusion of Section 3.1 for our simple SELECT language, SELECT statements in SQL always translate to tuple calculus expressions containing only positive existentially quantified tuple variables. For example, earlier we asserted that the SQL query

```
SELECT EMP.Name, EMP.Salary
   FROM EMPLOYEE EMP, DEPARTMENT DPT
  WHERE DPT.Manager = 888888888
     AND DPT.Dept = EMP.Dept
```

translates to the tuple calculus expression

$$\{t\colon [Name, Salary] \mid (\exists e)(\exists d)\ EMPLOYEE(e) \wedge DEPARTMENT(d) \wedge t[Name]=e[Name] \wedge t[Salary]=e[Salary] \wedge e[Dept]=d[Dept] \wedge d[Dept]=888888888\}$$

Observe how the SQL tuple variables EMP and DPT map to the existentially quantified tuple calculus variables e and d.

We therefore can conclude that the basic form of the SQL SELECT statement lacks the full power of the tuple calculus and relational algebra. Fortunately, there is a more complex form of the SELECT statement—one that includes **nested subqueries**—that overcomes the limitations of the basic statement. We shall illustrate the use of the nested subquery as its need arises in the following sequence of examples.

We begin illustrating SQL's power by again considering the relational algebra expressions used in Section 3.1 to illustrate the power of the tuple calculus.

Select: The relational algebra expression

$$\sigma_{(Name=\text{"Smith"}) \wedge (Salary>20000) \wedge (Dept=\text{"Toys"})}\ \text{EMPLOYEE}$$

can be expressed in SQL as

```
SELECT EMPLOYEE.SS, EMPLOYEE.Name, EMPLOYEE.Salary, EMPLOYEE.Dept
   FROM EMPLOYEE
  WHERE EMPLOYEE.Name = "Smith"
     AND EMPLOYEE.Salary > 20000
     AND EMPLOYEE.Dept = "Toys"
```

SQL permits the construct 'SELECT *' when all attributes of the tables referenced in the FROM clause are to be included in the result table. Hence, the preceding query can be written as

```
SELECT *
   FROM EMPLOYEE
  WHERE EMPLOYEE.Name = "Smith"
     AND EMPLOYEE.Salary > 20000
     AND EMPLOYEE.Dept = "Toys"
```

Project: The relational algebra expression

$\Pi_{<Name>}$ EMPLOYEE

is expressed in SQL as

```
SELECT EMPLOYEE.Name
  FROM EMPLOYEE
```

SQL permits an attribute to appear unqualified by a tuple variable when only one table appears in the FROM clause. Hence, the preceding query can be written as

```
SELECT Name
  FROM EMPLOYEE
```

In this query, the reference Name is shorthand for EMPLOYEE.Name.

Union: The relational algebra expression

$EMPLOYEE \cup EMPLOYEE2$

is expressed in SQL by means of the special UNION operator:

```
SELECT SS, Name, Salary, Dept
  FROM EMPLOYEE
    UNION
SELECT SS, Name, Salary, Dept
  FROM EMPLOYEE2
```

Difference: The relational algebra expression

$EMPLOYEE - EMPLOYEE2$

requires the use of a nested subquery. One form of an SQL query containing a nested subquery is as follows:

SELECT $tv_1.attname_1,...,tv_k.attname_k$
  FROM $T_1 tv_1, . . . , T_k tv_k$
  WHERE *op* (*SQL query*)

The operators that may play the role of *op* in this query include IN, EXISTS, and =ALL. Additionally, the logical operator NOT may be composed with each of these operators. We note also that a subquery may be one of several terms in a WHERE clause that are connected by logical connectives.

Now consider the following SQL query that expresses the relational algebra expression $EMPLOYEE - EMPLOYEE2$.

```
SELECT *
   FROM EMPLOYEE
  WHERE NOT EXISTS
          (SELECT *
              FROM EMPLOYEE2
```

```
WHERE EMPLOYEE2.SS = EMPLOYEE.SS
   AND EMPLOYEE2.Name = EMPLOYEE.Name
   AND EMPLOYEE2.Salary = EMPLOYEE.Salary
   AND EMPLOYEE2.Dept = EMPLOYEE.Dept)
```

Observe that the tuple variable EMPLOYEE appears in both the outer and inner query. As such, the outer and inner queries are said to be **correlated.** Such a construct, typically used in conjunction with the EXISTS operator, causes the query to be evaluated as follows:

> For each tuple *t* that could qualify for the outer query (e.g., *t* is formed from tuples coming from the correct tables; *t* satisfies any "simple" WHERE clause components that may be present), evaluate the inner query with values from tuple *t* replacing references to corresponding correlation variables. Determine whether this evaluation of the inner query results in an empty table. If EXISTS is applied to the inner query, then *t* is in the result of the outer query if and only if the evaluation of the inner query with respect to *t* results in a nonempty table. Similarly, if NOT EXISTS is applied to the inner query, then *t* is in the result of the outer query if and only if the evaluation of the inner query with respect to *t* results in an empty table.

Applying this algorithm to the preceding query, we see that the tuple <*ss*,*n*,*sl*,*d*> from table EMPLOYEE is in the result of the entire query exactly when the inner query evaluates to the empty set of tuples when, in the inner subquery, *ss* replaces EMPLOYEE.SS, *n* replaces EMPLOYEE.Name, *sl* replaces EMPLOYEE.Salary, and *d* replaces EMPLOYEE.Dept. Thus, the entire query evaluates to the set of tuples <*ss*,*n*,*sl*,*d*> that are in EMPLOYEE but are not in EMPLOYEE2.

Note that in a query such as the foregoing, the attributes selected for retrieval by the inner query have no effect on the entire query's result. Hence, it is common practice to use "*" in the construction of the inner query. We note also that an inner query itself may contain a nested subquery; later in this section we shall encounter an example of such a construct.

Before leaving the Difference operator, we consider several variations to the preceding query. Consider first the query

```
SELECT *
   FROM EMPLOYEE
  WHERE NOT EXISTS
         (SELECT *
            FROM EMPLOYEE2
         WHERE EMPLOYEE2.Name = EMPLOYEE.Name)
```

The result of this query differs from that of the original in that if EMPLOYEE contains a tuple such as <111111111, Jones, 30K, Toys>, this tuple will be in the result only if EMPLOYEE2 contains no tuple with name Jones; in particular, if EMPLOYEE2 contains a tuple such as <222222222, Jones, 30K, Toys>, tuple <111111111, Jones, 30K, Toys> will *not* be in the query's result. Hence, the query does not correctly implement the difference operator for all possible instances of tables EMPLOYEE and EMPLOYEE2.

Suppose now we are supplied with the semantic information that if a pair of tuples t and t' (whether they both be from one of EMPLOYEE and EMPLOYEE2 or whether one tuple be in each table) agree on SS, then t and t' must also agree on all their other attributes. In this case, the query

```
SELECT *
   FROM EMPLOYEE
  WHERE NOT EXISTS
         (SELECT *
            FROM EMPLOYEE2
           WHERE EMPLOYEE2.SS = EMPLOYEE.SS)
```

correctly implements the Difference operator with respect to instances of EMPLOYEE and EMPLOYEE2 that are consistent with this semantic information.

In fact, if the preceding semantic information regarding SS is valid, a simpler SQL construct can be used to implement the Difference operator. Consider the query

```
SELECT *
   FROM EMPLOYEE
  WHERE EMPLOYEE.SS NOT IN
         (SELECT SS
           FROM EMPLOYEE2)
```

The IN operator (or the NOT IN combination) is applied to a simple attribute value and a table with arity one; the operator simply tests set membership. That is, a table of arity one is a set of simple values, and the IN operator evaluates to true if and only if the value of the attribute operand is a member of this set of simple values. Hence, a tuple $<ss,n,sl,d>$ is in the result of the preceding query if and only if ss is not a member of the result of the inner query, namely the projection onto SS of table EMPLOYEE2.

Cartesian Product: The relational algebra expression

$$EMPLOYEE \times DEPARTMENT$$

is expressed in SQL as

```
SELECT *
  FROM EMPLOYEE, DEPARTMENT
```

We have now demonstrated that SQL is capable of expressing each of the five relational operators. Just as we were concerned in Section 3.1 with expressing relational expressions containing several operators in tuple calculus, we must be concerned with expressing such queries in SQL. The reader should specify a translation algorithm for this task analogous to the recursive translation algorithm Alg_To_Calc presented in Section 3.1. Here we illustrate how to express in SQL three of the queries considered in Section 3.1.

1. The Natural join query "Retrieve the name of each employee along with the employee's manager" is stated in SQL as

```
SELECT EMPLOYEE.Name, DEPARTMENT.Manager
   FROM EMPLOYEE, DEPARTMENT
  WHERE EMPLOYEE.Dept = DEPARTMENT.Dept
```

2. Consider the query "Retrieve the departments that do *not* stock the product with Prod# 555." (Assume that each department stocks at least one product.) A first attempt to state this query in SQL might be

```
SELECT STOCKS.Dept
   FROM STOCKS
  WHERE STOCKS.Prod<>555
```

   This SQL query is not correct since it will return each department that stocks at least one product different from 555, even if the department also stocks product 555. That is, this query is equivalent to the tuple calculus expression

   $$\{t\colon [Dept] \mid (\exists s)(Stocks(s) \wedge t[Dept]=s[Dept] \wedge s[Prod\#]\neq 555)\}$$

   Recall that this expression was constructed in the previous section in a failed attempt at stating the query under consideration. The query can be stated correctly in SQL as follows:

```
SELECT STOCKS.Dept
   FROM STOCKS
  WHERE STOCKS.Dept NOT IN
         (SELECT S.Dept
            FROM STOCKS S
           WHERE S.Prod = "555")
```

3. Consider the query "Retrieve the department that stocks *all* the products in the current instance of table PRODUCTS." To begin, we write an SQL expression that evaluates to a table containing all $<D, P>$ tuples such that D is a department in STOCKS that does *not* stock the product P from PRODUCTS.

```
SELECT ST.Dept, PRODUCTS.Prod
   FROM STOCKS ST, PRODUCTS
  WHERE NOT EXISTS (SELECT *
          FROM     STOCKS S
         WHERE     S.Dept = ST.Dept
           AND     S.Prod = PRODUCTS.Prod )
```

   Observe that the tuple $<D,P>$ is in the result of the entire query exactly when the inner query evaluates to the empty set of tuples when D replaces ST.Dept and P replaces PRODUCTS.Prod. Thus, the entire query evaluates to the set of tuples $<D,P>$ that are in the Cartesian product of STOCKS and PRODUCT but are not in the table STOCKS; that is, $<D,P>$ is in the result if and only if D is a department, P is a product, and D does not stock P.

To complete the query, we must write an expression that selects those departments from STOCKS that do not appear in the result of the preceding query. This can be accomplished by using the previous query as the basis for an inner subquery, obtaining

```
SELECT STOCKS.Dept
   FROM STOCKS
  WHERE NOT EXISTS
        (SELECT *
           FROM STOCKS ST, PRODUCTS
          WHERE ST.Dept = STOCKS.Dept
            AND NOT EXISTS (SELECT *
                              FROM STOCKS S
                             WHERE S.Dept = ST.Dept
                               AND S.Prod = PRODUCTS.Prod ) )
```

SQL provides Update operators as one would expect. Since these Update operators add little conceptually to the material already presented, we omit discussion of them. In Section 3.4, we shall return to SQL, using it to illustrate the concept of **aggregate operators.**

3.4 LANGUAGE EXTENSIONS

We have been using relational algebra (and, equivalently, tuple calculus) as our benchmark for the power of a query language. However, even relational algebra and tuple calculus lack the power necessary to perform certain important tasks. We now consider several such tasks.

Aggregate Operators

Often, one needs to pose queries such as "What is the average salary over all employees in the toys department?" "Which employees make less than the average salary of all employees?" "What is the maximum salary paid in each department?" These queries require that an aggregate quantity—such as average, sum, or maximum—be computed over some values contained in a collection of tuples. While the maximum and minimum aggregate operators can be expressed in relational algebra and tuple calculus, doing so is somewhat difficult (see exercise 3.14). What's more, other aggregate operators, such as Average, Sum, and Product, which compute arithmetic quantities, are outside the scope of relational algebra and tuple calculus. Consequently, most commercially available relational query languages provide a wide range of predefined aggregate operators. We shall illustrate the use of aggregate operators by constructing an SQL expression for each of the preceding three queries.

1. "What is the average salary over all employees in the toys department?"

```
SELECT Av_Sal = AVG(EMPLOYEE.Salary)
   FROM EMPLOYEE
  WHERE EMPLOYEE.Dept = "Toys"
```

This expression evaluates to an instance of the table scheme over the single attribute Av_Sal. The value of the table is the single tuple that represents the average of the Salary attributes over all the tuples that satisfy the qualification of the WHERE clause.

2. "Which employees make less than the average salary of all employees?"

```
SELECT Low_Emps = EMPLOYEE.SS
   FROM EMPLOYEE
  WHERE EMPLOYEE.Salary < (SELECT AVG(EMP.Salary)
                              FROM EMPLOYEE EMP )
```

This expression evaluates to an instance of the table scheme over the single attribute Low_Emps. The value of the table is the set of SS#s of those employees whose salaries are less than the average of all employee salaries—this latter quantity being the value of the inner subquery.

3. "What is the maximum salary paid in each department?"

```
SELECT EMPLOYEE.Dept, Max_Sal = MAX(EMPLOYEE.Salary)
   FROM EMPLOYEE
  GROUP BY EMPLOYEE.Dept
```

This query illustrates the SQL GROUP BY option. The expression evaluates to an instance of the table scheme over the attributes Dept and Max_Sal. The table instance contains a single tuple t for each department that appears in the EMPLOYEE table. Each of these t is such that t[Max_Sal] is the maximum salary paid to an employee in department t[Dept].

The Outer Join Operator

Consider the two table schemes[3]

PROFESSOR(Name, Dept, Phone, Research_Area)
STUDENT(Name, Major, GPA, Faculty_Advisor)

Suppose that the Board of Regents wishes to generate a listing of professors and the students advised by the professors, including with each professor-student pair all the information associated with the professor and student. The regents might construct the following relational algebra expression:

$$PROFESSOR \underset{Name=Faculty\_Advisor}{\bowtie} STUDENT$$

[3] From this point on, we often shall omit the domains of attributes when describing a table scheme.

The result of this query is a table over the attributes

(PROF.Name, Dept, Phone, Research_Area, STUD.Name, Major, GPA, Faculty_Advisor)

Of course, the result contains a good deal of redundancy since the information associated with each professor is repeated for each student that he or she advises. Let us suppose, however, that the regents, for ease of reference, desire the listing to be presented in this manner.

There is the potential for a problem in the listing. Suppose that some professor, call him Professor Lazy, advises *no* students. Observe that no entry for Professor Lazy will appear in the listing. That is, the listing omits all traces—Dept, Phone, Research_Area—of Professor Lazy. This is the case because Professor Lazy's tuple in the Professor table is a **dangling tuple** with respect to this Join (i.e., the value of the Join attribute Name has no matching value in the Faculty_Advisor attribute) and hence is "lost" in the result. It might well be that this effect is not what is desired by the regents. For example, suppose one of the regents' motivations for generating the listing is to identify professors who do not advise enough students. If the regents attempt to identify such professors by perusing the result of this query, they will overlook professors, like Professor Lazy, who advise no students at all!

In many cases, when performing a Join between a pair of tables, it is desirable to include in the result all dangling tuples. The modified Join operator with this behavior is known as the **outer join operator,** denoted here as $\underset{A=B}{OJ}$. Each tuple in R or S that dangles with respect to the join $R \underset{A=B}{\bowtie} S$ is "padded" with special values so that it can appear as a tuple in $R \underset{A=B}{OJ} S$. We call such special values **null values** and represent these values with the symbol $\perp$. Thus, for example, the result of the Outer join between instances

PROFESSOR

Name	Dept	Phone	Research_Area
Smith	CS	1234	Complexity
Luger	CS	2345	AI
Lazy	Math	3456	Stat
Harris	Math	9999	Algebra

and

STUDENT

Name	Major	GPA	Faculty_Advisor
Jones	CS	3.8	Lugar
Lee	CS	3.7	Harris
Long	Math	3.6	Smith
Drew	CS	3.2	Lugar
Feld	EE	3.1	Jennings

is

Prof.Name	Dept	Phone	Research_Area	Stud.Name	Major	GPA	Faculty_Advisor
Smith	CS	1234	Complexity	Long	Math	3.6	Smith
Lugar	CS	2345	AI	Drew	CS	3.2	Lugar
Lugar	CS	2345	AI	Jones	CS	3.8	Lugar
Lazy	Math	2345	Stat	⊥	⊥	⊥	⊥
⊥	⊥	⊥	⊥	Feld	EE	3.1	Jennings

Observe that, in the resulting table, Professor Lazy's tuple is padded with null values because he is the faculty advisor of no student in table STUDENT. Similarly, the student Feld's tuple is padded with null values because her faculty advisor Jennings is not in the table PROFESSOR.

The Outer join operator can be defined algorithmically as follows. To compute $R \underset{A=B}{OJ} S$,

1. Compute $ANSW = R \underset{A=B}{\bowtie} S$.
2. Compute $LEFT\_DIFF = (R - (\Pi_{<attributes\ in\ R>})ANSW))$.
3. Compute $RIGHT\_DIFF = (S - (\Pi_{<attributes\ in\ S>}ANSW))$.
4. Append to *ANSW* each tuple in *LEFT_DIFF* and *RIGHT_DIFF*, after padding with $\perp$.

See exercise 3.19 for a discussion of how we might attempt to state the Outer join operator within relational algebra.

The Outer join is a useful operator in many contexts, but a word of caution is in order. The null values used to pad dangling tuples in the result of the Outer join are a potential source of difficulty. For example, what values do null values match on Select and Join operations, and how are these values treated by aggregate functions? A consistent set of conventions for treating null values is required. Much research has been done on the "null value problem"; see, for example, Gallaire and Minker (1978); Gallaire, Minker, and Nicholas (1984); and Maier, Ullman, and Vard (1984).

Recursion

Suppose our RDM contains an instance of the table scheme

PARENT(Child, Par)

Suppose further that we wish to derive from this instance of PARENT the instance of table scheme *ANCESTOR(Desc,Ancs)*, which contains the tuple $<d,a>$ if and only if d is a descendant (as determined from the information contained in the given instance of table PARENT) of a. To see how the problem might be solved in relational algebra, first consider the problem of computing the "two-generation" table $ANCESTOR_2$, that is, the table instance that contains the tuple $<d,a>$ if and only if d is a child or grandchild of a.

$ANCESTOR_2$ can be expressed in relational algebra as

$$PARENT \cup (\Pi_{Child(1),\, Parent(2)}(PARENT \underset{Parent=Child}{\bowtie} PARENT))$$

[We use the notation *Child*(1) and *Parent*(2) to indicate that these attributes come, respectively, from the first and second PARENT table participating in the Join. Also, we assume that the attributes in the resulting table are renamed to *Desc* and *Ancs*.]

Similarly, if we wished to compute the three-generation ancestor relation $ANCESTOR_3$, we could write

$$PARENT \cup (\Pi_{Child(1),\, Parent(2)}(PARENT \underset{Parent=Child}{\bowtie} PARENT))$$

$$\cup\ (\Pi_{Child(1),\, Parent(2)}(\Pi_{Child(1),\, Parent(2)}(\mathrm{PARENT} \underset{Parent=Child}{\bowtie} \mathrm{PARENT})) \underset{Parent=Child}{\bowtie} PARENT)$$

In general, if we wish to compute $ANCESTOR_k$ in this manner, we will require an expression containing $k - 1$ Union operators. Consequently, we cannot write a single relational algebra expression (which, by definition, is of finite length) to compute the table ANCESTOR for arbitrary instances of table PARENT; if we write an expression of the preceding form containing k Union operators, the value of the expression on an instance of PARENT in which someone has ancestors $k + 2$ or more generations back will be incorrect. We conclude that relational algebra, and hence tuple calculus, lacks the power to express recursive queries.

Observe that we can express as a recurrence relation the required contents of the table ANCESTOR:

$$ANCESTOR_1 = PARENT$$
$$ANCESTOR_i = \mathrm{ANCESTOR}_{i-1} \cup (\pi_{<Child,\, Ancs>}(PARENT \underset{Par=Desc}{\bowtie} ANCESTOR_{i-1}))$$

Since any instance of the PARENT table contains only a finite number of tuples, there is for each instance of PARENT a k such that $ANCESTOR_k = ANCESTOR_{k+1} = \cdots$. A minimal instance $ANCESTOR_k$ with this property (i.e., no proper subset of $ANCESTOR_k$ has the property) is called a **least fixed point** of the recurrence relation and, by definition, is its solution for the given instance of the PARENT table. Observe that, while the exact value of the smallest k such that $ANCESTOR_k$ is a solution depends on the given instance of PARENT, the recurrence relation expresses correctly the contents of the ANCESTOR table for every instance of the table PARENT.

In Chapter 13, we shall further study recursive query languages as well as other extensions to the RDM.

Embedded Languages

Many commercial relational database systems support, in one form or another, the "embedding" of database interactions within a host programming language. At first blush, such a capability may seem to contradict our advocacy of high-level, standalone query languages; there are, however, several strong motivations for interfacing a high-level query language and a host programming language.

The extensions to the relational algebra and tuple calculus considered in the previous subsections illustrate that query languages based on these formalisms, while quite powerful, are not by themselves of sufficient power to perform certain very natural tasks. This observation can be construed as one motivation for a facility that supports the embedding of queries within the control structures of a host programming language. While one might argue that a better approach is to enhance a query language's inherent power, thereby obviating the need for the host programming language, this approach is practical to only a limited extent. If the query language is to provide for all the tasks that might potentially be required, it would have to become far more complex, both for the user to learn and for the query optimizer to process.

A second motivation for an embedding facility is that it provides a convenient tool for developing **persistent** database applications. Suppose, for example, that we have a population of noncomputer-literate users who wish to repeatedly perform one of a small number of predefined tasks. Rather than requiring these users to learn a relational query language, we would like to provide them with a menu-oriented interface that helps them specify their required tasks. To illustrate, suppose that, in a library application, the users need to perform the following tasks:

1. List a book's information by call number.
2. List a book's information by title.
3. List a book's information by author.
4. Update the catalog (authorized users only).

While a student of query languages should have little trouble composing the required queries, it is apparent that the typical library patron would far prefer to be presented with a sequence of menus, such as

```
                    Main Menus Options
1. List a book's information by call number.
2. List a book's information by title.
3. List a book's information by author.
4. Update the catalog (authorized users only).
Enter a choice, 1–4_
{ User enters choice 1 and the following prompt appears. }

                    Retrieve Book by Call Number
Enter a seven character call number, e.g., QA 076 D4 _______
```

The question then is, "How do we build software that allows the user to interact with a database via menus such as those depicted here?" Consider a high-level algorithm that supports this interaction:

```
Host-language print statements display main menu
Host-language read statements input user's choice
```

```
Error checking routine is invoked to verify syntax of response,
  possibly offering help in case of error
case: (user_response)
1: Host-language print statements display call number menu
   Host-language read statements input desired call number
   Error checking routine is invoked to verify syntax of call number,
     possibly offering help in case of error
   Special database interface retrieves appropriate catalog entry
   Host print statements display information in desired format
2:  .
    .
    .
```

This simple example illustrates the utility of a facility for embedding within a host programming language database interactions. We can identify three basic approaches to providing such a facility:

1. Supply a subroutine library of database routines. That is, provide routines such as Retrieve by attribute value, Delete by attribute value, and Insert a tuple. This interface resembles those rejected in Chapter 1 on the grounds of being too procedural.
2. Support the passing of "query strings." That is, provide a routine of the form

   ```
   CallDBMS(S)
   ```

   where S is a character array (a type in our host programming language) whose value at the time of the call is a string of characters that is a query in the relational query language. Thus, for example, we might make the call

   ```
   CallDBMS(S)
   ```

   where the value of *S* is the string

   ```
   'SELECT * FROM CATALOG WHERE CATALOG.CallNo = "QA 076 D4" '
   ```

   This approach improves greatly upon approach 1 in that it allows the programmer to use the same nonprocedural language used for interactive interrogations, which in turn allows a single query optimizer to process both interactive queries and queries passed from a host programming language.
3. Support the embedding of queries directly in the host code. This improvement over approach 2 leads to code of the form

   ```
   host statements
   read (InStr) { host statement reads desired call number }
   SELECT * FROM CATALOG WHERE CATALOG.CallNo = InStr
   host statements
   ```

   This direct embedding has at least two significant advantages over approach 2 *a.* *Ease of construction*: Note that, in the preceding example, we place in the WHERE clause a host-language variable containing the value of the desired call number. Consider how in the example from approach 2 the query string S would have to be constructed to reference the desired call number. The program would first input into a program variable the call number and then concatenate the contents of this variable to the remainder of the query string. This construction gets messy quickly if a query references several values, especially if some values are not character strings (e.g., if some values are integers).

b. *Optimization opportunities*: When queries are embedded directly into the code, an extended host-language compiler is required. Note that this extended compiler has the opportunity to do a significant amount of query optimization since much of the structure of a query can often be determined at compile time. Contrast this with approach 2, where little or no compile-time optimization is possible. (The value of the string S passed to CallDB generally cannot be determined at compile time.) The benefit of performing compile-time optimization is great since it is a one-time, offline task. Additionally, a great deal of current research addresses the multiple query optimization problem, where an optimizer attempts to construct a single efficient strategy for processing several of the queries appearing in a program. If these queries share common subtasks (e.g., Retrieve a common set of tuples), a good deal of the processing can be shared. Of the three approaches considered, only direct embedding potentially supports multiple query optimization.

A major issue that must be addressed in the design of a database/host-language interface is how to support communication between the host program and the database. We have already seen one aspect of this communication, the placement within the embedded query of host-language variables containing values that are part of the query's qualification. Similarly, for embedded Insert and Modify commands, we must be able to use program variables to communicate new values to the database. For example, the following is a sample embedded Insert command, where NewName, NewNum, NewSal, and NewDept are host-language variables.

```
INSERT INTO EMPLOYEE (SS=NewNum, Name=NewName
                      Salary=NewSal, Dept=NewDept)
```

Communication from the database to the host program is a bit more complex than the program-to-database communication considered earlier. This complexity is rooted in the fact that, in general, a query evaluates to a set of tuples of indeterminate size, while most programming languages provide no data type whose variables can hold an arbitrarily large number of tuples. Two solutions to this problem are

1. Interface the query language with a so-called object-oriented programming language that permits the definition of the appropriate data types. While this may be a clean solution in principle, it does not apply if our goal is to embed our queries in a more traditional host language (e.g., C, Pascal, FORTRAN). Chapter 4 further considers the object-oriented solution.
2. Modify the Retrieve command so that it returns one tuple at a time, allowing the host program to processes each tuple as it is returned. Consider, for example, the following SQL-like embedded SELECT statement:

```
SELECT(GetNum=EMPLOYEE.SS, GetName=EMPLOYEE.Name,
       GetSal=EMPLOYEE.Salary, GetDept=EMPLOYEE.Dept)
   FROM EMPLOYEE
  WHERE EMPOYEE.Dept = "Toys"
BEGIN_SELECT_LOOP
  host-language statements that process values held in
    host variables GetNum, GetName, GetSal, GetDept
END_SELECT_LOOP
```

In this approach, the SELECT statement has a processing loop associated with it. For each tuple *t* that qualifies, the attribute values of *t* are assigned to host variables as specified in the attribute list, and then the host statements contained in the scope of the select loop are executed.

SUMMARY AND ANNOTATED BIBLIOGRAPHY

This chapter developed nonprocedural query languages based on predicate calculus; for a thorough treatment of the predicate calculus, the reader is referred to Bridge (1977), and Chang and Lee (1979). The chapter first introduced tuple calculus, an abstract query language based on predicate calculus. A fundamental result is that tuple calculus and relational algebra have identical expressive power. We presented a proof of one direction of this theorem; for a complete proof, the reader is referred to Codd (1972); Maier, Ullman, and Vardi (1984); and Ullman (1982).

After studying tuple calculus, we introduced SQL, the most important commercial query language. We also considered several extensions to relational algebra– and predicate calculus–based languages, including aggregate operators, the Outer join operator [Codd (1979)], recursion [Agrawal (1988); Gallaire and Minker (1978); Gallaire, Minker, and Nicolas (1984); Henschen and Naqvi (1984); Ullman (1988); and Ullman (1989)], and embedded query languages. Recursion, as well as other extensions to the relational model, are studied in Chapter 13.

This chapter concludes Part One, Definition of the Relational Data Model Abstract Data Type. Part Two, Design of the Relational Data Model Abstract Data Type, considers the issue of how to design the table schemes comprising an RDM to maximize semantic integrity. Parts Three and Four, Implementations of the Relational Data Model Abstract Data Types, consider the problem of implementing an RDM in external memory. This study includes file structures, concurrency control, recovery, and query optimization.

EXERCISES

1. Consider the following two table instances:

R

A	B	C
a	x	y
a	z	w
b	x	k
b	m	j
c	x	y
f	g	h

S

D	E
x	y
z	w

Give the *exact* table instance that will result from each of the following queries:[4]

a.
```
SELECT R.A
FROM R, S
WHERE (R.B != S.D) AND (R.C != S.E)
```

b. $\{t{:}[A] \mid (\forall s)(\exists r)R(r) \wedge$
$[\ S(s) \Rightarrow (\ (r[B]=s[D]) \wedge (t[A]=r[A])\ )]\}$

c. $\{t{:}[A] \mid (\forall s)(\exists r)$
$[\ S(s) \Rightarrow (\ (r[B]=s[D]) \wedge (t[A]=r[A])\ )]\}$

d. $\{t{:}[A] \mid (\forall s)(\exists r)S(s) \wedge$
$(r[B]=s[D]) \wedge (t[A]=r[A])\}$

e. $\{t{:}[A] \mid (\forall s)(\exists r)$
$[\ (R(r) \wedge S(s)\ ) \Rightarrow (\ (r[B]=s[D]) \wedge (t[A]=r[A])\ )]\}$

f. $\{t{:}[A] \mid (\exists r)(\forall s)$
$[\ (\ R(r) \wedge S(s)\ ) \Rightarrow (\ (r[B]=s[D]) \wedge (t[A]=r[A])\ )]\}$

g. $\{t{:}[A] \mid (\exists r)(\forall s)R(r) \wedge$
$[\ S(s) \Rightarrow (\ (r[B]=s[D]) \wedge (t[A]=r[A])\ )]\}$

h. $\{t{:}[A] \mid (\exists r)(\forall s)$
$[\ S(s) \Rightarrow (\ (r[B]=s[D]) \wedge (t[A]=r[A])\ )]\}$

[4] If a query is not legal, state why.

2. Consider the following instances of table *R*:

R

A	B
x	1
x	2
x	3
y	3
w	2
w	5

S

C
1
2
3

Give the *exact* table instance that will result from each of the following queries:[5]

a. $\{t{:}[A] \mid (\forall s)(\exists r)(S(s) \Rightarrow [(t[A]=r[A]) \wedge (r[B]=s[C])])\}$

b. $\{t{:}[A] \mid (\exists r)(\forall s)(S(s) \Rightarrow [(t[A]=r[A]) \wedge (r[B]=s[C])])\}$

c. $\{t{:}[A] \mid (\exists r)(\forall s)(R(s) \Rightarrow [(t[A]=r[A]) \wedge (r[B]=s[C])])\}$

3. Consider the following two table instances:

R

A	B	C
a	b	c
a	d	g
x	b	f

S

D	E
b	f
d	f

Give the *exact* result of each of the following queries against these instances:

a. $\{t{:}[A] \mid (\forall s)(\exists r)(\ (R(r) \wedge (t[A]=r[A])) \wedge (S(s) \Rightarrow (r[B]=s[D]))\ )\}$

b. $\{t{:}[A] \mid (\exists s)(\forall s)(\ (R(r) \wedge (t[A]=r[A])) \wedge (S(s) \Rightarrow (r[B]=s[D]))\ )\}$

4. Consider the following two table instances:

R

A	B
a1	b1
a2	b2
a1	b3
a1	b3
a3	b4
a4	b4

S

A	C
a1	x
a1	y
a2	x
a3	y
a4	z

a. What is the exact result of the following query?

$$\{t{:}[B] \mid (\exists r)(\forall\ s)(R(r) \wedge (t[B]=r[B])) \\ \wedge [(S(s) \wedge (s[A]=r[A])) \Rightarrow (S[C] = \text{“x”})]\ \}$$

[5] If a query is not legal, state why.

b. For the same instances of R and S given in part a, show the exact result of the following query:

$$\{t{:}[B] \mid (\forall s)(\exists r)(R(r) \wedge (t[B] = r[B])) \\ \wedge [\, (S(s) \wedge (s[A] = r[A]))\Rightarrow(S[C] = \text{"x"})]\}$$

5. Consider the following two table instances:

S

A	B	C
a1	b1	c1
a2	b1	c1
a2	b2	e2
a3	b2	e2

R

D	E
b1	e1
b2	e2

Show the *exact* result of evaluating each of the following queries:[6]

a. $((\Pi_{<A>}S) - (\Pi_{<A>}(\Pi_{<A,D,E>}(S \times R)) - (\Pi_{<A,D,E>}(S \underset{B=D}{\bowtie} R))))$

b. $\{t{:}[A] \mid (\exists s)(\forall r)(S(s) \wedge (t[A]{=}s[A])) \\ \wedge [R(r) \Rightarrow (s[B]{=}r[D])]\}$

c. $\{t{:}[A] \mid (\forall r)(\exists s)(S(s) \wedge (t[A]{=}s[A])) \\ \wedge [R(r) \Rightarrow (s[B]{=}r[D])]\}$

d. $\{t{:}[A] \mid (\exists s)(\forall r)(S(s) \wedge (t[A]{=}s[A])) \\ \wedge [(R(r) \wedge (s[C]{=}r[E]))\Rightarrow (s[B] \neq r[D])]\}$

e.
```
SELECT S.A
FROM S,R
WHERE (S.C != R.E)
```

6. Consider the table schemes Student(Name, Co_Num) and Course(Co_Num, Prof) and the following pair of tuple calculus expressions:

$$\{t{:}\ [Name] \mid (\forall c)(\exists s)(Student(s) \wedge (t[Name]{=}s[Name])) \\ \wedge [\, (Course(c) \wedge (c[Prof]{=}Jones)) \Rightarrow (s[Co\_Num]{=}c[Co\_Num])\,]$$

$$\{t{:}\ [Name] \mid (\exists s)(\forall c)(Student(s) \wedge (t[Name] \Rightarrow s[Name])) \\ \wedge [\, (Course(c) \wedge (c[Prof]{=}Jones)) \Rightarrow (s[Co\_Num]{=}c[Co\_Num])\,]$$

a. Construct an instance of Student and an instance of Course such that the expressions evaluate to the same answer. Your instances must contain at least two tuples each.

b. Construct an instance of Student and an instance of Course such that the expressions evaluate to different answers. Your instances must contain at least two tuples each.

---

[6] If a query is not legal, state why.

7. Consider the following two table instances:

R

A	B	C	D
a	1	2	*x*
a	2	2	*x*
b	1	2	*x*
b	1	3	*x*
b	2	2	*x*
c	5	2	*x*

S

B	C	D	E
1	2	*x*	*p*
1	3	*x*	*q*
2	2	*x*	*r*

Translate each of the following SQL statements into an equivalent tuple calculus expression, and show the exact result of each query when evaluated against the preceding instances of *R* and *S*.

a.
```
SELECT R.A, S.E
FROM R, S
WHERE (R.B = 2) AND (R.C = S.C)
```

b.
```
SELECT R.A
FROM R, S
WHERE (R.B <> S.B)
```

8. Consider the following table schemes of an RDM:

```
EMPLOYEE(SS#, Name, Salary, Dept)
PERSONAL(SS#, Age, Highest_Degree)
DEPARTMENT(Dept, Manager, Location, D_Desc)
```

Assume that the semantics of these schemes are as discussed throughout Chapters 2 and 3. Express each of the following in tuple calculus and SQL:

a. Retrieve the SS# and name of all employees of the toys department who earn between $20,000 and $40,000.

b. Retrieve the SS# and name of all employees whose highest degree is a BA and who earn between $20,000 and $40,000.

c. Retrieve the SS# and name of all employees whose manager has SS# 444444444 and who earn between $20,000 and $40,000.

d. Retrieve the SS# and name of all employees whose highest degree is a BA, whose manager has SS# 444444444, and who earn between $20,000 and $40,000.

9. Consider the following table schemes of an RDM:

```
EMPLOYEE(Name, Dept, Salary)
DEPARTMENT(Dept, Manager)
```

Assume that managers are also employees, that every department has exactly one manager, that every manager manages exactly one department, and that no two employees have the same name. Express each of the following in tuple calculus and SQL:

a. Retrieve nonmanagers who earn more than at least one manager.

b. Retrieve nonmanagers who earn more than all managers.

c. Retrieve nonmanagers who earn more than their own manager.

10. Consider the following table schemes of an RDM:

```
PATIENT(Name, Disease, Treatment)
DOCTOR(Name, Specialty)
```

Assume that Names uniquely identify both patients and doctors and that some doctors may also be patients. Assume that diseases and specialties are the same kinds of things (e.g., Flu might be both a disease and a specialty). A doctor may have more than one specialty, a patient may have more than one disease, and each disease a patient has may be treated in more than one way. Express each of the following in tuple calculus and SQL:

a. Retrieve the names of doctors who have a disease that is one of their specialties.

b. Retrieve the names of doctors who have all the diseases that are their specialties.

c. Retrieve the diseases for which there is only one treatment.

d. Retrieve the names of the patients *P* with some disease (call it *D*) such that if any other patient *P'* is receiving some treatment *T* for *D*, then *P* also is receiving *T* for *D*. That is, we want those patients with some disease who are receiving all known treatments for that disease.

11. Assume the following table schemes:

```
SHIP(S_Name, Captain)
CREW(C_Name, Planet, S_Name)
GROWS(Planet, Flower)
ALLERGIES(C_Name, Flower)
```

Translate each of the following queries into relational algebra, tuple calculus, and SQL:

a. Get the names of crewmembers allergic to no flowers that grow on their home planet.

b. Get the names of crewmembers allergic to all flowers that grow on their home planet.

c. Get the names of crewmembers allergic only to flowers that grow on their home planet (and possibly grow elsewhere).

d. Get the names of crewmembers allergic to all the flowers that do not grow on their home planet.

e. Get the names of crewmembers allergic to exactly the same flowers as their captains are allergic to.

12. Refer to the table schemes of exercise 10 and consider the expressions

$$\text{(E1) } \{t{:}[Name] \mid (\exists p(PATIENT(p) \wedge t[Name]=p[Name])\}$$
$$\text{(E2) } \{t{:}[Name] \mid (\exists p)(\exists d)(PATIENT(p) \wedge DOCTOR(d) \wedge t[Name]=p[Name] \wedge p[Name]=d[Name]) \}$$

Construct nonempty instances of PATIENT and DOCTOR such that

a. The expressions evaluate to the same value.

b. The expressions evaluate to different values, but the second expression does not evaluate to an empty set of tuples.

c. The second expression evaluates to an empty set of tuples.

13. Describe the set of departments returned by the following query:

$$\{t{:}\ [Dept] \mid (\forall s')(\exists s)(STOCKS(s) \wedge (t[Dept]=s[Dept]) \wedge (STOCKS(s') \wedge (s'[Dept]=s[Dept]) \Rightarrow (s'[Prod\#] \neq 555))\}$$

14. Consider the relation EMPLOYEE(Name, Salary). Write expressions that will return the names of all lowest paid employees (i.e., all employees who earn less than or equal to all other employees) in tuple calculus and relational algebra. Do *not* use aggregate functions. You may assume that attribute Name uniquely identifies an employee.

15. Give the tuple calculus expression that would result from application to each of the following relational algebra expressions of the translation algorithm Alg_To_Calc:

a. $\Pi_{<Name,\ Manager>}(EMPLOYEE \underset{Dept=Dept}{\bowtie} DEPARTMENT)$

b. $(\Pi_{<Dept>}(STOCKS) - \Pi_{<Dept>}(\sigma_{Prod\#=555}STOCKS))$

16. Consider the following relational algebra expression:

$$\Pi_{<Dept>}(STOCKS \div (\Pi_{<Prod\#>}PRODUCTS))$$

a. Express the expression in terms of the five basic relational operators.

b. Give the tuple calculus expression that would result from application to your expression in part a of the translation algorithm Alg_To_Calc.

17. Develop a translation algorithm Alg_To_SQL analogous to the Alg_To_Calc algorithm.

*18. Develop a translation algorithm SQL_To_Calc.

19. Attempt to develop an algorithm that maps a relational expression containing the Outer join operator into an equivalent relational expression not containing the Outer join operator. You will find that the current instance of the database must be assumed to contain certain "constant table instances." Explain.

20. Using the embedded query language of Section 3.4, construct a pseudocode program to compute the ANCESTOR table of Section 3.4.

PART ***TWO***

Design of the Relational Data Model Abstract Data Type

Chapter ***4***
Data Models and Data Modeling

Chapter ***5***
Semantic Design and Normalization for the Relational Data Model

Chapter ***6***
Dependencies and Normalization: A Further Study

CHAPTER **4**

Data Models and Data Modeling

This chapter begins our study of the process by which the informational requirements of an application are represented within the framework of a particular data model. Chapter 1 informally introduced the entity relation (E/R) diagram as our first data model and then began our study of the relational data model (RDM). In this chapter, we formalize the definition of the E/R data model and demonstrate how the model is used to represent several complex real-world situations. We then consider the problem of mapping information originally represented in the E/R model to the tables of an RDM and, in so doing, discover several limitations of the RDM, most notably its lack of support for a strong notion of object identity. These limitations lead us to introduce the **object-oriented data model,** a relatively new model that enhances the RDM in several important ways.•

Chapters 5 and 6, with the introduction of the theory of **normalization,** continue our study of the problem of representing the informational requirements of an application in the RDM. Chapters 7 through 12 then study physical implementations for the RDM, including external file structures, transaction management, and query optimization. Chapter 13 resumes our study of alternative data models (including the object-oriented model) by considering additional representational issues and by exploring how RDM implementations serve as the foundation for implementations of the alternative models.

4.1 A FORMAL LOOK AT THE E/R MODEL

The E/R data model serves as the point of departure for many of the topics treated in this chapter. Although the E/R model has been implemented successfully by a variety of experimental database management systems (DBMSs) the E/R model's greatest value is as an intuitive and general-purpose information representation tool, often serving as the framework for an initial representation of the informational requirements of an application. This initial representation then is mapped by database designers to the data model supported by the particular commercial DBMS available at the target computing system (e.g., a relational, object-oriented, network, or hierarchical data model). In fact, careful analysis of the initial E/R representation often indicates which data model is most appropriate for the application and, ideally, influences the acquisition of the commercial DBMS.

In the three previous chapters, we used E/R diagrams informally, as an intuitive means of conceptualizing the informational content of an application of interest. This section presents a more rigorous definition of the E/R model. As E/R definitions and concepts are developed, we shall discover a high degree of similarity between the E/R and relational models. The section that follows pursues the correspondence between the two data models by considering the process of mapping information originally represented within the E/R framework to an RDM.

Entity Sets and Attributes

The E/R model assumes the existence of a **universe *E* of entities.** An entity is a primitive of the model, which is to say we make no attempt to define it formally. Intuitively, the universe *E* is inclusive enough to encompass all objects that might ever be relevant to our application. An **entity set** is a construct of the E/R model that corresponds to a condition that, at any point in time, defines a subset of the the universe *E*, namely, the subset of *E* consisting of exactly those entities that satisfy the condition. For example, we can define the entity set EMPLOYEE to correspond to the condition *e is an entity that currently works in our store*. Note that the definition of an entity set is invariant over time, while the actual set defined by the condition changes over time. The current value of the entity set (i.e., the set that is currently defined) is often called the current **instance** of the entity set.

The formalism used to express an entity set's membership condition is a unary **membership predicate,** a function $P(\cdot)$ that evaluates to either true or false when applied to any entity $e \in E$. The membership predicate for an entity set is typically given the same name as the entity set itself. Hence, for example, we might define the entity set EMPLOYEE in terms of the membership predicate

> *EMPLOYEE*(*e*)=*True* if and only if $e \in E$ and *e* is a person who currently works in our store.

The current instance of entity set *ES* with membership predicate *P* is the set of entities on which *P* currently evaluates to true. Any entity *e* on which the membership predicate for entity set *ES* evaluates to true is said to be a **member** of the current instance of entity set *ES*, a situation frequently denoted by $e \in ES$. In the previous example, any entity *e* for which *EMPLOYEE*(*e*) evaluates to true (i.e., any entity that is a current employee of our store) is a member of the current instance of the entity set EMPLOYEE, and we would write $e \in EMPLOYEE$.

There are many different mechanisms for specifying a membership predicate. Recall from Chapter 3, for example, the tuple calculus's use of a predicate *T* in the atom $T(t)$. In this construct, *t* is a tuple variable that ranges over vectors of database values and the atom $T(t)$ asserts that *t* is a member of the current instance of table *T*, and, hence, for any substitution for *t* of database values *v*, the truth value of $T(v)$ can be established by simple inspection of the current (finite) instance of table *T*. In contrast, the E/R model does not restrict, to any specific mechanism, the procedure for determining the truth value of membership predicate $P(e)$ on entity $e \in E$. In its full generality, the E/R model assumes only that a membership predicate is **decidable,** that is, that there exists a finite procedure for determining the truth value of $P(e)$ for every $e \in E$.

In previous chapters, we informally associated attributes with our entities. For example, with the entity EMPLOYEE, we associated the attributes Name, SS#, Salary, and Dept, and we depicted this association as shown in Figure 4.1.

Figure 4.1 EMPLOYEE with attributes

The E/R model formalizes the association between an entity set *ES* and its attributes in much the same way as the relational model formalizes the definition of a tuple. Recall from Section 2.2 that a tuple *t* is consistent with table scheme *T*(<attribute_list>) if *t* maps each attribute name *A* in attribute_list into a value from the domain of *A*. In the E/R model, an entity set's attribute *A* is viewed as mapping each current member *e* of the entity set to the *A*-value associated with *e*. The E/R model uses the term **value set** (similar in the relational model to an attribute's domain) to describe the set of underlying values to which an attribute maps. For example, the value set of attribute Age, which is associated with entity set EMPLOYEE, might be

POSINT = {integer n | n > 0}

In this case, Age is a function,

Age: {instances of entity set EMPLOYEE} → POSINT

and if *e* is a member of the current instance of the EMPLOYEE entity set (i.e., EMPLOYEE(*e*) is true), Age(*e*)=30 specifies that the age of entity *e* is 30.

One important difference between the E/R and relational models concerns the type of values that attributes can assume. Recall from Chapter 2 that in the RDM, there is a restriction that attributes be scalar valued. As we shall begin to discover in Chapter 5, this restriction, known as **first normal form (1NF),** has strong justifications of both practical and theoretical natures. Unfortunately, the 1NF restriction, in several common situations, makes the modeling of information difficult. In contrast, the E/R model, intended more as a representational tool than as a data model to be implemented, places no such restriction on attribute values and, hence, can model information more naturally in these problem situations.

In the E/R model, an attribute, in addition to being a simple-valued function, may be either set valued or vector valued. A set-valued attribute A is defined over an underlying values set VS but assumes as its values *subsets* of VS. That is, in this case, attribute A of entity set ES is a function

$$A\text{: \{instances of } ES\} \rightarrow POWER\_SET(VS)$$

To illustrate the utility of a set-valued attribute, suppose that, as in Figure 4.1, we wish to associate with the entity set EMPLOYEE the attribute Dept. Suppose, however, that an employee could be assigned to several departments simultaneously. This situation is modeled most naturally by allowing function Dept to map each EMPLOYEE entity to the *set* of departments to which that employee is assigned. Hence, Dept is a function

$$Dept\text{: \{instances of EMPLOYEE\}} \rightarrow \text{POWER\_SET(\{strings\})}$$

If, for example, $e \in EMPLOYEE$ is assigned to the toys, books, and software departments, we would have

$$Dept(e) = \{Toys, Books, Software\}$$

The reader should consider how the tables of the RDM scheme introduced in Chapter 2 would need to be modified to handle this situation. We shall return to such issues in Section 4.2 and in the exercises.

As a second illustration of nonscalar-valued attributes, suppose we wish to associate employees with the names of their dependents. One solution is to define the set-valued attribute

$$Dependents\text{: \{instances of EMPLOYEE\}} \rightarrow \text{POWER\_SET(\{strings\})}$$

This is a satisfactory solution for the situation described, but suppose that we wish to also associate with each dependent the dependent's sex and the dependent's date of birth (DOB). One way to address this problem is to change the underlying value set of attribute Dependents from strings to the Cartesian product

$$\text{\{strings\}} \times \text{\{M,F\}} \times \text{\{dates\}}$$

If every employee had exactly one dependent, we would define Dependents to be a vector-valued function

$$Dependents\text{: \{instances of EMPLOYEE\}} \rightarrow \text{\{strings\}} \times \text{\{M,F\}} \times \text{\{dates\}}$$

Hence, for example, we might have Dependents(e)=(John, M, 01-07-1991). This definition of the function Dependents, however, is not sufficient under the more realistic assumption that each employee can have any number of dependents. (Note that, as just defined, Dependents maps to a single element of—rather than a subset of—the Cartesian product {strings} × {M,F} × {dates}.) To accommodate the arbitrary number of dependents that each employee has, we must modify the definition of the function Dependents as follows so that it becomes set valued:

Dependents: {instances of EMPLOYEE} $\rightarrow$
Power_Set({strings} $\times$ {M,F} $\times$ {dates})

Hence, for example, if employee entity *e* has multiple dependents, we would have a mapping such as Dependents(*e*)={(Bill, M, 06-07-1988), (Sue, F, 01-04-1985), (Jane, F, 10-07-1992)}. The reader should consider how such a situation could be handled in the RDM.

Relationship Sets

As we have seen in the previous chapters, the third critical component of the E/R model (entity sets and attributes being the first two) is **relationships.** The most important type of relationship is between entity sets, although relationships between attributes can be defined also. A **relationship set** *RS* between entity sets specifies a list $ES_1, ES_2, \ldots, ES_k$ of the entity sets involved in the relationship it models. Like an RDM table scheme, this list specifies the structure of the relationship, and we say that *RS* is a relationship set **over** entity sets $ES_1, ES_2, \ldots, ES_k$. A relationship over a list of *k* (*not* necessarily distinct) entity sets is called a *k*-ary relationship set.

A *k*-ary relationship set *RS* specifies also a *k*-ary membership predicate, typically given the same name as the relationship set, which, at any point in time, defines the current **instance** of relationship set *RS*. Assuming that *RS* is a relationship set defined over the list $ES_1, ES_2, \ldots, ES_k$ of entity sets, membership predicate $RS(\cdot,\cdot,\ldots,\cdot)$ is applied to a vector $<e_1, \ldots, e_k>$ of entities, where each entity e_i is a member of the current instance of ES_i. The current instance of relationship set *RS* then is the set

$$\{<e_1, \ldots, e_k> \mid e_i \in ES_i, 1 \leq i \leq k \text{ and } RS(<e_1, \ldots, e_k>)=True\}$$

Hence, the current instance of a relationship set over the list $ES_1, ES_2, \ldots, ES_k$ of entities is precisely a mathematical relation (see Section 2.4) on the current instances of the entity sets $ES_1, ES_2, \ldots, ES_k$ (i.e., it is a subset of the Cartesian product of the current instances of these entity sets) and resembles somewhat an instance of an RDM's table scheme. When $<e_1, \ldots, e_k>$ is a member of the current instance of entity set *RS*, we frequently write $<e_1, \ldots, e_k> \in RS$.

To illustrate the concept of a relationship set, consider first a binary relationship set, that is, a relationship set over two entity sets. Suppose that our application includes EMPLOYEE and DEPARTMENT entity sets and that, as in Figure 1.3, we wish to model a relationship Assigned_To between EMPLOYEE and DEPARTMENT. In terms of the E/R model's formalism, relationship set Assigned_To is defined over EMPLOYEE and DEPARTMENT, and membership in the current instance of the relationship set can be expressed as

Assigned_To(*e,d*)=*True* iff ($e \in EMPLOYEE$) $\wedge$ ($d \in DEPARTMENT$) $\wedge$
(*e* currently is assigned to department *d*)

Hence, if, for example, at the current point in time, employee e is assigned to the department d, we would have $(e,d) \in Assigned\_To$. Equivalently, we have $Assigned\_To(e,d)=True$ for such e and d.

While binary relationship sets are by far the most common type of relationship sets, k-ary (for $k > 2$) relationship sets often are useful modeling tools also. Suppose, for example, that a university application includes the entity sets STUDENT, FACULTY, and STAFF and that, in the university being modeled, each student has a faculty advisor (who is a faculty member) and an administrative advisor (who is a staff member). In this case, the relationship Advises might be modeled as a tertiary relationship set over STUDENT, FACULTY, and STAFF. In particular, we could define the membership predicate

Advises(s,f,st)=True iff $(s \in STUDENT) \wedge (f \in FACULTY) \wedge (st \in STAFF) \wedge$
(f is the faculty advisor of s) $\wedge$ (st is the staff advisor of s)

We now turn to the notion of a **recursive** relationship set. Inspection of the definition of a relationship set reveals that the entity sets ES_i appearing in the list over which relational set *RS* is defined need not be distinct. We say that a relationship set *RS* is recursive if the entity set list over which *RS* is defined contains multiple occurrences of one or more entity sets. Consider, for example, an entity set PERSON along with the recursive relationship set Ancestor defined on the entity set list PERSON, PERSON and depicted in Figure 4.2. The membership predicate for relationship Ancestor can be defined as

Ancestor(p,p')=True iff $(p \in PERSON) \wedge (p' \in PERSON) \wedge$ (p' is a genealogical ancestor of p)

The pair p,p' is a member of the current instance of this relationship set if and only if person p' is an ancestor of person p. The reader should contrast the recursive relationship set Ancestor with the recursive definition given in Section 3.4 of table scheme ANCESTOR.

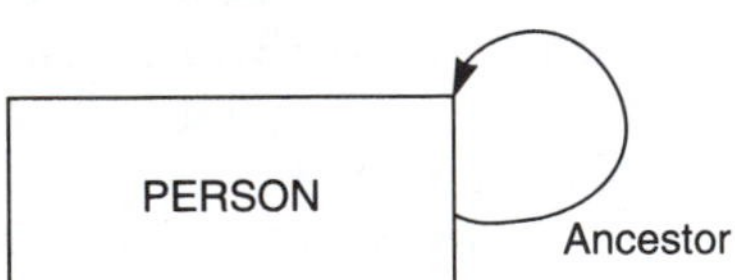

Figure 4.2 Recursive Ancestor relationship set

As the closing points of this subsection, we note that relationship sets can be defined between attributes and that attributes can be associated with relationship sets. The first of these constructs is explored in exercise 4.5. To illustrate the utility of associating attributes with relationship sets, suppose again that our university application includes entity sets FACULTY and STUDENTS and that the relationship set Taught is defined over these entities with membership predicate

Taught(f,s)=True iff ($f \in FACULTY$) $\wedge$ ($s \in STUDENT$) $\wedge$ (*s* has completed a class taught by *f*)

It is natural that we might wish to capture information—for example, course number and grade—associated with each member of this relationship set. This task can be accomplished via the attribute Class_Record defined by

Class_Record: {instances of Taught} $\rightarrow$ Power_Set({strings} $\times$ {A,B,C,D,F})

If, for example, student *s* has taken two courses from faculty member *f*—CS 100, earning a grade of A, and CS 200, earning a grade of B—we would have *Class_Record*($<s,f>$) = {(CS 100, A), (CS 200, B)}.

Relationship Set Properties and Other Data Constraints

The E/R model includes facilities for asserting various properties that *describe* the information being modeled, so called **meta-data.** Two of the primary motivations for such a facility are as follows:

1. As we have indicated earlier in this chapter, the E/R model is typically used as a starting point in the database design process. Once the informational requirements of an application have been represented in the E/R framework, the next step often is to map the E/R representation to the data model (e.g., to an RDM) supported by the target DBMS. As we shall see in the following section, certain descriptive information supplied by the user is critical to this mapping process.
2. Some descriptive information translates to **integrity constraints.** That is, the DBMS (whether it directly implements the E/R model or some other data model) should allow an update to the database only after the DBMS has verified that the result of the update leaves the database in a state consistent with all relevant integrity constraints. Chapter 6 briefly considers the task of integrity enforcement.

Several important properties can be specified for relationship sets, and these properties play a critical role in determining how to model as RDM tables the entity sets involved in the relationships. A relationship set's **functionality** is one such property. Here, we consider the functionality of binary relationship sets over entity sets; the exercises consider the functionality of nonbinary relationship sets and of relationship sets over attributes.

The functionality of a relationship set *RS* over entity sets *A* and *B* is either **1 : 1** (also called **one-to-one**), **1 : *n*** (also called **one-to-many**), or ***n* : *m*** (also called **many-to-many**). Relationship set *RS* is 1 : 1 between entity sets *A* and *B* if, at any point in time,

1. For each $a \in A$, there exists exactly one $b \in B$, such that $<a,b> \in RS$, and
2. For each $b \in B$, there exists exactly one $a \in A$, such that $<a,b> \in RS$.

In other words, at any point in time, each member a of the current instance of A is related by RS to exactly one member b of the current instance of B, and each member b of the current instance of B is related by RS to exactly one member of the current instance of entity set A. In our department store application, we might assert that the relationship set Describes over PERSONAL and EMPLOYEE is 1 : 1, a situation we would depict as shown in Figure 4.3.

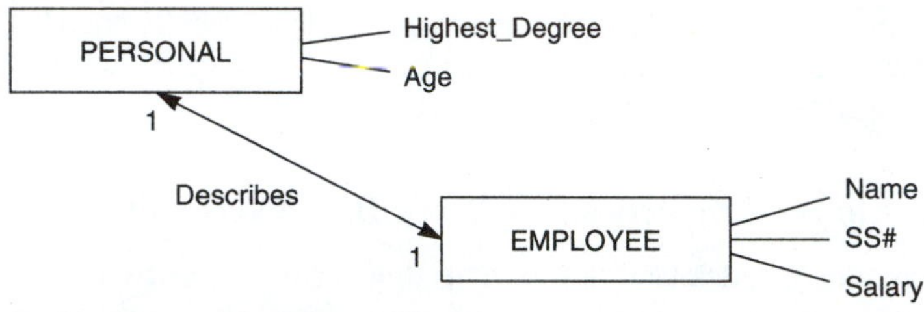

Figure 4.3 E/R diagram showing 1 : 1 relationship

Relationship set RS is $1:n$ from entity set A to entity set B if, at any point in time,

For each $b \in B$, there exists exactly one $a \in A$, such that $<a,b>\in RS$.

In other words, at any point in time, each member of the current instance of entity set A is related by RS to zero or more members of the current instance of entity set B, and each member of the current instance of entity set B is related by RS to exactly one member of the current instance of entity set A. In our department store application, we might assert that the relationship set Assigned_To is $1:n$ from DEPARTMENT to EMPLOYEE, a situation we would depict as shown in Figure 4.4.

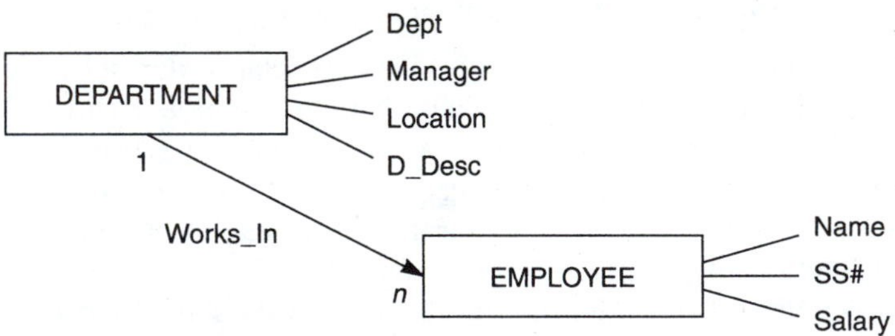

Figure 4.4 E/R diagram showing $1:n$ relationship

Observe that if a relationship set RS is 1 : 1 between A and B, it is necessarily also $1:n$ from A to B and $1:n$ from B to A. However, since the condition that RS is 1 : 1 between A and B is stronger than either of the $1:n$ conditions (although it is equivalent to the two $1:n$ conditions taken together), it is the 1 : 1 condition that should be specified when it indeed is known to hold.

When the functionality of a relationship set *RS* over entity sets *A* and *B* is left unspecified by the user (and no other properties are specified), no restrictions may be assumed on *RS*, and, hence, in a given instance of *RS*, $a \in A$ may be related to zero or more members of *B*, and $b \in B$ may be related to zero or more members of *A*. The functionality of such a relationship set is said to be $n:m$, a situation we would depict as shown in Figure 4.5.

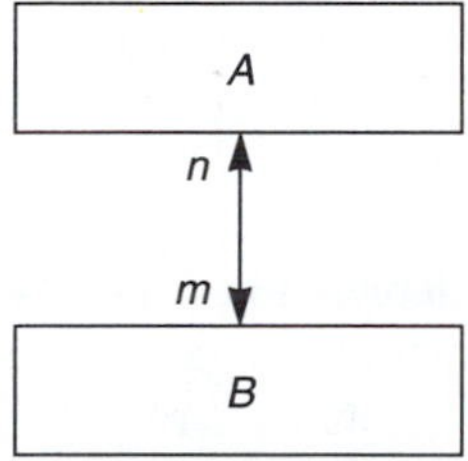

Figure 4.5 $n:m$ relationship set

It is important to emphasize that the functionality of a relationship set pertains to the *nature* of the relationship and is "instance independent." That is, the functionality of a relationship set does not pertain to a particular instance of the information that is being modeled (e.g., to the information that describes our department store at some single instance in time) but rather to all possible instances of the information. We cannot deduce from inspection of an E/R diagram, nor from an instance of the information that it models, the functionality of the relationships. Rather, *the functionality of a relationship set is information that must be supplied to us by people familiar with the nature of the application.*

Another type of information we can associate with a relationship set is an **existence dependency.** Note that our definition of a $1:n$ relationship set (and, hence, of a $1:1$ relationship set) from *A* to *B* implies that, at any point in time, each *b* in the current instance of *B* must be related to some member of the current instance of *A*. In other words, a member of *B* *cannot exist* without the member *A* that corresponds to it under the $1:n$ relationship. Such an entity set *B* is said to be a **weak** entity set.

While the definition of a $1:n$ relationship set (and, hence, of a $1:1$ relationship set) implicitly includes an existence dependency, such is not the case when the functionality of a relationship set is $n:m$. However, by explicitly asserting an existence dependency on a relationship set over *A* and *B*, we can specify that the existence of a member of the current instance of entity set *B* requires the existence of at least one member of the current instance of entity set *A* that is related to *B* by means of *RS*. For example, if Treats is an $n:m$ relationship set between DOCTOR and PATIENT, it may be appropriate (depending on the policies of the hospital being modeled) to assert on Treats an existence dependency, with PATIENT designated as the weak entity set. Such an assertion forces a new patient to be assigned to one or more doctors immediately upon admission. Note, however, that such an existence dependency would not be appropriate if the hospital uses the PATIENT entity set to model patients once they are dismissed and no longer under the care of a particular doctor.

It is instructive to note that if a DBMS implementing the E/R model enforces existence dependencies, it must allow "simultaneous" (or **atomic**) updating of certain entity and relation sets. For example, if there is a 1 : 1 relationship set over entity sets *A* and *B*, the DBMS must support the simultaneous updating of entity sets *A* and *B* and of relationship set *RS*, or else we will at some point have a violation of the implicit existence dependency. That is, since a 1 : 1 relationship set *RS* between *A* and *B* is also a 1 : *n* relationship set both from *A* to *B* and *B* to *A*, a pair of existence dependencies is implied. In terms of the Describes relationship set depicted in Figure 4.3, the DBMS would have to support the simultaneous insertions of new members into EMPLOYEE and PERSONAL and into Describes of the entity pair that relates the new members, or else Describes's implicit existence dependency would be temporarily violated when we attempt to perform the first of these insertions. Similarly, in the case of a 1 : *n* relationship set and an *n* : *m* relationship set with explicit existence dependencies, the DBMS must support simultaneous insertions into the weak entity set and the relationship set.

In addition to constraints on relationship sets, the E/R model provides for certain kinds of constraints on attribute values. Typical constraints are that the value of an age is positive, that one salary be greater than another (e.g., that a manager earn more than each employee who works in the department that she manages), or that no distinct EMPLOYEE entities have the same social security number. These types of constraints are not unique to the E/R model, and we shall take them up later in the context of the RDM (see also exercise 4.8).

Operations

The E/R model's primary value has been to provide a framework for an initial representation of an application's informational requirements. As such, far more attention has been paid to the model's representational constructs than to operations for interfacing with the data. The first generation of E/R operations resembled the procedural operations of Chapter 1. More recent research has proposed less procedural languages for the E/R model, resembling those studied in Chapters 2 and 3 for the RDM. The exercises and references in the annotated bibliography explore further E/R operations.

4.2 MAPPING FROM THE E/R MODEL TO THE RDM

In the previous section, we discovered several points of commonality between the E/R model and the RDM. This section pursues the relationship between these models by illustrating how information in the E/R representation can be mapped to an RDM scheme.

To begin, consider the E/R diagram of Figure 4.6. This E/R diagram is a somewhat more natural and detailed representation of the informational requirements of the department store application than is the E/R diagram of Figure 1.3. Many of the modeling improvements seen in Figure 4.6 are made possible by the definitions and conventions introduced in the previous section.

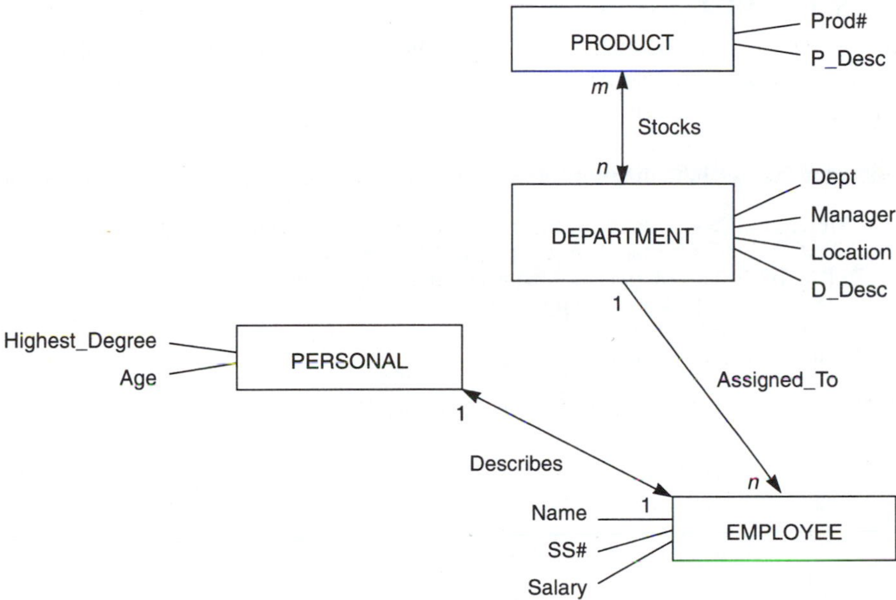

Figure 4.6 E/R diagram without migrated keys and entity STOCKS

It will be instructive to compare the E/R diagrams of Figures 1.3 and 4.6. In the new E/R diagram, we have removed the entity set STOCKS and certain attributes: from the PERSONAL entity set, we have removed the SS# attribute, and from the EMPLOYEE and PRODUCT entity sets, we have removed the Dept attribute. Observe that the relationship sets Stocks, Describes, and Assigned_To make entity set STOCKS and each of these attributes redundant. For example, the Dept attribute in the EMPLOYEE entity set is redundant because the relationship Works_In connects an EMPLOYEE entity to a DEPARTMENT entity, thereby determining the value of this attribute. Similarly, entity set STOCKS now appears to be unnatural because information about which departments stock which products can be captured by a direct relationship set (denoted Stocks in Figure 4.6) between entity sets DEPARTMENT and PRODUCT. Additionally, as the new E/R diagram indicates, we have asserted functionalities for each of the relationship sets.

In all likelihood, an experienced analyst would construct an E/R diagram resembling that of Figure 4.6 as an initial representation of the department store application. The two sections that follow use this E/R diagram as the starting point of our design process and illustrate how the diagram is mapped to an RDM scheme.

An Introduction to Semantic Design Issues: The Problems of Redundancy

There are, in general, many ways to use the RDM to model a given collection of information. For example, in the previous chapters, we proposed the following RDM scheme for modeling the informational requirements of the department store application depicted originally by the E/R diagram of Figure 1.3 and now by the E/R diagram of Figure 4.6:

```
EMPLOYEE(SS#=integer, Name=string, Salary=real, Dept=string)
PERSONAL(SS#=integer, Age=integer, Highest_Degree=string)
DEPARTMENT(Dept=string, Manager=integer, Location=string,
           D_Desc=string)
PRODUCT(Prod#=integer, P_Desc=string)
STOCKS(Prod#=integer, Dept=string)
```

While this seems to be a natural way to model the information described by the E/R diagrams, many other natural ways are possible also. For example, Chapter 1 briefly considered the universal relation model, which would present the user with the single table

```
U(SS#=integer, Name=string, Salary=real, Highest_Degree=string,
   Age=integer, Dept=string, Manager=integer, Location=string,
   D_Desc=string, Prod#=integer, P_Desc=string)
```

This modeling of the information is appealing since, from the user's perspective, intertable operators such as joins are not required—all relevant information is contained in a single table.

In Chapter 1, we pointed out that to avoid massive redundancy, we would not implement table *U* as a single file in which there is a one-to-one correspondence between tuples in *U* and records in the file. Rather, the implementation of table *U* probably would be built on top of an RDM consisting of smaller tables, such as EMPLOYEE, DEPARTMENT, PRODUCT, PERSONAL, and STOCKS, and each of these tables would then be implemented as a single file in which tuples of the table correspond directly to file records (see Figure 4.7). To dramatize the problems that can arise from a careless mapping of an E/R diagram to an RDM scheme, however, suppose for the moment that we have decided to map the E/R diagram to table *U* and (foolishly) to implement this table directly as a single file. There are several disastrous consequences inherent in such a design:

- *Redundancy:* There is the potential for massive redundancy within table *U*. For example, if there are 100 employees in the toys department, there will be at least 100 tuples in table *U* with Dept = Toys. That is, the infor-

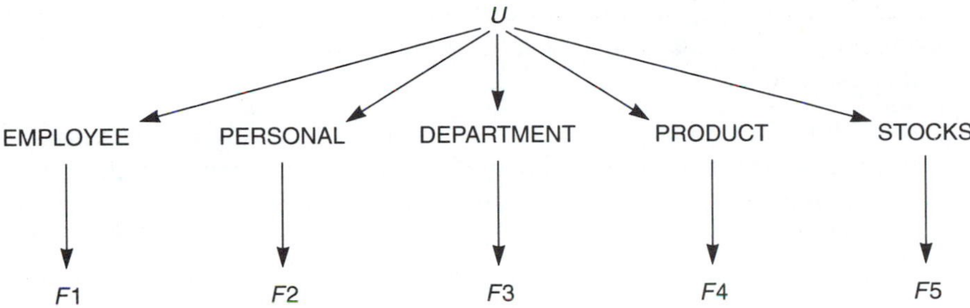

Figure 4.7 Implementation of table *U*

mation associated with the toys department (i.e., its Manager, Location, and D_Desc) must be repeated for each employee who works in this department. The problem is likely far worse than this, however. Suppose that the toys department stocks 1,000 different products. In this event, there would be 100,000 tuples in table *U* that repeat the information associated with the toys department. That is, the information associated with the toys department must be repeated for each of its 100 employees, and each of the resulting 100 "subtuples" <ss#, name, salary, age, highest_degree, TOYS, manager, location, d_desc> must be repeated for each of the 1,000 products stocked by the department! In most imaginable applications, this much redundancy is prohibitive.

- *Inconsistencies and update overhead:* There is the likelihood that user updates to table *U* will introduce inconsistencies to the data. Suppose, for example, that the manager of the toys department should change. It is quite possible that the user will make this change to a single tuple, leaving the remaining 99,999 toy department tuples unchanged and thus out of date. This problem is known as an **update anomaly.** Further, even if the update were performed correctly (i.e., by applying it to all tuples corresponding to the toys department), it would be very inefficient—100,000 tuples have to be modified to effect this single change! Observe that *both of these problems are direct consequences of the redundancy* that results from representing the information as a single, large table.
- *Unavailable/not applicable field values:* Suppose that we have just created a new department and assigned it a manager. The manager, however, has yet to decide what products the department will stock. How can information for this new department be represented in table *U*? There is no facility for storing information about a department if the department does not have at least one product (and one employee) associated with it. The only way to use table *U* to represent information about our new department is to introduce special null values to fill out the tuple. However, as was discussed in Section 3.4, there are many difficult problems associated with the use of null values (see Figure 4.8).

<Λ, Λ, Λ, Λ, Software, Jones, 10C, Computer stuff, Λ, Λ>

Figure 4.8 Tuple padded with null values

These observations make clear the desirability of modeling the information represented by our initial E/R diagram of Figure 4.6 as several small tables. The question remains, however, of exactly how to design our table schemes so that they are as free as possible of the types of problems discussed earlier. The following section begins to address this question, and Chapters 5 and 6 present a rigorous design methodology known as normalization.

Semantically Sound RDM Modeling of an E/R Diagram

We now consider the process of mapping the information represented initially by an E/R diagram to a semantically sound RDM scheme. We are particularly interested in how the functionalities of the relationship sets impact on this mapping process.

Return to the E/R diagram of Figure 4.6, which depicts the way an experienced database designer might represent in the E/R model our department store's informational requirements. Consider first the Describes relationship set between the entity sets EMPLOYEE and PERSONAL. Because this relationship set is 1 : 1, it is semantically sound to model the information from these entity sets as a single table:

```
EMP_PERS(SS#, Name, Salary, Age, Highest_Degree)
```

Observe that table EMP_PERS, which combines the information of entity sets EMPLOYEE and PERSONAL, does not seem to suffer the redundancy problems that plagued table *U*. A general rule of thumb is: *Entity sets related by a 1 : 1 relationship may be modeled as a single table without causing redundancy to be introduced.*

While the table EMP_PERS appears acceptable on semantic grounds, there are potential motivations for modeling the entity sets EMPLOYEE and PERSONAL as two or more tables. These potential motivations include efficiency, security (e.g., suppose we wish to allow the typical user to access attributes SS#, Name, and Salary but not attributes Age and Highest_Degree), and user convenience. It therefore will be instructive to consider how we would model these entities as more than one table. If we attempted to directly define the two tables

```
EMPLOYEE(SS#, Name, Salary)
PERSONAL(Age, Highest_Degree)
```

from the entity sets EMPLOYEE and PERSONAL, we would find that we have lost the relationship set Describes since there is no attribute common to the tables that can be used to join tuples that correspond under the Describes relationship set. (For example, attempt to write a relational algebra or tuple calculus expression to answer the query "Find the age of the employee with SS#=999999999.") To support the Describes relationship, it is necessary to **migrate** from one table to the other an attribute on which a Join that realizes the relationship Describes can be based. In this example, we must migrate the SS# attribute into the PERSONAL table to form the tables

EMPLOYEE(SS#, Name, Salary)
PERSONAL(SS#, Age, Highest_Degree)

The query "Find the age of the employee with SS#=999999999" can now be answered as $\Pi_{<Age>}((\sigma_{SS\#=999999999}\, EMPLOYEE) \underset{SS\#=SS\#}{\bowtie} PERSONAL)$. Observe that the design process has led us to two table schemes quite similar to the corresponding schemes of the RDM presented in Section 4.2.

If each of the relationship sets in the E/R diagram were 1 : 1, many of the problems discussed in association with the table U would not arise. However, the E/R diagram of Figure 4.6 specifies that neither the relationship set Works_In nor Stocks is 1 : 1. Consider first the relationship set Works_In, which the E/R diagram specifies is 1 : n from DEPARTMENT to EMPLOYEE, implying that the department store has a policy that each employee works in exactly one department but, of course, allows many employees to work in any single department.

Suppose first that we attempt to model the entity sets EMPLOYEE and DEPARTMENT as a single table:

EMP_DEPT(SS#, Name, Salary, Dept, Manager, Location, D_Desc)

We see immediately that this table is plagued by the same problem of redundancy that plagued the table U. For any given department D, the subtuple

<Manager = *M* , Dept = *D*, Location = *L*, D_Desc=DD>

corresponding to department D must be repeated for each employee who works in department D. A general rule of thumb is: *Modeling two entity sets related by a 1 : n or n : m relationship as a single table will introduce redundancy.*

To address the problem of redundancy, we consider modeling the EMPLOYEE and DEPARTMENT entity sets as two tables:

EMPLOYEE(SS#, Name, Salary)
DEPARTMENT(Dept, Manager, Location, D_Desc)

As we discovered in the context of the relationship set Describes, to preserve a relationship between entities, an attribute may have to be migrated into one of the two tables. In the current example, to preserve the relationship Works_In, we might consider migrating either SS# into DEPARTMENT or Dept into EMPLOYEE.

If we attempt to migrate SS# into DEPARTMENT, we obtain the tables

EMPLOYEE(SS#, Name, Salary)
DEPARTMENT(Dept, SS#, Manager, Location, D_Desc)

Although these tables do support the relationship Works_In [the query "Find the employees who work in a department managed by the manager with SS# 888888888" is answered as $\Pi_{<Name,SS\#>}(EMPLOYEE \underset{SS\#=SS\#}{\bowtie} \sigma_{Manager=888888888}(DEPARTMENT))$], the table DEPARTMENT suffers from the same problem of redundancy as the table EMP_DEPT. On the other hand, migrating Dept into EMPLOYEE results in the tables

EMPLOYEE(SS#, Name, Salary, Dept)
DEPARTMENT(Dept, Manager, Location, D_Desc)

These tables also support the relationship Works_In [the query "Find the employees who work in a department managed by the manager with SS# 888888888" is answered as $\Pi_{<Name,SS\#>}(EMPLOYEE \underset{Dept=Dept}{\bowtie} \sigma_{Manager=888888888}(DEPARTMENT))$] and do not suffer from the redundancy problems of the previous schemes. A general rule of thumb is: *To support a 1 : n relationship set from entity set A to entity set B, we should migrate from the table corresponding to entity set A into the table corresponding to entity set B an attribute on which a join that realizes the relationship can be based.*

The notion of "an attribute on which a join that realizes the relationship" needs some elaboration. As an example, consider the DEPARTMENT entity. It is quite plausible that the same department (i.e., a department with one name and one description) has several locations, with each location having its own manager. If this were the case, the following tuples are part of a possible instance of table DEPARTMENT:

DEPARTMENT

Dept	Manager	Location	D_Desc
Toys	888888888	10C-NY	This department stocks toys for ages 2–15
Toys	777777777	5F-LA	This department stocks toys for ages 2–15
Toys	222222222	9B-SF	This department stocks toys for ages 2–15

Consider now part of a possible instance of the proposed EMPLOYEE table:

EMPLOYEE

SS#	NAME	Salary	Dept
444444444	Kline	30,000	Toys
555555555	Ray	40,000	Toys
666666666	Garcia	50,000	Toys

It is apparent that this representation fails to capture information regarding the specific location in the Toys department in which each employee works. For example, the result of the query $\Pi_{<Manager,SS\#,Name\#>}((\sigma_{SS\#=444444444} EMPLOYEE) \underset{Dept=Dept}{\bowtie} DEPARTMENT)$ would imply that the employee with SS# 444444444 works for three different managers.

This example illustrates that to support a $1:n$ (or $1:1$) relationship from entity set A to entity set B, the attribute migrated from table A to table B must *uniquely identify tuples in table A*. Such an attribute is known as a **key.** In the current example, the attribute Dept does not uniquely identify tuples in DEPARTMENT. On the other hand, if we can be sure that there can never be more than one department per location, the Location attribute does uniquely identify tuples in the DEPARTMENT table and can be migrated into the EMPLOYEE table, resulting in the tables

```
EMPLOYEE(SS#, Name, Salary, Location)
DEPARTMENT(Dept, Manager, Location, D_Desc)
```

As a final observation, we note that sometimes a *set* of attributes, rather than a single attribute, must be migrated between tables. For example, if more than one department can be assigned to a single location and if a manager can manage more than one department, no single attribute of the table DEPARTMENT uniquely identifies tuples. However, the set of attributes {Dept, Location} does uniquely identify tuples (at most one DEPARTMENT tuple contains any single combination of values for the attributes Dept and Location), and the relationship between EMPLOYEE and DEPARTMENT can be supported by migrating the set of attributes {Dept, Location} into EMPLOYEE, resulting in the tables

```
EMPLOYEE(SS#, Name, Salary, Dept, Location)
DEPARTMENT(Dept, Manager, Location, D_Desc)
```

In the discussion that follows, we shall assume that the Location attribute by itself uniquely identifies DEPARTMENT tuples, and, therefore, we shall assume the tables

```
EMPLOYEE(SS#, Name, Salary, Location)
DEPARTMENT(Dept, Manager, Location, D_Desc)
```

Finally, we consider the $n:m$ relationship set Stocks between the entity sets DEPARTMENT and PRODUCT. If we attempted to model these entity sets as the table DEPT_PROD(Dept, Manager, Location, Desc, Prod#, P_Desc), we would create an enormous amount of redundancy. Observe how the fact that Stocks is $n:m$ rather than simply $1:n$ exasperates the redundancy problem.

To avoid the problems of redundancy, we model the entity sets with tables of the form

```
DEPARTMENT(Dept, Manager, Location, D_Desc)
PRODUCT(Prod#, P_Desc)
```

Next, we must choose an attribute to migrate between the tables to support the Stocks relationship. The fact that the Stocks relation is $n:m$, however, presents us with a new challenge. If we migrate the Location attribute from DEPARTMENT into PRODUCT, obtaining the tables

```
DEPARTMENT(Dept, Manager, D_Desc, Location)
PRODUCT(Prod#, Location, P_Desc)
```

we see that a product's information <Prod#, P_Desc> is repeated for each department location that stocks the product. On the other hand, if we migrate the Prod# attribute from PRODUCT into DEPARTMENT, obtaining the tables

DEPARTMENT(Dept, Prod#, Manager, Location, D_Desc)
PRODUCT(Prod#, P_Desc)

we see that a department's information <Dept, Manager, Location, D_Desc> is repeated for each product the department location stocks. Neither of these situations is acceptable.

The solution is to model the DEPARTMENT and PRODUCT entity sets and the Stocks relationship set between them as three tables:

DEPARTMENT(Dept, Manager, Location, D_Desc)
PRODUCT(Prod#, P_Desc)
STOCKS(Location, Prod#)

Note that the sole purpose of table STOCKS is to capture the relationship Stocks by specifying which products are stocked by which department locations. Although many common queries now require a complex Join involving the three tables [e.g., the query "List the description of each product stocked by the department located at 10C-NY" is answered by $\Pi_{<P\_Desc>}((\sigma_{Location=\text{“10C-NY”}}\ DEPARTMENT) \bowtie_{Location=Location} STOCKS \bowtie_{Prod\#=Prod\#} PRODUCT)$], we have overcome the redundancy problems of the previous schemes. A general rule of thumb is: *To support an n : m relationship set between entity set A and entity set B, create three tables:*

1. *Table A corresponding to entity set A.*
2. *Table B corresponding to entity set B.*
3. *A third table to support the relationship set between the two entity sets.*

The third table contains only attributes from entity sets A and B sufficient to support a join that realizes the relationship set between the two entity sets.

To summarize, in this section we have mapped the E/R diagram of Figure 4.6 into the following five tables:

EMPLOYEE(SS#, Name, Salary, Location)
PERSONAL(SS#, Age, Highest_Degree)
DEPARTMENT(Dept, Manager, Location, D_Desc)
PRODUCT(Prod#, P_Desc)
STOCKS(Location, Prod#)

At this juncture, it is appropriate to raise two points of perspective. First, although our discussion has covered many of the major considerations for mapping from the E/R model to the RDM, the E/R diagram of Figure 4.6 from which we began contained only the basic constructs of the E/R model. The subsection that follows considers mapping more complex E/R constructs to the relational model. In this context, we shall explore certain limitations of the RDM and thereby find motivations for new, more powerful data models, such as the object-oriented data model, which is introduced in Section 4.3. The second point of perspective is that, while the mapping techniques of the current section generally yield a reasonable RDM scheme, the resulting scheme often requires further refinement before a completely satisfactory design is obtained. **Normalization** is a rigorous, mathematically based technique that allows us to identify and rectify many problems that may be present in a proposed RDM design. Chapters 5 and 6 study in detail the theory and practice of normalization.

Complex E/R Constructs, RDM Limitations, and Object Identity

Recall that the E/R model permits attributes to be associated with relationship sets as well as with entity sets. Suppose, for example, that in our department store E/R diagram of Figure 4.6, we wish to specify, for each department and product stocked by the department, the quantity of this product currently on hand in the department. This information can be modeled by associating with the Stocks relationship set the attribute Quantity, defined by

Quantity: {instances of Stocks} $\rightarrow$ integer

If, for example, department d has 20 units of product p, we would have Quantity($<d,p>$)=20.

This construct can be mapped to the relational model by modifying the table STOCKS that was created to model the $n:m$ stocks relationship set Stocks. In particular, we could define the table STOCKS(Location, Prod#, Quantity), and if, for example, the department at location 10-C NY currently has 20 units of product number 234, the current instance of table STOCKS would contain the tuple <10-C NY, 234, 20>.

Now consider the modeling of nonbinary relationship sets in the relational model. The previous section considered, as an example of a nonbinary relationship set, the relationship set Advises, defined by the membership predicate

Advises(s,f,st)=True iff ($s \in STUDENT$) $\wedge$ ($f \in FACULTY$) $\wedge$ ($st \in STAFF$) $\wedge$
(f is the faculty advisor of s) $\wedge$ (st is the staff advisor of s)

Assuming that the entity sets STUDENT, STAFF, and FACULTY have mapped to tables

STUDENT(Stud_Id#, Name, Major, GPA)
FACULTY(Prof_Id#, Name, Dept, Phone, Office_Hrs)
STAFF(Staff_Id#, Name, Dept, Phone, Office_Hrs)

relationship set Advises can be mapped to the RDM by creating a table scheme ADVISES(Stud_Id#, Prof_Id#, Staff_Id#). Alternatively, if it is university policy that each student have exactly one faculty advisor and exactly one staff advisor, we could migrate into the STUDENT table the Prof_Id# and Staff_Id# attributes, obtaining the table STUDENT(Stud_Id#, Name, Major, GPA, Prof_Id#, Staff_Id#).

These examples highlight the somewhat unnatural modeling of certain E/R relationship sets provided by the RDM. The sole purpose of tables STOCKS and ADVISES is to model relationship sets Stocks and Advises. For example, table ADVISES is defined to contain **migrated keys**—each Id attribute in ADVISES is a key of one of the tables involved in the relationship. A tuple in ADVISES containing values for these migrated keys identifies the tuples representing the entities involved in a relationship set instance; because the sole purpose of table ADVISES is to model a relationship set, it may be considered somewhat artificial. Further, the modeling is less than elegant in that Joins are required to realize the relationship since no single table contains all information describing the entities involved in the relationship. For example, answering the query "Retrieve the office hours of all faculty and staff who advise computer science majors" requires an expression such as

$$\Pi_{<Office\_Hrs>}((\sigma_{Major="CS"}\ STUDENT) \underset{Prof\_Id\#=Prof\_Id\#}{\bowtie} FACULTY)$$
$$\cup\ \Pi_{<Office\_Hrs>}((\sigma_{Major="CS"}\ STUDENT) \underset{Staff\_Id\#=Staff\_Id\#}{\bowtie} STAFF)$$

While this example illustrates the RDM's unnatural modeling of nonbinary relationship sets, similar problems are also present even when, as in the previous section, we modeled simple relationship sets. For example, even in the simple case that there is a binary $1:n$ relationship set from entity set A to B, a key must be migrated from the table representing A into the table representing B. Similar comments apply to the second modeling described of the Advises relationship set in which keys were migrated into table STUDENTS. To one unfamiliar with the relational model, the modeling of even these relatively simple relationship sets may appear unnatural and inconvenient. To a large extent, the limitation of the relational model that often forces unnatural modelings can be traced to *the RDM's lack of support for complex attribute types*.

How would the support of complex attribute types allow for more natural modelings of relationships? As a first step in answering this question, consider the modeling of the Stocks relationship provided by the table

PRODUCTS(Prod#, Prod_Desc, Inventory)

where Inventory assumes values that are *sets* of <Location, Quantity> pairs. Under this modeling, if Prod# 333 currently is stocked in three departments, the current instance of PRODUCTS would contain a tuple such as

<333, Game for children 2-5 years, {(10-C NY, 10), (6-B NY, 2), (3-A LA, 5)}

Observe that since each value of attribute Inventory is a *set of pairs,* the attribute can be viewed as a *table embedded within table PRODUCTS.* A table such as PRODUCTS obviously violates our restriction that attributes be simple valued but, in some situations, provides an attractive modeling.

Even if the RDM were extended as illustrated to allow nonsimple attributes, the modelings supported still might appear unnatural in that they force Joins (or some generalization of the Join operator) to pose many frequent queries. Consider, for example, the query "Retrieve the managers of the departments that currently stock product 333." Posing this query requires an expression such as

$$DEPARTMENT \underset{Location \in Inventory\,set}{\bowtie} (\sigma_{Prod\#=333}\, PRODUCTS)$$

This expression contains a generalized Join operator, which must "expand" the attribute Inventory so that a connection is made between each Location appearing in the Inventory set of Product 333 and the corresponding tuple in table DEPARTMENT. The following section and the exercises consider extended relational operators such as this.

That the preceding query requires a Join operator can be traced to the fact that table PRODUCTS, although it contains sufficient information to relate products to departments, does not contain all the required information about the departments involved in the relationship. This and similar queries would be easier to express under a modeling that actually records all information about related departments within the Inventory attribute of a particular product. It is clear, however, that doing so directly would introduce too much redundancy: If a department stocks *n* different products, a direct implementation of the proposed modeling would repeat *n* times as part of Inventory attributes all the information associated with that department.

Abstractly, the RDM's modeling limitation that forces us to choose between Joins that realize relationships and unacceptable redundancy can be attributed to the fact that the RDM supports only a weak notion of **object identity.** Migrating the key Location into the Inventory attribute of PRODUCTS allows a Join to make the connection between products and departments but places on the user the burden of realizing the relationship with appropriate Joins. Researchers have proposed extending the relational model with stronger notions of object identity, notions that, for example, would allow the user to pose queries as if the entire department object were stored within the Inventory attribute. To realize such a notion of object identity without introducing unacceptable redundancy, a "surrogate" for a department object could be stored as part of an Inventory value, and the data model's mapping algorithms would support querying the surrogate as if the department tuple, with all its attributes, were stored within the Inventory value. Support of complex attribute types and of a strong notion of object identity are two of the motivating factors behind the **object-oriented data model,** an emerging model that we now survey.

4.3 THE OBJECT-ORIENTED DATA MODEL[1]

The object-oriented data model supports both complex attribute types and a strong notion of object identity. In addition to these capabilities, the object-oriented model includes several other features that, its proponents argue, combine to make it an attractive enhancement of the relational model. Since many of the object-oriented model's most important features are closely intertwined,

[1] This section may be skipped without a loss of continuity.

in this section we survey not only the features that address the RDM limitations discussed in the previous sections but also consider other key features of the object-oriented model. In particular, the following subsections discuss four of the central concepts of the object-oriented data model: extensibility and encapsulation (a facility that supports complex attribute types), type hierarchies and inheritance (facilities that also support complex attribute types), object identity, and a clean programming language/database interface.

We point out at the onset that, currently, the term *object oriented* is highly nonstandardized. Each school of researchers has its own notion of what *the* object-oriented model is. Therefore, rather than focusing on the details of particular versions of the model, we shall explore concepts that are central to the object-oriented approach.

Extensibility and Encapsulation

Database researchers, practitioners, and users have concluded that, for many applications, the simple attribute types supported by the relational model are too restrictive. In the previous section, for example, we encountered situations where we would like attributes to take on values that are sets of simple values or even embedded tables. Such complex attribute types violate most notions of what the RDM supports.

A central feature of the object-oriented database model is **extensibility**—the ability for the users themselves to define new kinds of data types as needed for a given application. Not only does this capability allow the user to define an attribute to be a set or table over standard types (e.g., a list of strings or a collection of <string, integer> pairs) and operations for manipulating values of these types, but it also allows users to define highly application-specific data types and operations. This latter capability often is quite useful. A classic example from computer-aided design (CAD) is that we wish to model information about spatial objects, such as **boxes.** A box might represent, for example, a chip in very large-scale integration (VLSI) design or certain assembly components in aircraft design. We wish to store, in addition to traditional information (e.g., the box's name, creator, and creation date), specialized spatial information about the box. For example, we may wish to store the box's location relative to a coordinate grid. While such spatial information can be forced into the representation of a standard RDM tuple with several scalar values, doing so is quite unnatural. Not only would this not be an intuitive way for the user to conceptualize the data but, even more importantly, the operations we might wish to perform on boxes (e.g., find a box's area, determine if two boxes intersect, rotate a box) are not naturally mapped to the operations provided by the relational algebra. A more elegant solution allows the user to define a new type **box,** including a collection of operations that can be performed on boxes.

In an extensible database model, the users, with the aid of a person referred to as the **DBI** (**database implementor**), can construct specialized types to suit the application from the model's predefined types and **type constructors.** For example, the definition

```
Type
  Set_of_Strings = set of string
```

defines the user type Set_of_Strings in terms of the predefined type *string* and the type constructor *set of*. The type EMPLOYEE, which can be used to model a situation in which an employee can work in more than one department, then can be defined as:

```
Type
  EMPLOYEE = (SS#=integer, Name=string, Salary=real,
              Location=Set_of_Strings)
```

Each **object** (i.e., instance) from the EMPLOYEE type corresponds to the RDM notion of an EMPLOYEE tuple, except that the field Location is a nonscalar, user-defined type. The collection of all EMPLOYEE objects corresponds to the notions of table instance and entity set instance.

The type constructor facility can be used to model even more complex attributes, such as the Inventory attribute of PRODUCTS considered in the previous section. For this modeling, we define

```
Type
  Inv_Pair = (Location=string, Quantity=integer)
Type
  Inv_Set = set of Inv_Pair
Type
  PRODUCTS = (Prod#=integer, Inventory=Inv_Set)
```

As an example of the use of type constructors in the modeling of highly speciailized applications, consider the following definitions, which can be used to represent spatial objects in a VLSI design application:

```
Type
  Coordinate = (X_val=real, Y_val=real)
Type
  Box = (Vertex1=Coordinate, Vertex2=Coordinate, Vertex3=Coordinate,
         Vertex4=Coordinate)
Type
  Chip = (Name = string, Creator= string, Creation_Date = Date,
          Spatial_Desc = Box)
```

The ability to define the logical structure of a new type is only one aspect of extensibility; additionally, we must be able to specify operations on objects of the new type. Recall, for example, that the previous section introduced informally a generalized Join operator, allowing us to pose the query "Retrieve the managers of the departments that currently stock product 333" as follows:

$$DEPARTMENT \underset{Location \in Inventory\ set}{\bowtie} (\sigma_{Prod\#=333}\ PRODUCTS)$$

Now we shall see how the object-oriented model allows the definition of primitive operations on user-defined types and how these primitives can be used to pose high-level queries such as the foregoing.

Operations on Objects of Type Set_of_Strings

Is_Present_Str(x : string; S : Set_of_Strings) : Boolean
{ Determine if x is a member of S. }

Add_Str(x : string; S : Set_of_Strings) : Set_of_Strings
{ Return the set which results from adding to S a new member x. }

Operations on Objects of Type Set_of_Inv_Pair

Is_Present_Pair_1(x : string; P : Inv_Set) : Boolean
{ Determine if x is a first coordinate of a pair in P. }

Is_Present_Pair_2(x : integer; P : Inv_Set) : Boolean
{ Determine if x is a second coordinate of a pair in P. }

Operations on Objects of Type Box

Area(b : box) : Real
{ Compute the area of box. }

Intersect(b1, b2 : box) : Boolean
{ Determine if boxes b1 and b2 overlap. }

Rotate(b : box; d : real) : box
{ Return the box which results from rotating box b d degrees. }

Assuming the existence of a relational-like interface to a database of objects, we can state the following queries:

```
{ Retrieve all EMPLOYEE objects, such that the employee works at location 10-C
  NY. }
  SELECT EMPLOYEE
    WHERE Is_Present_Str("10-C NY", EMPLOYEE.Locations)

{ Add employee with SS# 999999999 to the department at 10-C. }
  MODIFY (EMPLOYEE.Locations=Add_Dept("10-C", EMPLOYEE.Locations))
    WHERE EMPLOYEE.SS#=999999999

{ Retrieve the DEPARTMENT objects for each department in which employee
  with SS# 999999999 works. }
  SELECT DEPARTMENT
    WHERE EMPLOYEE.SS#=999999999
      AND Is_Present_Str(DEPARTMENT.Location, EMPLOYEE.Locations)

{ Retrieve the managers of the departments that currently stock product 333. }
  SELECT DEPARTMENT.Manager
    WHERE PRODUCTS.Prod#=333
      AND Is_Present_Pair_1(DEPARTMENT.Location, PRODUCT.Inventory)
```

We shall see shortly how the concept of object identity provides us with a modeling alternative that eliminates the need for Joins such as those required by the two previous queries.

```
{ Retrieve big chips. }
  SELECT CHIP
    WHERE Area(CHIP) > 500
```

```
{ Retrieve all chips which overlap chip Xchip. }
  SELECT C2
    WHERE C1.Name = Xchip
       AND Intersect(C1.Location, C2.Location)

{ Rotate Xchip 25 degrees. }
  MODIFY (CHIP.Location = Rotate(CHIP.Location, 25))
    WHERE CHIP.Name = Xchip
```

It is important to emphasize that an EMPLOYEE or CHIP is a *single* object, analogous to a single tuple in the RDM or an entity set member in the E/R model. In the preceding examples, we used a relational-like language to pose queries and to state updates against the *collection* of all EMPLOYEE and CHIP objects in the database. In addition to such a query facility that operates on a collection of objects, we often wish to define *types* that themselves are *collections of objects,* analogous to the way tables are collections of tuples. The motivation here is that, as part of the definition of such types, we can specify frequent operations, thus freeing the user of the burden of constructing query language statements for these operations. For example, we might specify the following definition:

```
Type
  EMPLOYEE_Collection = set of EMPLOYEE
```

Operation on EMPLOYEE_Collection

```
Assign_To_Dept(ss : integer; newdept : string) : EMPLOYEE_Collection
{ Add newdept to the department list of the employee object with SS# ss.
  The result of this operation is new instance of the type
  EMPLOYEE_Collection. }
```

Along with the definition of a type's logical structure and a specification of its operations, the DBI must specify an implementation. In particular, the DBI specifies the physical structures used to store the objects of a type and supplies procedures, or **methods,** for performing the operations. The notion of **encapsulation** is that, while the DBI specifies implementation details, only the type's logical structure and operation specifications are visible to the typical user. Thus, encapsulation closely parallels our perspective of high-level abstract data types (ADTs) serving as the user interface, with a query optimizer mapping operations and queries stated against the interface to implementation programs to hide the physical-level implementation from the user. What is new in the object-oriented data model is that the users have the ability, in the context of an *existing system,* to define new types and operations *as they are required.*

Whenever a new type is added to an object-oriented database, methods for performing the operations are supplied; hence, it might appear that nothing else is required to extend the processing capabilities of the system to account for extensions to the data model. However, a critical problem is to extend the query optimizer's search strategies whenever new operations and their methods are added to the data model. Suppose, for example, that alternative methods are supplied for performing a new operation. How does the optimizer choose a method at the time this operation must be applied? Or suppose that a query composes a new user-defined operator with a primitive, predefined operator (e.g., a Select)—how does the query optimizer perform the processing? These problems are aspects of the problem area known as **extensible query optimization,** which is considered in Chapter 13.

Type Hierarchies and Inheritance

When constructing the type definitions to support a particular application, we often find that one or more types *specialize* one supertype. For example, there might exist in our application the following types:

```
Type
  PERSON = (Name=string, Age=integer, Sex={M,F})
Type
  STAFF = (Name=string, Age=integer, Sex={M,F}, Salary=real,
           Supervisor=string, Dependents = Set_of_Strings)
Type
  MANAGER = (Name=string, Age=integer, Sex={M,F}, Salary=real,
             Departments=Set_of_Strings,
             Dependents=Set_of_Strings)
Type
  OFFICER = (Name=string, Age=integer, Sex={M,F}, Salary=real,
             Departments=Set_of_Strings,
             Regional_Offices=string, Dependents=Set_of_Strings)
Type
  DEPENDENT = (Name=string, Age=integer, Sex={M,F},
               Dependent_Of=string)
```

Observe that each of STAFF, MANAGER, OFFICER, and DEPENDENT is a special case of PERSON and that OFFICER additionally is a special case of MANAGER. That is, each of STAFF, MANAGER, OFFICER, and DEPENDENT have all the attributes of PERSON, plus additional attributes, and OFFICER has all the attributes of MANAGER, plus an additional attribute. This relationship between the logical structures of the types is conceptualized as the type hierarchy in Figure 4.9.

In addition to aiding our conceptualization of the relationships between the logical structures of an application's types, a type hierarchy can be an aid in defining and using the types. For example, many object-oriented data models support the use of an *isa facility* in a type definition. With such a facility, the

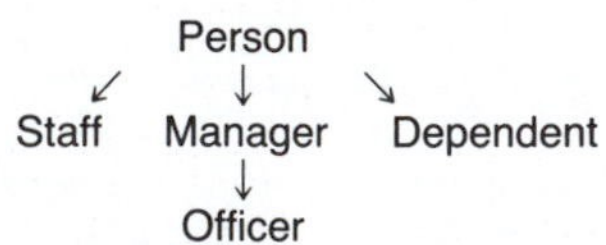

Figure 4.9 Type hierarchy

type STAFF could be defined as follows:

```
Type
  STAFF = isa(PERSON) | (Salary=real, Supervisor=string,
                         Dependents = Set_of_Strings)
```

This definition of STAFF specifies that the type is a subtype of type PERSON and hence has all the attributes that PERSON has and, additionally, has attributes Supervisor and Dependent. We say that type STAFF **inherits** as part of its logical structure the logical structure of PERSON.

The use in type definitions of the isa facility saves us a bit of work, but this alone is hardly a major benefit. Of far more importance is the assertion that type X isa(Y) specifies that type X inherits type Y's *operations*. That is, any operation specified for type Y automatically is applicable to type X. More generally, the **principle of substitutability** asserts that any expression that references an object of type Y automatically may reference also an object of its subtype X. Such an inheritance facility eliminates the need for redundant code that otherwise would be required to implement identical operations for distinct types and eliminates the need in application programs for special cases that otherwise would be required to handle expressions that can reference objects of either a supertype or its subtypes.

Object Identity

Object identity is a powerful concept that is an integral part of the object-oriented model. Object identity provides us with a mechanism for defining relationships between objects in a manner that elegantly addresses one of the most fundamental shortcomings of the RDM, namely that the RDM's lack of support for object identity often forces unnatural modelings and Joins. Consequences of this shortcoming were illustrated in Section 4.2; here, we consider additional motivations for a strong notion of identity and discuss how these notions can be realized.

Consider again the type definition

```
Type
  STAFF = isa(PERSON) | (Salary=real, Supervisor=string,
                         Dependents = Set_of_Strings)
```

The role of the attribute Supervisor is to model the relationship between staff members and their supervisors. Similarly, the role of the attribute Dependents is to model the relationship between staff members and their dependents. In both cases, these attributes are strings (or sets of strings) that represent the *names* of the supervisor and dependents. These methods of modeling such relationships reflect an RDM mind set. To have a STAFF member's object refer to the staff member's supervisor, we migrate into the STAFF member's tuple a *key* that identifies a supervisor tuple; to have a STAFF member's tuple refer to the staff member's dependents, we migrate into the staff member's tuple a list of keys that identify dependent tuples. (Of course, in a pure relational model, we could not have a list of dependents; rather, a separate table made up of <Sname, Dname> tuples would be required.) To follow the relationships, Joins are required. For example, posing the query "Retrieve the salary of Smith's Supervisor" requires an expression such as

```
SELECT MANAGER.Salary
  WHERE MANAGER.Name=STAFF.Supervisor
    AND STAFF.Name="Smith"
```

Note that such a query becomes even more difficult to state if a staff member's supervisor could be either a MANAGER or an OFFICER since, in this case, we would not know with which table STAFF must be joined.

As a result of the RDM's difficulties in modeling such relationships, researchers have sought an alternative approach. Observe that what we wish to do is conceptually quite simple. For example, we wish to include the *Supervisor object, rather than just the name,* as part of the staff member's object. We could do this in the RDM (ignoring for the moment the problems caused by the supervisor's lists of dependents) by defining the scheme for table STAFF to include all attributes associated with a supervisor. This, however, is a poor design because of the redundancy introduced—a supervisor's information is repeated for each employee who reports to that supervisor. Not only would the design require much storage, but the potential for update problems is great—if the information associated with supervisor *S* should change, modifications must be made to the tuples of each staff member who reports to *S*. Additionally, if some supervisors can be MANAGERs and others can be OFFICERs, the situation would be complicated further since the structure of the STAFF tuples could then not be uniform.

The concept of object identity provides the means of modeling relationships in a semantically natural manner while avoiding the problems associated with redundancy. The concept of object identity is that every object in the database has a unique identity that can be encoded as an **identifier value** that can be assigned and referenced. We use the term "value" loosely as, in general, an identifier value will have no meaning to the user and, in fact, might even be a procedure that the system uses to locate the referenced object.

To realize the concept of object identity, we can stipulate that every object *obj*, of every type, contain an attribute *id* whose "value" uniquely identifies *obj* and that can be referenced as *obj.id*. We assume that when a new object *obj* is created, the system assigns to *obj.id* a unique identifier value and that this "value" can be used to refer to the object. For example, if *X* is a variable of the appropriate type, we can make the assignment $X \leftarrow obj.id$. After such an assignment, we can reference the attributes of *obj* through *X*; that is, if *A* is an attribute of *obj*, the meanings of *X.A* and *obj.A* are identical, each evaluating to the *A*-value associated with object *obj*.

We now have an elegant means of modeling relationships. Consider, for example, the following definition of the STAFF type:

```
Type
  STAFF = isa(PERSON) | (Salary=real, Supervisor=object_identifier,
                         Dependents=(set of object_identifier))
```

When a staff member reports to a given supervisor, we simply set the attribute Supervisor to the object identifier of the supervisor. For example, if the STAFF member with name Smith is to report to the MANAGER with name Jones, we can use the statement

```
MODIFY (STAFF.Supervisor = MANAGER.id)
  WHERE STAFF.name = "Smith"
    AND MANAGER.name = "Jones"
```

to reflect the relationship. We can then pose the query "Retrieve the salary of Smith's Supervisor" with the expression

```
SELECT STAFF.Supervisor.Salary
  WHERE STAFF.Name="Smith"
```

Note that this query is valid regardless of whether Smith's supervisor is a MANAGER or an OFFICER.

It is instructive to contrast the concept of an object identifier with more familiar RDM concepts:

- *An object identifier is not simply a key for a table scheme:* A set of attributes K is a key for table T if no two distinct tuples in a given instance of T can agree on their values for all the attributes in K. However, key values are not unique across tables (a tuple in table S can have the same values in K as does a tuple in T), and, hence, a key value need not identify a unique tuple in the database. Even if this problem were overcome (e.g., by appending to a key value a table name), the user could not refer to the attributes of the tuple with key value k simply as $k.A$; that is, it is the user's burden to follow relationships. Further, if a key value should change, the change would have to be reflected by the user in all tuples that include the key value.
- *An object identifier is not simply a tuple address:* While a tuple's physical address does uniquely identify a tuple across tables in the database, it does not directly support easy access through the query language to the attributes of the referenced tuple. Further, if the referenced tuple should move, all copies of its address would have to be updated.
- *An object identifier is not simply a copy of the tuple:* Conceptually, we might think of an attribute (e.g., Supervisor) that is assigned a tuple identifier as receiving an actual copy of the referenced tuple. The difficulty with this perspective is that a modification to the referenced tuple would have to be reflected in all of its copies.

While these familiar concepts fail to realize object identity, implementations of object identity may utilize variations of the concepts. For example, a tuple address can realize object identity if the query processor is extended appropriately. The query processor would have to interpret a reference such as Supervisor.Salary as

```
retrieve the tuple from the address stored in the Supervisor attribute
return the Salary attribute of this tuple
```

Further, whenever a tuple is moved (e.g., to accommodate insertions), all attributes that contain references to the tuple must be updated. Unfortunately, such updating of references is a nontrivial task. The experimental system POSTGRESS [see Rowe and Stonebraker (1986)] employs an alternative scheme in which *logical queries* are the values of object identifiers. For example, if a staff member's supervisor is manager Smith, the Supervisor attribute of this staff member's tuple would be assigned the value

```
'SELECT *
  WHERE (MANAGER.Name="Smith")'
```

That is, the value of attribute Supervisor is an actual query string or some other representation of the query. When a user query contains a reference such as Supervisor.Salary, the query processor evaluates the query stored in the Supervisor attribute, retrieves the referenced tuple t, and returns the value t.Salary.

Whatever method is chosen to implement object identity, it is the responsibility of the DBMS to properly interpret object references. *Data abstraction thus hides from the user the implementation mechanism employed, allowing him or her to query attributes representing objects as if the objects actually were stored as attribute values.*

The exercises explore how the object-oriented model's support of user-defined types and object identity can be used to naturally model several of the E/R model constructs from Section 4.2 that we found difficult to model in the RDM.

The Programming Language/Database Interface

Although not directly related to the modeling issues discussed in this chapter, supporting a clean host programming language interface is one of the object-oriented database model's primary goals. For completeness, we conclude our introductory survey by considering such an interface.

In Chapter 3, we considered the problem of interfacing a relational database with a host programming language. Several alternative solutions were presented, the best of which, we argued, was embedding a nonprocedural query language, such as SQL, into the host language. But even this approach has at least one inherent shortcoming: Data transfer is clumsy. For example, while an embedded query evaluates to an indeterminate-sized collection of tuples, the constructs of most languages are fixed-sized structures (e.g., arrays of records). The solution proposed (and implemented by many systems) is a looping mechanism that allows tuple-at-a-time processing. Consider, for example, the embedded SQL-like statement

```
SELECT (var1=EMPLOYEE.Name, var2=EMPLOYEE.Salary)
    FROM EMPLOYEE
  WHERE EMPLOYEE.Dept = "Toys"
BEGIN_SELECT_LOOP
  { Host language processing loop }
END_SELECT_LOOP
```

where var1 and var2 are host language variables. The processing loop is executed once for each tuple retrieved; at the start of each iteration, the retrieved tuple's attribute values are assigned to host variables as specified in the selection clause.

While this solution may be satisfactory in many situations, it still does not allow the data to be transferred from the database to the program in a clean manner. The ideal solution would be a statement that says "Take the data that results from the query, and place it in a host variable that the program can later manipulate as it requires." But what programming language structure is appropriate for holding such data? Even if we can define a dynamically sized structure (e.g., a linked list of records) in a traditional host language such as PASCAL, C, or FORTRAN, the structure differs from the data model's structure and perhaps is not the most convenient type of structure to manipulate. Generally speaking, good software design practices mandate common structures for database data and for the program variables holding the data for manipulation.

Given that supporting common structures for database data and program data is a central objective of the object-oriented database model, it is natural that the focus of much current research is on techniques for making the database model compatible with the model of an **object-oriented programming language.** One reason that object-oriented languages appear to be an appropriate language to interface with an object-oriented database model is that, like the database model, object-oriented languages are **extensible** in the sense that they allow users to define new data types and operations to suit a given application. Hence, object-oriented programs can be kept compatible with the database, even as database users introduce new data types and operations for the application at hand.

It is interesting to note that, historically, object-oriented programming languages were the precursors of object-oriented database models. Researchers and users of object-oriented programming languages sought ways to extend the capabilities of their languages to make the languages more conducive to their applications. It quickly became apparent to these researchers that many of the enhanced capabilities desired are best provided within a database environment, thereby motivating the development of object-oriented database models. The enhancements to object-oriented programming languages that motivated object-oriented database models include the following:

- *Data persistence:* A program's data lives when the program executes and dies when the program terminates. In a traditional programming language, the only persistent data structure is the file, and files generally are even less compatible with the programming language's data model than is a relational database.

- *Reliability:* If a program is performing a computation on its data and the computer crashes, much work may be lost. In some applications, computations are based on interactive user input that cannot be reproduced easily. Recovery techniques such as those discussed in Chapter 10 should be employed.
- *Concurrent access:* Several application programs may need to access the same data at the same time. Concurrency control techniques such as those discussed in Chapter 10 should be employed.
- *Efficiency:* If an application requires large quantities of data, portions of the data will be stored on disk, even if this fact is invisible to the user. For example, in a virtual computing system, portions of a program's data will be swapped to the disk by the operating system when the program is not referencing the data and will be swapped back to internal memory when the data is needed. Generally, this swapping may not be as efficient as if a DBMS organizes the data on disk and controls access to it.

Typical applications of object-oriented languages (e.g., CAD and graphics) are applications that very much require the aforementioned database capabilities.

This completes our introduction to the object-oriented database model. We shall return to the model when, in Chapter 13, we explore issues arising in its implementation. Until then, as we study RDM design and implementation, the reader should keep in mind that many of the techniques developed in the RDM context form the foundations of implementations for more complex data models, such as the object-oriented model. As depicted in Figure 4.10, the object-oriented model can be viewed as adding an additional level of abstraction to our RDM implementation; hence, implementations of the object-oriented and relational models share a common foundation. While the object-oriented data model currently is receiving much attention, we must realize that much more work is needed before its design and implementation issues are as well understood as are those of the RDM.

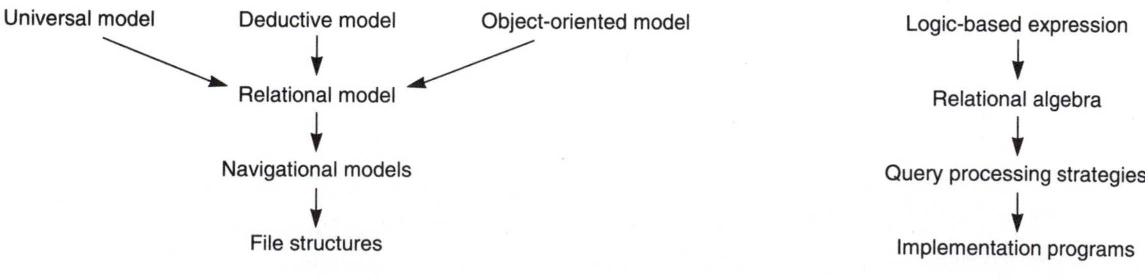

Figure 4.10 Levels of abstraction

SUMMARY AND ANNOTATED BIBLIOGRAPHY

This chapter studied several data models and techniques for data modeling—the process of using a data model to represent the information required by an application.

We began our study of data models with a more rigorous look at the entity/relation model, a data model we used informally in the first three chapters. Chen (1976) is generally credited with formalizing the E/R model, which has become a standard framework for stating an initial representation of an application's informational requirements. Much has been written on the processes of creating E/R diagrams from the information supplied by a user community. Some of the presentations on this subject include Chen (1976); Chen (1980); Teorey and Fry (1982); and Tsichritzis and Lochovsky (1982). Chapter 9 presents a sample design problem in which the first step employs an E/R diagram to represent an application's informational requirements.

The chapter considered the problem of mapping a user-supplied E/R diagram into an RDM scheme, and of developing principles for handling interentity relationships of various functionalities. Our study of this problem led to the discovery of several shortcomings of the RDM, most notably its lack of support for complex attribute types and its lack of a strong notion of object identity. The object-oriented data model extends the RDM in ways that address many of these shortcomings. Researchers in both programming languages and databases have proposed numerous different object-oriented models. Attempts to unify the concepts and terminology are found in Bancilhon (1986), and Kim and Lochovsky (1989). Most researchers agree that four features central to an object-oriented database model are extensibility and encapsulation, type hierarchies and inheritance, object identity, and clean host language/database interface. Chapter 13 revisits the object-oriented model by considering problems involved in its implementation.

This chapter serves as an introduction to RDM design. The next two chapters study dependencies and normalization, the main ingredients of an algorithmic methodology for RDM design. We emphasize that since enhanced data models, such as the object-oriented model, are often realized as abstraction levels placed above an RDM foundation, the RDM design and implementation techniques presented in Chapters 5 through 12 are highly relevant to the study of the enhanced data models as well as to the RDM.

EXERCISES

1. Define the following modeling constructs: entity set, relationship set, attribute, $1:1$, $1:n$, $n:m$, existence dependency, key, user-defined type, type hierarchy, and object identifier.
2. Give examples of $1:1$, $1:n$, and $n:m$ relationship sets. Model these relationship sets in both the RDM and the object-oriented model.
3. Consider the E/R diagram in Figure 4.11 for a professional baseball

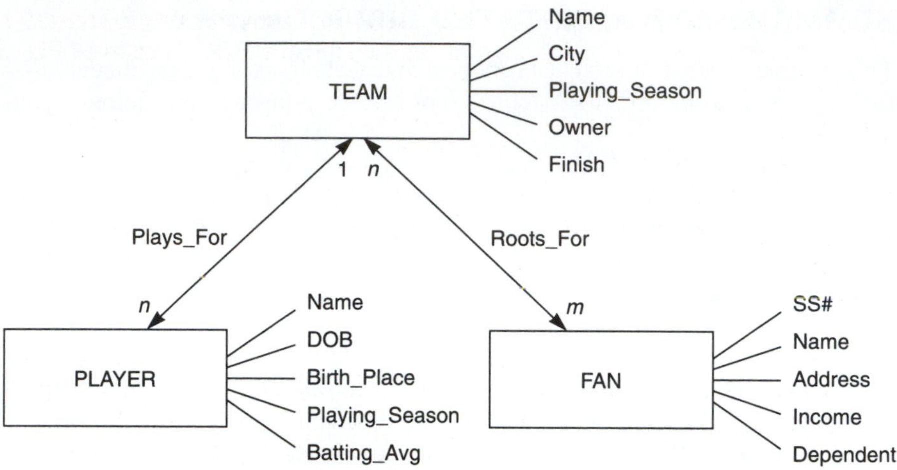

Figure 4.11 Sports E/R diagram

team and its fans. Construct an RDM that soundly implements the informational requirements conveyed by the diagram.

4. Section 4.1 models the relationship Advises as a tertiary relationship set. Demonstrate how the same information can be modeled as a pair of binary relationship sets.
5. Section 4.1 presents a modeling of the EMPLOYEE entity set in which an employee has many dependents and each dependent has an associated name, sex, and DOB. Propose an alternative modeling of the dependent information in which we define individual attributes related by a relationship set.
6. Section 4.1 defines the functionality of a binary relationship set. Generalize the definition to *k*-ary relationship sets. Discuss the various options available in these definitions, and indicate what information is useful when mapping to RDB schemes.
7. Define the functionality of relationship sets over attributes. Illustrate your definitions with examples.
8. One type of constraint that can be applied to an attribute of an entity set is a **key constraint,** specifying that no two members of any instance of the entity set can map the attribute to the same value. Discuss how this and similar attribute constraints can influence the mapping of an E/R diagram to the RDM.
9. Modify the procedural operations of Chapter 1 so that they can be applied in the context of the E/R model. In particular, refine the operations so that they allow easy navigation of relationship sets.

*10. Propose a nonprocedural, self-contained query language for the E/R model.

11. Using the operations and query language of the previous two exercises, state the queries preceding exercise 1.3 against the E/R diagram of Figure 1.14.
12. Model the E/R diagram of Figure 1.14 in terms of an object-oriented model. Be sure to fully utilize the model's facilities for complex types and object identity.
13. State against your objects of the previous exercise the queries preceding exercise 1.3.
14. Demonstrate how the complex E/R constructs of Section 4.2 can be modeled in terms of an object-oriented model. Be sure to utilize fully the model's facilities for complex types and object identity.
15. Section 4.2 considered a generalized Join operator that "expands" the attribute Inventory so that a connection is made between each location appearing in the set and the tuple in table DEPARTMENT. Supply a more formal definition of this operator. How must the other relational operators be generalized to interface with the complex attribute types supported by an object-oriented model?
16. Propose an internal memory implementation for a table containing a set-valued attribute such as Dependents.
17. In Section 4.3, we discussed several methods for implementing object identifiers. Analyze the relative advantages and disadvantages of a method that stores a pointer address to the referenced object and a method that stores a logical query that identifies the referenced object.

CHAPTER 5

Semantic Design and Normalization for the Relational Data Model

In this and the chapter that follows, we consider the question of how best to utilize the RDM to model the information of a given application. Whereas Chapter 4 introduced a set of guidelines for deriving an RDM scheme from an E/R diagram, we consider here a rigorous mathematical theory that allows us to analyze and improve on the design of an RDM scheme, regardless of how this scheme was originally obtained. The issues considered in these chapters are of the utmost importance since a poorly designed scheme can make a database both inconvenient to use and susceptible to problems that undermine the very integrity of the database. Additionally, a poorly designed scheme can negatively affect the efficiency of the database since the definition of a scheme to some extent determines the implementation options that are available. The reader should note further that the issues discussed in these chapters have implications beyond the RDM since data models (e.g., the object-oriented data model) that enhance the capabilities of the RDM are often implemented on top of an RDM foundation.•

We begin with a data abstraction perspective of the design process and a summary of the E/R design principles introduced in the previous chapter. We then define functional dependencies and demonstrate how they are used to formalize the semantic design processes by introducing several basic normal forms, the definitions of which are based on functional dependencies. We also introduce the concept of a lossless decomposition, another concept crucial to the design process. The chapter culminates with a simple yet efficient normalization algorithm. Chapter 6 considers more advanced semantic design issues, including the concept of *F*-enforceable decompositions, methods for deriving logical consequences of a set of functional dependencies, and multivalued dependencies, a formalism for capturing additional types of semantic information about a table scheme.

5.1 A DATA ABSTRACTION PERSPECTIVE ON THE DESIGN PROCESS

The previous chapter considered the problem of deriving semantically sound table schemes from an E/R diagram, focusing on guidelines based on relationship set functionalities for avoiding redundancy. In this chapter, our perspective is slightly different. We shall assume that we, the database designers, are given the tables that define the RDM scheme with which the user community wishes to interact (called the **interface-level** tables) and that it is our our responsibility to design a collection of tables schemes at the **implementation level** that reflect how tuples are to be stored physically in files.

The principles of data abstraction support the independence of interface- and implementation-level tables suggested by Figure 5.1. That is, a table scheme that is presented to the user need not reflect how the table's data actually is stored—a DBMS's query processing algorithms have the responsibility of mapping a user's query stated against interface-level tables first into queries against the implementation-level tables and then into operations against the files that implement these tables. Consequently, if we identify a potential problem with a table scheme at the interface level, we can attempt to map the interface-level table to one or more implementation-level tables in such a way that this problem does not materialize at the physical level of actual, stored data.

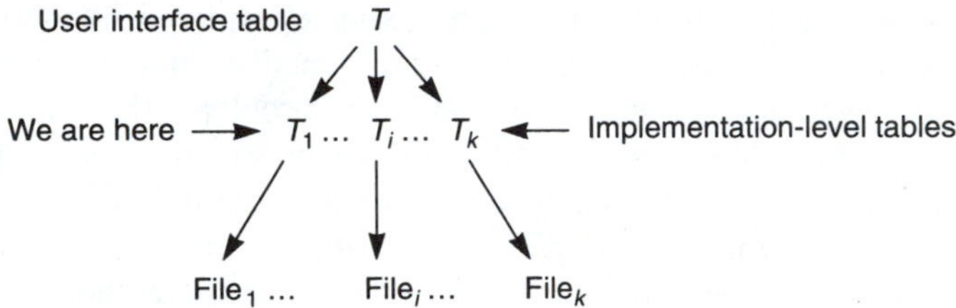

Figure 5.1 Designing tables to be implemented as files

The best perspective for the material in this chapter and the next, therefore, is that *we are given the table schemes with which the users will interact, and we are to design table schemes to be used in the implementation of these interface-level schemes*. It may be the case that the interface-level tables given to us were derived from an E/R diagram by careful application of techniques such as those outlined in the previous chapter (see Figure 5.2). Even if this is the case, the potential exists that some redundancy would be present if these tables were used at the implementation level. What's more, many database de-

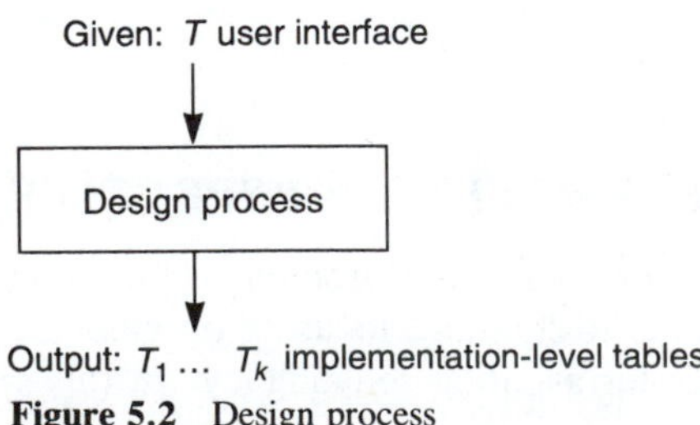

Figure 5.2 Design process

signers completely bypass the E/R model and construct interface-level tables as an initial representation of their informational requirements, paying little attention to the redundancy that these initial table definitions may imply. Hence, we have ample motivation for a design theory that can be applied to a collection of interface-level tables, independent of how those tables were created.

One final point of perspective is in order before we begin to develop the design theory. It turns out that, in practice, the techniques we develop to design implementation-level tables are very often also applied to the design of tables that are ultimately used at the interface level as well. That is, in practice, the tables designed by the process described here often replace the original tables at the interface level, and hence the definition of tables at the interface level and the definition of tables at the lower levels of abstraction are often one and the same. As will be seen at various points in the book, there are strong theoretical reasons for this correspondence in definitions, and, besides, most commercial relational database systems insist on it. It should be kept in mind, however, that there is nothing inherent in the RDM itself that says this must be the case. Hence, although it may be natural to view the material in this chapter and the next as addressing the design of tables at the user interface level, as well as at the implementation level, data independence implies that the two designs need not be the same.

5.2 THE ROOTS OF REDUNDANCY

We begin by summarizing some of the observations of Section 4.2 regarding the effect of relationship set functionalities on the mapping of an E/R diagram to table schemes. This discussion will lead us to functional dependencies, the cornerstone of a mathematical theory of semantic design for the relational model.

Recall that when mapping from the E/R model to the RDM, we must carefully consider the functionalities of relationships sets. In so doing, we hope to avoid the introduction of redundancy and the severe problems often associated with it. Section 4.2 presented rules of thumb, which we now summarize, for mapping from entity sets to table schemes:

1. Entities related by a $1:1$ relationship set may be modeled as a single table without causing redundancy to be introduced.
2. Modeling two entities related by a $1:n$ or $n:m$ relationship as a single table set will introduce redundancy. To support a $1:n$ relationship set from entity A to entity B, we should migrate from the table corresponding to entity A into the table corresponding to entity B an attribute on which a Join that realizes the relationship can be based.
3. To support an $n:m$ relationship set between entity A and entity B, create three tables:
   a. Table A corresponding to entity A.
   b. Table B corresponding to entity B.
   c. A third table to support the relationship between the two entities.

The discussion of the previous chapter should strengthen our intuition as to what constitutes a well-designed relational scheme and what constitutes a poorly designed one and should give us guidance in deriving a good relational scheme from an E/R diagram. A major flaw with deriving table schemes directly from E/R diagrams, however, is that the approach relies too heavily on the soundness of the original E/R diagram. If the entities in the original E/R diagram themselves suffer from semantic problems, these problems may well be inherited by the relational scheme that results from applying the design techniques.

For example, consider the DEPARTMENT entity. In the previous chapter, we allowed for the possibility that one department might have several locations. We have already observed that in this case it is not sufficient to migrate the Dept attribute from table DEPARTMENT into table EMPLOYEE. Unfortunately, our E/R diagram fails to capture the information required to determine what attribute, or set of attributes, should be migrated. Further, the failure of the E/R diagram to capture this kind of information results in an even more fundamental problem: If one department can have several locations, the table DEPARTMENT(Dept, Manager, Location, D_Desc) itself suffers from problems of redundancy. To see this, recall that if a department can have several locations, the following tuples are part of a possible instance of table DEPARTMENT:

DEPARTMENT

Dept	Manager	Location	D_Desc
Toys	888888888	10C-NY	This department stocks toys for ages 2–15
Toys	777777777	5F-LA	This department stocks toys for ages 2–15
Toys	222222222	9B-SF	This department stocks toys for ages 2–15

Observe that the description of the toys department is repeated for each of the department's locations. The problem with this table is identical to the problem we would likely encounter if we collapsed a pair of entities related by a $1:n$ relationship into a single table. Our design techniques were unable to avoid this problem because the $1:n$ relationship that exists between departments and locations is *hidden within* the DEPARTMENT entity.

Thus, we see that the problem of redundancy can arise not only when a single table is formed by improperly collapsing multiple entities but also when a table is formed directly from a single entity. In light of this fact, we would like a means of characterizing semantic problems in a table scheme, independent of the processes that created the table scheme. More specifically, we would like to develop methods that allow us to examine a table scheme, with no knowledge of the origins of that scheme, and determine whether or not the scheme is semantically sound. Additionally, we would like to develop methods that can be used to redesign an unsound table scheme.

To begin, we consider two relationships captured by the table DEPART-

MENT. These relationships are somewhat different from the relationships we have considered previously in that the relationships are between attributes contained in a single table.

1. There is a 1 : 1 relationship between the Dept attribute and the D_Desc attribute. For each Dept value V that appears in an instance of the DEPARTMENT table, there is exactly one D_Desc value V' such that V and V' appear together in tuples of the instance. Similarly, for each D_Desc value V' that appears in an instance of the DEPARTMENT table, there is exactly one Dept value V such that V' and V appear together in tuples of the instance.
2. There is a 1 : n relationship from the Dept attribute to the Location attribute. For each Location value W that appears in an instance of the DEPARTMENT table, there is exactly one Dept value W' such that W and W' appear together in tuples of the instance. In contrast, for each Dept value W' that appears in an instance of the DEPARTMENT table, there are *one or more* Location values W such that W and W' appear together in tuples of the instance.

The root of the redundancy in table DEPARTMENT, and, in fact, in all the poorly designed tables we have encountered, is that the tables *capture interattribute relationships whose functionalities are of a bad mix*. What, specifically, is this "bad mix" of functionalities? The bad mixes we have encountered are of the following form: A table contains attributes (or sets of attributes) X, Y, and Z such that

1. There exists a relationship from Y to X that is either 1 : n or 1 : 1, and
2. There exists a relationship from X to Z that is either m : n or 1 : n.

In other words, there exists a pair of relationships of the form Y 1 : _ X and X _ : n Z. This combination of relationships will cause problems, regardless of how the '_'s (spaces) are filled in. For example, in the DEPARTMENT table, there is a pair of relationships D_Desc 1 : 1 Dept and Dept 1 : n Location. Hence, letting D_Desc play the role of Y, Dept play the role of X, and Location play the role of Z, we see that these relationships fit the general pattern of a bad mix described earlier.

Why does such a mix of relationships *necessarily* lead to redundancy? Each value of attribute X (e.g., each Dept value) must appear in a separate tuple with each of the many values of attribute Z (e.g., Location) with which it is associated. Further, across all of these tuples that contains a given X value, there is a *single* value for attribute Y (e.g., a D_Desc value). Consequently, the association between a given X value and its (uniquely) associated Y value is *repeated for each of the many Z values with which this X value is associated*.

In contrast to these poorly designed tables, *a semantically sound table captures interattribute relationships whose functionalities are of a restricted mix*. This observation, while intuitively satisfying, relies on our informal concepts of interattribute relationships and their functionalities. Before we can put the observation to use, we must formalize the concepts, and then, in light of the formalization, we must specify the restrictions we wish to place on the interattribute relationships that a table may contain. In the following sections, we begin to develop a mathematically precise formalization that is the cornerstone of a theory for the semantic design of RDM schemes.

5.3 FUNCTIONAL DEPENDENCIES: THE CORNERSTONE OF A FORMAL THEORY OF SEMANTIC DESIGN

To begin, we make precise the perspective from which we wish to confront the problem of designing RDM schemes. We shall assume that we are presented with an RDM scheme $\mathcal{R}$ and some auxiliary information that describes the semantics of each table scheme in $\mathcal{R}$. Thus, the semantic design process takes $\mathcal{R}$ and its auxiliary information as input and produces a new RDM scheme $\mathcal{R}'$ as output. $\mathcal{R}'$ will have an informational content equivalent to that of $\mathcal{R}$, but hopefully will be more semantically sound than $\mathcal{R}$. To summarize,

INPUT: Original RDM Scheme $\mathcal{R}$: $T_1, T_2, \ldots, T_N$; $AuxInfo_1, AuxInfo_2, \ldots, AuxInfo_N$

↓

Design Process

↓

OUTPUT: New RDM Scheme $\mathcal{R}'$: $T'_1, T'_2, \ldots, T'_M$

This description of the design process relies on concepts that must be explored: "auxiliary information," "equivalent informational content," and "more semantically sound." We begin with the concept of *auxiliary information*. Observe that an RDM scheme is nothing more than a syntactic construct—a collection of table schemes, each of which is a name and an attribute list. The problems associated with a poor design, on the other hand, are semantic in nature, arising from the *meanings* of the attributes in the table schemes, in particular from how the attributes relate to one another. The role of the auxiliary information in the design processes is to capture, in a mathematically precise way, the relevant semantics of a table scheme, thereby allowing us to detect and correct problems in the scheme's definition.

For the moment, we shall assume that the auxiliary information associated with each table scheme is a collection of **functional dependencies.** Intuitively, a functional dependency for table scheme $T(A_1, A_2, \ldots, A_N)$ describes potential relationships between the values of one subset $X \subseteq \{A_1, \ldots, A_N\}$ of the attributes and another subset $Y \subseteq \{A_1, \ldots, A_N\}$. The formal definition of a functional dependency uses the tuple-as-mapping perspective introduced in Section 2.2.

Definition 5.1 Let $T(A_1, A_2, \ldots, A_N)$ be a table scheme and let $X, Y \subseteq \{A_1, A_2, \ldots, A_N\}$. The functional dependency $X \rightarrow Y$ (read "X functionally determines Y") is an assertion on table scheme T that if t and t' are tuples present in *any single* instance of table scheme T, then

$$t[X]=t'[X] \Rightarrow t[Y]=t'[Y]$$

In other words, if *any* instance of table scheme T contains a pair of tuples that agree on each attribute in the set X, then the pair of tuples *necessarily* agrees on each attribute in the set Y.

Definition 5.2 An instance of table scheme T **obeys a functional dependency** f if the instance contains no pair of tuples that violates the assertion made by f. An instance of table scheme T **obeys a set** $F = \{f_1, \ldots, f_k\}$ of functional dependencies if the instance obeys each $f_i \in F$. If an instance does not obey a functional dependency f, or a set of functional dependencies F, the instance is said to **violate** f or F.

To illustrate these definitions, consider the table scheme $T(A,B,C,D,E,G)$ and the set $F = \{A \rightarrow C, AB \rightarrow DE\}$ of functional dependencies. (Note that we have written the attributes involved in the functional dependencies without set brackets, e.g., $AB \rightarrow DE$ rather than $\{AB\} \rightarrow \{DE\}$. This is a notational liberty, and it should be remembered that *sets of attributes* appear on each side of the $\rightarrow$ symbol.) The table instance

A	B	C	D	E	G
a1	b1	c1	d1	e1	g1
a2	b1	c1	d1	e1	g1
a1	b2	c2	d2	e2	g1

violates F since the pair of tuples

a1	b1	c1	d1	e1	g1
a1	b2	c2	d2	e2	g1

violates the functional dependency $A \rightarrow C$. The table instance

A	B	C	D	E	G
a1	b1	c1	d1	e1	g1
a1	b2	c1	d2	e2	g1
a1	b1	c1	d1	e2	g1

violates F since the pair of tuples

a1	b1	c1	d1	e1	g1
a1	b1	c1	d1	e2	g1

violates the functional dependency $AB \rightarrow DE$. On the other hand, the table instance

A	B	C	D	E	G
a1	b1	c1	d1	e1	g1
a1	b2	c1	d2	e2	g1
a2	b1	c1	d2	e2	g1
a2	b2	c1	d3	e3	g1
a3	b2	c2	d3	e3	g1
a3	b2	c2	d3	e3	g2

obeys F.

It is crucial to emphasize that a functional dependency, like the functionality of a relationship in an E/R diagram, is associated with the nature of a table scheme and *not* with particular instances of the table. From inspection of a particular table instance, we can conclude that the instance obeys or violates a functional dependency, but we can never conclude from inspection of one instance, or of a million instances, of a table that a functional dependency correctly captures the semantics of a table scheme. Functional dependencies are supplied by the users along with the table scheme definition, and convey to us semantic information that *the user asserts* about the table scheme.

Functional dependencies play two roles in database theory: They are part of the auxiliary information that helps us to design the RDM scheme, and, in addition, they serve as **integrity constraints** that are checked in the course of transaction processing. Functional dependencies serve as constraints in that they restrict the legal instances of a table scheme. For example, if $T(A_1 = D_1, A_2 = D_2, A_3 = D_3, A_4 = D_4)$ is a table scheme with no associated functional dependencies, then any subset of the $|D_1| * |D_2| * |D_3| * |D_4|$ tuples consistent with T's scheme is a legal instance of T. On the other hand, if $A_1 \rightarrow A_2$ is a functional dependency the user associates with scheme T, then any instance which contains a pair of tuples such as

A_1	A_2	A_3	A_4
a	b	c	d
a	b'	c	d

is illegal and not a potential instance. In many contexts, it is desirable to explicitly check each user update to verify that the result of the update is a legal (with respect to a given set of functional dependencies) instance of the effected table. For example, suppose that table scheme PERSONAL(SS#, Age, Highest_Degree) has associated with it the functional dependency SS# → Age Highest_Degree and that the current instance of PERSONAL is

SS#	Age	Highest_Degree
111111111	35	PhD
222222222	30	MS
333333333	22	BA

(Observe that this instance of PERSONAL obeys the functional dependency SS# → Age Highest_Degree.) A user update such as ADD(PERSONAL, <222222222, 30, PhD>) should be disallowed on the grounds that the resulting instance of PERSONAL is illegal since it violates the functional dependency SS# → Age Highest_Degree.

Of more immediate interest to us than the role of functional dependencies in update processing is their role in table scheme design. We again consider the table scheme DEPARTMENT(Dept, Manager, Location, D_Desc). Suppose the user asserts that the set

F={Dept → D_Desc, D_Desc → Dept, Location→ Dept Manager D_Desc }

of functional dependencies applies to the table scheme DEPARTMENT. In general, a set of functional dependencies for a table scheme conveys two critical pieces of information. First, a set *F* of functional dependencies specifies that the only instances of the table scheme that we need concern ourselves with are those instances that obey *F*. (We assume that if a careless user should attempt to perform an update that would cause *F* to be violated, the database system will disallow the update.) Second, a set *F* of functional dependencies specifies that we must concern ourselves with *every* instance of the table scheme that obeys *F*. That is, a designer must act as if *any* table instance that obeys the set of functional dependencies will occur.

Let us see how the set *F* of functional dependencies for the table DEPARTMENT captures the same kind of information that was specified informally in terms of interattribute relationships:

1. Consider the functional dependencies Dept → D_Desc and D_Desc → Dept. The functional dependency Dept → D_Desc asserts that if an instance of DEPARTMENT contains a pair of tuples that have the same Dept value *V*, then the pair of tuples has the same D_Desc value *V'*. Similarly, the functional dependency D_Desc → Dept asserts that if an instance of DEPARTMENT contains a pair of tuples that has the same D_Desc value *V'*, then the pair of tuples has the same Dept value *V*. Taken together, these two functional dependencies capture the same information we specified informally by saying there was a 1 : 1 relationship between attributes Dept and D_Desc.

More generally, the functional dependency *X → Y formalizes the notion that there is either a 1 : 1 or 1 : n relationship from the set of attributes Y to the set of attributes X*. If we also have a functional dependency *Y → X*, we know that the relationship between *Y* and *X* must be 1 : 1. If, on the other hand, the functional dependency *Y → X* need not hold, a potential table instance contains a pair of tuples that has the same values for the attributes in *Y* yet different values for the attributes in *X*. In this case, the relationship from *Y* to *X* must be 1 : *n*.

2. Consider the functional dependency Location → Dept Manager D_Desc. Observe first that this dependency is equivalent to the three functional depen-

dencies Location → Dept, Location → Manager, and Location → D_Desc taken together. That is, an instance of table DEPARTMENT obeys the functional dependency Location → Dept Manager D_Desc if and only if the instance obeys each of the three dependencies Location → Dept, Location → Manager, and Location → D_Desc. In Chapter 6, we shall see how to formally establish this and other equivalences between functional dependencies. Consequently, the functional dependency Location → Dept Manager D_Desc captures the information that there is a 1 : *n* relationship from each of Dept, Manager, and D_Desc to Location.

3. Consider the consequences of the absence from *F* of certain functional dependencies. Recall that if an instance of table DEPARTMENT does not violate any functional dependency in *F*, then it must be assumed that this is an instance that will occur. For example, because the set *F* of functional dependencies contains no information to the effect that Dept → Location, we must act as if an instance such as

Toys	888888888	10C-NY	This department stocks toys for ages 2–15
Toys	777777777	5F-LA	This department stocks toys for ages 2–15
Toys	222222222	9B-SF	This department stocks toys for ages 2–15

will occur. Consequently, the relationship identified earlier from Dept to Location indeed must be assumed to be 1 : *n* rather than 1 : 1. For the same reason, the relationships from Manager and D_Desc to Location also must be assumed to be 1 : *n*.

Observe that functional dependencies capture the same kind of information as interattribute relationships while avoiding the semantic vagueness and subjectivity inherent in any attempt at defining what such relationships "mean." Functional dependencies accomplish this task by speaking of potential table instances, bypassing the need to explain why an instance is possible or why it is not. In this sense, functional dependencies are a mathematical bridge between syntax and semantics, conveying in a formal manner the information required to detect semantic problems associated with a table scheme.

5.4 NORMALIZATION

At the conclusion of Section 5.2, we developed guidelines based on interattribute relationships for detecting poorly designed table schemes. We asserted that a table scheme is poorly designed if it contains sets of attributes *X*, *Y*, and *Z* such that there exists a pair of relationships of the form *Y* 1 : _ *X* and *X* _ : *n* *Z*. We now can state this rule in terms of functional dependencies:

> A table scheme is poorly designed if it contains sets of attributes *X*, *Y*, and *Z* ($Y \not\subseteq X$) such that $X \rightarrow Y$, but it is not the case that $X \rightarrow Z$. In other words, a set of attributes should determine either all the other attributes in the table scheme or none of the other attributes in the table scheme.

For example, consider again the table scheme

DEPARTMENT(Dept, Manager, Location, D_Desc)

and the set

F = {*Dept* → *D_Desc*, *D_Desc* → *Dept*, *Location* → *Dept Manager D_Desc*}

of functional dependencies. According to the preceding rule, the table scheme is poorly designed. We have that Dept → D_Desc, while Dept does not functionally determine any of the other attributes in the table. (Similar comments apply to the functional dependency D_Desc → Dept.) Consequently, if an instance of table DEPARTMENT contains *n* tuples with the same value *D* for the Dept attribute, the association of department *D* with its D_Desc will be repeated *n* times. Therefore, we are led to conclude once again that table DEPARTMENT may be plagued by problems of redundancy.

Once a semantic problem with a table is detected, it often is possible to **decompose** the table into a collection of semantically sound tables. For example, we can decompose the table

DEPARTMENT(Dept, Manager, Location, D_Desc)

into the pair of tables

DEPT1(Dept, Manager, Location)
DEPT2(Dept, D_Desc)

Intuitively, this is a superior design because the two pieces of information captured by table DEPARTMENT are split between the two smaller tables. Table DEPT1 captures information associating a location with a department and its manager, while table DEPT2 captures information associating a department with its description. The semantic problems inherent in table DEPARTMENT result from the fact that the table captures both these pieces of information, as is evident from the fact that the dependencies Dept → D_Desc and Location → Dept Manager each applies to table DEPARTMENT. On the other hand, only Location → Dept Manager applies to table DEPT1, while only Dept → D_Desc applies to table DEPT2. Observe that, in each of DEPT1 and DEPT2, if a set of attributes determines some other attribute in the table, it determines all the other attributes in the table.

The tasks at hand are to formalize what it means for a decomposition to be a satisfactory design and to develop algorithmic methods for obtaining satisfactory designs.

Logical Closures, Keys, and Prime Attributes

In this section, we define some basic concepts that are necessary for the design theory that follows. All of these concepts pertain to a single table scheme *T* and its associated set *F* of functional dependencies.

We begin by observing that a set *F* of functional dependencies may **imply** one or more functional dependencies that are not explicitly listed in *F*.

Definition 5.3 Let F be a set of functional dependencies for table scheme T. The set F **logically implies** the functional dependency f if any instance of T that obeys F necessarily obeys f also.

For example, consider table scheme $T(A, B, C)$ with associated set $F = \{A \rightarrow B, B \rightarrow C\}$ of functional dependencies. The following are among the functional dependencies logically implied by F:

1. F logically implies each functional dependency $f \in F$.
2. F logically implies the functional dependency $A \rightarrow A$. In fact, for *any* table scheme $T(U)$ and *any* set F of functional dependencies, each dependency of the form $X \rightarrow Y$, where $Y \subseteq X \subseteq U$, is logically implied by F. This is the case because every instance of T obviously obeys the functional dependency $X \rightarrow Y$, when $Y \subseteq X$. Consequently, if an instance of T obeys F, it certainly obeys $X \rightarrow Y$, thus satisfying the preceding definition of logical implication. Dependencies of this form are not very interesting and are referred to as **trivial dependencies**.
3. F implies the functional dependency $AC \rightarrow B$. To see this, consider an arbitrary instance I of table T that obeys F. Then I must obey the functional dependency $A \rightarrow B \in F$. Suppose now that I contains a pair of tuples t_1 and t_2 such that $t_1[AC] = t_2[AC]$. Then it certainly is the case that $t_1[A] = t_2[A]$. But since instance I obeys the functional dependency $A \rightarrow B$, $t_1[B] = t_2[B]$. Therefore, instance I obeys the functional dependency $AC \rightarrow B$.
4. F implies the functional dependency $A \rightarrow C$. The reader is encouraged to establish this by supplying an argument along the lines of the one just given.

Definition 5.4 The **logical closure** of a set F of functional dependencies for table scheme T is the set of functional dependencies $F^* = \{f \mid F$ logically implies $f\}$.

It is crucial to emphasize that in considering the logical closure F^* of F we are not discovering new functional dependencies from inspection of table instances. Rather, we are making explicit functional dependencies that must hold because the dependencies in F are known to hold. The significance of logical closures is that we wish to design a table scheme that is sound with respect to the logical closure of a user-supplied set of functional dependencies rather than simply with respect to the set itself. To accomplish this, of course, we will require some way to obtain from the user-supplied set F the logical closure F^*, or at least a representation of relevant aspects of F^*. We put off this problem until Chapter 6, and until then we shall proceed under the assumption that a method exists for obtaining F^*.

Our next concept is that of a **key** of a table scheme. The term *key* has developed various informal meanings in several different contexts. One common meaning is that a key is a record field that uniquely identifies the record; that is, no two distinct records in a file have the same value for the key field. The key of a table scheme has meaning similar to this.

Definition 5.5 Let $T(A_1, A_2, \ldots, A_n)$ be a table scheme with associated set F of functional dependencies. A **key of T** is any subset $K \subseteq \{A_1, A_2, \ldots, A_n\}$ with the following two properties:

a. (Superkey property) F^* contains the functional dependency $K \rightarrow A_1 A_2, \ldots, A_n$. That is, K functionally determines all the attributes in the table. The superkey property implies that no two tuples in any legal instance of table T agree on all the attributes in K.

b. (Minimality property) K is a minimal set with property *a*. That is, no proper subset of K functionally determines all the attributes in table T.

A set of attributes that obeys the superkey property, whether the set be minimal or not, is called a **superkey.** Thus *all keys are superkeys, but not all superkeys are keys.*

We now consider two questions regarding keys:

1. Can a table have more than one key?
2. Do all tables have at least one key?

The answer to the first question is yes, as can be demonstrated by considering the table scheme T(SS#, Name, Salary, Address) and the associated set F = {SS# → SS# Name Salary Address, Name Address → SS# Name Salary Address} of functional dependencies. Clearly, {SS#} and {Name, Address} each is a superkey of table scheme T. Further, it can be shown that F^* does *not* contain any of the following functional dependencies: $\emptyset$ → SS# Name Salary Address, Name → SS# Name Salary Address, or Address → SS# Name Salary Address. Consequently, each of the superkeys {SS#} and {Name, Address} obeys the minimality property, and each is thus a key. It also can be shown that table scheme T has no other keys.

The answer to the second question, Do all table schemes have a key? is yes also. To see this, consider the following algorithm:

```
FindKey( T(A1,A2, . . . , An), F, K )
  { Return in K a key for table scheme T which has associated set F
    of functional dependencies. }
  K ← {A1,A2, . . . , An}
  { K is now a superkey }
  for (each Ai in K)
    if (K − {Ai} is a superkey)
      K ← K − {Ai}
    endif
  end for
end FindKey
```

This algorithm always will return a key of table scheme T. The algorithm is based on the fact that the set of all attributes in table scheme T is a superkey. If this set is not a minimal set with the superkey property, we can remove attributes, one at a time, until we obtain a superkey with the minimality property. Note that the algorithm assumes that we have a method for determining whether a set X of attributes is a superkey. While the problem is not difficult, we shall not present a method for making this determination until the next chapter. Observe also that, while the order in which the attributes are selected in the **for** loop has no effect on the correctness of algorithm FindKey, the selection order does determine the identity of the key constructed when more than one key exists.

We have one final definition pertaining to table scheme keys.

Definition 5.6 Let $T(A_1, A_2, \ldots, A_n)$ be a table scheme. Attribute A_i is **prime** if there exists a key K of T such that $A_i \in K$. If an attribute is not prime it is called **nonprime**.

The Basic Normal Forms

In this section, we define four basic normal forms that successively place more severe restrictions on allowable table schemes. The more restrictive, or higher, the normal form is, the fewer are the semantic problems that can potentially be associated with a table scheme obeying the normal form. In the sections that follow, we consider the problem of obtaining from a given table scheme and associated set of functional dependencies a collection of table schemes that represents the same information as the original table scheme, such that each table scheme in the collection is in a higher normal form than the original table scheme. This process is known as **normalization**.

The definition of a table scheme given in Chapter 2 incorporates the restriction of first normal form.

Definition 5.7 A table scheme is in **first normal form (1NF)** if the domain of each attribute in the scheme is scalar valued.

Forbidden by 1NF are attributes that can take on values that are, for example, vectors or lists. The primary motivation for 1NF is that without its restrictions, each attribute of a table scheme could be, in effect, a table scheme itself. In this case, all the problems that can occur "between" the attributes of a table scheme potentially could occur "within" a nonscalar attribute (e.g., there could be unsound mixes of dependencies between the coordinates of a vector-valued attribute). Addressing such problems would require that we extend the theories of functional dependencies and normalization to apply within a single attribute. Of course, each coordinate of a vector could itself be nonscalar, causing this "recursion" to continue. The standard practice in database theory simply is to "stop the recursion" at the table scheme level, and hence the rational for 1NF. We shall continue to assume that all table schemes are in 1NF, and the definitions of the higher normal forms will assume implicitly that the table scheme in question is in 1NF. Chapter 13 considers data models that relax the 1NF restriction.

Second normal form deals with **partial dependencies** of *nonprime* attributes.

Definition 5.8 Suppose X is a key of the table scheme T, Y is a proper subset of X, and A is an attribute not in Y. Then

$$Y \rightarrow A$$

is a *partial dependency*.

Definition 5.9 A table scheme T with associated set F of functional dependencies is in **second normal form (2NF)** if F^* contains no partial dependency

$$Y \rightarrow A$$

where A is nonprime.

Note that in this definition, and in the definitions that follow, we consider only functional dependencies in which the right side is a single attribute. It should be noted, however, that if F contains as well a functional dependency $X \rightarrow Z$, where Z is a set of attributes, then F^* contains the functional dependency $Z \rightarrow A$, for every $A \in Z$.

To illustrate the definition of 2NF, consider the table scheme

SCHEDULE(Prof, Course, Room, Office_Hrs)

with associated set

F={Prof → Office_Hrs, Prof Course → Prof Course Room Office_Hrs}

of functional dependencies. The functional dependency Prof → Office_Hrs is a partial dependency since {Prof} is a proper subset of the key {Prof,Course}. Further, it can be shown that {Prof,Course} is the only key of table scheme SCHEDULE, and thus Office_Hrs is a nonprime attribute. Consequently, the table scheme SCHEDULE is *not* in 2NF.

That table scheme SCHEDULE is not in 2NF is a tipoff to the types of problems we identified earlier. For example, the association between a professor and her or his office hours is repeated for every course the professor teaches. As a possible solution to this problem, we might *decompose* the table scheme SCHEDULE into two smaller table schemes:

CLASS(Prof, Course, Room)
TIMES(Prof, Office_Hrs)

We would like to conclude that this decomposition of table scheme SCHEDULE represents, in a manner that is semantically sound, the same information that is represented in the original table. Although intuitively this seems to be a valid conclusion, we shall not be able to give precise meaning to this conclusion until later in this chapter.

While a table scheme that is not in 2NF is prone to redundancy problems, that a table scheme is in 2NF is *not* a condition sufficient to ensure that the table scheme is free of redundancy problems. Consider, for example, the table scheme DIRECTORY(Professor, Department, Building) with associated set F={Professor → Department Building, Department → Building} of functional dependencies. The only key of table scheme DIRECTORY is {Professor}. Because ∅, the only proper subset of key {Professor}, does not determine any attribute, relation DIRECTORY is in 2NF. Observe, however, that the association between a department and the building that houses it will be repeated for each professor in that department.

The preceding example demonstrates that a 2NF table scheme may be vulnerable to redundancy problems. The problem with table scheme DIRECTORY is that it has a **transitive dependency**.

Definition 5.10 Let Y be a set of attributes from table scheme T and A be an attribute not contained in Y. The functional dependency

$$Y \rightarrow A$$

is a **transitive dependency** if Y is neither a superkey of T nor a proper subset of a key of T.

Definition 5.11 A table scheme is in **third normal form (3NF)** if it is in 2NF and if F^* contains no transitive dependencies

$$Y \rightarrow A$$

where A is nonprime. Equivalently, a table scheme is in 3NF if, for each nontrivial functional dependency $Y \rightarrow A$, Y is a superkey or A is prime.

We observe that table scheme DIRECTORY is not in 3NF, since Department → Building is a transitive dependency and Building is nonprime. As we did earlier in the context of the table scheme SCHEDULE, we might decompose the table scheme DIRECTORY into two smaller table schemes:

ASSIGNMENT(Professor, Department)
HOUSES(Department, Building)

and conclude intuitively that the decomposition represents, in a manner that is semantically sound, the same information that is represented in the original table.

The distinction between 2NF and 3NF is essentially a definitional convenience. The types of problems inherent in a table scheme not in 2NF completely parallel those inherent in a table scheme in 2NF but not 3NF. Further, as we soon shall see, it is a simple matter to algorithmically decompose an arbitrary table scheme so that each resulting table scheme is in 3NF. Consequently, there is little justification for a general design criterion based on 2NF, that is, for a design criterion requiring table schemes to be in 2NF while permitting them not to be in 3NF. This, however, is not to say that we should *always* insist on 3NF table schemes. Rather, on a case-by-case basis, decisions must be made as to whether the price of requiring joins in certain queries stated against the decomposition is higher than the price of having a partial or transitive dependency.

While there is little practical reason for distinguishing between 2NF and 3NF, the next normal form to be considered has characteristics that, in fact, make its applicability to the design process quite different from that of 2NF and 3NF. To motivate this new normal form, we observe that both 2NF and 3NF restrict attention to nonprime attributes. That is, these normal forms allow partial and transitive dependencies

$$Y \rightarrow A$$

whenever A is prime. It is natural to ask why the definitions of these normal forms include the caveat permitting prime attributes on the right side of a partial or transitive dependency. A traditional justification for allowing partial and transitive dependencies involving prime attributes is that there are few "natural" examples of 3NF table schemes that exhibit serious semantic problems. While perhaps rare, such 3NF table schemes in fact do arise in practice. For example, consider the table scheme

POSTOFFICE=(City, Street_Addr, Zip)

with associated set F = {City Street_Addr → Zip, Zip → City} of functional dependencies. This example is from Ullman (1982), and the set of functional dependencies F associated with table scheme POSTOFFICE appears to be realistic.

It can be shown that POSTOFFICE has exactly two keys, {City, Street_Addr} and {Zip, Street_Addr}; since all attributes are prime, POSTOFFICE is in 3NF. Despite the fact POSTOFFICE is in 3NF, it suffers from problems of redundancy as Zip → City is a partial dependency, and, hence, many identical (Zip, City) pairs may appear in an instance of the table scheme. For example, if 1,000 street addresses in New York City have the zip code 10015, the association between zip code 10015 and New York City will be repeated 1,000 times.

A possible decomposition of table scheme POSTOFFICE is into the table schemes

P1=(Street_Addr, Zip)
P2=(Zip, City)

While this decomposition eliminates the redundancy problems, we shall see in the following chapter that the decomposition suffers from subtle, but serious, problems of its own.

Boyce-Codd normal form (BCNF) is a strengthening of 3NF that addresses table schemes such as POSTOFFICE that are in 3NF but suffer from semantic problems.

Definition 5.12 A table scheme is in BCNF if F^* contains no partial or transitive dependencies. Equivalently, a table scheme is in BCNF if the left side of each nontrivial functional dependency in F^* is a superkey.

We observe that table scheme POSTOFFICE is not in BCNF since associated with it is the functional dependency Zip → City, and {Zip} is not a superkey.

It is apparent that BCNF detects problems not detected by 3NF. Observe, in fact, that the restrictions of BCNF coincide with the design rule we derived intuitively at the beginning of this section:

> A table scheme will have semantic problems if it has a functional dependency $X \rightarrow A_1$ but it is not the case that $X \rightarrow A_2$. (Observe that because it is not the case that $X \rightarrow A_2$, X is not a superkey.)

An obvious question, therefore, is, Why should we concern ourselves with 3NF when BCNF is safer? That is, rather than concentrating on 3NF, why not develop algorithms for decomposing table schemes into BCNF? The short answer is that a "satisfactory" decomposition of a table scheme into BCNF does not always exist, and, even when one does exist, it may be very difficult to find. A more detailed answer must wait for the results of the remainder of this chapter and of the following chapter.

5.5 DECOMPOSITIONS OF A TABLE SCHEME

The previous sections identified important design issues for RDM schemes and introduced functional dependencies and four normal forms as a means of addressing these issues. This section begins to consider the normalization processes in which an initial table scheme T is decomposed into a collection D of tables, such that D provides a semantically sound implementation of T.

The **normalization process** begins with a table scheme T and associated set F of functional dependencies and produces a **decomposition** of T into one or more table schemes $T_1, T_2, \ldots, T_k$. The goal is to produce a decomposition in which each T_i is in a higher normal form than the original table scheme T.

We first must define formally a decomposition of a table scheme.

Definition 5.13 Let $T(A_1, A_2, \ldots, A_n)$ be a table scheme. A **decomposition D of T** is a set of table schemes

$$D = \{T_1(X_1), \ldots, T_k(X_k)\}$$

such that $\bigcup_{i=1}^{k} X_i = \{A_1, A_2, \ldots, A_n\}$.

We note that the attribute sets X_i need not be pairwise disjoint, and, typically, they will not be.

As we have stated, the goal of the normalization process is to produce a decomposition D for table scheme T such that each $T_i \in D$ is in a higher normal form than T. Observe, however, that while table scheme T may have associated with it a set F of functional dependencies, each $T_i \in D$ has no set of functional dependencies explicitly associated with it, and, therefore, any assertion that T_i is in some normal form or other is not entirely well defined. To address this and other equally important issues, we return to the perspective of the design process that was described in Section 5.1.

In Section 5.1, we agreed that the table schemes we design would correspond to implementation-level structures, that is, that each table resulting from the design process would correspond to a file, with each tuple in the table mapping to a record in the file. We observe further that the starting point of our design process is one or more user-supplied table schemes, each with an associated set of functional dependencies. It is natural to take the perspective that each of the user-supplied table schemes *T* and its associated set *F* of functional dependencies model some aspect of "reality," that is, some aspect of the information of the application under consideration. Consequently, a decomposition *D* of table scheme *T* must model *the same information* as table scheme *T*, but hopefully in a more semantically sound manner.

T <aspects of user-perceived reality, table *T*>
↓
D <implementation of *T* as collection of table schemes>
↓
Files

We observe further that if decomposition *D* has the properties we shall describe shortly, the users can continue to interact with table scheme *T* and be oblivious to the fact that it is a decomposition of *T* that actually is implemented. That is, users can pose queries and updates against table scheme *T*, while implementation algorithms map these queries and updates first into operations against decomposition *D* and then into operations against the files that implement the table schemes in *D*. To illustrate, consider again the table scheme

SCHEDULE(Prof, Course, Room, Office_Hrs)

and the proposed decomposition

CLASS(Prof, Course, Room)
TIMES(Prof, Office_Hrs)

From the perspective just described, the users can interact with table scheme SCHEDULE while table schemes CLASS and TIMES reflect how the data actually is stored.

SCHEDULE
↙ ↘
CLASS TIMES
↓ ↓
*F*1 *F*2

Suppose that at the time the database begins operation, "reality" is reflected by the instance of table scheme SCHEDULE shown in Figure 5.3a. Under our im-

SCHEDULE			
Handly	720	100	10-11
Handly	463	305	10-11
Smith	463	210	3-4
Jones	144	305	10-11

a. Instance of SCHEDULE

CLASS		
Handly	720	100
Handly	463	305
Smith	463	210
Jones	144	305

b. Projection onto CLASS

TIMES	
Handly	10-11
Smith	3-4
Jones	10-11

c. Projection onto TIMES

Figure 5.3 Implementation of instance of SCHEDULE

implementation of table scheme SCHEDULE, this instance is mapped into the instances of table schemes CLASS and TIMES shown in Figures 5.3b and 5.3c, which reflect how the data actually is stored. That is, the instances of CLASS and TIMES that we intend to store are the projections onto CLASS and TIMES of the user-perceived instance of SCHEDULE.

To generalize and formalize the concepts in this example, we introduce the following definitions.

Definition 5.14 Let $T(A_1, \ldots, A_n)$ and $T_i(X_i)$, with $X_i \subseteq \{A_1, \ldots, A_n\}$, be table schemes, with I_T denoting an instance of table scheme T. $\Pi_{T_i}(I_T)$ denotes the instance of table scheme T_i that results from projecting onto the attributes of T_i the instance I_T; that is, $\Pi_{T_i}(I_T) = \Pi_{X_i}(T)$, where the current instance of table scheme T is I_T.

For example, if $I_{SCHEDULE}$ is the instance of table scheme SCHEDULE shown in Figure 5.3a, then $\Pi_{CLASS}(I_{SCHEDULE})$ and $\Pi_{TIMES}(I_{SCHEDULE})$ are the instances of table schemes CLASS and TIMES shown in Figures 5.3b and 5.3c.

Definition 5.15 Let T be a table scheme and $D = \{T_1, T_2, \ldots, T_k\}$ a decomposition of T. The **D-Projector** of T is a map

$$\text{D-Proj: \{instances } I_T \text{ of } T\} \rightarrow \{\langle I_{T_1}, \ldots, I_{T_k} \rangle \mid I_{T_i} \text{ is an instance of } T_i\}$$

defined by

$$\text{D-Proj}(I_T) = \langle \Pi_{T_1}(I_T), \ldots, \Pi_{T_k}(I_T) \rangle$$

As Figure 5.4 illustrates, the implementation of table scheme T by its decomposition D utilizes the D-Proj mapping.

Consider now the processing of a query Q posed against table scheme T. If all the attributes referenced in the query are contained entirely in the attribute set X_i of one of the $T_i \in D$, Q can be mapped straightforwardly into a query

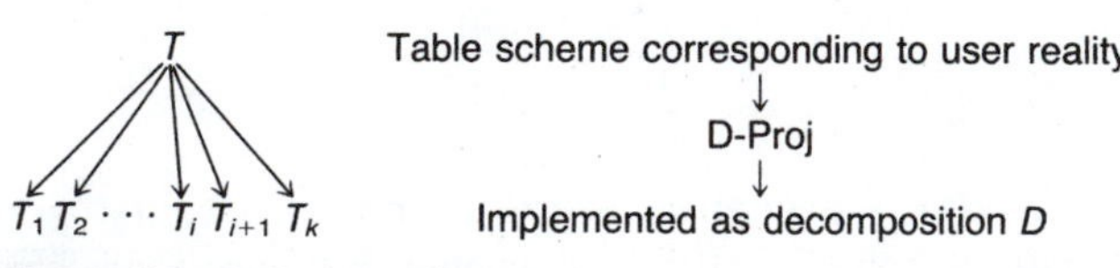

Figure 5.4 D-Proj mapping

against T_i. For example, the query $\Pi_{<Prof, Office\_Hrs>}(\sigma_{Prof=\text{"Handly"}} SCHEDULE)$ maps to the query $\sigma_{Prof=\text{"Handly"}}(TIMES)$.[1] Observe that as long as the instance of table scheme TIMES is derived from the user-perceived instance of table scheme SCHEDULE as specified by the D-Proj mapping [i.e., the instance is $\Pi_{TIMES}(I_{SCHEDULE})$], the query against TIMES yields the same result as the original query against SCHEDULE. In general, the implementation map for a query whose referenced attributes are contained entirely in one of the X_i is simple:

```
{ map Q against T into Q' against one of the Ti ∈ D—it is assumed that the
  attributes referenced by Q are contained entirely in one of the Xi }
find an Xi that contains all the referenced attributes
replace in Q all references to T with Ti
let Q' denote the result of this mapping
```

Algorithm 5.1

It is clear that Q', when processed against T_i, gives the "correct" answer; that is,

$$Q(I_T) = Q'(\Pi_{T_i}(I_T))$$

where $Q(I)$ denotes the value of the relational expression Q when the (single) table it references has value I.

As is seen in Figure 5.5, the implementation of the table T has two levels of abstraction. The preceding algorithm maps a query Q (of the simple form described) into a query Q' against one of the T_i and then other query-processing algorithms map Q' into file-level operations.

T, user query Q	
↓	Algorithm 5.1 maps Q to Q'
T_i, Q'	
↓	Other query-processing algorithms
F, file level operation	

Figure 5.5 Map for simple query

The mapping of queries posed against table scheme T in which the referenced attributes are not contained in any one X_i, and the mapping of updates, are more complex than the preceding mapping. Before considering the issues involved there, however, let us return to a question asked earlier: If the goal of decomposing table scheme T is to produce table schemes T_i in a higher normal form than T, with respect to what functional dependencies should T_i be considered? To answer this question, recall that the purpose of a set of functional dependencies is to characterize the instances of a table scheme that possibly can occur. The normal forms, in turn, use this characterization to determine if any

[1] In the following development, we shall state queries in relational algebra; of course, parallel results hold for queries stated in tuple calculus and commercial query languages such as SQL.

of the possible instances of a table scheme are semantically unsound. We thus wish to normalize table scheme T_i with respect to a set F_i of functional dependencies that characterize the instances of T_i that possibly can occur.

Observe that the instances of a table scheme T_i in a decomposition of table scheme T that possibly can occur (assuming the mapping perspective described earlier) are exactly those instances that arise from projecting an instance of table scheme T onto the attributes X_i of T_i. With this observation in mind, consider the following definitions.

Definition 5.16 The functional dependency $Y \rightarrow Z$ **applies** to table scheme $T(X)$ if $YZ \subseteq X$.

Definition 5.17 Let $T(X)$ be a table scheme with associated set F of functional dependencies, and let $T(X_i)$, with $X_i \subseteq X$, be a table scheme. The **projection of F onto** T_i is the set

$$F_{T_i} = \{ \text{functional dependencies } Y \rightarrow Z \in F^* \mid Y \rightarrow Z \text{ applies to } T_i \}.$$

In context, we often shall write F_i rather than F_{T_i}. If $D = \{T_1, \ldots, T_k\}$ is a decomposition of T, define $F_D = \bigcup_{i=1}^{k} F_i$.

Observe that in the preceding definition of F_{T_i}, the functional dependencies $Y \rightarrow Z$ that project onto T_i are required to be in only F^* rather than in F. One consequence of this fact is that it is always the case that $F_{T_i} = (F_{T_i})^*$.

It is fairly easy to see that if I_{T_i} is an instance of T_i that is the projection of an instance I of T that obeys F, then I_{T_i} obeys F_i. Thus, the only instances of T_i that can occur are those that obey F_i.[2] Thus, in the context of the mapping perspective we have been describing, it is "safe" to normalize T_i with respect to F_i since this would account for all instances of T_i that can occur as projections of instances of T that obey F. Further, in the next chapter, we shall discover additional motivations (that do not directly depend on the mapping perspective) for allowing only instances of T_i that obey F_i.

Consequently, we are led to the following definition.

Definition 5.18 Let T be a table scheme with associated set F of functional dependencies and $D = \{T_1, \ldots, T_k\}$ a decomposition. D is in *XNF* (where *XNF* is either 2NF, 3NF, or BCNF) if each T_i is in *XNF* with respect to F_i.

To summarize the design process under consideration, we begin with a user-supplied table scheme T and associated set F of functional dependencies, and we decompose T into $T_1, \ldots, T_k$ so that each T_i is in a high normal form (usu-

---

[2] Interestingly, however, there may be instances of the T_i that obey the F_i that are not projections of instances of T that obey F. Generally speaking, functional dependencies by themselves are not sufficient to characterize exactly the instances of the T_i that are projections of instances of T that obey F. See exercise 5.19.

ally 3NF) with respect to F_{T_i}. This is the goal, but there remain several important issues to consider:

1. To be of use, a decomposition must possess properties in addition to the property that each T_i is in a high normal form. The following section considers one such property, that the decomposition and the original table have "equivalent" information content.
2. We require efficient algorithms for deriving a satisfactory decomposition from a user-supplied table scheme and associated set of functional dependencies.
3. Do the four basic normal forms address satisfactorily all important design issues?

In the remainder of this chapter, and in the next chapter, we shall address these issues.

5.6 LOSSLESS DECOMPOSITIONS

We now come to a crucial concept. In the previous section, we presented an algorithm used to map a query Q posed against table scheme T, *whose referenced attributes are contained in one of the X_i*, into a query against one $T_i \in D$. We now consider the issue of mapping an *arbitrary query Q* posed against T into a query against the decomposition D:

$$\begin{array}{ccl} T & Q & \\ \downarrow & \downarrow & \text{Required mapping} \\ T_1 T_2 \cdots T_k & Q' & \end{array}$$

Let us consider the most general case, that a user wishes to see the instance of table scheme T that is represented by the decomposition. Therefore, from the current instances of the $T_1, T_2, \ldots, T_k$ (which, recall, are stored in place of the instance of T) we need to reconstruct the current instance of T. The mechanism for reconstructing T from its decomposition D is to take the natural join of the T_i. For example, consider again the instance of SCHEDULE and the projections of this instance that actually are stored:

SCHEDULE

Handly	720	100	10-11
Handly	463	305	10-11
Smith	463	210	3-4
Jones	144	305	10-11

a.

CLASS

Handly	720	100
Handly	463	305
Smith	463	210
Jones	144	305

b.

TIMES

Handly	10-11
Smith	3-4
Jones	10-11

c.

To reconstruct the instance of SCHEDULE that is represented by the instances of CLASS and TIMES, we need only take the Natural join CLASS $\bowtie$ TIMES. The reader can verify that this Natural join indeed does result in the correct instance of SCHEDULE.

More generally, suppose that table scheme T is decomposed into $D = \{T_1, \ldots, T_k\}$. As we have described, if I_T is the instance of T that represents the current state of reality, the instances of T_i that are stored is given by the D-Projector map

$$\text{D-Proj}(I_T) = <\Pi_{T_1}(I_T), \ldots, \Pi_{T_k}(I_T)>$$

The way to reconstruct from the instances I_{T_i} of T_i the instance I_T of T is to take the Natural join

$$I_{T_1} \bowtie I_{T_2} \bowtie \cdots \bowtie I_{T_k}$$

We now make a critical observation. A decomposition must have a certain property before we can guarantee that the natural join of the the instances I_{T_i} really results in the instance of T that is being represented. What's more, without this property, there is *no way at all* to reconstruct the instance of T that the decomposition is supposed to represent. As an example of what can go wrong, consider the table scheme T(Emp_Name, Division, Boss) and its decomposition into the two table schemes

T_1(Emp_Name, Division)
T_2(Division, Boss)

Suppose that at some point in time the stored instances of T_1 and T_2 are as shown in Figures 5.6a and b. In order for this decomposition to be a satisfactory representation of the table scheme T, we must be able to deduce from the above instances of T_1 and T_2 the instance of T that is being represented (e.g., so that we can answer a user query such as "Who is the boss of employee Smith?").

Emp_Name	Division
Smith	A
Jones	B
Harris	A

Figure 5.6a Stored instance of T_1

Division	Boss
A	Mr. Big
B	Mr. Very Big
A	Mr. Moderately Large

Figure 5.6b Stored instance of T_2

From our previous discussion, we see that the way to reconstruct the instance of T that is represented by these instances of T_1 and T_2 is to take the Natural join of T_1 and T_2. If we do this, we get the instance of T shown in Figure 5.6c. Can we be sure that this is the instance of T that is represented by the preceding instances of T_1 and T_2? Unfortunately, the answer is *no*! This *could* be the instance of T that the instances of the decomposition represent—note

Emp_Name	Division	Boss
Smith	A	Mr. Big
Smith	A	Mr. Moderately Large
Jones	B	Mr. Very Big
Harris	A	Mr. Big
Harris	A	Mr. Moderately Large

Figure 5.6c Instance of T resulting from $T_1 \bowtie T_2$

that if we project this instance of T onto T_1 and T_2, we indeed get the instances of the decomposition shown previously. Thus, the assertion that the preceding instance of T is the one being represented by the decomposition is consistent with our convention of representing an instance of T by its D-Projection.

Observe, however, that the D-Projection of other instances of T result in *exactly the same* instances of T_1 and T_2 being stored. For example, the instance shown in Figure 5.6d also has the preceding instances of T_1 and T_2 as its D-Projection. (Observe also that for this instance, it is not the case that the join of the projections yields the original instance; we have already observed that it yields the instance in Figure 5.6c.) In other words, in this example, we have no way of determining what instance of T was projected onto the decomposition to yield the instances of T_1 and T_2 that have been stored.

Emp_Name	Division	Boss
Smith	A	Mr. Big
Jones	B	Mr. Very Big
Harris	A	Mr. Moderately Large

Figure 5.6d Second instance of T with same projections

To further explore this problem, consider the following general scenario:

1. From the user's perspective, table T exists and currently has value I_T.
2. Table T is represented by decomposition $D = \{T_1, \ldots, T_k\}$, with each T_i currently having value $I_{T_i} = \Pi_{T_i}(I_T)$.
3. To recover the current instance of T, we join the T_i and get instance $I = I_{T_1} \bowtie \cdots \bowtie I_{T_k}$ of T. Instance I, however, is not necessarily the instance of T that the projections I_{T_i} are representing—another instance I' could have projected onto these same I_{T_i}. That is, we cannot determine if the original instance I_T of T is I or I' (or possibly some other instance).

This scenario is depicted in the diagram in Figure 5.7.

I — D-Proj → $I_{T_1}, I_{T_2}, \ldots, I_{T_k}$ — join → I

but also

I' — D-Proj → $I_{T_1}, I_{T_2}, \ldots, I_{T_k}$ — join → I

Figure 5.7 The lossy join problem

The problem we are encountering is rooted in the fact that the D-Proj map need not be *injective;* that is, for distinct instances I and I' of T, it may be the case that D-Proj(I) = D-Proj(I'). When this is the case, it is not possible to define an inverse mapping of D-Proj (e.g., join) from instances of the decomposition to the instance of T that is being represented.

To arrive at a resolution of our problem, we must better understand the relationship between the D-Proj and join mappings. To this end, consider the following lemma.

Lemma 5.1 Let T be decomposed into $D = \{T_1, T_2, \ldots, T_k\}$. Let I be any instance of T and let

$$\gamma_D(I) = \Pi_{T_1}(I) \bowtie \cdots \bowtie \Pi_{T_k}(I)$$

Then $\gamma_D(I) \supseteq I$. Further, D-Proj($\gamma_D(I)$) = D-Proj(I).

Proof Left as exercise 5.17.□

The lemma states that if we begin with instance I of T, store its D-Projection, and then attempt to reconstruct instance I by taking the natural join of the projections, we get back an instance $\gamma_D(I)$ of T that contains at least the tuples in I, *but possibly additional tuples that are not in* I. Further, the extraneous tuples cannot be detected because instance $\gamma_D(I)$, like instance I, has as its D-Projection the stored instances $\Pi_{T_i}(I)$, as shown in Figure 5.8.

$$I \text{ — D-Proj} \rightarrow I_{T_1}, I_{T_2}, \ldots, I_{T_k} \text{ — join} \rightarrow \gamma_D(I) \text{ — D-Proj} \rightarrow I_{T_1}, I_{T_2}, \ldots, I_{T_k}$$

Figure 5.8 Gaining tuples and looping back

Our previous example illustrates this phenomenon. Suppose our original instance I of table T is

Emp_Name	Division	Boss
Smith	A	Mr. Big
Jones	B	Mr. Very Big
Harris	B	Mr. Moderately Large

The D-Projection of instance I consists of the instances

Emp_Name	Division
Smith	A
Jones	B
Harris	A

Division	Boss
A	Mr. Big
B	Mr. Very Big
B	Mr. Moderately Large

The instance $\gamma_D(I)$ that results from the Natural join of the D-Projection is

Emp_Name	Division	Boss
Smith	A	Mr. Big
Smith	A	Mr. Moderately Large
Jones	B	Mr. Very Big
Harris	A	Mr. Big
Harris	A	Mr. Moderately Large

We thus have gained the tuples

Smith	A	Mr. Moderately Large
Harris	A	Mr. Big

which are not in the original instance I. Observe further that, since D-Proj(I) = D-Proj($\gamma_D(I)$), there is no way to deduce from the instances in the D-Projection which instance of T is being represented.

As a first attempt at resolving this dilemma, suppose that for some decomposition $D = \{T_1, \ldots, T_k\}$ of T we could ensure that, for all instances I of T,

$$\gamma_D(I) = I$$

That is, whenever we take the natural join of the D-Projections of an instance I, we get back instance I (i.e., we don't gain extraneous tuples). If this were the case, the D-Projector and join mappings would be inverses, and the D-Proj mapping would therefore be injective (only injective functions have inverses). This condition is sufficient to support the implementation scenario we have been describing: We store the D-Projection of an instance I and reliably reconstruct the instance I by taking the natural join of the instance in the D-Projection (see Figure 5.9).

$$I \text{ — D-Proj} \rightarrow I_{T_1}, \ldots, I_{T_k} \text{ — join} \rightarrow \gamma_D(I) = I$$

Figure 5.9 Lossless join

Unfortunately, in general, we shall not be able to ensure that $\gamma_D(I) = I$ for all instances I of T. Our design process, however, has something more to bring to bear on the problem: Associated with table scheme T is a set F of functional dependencies. Since the role of F is to characterize those instances of table scheme T that possibly can occur, in the current context we can use F to limit the instances of table scheme T with which we need concern ourselves. That is, it suffices to ensure that $\gamma_D(I) = I$, *for all instances I of T that obey F*. We need not concern ourselves with other instances of T because our entire design process is predicated on the fact that instances that violate a given set of functional dependencies will not be allowed to occur. This observation leads us to the following definition.

Definition 5.19 Let T be a table scheme with associated set F of functional dependencies. The decomposition D of T is **lossless** (with respect to F) if, for every instance I of T that obeys F,

$$\gamma_D(I) = I$$

A decomposition that is not lossless is said to be **lossy**.

Thus any instance I of T that satisfies F (and these are the only instances we care about) can be recovered from the D-Projection of I onto the lossless decomposition D. When this is the case, the project and join mappings are inverses, a situation illustrated in Figure 5.10.

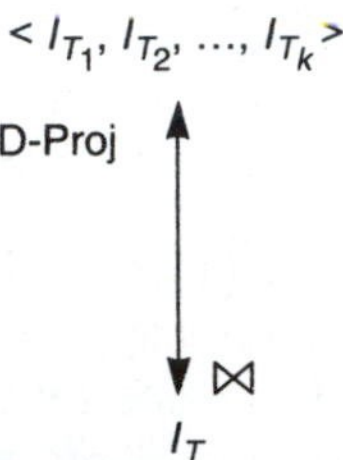

Figure 5.10 Inverse mappings

It should be emphasized that the terms *lossless* and *lossy* refer to information and not to tuples. That is, a lossless decomposition preserves information about what instance of the original table scheme the instances of the decomposition are representing. On the other hand, a lossy decomposition loses this information. The terminology is perhaps bit confusing since when D is a lossy decomposition, $\gamma_D(I)$ actually *gains* tuples over instance I.

An important question to be able to answer is,

Given A table scheme T, an associated set F of functional dependencies, and a decomposition D of T.

Question Is decomposition D lossless?

In Chapter 6, we shall present an algorithm for answering this question for any decomposition D. The question is substantially easier to answer in the special case in which the decomposition D consists of only two tables.

Theorem 5.1 Let $T(A_1, A_2, \ldots, A_k)$ be a table scheme, F an associated set of functional dependencies, and $D = \{T_1(X_1), T_2(X_2)\}$ a decomposition of T, with $Y = X_1 \cap X_2$. Decomposition D is lossless with respect to the set F of functional dependencies iff either $Y \rightarrow X_1$ or $Y \rightarrow X_2$ is in F^*.

Proof Left as exercise 5.17.□

To illustrate this theorem, suppose that in our previous example is the set $F = \{Division \rightarrow Boss\}$ of functional dependencies associated with the table scheme T(Emp_Name, Division, Boss). In this case, since *Division* → *Boss Division* $\in F_2$, the decomposition of T into T_1(Emp_Name, Division) and T_2(Division, Boss) is lossless. Observe that the instances of table scheme T

shown in Figures 5.6c and 5.6d violate F, so our previous difficulties with this decomposition are of no consequence in the context of the the set F of functional dependencies.

5.7 AN ALGORITHM FOR 3NF

We conclude this chapter by presenting a simple yet efficient algorithm that takes a table scheme T and set F of functional dependencies as input and produces a lossless 3NF decomposition of T as output.

Before presenting the core of the 3NF algorithm, it is necessary to describe a preprocessing step that converts the user-supplied set F of functional dependencies to a **minimal cover** F_M of F. A minimal cover F_M is a set of functional dependencies **equivalent** to F and possessing certain desirable properties. Equivalence between sets of functional dependencies is defined as follows with respect to equality of the sets' logical closures.

Definition 5.20 Let F and G be sets of functional dependencies applying to the same table scheme T. We say F and G are **equivalent** if $F^* = G^*$. In this case, we write $F \equiv G$.

Note that if $F \equiv G$, the two sets of functional dependencies are essentially different representations of the same information. We define as follows a minimal cover for a set F of functional dependencies.

Definition 5.21 F_M is a minimal cover for F if $F \equiv F_M$ and F_M is a **minimal set of functional dependencies** in the following sense:

1. Each right side of a functional dependency in F_M is a single attribute.
2. Each left side of a functional dependency in F_M is reduced as much as possible. That is, if $X \rightarrow A \in F_M$, Y is any proper subset $Y \underset{\neq}{\subset} X$, and $F' = F_M - \{X \rightarrow A\} \cup \{Y \rightarrow A\}$, then it is *not* the case that $F_M \equiv F'$. (Observe that for any F' formed from F_M as described earlier, $(F')^* \supseteq F_M^*$. Condition 2 states that for no such F' is the containment proper.)
3. No functional dependency in F_M is redundant. That is, there is no $f \in F_M$ such that the removal of f from F_M results in an $F' \equiv F_M$. (Observe that for any F' formed from F_M as described earlier, $(F')^* \subseteq F_M^*$. Condition 3 states that for no such F' is the containment proper.)

Example

Let $T(A,B,C,D,E,F)$ be a table scheme with associated set $F = \{A \rightarrow B, B \rightarrow C, A \rightarrow C, AB \rightarrow D, B \rightarrow EF\}$ of functional dependencies. The functional dependency $B \rightarrow EF$ violates the first condition of a minimal cover and can be replaced by the pair of functional dependencies $B \rightarrow E$ and $B \rightarrow F$; that such a replacement results in an equivalent set of functional dependencies is established in the next chapter. The functional dependency $AB \rightarrow D$ violates the second condition of minimal cover. To see this, observe that, since $A \rightarrow B$ is in the set of functional dependencies, the functional dependency $AB \rightarrow D$ can be replaced by the functional dependency $A \rightarrow D$ without altering the logical closure of the set. The functional dependency $A \rightarrow C$ violates the third condition (it is redundant since the set contains $A \rightarrow B$ and $B \rightarrow C$) and hence must be removed. The set F_M resulting from these modifications is $F_M = \{A \rightarrow B, B \rightarrow C, A \rightarrow D, B \rightarrow E, B \rightarrow F\}$, and this can be shown to be a minimal cover of F.

The next chapter presents a general algorithm

```
Procedure MinCov(F, F_M)
{ Return in F_M a minimal cover for F }
```

for computing minimal covers. For now, we assume the existence of such an algorithm and remark that the algorithm to be presented runs in time bounded by a low-order polynomial in the size of F.

The motivation for insisting that the 3NF algorithm run on a minimal set of functional dependencies is as follows. Conditions 1 and 2 are required for the algorithm's correctness. Condition 3, although not necessary for the algorithm's correctness, is highly desirable because both the algorithm's running time and the number of table schemes that are in the decomposition produced by the algorithm (the fewer the better, in general) are determined by the cardinality of the input set of functional dependencies. We note that a set F may have more than one minimal cover, but we shall not be concerned here with which minimal cover procedure MinCov returns.

We now are ready to state the 3NF algorithm. The input/output behavior of procedure 3NF is summarized as follows.

- INPUT: Table scheme $T(A_1, \ldots, A_n)$ and a set F of functional dependencies.
- OUTPUT: Lossless decomposition D of T such that each $T_i \in D$ is in 3NF with respect to F_i, the projection of F onto T_i.

```
Procedure 3NF(T(A_1, . . . , A_n),F,D)
  { Preprocessing step—obtain a minimal cover for F }
  MinCov(F,F_M)

  { Special Case }
  if (F_m contains X → A such that X ∪ {A}={A_1, A_2, . . . , A_n})
    { T is in 3NF }
    return with D={T(A_1, . . . , A_n)}
  endif

  D ← ∅
  i ← 1
```

```
for (each X → A in F_M)
  { Add to the decomposition a table scheme over the attributes XA. }
  D ← D ∪ {T_i(XA)}
  i←i+1
end for
{ At this point D is in 3NF, but it may not be lossless. The following step
  ensures the decomposition is lossless. }
Let K be any key of T
D ← D ∪ {T_i(K)}
end 3NF
```

Example of the 3NF Algorithm

Let $T(A,B,C,D,E,F)$ be a table scheme with associated set $F = \{A \rightarrow B, C \rightarrow DF, AC \rightarrow E, D \rightarrow F\}$ of functional dependencies. It can be shown that $\{A,C\}$ is the only key of table scheme T. Therefore, T has both partial and transitive dependencies involving nonprime attributes and is thus not in 2NF (and thus not in 3NF).

We apply procedure 3NF to obtain a decomposition for T.

Step 1: Apply algorithm MinCov(F, F_M) to obtain a minimal cover. Let $F_M = \{A \rightarrow B, C \rightarrow D, AC \rightarrow E, D \rightarrow F\}$ be the minimal cover returned by MinCov.

Step 2: Place in decomposition D a table scheme corresponding to each functional dependency in F_M. The following are the table schemes placed in D:

$T_1(A,C,E)$
$T_2(C,D)$
$T_3(D,F)$
$T_4(A,B)$

Step 3: Add to D the table scheme $R_5(A,C)$, corresponding to table T's only key $\{A,C\}$.

It can be verified (tediously) that each T_i is in 3NF with respect to the projection F_i of F.

The following theorem, proved in the next chapter, establishes the correctness of procedure 3NF.

Theorem 5.2 Procedure 3NF is correct.

Efficiency of the 3NF Algorithm

The time required by the 3NF algorithm is dominated by the call to MinCov, which converts the user-supplied set of functional dependencies to a minimal cover and by the time required to find a key K of table scheme T. In the next chapter, we demonstrate that both of these steps can be performed in time bounded by a low-order polynomial in the size of F. Exclusive of these two steps, algorithm 3NF is linear in the size of F since the algorithm's main loop considers each functional dependency in F exactly once.

In the following chapter, we refine and improve the statement of the 3NF algorithm. As already mentioned, two necessary refinements are to fully specify the algorithm MinCov and an algorithm for finding a key K of table scheme T. We also offer a potential improvement to the algorithm by developing a test that generalizes the result of Lemma 5.1, allowing us to determine whether an arbitrary decomposition is lossless. In the context of the 3NF algorithm, the utility of this test is that it can be applied to the decomposition created by the 3NF algorithm before the step that adds the "key table" $T_i(K)$; if the decomposition already is lossless, the final step can be omitted.

In Chapter 6, we shall discover that algorithm 3NF presented earlier has a highly desirable property not yet discussed. This additional property pertains to the role of functional dependencies in integrity checking. As we shall see in Chapter 6, it will be necessary to perform updates to the table schemes of a decomposition while ensuring that the instance of the original table scheme being represented by the decomposition obeys its integrity constraints. In Chapter 6, we shall demonstrate that the decomposition D produced by the 3NF algorithm has the property that such integrity checking can be performed on D in a highly efficient manner.

SUMMARY AND ANNOTATED BIBLIOGRAPHY

In this chapter, we introduced principles fundamental to the design of semantically sound RDM schemes. We introduced functional dependencies as a means of formalizing the process of RDM design. We viewed functional dependencies as a mathematical bridge between syntax and semantics, conveying in a formal manner the information required to detect semantic problems with a table. Three normal forms—2NF, 3NF, and BCNF—were introduced as a means of specifying design criteria using functional dependencies as the building blocks. These normal forms were originally proposed in Codd (1970) and Codd (1974). Another critical concept introduced in this chapter is that of a lossless join decomposition. We demonstrated that not all decompositions are lossless and illustrated that when such is not the case, information is lost, and hence, the decomposition is not an acceptable representation of the information being modeled.

The chapter concluded with a simple but efficient algorithm for creating a lossless 3NF decomposition from an arbitrary table scheme. This algorithm is based on the concept of table scheme synthesis, as described in Bernstein (1976). An alternative method of normalizing, not considered here, is known as decomposition. Generally speaking, decomposition often produces more natural table schemes than does synthesis, although all known algorithms based on decomposition have exponential worst-case running time. The reader is referred to Fagin (1977) for more details of the decomposition approach.

This chapter leaves several loose ends to be tied in Chapter 6. First, the 3NF algorithm is only partially specified since we have postponed solving the problems of obtaining a minimal cover for the user-supplied set of functional dependencies and of finding a key for a table scheme. Further, we still lack the techniques required to prove the 3NF algorithm correct. Chapter 6 supplies these missing pieces. Chapter 6 additionally considers the behavior under Update operations of a decomposition and, in that context, introduces the notion of an F-enforceable decomposition and demonstrates that the 3NF algorithm produces F-enforceable decompositions. Chapter 6 explores also BCNF (demonstrating limitiations on our ability to obtain a satisfactory BCNF decomposition) and 4NF, a higher normal form based on multivalued dependencies.

EXERCISES

1. Define the terms *functional dependency, logical consequence, logical closure, key, superkey,* and *lossless join decomposition.*
2. Define the four normal forms: 1NF, 2NF, 3NF, and BCNF. Give natural examples of table schemes that obey each normal form but do not obey the next higher normal form.
3. Prove that if functional dependencies $X \rightarrow Y$ and $Y \rightarrow Z$ hold for table scheme T, then so does the functional dependency $X \rightarrow Z$.
4. Let $T(A,B,C,D)$ be a table scheme and $F = \{AB \rightarrow C, C \rightarrow D, A \rightarrow B, B \rightarrow D\}$ an associated set of functional dependencies. The functional dependency $B \rightarrow C$ is *not* a logical consequence of F. Demonstrate this by constructing an instance of T that obeys F but violates $B \rightarrow C$.
5. Argue for or against each of the following implications:
   a. Functional dependency $A \rightarrow B$ implies functional dependency $B \rightarrow A$.
   b. Functional dependency $AB \rightarrow C$ implies functional dependency $A \rightarrow C$.
   c. Functional dependency $AB \rightarrow C$ implies at least one of the two functional dependencies $A \rightarrow C$ or $B \rightarrow C$.
6. Demonstrate that, for any integer $k > 1$, there exists a table scheme $T(A_1, \ldots, A_N)$ (with $n \leq k$) and a set F of functional dependencies such that $|F| = k$ and $|F^*| \geq 2^k$.
7. Give an example of a table scheme T with set F of functional dependencies and a decomposition D of T, such that the set

$\{f \mid f \in F \text{ and } f \text{ applies to } T_i\}$

differs from the projection F_{T_i} of F onto T_i.

8. Consider algorithm FindKey. Demonstrate that the order in which attributes A_i are considered for removal from the set K can affect both the identity and the cardinality of the resulting key.
9. Let $T(A,B,C,D)$ be a table scheme. For each of the following sets of functional dependencies, tell what is the highest normal form that table T is in. For example, if the table is in 3NF but not BCNF, your answer should be 3NF. Also, identify the reason that the relation is not in the next higher normal form.

   a. $F = \{ AB \rightarrow CD, B \rightarrow C \}$

   b. $F = \{ AB \rightarrow CD, C \rightarrow A \}$

   c. $F = \{ AB \rightarrow CD, B \rightarrow A \}$

   d. $F = \{ AB \rightarrow CD, C \rightarrow D \}$

   e. $F = \{ AB \rightarrow CD, D \rightarrow ABC \}$

   f. $F = \{ AB \rightarrow C, D \rightarrow ABC \}$

   g. $F = \{ AB \rightarrow CD, C \rightarrow B, C \rightarrow D \}$

10. Suppose $T(U)$ is in 3NF but not BCNF with respect to F. Let f be some functional dependency that applies to T. Is it possible that T is in BCNF with respect to $(F \cup \{f\})$?
11. The restriction of 1NF requires that all attributes of a relation scheme be simple valued. Describe an application in which such a restriction may be undesirable. In the application you describe, how might you use a traditional (1NF) relational database system to implement a non-1NF table scheme? What modifications must be made to our query languages and design theory to accommodate non-1NF table schemes?
12. Let $T(A,B,C,D)$ be a table scheme with associated set $F = \{AB \rightarrow C, B \rightarrow D, D \rightarrow A\}$ of functional dependencies. Is $T_1(A,B,D)$, $T_2(B,C)$ a lossless decomposition of T?
13. Let $T(A,B,C,D,E,F)$ be a table scheme with associated set $F = \{B \rightarrow D, C \rightarrow A, AD \rightarrow F\}$ of functional dependencies. Is the decomposition $T_1(A,B,C,F)$, $T_2(B,C,D,E)$ lossless?
14. Let $T(A,B,C,D)$ be a table scheme and $F = \{A \rightarrow B, B \rightarrow D, C \rightarrow A\}$ an associated set of functional dependencies. Consider the following two decompositions:

    Decomposition 1: $T_1(A,B,C)$ $T_2(C,D)$
    Decomposition 2: $T_1(A,B,D)$ $T_2(C,D)$

    One of the decompositions is lossless with respect to F, and the other is not. Identify the decomposition that is *not* lossless and support your contention by constructing an instance I of T such that I obeys F but when we join the projections of I onto T_1 and T_2, we do not get back I.

15. Suppose we are given the table scheme

    COMP(Employee, Title, Salary)

    and that we decide to decompose COMP into

    $COMP_1$(Employee, Title)
    $COMP_2$(Title, Salary)

    What query might be impossible to answer against $COMP_1$ and $COMP_2$ that previously could have been answered against COMP? Illustrate the problem by constructing an instance of the table COMP. What additional information about the table COMP might we have that would make valid the decomposition into $COMP_1$ and $COMP_2$?

16. Consider the table scheme SCHEDULE(Course, Section, Time, Student) with the associated set F = {Student Course $\rightarrow$ Section} of functional dependencies. The semantics of SCHEDULE are as follows: For every section of every course in our university, the relation gives the meeting time(s) of that section and the student(s) enrolled in that section.

    a. Does the following instance of SCHEDULE obey f?

Course	Section	Time	Student
463	001	9M	Jones
463	001	9W	Jones
463	001	9M	Smith
463	001	9W	Smith
563	001	3T	Harris
563	002	3F	Smith

    b. Find all the keys of relation scheme SCHEDULE.

    c. What is the highest normal form that relation scheme SCHEDULE is in?

    d. What are the potential redundancy problems associated with relation scheme SCHEDULE? Propose a decomposition that will improve the situation. In what way is your decomposition not a completely satisfactory solution? Can you develop a better solution?

17. Prove Lemma 5.1 and Theorem 5.1.

18. Let D be any decomposition of table T, let tables T_i and T_j of D share at least one attribute, and suppose that F_{T_i} contains at least one nontrivial functional dependency. Demonstrate that there exists an instance I_D of the decomposition such that I_{T_i} violates F_{T_i} yet instance $I_{T_1} \bowtie I_{T_2} \bowtie \cdots \bowtie I_{T_i} \cdots \bowtie I_{T_k}$ of T obeys F.

*19. Demonstrate that there exist table schemes T, associated set F of functional dependencies, and a decomposition $D = \{T_1, \ldots, T_k\}$ of T such that there is an instance of at least one of the T_i that obeys F_{T_i} but is not the projection of any instance of T that obeys F.

20. Suppose you are designing a relational database. Since you have just completed a course in database management, you tell your boss that the relations in the database should be normalized. However,
    a. Your boss says that the database is read only; that is, the users will be using only the Select command. What justifications can you give your boss for normalizing the database?
    b. Your boss says that although the database will be updated, it will be updated only by people "who know what they are doing." In other words, the people who update the database can be trusted not to introduce inconsistencies into the data. What justifications (in addition to the ones in part *a*) can you give your boss for normalizing the database?

CHAPTER 6

Dependencies and Normalization: A Further Study

The previous chapter identified important design issues for RDM schemes and introduced functional dependencies and four normal forms as a means of addressing these issues. This chapter begins by considering Update processing in the context of a decomposition, deriving the condition known as F-enforceability. The chapter then considers normal forms beyond 3NF. In particular, we consider the problem of decomposing a table scheme into BCNF, introduce multivalued dependencies, and define 4NF. The chapter's final three sections[1] present algorithms for computing the logical closure of a set of functional dependencies and for testing whether a decomposition is lossless and F-enforceable, and it culminates with a refinement of the 3NF algorithm and a proof of its correctness.•

6.1 UPDATE PROCESSING AND DECOMPOSITIONS

The results of the previous chapter address the problem of processing a query Q, posed against a table scheme T, when T is implemented in terms of a decomposition D. When the attributes referenced by Q are contained in one of the X_i, Algorithm 5.1 suffices. When this is not the case, the instance of T being represented by the decomposition may have to be reconstructed. As long as the decomposition is lossless, this is accomplished by taking the Natural join of the instances of the decomposition. These query-processing methods should be viewed as components of the algorithms that map between the levels of implementation shown in Figure 5.5.

There is another type of mapping required for the implementation depicted in Figure 5.5. This is the mapping of *Updates* the user poses against table T to Updates against the decomposition D that implements T. For example, suppose again that table T(Emp_Name, Division, Boss) (with associated set F = {Division → Boss} of functional dependencies) is implemented by the decomposition T_1(Emp_Name, Division) and T_2(Division, Boss). Suppose that a user requests an Update such as ADD(T, <Clark, C, Mr. Big>) or DELETE(T, <Smith, A, Mr. Big>).[2] How are these operations mapped into operations against the decomposition T_1 and T_2?

[1] Sections 6.4, 6.5, and 6.6 may be omitted without loss of continuity.

[2] In this chapter we assume that the second argument to DELETE is a complete tuple. In the current context, any multi-tuple DELETE can be treated conceptually as zero or more of these DELETEs.

We now consider four aspects of the Update problem:

1. The desired effect of the Update.
2. Considerations in the implementation of the ADD operation.
3. Considerations in the implementation of the DELETE operation.
4. Updating the decomposition directly.

The discussion of these four aspects of Update processing will lead us into the next section where we discuss the notion of an F-enforceable decomposition.

The issues raised, although illustrated in the specific context of a lossless decomposition $D = <T_1, T_2>$ of table scheme T, apply to any lossless decomposition into any number of table schemes.

The Desired Effect of the Update

Suppose instance I_T, which obeys F, is implemented as its D-Projection D-Proj $(I_T) = <I_{T_1}, I_{T_2}>$. Although only instances I_{T_1} of T_1 and I_{T_2} of T_2 are stored, we can reconstruct the instance I_T of T that is being represented by taking the Join $I_{T_1} \bowtie I_{T_2}$. Thus, the desired effect of the Update is clear: Add to or delete from instance I the specified tuple. Logically, this task can be accomplished as

construct I by taking the join $I_{T_1} \bowtie I_{T_2}$
add to or delete from I the desired tuple, obtaining instance I' of T
represent I' as instances $\Pi_{T_1}(I')$ and $\Pi_{T_2}(I')$ of T_1 and T_2

Algorithm 6.1

The algorithm is illustrated by the **commutativity diagram** of Figure 6.1. We begin at the northwest corner, take the Join to the southwest corner, Add or Delete the tuple to arrive at the southeast corner, and Project to the northwest corner, which corresponds to the desired instances of T_1 and T_2.

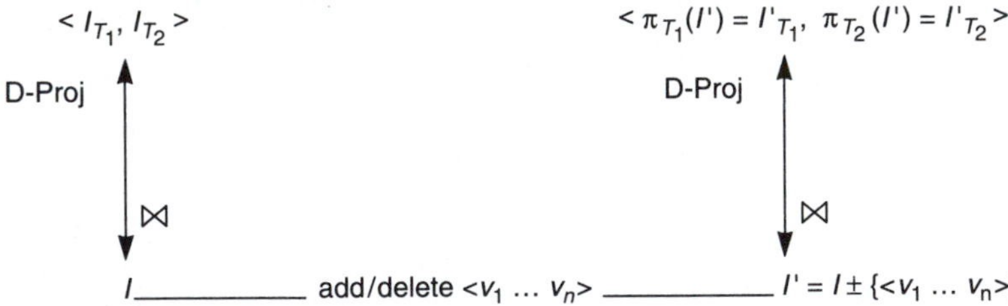

Figure 6.1 Commutativity diagram

Observe that, since the decomposition is lossless, as long as instance I' obeys the functional dependencies in F, instance I' in the future can be reconstructed as $\Pi_{T_1}(I') \bowtie \Pi_{T_2}(I')$. In terms of the diagram, the Project and Join maps at the east end are inverses. Note well, however, that the validity of our Update procedure depends on the fact that I' *obeys the functional dependencies* F. Thus, we must modify the Update algorithm as follows:

```
construct I by taking the join I_T1 ⋈ I_T2
if (adding or deleting the specified tuple results in an instance
      I' that obeys the functional dependencies F)
   represent I' as instances Π_T1(I') and Π_T2(I') of T1 and T2
else
   disallow the update {leave I_T1 and I_T2 unchanged }
endif
```

Algorithm 6.2

We emphasize that it is necessary to check that I' obeys the functional dependencies, not only to ensure that the instance I' can be reconstructed from its D-Projection but, more fundamentally, because we should disallow any Update that violates the user-supplied integrity constraints in F.

While the preceding update algorithm is logically correct, in general it will be rather inefficient. Thus, we consider whether the same effect can be obtained by a more efficient procedure, e.g., by a procedure that does not require the joining of the instances of the D-Projection.

Considerations in the Implementation of the ADD Operation

Consider a proposed algorithm for implementing the Update ADD(T, $<v_1, v_2, \ldots, v_n>$).

```
{ proposed efficient implementation of ADD(T, <v1,v2, . . . , vn>) }
Let t1=Π_T1{<v1,v2, . . . , vn>}
ADD(T1, t1)
Let t2=Π_T2{<v1, v2, . . . , vn>}
ADD(T2, t2)
```

Agorithm 6.3

The obvious advantage of Algorithm 6.3 is that it does not require the joining of instances of the decomposition. We must consider, however, whether the algorithm is guaranteed to have the desired effect. That is, if I_{T_1} and I_{T_2} are instances of T_1 and T_2 that represent instance $I = I_{T_1} \bowtie I_{T_2}$ of T, do the instances $I_{T_1} \cup \{t_1\}$ and $I_{T_2} \cup \{t_2\}$ necessarily represent the instance $I' = I \cup \{<v_1, v_2, \ldots, v_n>\}$ of T?

In terms of the commutativity diagram of Figure 6.2, we wish to ensure that the instances of T_1 and T_2 obtained by following the Add at the north end of the diagram are the same instances we would obtain by the brute force algorithm of first joining, then adding to I to obtain I', and then projecting. The following theorem addresses this concern.

Theorem 6.1 Suppose $I_T = I_{T_1} \bowtie \cdots \bowtie I_{T_k}$. Then

$$D\text{-}Proj(I_T \cup \{t\}) = <I_{T_1} \cup \{\Pi_{T_1}(t)\}, \ldots, I_{T_k} \cup \{\Pi_{T_k}(t)\}>$$

Proof The theorem is implied by the following easily verifiable identity:

$$\Pi_{<X_i>}(I_T \cup I'_T) = \Pi_{<X_i>}(I_T) \cup \Pi_{<X_i>}(I'_T) \Box$$

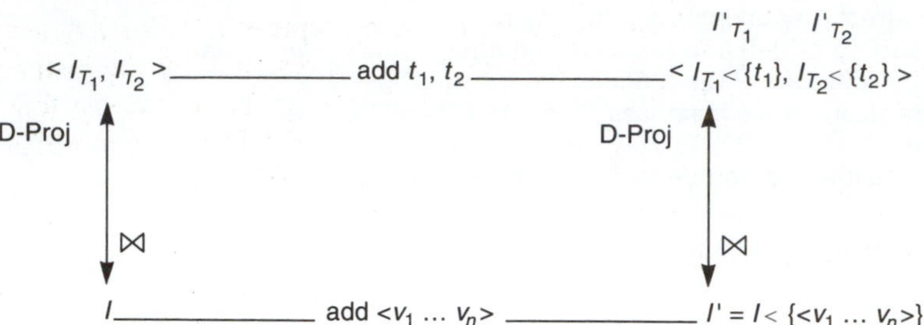

Figure 6.2 Commutativity diagram

This theorem only partially establishes the validity of the proposed Update algorithm. We need to ensure also that, as the commutativity diagram implies, the Project and Join maps at the east end of the diagram are inverses; that is, we need to ensure that $\gamma_D(I') = I'$. [Recall from Section 5.6 that γ_D is defined by $\gamma_D(I) = \Pi_{T_1}(I) \bowtie \cdots \bowtie \Pi_{T_k}(I)$.] Even though the decomposition of T into D is lossless, we can be sure that the D-Proj of I' correctly represents I' only if I' obeys F. Further, if I' violates F, we do not want to permit the Update at all. Observe that this problem really is not new—it is not a consequence of the proposed Update algorithm but is the same problem we had to consider for the brute force Update algorithm: Is the Update legal in that it results in an instance of T that obeys F? The new twist to the problem is that, since the proposed Update algorithm has so far avoided joining instances of the decomposition, we would very much like to verify the legality of the Update without explicitly constructing an instance of T. That is, the question at hand is whether we can construct an algorithm of the form:

```
{ efficient implementation of ADD(T,<v1,v2, . . . , vn>) }
Let t1=ΠT1{<v1,v2, . . . , vn>}
ADD(T1, t1), call the resulting instance I'T1
Let t2=ΠT2{<v1,v2, . . . , vn>}
ADD(T2, t2), call the resulting instance I'T2
{ verify the functional dependencies without taking a join }
if (instances I'T1 and I'T2 are such that I'T1 ⋈ I'T2 obeys F)
  allow the Update by storing I'T1 and I'T2
else
  disallow the Update by restoring the previous instances of T1 and T2
endif
```

Algorithm 6.4

Shortly, we shall consider the problem of checking the functional dependencies without joining the instances of the decomposition. But even assuming for the moment that this problem can be resolved successfully, there remains one final concern that must be addressed before we can conclude that the preceding Update procedure is valid. Theorem 6.1 assures us that instances $I'_{T_1} = I_{T_1} \cup \{t_1\}$ and $I'_{T_2} = I_{T_2} \cup \{t_2\}$ of T_1 and T_2 indeed are the D-Projection of the instance I'_T of T that results from adding tuple $<v_1, \ldots, v_n>$ to the current instance I_T of T (i.e., the instance of T represented by the instances of I_{T_1} and I_{T_2} of T_1 and T_2 before the Update). Consider, however, the following possibility. Although we know that I'_{T_1} and I'_{T_2} are the D-projection of the instance I' (this follows from Theorem 6.1), is it possible that $I'_{T_1} \bowtie I'_{T_2}$ is equal to some instance I'' of T different from I' (see Figure 6.3)? Note that if this were the case, the proposed Update algorithm would be checking the validity of instance I'' rather than that of the instance I' that results from the Update, and if the validity of I'' were established, the wrong instance of T would be represented!

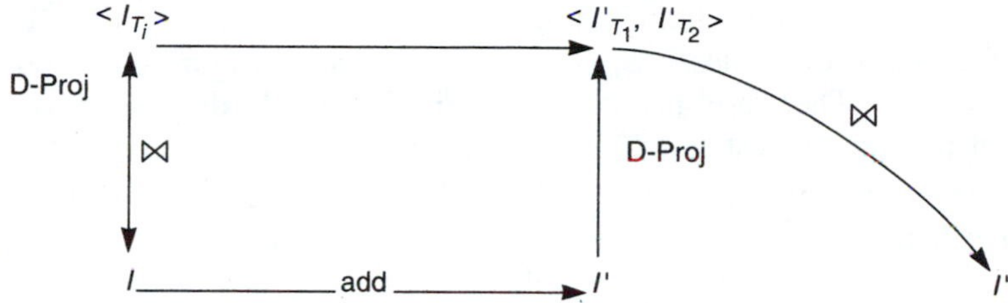

Figure 6.3 An impossible situation

We must consider if Figure 6.3 is possible, given that the decomposition is lossless. Observe first that it follows directly from the definition of a lossless decomposition that Figure 6.3 is not possible if both I' and I'' obey F. Consider, however, two other possibilities:

1. We determine that instance $I'_{T_1} \bowtie I'_{T_2}$ of T violates the set F of functional dependencies and therefore disallow the Update. Can we be sure that $I'_{T_1} \bowtie I'_{T_2}$ is actually instance I' rather than instance I'' as in Figure 6.3? In particular, if $I'_{T_1} \bowtie I'_{T_2} = I''$, have we made the correct decision in disallowing the Update that really results in instance I' of T (see Figure 6.4)? The answer has two parts:
   a. If the instance I' violates F as well, then clearly we have correctly disallowed the Update (although it in fact is possible that $I'_{T_1} \bowtie I'_{T_2}$ is not the instance $I' = I \cup \{t\}$).

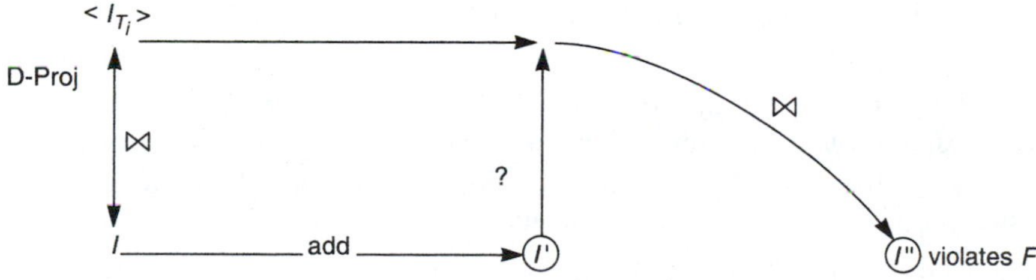

Figure 6.4 I'' violates F

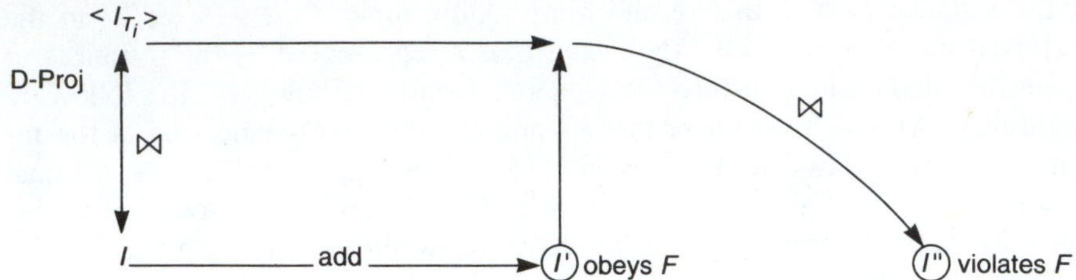

Figure 6.5 I'' violates F but I' obeys F

b. If the instance I' obeys F (see Figure 6.5), we note that it follows from Theorem 6.1 that *D-Proj* $(I') = <I'_{T_1}, I'_{T_2}>$ and thus, since the decomposition is lossless, $I'_{T_1} \bowtie I'_{T_2} = I'$; that is, Figure 6.5 is not possible. Therefore, it is correct to disallow the Update whenever we determine the instance $I'_{T_1} \bowtie I'_{T_2}$ violates F.

2. We determine that instance $I'_{T_1} \bowtie I'_{T_2}$ of T obeys the set F of functional dependencies and therefore allow the Update. But suppose, as in Figure 6.6, $I'_{T_1} \bowtie I'_{T_2} = I''$ obeys F while I' *violates* F. Observe that the definition of a lossless decomposition does not seem to directly rule out the situation depicted in Figure 6.6. If this situation indeed is possible, it could be that I'' is a legal instance, but instance I' that results from the Update is illegal and thus the Update should be disallowed.

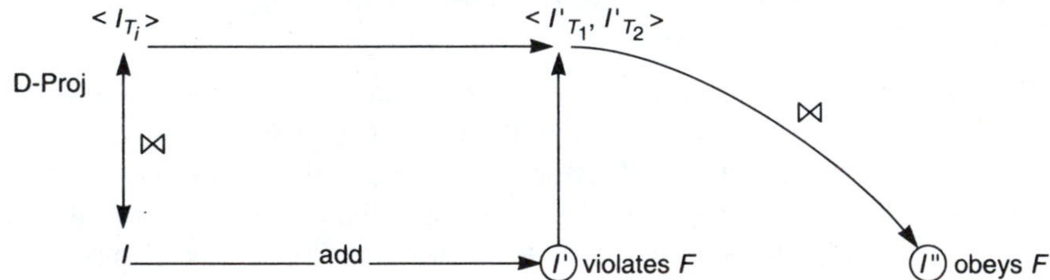

Figure 6.6 I'' obeys F but I' violates F

Fortunately, however, we can prove the following theorem:

Theorem 6.2 Let D be a lossless decomposition of T with respect to functional dependencies F. If $D\text{-}Proj(I_1) = D\text{-}Proj(I_2) = <I_{T_1}, I_{T_2}>$, then neither I_1 nor I_2 obeys F.

Proof Clearly, both instances can't obey F by definition of lossless decomposition. Suppose I_1 obeys F while I_2 violates F. By the lossless property, $I_{T_1} \bowtie I_{T_2} = I_1$. By properties of Project and Join, $I_{T_1} \bowtie I_{T_2} \supseteq I_2$. Thus, we have $I_1 \supseteq I_2$. Thus, I_2 violates $F \Rightarrow I_1$ violates F.□

The theorem satisfactorily addresses our final concern regarding the validity of the ADD algorithm. Because Lemma 5.1 implies that if $I'_{T_1} \bowtie I'_{T_2} = I''$, then

$D\text{-}Proj(I'') = <I'_{T_1}, I'_{T_2}>$, and since Theorem 6.1 tells us that $D\text{-}Proj(I') = <I'_{T_1}, I'_{T_2}>$, Theorem 6.2 tells us that I'' cannot obey F while I' violates it. Consequently, if our ADD algorithm establishes that $I'_{T_1} \bowtie I'_{T_2}$ obeys F, then $I'_{T_1} \bowtie I'_{T_2}$ is in fact the "correct" instance of T (i.e., instance I' in Figure 6.2), and hence it is correct to allow the Update.

We therefore have established that our ADD procedure in Algorithm 6.4 is valid. The procedure, of course, relies on the assumption that we can verify the functional dependencies of T without joining the instances of the D-Proj. The primary unresolved issue of this section thus is,

Can we, without explicitly joining instances I'_{T_1} and I'_{T_2}, determine if the instance $I'_{T_1} \bowtie I'_{T_2}$ of T obeys T's functional dependencies?

We shall begin to answer this critical question shortly.

Considerations in the Implementation of the DELETE Operation

Deletions are more difficult than insertions in one regard and easier than insertion in another regard. Consider the proposed Deletion algorithm:

```
{ proposed efficient implementation of DELETE(T,<v1,v2, . . . , vn>) }
Let t1=ΠT1{<v1, v2, . . . ,vn>}
DELETE(T1, t1)
Let t2=ΠT2{<v1, v2, . . . , vn>}
DELETE(T2, t2)
```

Algorithm 6.5

To see the problem with this algorithm, consider the table scheme $T(A,B,C,D)$ with associated set $F = \{A \rightarrow D\}$ of functional dependencies and the lossless decomposition $D = \{(T_1(A,B,C), T_2(A,D)\}$ of T. Suppose instances

T_1

A	B	C
a1	b1	c1
a2	b2	c2
a2	b3	c3

T_2

A	D
a1	d1
a2	d2

of T_1 and T_2 are representing instance

T

A	B	C	D
a1	b1	c1	d1
a2	b2	c2	d2
a2	b3	c3	d2

of T. If we apply the preceding Deletion algorithm to DELETE(T,

<*a*1,*b*1,*c*1,*d*1>), we obtain instances

T₁

A	*B*	*C*
*a*2	*b*2	*c*2
*a*2	*b*3	*c*3

T₂

A	*D*
*a*2	*d*2

of T_1 and T_2, which represent the correct instance of T (see Figure 6.7). That is, instances I'_{T_1} *and* I'_{T_2} of T_1 and T_2 are the D-Projection of I', the original instance I minus the tuple <*a*1,*b*1,*c*1,*d*1> (and also, I' obeys F). However, if

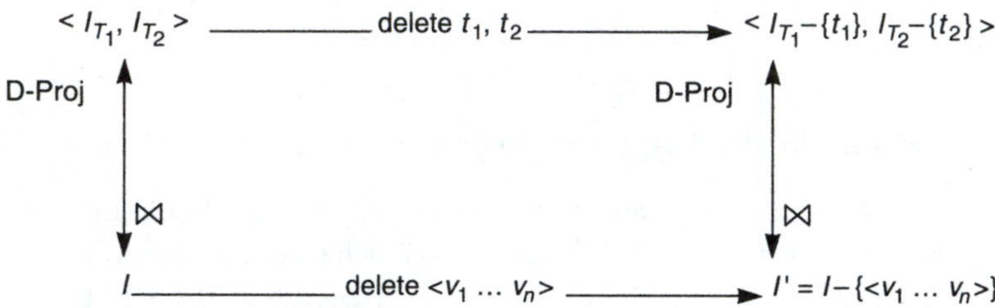

Figure 6.7 Deletion commutativity

(starting with the original instances T, T_1, and T_2) we apply the Deletion algorithm to DELETE(T,<*a*2,*b*2,*c*2,*d*2>), we obtain instances

T₁

A	*B*	*C*
*a*1	*b*1	*c*1
*a*2	*b*3	*c*3

T₂

A	*D*
*a*1	*d*1

of T_1 and T_2, which do *not* represent the correct instance of T (see Figure 6.8). That is, instances I'_{T_1} and I'_{T_2} of T_1 and T_2 are *not* the D-Projection of I', the original instance I minus the tuple <*a*2,*b*2,*c*2,*d*2> (and $I'_{T_1} \bowtie I'_{T_2}$ is not I').

The second deletion illustrates that a simple Deletion algorithm, such as Algorithm 6.5, does not work in general. The correct way to implement the second deletion is to delete <*a*2,*b*2,*c*2> from T_1, leaving T_2 unchanged. (Observe

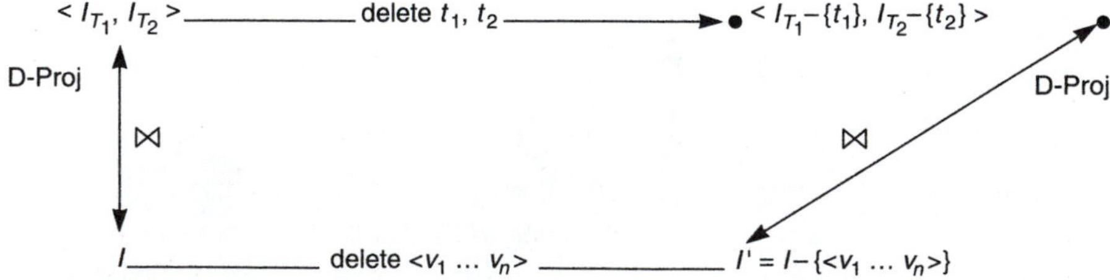

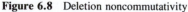

Figure 6.8 Deletion noncommutativity

that deleting tuple <*a*2,*d*2> from T_2 does *not* give the correct result.) We conclude that the correct course of action depends on cross-table "matching characteristics" of the projections of the tuple of T to be deleted (see exercise 6.4). Despite this difficulty, algorithms can be developed for deleting from a decomposition in a manner that typically will be far faster than the brute force algorithm discussed earlier.

In another regard—a regard that has greater significance for the material in this section—the deletion problem is easier than the insertion problem. This is in regard to verifying functional dependencies. It is easy to see that if I is any instance of table scheme T that obeys the set F of functional dependencies, and if t is any tuple, then the instance I-$\{t\}$ of T also obeys F. Consequently, there is never a need to verify that a deletion results in an instance that obeys a set of functional dependencies, assuming we know that the original instance obeyed F. Thus, for example, it suffices to develop a Deletion algorithm that removes tuple(s) from instance(s) of decomposition D to obtain the instances of D that correspond to the D-Projection of the original instance of T minus the tuple to be deleted. The new instance of T obeys F (assuming the original instance of T did) and thus is correctly represented by its D-Projection. Since the problem of verifying functional dependencies against a decomposition is the focus of this section, and since this problem does not arise in the context of deletions, we shall not consider deletions in the remainder of this section.

Updating the Decomposition Directly

In practice, updates often are posed directly against a decomposition. While almost all database systems allow queries to be stated against T and processed against the decomposition D that implements T, many systems require updates to be stated directly against D. Further, even when a system does allow Updates to be posed against T, it is often desirable to allow some users to interact directly with the decomposition D. We observe that, when interacting directly with a decomposition, we encounter part of the problem described earlier: How can we check if an Update is legal, without reconstructing the instance of T that is being represented? That is, because it is T for which we have functional dependencies, it is in terms of T and its functional dependencies that we must judge the legality of an Update.

We are now ready to address the problem of checking functional dependencies against a decomposition D of T, without reconstructing the instance of T that D represents.

6.2 *F*-ENFORCEABLE DECOMPOSITIONS

To summarize the observations of the previous subsections, the major unresolved problem in processing an Update against decomposition D is verifying efficiently that the resulting instance $I'_D = \langle I'_{T_1}, \ldots, I'_{T_k}\rangle$ of D is such that $I'_{T_1} \bowtie \cdots \bowtie I'_{T_k}$ is an instance of T that obeys T's functional dependencies.

That is, whether we begin with an ADD operation posed against T and map the operation into operations against the D-Projection or with a tuple to be inserted directly into some $T_i \in D$, we have the problem of verifying that the instance $I'_{T_1} \bowtie \cdots \bowtie I'_{T_k}$ of T obeys T's functional dependencies. Efficiency consider ations lead us to the following problem:

> *Determine if instance $I_{T_1} \bowtie \cdots \bowtie I_{T_k}$ of T obeys F, while inspecting only the instances $I_{T_1}, \ldots, I_{T_k}$ of the decomposition, that is, without joining the instances.*

We now begin to consider how we might determine whether an instance $I_{T_1} \bowtie \cdots \bowtie I_{T_k}$ of T obeys F, while inspecting only the instances $I_{T_1}, \ldots, I_{T_k}$ of the decomposition. Recall that in Section 5.5, we defined the projection F_i of F onto each member T_i of T's decomposition to be

$$F_i = \{ \text{functional dependencies } Y \rightarrow Z \in F^* \mid Y \rightarrow Z \text{ applies to } T_i \}$$

It seems natural to attempt to determine whether the instance $I_{T_1} \bowtie \cdots \bowtie I_{T_k}$ obeys F by determining whether each instance I_{T_i} obeys F_i. Unfortunately, as the following example demonstrates, it is possible for each instance I_{T_i} of the T_i to obey F_i while the instance $I_{T_1} \bowtie \cdots \bowtie I_{T_k}$ violates F.

Consider again the table scheme POSTOFFICE(City, Street_Addr, Zip) with functional dependencies F = {City Street_Addr → Zip, Zip → City}. In Section 5.4, we observed that this table scheme is not in BCNF. Therefore, we considered decomposing POSTOFFICE into

P_1(Street_Addr, Zip)
P_2(City, Zip)

It is verified easily that F_1 contains only trivial dependencies, while F_2 contains only trivial dependencies, Zip → City, and logical consequences of this dependency. As a result, we observe that (since *Zip → City* $\in F_2$) Theorem 5.1 implies that this decomposition is lossless. We also observe that P_1 is in BCNF with respect to F_1 and that P_2 is in BCNF with respect to F_2.

Consider now the following instances of P_1 and P_2:

P_1

Street_Addr	Zip
1 Main	20
1 Main	30

P_2

City	Zip
Albuquerque	20
Albuquerque	30

Note that each of these instances obeys its projection F_i of F. The instance $P_1 \bowtie P_2$ of P, however, is

City	Street_Addr	Zip
Albuquerque	1 Main	20
Albuquerque	1 Main	30

and this instance *violates* the functional dependency City Street_Addr → Zip in F. Intuitively, we cannot detect that it is a problem that in P_1 1 Main Street has zips 20 and 30 without inspecting P_2 and seeing that zips 20 and 30 are in the same city.

This example illustrates that it is possible for instances of the individual tables T_i of a lossless decomposition to obey their F_i, while the instances taken together (e.g., joined) violate F. In this sense, the F_i, *in general,* provide only a weak characterization of F. This observation leads us to attempt to identify those decompositions that, by means of their F_i, characterize F in a manner stronger than do decompositions in general.

Definition 6.1 Let T be a table scheme with associated set F of functional dependencies, and $D = \{T_1, \ldots, T_k\}$ a decomposition of T. D is **functional dependency enforceable with respect to F (F-enforceable)** if

$$[\text{each instance } I_{T_i} \text{ of } T_i \text{ obeys } F_i] \Rightarrow [\text{instance } I_{T_1} \bowtie I_{T_2} \bowtie \cdots \bowtie I_{T_k} \text{ of } T \text{ obeys } F]$$

The previous example illustrates that the decomposition into P_1 and P_2 of POSTOFFICE is not F-enforceable since the instances of P_1 and P_2 obey F_1 and F_2, respectively, while the Join of these instances does not obey F.

To motivate the desirability of an F-enforceable decomposition, suppose for the moment that table T (with associated set F of functional dependencies) is decomposed into $D = \{T_1, \ldots, T_k\}$, which is a lossless and F-enforceable decomposition. Let us consider if we are now able to support the Update implementations described in the previous section. Specifically, suppose that after performing an ADD operation using Algorithm 6.4, we arrive at the instance $<I'_{T_1}, \ldots, I'_{T_k}>$ of D. If we determine that each instance I'_{T_i} obeys F_i, it follows from our previous results and the definition of an F-enforceable decomposition that $<I'_{T_1}, \ldots, I'_{T_k}>$ represents the correct instance of T, an instance which obeys F. Hence, the F-enforceability of the decomposition allows us to conclude—without joining the instances of the decomposition—that the ADD operation respects the functional dependencies. On the other hand, suppose we determine that some instance I'_{T_i} violates F_i. Can we conclude that the instance $I'_{T_1} \bowtie I'_{T_2} \bowtie \cdots \bowtie I'_{T_k}$ violates F and therefore correctly disallow the Update? Observe that while the definition of an F-enforceable decomposition ensures that

$$[\text{each instance } I_{T_i} \text{ of } T_i \text{ obeys } F_i] \Rightarrow [\text{instance } I_{T_1} \bowtie I_{T_2} \bowtie \cdots \bowtie I_{T_k} \text{ of } T \text{ obeys } F]$$

it does *not* follow from the definition of an F-enforceable decomposition that

$$[\text{some instance } I_{T_i} \text{ of } T_i \text{ violates } F_i] \Rightarrow [\text{instance } I_{T_1} \bowtie I_{T_2} \bowtie \cdots \bowtie I_{T_k} \text{ of } T \text{ violates } F]$$

[In fact, given *any* (nontrivial) decomposition D of T, it is a simple matter to construct an instance I_D of the decomposition such that some I'_{T_i} violates F_i yet $I_{T_1} \bowtie I_{T_2} \bowtie \cdots \bowtie I'_{T_i} \cdots \bowtie I_{T_k}$ obeys F (see exercise 5.18).]

Observe, however, that since I'_{T_i} violates F_i, there is no instance I of T obeying F such that $\Pi_{x_i}(I) = I'_{T_i}$. Therefore, any instance I such that $D\text{-}Proj(I) = \langle I'_{T_1}, \ldots, I'_{T_i}, \ldots, I'_{T_k} \rangle$ violates F. With this observation in mind, consider the instance I'_T of T that results from applying the Update to instance I'_T of T (see Figures 6.1 and 6.2). Since I'_T D-Projects to $\langle I'_{T_1}, \ldots, I'_{T_i}, \ldots, I'_{T_k} \rangle$, we can conclude that the instance I'_T of T that results from the Update does not obey F, and therefore, it indeed is correct to disallow the Update.[3]

Consequently, if we have a lossless decomposition of T that is functional dependency enforceable, the final piece of the implementation method described in this section is in place. Algorithm 6.4 can be completed simply by replacing the condition

(instances I'_{T_i} are such that $\bowtie I'_{T_i}$ obeys F)

with the (easily verifiable) condition

(each I_{T_i} obeys F_i)

This discussion makes clear that, for practical reasons regarding the efficiency of Update processing, it is highly desirable that any decomposition used to implement a table scheme T be F-enforceable. Fortunately, the simple 3NF algorithm presented in the previous chapter always produces an F-enforceable decomposition. In Section 6.5, we shall develop the tools necessary to demonstrate this fact (as well as the fact that the decomposition produced by the 3NF algorithm is lossless), and in Section 6.6, we shall restate the 3NF algorithm and prove that the decomposition it produces is both F-enforceable and lossless.

6.3 HIGHER NORMAL FORMS AND MULTIVALUED DEPENDENCIES

In this section, we consider two normal forms more restrictive than 3NF. We start by reconsidering the Boyce-Codd Normal Form (BCNF), first introduced in Section 5.4. We then consider Fourth Normal Form (4NF), which is based on a new kind of dependency known as a multivalued dependency.

[3] While we have been assuming in this chapter that we shall encounter only instances of a decomposition that are the images under D-Proj of instances of the original table T, there are situations where we may wish to drop this assumption (e.g., when the decomposition can be updated directly). See exercise 6.5 for a discussion of motivations for, and consequences of, this possibility.

Boyce-Codd Normal Form

In Chapter 5, we considered BCNF, a normal form stronger than 3NF. For convenience, we review here the definition of BCNF.

> **Definition 6.2** A table scheme is in BCNF if F^* contains no partial or transitive dependencies. Equivalently, a table scheme is in BCNF if the left side of each nontrivial functional dependency in F^* is a superkey.

Recall that BCNF strengthens 3NF by disallowing all partial and transitive dependencies $Y \rightarrow A \in F^*$, *even when A is a prime attribute*.

A motivation for BCNF was found in the post office example. Consider again the table scheme POSTOFFICE(City, Street_Addr, Zip) with associated set $F = \{Zip \rightarrow City,\ CityStreet\_Addr \rightarrow Zip\}$ of functional dependencies. Since all attributes are prime (both {Zip, Street_Addr} and {City, Street_Addr} are keys), POSTOFFICE is in 3NF. However, as was observed in Chapter 5, the table suffers from the classic redundancy problems of an unnormalized table scheme. BCNF, on the other hand, detects the redundancy problem in the POSTOFFICE table—the functional dependency $Zip \rightarrow City$ is a partial dependency and hence the table scheme is not in BCNF.

Since BCNF identifies semantic problems of a table scheme not identified by 3NF, it might seem that, given any table scheme T and functional dependencies F, we would want to decompose T into $D = \{T_1, \ldots, T_k\}$ such that each T_i is in BCNF with respect to F_i. There are, however, at least two factors that preclude the ideal of decomposing an arbitrary table scheme into BCNF.

The first factor precluding the decomposition of an arbitrary table scheme into BCNF is that there exist table schemes with associated sets F of functional dependencies that have no F-enforceable decomposition into BCNF. In fact, it can be shown that POSTOFFICE is such a table scheme. Intuitively, if a decomposition of POSTOFFICE is in BCNF, no table scheme of the decomposition can contain all three attributes City, Street_Addr, and Zip. On the other hand, if the three attributes do not appear together in a table scheme, the only nontrivial dependency that any F_i will contain is Zip → City, and there is no way to enforce the functional dependency City Street_Addr → Zip by enforcing on individual tables the functional dependency Zip → City. In Section 6.5, we shall see how to formalize this argument, and exercise 6.6 proves the theorem that some table schemes do not possess F-enforceable decompositions into BCNF.

A further negative result regarding the ideal of decomposing an arbitrary table scheme into BCNF concerns the complexity of the process. While it can be shown that there always exists a lossless (though not necessarily F-enforceable) decomposition of any given table scheme into BCNF, the problem of obtaining such a decomposition is NP-hard, implying that all known algorithms will require time exponential in the size of F to obtain the decomposition. We conclude that, although BCNF is of much theoretical interest and is potentially useful on a case-by-case basis, we must be content with 3NF as our general design goal.

Multivalued Dependencies

Of the four normal forms considered, BCNF places the strongest restrictions on the set of functional dependencies that can be associated with a table scheme. To explore the question of whether a table scheme being in BCNF ensures that it has no redundancy problems, consider the table scheme MEDICAL(Patient, Disease, Drug). Suppose that the user-supplied set F of functional dependencies is empty. Since, in this case, every functional dependency in F^* is of the form $X \rightarrow Y$, where $Y \subseteq X$, MEDICAL is in BCNF.

Suppose the instance of table scheme MEDICAL in Figure 6.9 reflects the current state of reality. Consistent with the fact that the set F of functional dependencies is empty, we see that a patient can have more than one disease, that a disease can be treated with more than one drug, and that a drug can be used in the treatment of more than one disease. The semantics of the table

Patient	Disease	Drug
Smith	Cold	Aspirin
Smith	Cold	Nose Spray
Smith	Cold	Tissue
Jones	Pneumonia	Penicillin
Jones	Pneumonia	Aspirin
Harris	Cold	Aspirin
Harris	Cold	Nose Spray
Harris	Cold	Tissue
Harris	Pneumonia	Penicillin
Harris	Pneumonia	Aspirin

Figure 6.9 Instance of table scheme MEDICAL

scheme MEDICAL, however, lead us to suspect that there are some restrictions on the legal instances of the table scheme. In particular, we suspect that *any patient P who has disease D should be given all the drugs that are used to treat disease D.*[4] Indeed, the preceding instance of MEDICAL is consistent with this suspicion. Further, if, for example, the preceding instance of MEDICAL contained the single additional tuple

Rogers	Cold	Tissue

[4] Ignore for the moment the possibility that we might treat some patients who have disease *D* differently from other patients with disease *D*.

we would suspect an error. Why is Rogers not given Aspirin and Nose Spray, drugs used in the treatment of other patients' colds?

The discussion to follow will demonstrate that (1) the suspected semantic property that any patient *P* who has disease *D* should be given all the drugs that are used to treat disease *D* cannot be captured with functional dependencies; (2) if the table scheme MEDICAL has this suspected semantic property, then it is prone to redundancy problems analogous to those we have encountered previously; and (3) it is desirable to rigorously capture semantic properties such as the one under consideration, both for reasons of design and integrity checking.

Suppose that the user wishes to supply us with the information that any patient *P* who has disease *D* should be given all the drugs that are used to treat disease *D*. One issue we will need to address is how to rigorously capture such information. Observe that there is no functional dependency, or collection of functional dependencies, for MEDICAL that exactly conveys this information. For example, the functional dependency Disease → Drug forces every disease to be treated with a single drug. While this restriction has the incidental effect of forcing a patient who has a given disease to be treated with all the drugs that are used to treat that disease (since there can be only one such drug), the restriction imposed by the functional dependency is too severe. For example, it makes illegal the instance of MEDICAL in Figure 6.9, although this instance is consistent with the semantics of the reality that the table scheme is attempting to model. In general, functional dependencies are too coarse to capture by themselves certain types of semantic information that often are associated with table schemes.

Putting aside for the moment the issue of how we might rigorously convey information such as any patient *P* who has disease *D* should be given all the drugs that are used to treat disease *D*, we consider two consequences of such semantic information for a table scheme:

1. Table scheme MEDICAL, while in BCNF, is prone to redundancy problems. For example, if there are 1,000 patients with a cold, the information that this disease is treated with Aspirin, Nose Spray, and Tissue is repeated 1,000 times. (And, of course, the information that patient Smith has a cold is repeated for each drug that is used to treat the disease.) This problem is completely analogous to the problems that led us to decompose table schemes in the past. We can attempt to address the problem by decomposing table scheme MEDICAL into

   HAS(Patient, Disease)
   TREAT(Disease, Drug)

   While this decomposition intuitively seems to solve the problem, there is nothing in the previously presented theory that allows us to conclude that this decomposition is lossless with respect to the admissible instances of table scheme MEDICAL. (Note that Disease functionally determines neither Patient nor Drug.)

2. The semantic information that any patient P who has disease D should be given all the drugs that are used to treat disease D should be enforced as an integrity constraint. For example, a user's attempt to add the single tuple

   Rogers Cold Tissue

   to the instance of MEDICAL in Figure 6.9 should be disallowed.

Thus, we have ample motivation for a mechanism that can capture semantic information of the type we have been discussing. A **multivalued dependency** is such a mechanism.

We can view a multivalued dependency as a relaxation of a functional dependency. Suppose that functional dependency $X \rightarrow Y$ applies to table scheme $T(U)$ and that I_T is a legal instance of T. The functional dependency $X \rightarrow Y$ asserts that with each X value V (i.e., the collective values $t[X]$ in some single tuple t) that appears in I_T there is in I_T *exactly one* associated Y value, $Y(V) = V'$. That is, for any tuple t in I_T, if $t[X] = V$ then $t[Y] = Y(V)$. The multivalued dependency $X \rightarrow\rightarrow Y$ (read X **multivalued determines** Y) asserts that with each X value V that appears in I_T there is in I_T *a set* of associated Y values $Y(V) = \{V'_1, V'_2, \ldots, V'_k\}$. Further, as the notation $Y(V)$ suggests, *the other attributes in table scheme T have no effect on the association of an X value with its set of Y values.*

The last provision in the preceding description of the multivalued dependency $X \rightarrow\rightarrow Y$ is crucial and requires elaboration. Let $Z = (U-(X \cup Y))$. The provision asserts that if instance I_T contains a tuple t with $t[X] = V$ and $t[Z] = W$, for any W, then I_T must contain a tuple t_i for each member V'_i of the "Y set" $Y(V) = \{V'_1, V'_2, \ldots, V'_i, \ldots, V'_k\}$, such that $t_i[X] = V$, $t_i[Z] = W$, and $t_i[Y] = V'_i$.

Before formalizing the definition of a multivalued dependency, we further explore the analogy between it and functional dependencies and present an illustration. Let $T(X\ Y\ Z)$ be a table scheme. That is, the attributes in T are partitioned into three sets: X, Y, and Z. If an instance of T contains the tuples

X	Y	Z
x_1	y_1	z_1
x_1	y_2	z_2

and obeys the functional dependency $X \rightarrow Y$, we can conclude that $y_1 = y_2$. Note that this is true regardless of the Z values of the tuples in question.

If an instance of T contains the tuples

X	Y	Z
x_1	y_1	z_1
x_1	y_2	z_2

and obeys the multivalued dependency $X \twoheadrightarrow Y$, we can conclude that the instance must also contain the tuples

X	Y	Z
x_1	y_2	z_1
x_1	y_1	z_2

This is true regardless of the Z values of the tuples in question.

The following reasoning is used to reach the conclusion that the two tuples

X	Y	Z
x_1	y_2	z_1
x_1	y_1	z_2

must be present in the previous instance of T. Because the values of the attributes not in XY cannot affect the association of X value x_1 with its set of Y values, if x_1 and y_1 appear together in *any* tuple of an instance I_T and if x_1 and y_2 appear together in *any* other tuple of I_T, we can conclude, independent of the values of the other attributes in these tuples, that the set $Y(x_1)$ of Y values associated with the X value x_1 includes y_1 and y_2. The consequence of $Y(x_1)$ including y_1 and y_2 is that if x_1 appears in a tuple that has the value z_1 for the Z attributes, x_1 must appear in a tuple with z_1 for each of the values y_1 and y_2. In general, if x and z appear together in some tuple of a legal instance I_T, then each member of x's Y set $Y(x)$ must appear with x and z in some tuple of I_T.

We further illustrate the concept of a multivalued dependency by applying it to the table scheme MEDICAL. We shall demonstrate that the multivalued dependency Disease $\twoheadrightarrow$ Drug captures the semantic information that any patient P who has disease D should be given all the drugs that are used to treat disease D. Consider again the following table instance, which is consistent with this semantic information:

Patient	Disease	Drug
Smith	Cold	Aspirin
Smith	Cold	Nose Spray
Smith	Cold	Tissue
Jones	Pneumonia	Penicillin
Jones	Pneumonia	Aspirin
Harris	Cold	Aspirin
Harris	Cold	Nose Spray
Harris	Cold	Tissue
Harris	Pneumonia	Penicillin
Harris	Pneumonia	Aspirin

By inspection, we determine that for this instance of table scheme MEDICAL, the Drug set Drug(Cold) = {Aspirin, Nose Spray, Tissue}, and that the

Drug set Drug(Pneumonia) = {Penicillin, Aspirin}. Consequently, if the multivalued dependency Disease $\rightarrow\!\!\!\rightarrow$ Drug is to be obeyed, then (for example) if any tuple t in this instance is such that t[Disease] = Cold and t[Patient] = P, then there must exist in this instance tuples t_1, t_2, and t_3 such that t_1[Disease] = Cold, t_1[Patient] = P, and t_1[Drug] = Aspirin; t_2[Disease] = Cold, t_2[Patient] = P, and t_2[Drug] = Nose Spray; and t_3[Disease] = Cold, t_3[Patient] = P, and t_3[Drug] = Tissue. Observe that this requirement captures the semantic information that any patient P who has disease D should be given all the drugs that are used to treat disease D, by forcing every patient who has a Cold to be treated with every Drug in the Drug set Drug(Cold).

Before leaving this example, we consider instances of table scheme MEDICAL that violate the multivalued dependency Disease $\rightarrow\!\!\!\rightarrow$ Drug. First, suppose that to the preceding instance of table scheme MEDICAL we add the single tuple

Rogers	Cold	Tissue

obtaining the instance

Patient	**Disease**	**Drug**
Smith	Cold	Aspirin
Smith	Cold	Nose Spray
Smith	Cold	Tissue
Jones	Pneumonia	Penicillin
Jones	Pneumonia	Aspirin
Harris	Cold	Aspirin
Harris	Cold	Nose Spray
Harris	Cold	Tissue
Harris	Pneumonia	Penicillin
Harris	Pneumonia	Aspirin
Rogers	Cold	Tissue

We have already observed that this instance violates the semantic information that any patient P who has disease D should be given all the drugs that are used to treat disease D because Rogers is not treated with Aspirin or Nose Spray. In terms of the multivalued dependency Disease $\rightarrow\!\!\!\rightarrow$ Drug, the values Aspirin and Tissue, which are members of the set Drug(Cold), fail to appear in tuples with Cold and Rogers.

Suppose now that in addition to the preceding tuple, we add the tuples

Rogers	Cold	Aspirin
Rogers	Cold	Nose Spray
Rogers	Cold	New Drug

to the instance of table scheme MEDICAL, obtaining the instance

Patient	Disease	Drug
Smith	Cold	Aspirin
Smith	Cold	Nose Spray
Smith	Cold	Tissue
Jones	Pneumonia	Penicillin
Jones	Pneumonia	Aspirin
Harris	Cold	Aspirin
Harris	Cold	Nose Spray
Harris	Cold	Tissue
Harris	Pneumonia	Penicillin
Harris	Pneumonia	Aspirin
Rogers	Cold	Tissue
Rogers	Cold	Aspirin
Rogers	Cold	Nose Spray
Rogers	Cold	New Drug

Note that for this instance, the Drug set Drug(Cold) = {Aspirin, Nose Spray, Tissue, New Drug}. Thus, this instance is in violation of the multivalued dependency Drug $\twoheadrightarrow$ Disease because the Colds of patients Smith and Harris are not treated with every drug in Drug(Cold).

As a final point, suppose that patient Smith is allergic to Aspirin. In this case, we would want to permit an instance of table scheme MEDICAL such as the following:

Patient	Disease	Drug
Smith	Cold	Nose Spray
Smith	Cold	Tissue
Jones	Pneumonia	Penicillin
Jones	Pneumonia	Aspirin
Harris	Cold	Aspirin
Harris	Cold	Nose Spray
Harris	Cold	Tissue
Harris	Pneumonia	Penicillin
Harris	Pneumonia	Aspirin

Clearly, this instance of table scheme MEDICAL is in violation of the multivalued dependency Disease $\twoheadrightarrow$ Drug. However, if we wish to allow for the possibility that some patients are to be treated differently from other patients with the same disease, we must renounce the assertion that any patient P who has disease D should be given all the drugs that are used to treat disease D. That is, the newly proposed semantics of the table scheme MEDICAL allowing the treatment of a disease to be patient specific are not consistent with the multivalued dependency Disease $\twoheadrightarrow$ Drug.

While our working definition of a multivalued dependency (hopefully) is intuitively pleasing, it nevertheless is a bit cumbersome. The following more concise definition is standard.

Definition 6.3 Let $T(U)$ be a table scheme with $U = X \cup Y \cup Z$, and X, Y, and Z pairwise disjoint. T **obeys the multivalued dependency** $X \twoheadrightarrow Y$ if, whenever a single instance I_T of T contains tuples t and s with $t[X] = s[X]$, I_T also contains a tuple u such that

1. $u[X] = t[X] = s[X]$.
2. $u[Y] = t[Y]$ and $u[Z] = s[Z]$.

The following observations are easily verified.

Observations

1. The formal definition of a multivalued dependency agrees with our intuitive definition based on Y sets (see Exercise 6.7).
2. The definition of $X \twoheadrightarrow Y$, in addition to asserting the presence in I_T of the tuple u, implies the presence in I_T of a tuple v such that
   a. $v[X] = t[X] = s[X]$.
   b. $v[Y] = s[Y]$ and $v[Z] = t[Z]$.
3. If $T(U)$ is a table scheme with $U = X \cup Y \cup Z$ and T obeys the multivalued dependency $X \twoheadrightarrow Y$, then T obeys $X \twoheadrightarrow Z$ also.
4. If table scheme T obeys the functional dependency $X \rightarrow Y$, then T obeys the multivalued dependency $X \twoheadrightarrow Y$ also, although the converse is not true. This is the sense in which a multivalued dependency is a relaxation of a functional dependency.

Now that we have a concise definition of multivalued dependencies, we consider how they can be used to address the issues of table scheme design and integrity checking. Suppose that we allow the user-supplied semantic information associated with a table scheme T to be a set Φ containing both functional and multivalued dependencies. The consequences for integrity checking are clear. If, for example, the user-supplied set Φ associated with table scheme MEDICAL contains the multivalued dependency Disease $\twoheadrightarrow$ Drug, then an attempt to add to the instance

Patient	Disease	Drug
Smith	Cold	Aspirin
Smith	Cold	Nose Spray
Smith	Cold	Tissue
Jones	Pneumonia	Penicillin
Jones	Pneumonia	Aspirin
Harris	Cold	Aspirin
Harris	Cold	Nose Spray
Harris	Cold	Tissue
Harris	Pneumonia	Penicillin
Harris	Pneumonia	Aspirin

the single tuple

Rogers	Cold	Tissue

should be disallowed on the grounds that the resulting instance of table scheme MEDICAL does not obey Φ.

Observe that when the set Φ of integrity constraints contains multivalued dependencies, *deletions,* as well as insertions, can lead to violations of these constraints. That is, even if instance I of table scheme T obeys a multivalued dependency, it may be the case that $I - \{t\}$ violates this multivalued dependency. (Earlier, we observed that this cannot happen when the only dependencies are functional dependencies.) For example, if we delete the single tuple

Harris	Pneumonia	Aspirin

from the preceding instance of table scheme MEDICAL (which obeys the multivalued dependency Disease $\twoheadrightarrow$ Drug), the resulting instance of table scheme MEDICAL would violate the multivalued dependency Disease $\twoheadrightarrow$ Drug.

As a final point regarding the role of multivalued dependencies in integrity checking, observe that we now require facilities for inserting and deleting *sets* of tuples. That is, if we could insert or delete only a single tuple at a time, we in general would not be able to update a table instance without violating a multivalued dependency. For example, consider again the foregoing instance of table scheme MEDICAL. Suppose that we wish to delete from this instance the tuples corresponding to patient Harris. If we could delete tuples only one at a time, we would not be able to accomplish our task because any initial deletion of a Harris tuple would violate the multivalued dependency Disease $\twoheadrightarrow$ Drug and would thus be disallowed. However, if we have a facility for deleting the *set of tuples* corresponding to the patient Harris, our task can be accomplished since we can go directly from the foregoing instance of MEDICAL to the instance with all Harris tuples removed—an instance that obeys the multivalued dependency Disease $\twoheadrightarrow$ Drug.

The consequences for design of multivalued dependencies are more involved than for integrity checking. Recall that 2NF, 3NF, and BCNF identify *bad mixes of functional dependencies* that may be associated with a table scheme. Now that we allow the user to supply multivalued, as well as functional, dependencies, we must characterize when a set of such dependencies spells trouble for a table scheme.

To illustrate, consider again the table scheme MEDICAL with associated set $\Phi = \{\text{Disease} \twoheadrightarrow \text{Drug}\}$ of dependencies. We have observed that in instances of this table scheme, a disease's treatment is repeated for each patient with the disease. This is the case *despite the fact that table scheme MEDICAL is in BCNF*. (The user-supplied set Φ contains no functional dependencies.) The user, by asserting that the the multivalued dependency Disease $\twoheadrightarrow$ Drug applies to table scheme MEDICAL, guarantees that in *all instances* of table scheme MEDICAL, the association between *every* disease and the drugs used to treat that disease will be repeated for each patient with the disease (i.e., the treatment of every disease is patient independent). This user-supplied piece of information thus indicates that legal instances of MEDICAL may suffer from problems of redundancy and is a tipoff that we should consider decomposing the table scheme.

These observations motivate fourth normal form.

Definition 6.4 Table scheme $T(U)$ with associated set Φ of functional and multivalued dependencies is in **fourth normal form (4NF)** if, whenever we have $X \twoheadrightarrow Y$, at least one of the following holds:

1. $Y \subseteq X$.
2. $X \cup Y = U$.
3. X is a superkey of table scheme T.

When either condition 1 or 2 holds, $X \twoheadrightarrow Y$ is said to be a **trivial** multivalued dependency.

We note that, as is the case for the normal forms defined previously, the definition of 4NF is with respect to the functional and multivalued dependencies in the logical closure Φ^* of Φ, where $\Phi^* = \{d \mid d$ is a functional or multivalued dependency that is obeyed by all instances of table scheme T that obey $\Phi\}$.

The only nontrivial type of multivalued dependency permitted by 4NF is a multivalued dependency whose left side is a superkey. This leads us to suspect that 4NF is a direct strengthening of BCNF. The following theorem demonstrates that this indeed is the case.

Theorem 6.3 Let $T(U)$ be a table scheme with associated set Φ of multivalued and functional dependencies. If T is in 4NF with respect to Φ, then T is in BCNF with respect to Φ.

Proof Suppose that T violates BCNF. Then Φ^* contains a nontrivial functional dependency $X \rightarrow Y$, such that X is not a superkey of T. Note that X not a superkey, and $X \rightarrow Y$ implies that $X \cup Y \neq U$. But we already have observed that $X \rightarrow Y$ implies that $X \twoheadrightarrow Y$, and hence, Φ^* contains a multivalued dependency of a type disallowed by the definition of 4NF.□

This result implies that it is at least as difficult to obtain satisfactory 4NF decompositions of table schemes as it is to obtain satisfactory BCNF decompositions of table schemes. Consequently, 4NF, like BCNF, must be viewed as a heuristic design criterion rather than as an absolute design requirement.

Observe that table scheme MEDICAL with associated set $\Phi = \{Disease \twoheadrightarrow Drug\}$, while in BCNF, is not in 4NF. (Establishing this fact formally requires showing that $Disease \rightarrow Patient\ Drug \notin \Phi^*$, and hence that $\{Disease\}$ is not a superkey of table scheme MEDICAL.) To address the redundancy problems associated with table scheme MEDICAL, consider the decomposition of MEDICAL into a collection of 4NF table schemes. Intuitively, it seems reasonable to decompose table scheme MEDICAL into the pair

HAS(Patient, Disease)
TREAT(Disease, Drug)

of table schemes. This decomposition seems consistent with the semantics of table scheme MEDICAL in that a patient is associated with one or more diseases and that a disease is associated with one or more drugs in a manner that *does not depend on the patient who has that the disease*. Further, it can be shown that the only multivalued dependencies from Φ^* applying to either HAS or TREAT are of a form permitted by condition 1 or 2 of the definition of 4NF.

While each of HAS and TREAT is a 4NF table scheme, we should be concerned with whether or not we have a lossless decomposition of table scheme MEDICAL. A seeming cause for concern is Theorem 5.1, which was originally stated in Section 5.6:

Theorem 5.1 Let $T(A_1, A_2, \ldots, A_k)$ be a table scheme, F an associated set of functional dependencies, and $D = \{T_1(X_1), T_2(X_2)\}$ a decomposition of T, with $Y = X_1 \cap X_2$. Decomposition D is lossless with respect to the set F of functional dependencies iff either $Y \rightarrow X_1$ or $Y \rightarrow X_2$ is in F^*.

Since we have observed that only trivial functional dependencies in Φ^* apply to either HAS or TREAT, we know that *Disease* $\rightarrow$ *Patient* $\notin \Phi^*$ and *Disease* $\rightarrow$ *Drug* $\notin \Phi^*$. Does this not imply that the decomposition is *lossy* with respect to Φ^*? The answer is, no, the theorem does *not* imply that the decomposition is lossy with respect to Φ^*. To see why, we must consider carefully the theorem's statement.

The theorem characterizes when a decomposition is lossless with respect to a set F of *functional dependencies*. Specifically, suppose that the set F contains only functional dependencies and let $INST(F) = \{I \mid I \text{ obeys } F\}$. The theorem asserts that every instance $I \in INST(F)$ has the property that

$$\gamma_D(I) = I$$

if and only if F^* contains *Disease* $\rightarrow$ *Patient* or *Disease* $\rightarrow$ *Drug*. However, the theorem does *not* assert that there are no instances I violating both *Disease* $\rightarrow$ *Patient* and *Disease* $\rightarrow$ *Drug* for which

$$\gamma_D(I) = I$$

For example, the instance $I_{MEDICAL}$ of MEDICAL in Figure 6.9 violates both *Disease* $\rightarrow$ *Patient* and *Disease* $\rightarrow$ *Drug*, yet $\gamma_D(I_{MEDICAL}) = I_{MEDICAL}$. In fact, as is illustrated by Figure 6.10, the set of instances that have the lossless Join property may properly contain $INST(F)$ for *every* F that satisfies the condition of Theorem 5.1.

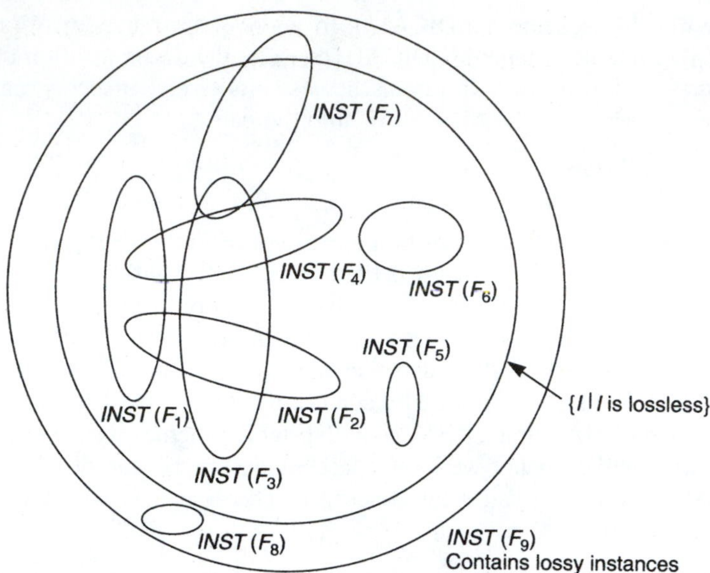

Figure 6.10 Instances that decompose losslessly and lossy

We once again are discovering a sense in which functional dependencies alone are too coarse a tool for modeling the semantics of a table scheme. If we have a set F of functional dependencies that satisfies the condition of the theorem, $INST(F)$ may be properly contained in the set of instances I with the property that

$$\gamma_D(I)=I$$

On the other hand, if F does not satisfy the theorem's condition, there will be instances I' in $INST(F)$ with the property that

$$\gamma_D(I') \supseteq I'$$

In general, there may not exist a set F of functional dependencies such that

$$INST(F)=\{I \mid \gamma_D(I)=I\}$$

How, then, can we characterize the instances I for which

$$\gamma_D(I)=I$$

The following theorem provides the desired characterization when D is a binary decomposition.

Theorem 6.4 Let $T(A_1, A_2, \ldots, A_k)$ be a table scheme and $D = \{T_1(Y\,X_1),T_2(Y\,X_2)\}$ a decomposition of T, with $X_1 \cap X_2 = \emptyset$. Instance I of T has the property that

$$\gamma_D(I)=I$$

if and only if I obeys the multivalued dependency $Y \twoheadrightarrow X_1$ (equivalently, if and only if I obeys the multivalued dependency $Y \twoheadrightarrow X_2$).

A consequence of this theorem is that instances of table scheme MEDICAL that satisfy the multivalued dependency Disease $\twoheadrightarrow$ Drug have the lossless Join property. Hence, the proposed decomposition of MEDICAL is lossless with respect to $\Phi = \{\text{Disease} \twoheadrightarrow \text{Drug}\}$. (It will be instructive for the reader to consider the consequences of an instance of MEDICAL that violates this multivalued dependency because the treatment of some disease is patient specific.)

Observe that Theorem 6.4 applies only to binary decompositions. A mechanism called **Join dependencies** is needed to characterize the set of instances that have the lossless Join property when a decomposition is nonbinary. And, as you may have guessed, there are normal forms that are defined with respect to Join dependencies. A discussion of Join dependencies is beyond our scope; the interested reader is referred to Aho, Beeri, and Ullman (1979); and Rissanen (1977).

6.4 COMPUTING AND REPRESENTING LOGICAL CLOSURES[5]

In this section and the next we present algorithms and theorems that allow us to fully specify and prove correct the 3NF algorithm originally presented in Section 5.7. Specifically, the results we require are

1. An algorithm for obtaining a minimal cover of a set F of functional dependencies. Such an algorithm is required as a preprocessing step for the 3NF algorithm.
2. An algorithm for obtaining a key of a table scheme, given a set of functional dependencies applying to that table scheme. Such an algorithm is required as the last step of the 3NF algorithm.
3. Algorithms for testing whether a decomposition is lossless and F-enforceable. Such algorithms are required to prove correct the 3NF algorithm.

The first two of these tasks require that we be able to compute, or at least test membership in, the logical closure F^* of a set F of functional dependencies. Methods for addressing this problem are presented in this section. Algorithms for testing losslessness and F-enforceability are presented in Section 6.5. The chapter culminates with a proof of correctness for the 3NF algorithm. We note that the algorithms presented in these sections, in addition to having much importance in the context of the 3NF algorithm, have significant independent importance, as the problems they solve must be confronted in a variety of contexts.

We begin by considering the problem of computing the logical closure of a set of functional dependencies. Recall from Chapter 5 the following definitions:

---

[5] This section may be omitted without loss of continuity.

Definition 5.3 Let F be a set of functional dependencies for table scheme T. The set F **logically implies** the functional dependency f (which applies to T) if any instance of T that obeys F necessarily obeys f also.

Definition 5.4 The **logical closure** of a set F of functional dependencies for table scheme T is the set of functional dependencies $F^* = \{f \mid F \text{ logically implies } f\}$.

The logical closure F^* of a set F of functional dependencies is typically far larger than F. For example, if $T(A,B,C)$ is a table scheme with functional dependencies $F = \{A \rightarrow B, B \rightarrow C\}$, it can be shown that

$$\begin{aligned}F^* = \{&A \rightarrow \emptyset, B \rightarrow \emptyset, C \rightarrow \emptyset, AB \rightarrow \emptyset, AC \rightarrow \emptyset, BC \rightarrow \emptyset, ABC \rightarrow \emptyset,\\ &A \rightarrow A, B \rightarrow B, C \rightarrow C, AB \rightarrow A, AB \rightarrow B,\\ &AC \rightarrow A, AC \rightarrow C, BC \rightarrow B, BC \rightarrow C, ABC \rightarrow A, ABC \rightarrow B, ABC \rightarrow C,\\ &AB \rightarrow AB, AC \rightarrow AC, BC \rightarrow BC, ABC \rightarrow AB, ABC \rightarrow AC, ABC \rightarrow BC, ABC \rightarrow ABC,\\ &A \rightarrow B, B \rightarrow C, AC \rightarrow B, AC \rightarrow AB, AC \rightarrow BC, AC \rightarrow ABC,\\ &AB \rightarrow C, AB \rightarrow BC, AB \rightarrow AC, AB \rightarrow ABC, AB \rightarrow C, A \rightarrow AC\}\end{aligned}$$

The following arguments can be used to show that F^* contains these functional dependencies.

1. The functional dependencies

$$\begin{aligned}&A \rightarrow \emptyset, B \rightarrow \emptyset, C \rightarrow \emptyset, AB \rightarrow \emptyset, AC \rightarrow \emptyset, BC \rightarrow \emptyset, ABC \rightarrow \emptyset,\\ &A \rightarrow A, B \rightarrow B, C \rightarrow C, AB \rightarrow A, AB \rightarrow B,\\ &AC \rightarrow A, AC \rightarrow C, BC \rightarrow B, BC \rightarrow C, ABC \rightarrow A, ABC \rightarrow B, ABC \rightarrow C,\\ &AB \rightarrow AB, AC \rightarrow AC, BC \rightarrow BC, ABC \rightarrow AB, ABC \rightarrow AC, ABC \rightarrow BC, ABC \rightarrow ABC\end{aligned}$$

   are of the form $X \rightarrow Y$, where $Y \subseteq X$; that is, these are trivial dependencies, meaning that they are obeyed by all instances of all table schemes to which they apply. Clearly, all trivial dependencies applying to $T(A,B,C)$ are in F^*.
2. The functional dependencies $A \rightarrow B$ and $B \rightarrow C$ are in F. Since any instance of T that obeys F obeys each functional dependency in F, F^* always contains F.
3. The functional dependencies

$$\begin{aligned}&AC \rightarrow B, AC \rightarrow AB, AC \rightarrow BC, AC \rightarrow ABC,\\ &AB \rightarrow C, AB \rightarrow BC, AB \rightarrow AC, AB \rightarrow ABC, A \rightarrow C, A \rightarrow AC\end{aligned}$$

   are a bit more interesting. It may not be immediately obvious that any instance of T that obeys F necessarily obeys each dependency listed earlier, but this is the case. We shall develop methods for establishing this fact in this section.

The notion of logical closure is central to the theory previously presented. Given a table scheme T and a user-supplied set F of functional dependencies that apply to T, we design T, not with respect to just F, but with respect to F^*. For example, our definitions of the normal forms are with respect to the functional dependencies in the logical closure F^* of F rather than with respect to F

itself. Further, we say that a decomposition $D = \{T_1, \ldots, T_k\}$ of T is in 3NF provided that each T_i is in 3NF with respect to the functional dependencies of F^* that apply to T_i. What's more, as noted at the beginning of this section, the 3NF algorithm requires that we compute a minimal cover for the user-supplied set of functional dependencies and that we be able to find a key for the original table scheme; the solution developed for each of these problems is based on an algorithm for testing membership in the logical closure of a set of functional dependencies.

We first shall develop a systematic method for constructing F^* for any given set F of functional dependencies. We shall then consider an alternative to constructing explicitly logical closures. This alternative has significant computational advantages over any method that explicitly materializes logical closures.

Inference Axioms for Functional Dependencies and an Algorithm for Computing F^*

To begin, we verify that F^* is finite. Let F be any set of functional dependencies that applies to table scheme $T(A_1, \ldots, A_n)$. Observe that any functional dependency applying to T is of the form $S_1 \rightarrow S_2$, where $S_1, S_2 \subseteq \{A_1, \ldots, A_n\}$. Therefore, there are $2^n * 2^n = 2^{2n}$ functional dependencies that apply to T. This implies that the original set F of functional dependencies, as well as its logical closure F^*, is finite.

The finiteness of F^* gives us hope of being able to construct it. We consider first an approach that *generates* the functional dependencies in F^*.

```
Procedure Closure(F,ANS)
  { Return in ANS the logical closure F* of F }
   ANS ← F
   done ← false
   while (not done)
     Attempt to generate an f ∉ ANS such that F logically implies f
     if (such an f exists)
        ANS ← ANS ∪ {f}
     else
        done ← true
     endif
   end while
 end Procedure Closure
```

Except for the statement

attempt to generate an $f \notin ANS$ such that F logically implies f

the algorithm is well specified. It is clear that if, at each iteration, we can always find an $f \notin ANS$ such that F logically implies f when such an f exists (and determine that no such f exists whenever this is the case), Procedure Closure would correctly construct F^*. Further, our previous discussion on the finiteness of F^* guarantees that Procedure Closure would terminate within 2^{2n} iterations.

The task at hand then is to devise a method for finding, at each iteration, an $f \notin ANS$ such that F logically implies f, provided that such an f exists. The method we shall develop is based on a collection of **inference axioms.** Inference axioms for functional dependencies are rules that, when applied to a set F of functional dependencies, produce new functional dependencies. The inference axioms of interest to us have the property that their application to a set F of functional dependencies produces only functional dependencies that are logically implied by F.

Consider the following collection of inference axioms, known as **Armstrong's axioms (AA).** The table scheme in question is $T(A_1, A_2, \ldots, A_n)$.

A1: Obtain $X \rightarrow Y$ for any $Y \subseteq X \subseteq \{A_1, \ldots, A_n\}$.

A2: From $X \rightarrow Y$, obtain $XZ \rightarrow YZ$ for any $Z \subseteq \{A_1, \ldots, A_n\}$.

A3: From $X \rightarrow Y$ and $Y \rightarrow Z$, obtain $X \rightarrow Z$.

Each of these axioms is a rule for generating new functional dependencies from a given set F of functional dependencies. For example, if the table scheme is $T(A,B,C,D)$ and F is $\{A \rightarrow B, B \rightarrow C\}$, we can apply each rule as follows:

1. We apply $A1$ and obtain $CD \rightarrow C$. Note that axiom $A1$ applies independent of the set F (i.e., it does not matter what functional dependencies are in F) and generates the trivial dependencies that apply to the table scheme.
2. We apply $A2$ to $A \rightarrow B \in F$ and obtain $ACD \rightarrow BCD$.
3. We apply $A3$ to $A \rightarrow B$, $B \rightarrow C \in F$ and obtain $A \rightarrow C$.

As we have stated, we are interested in an inference axiom Ax if it has the property that the application of Ax to F yields only functional dependencies that are logical consequences of F. Of course, not all inference axioms have this property. Consider, for example, the inference axiom:

Bogus: From $X \rightarrow Y$, deduce $Z \rightarrow Y$ for any $Z \subseteq X$.

Observe that if, for example, $T(A,B,C)$ and $F = \{AB \rightarrow C\}$, we can obtain the functional dependency $A \rightarrow C$ by applying Bogus to F. It is easy to demonstrate, however, that $A \rightarrow C$ is *not* a logical consequence of F. To see this, consider the following instance of T:

A	B	C
a	b	c
a	b'	c'

Since this instance obeys F but violates $A \rightarrow C$, f is not a logical consequence of F, and inference axiom Bogus indeed is bogus.

The previous example demonstrates that only special inference axioms are of value in computing logical closures, motivating us to formulate the following essential property for an inference axiom.

Definition 6.5 Inference axiom *Ax* is **sound** if any application of *Ax* to any set *F* of functional dependencies generates only a logical consequence of *F*. A collection *C* of inference axioms is **sound** if each of its members is sound.

The previous example demonstrates that the inference axiom Bogus is not sound. On the other hand, each of Armstrong's axioms is sound.

Theorem 6.5 Each of Armstrong's axioms is sound.

Proof Left as exercise 6.9.□

The result of Theorem 6.5 allows us to refine the strategy of algorithm Closure.

```
Procedure Closure(F,ANS)
  { Return in ANS the logical closure F* of F }
    ANS ← F
    done ← false
    while (not done)
      { Function ApplyAA is defined below }
      newf ← ApplyAA(ANS)
      if (newf is not NULL)
        ANS ← ANS ∪ {newf}
      else
        done ← true
      endif
    end while
  end Procedure Closure
Function ApplyAA(S)
  { Return some functional dependency f ∉ S that can be obtained
    from the set S of functional dependencies by a single application
    of one of Armstrong's axioms. Return NULL if no such functional
    dependency exists. }
  for (each Armstrong axiom A in {A1, A2, A3}) { taken in any order }
    for (each way to apply A to S) { tried in any order }
      if (f ∉ S is generated)
        return(f)
      endif
    end for
  end for
  { Arriving at this point in the function's execution implies no f ∉ S can be
    generated. }
  return(NULL)
end Function ApplyAA
```

At each iteration of the **while** loop, function ApplyAA is invoked to generate from the current value of the set *ANS* a new functional dependency, which is then added to *ANS*. We observe first that function ApplyAA leaves unspecified the order in which Armstrong's axioms are applied to its formal argument *S*. Consequently, function ApplyAA does not specify which functional dependency will be returned when more than one functional dependency can result from different applications of Armstrong's axioms to S. This vagueness is of little import, however, since we shall demonstrate that

Algorithm Closure will be correct regardless of which functional dependency function ApplyAA returns when more than one functional dependency can be generated by different applications of Armstrong's axioms.

Consequently, removal of the vagueness from function ApplyAA is a mere implementation detail that does not affect correctness.

To prove the correctness of algorithm Closure(F,ANS), we first establish that the algorithm maintains the invariant that ANS at all times is a subset of the logical closure of F, and hence that the set ANS returned by Closure is a subset of the logical closure of F, that is, that every member of ANS is a logical consequence of F.

Theorem 6.6 At all times during the execution of procedure Closure, $ANS \subseteq F^*$.

Proof Left as exercise 6.13.□

Theorem 6.6 guarantees that the set ANS returned by algorithm Closure contains only functional dependencies that are logical consequences of F. This result moves us halfway to establishing the correctness of algorithm Closure. To complete the proof of correctness of algorithm Closure, we must establish that the set ANS it returns contains *all* the logical consequences of F. In other words, Theorem 6.6 implies that $ANS \subseteq F^*$; it remains to be established that $F^* \subseteq ANS$.

To complete the proof of algorithm Closure's correctness, it is convenient to view its action as generating **derivations.** Given a collection C of inference axioms (such as $AA = \{A1,A2,A3\}$) and a set F of functional dependencies, a **derivation using C** of functional dependency f from F is a finite sequence of functional dependencies $f_1, \ldots, f_k$, such that

1. $f_i \in F$, or f_i can be generated by application of one of the inference axioms in C to zero or more of the preceding functional dependencies f_j, $1 \leq j \leq i - 1$.
2. The last functional dependency f_k in the sequence is f.

If there exists a derivation using C of f from F we write $F \vdash_{C} f$.

For example, the following is a derivation using AA of $ABCG \rightarrow H$ from $F = \{AB \rightarrow DE,\ DEG \rightarrow H\}$. The table scheme in question is $T(A,B,C,D,E,G,H)$.

f_1:$ABC \rightarrow AB$ (by $A1$)
f_2:$AB \rightarrow DE$ (member of F)
f_3:$ABC \rightarrow DE$ (by $A3$ applied to f_1 and f_2)
f_4:$ABCG \rightarrow DEG$ (by $A2$ applied to f_3)
f_5:$DEG \rightarrow H$ (member of F)
f_6:$ABCG \rightarrow H$ (by $A3$ applied to f_4 and f_5)

This derivation establishes it is the case that $F \vdash_{AA} (ABCG \rightarrow H)$.

Procedure Closure can be viewed as implicitly generating a derivation for each functional dependency it places in *ANS*. In particular, when *ANS* is initialized to $F = \{f_1, \ldots, f_n\}$, the following derivation is generated implicitly for each $f_i \in F$.

f_1 (member of F)
f_2 (member of F)
.
.
.
f_i (member of F)

If g_1 is returned by the 1st call to function ApplyAA, the derivation

f_1 (member of F)
f_2 (member of F)
.
.
.
f_i (member of F)
.
.
.
f_n (member of F)
g_1 (application of axiom A to zero or more functional dependencies in $\{f_1, \ldots, f_n\}$)

of g_1 is generated implicitly where the justification for g_1 is the particular application of Armstrong's axioms made by ApplyAA ($\{f_1, \ldots, f_n\}$). If g_i is returned by the ith ($i > 1$) call to function ApplyAA, the derivation

f_1 (member of F)
f_2 (member of F)
.
.
.
f_i (member of F)
.
.
.
f_n (member of F)
g_1 (application of axiom A to zero or more functional dependencies in $\{f_1, \ldots, f_n\}$)
.
.
.
g_i (application of axiom A to zero or more functional dependencies in $\{f_1, \ldots, f_n, g_1, \ldots, g_{i-1}\}$)

of g_i is generated implicitly where the justification for g_i is the particular application of Armstrong's axioms made by ApplyAA($\{f_1, \ldots, f_n, g_1, \ldots, g_{i-1}\}$).

This correspondence between algorithm Closure and derivations has several important consequences. We first demonstrate that not only does algorithm

Closure generate derivations, but that if any derivation for f from F exists, Closure will place f in ANS, thereby implicitly generating one such derivation for f. This fact is true, regardless of which functional dependency function ApplyAA returns when more than one functional dependency can be generated by different applications of Armstrong's axioms.

Theorem 6.7 If $F \vdash_{AA} f$, then Closure(F, ANS) will return ANS containing f. This is true regardless of which functional dependency function ApplyAA returns when more than one functional dependency can be generated by different applications of Armstrong's axioms.

Proof Suppose not, that $F \vdash_{AA} f$ yet Closure terminates with $f \notin ANS$. When Closure terminates, the final call to ApplyAA(ANS) returns NULL, implying that no application of Armstrong's axioms to ANS generates a functional dependency not in ANS. Observe, however, that since $ANS \supseteq F$, $ANS \vdash_{AA} f$ (any derivation of f from F also is a derivation of f from ANS). Consider any derivation of f from ANS. Since $f \notin ANS$, the derivation must include at least one functional dependency not in ANS. Consider the first occurrence in the derivation of a functional dependency $f \notin ANS$. The justification allowing f to appear in the derivation is the application of one of Armstrong's axioms to zero or more preceding functional dependencies. But by the way f was selected, all functional dependencies preceding f in the derivation are in ANS. This contradicts that ApplyAA(ANS) will return NULL.□

The following is an important corollary to Theorems 6.6 and 6.7.

Corollary 6.1 If $F \vdash_{AA} f$, then f is a logical consequence of F.

Proof By Theorem 6.7, if $F \vdash_{AA} f$, then Closure places f in ANS. That f is a logical consequence of F then follows immediately from Theorem 6.6.□

There remains one final result to be established before we can conclude that $ANS = F^*$ upon algorithm Closure's termination. Theorem 6.7 tells us that if $F \vdash_{AA} f$, then Closure will place f in ANS; it remains to be established that if $f \in F^*$, then $F \vdash_{AA} f$. At first glance, establishing this result may appear to be a formidable task. We must show for *any* set F of functional dependencies applying to *any* table scheme T and *any* functional dependency f applying to T, that if f is a logical consequence of F, then there is a derivation of f from F using Armstrong's axioms. The proof strategy is to show that if there is no derivation of f from F using Armstrong's axioms, then it cannot be the case that f is a logical consequence of F. The way we show that a *particular* f is not a logical consequence of a *particular* F is to construct an instance of the table scheme in question that obeys F but violates f. Our task is to specify a method of construction that will be valid for *any* F and *any* f such that $F \not\vdash_{AA} f$.

The following lemma is required to support the construction. The proof is simple and is left as an exercise.

Lemma 6.1 Let F be any set of functional dependencies, X any set of attributes, and $y_1, y_2, \ldots, y_k$ individual attributes. Then $F \vdash_{AA} (X \rightarrow y_i)$ for $1 \leq i \leq k$ if and only if $F \vdash_{AA} (X \rightarrow y_1 y_2 \cdots y_k)$.

We now are in a position to prove the following theorem.

Theorem 6.8 Let F be any set of functional dependencies applying to table scheme $T(U)$ and f any functional dependency applying to table scheme $T(U)$. If f is a logical consequence of F, then $F \vdash_{AA} f$.

Proof Suppose there is no derivation of f from F using Armstrong's axioms. We shall establish that f is not a logical consequence of F. Let f be $X \rightarrow Y$, $X, Y \subseteq U$. Let X^+ denote the set of attributes $\{z \mid F \vdash_{AA} (X \rightarrow z)\}$. It follows from Lemma 6.1 that $Y \not\subseteq X^+$; otherwise, Lemma 6.1 would imply that $F \vdash_{AA} (X \rightarrow Y)$, in contradiction to our assumption.

Consider now the following instance of table T.

X^+	OTHERS
0 0 0 0 0 0	0 0 0 0 0
0 0 0 0 0 0	1 1 1 1 1

We first shall establish that this instance obeys F. The only functional dependencies this instance can violate are of the form $Z \rightarrow W$, where $Z \subseteq X^+$. (If the left side contains attributes from OTHERS, then the two tuples in the instance do not agree on the left side of the functional dependency, and, hence, the functional dependency is obeyed.) But if such a $Z \rightarrow W \in F$ and $Z \subseteq X^+$, there is a derivation from F of $X \rightarrow W$—this derivation is a derivation from F of $(X \rightarrow Z)$ (the existence of which follows from Lemma 6.1 since $Z \subseteq X^+$), followed with the functional dependency $Z \rightarrow W$ (a member of F by assumption), followed with the functional dependency $X \rightarrow W$ by $A3$. But it then follows from Lemma 6.1 that W is contained in X^+, and thus the instance obeys the functional dependency $(X \rightarrow W)$ since the two tuples agree on each attribute in W. Hence, the instance obeys F.

To complete the proof, we establish that this instance of T violates $f = X \rightarrow Y$, and thus f is not a logical consequence of F. Observe that $X \subseteq X^+$. We thus can establish the result by showing $Y \not\subseteq X^+$ (and thus that $Y \cap OTHERS \neq \emptyset$). If, to the contrary, $Y \subseteq X^+$, it follows from the definition of X^+ and Lemma 6.1 that $F \vdash_{AA} (X \rightarrow Y)$, in contradiction to our assumption.□

Theorems 6.6, 6.7, and 6.8 taken together establish that the procedure Closure(F,ANS) returns ANS equal to the logical closure F^* of F. In addition, Theorem 6.8 establishes that if f is in the logical closure of F then $F \vdash_{AA} f$. This property of Armstrong's axioms is known as **completeness.**

Definition 6.6 A collection C of inference axioms is **complete** if for any set F of functional dependencies and any functional dependency f that is a logical consequence of F, $F \vdash_{AA} f$.

While procedure Closure gives us a method for computing logical closures, we need to be concerned with its efficiency. We have already observed that for table scheme $T(A_1, \ldots, A_n)$ there are 2^{2n} functional dependencies that syntactically apply to T. In fact, it can be shown (see exercise 5.6) that for any integer $k > 1$ there exists a table scheme $T(A_1, \ldots, A_n)$ (with $n \leq k$) and a set F of functional dependencies such that $|F| = k$ and $|F^*| \geq 2^k$. As a consequence, procedure Closure, as well as *any* other algorithm that takes as input a set F of functional dependencies and produces as output F^*, will require in the worst-case time exponential in $|F|$.

This result might dampen our enthusiasm for procedure Closure and, more fundamentally, our enthusiasm for the idea of designing table schemes with respect to the logical closure of a given set of functional dependencies. Fortunately, however, it is possible to design a table scheme with respect to F^* without ever explicitly constructing F^*. In particular, we shall demonstrate that algorithm 3NF requires only a *membership algorithm* for F^*. That is, algorithm 3NF requires only an algorithm Memb_Clos?(F, f) that determines whether or not $f \in F^*$. In the next section, we shall develop an efficient membership algorithm that is built on the foundations developed in this section.

An Efficient Algorithm for Testing Membership in F^*

We wish to develop an efficient algorithm for computing the following Boolean function:

```
Memb_Clos?(F, f)
  { Return true if f ∈ F* and false otherwise. }
```

The central concept of our algorithm was introduced in the proof of Theorem 6.8. Recall that X^+ was used to denote the set of attributes $\{z \mid F \vdash_{\overline{AA}} (X \rightarrow z)\}$. Observe that it follows from Lemma 6.1 that $Z \subseteq X^+$ if and only if $F \vdash_{\overline{AA}} (X \rightarrow Z)$. It follows from Corollary 6.1 and Theorem 6.8 that $F \vdash_{\overline{AA}} (X \rightarrow Z)$ if and only if $(X \rightarrow Z) \in F^*$. Combining these results we obtain

Corollary 6.2 $(X \rightarrow Z) \in F^*$ if and only if $Z \subseteq X^+$.

The result of this corollary is of great potential value. If we can devise an efficient means of computing X^+, we will have an efficient means of determining, for any Z, whether $(X \rightarrow Z) \in F^*$. Consider the following algorithm for computing X^+, where F is the user-supplied set of functional dependencies for table scheme $T(U)$ and X is any subset of U.

```
Procedure X_Plus(F, X, ANS)
  X_prev ← ∅
  X_cur ← X

  while(X_cur ≠ X_prev)
    X_prev ← X_cur
```

```
    X_cur ← X_cur ∪ Z, where Z is any set of attributes such that (Y → Z) ∈ F
                 and Y ⊆ X_cur
  end while
  ANS ← X_cur
end Procedure X_Plus
```

We first establish the correctness of procedure X_Plus.

Theorem 6.9 Procedure X_Plus returns $ANS = X^+$. This is true regardless of which set Z is added to X_cur at each iteration of the **while** loop, if more than one set qualifies.

Proof The proof has three steps: (a) establishing that the procedure terminates in a finite number of iterations of the **while** loop, (b) establishing that $ANS \subseteq X^+$, and (c) establishing that $X^+ \subseteq ANS$.

a. Finite termination: Since only members of U are ever placed in X_cur, $|X\_cur| \leq |U|$. Each iteration of the **while** loop adds to X_cur at least one member of U, else the **while** loop terminates. Therefore, the number of iterations of the **while** loop is bounded by $|U|$.

b. $ANS \subseteq X^+$*:* We shall establish the invariant that $X\_cur \subseteq X^+$. Before the first iteration of the **while** loop, X_cur is equal to X, and we already have observed that $X \subseteq X^+$. Suppose that before the kth iteration of the **while** loop $X\_cur \subseteq X^+$ and at the kth iteration, Z is added to X_cur. It suffices to establish that $F \vdash_{\overline{AA}} (X \to Z)$. If at iteration k, Z is added to X_cur, $Y \to Z \in F$ and $Y \subseteq X\_cur$. But since we assume the invariant holds before the kth iteration and $Y \subseteq X\_cur$, it must be that $F \vdash_{\overline{AA}} (X \to Y)$. We form a derivation for $X \to Z$ by appending to a derivation for $(X \to Y)$ the functional dependency $(Y \to Z)$ (member of F) followed by the functional dependency $(X \to Z)$ [A3 applied to $(X \to Y)$ and $(Y \to Z)$]. Thus $F \vdash_{\overline{AA}} (X \to Z)$. We conclude the invariant is preserved.

c. See exercise 6.14.□

With the correctness of algorithm X_Plus established, we use it as follows to implement the membership function Memb_Clos?:

```
Function Memb_Clos?(F,f)
  { Return true if f ∈ F* and false otherwise. }
  Let f be X → Y
  X_Plus(F,X,ANS)
  if (Z ⊆ ANS)
    return(true)
  else
    return(false)
  endif
end Function Memb_Clos?
```

The time requirement of algorithm Memb_Clos? is dominated by the time to compute X_Plus(F,X,ANS). We sketch here a straightforward implementation of X_Plus that allows it to run in $O(|F| * |U|^2)$ time, where U is the attribute set of the underlying table scheme T. We observed in part a of the proof of Theorem 6.9 that the algorithm terminates within $|U|$ iterations. At each iteration, the algorithm checks if each $f \in F$ is such that the $LHS(f) \subseteq X\_Cur$ and that $RHS(f) \not\subseteq X\_Cur$. This check can be implemented (straightforwardly) in time bounded by $O(|U|)$. Since at each of the at most $|U|$ iterations we must make this test for each $f \in F$, this implementation is $O(|F| * |U|^2)$ time.

The preceding implementation of X_Plus allows membership in F^* to be tested in $O(|F| * |U|^2)$ time, a significant improvement over the potentially exponential (in $|F|$) time required to compute explicitly F^*. However, since we will be extensively using algorithms Memb_Clos? and X_Plus, it is good to know that an even more efficient implementation of X_Plus is available. Algorithm X_Plus can be implemented to run in time linear in $Len(F)$, where $Len(F)$ denotes the total number of attribute occurrences in F [e.g., if $F = \{A_1A_2 \rightarrow A_3, A_1 \rightarrow A_1A_3\}$, $Len(F) = 6$].

Lemma 6.2 Algorithm X_Plus can be implemented to run in time $O(Len(F))$.

Proof See exercise 6.15.□

Another important application of algorithm X_Plus is its use in testing the equivalence of two sets of functional dependencies. Recall from Chapter 5 the following definition.

Definition 5.20 Let F and G be sets of functional dependencies applying to the same table scheme T. We say F and G are **equivalent** if $F^* = G^*$. In this case, we write $F \equiv G$.

It often is necessary to test two sets F and G of functional dependencies for equivalence. The following algorithm performs this task:

```
Function Equiv?(F,G)
  { Return true if F≡G, false otherwise}
   for (each X→ Y in F)
     X_Plus(G,X,ANS)
     if (Y ⊄ ANS) return(false)
   end for
   for (each X→ Y in G)
     X_Plus(F,X,ANS)
     if (Y ⊄ ANS) return(false)
   end for
   return(true)
end Function Equiv?
```

Function Equiv? clearly runs in time polynomial in $(Len(F),Len(G))$. The first **for** loop tests if $F^* \subseteq G^*$. To see this, observe that if $Y \subseteq X^+$ (X^+ computed with respect to G), then $X \rightarrow Y$ is in G^*. If this is the case for every $X \rightarrow Y$ in F, then $F \subseteq G^*$. But this implies that $F^* \subseteq G^*$. (Why?) Further, if $Y \not\subseteq X^+$ (X^+ computed with respect to G), then $X \rightarrow Y \notin G^*$. If this is the case for some $X \rightarrow Y \in F$, then clearly $F^* \not\subseteq G^*$. By a symmetric argument, the second **for** loop is seen to test if $G^* \subseteq F^*$, and thus, function Equiv? is correct.

As a simple application of the Function Equiv?, consider the following lemma.

Lemma 6.3 Let F be any set of functional dependencies. Let F' denote the set of functional dependencies obtained by replacing each $X \rightarrow A_1 \cdots A_i \cdots A_k$ in F with the k functional dependencies $X \rightarrow A_i$ containing single attributes on the right side. Then $F \equiv F'$.

Proof We obtain F' from F by replacing each compound functional dependency $X \rightarrow A_1 \cdots A_k$ in F with k functional dependencies $X \rightarrow A_i$. When we run Equiv?(F,F'), the function will first make the call X_Plus(F', X, ANS) for each $X \rightarrow A_1 \cdots A_k \in F$; it follows from the construction of F' and Lemma 6.1 that ANS will be returned containing $A_1, \ldots, A_k$. This establishes that $F^* \subseteq F'^*$. Equiv? will next make the call X_Plus(F, X, ANS) for each $X \rightarrow A_i \in F'$; it follows from the construction of F' and Lemma 6.1 that ANS will be returned containing A_i. This establishes that $F'^* \subseteq F^*$.□

Observe that this lemma provides the formal justification for our previous assumption that we can convert any set of functional dependencies into an equivalent set containing only functional dependencies whose right sides are single attributes.

Applying the Logical Closure Techniques to the 3NF Algorithm

We now consider how the techniques of the previous section can be used as the basis for two of the algorithms required by Procedure 3NF of Section 5.7, namely

1. The algorithm for obtaining a minimal cover of a set F of functional dependencies. This algorithm will be used in the preprocessing step for the 3NF algorithm.
2. The algorithm for obtaining a key of a table scheme, given a set of functional dependencies applying to that table scheme. This algorithm will be used in the last step of the 3NF algorithm.

The key construction algorithm is the simpler of the two. Recall that in Chapter 5 we presented the following high-level algorithm for constructing a key.

```
FindKey( T(A1,A2, . . . , An ), F, K )
  { Return in K a key for table scheme T which has associated set F
    of functional dependencies. }
    K ← {A1, A2, . . . , An}
    { K is now a superkey }
    for (each Ai in K)
```

```
        if (K-{A_i} is a superkey)
            K ← K-{A_i}
    end for
end FindKey
```

As was observed in Chapter 5, this algorithm assumes that we have a method for determining whether a set X of attributes is a superkey. The X_Plus algorithm provides a simple and efficient test of the superkey property:

```
Invoke X_Plus(F,X, ANS) to compute X+ = ANS
if X+ is equal to the set of all attributes
    X is a superkey
else
    X is not a superkey
endif
```

Since the X_Plus algorithm can be implemented to run in time linear in $Len(F)$, the total running time of algorithm FindKey on table $T(U)$ is $O(|U|*Len(F))$.

We now turn to the problem of obtaining a minimal cover for a set F of functional dependencies. Recall from Chapter 5 that F_M is a minimal cover for F if $F \equiv F_M$, and F_M is a **minimal set of functional dependencies** in the following sense:

1. Each right side of a functional dependency in F_M is a single attribute.
2. If $X \rightarrow A \in F_M$, Y is any proper subset $Y \subsetneq X$, and $F' = F_M - \{X \rightarrow A\} \cup \{Y \rightarrow A\}$, then it is *not* the case that $F_M \equiv F'$. (Observe that for any F' formed from F_M as described previously, $(F')^* \supseteq F_M^*$. Condition 2 states that for no such F' is the containment proper.)
3. No functional dependency in F_M is redundant. That is, there is no $f \in F_M$ such that the removal of f from F_M results in an $F' \equiv F_M$. (Observe that for any F' formed from F_M as described earlier, $(F')^* \subseteq F_M^*$. Condition 3 states that for no such F' is the containment proper.)

The following simple method for obtaining a minimal cover F_M for an arbitrary set F of functional dependencies is based on the results of the previous section.

Step 1, Decompose

Replace each functional dependency $(X \rightarrow \{A_1, A_2, \ldots, A_k\}) \in F$, where $k > 1$, with the k functional dependencies $X \rightarrow A_1, X \rightarrow A_2, \ldots, X \rightarrow A_k$. Call the resulting set F_{M_1}. It follows from Lemma 6.3 that $F \equiv F_{M_1}$.

Step 2, Left Reduce

```
F_M2 ← F_M1
for (each X → A ∈ F_M2)
    { find a minimal Z ⊆ X that can serve as LHS }
    Z ← X
    for (each x ∈ X)
        F' ← F_M2 - {Z → A} ∪ {Z - {x} → A}
        if (Equiv?(F_M2 , F')
            Z ← Z - {x}
```

```
            F_M2 ← F'
        endif
    end for
end for
```

Several comments are in order. First, it is clear that since a change is made to F_{M_2} only when equivalence is preserved, we have at all times $F \equiv F_{M_1} \equiv F_{M_2}$. As described in exercise 6.17, it can be shown that regardless of the order in which functional dependencies are considered in the outer **for** loop and regardless of the order in which the attributes are considered in the inner **for** loop, at the conclusion of the procedure, F_{M_2} will obey property 2 of minimality. (However, different sets of functional dependency will result from different orders.) Also, we observe that the call to Equiv? can be replaced by a one-sided containment test as described in the parenthetical of property 2.

Step 3, Remove Redundant Functional Dependencies

```
F_M ← F_M2
for (each f ∈ F_M)
    { See if f is redundant }
    if (Equiv?(F_M , F_M − {f})
        F_M ← F_M − {f}
    endif
end for
```

Comments analogous to those following step 2 apply to step 3. We observe additionally that when step 3 is applied to a set of functional dependencies that is left reduced, step 3 produces a set of functional dependencies that itself is left reduced. Hence, the required minimal cover results from the three-step algorithm. It is interesting to note that the ordering of steps 2 and 3 must not be inverted, for step 2, when applied to a set of functional dependencies that contains no redundant dependencies, could produce a set that, although left reduced, contains redundant functional dependencies (see exercies 6.17 and 6.18).

We combine the three steps to form the procedure

```
Procedure MinCov(F,F_M)
    { Return in F_M a minimal cover for F }
```

Procedure MinCov runs in time polynomial in $Len(F)$ and produces a minimal cover F_M such that $|F_M|$ is polynomial in $|F|$ (and in the number of attributes in the relation scheme). See exercise 6.16 for a more detailed analysis.

6.5 TESTING FOR LOSSLESS AND F-ENFORCEABLE DECOMPOSITIONS[6]

In this section, we present algorithms for checking whether an arbitrary decomposition is lossless and F-enforceable. Recall that, given a table scheme $T(A_1, A_2, \ldots, A_n)$ and set F of functional dependencies, the decomposition

[6] This section may be omitted without loss of continuity.

$D = \{T_1(X_1), \ldots, T_k(X_k)\}$ of T is

1. **Lossless** with respect to F if, for every instance I of T that obeys F,

   $\gamma_D(I)=I$

2. **F-enforceable** if, for any instances $I_1, I_2, \ldots, I_k$ of $T_1, T_2, \ldots, T_k$,

   [each instance I_i of T_i obeys the projection F_i of F]

   $\Rightarrow$

   [instance $I_{T_1} \bowtie I_{T_2} \bowtie \cdots \bowtie I_{T_k}$ of T obeys F]

Algorithms for verifying these properties of a decomposition are useful in many contexts. One such context is establishing the correctness of our 3NF algorithm, which takes as input an arbitrary table scheme T and associated set F of functional dependencies and produces a decomposition D that is 3NF, lossless, and F-enforceable. The algorithms developed in this section are instrumental in verifying that the second and third properties hold for any decomposition produced by the 3NF algorithm.

Testing Losslessness

In Section 5.6, we presented the following theorem characterizing the losslessness of a decomposition of an arbitrary table scheme T into two tables schemes T_1 and T_2.

> **Theorem 5.1** Let $T(A_1, A_2, \ldots, A_n)$ be a table scheme, F an associated set of functional dependencies, and $D = \{T_1(X_1), T_2(X_2)\}$ a decomposition of T, with $Y = X_1 \cap X_2$. Decomposition D is lossless with respect to the set F of functional dependencies iff either $Y \rightarrow X_1$ or $Y \rightarrow X_2$ is in F^*.

Observe that the X_Plus algorithm allows us to apply the theorem efficiently. Let Y denote $X_1 \cap X_2$. To apply the theorem, we must determine if either $Y \rightarrow X_1$ or $Y \rightarrow X_2$ is in F^*. This is accomplished by computing Y^+ and testing whether Y^+ contains either X_1 or X_2.

While Theorem 5.1 can be quite useful, we must be able to test the losslessness of a decomposition of a table scheme T into any number of table schemes $T_1, T_2, \ldots, T_k$. The testing procedure for a general decomposition is far more complex than for the binary case. We now describe an algorithm for performing this test.

The algorithm utilizes a very important tool of relational database theory: a **tableaux.** A tableaux is a tool that allows us to study many important properties of a given collection $T_1(X_1), T_2(X_2), \ldots, T_k(X_k)$ of table schemes. A tableaux is a matrix that, in general, contains a row T_i for each table in the collection of interest and a column A_j for each attribute in $\bigcup_{i=1}^{k} X_i$.

For example, suppose that table scheme $T(A_1,A_2,A_3,A_4)$ is decomposed into $D = \{T_1(A_1,A_2), T_2(A_1,A_3), T_3(A_2,A_3,A_4)\}$. The tableaux for D is the 3×4 matrix M_D shown in Figure 6.11.

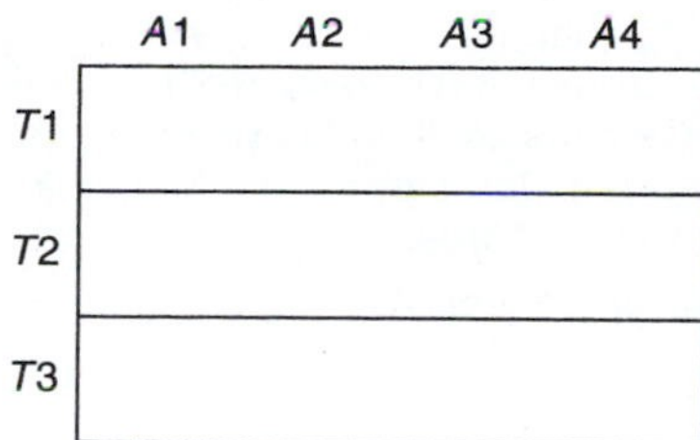

Figure 6.11 Tableaux M_D for $D = \{T_1(A_1, A_2), T_2(A_1, A_3), T_3(A_2, A_3, A_4)\}$

The algorithm for testing whether a decomposition D of T is lossless with respect to the set F of functional dependencies is as follows:

```
Function Lossless(T,D,F)
  { Return true if decomposition D is lossless with respect to F and
    false otherwise. It is assumed that the RHS of each dependency in
    F is a single attribute. }
  { Initialize tableaux M_D }
  for (each row T_i in M_D)
      for (each column A_j in M_D)
         if A_j ∈ X_i
            M_D [i,j] ← a_j
         else M_D [i,j] ← b_ij
         endif
      end for
  end for
  done ← false
  while (not done)
      change ← false
      mark all f ∈ F as "untried"
      while (not change) and (F contains at least one untried f)
         select any untried X → A_j from F and mark it "tried"
         for (each collection S of rows of M_D that agree on all of X)
            { Procedure Equate is defined below }
            Equate(M_D, S, A_j, change)
            if (any row of M_D contains all a's)
               {D is a lossless decomposition }
               return(true)
            endif
         end for
      end while
      done ← (not change)
  end while
  { Algorithm was unable to transform any row of M_D to all a's—
    D is a lossy decomposition }
  return(false)
end Function Lossless
```

```
Procedure Equate(M, S, A_j, change)
  { Change all column A_j entries in the rows in S to a common
    value. If these entries are the same value when the procedure is
    invoked, no action is taken, and parameter change is not altered; otherwise,
    parameter change is returned true. }
   if (all rows in S agree on column A_j)
     return
   else
     change ← true
     if (any row in the collection S has the value a_j in column A_j)
       comm_val ← a_j
     else
       let k be the smallest row number in the collection S
       comm_val ← b_kj
     endif
     for (each row r_i ∈ S)
       M_D [i,j] ← comm_val
     end for
   endif
 end Procedure Equate
```

Example

Suppose we wish to determine whether $D = \{T_1(A_1,A_2), T_2(A_1,A_3), T_3(A_2,A_3,A_4)\}$ is a lossless decomposition of table scheme $T(A_1,A_2,A_3,A_4)$ with respect to the set $F = \{A_1 \rightarrow A_3, A_3 \rightarrow A_4\}$ of functional dependencies.

After initialization, M_D is as shown in Figure 6.12. Suppose the lossless algorithm first considers functional dependency $A_1 \rightarrow A_3$. Equate will be called

	A_1	A_2	A_3	A_4
T_1	a_1	a_2	b_{13}	b_{14}
T_2	a_1	b_{21}	a_3	b_{24}
T_3	b_{31}	a_2	a_3	a_4

Figure 6.12 M_D after initialization

	A_1	A_2	A_3	A_4
T_1	a_1	a_2	a_3	b_{14}
T_2	a_1	b_{21}	a_3	b_{24}
T_3	b_{31}	a_2	a_3	a_4

Figure 6.13 M_D after first call to Equate

	A_1	A_2	A_3	A_4
T_1	a_1	a_2	a_3	a_4
T_2	a_1	b_{21}	a_3	a_4
T_3	b_{31}	a_2	a_3	a_4

Figure 6.14 M_D after second call to Equate

on the first two rows, producing the new tableaux in Figure 6.13. The lossless algorithm next considers functional dependency $A_3 \rightarrow A_4$. Equate will be called on all three rows, producing the new tableaux in Figure 6.14. Since row T_1 is all a's, the function terminates and reports that the decomposition D is lossless.

Theorem 6.10 Function Lossless correctly determines if a decomposition is lossless.

Proof We shall establish that if Lossless terminates before any row becomes all a's, then the decomposition is lossy. The proof that Lossless terminating with a row containing all a's implies that the decomposition is lossless is beyond the scope of this discussion.

The strategy is to view the final state of the tableaux as an instance I of T. We shall show that if at termination there is no row of all a's, we will have an instance that obeys F but violates the lossless property. More precisely, the proof relies on the fact that an instance of T over the proper domains can be constructed to correspond with the final state of the tableaux; this is the case, provided that the attribute domains have sufficient numbers of distinct elements.

Suppose there is no row in I that contains all a's. Then the algorithm terminated because there were no more equates to make. This instance I clearly obeys F, because if there is an $X \rightarrow A$ such that two rows agree on X but disagree on A, these rows can be equated.

Now this instance of I projects onto the T_i in such a way that the Join of the resulting instances contains a row that is all a's. Each projection contains a row that is all a's (the ith row of the projection onto T_i). When we join any pair of instances

I_i
row i: $aaaa$

I_j
row j: $aaaaa$

either they have no attributes in common, in which case the row $aaaaaaaaa$ is certainly in the Join or each A_i in common has the value a_i, in which case $aaaaaaaaa$ again is in the Join. Hence, the Join has a row that is all a's, and this row is not in I.□

When function Lossless is called on a table scheme T containing n attributes and a decomposition D containing k table schemes, the tableaux M_D is an $n \times k$ matrix. One way to see that algorithm Lossless terminates is to observe that the quantity

$$\sum_{\{i \mid b_{ij} \text{ appears in } M_D\}} i$$

decreases at each iteration of the **while** loop until the termination condition is reached. Since, initially, this sum is less than $n^2 * k$, it not difficult to implement function Lossless so that it runs in time bounded by a low-order polynomial in n,k and $|F|$. See exercise 6.19 for details.

Testing for F-Enforceability

Recall that if F is a set of functional dependencies applying to table scheme T and D is a decomposition of T, then for $T_i \in D$, the projection of F onto T_i is

F_{T_i} = {functional dependencies $Y \rightarrow Z \in F^* \mid Y \rightarrow Z$ applies to T_i}, and F_D denotes the union $\bigcup_{T_i \in D} F_{T_i}$ of the projections of F.

We first prove the following theorem characterizing when a decomposition D is F-enforceable.

Theorem 6.11 D is an F-enforceable decomposition of T if and only if $F \equiv F_D$.

Proof We first establish that if $F \equiv F_D$, then D is F-enforceable. Suppose $I_1, I_2, \ldots, I_k$ are instances of the table schemes T_i in D, and suppose that each I_i obeys F_i. Suppose, contrary to the theorem, that $I = I_1 \bowtie I_2 \bowtie \cdots \bowtie I_k$ violates some functional dependency in F. Since $F \equiv F_D$, I must violate also some functional dependency in F_D, call it $W \rightarrow Z$. Hence, instance I of T contains tuples t and t' such that $t[W] = t'[W]$ and $t[Z] \neq t'[Z]$. But since $W \rightarrow Z \in F_D$, some table scheme $T_j(X_j)$ in D must be such that $WZ \subseteq X_j$. Therefore, the only way t and t' can be in the instance $I = I_1 \bowtie I_2 \bowtie \cdots \bowtie I_j \bowtie \cdots \bowtie I_k$ is if I_j contains tuples s and s' such that $s[WZ] = t[WZ]$ and $s'[WZ] = t'[WZ]$. But then I_j violates $W \rightarrow Z \in F_i$, a contradiction.

To complete the proof, we establish that if D is an F-enforceable decomposition of T, then it must be the case that $F \equiv F_D$. Suppose that D is F-enforceable, but, contrary to the theorem, F and F_D are not equivalent. Thus, there is a $W \rightarrow Z \in F$ that is not in F_D. Construct an instance I of T that obeys each member of F_D and violates $W \rightarrow Z$. (It is always possible to construct such an instance I; see exercise 6.12.) Consider now the instances $I_1, \ldots, I_k$ obtained by projecting onto D this instance I. Clearly, each I_i obeys F_i. Let $I' = I_1 \bowtie \cdots \bowtie I_k$ and observe that $I' \supseteq I$. Hence, it follows from the fact that I violates $W \rightarrow Z$ that I' violates this functional dependency in F. This contradicts that D is F-enforceable.□

Algorithm Equiv? presented in Section 6.4 can be used to test whether $F \equiv F_D$. Note, however, that Equiv? would require X_Plus to be called to compute closures with respect to F_D. X_Plus, in this case, requires that F_D be available and runs in time proportional to $Len(F_D)$. This is a potential problem since $Len(F_D)$ can be exponential in $Len(F)$. We therefore ask whether we can test by some more efficient means whether $F \equiv F_D$. The answer to this question is yes, we can perform this test in time polynomial in $Len(F)$. The algorithm is discussed in exercise 6.20.

Assuming we have available the algorithm discussed in exercise 6.20, we can test efficiently whether a decomposition is F-enforceable. However, there remains a subtle problem. The reason that we want our decomposition D to be F-enforceable is so that we can verify the validity of Updates by checking instances of each T_i against the corresponding F_{T_i}. This method, however, requires that we make explicit the F_{T_i}, which is just what the efficient algorithm of exercise 6.20 is attempting to avoid. Not only might it be expensive to make explicit the F_{T_i}, but once we have them, it may be too expensive to enforce F_{T_i} after each Update to table T_i, since these sets of functional dependencies in general will be enormous. A partial solution to this problem is found in the following lemma.

Lemma 6.4 Let T be a table scheme with associated set F of functional dependencies. Suppose D is a decomposition of T and that G is a set of functional dependencies such that $F \equiv G$ and such that each functional dependency in G applies to at least one of the T_i in D. Then D is F-enforceable and it suffices to enforce G on D. That is, if each T_i obeys all the functional dependencies in G that apply to it, then the Join of these instances obeys F.

This result is of potential value because we may be able to find a set G, far smaller than F_D, that satisfies the conditions of the lemma. But how can we find such a G? It can be shown that if D is F-enforceable, then such a G can be constructed in time polynomial in $|F|$ (see Maier, Ullman, and Vardi, 1984). This result implies not only that we can find a satisfactory G quickly, but also that this G can contain only polynomially (in $|F|$) many functional dependencies. Of more immediate interest to us than the existence of a procedure for constructing such a set G is Lemma 6.4 applied to our 3NF algorithm. Observe that the decomposition produced by the 3NF algorithm has the property that each functional dependency in the minimal cover F_M of the user-supplied set F applies to at least one table scheme in the decomposition. Consequently, since $F \equiv F_M$, F can be enforced by enforcing F_M on the table schemes of the decomposition. In other words, we need not search for a compact set of functional dependencies to enforce on the decomposition—the algorithm itself produces the required set of functional dependencies.

6.6 THE 3NF ALGORITHM REVISITED[7]

We now use the results of the previous sections to refine the statement of the 3NF algorithm and prove it correct.

We first refine the statement of the 3NF algorithm. The input/output behavior of procedure 3NF is summarized as follows:

[7] This section may be omitted without loss of continuity.

- INPUT: Table scheme $T(A_1, \ldots, A_n)$ and a set F of functional dependencies.
- OUTPUT: Decomposition D of T and a minimal cover F_M of F. Each $T_i \in D$ is in 3NF with respect to F_i, the projection of F onto T_i. D is lossless and F-enforceable, and F can be enforced by enforcing F_M on D.

```
Procedure 3NF(T(A1 , . . . , An),F,D,FM)
  { Preprocessing step—obtain a minimal cover for F }
  MinCov(F,FM)
  { Special Case }
  if (FM contains X → A such that X ∪ {A}={A1, A2 , . . . , An})
    { T is in 3NF }
    return with D={T(A1, . . . , An)}
  endif
  D ← ∅
  i ← 1
  for (each X → A in FM)
    { Add to the decomposition a table scheme over the attributes XA. }
    D ← D ∪ {Ti (XA)}
    i ← i+1
  end for
  { At this point D is in 3NF and is F-enforceable.
  D, however, may not be a lossless decomposition. }
  { Test D for losslessness. Since FM≡F, D is lossless
    with respect to F if and only if it is lossless with respect to FM. }
  if (not Lossless(D, FM))
    FindKey( T(A1, A2, . . . , An), F, K )
    D ← D ∪ {Ti (K) }
  endif
end 3NF
```

Note: We have modified the algorithm from its previous statement so that a test of losslessness is made before adding the key table. In some contexts, however, it may be desirable to add $T_i(K)$ without first testing for losslessness because the time to compute the function Lossless will dominate the running time of the algorithm when F_M is large. The disadvantage of adding $T_i(K)$ without first testing for losslessness, of course, is that the resulting decomposition may contain an unnecessary table scheme. The proof of the following theorem includes a demonstration that once the key table is added, the resulting decomposition is guaranteed to be lossless.

Example of the 3NF Algorithm

We revisit the example from Chapter 5. Let $T(A,B,C,D,E,F)$ be the original table scheme with associated set $F = \{A \to B,\ C \to DF,\ AC \to E,\ D \to F\}$ of functional dependencies. Observe that the only key of table scheme T is $\{A,C\}$. Therefore, T has both partial and transitive dependencies involving nonprime attributes and is thus not in 2NF (and thus not in 3NF).

We apply procedure 3NF to obtain a decomposition for T.

Step 1: Apply algorithm MinCov(F,F_M) to obtain a minimal cover. Let $F_M = \{A \rightarrow B,\ C \rightarrow D,\ AC \rightarrow E,\ D \rightarrow F\}$ be the minimal cover returned by MinCov.

Step 2: Place in decomposition D a table scheme corresponding to each functional dependency in F_M. The following are the table schemes placed in D:

$T_1(A,C,E)$
$T_2(C,D)$
$T_3(D,F)$
$T_4(A,B)$

Step 3: Evaluate function Lossless(D,F_M). We find that D in fact is lossless, so procedure 3NF can terminate with D containing the four tables listed previously. Alternatively, we could bypass the lossless test and simply add to D the table scheme $T_5(A,C)$.

It can be verified (tediously) that each T_i is in 3NF with respect to the projection F_i of F. Further, F can be enforced on D by enforcing F_M on the T_i since $F_M \equiv F$ and each member of F_M applies to at least one of the T_i (see Lemma 6.4.).

We now establish the correctness of procedure 3NF.

Theorem 6.12 Procedure 3NF is correct. That is, the procedure has the following input/output behavior:

- Input: Table scheme $T(A_1, \ldots, A_n)$ and a set F of functional dependencies.
- Output: Decomposition D of T and a minimal cover F_M of F. Each $T_i \in D$ is in 3NF with respect to F_i. D is lossless and F-enforceable, and F can be enforced by enforcing F_M on D.

Proof First consider the special case in which F_M contains a functional dependency involving all the attributes of T. That is, suppose the table scheme is $T(A_1, A_2, \ldots, A_n)$, and F_M contains the functional dependency $X \rightarrow A$, where $X = \{A_1, A_2, \ldots, A_n\} - \{A\}$, and A is one of the A_i. We must establish that T is in 3NF.

Observe that X must be a key for T because no proper subset $Y \underset{\neq}{\subset} X$ could functionally determine A. To see this, suppose to the contrary that $Y \rightarrow A \in F^*$. Then F_M could not have been minimal because if we let $F' = F_M - \{X \rightarrow A\} \cup \{Y \rightarrow A\}$, it is easy to see that $F_M \equiv F'$.

Suppose now that T is not in 3NF. There are two cases to consider:

1. T has a partial dependency involving a nonprime attribute as the right side. Since A is the only potential nonprime attribute, this

means that F^* contains a functional dependency $Y \rightarrow A$ for some $Y \subsetneq X$. But the previous argument showed that this contradicts the fact that F_M is minimal.

2. T has a transitive dependency involving a nonprime attribute as the right side. Since A is the only potential nonprime attribute, this means that F^* contains a functional dependency $Y \rightarrow A$, where Y is neither a superkey nor a proper subset of a key and $A \in Y$. But this does not leave anything for Y to be.

Since the decomposition $D = \{T\}$ of T is lossless and F-enforceable, we have established that the special case of the algorithm is correct.

Consider now the general case of the algorithm. First we establish that each T_i in the decomposition is in 3NF (with respect to the projection F_i of F). If $T_i(X_i)$ is placed in the decomposition then either:

1. F_M contains the functional dependency $X_i' \rightarrow A$, where A is some member of X_i and $X_i' = X_i - \{A\}$. Since $X_i' \rightarrow A \in F_M$ and applies to T_i, $X_i' \rightarrow A \in F_i$. As in the special case, it follows that X_i' is a key of T_i. To see this, suppose to the contrary that $Y \rightarrow A \in F_i$ for $Y \subsetneq X$. Then $Y \rightarrow A \in F^*$. Therefore, F_M could not have been minimal because if we let $F' = F_M - \{X_i \rightarrow A\} \cup \{Y \rightarrow A\}$, it is easy to show that $F_M \equiv F'$.

   There are two subcases to consider in establishing that T_i is in 3NF with respect to F_i:

   a. T_i has a partial dependency involving a nonprime attribute as the right side. Since A is the only potential nonprime attribute, this means that F_i contains a functional dependency $Y \rightarrow A$ for some $Y \subsetneq X$. But then F^* also contains $Y \rightarrow A$. Thus (constructing F' as in special case), $F_M \equiv F'$, and F_M could not have been minimal.

   b. T_i has a transitive dependency involving a nonprime attribute as the right side. Since A is the only potential nonprime attribute, this means that F_i contains a functional dependency $Y \rightarrow A$, where Y is neither a superkey nor a proper subset of a key and $A \notin Y$. But this does not leave anything for Y to be.

2. $T_i(X_i)$ was added to the decomposition following the lossless test, and thus X_i is a key of T. Thus, $X_i \rightarrow A_1 \cdots A_n \in F^*$. It follows that X_i is a key for T_i. (If some proper subset $Y \subsetneq X_i$ is a key for T_i, we must have that $Y \rightarrow X_i$ is in F_i and thus in F^* also. Thus F^* also contains $Y \rightarrow A_1 \cdots A_n$, which contradicts that X_i is a key of T). Since X_i is a key of T_i, T_i contains no nonprime attributes and thus is in 3NF.

We thus have established that each T_i in the decomposition is in 3NF with respect to F_i. It remains to establish that the decomposition is lossless and F-enforceable and that F can be enforced by enforcing F_M on D. First consider F-enforceability. Since $F_M \equiv F \equiv F^*$ and F_M contains only functional dependencies that apply to at least one of the T_i, it must be that $F_M \equiv F_D$. Thus, $F_D \equiv F$, and by Theorem 6.11, D is F-enforceable. That F can be enforced by enforcing F_M on D then follows from Lemma 6.4.

To establish that the decomposition is lossless, we must show that adding a scheme $T_K(K)$, where K is any key of T, to the preliminary result $\{T_1(X_1), T_2(X_2), \ldots, T_k(X_k)\}$ of the algorithm creates a decomposition that is necessarily lossless. We shall establish this fact by demonstrating that algorithm Lossless?, when run on the decomposition $D = \{T_1(X_1), T_2(X_2), \ldots, T_k(X_k), T_K(K)\}$ (and set F_M of functional dependencies), terminates with some row containing all a's. Suppose not. Consider the row corresponding to T_K and the collection of A_j, which in row T_K are not a_j at termination. Consider the order in which the attributes are placed in *ANS* by algorithm X_Plus(F_M,K,*ANS*), which computes K^+. (Since K is a key, at termination, *ANS* will contain all the attributes of T.) Let A be the attribute among these A_j that is added to *ANS first*, say at iteration i. But then there is a functional dependency $Y \rightarrow A \in F_M$ such that $Y \subseteq ANS$ at the beginning of this iteration. Further, by the way A was chosen, all columns for Y in T_K's row are a's. All Y columns in $T(YA)$ are also a's from initialization, as is A. Thus, before termination of Lossless?, EQUATE would set to a the A column of T_K. It then follows from Theorem 6.10 that the decomposition is lossless with respect to F_M and, hence, with respect to F.□

Efficiency of 3NF Algorithm

The time for 3NF is dominated by the calls to MinCov, Lossless, and FindKey. The efficiency of these algorithms was analyzed previously. Exclusive of these calls, algorithm 3NF is linear in $Len(F_M)$ since each functional dependency in F_M is considered exactly once.

SUMMARY AND ANNOTATED BIBLIOGRAPHY

This chapter completes our study of normalization and decomposition begun in Chapter 5. The chapter presented the algorithms and theory necessary for specifying completely the 3NF algorithm and for proving the 3NF algorithm correct. Specifically, the results presented in this chapter most relevant to the 3NF algorithm were an algorithm for computing the logical closure X^+ of a set of attributes, an algorithm for testing membership in F^*, an algorithm for testing the losslessness of an arbitrary decomposition, and an algorithm for testing the F-enforceability of an arbitrary decomposition.

Algorithm Lossless? is based on the algorithm of Aho, Beeri, and Ullman (1979). We presented here one direction of proof of the algorithm's correctness; proof of the other direction requires much development, and the interested reader is referred to Aho, Beeri, and Ullman (1979); and Maier, Ullman, and Vardi (1984). The techniques for determining whether a decomposition is F-enforceable and the discussions of the algorithmic issues are derived from Beeri and Honeyman (1981).

One technique central to much of the theory in this chapter is that of computing logical closures of sets of functional dependencies and of testing membership in the logical closure. We presented Armstrong's axioms as a sound and complete set of inference axioms for functional dependencies and developed the notion of a derivation. The presentation follows model-theoretic conventions for any logic system; for a general presentation of such concepts, the reader is referred to Bridge (1977), and Chang and Lee (1979).

The chapter considered also 4NF, a design criterion based on multivalued dependencies. Many of the algorithmic considerations developed here for functional dependencies have analogues for multivalued dependencies. For example, methods for deriving the logical closure Φ^* from Φ and for testing a multivalued dependency for membership in Φ^* parallel those developed in the context of functional dependencies. The interested reader is referred to Beeri, Fagin, and Howard (1977). Many other types of dependencies have been studied as well. These include dependencies that capture additional types of information within a table, including Join, embedded, and generalized dependencies (see Aho, Beeri, and Ullman, 1979; Rissanen, 1977; and Sadri and Ullman, 1980), and even dependencies for capturing intertable constraints.

The first six chapters of the book have considered the definition of, and semantic design for, the relational data model. The remainder of the book focuses on the implementation of the RDM. The implementation issues studied include file structure design, query optimization, concurrency control, and recovery.

EXERCISES

1. Construct natural examples of table schemes that are in BCNF but not 4NF.
2. Describe the problems you might anticipate from the table schemes of exercise 1.
3. Attempt to construct lossless 4NF decompositions of the table schemes of exercise 1.
4. Construct an algorithm for implementing the operation Delete(T, $<v_1, v_2, \ldots, v_k>$) against a decomposition $D = <T_1,T_2>$ of T (see Section 6.1 and the naive strategy of Algorithm 6.5). What is the efficiency of your algorithm in the worst case and in "typical" cases?
5. In some environments, it may be desirable to allow certain users to update the tables of a decomposition directly rather than requiring that all

updates be posed against the original table. For example, if table UNIVERSITY(P_Name, Dept, Salary, Student, Major) is decomposed into tables PROF(P_Name, Dept, Salary), TEACHES(P_Name, Student), and STUD(Student, Major), we may wish to allow updates such as ADD(PROF, <Jones, CS, 40K>). What are the primary benefits of allowing such a direct Update? Analyze the effects on the results of Section 6.1 of allowing direct Updates.

6. Demonstrate that there exist table schemes that do not possess F-enforceable decompositions into BCNF.
7. In Section 6.3, we presented two definitions of the multivalued dependency $X \twoheadrightarrow Y$. The first definition is based on the concept of a Y set, the second is Definition 6.3. Demonstrate that the two definitions are equivalent by showing that instance I of $T(XYZ)$ obeys $X \twoheadrightarrow Y$ by the first definition if and only if I obeys $X \twoheadrightarrow Y$ by the second definition.
8. Prove Lemma 6.1 by exhibiting the required derivations for each direction of the assertion.
9. Prove Theorem 6.5 that each of Armstrong's axioms is sound.
10. Prove that the following inference axiom for functional dependencies is not sound:

    From $X \rightarrow Y$ conclude $Z \rightarrow Y$ for any $Z \subseteq X$

11. Prove that Armstrong's axioms are **independent** in the sense that if any one of the three axioms were eliminated, the remaining two axioms would not form a complete set.
12. Let T be any table scheme with associated set F of functional dependencies. Construct a (single) instance I of T that obeys each member of F yet (simultaneously) violates *every* functional dependency applying to T that is not in F^*. *Hint:* Modify the construction used in the proof of Theorem 6.8.
13. Prove Theorem 6.6 that at all times during the execution of procedure Closure, $ANS \subseteq F^*$.

*14. Complete the proof of Theorem 6.9 establishing the correctness of algorithm X_Plus. *Hint:* Equate the action of algorithm X_Plus with some procedure that is known to generate all of X^+.

15. Describe an implementation of algorithm X_Plus that runs in $O(Len(F))$ time. *Hint:* The key to an efficient implementation is data structures that allow the algorithm at each iteration to determine quickly which new attributes can be added to the set X_cur.
16. Derive a tight bound on the running time of algorithm MinCov.
17. Demonstrate that algorithm MinCov is correct regardless of the order in which functional dependencies are considered within each of steps 2 and 3. Demonstrate additionally that this ordering can affect both the identity and cardinality of the minimal cover F_M produced. Be sure to demonstrate that for $1 < k \leq 3$, the set of functional dependencies that

results from step k obeys properties $i \leq k$ of the definition of a minimal cover.

18. Demonstrate that algorithm MinCov would not be correct if the ordering of steps 2 and 3 were inverted.
19. Derive a tight bound on the running time of algorithm Lossless.

**20. Algorithm Equiv? presented in Section 6.4 can be used to test whether a given decomposition is F-enforceable by testing whether $F \equiv F_D$. However, such an application of Equiv? requires X_Plus to be called to compute closures with respect to F_D, a task requiring time proportional to $Len(F_D)$, which can be exponential in $Len(F)$. Modify algorithm Equiv? so that it can in time polynomial in $Len(F)$ test whether $F \equiv F_D$.

21. Let $T(A,B,C,D)$ be a table scheme with associated set $F = \{AB \rightarrow C, B \rightarrow D, D \rightarrow A\}$. Determine whether the decomposition

    $T_1(B,D)$, $T_2(A,D)$, $T_3(B,C)$

    is lossless.
22. *a.* Suppose T is decomposed losslessly (with respect to a set Φ of functional and multivalued dependencies) into T_1 and T_2. Suppose T_2 is then decomposed losslessly (with respect to the dependencies from Φ that apply to it) into T_3 and T_4. Is T_1, T_3, T_4 necessarily a lossless decomposition of T with respect to Φ?

    b. Can every lossless decomposition T_1, T_2, T_3 of T be obtained by some sequence of binary lossless decompositions, starting with T?
23. Let $T(A,B,C,D)$ be a table scheme and $F = \{A \rightarrow BC, B \rightarrow D, BC \rightarrow D, A \rightarrow D\}$ be an associated set of functional dependencies. Obtain a lossless, F-enforceable 3NF decomposition for T.
24. Let $T(A,B,C,D)$ be a table scheme with associated set $F = \{A \rightarrow B, B \rightarrow CD, C \rightarrow D\}$ of functional dependencies. Construct a 3NF decomposition of T that is lossless and functional dependency preserving.
25. Let $T(A,B,C,D)$ be a table scheme and $F = \{AB \rightarrow C, C \rightarrow D, A \rightarrow B, B \rightarrow D, B \rightarrow C\}$ be an associated set of functional dependencies. Consider the following two decompositions:

    Decomposition 1: $T_1(A,B,D)$ $T_2(C,D)$
    Decomposition 2: $T_1(A,B)$ $T_2(B,C,D)$

    One of the decompositions is F-enforceable, and the other is not. Identify the decomposition that is *not* F-enforceable, and support your contention by constructing an instance I_1 of T_1 obeying F_1 and I_2 of T_2 obeying F_2 such that instance $I_1 \bowtie I_2$ of T violates F.
26. Show that algorithm 3NF may fail to produce the required decomposition if run on a set of functional dependencies F that violates either condition 1 or 2 in the definition of a minimal set of functional dependencies. (That is, we neglect to use MinCov to preprocess the set F.)

27. Demonstrate that the technique employed by the 3NF algorithm of adding a table scheme T_K corresponding to a key of table T is not valid in general contexts. In particular, demonstrate that if $T(X)$ is an arbitrary table scheme, F an arbitrary set of functional dependencies, K a key of scheme T, and $T_1(X_1), \ldots, T_m(X_m)$ an arbitrary decomposition of T, then it need *not* be the case that $T_1(X_1), \ldots, T_m(X_m), T_{m+1}(K)$ is a lossless decomposition of T.
28. Let $T(A,B,C,D)$ be a table scheme with associated set $F = \{A \rightarrow BC, B \rightarrow D, BC \rightarrow D, A \rightarrow D\}$. Construct a 3NF decomposition of T that is lossless and functional dependency preserving.

PART ***THREE***

Implementations of the Relational Data Model Abstract Data Type—The Structures

CHAPTER 7

The External Environment

Chapters 1, 2, and 3 introduced the RDM abstract data type, focusing on its *definition*. Chapters 4, 5, and 6 focused on how to *design* an RDM to best meet the semantic requirements of a given application. We begin now the third part of the book, which focuses on the *implementation* of the RDM ADT.

This chapter introduces the concepts necessary for the subsequent development of external memory implementations of the RDM. Section 7.1 outlines the perspective for the chapter's material, Section 7.2 introduces a simple model of external memory, and Sections 7.3 and 7.4 illustrate how this model is used to describe some primitive, but essential, tasks performed on data residing in external memory. Chapters 8 through 13 then use the model to describe the complex algorithms and file structures that are at the heart of correct and efficient implementations of the RDM.•

7.1 PERSPECTIVE: THE RDM, EXTERNAL STORAGE, AND THE DBMS

The material presented in the first six chapters is, for the most part, independent of the issues of how and where an RDM's data is stored. Certainly, the theory of normalization and the definitions of query languages are completely independent of such implementation issues. The data abstraction approach allows—in fact, forces—this independence. On several occasions in the first six chapters, however, we briefly peeked at the implementation side of the wall. For example, in Chapter 2 we briefly considered internal memory implementations for the search table and RDM ADTs. Also in Chapter 2, and at several later junctures, we considered some basic query optimization principles.

It is the case that the vast majority of today's applications require that an RDM's data be stored in external memory devices, such as a disk. Recall from our discussion in Chapter 1 that the factors mandating an external implementation include

1. *Massive quantities of data:* Many of today's applications utilize RDMs containing huge quantities of data, sometimes on the order of several billion tuples. This much data far exceeds the capacities of the internal memories of today's computers. While hardware trends point to cheaper and more plentiful internal memory, future computer applications doubtless will require the management of far larger quantities of data than at present. Therefore, there is every reason to believe that, even in the future, many applications will require RDM implementations

on storage devices possessing characteristics resembling those modeled in this chapter.

2. *Shared and persistent nature of the data:* In a typical application, the data of an RDM must be accessed by many different programs and users, often concurrently. Further, this data must be capable of existing reliably over long periods of time and be immune to processor failure. Today's technologies best support these requirements with external storage devices.

In Chapters 7 through 13 we shall spend most of our time on the implementation side of the wall. We shall assume that the RDM's data must be stored externally and shall develop techniques for addressing this requirement. We shall discover that many of the implementation techniques presented in earlier chapters serve as good starting points for the techniques we must develop for external implementations. Two prime examples of the techniques that will prove useful are (1) the internal 2–3 tree and hashing implementations, as well as the indexing methods used to support multiple organizations of the data, and (2) the query optimization techniques for mapping high-level queries, first into relational algebra expressions and then into implementation-level programs. Additionally, in Chapter 10 we shall discover that the need to provide concurrent access to the database and protection from system failure lead to important techniques known collectively as **transaction management.**

The material pertaining to the RDM's definition (relational algebra in particular) and the theory of normalization also will come into play in Chapters 7 through 13. The specification of how the data in an RDM is to be used, which in part is captured by the definition of its operators, greatly influences our choice of implementation structures and algorithms. Additionally, once we become familiar with the alternative techniques for implementing the RDM ADT, it will become apparent that efficiency considerations should somewhat temper our zeal for applying to the design of RDM schemes the theory of normalization.

We conclude these introductory remarks with a few words of perspective regarding how commercial DBMSs fit into our development of topics. A relational DBMS is software that bridges the user's interface to the RDM ADT and the RDM's implementation. The most critical aspects of this bridge are the file structures the DBMS uses to store the RDM's data, the query optimization algorithms the DBMS uses to map high-level queries into programs that execute against these file structures, and the transaction management algorithms it employs to guarantee the database's integrity in light of concurrent access and possible system failure. The quality of these three DBMS components go a long way toward determining the DBMS's overall quality. While many software packages can provide a good user interface (e.g., by implementing a version of tuple calculus or relational algebra), the really difficult and critical task for an RDM implementation is to provide high-quality storage structures and high-quality query optimization and transaction management algorithms.

7.2 A SIMPLE MODEL OF EXTERNAL STORAGE

Figure 7.1 presents a high-level model of two types of computer memories—**internal memory** and **external memory**—and their interaction. Because hardware-oriented definitions of these two types of memories change so rapidly, we shall describe internal and external memory primarily in terms of their relative characteristics, typical applications, and interaction. This approach allows our model of the memories to automatically adapt to technological advances. For example, we currently think of a direct-access disk as the archetypical external memory device. However, there is reason to believe that current disk technology will become outdated within the foreseeable future. In contrast, the relative characteristics (e.g., speed and cost) that we use to distinguish between internal and external memory most likely always will be applicable. That is, there will always be classes of memory that are faster and more expensive than other classes. The fastest and most expensive classes of memories will fall into the category of internal memory, while the cheaper but slower memories will fall into the category of external memory.

Internal Memory		External Memory
Programs		
Internal data		
System I/O Buffers	⟷	External Device

Figure 7.1 High-level memory model

Characteristics of the Memories

1. Internal memory provides *faster access* than does external memory. While accessing data in internal memory (reading or writing it) requires roughly the same amount of time required to execute a machine-level instruction (e.g., branch to a segment of the code), the time required to access data in external memory is many times greater than this. For example, in today's typical computing environment, the time required to access data on a direct-access disk is comparable to that of executing tens of thousands of machine-level instructions. Some of the factors that contribute to this disparity in memory speeds are discussed later.

2. Internal memory is *more finely addressable* than is external memory. Consider, for example, a program that references a variable x that is associated with a cell of internal memory. The reference to x retrieves (or writes to) the single memory cell associated with x. While the size of the cell depends on the type of variable that x is, the cell associated with the variable x is the only portion of memory that participates in the operation. In contrast, when a program references a piece of data (a record, for example) that is stored in external memory, a portion of the external memory that may be far larger than the record in question is retrieved (or written to). This difference in addressability

is one of the factors that contributes to the disparity in the speeds of internal and external memory.

3. The availability of internal memory is *more constrained* than that of external memory. In a typical computing environment, much external memory is available, while the amount of internal memory available is severely limited. One factor contributing to this situation is that internal memory is more desirable for many tasks (primarily because of its speed) and hence is more in demand. A second contributing factor is that the hardware for external memory is cheaper and hence is likely to be more plentiful.

4. External memory is *persistent and sharable,* while internal memory generally is not.

Applications of the Memories

The characteristics just described lead to different utilizations of internal and external memory. Internal memory typically contains segments of executing user and system programs (e.g., segments of an operating system or a database management system), the data associated with the variables of an executing program, and any system information that is accessed frequently (e.g., directories to external files). External memory typically contains text files, program source codes, and the data that constitutes a database (e.g., the tuples in the current instances of an RDM table, as well as indices and table schemes). As Figure 7.1 indicates, internal memory also contains system input/output (I/O) buffers that play a central role in the interaction of internal and external memory. I/O buffers are considered later.

It must be pointed out that the division of the functions of internal and external memory is not quite as sharp as the preceding discussion indicates. One reason for this is that some state-of-the-art computer systems have a sufficient amount of internal memory that they can internally store portions of the data that traditionally have been stored externally. Another reason that the division is not as sharp as we have indicated is that in **virtual** computer systems, the location at which a particular piece of a program or piece of data currently resides is highly variable over time and is transparent to the user. For example, parts of an executing program that are not currently needed (e.g., the code for a subroutine that is not currently executing) may be stored externally and "brought in" to internal memory only as needed (e.g., when the subroutine is called). Similarly, some RDM tuples may be in internal memory (e.g., because they were accessed recently) at the time a program or user query needs to access them.

Interaction between the Memories

A fundamental precept in our modeling of memory is that *data can be inspected and modified only when it is in internal memory*. The implication of this precept is that data that resides externally must be transferred temporarily into internal memory before it can be inspected or modified.

Our model assumes that the atomic level of data transfer is the **block.** We do not specify the size of a block here, but typical block sizes are 1,024, 2,048, and 5,096 bytes. As indicated previously, in order to access a record stored externally, a portion of memory larger than that which contains the desired record often must be transferred into internal memory. In particular, to access a record, *the entire contents of the block containing the record must be transferred.* Our model assumes that, to facilitate such data transfer, a portion of internal memory is partitioned into a collection of **system I/O buffers,** each capable of holding a block of data. When a block of data residing in external memory is required, it is read into one of the system I/O buffers. Similarly, when a collection of data must be written to external memory, it first is placed in a system I/O buffer, and the contents of this buffer are then written to a block of external memory.

Our model abstracts a block's location, or address, in external memory as a simple integer. In reality, a block's address typically specifies information such as a device identifier (e.g., disk 232) and a physical location within the device (e.g., sector 21 of track 14 of platter 88). Our model assumes simply that the software managing the computing system's I/O can translate a block number into a full address; for our purposes, there is no need to look beyond a block number. We assume further that block i is physically "adjacent" to block $i - 1$ and hence that blocks numbered sequentially are physically contiguous in external memory.

While the preceding discussion postulates a model for the hardware-level interaction between internal and external memories, we model a program's interaction with external memory in terms of a collection of ADT operations. Three of these ADT operations are defined as follows:

```
CreateBuffers(n, suc)
  { Create for use by the calling program n program buffers named
    Buff1,Buff2, . . . ,Buffn. Each program buffer coincides in size with a system
    buffer (and hence with the block size). If system constraints do not allow the
    allocation of n program buffers, suc is returned false; suc is returned true
    otherwise. It is assumed that this operation is called only once in the course
    of a program's execution. }
ReadBlock(blocknum, Buffi)
  { Read into program buffer Buffi the contents of block blocknum.
    It is assumed that program buffer Buffi exists. }
WriteBlock(blocknum, Buffi)
  { Write to block blocknum the contents of program buffer Buffi.
    It is assumed that program buffer Buffi exists. }
```

A program references the contents of its buffers as it would reference an array of records. Thus, for example, once a ReadBlock operation has filled program buffer $Buff_i$, the expression

$Buff_i[q]$

is used to reference the qth record in this buffer, and the expression

$Buff_i[q].Name$

is used to reference the field *Name* of this record.

The operations CreateBuffers, ReadBlock, and WriteBlock describe how a program interacts functionally with external memory. In this sense, the operations refine our picture of how the ADT RDM, with its nonprocedural interface, is implemented by a sequence of mappings between successively lower level and more procedural ADTs (see Figure 7.2). Of course, the speed with which an implementation program processes a high-level query depends in part on the speed with which the computing system supports the ReadBlock and WriteBlock operations. This in turn depends on the interaction of the program buffers and system buffers and on the nature of the external memory devices. We now briefly explore these factors.

Predicate calculus interface to RDM ADT
↓
Relational algebra interface to RDM ADT
↓
Processing algorithms
↓
Implementation programs in terms of ReadBlock/WriteBlock

Figure 7.2 Levels of abstraction

Paging and the Interaction between Program Buffers and System Buffers

It is first necessary to reconcile some potentially confusing terminology. Many computing systems use the term **page** to refer to the system's atomic unit of data transfer. Further, a page often is subdivided into *several* blocks, each of which has its own address in external memory. Note that the model we have adopted agrees with this terminology in that blocks are addressable but disagrees with this terminology in that we always allow single blocks to be transferred. For the purpose of describing the algorithms in this book, there is no need to introduce aggregations of blocks into pages, and hence we shall continue to use the term *block* to refer to the atomic unit of data transfer; equivalently, we adopt the convention that the page size is one block.

While the concept of a page has little import for our presentation, the concept of **paging** does have some important consequences. There are in our model two types of buffers: program buffers and system buffers. Program buffers help model the actions of the ADT operations ReadBlock and WriteBlock, while system buffers are the hardware-level constructs that actually interface internal and external memory (see Figure 7.3).

While program buffers are the private reserve of the program that creates them, system buffers are utilized by many programs. Operationally, a ReadBlock operation has two potential effects: (1) transfer into a system buffer the contents of an external memory block, and (2) copy into a program buffer the

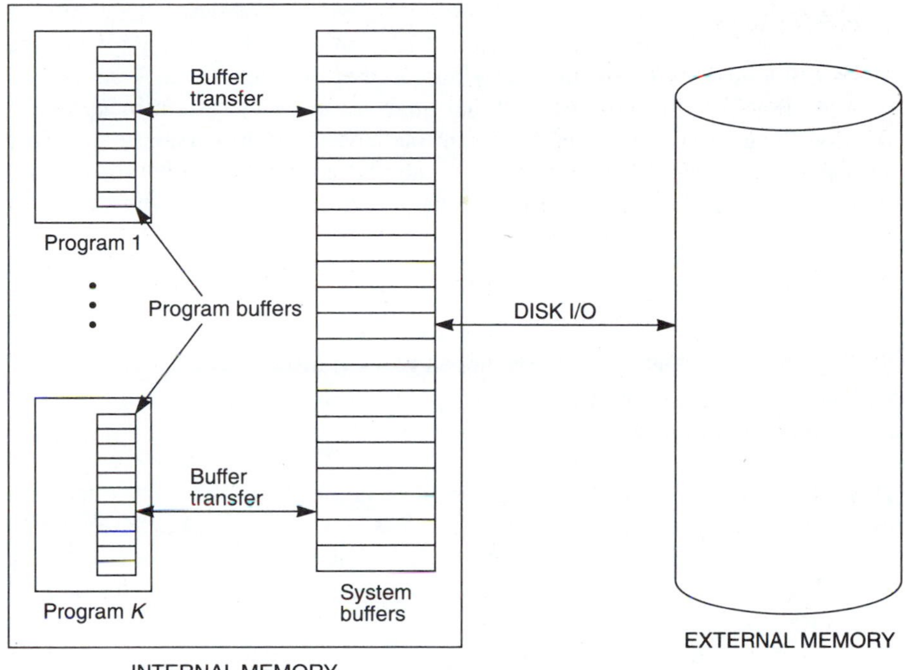

Figure 7.3 Interaction of memories and buffers

contents of a system buffer. The WriteBlock operation has the dual effects. The main consequence of the two levels of buffering is that it may be the case that some ReadBlock operations do not actually require data to be transferred from external to internal memory. For example, suppose that program *A* performs the operation

ReadBlock(5, $Buff_1$)

It may be the case that one of the system buffers already contains block 5 because program *A*, or some other program running on the computing system, has recently read block 5, and the system can determine that no subsequent modifications have been made to this block. If this is the case, the preceding ReadBlock requires only the copying of a system buffer to program *A*'s buffer $Buff_1$ and does not require data to be transferred from external to internal memory. Whether or not any given ReadBlock operation requires actual data transfer depends on what I/O has been performed recently and on the computing system's **paging algorithms.** A paging algorithm determines which block in the system buffers must be overwritten when a new block must be read. Paging algorithms can be as simple as *overwrite the block that's been in the system buffers the longest* (i.e., treat the system buffers as a finite queue), or the paging algorithm may utilize complex decision rules that attempt to anticipate future ReadBlock requests.

The variety of paging algorithms and the sensitivity of these algorithms to the activities of the various processes that may be executing at any given time make it impossible to analyze exactly the number of external block accesses a program requires. Because we wish our analyses to be as system independent as possible, we shall, in general, content ourselves with a worst-case analysis. That is, our analyses generally shall assume that each time a program issues a ReadBlock or WriteBlock request an actual block transfer is performed.

Three Common External Memory Devices

The work involved to implement a ReadBlock or WriteBlock operation (assuming that the ReadBlock actually requires a block transfer) depends on the characteristics of the external memory device. We now consider the characteristics of three common memory devices.

Direct-Access Disk: The direct-access disk is currently the most important external memory device. In this book, unless stated otherwise, the appropriateness of our algorithms (with regard to their efficiencies) will be based on the assumption that a direct-access disk is the external memory device against which ReadBlock and WriteBlock operate.

An idealized description of a direct-access disk equates its behavior with that of an array. The block number passed to a ReadBlock or WriteBlock command is treated very much like an array subscript. Like an array (and unlike a linked list, for example), block number i can be accessed without first "passing through" block numbers $1, 2, \ldots, i - 1$. It is this behavior that the term *direct access* describes. While this idealized description of a disk's behavior is not far from reality, we consider the two main factors that contribute to the time required to access a given disk block in a bit more detail.

- *Access delay:* The **disk head** must be moved to the desired location on the disk before the block can be read or written. While the idealized description of a disk's behavior postulates that the head can be moved "instantaneously" to the desired location, there is, in fact, some delay. Further, there is some dependence between the length of this delay and the current location of the disk head. It should come as no surprise, after all, that the closer the head is to the desired location, the less time it takes to get there! Thanks to the hardware characteristics of a disk, however, the disk head typically must "pass over" only a small fraction of the disk's blocks, even if many block numbers lie between the current block number and the desired block number. The hardware characteristics of a disk are not unlike those of a phonograph record or an audio compact disk. Thus, both the overall access delay and the dependence of this delay on the disk head's location are typically quite small, particularly when compared with those of other devices such as sequential tape. Therefore, the term *direct access,* although not completely accurate, is fairly descriptive of the behavior of a disk.

- *Transmission delay:* Once the disk head has moved to the appropriate location, the data in the desired block must be transmitted from the disk to an I/O buffer (in the case of ReadBlock) or from an I/O buffer to the disk (in the case of WriteBlock). The amount of time required for this transmission depends on the amount of data transmitted (as is determined by the block size) and on the characteristics of the **hardware channels** that connect internal and external memory.

Sequential Tape: The **sequential-access tape** is a memory device that in the past has had far more importance than it does today. Whereas the behavior of a direct-access disk resembles that of an array (or a phonograph record), the behavior of a sequential-access tape resembles that of a linked list (or an audio- or videocassette). In particular, in order to access block i, the tape head must "pass over" each block between its present location and block i. As a result, the access delay and the dependence on the current location of this delay both are great in comparison with those of a disk. Consequently, sequential tape's primary use in a modern computing environment is as an archival storage device, and it is rather inappropriate for supporting real-time database systems.

Read-Only Devices: So called read-only memory devices, such as the optical disk, are better termed **write once/read many (WORM)** devices. That is, we may write data to the disk but may not modify the data once written. The advantages offered by such devices are that, with respect to today's technology, they provide higher reliability and allow data to be read faster than their best read/write counterparts, such as traditional direct-access disks. WORM devices, however, are of limited use as they do not directly support the full range of operations we have attributed to the RDM. Exercise 7.10 considers how we might implement an RDM that requires only limited updating with a WORM device; beyond this, this text will not consider WORM devices.

7.3 ORGANIZING BLOCKS INTO FILES AND SYSTEM-LEVEL CONSIDERATIONS

Building a File

A block is the atomic data construct of an external memory device. Most users and user programs have no control over the block size, which, in general, is determined by system software and hardware configurations. Within the constraints of a predetermined block size, user programs can use the ReadBlock and WriteBlock operations to build rather sophisticated implementations of higher level ADTs. Typically, an application utilizes an external memory device by aggregating one or more blocks into **files.** For example, in a typical RDM implementation, each table scheme corresponds to a file, and the tuples of a table scheme instance correspond to **data records** within the file.

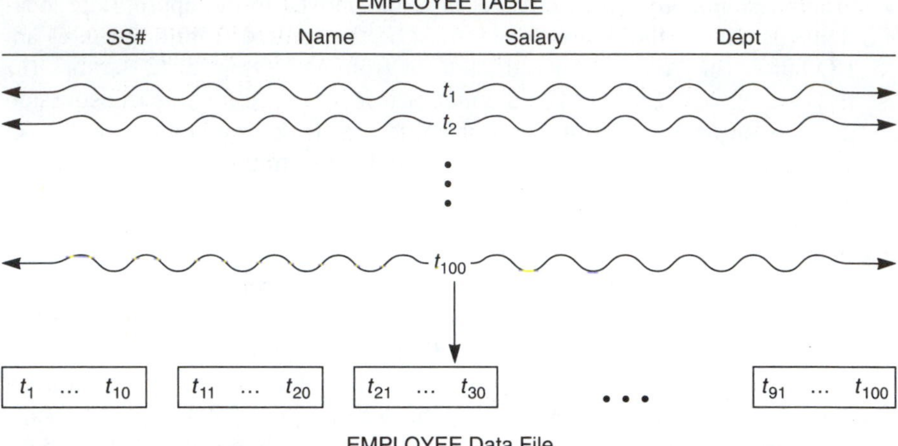

Figure 7.4 Tuples mapping to blocks

Figure 7.4 depicts the disk storage of a file. We see from the figure that several data records are stored in one disk block, with the number of records per block depending on the block and record sizes. Usually, the records from only a single file are stored in any single block, and the records are aggregated into blocks so that no record spans two blocks. Of course, if the record size exceeds the block's size, the latter restriction must be lifted.

We see also from Figure 7.4 that a file may be spread over a collection of disk blocks that are not physically contiguous. This observation brings us to the important issue of memory management. Our model of external storage assumes the existence of the following two additional operators:

```
Allocate(c,i)
  { Request c physically contiguous blocks. i is returned such that block
    numbers i, i+1, . . . , i+(c−1) are allocated by the system for use by the
    calling program. }
DeAllocate(i)
  { Deallocates block number i. This block is returned to the system and later
    may be reallocated by the system. }
```

Note that when a program makes the call Allocate(c,i), the blocks allocated are not automatically transferred into I/O buffers for immediate use by the program; rather, the only effect of the call is to *reserve* the blocks for future use by the program. It is the responsibility of the program to keep track of the blocks allocated to it and to use them as it requires.

To illustrate the use and effects of the Allocate operation, we consider two procedures, each of which reads (e.g., from a data entry terminal) a sequence of tuples and stores them in an external file. It is assumed that the calling program has used the CreateBuffer operation to create for the procedure's use at least one program buffer B.

```
procedure ContigFile(size, firstblock, lastblock, success)
  { Create a file over contiguous blocks of external storage to store the input
    tuples. Parameter size estimates the number of blocks required—if this
    number is not sufficient, success is returned false and returned true
    otherwise. Parameter firstblock returns the address of the first block of the
    resulting file, and parameter lastblock returns the address of the last block. }

  { Initialize }
  Allocate(size,firstblock)
  initialize buffer B to empty
  moreblocks ← true
  curblocknum ← firstblock

  while (more tuples to process) and (moreblocks)
    read the next tuple t
    if (Buffer B is not full)
      append to buffer B the tuple t
    else
      WriteBlock(curblocknum,B)
      if (curblocknum < (firstblock+size−1) )
        curblocknum ← curblocknum + 1
        initialize buffer B to empty
        append to buffer B the tuple t
      else
        moreblocks ← false
      endif
    endif
  end while

  if (more tuples to process)
    success ← false
    { return address of last block of the incomplete file }
    lastblock ← curblocknum−1
  else
    WriteBlock(B, curblocknum)
    lastblock ← curblocknum
    success ← true
    { DeAllocate any remaining blocks }
    for i: = lastblock+1 to (firstblock+size−1)
      DeAllocate(i)
  endif
end ContigFile
```

Assuming that *size* blocks suffice to hold all the tuples that must be read, the procedure segment creates a file spread over physically contiguous blocks of storage, as is depicted in Figure 7.5. To process the tuples in this file, we use a loop of the following form:

```
for blocknum: = firstblock to lastblock
  ReadBlock(blocknum,B)
  process tuples in buffer B
end for
```

Because the file is spread over contiguous blocks of storage, the delay due to disk head movement that is incurred in the course of sequential file processing

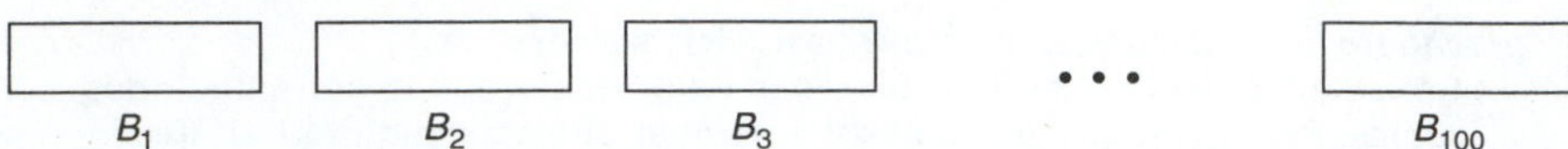

Figure 7.5 Contiguous blocks file

(as illustrated previously) is minimized. Unfortunately, it is not always possible to ensure that a file is spread over contiguous blocks of storage. If, for example, the initial invokation of procedure ContigFile is unable to complete the processing of the input tuples (because *size* blocks did not suffice), any subsequent calls to Allocate would almost certainly allocate blocks not adjacent to the original group of *size* blocks. The problem is compounded in a database environment, where blocks continually must be added to and deleted from a file (e.g., as tuples are added to and deleted from RDM tables). Generally speaking, we rarely are able to store a file over physically contiguous blocks of storage and, hence, require a more flexible scheme for storing our data.

Our strategy for developing such a flexible scheme is to use pointers to organize "randomly" located blocks into a file. Initially, our scheme will use pointers to organize blocks into a linear structure; in the following chapters, we shall consider more complex structures, such as trees. The scheme requires that we reserve enough space at the beginning of each block for a NextBlock pointer field. We use the expression *B*[NextBlock] to reference this field of the block residing in buffer *B*. The contents of the NextBlock pointer field of block number *i* is simply the number of the block that follows block *i* in the file. The constant NIL is any integer (e.g., 0) that is not a valid block number and is used to indicate that a pointer field points to no block. Under these conventions, the following procedure is an alternative to procedure ContigFile:

```
procedure FragFile(firstblock)
  { Create a file over scattered blocks of external storage to store the input
    tuples. Parameter firstblock returns the address of the first block of the
    resulting file. The NextBlock field of the last block of the file is set to NIL. }

  { Initialize }
  Allocate(1,firstblock)
  initialize buffer B to empty
  B[NextBlock] ← NIL
  curblocknum ← firstblock

  while (more tuples to process)
    read the next tuple t
    if (buffer B is not full)
      append to buffer B the tuple t
    else
      Allocate(1,newnum)
      B[NextBlock] ← newnum
      WriteBlock(curblocknum,B)
      curblocknum ← newnum
      initialize buffer B to empty
      B[NextBlock] ← NIL
      add to buffer B the tuple t
```

```
      endif
    end while
    WriteBlock(curblocknum,B)
  end FragFile
```

This procedure in general results is a **fragmented** file, as is depicted in Figure 7.6. To process the tuples in such a file, we use a loop of the form

```
blocknum ← firstblock
while (blocknum ≠ NIL)
  ReadBlock(blocknum,B)
  process tuples in buffer B
  blocknum ← B[NextBlock]
end while
```

Because of the hardware characteristics of a disk, sequential processing of a fragmented file is somewhat slower than for a physically contiguous file. In most contexts, however, the difference is not significant, and the flexibility afforded by pointers is essential for many applications.

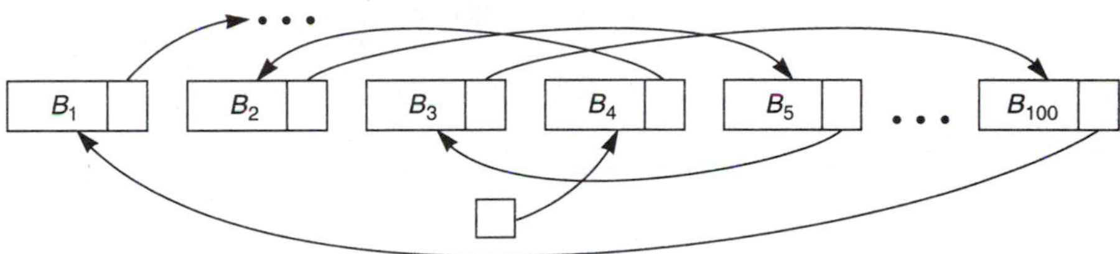

Figure 7.6 Fragmented file

7.4 SORTING A DISK FILE

The chapters that follow explore complex organizations of disk blocks into file structures and complex algorithms for operating on these file structures. Often, sorting must be performed as a subtask in support of these file structures and algorithms. For example, many file structures require that a data file be sorted as part of the structure's initialization or maintenance. In query processing, it is often beneficial as part of the implementation of a relational Join operation to sort one or both operand relations on the Join attributes. In this section, we develop an algorithm that can be used to sort a disk file, emphasizing how the algorithm coordinates calls to ReadBlock and WriteBlock and how hardware and system software constraints limit our options for implementing the algorithm as well as offering considerations for selecting the best implementation subject to these constraints.

The specification of our sorting problem is as follows. Disk file F contains R data records that we wish to sort on the field *Keyfield*. The sizes of a data record and of a block are such that M records fit per block, and thus, the file is spread over N = ceiling(M/R) blocks. For simplicity, we shall assume that M/R is integral, that the blocks of F are physically contiguous, numbered $F + 1, \ldots, F + N$, and that N physically contiguous blocks, numbered $S + 1, S + 2, \ldots, S + N$, are available for our use as a "scratch file." We further assume that the sorting program has created a private reserve of three I/O buffers, each capable of holding a single block of M records.

Before developing our sorting algorithm, it is instructive to note why the problem as described cannot be solved directly by application of the techniques typically employed to sort an internal data structure such as an array. The difficulty inherent in our problem results from the fact that at any one time we can fit only a very small fraction of the records to be sorted in internal memory. Therefore, a sorting technique must be developed that can complete the task while operating on only small pieces of the file at any one time. If the reader reviews the standard sorting techniques (e.g., Bubble sort, Heapsort, Insertion sort, Mergesort, and Quicksort), he or she perhaps will reach the conclusion that the strategy of Mergesort holds the most promise of being successfully modified to meet the constraints of the external sorting problem.

Recall that a key step in the Mergesort algorithm is the merging of two independently sorted lists into a single, sorted list. Suppose, for example, that L_1 and L_2 are sorted arrays as shown in Figure 7.7 and that we wish to combine the records of this array into a single sorted array L_3. The following simple procedure performs the merge.

```
procedure Merge(L1, L2, L3)
  cur1 ← 1
  cur2 ← 1
  cur3 ← 1
  while (cur1 ≤ | L1 |) and (cur2 ≤ | L2 |)
    if (L1[cur1] ≤ L2[cur2])
      L3[cur3] ← L1[cur1]
      cur1 ← cur1 +1
    else
      L3[cur3] ← L2[cur2]
      cur2 ← cur2 +1
    endif
    cur3 ← cur3 + 1
  end while
  { At this point, exactly one of L1 and L2 has elements which remain to be
    copied. }
  append to L3 any remaining elements from either L1 or L2
end Merge
```

Consider two important characteristics of this Merge algorithm. First, if there are a total of v values in lists L_1 and L_2 combined, the algorithm requires $O(v)$ time. Second, the algorithm operates by inspecting only the *leading edge* of each list. That is, at any point in the algorithm's execution, only the values of $L_1[\text{cur}_1]$ and $L_2[\text{cur}_2]$ are relevant to determining the algorithm's next action. These two characteristics of algorithm Merge give us hope that it can form the basis of an efficient sorting algorithm capable of operating within the constraints of our external sorting problem.

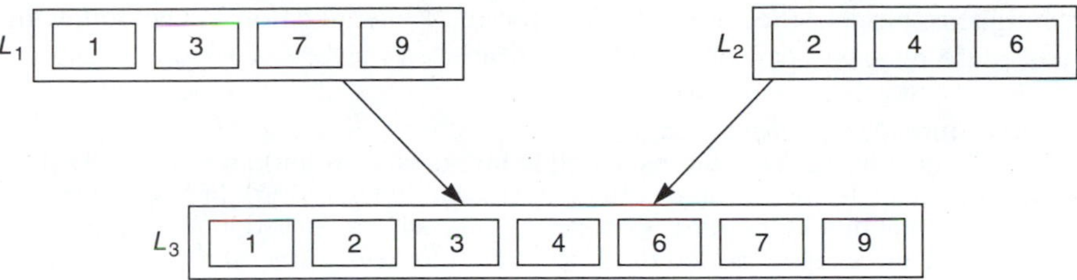

Figure 7.7 L_1, L_2, L_3 for Mergesort

Suppose now that L_1 and L_2 are each a list of records sorted on *Keyfield* and stored, respectively, in blocks B_1 and B_2 of external storage. We wish to merge these lists into a list sorted on *Keyfield* and stored in blocks B_3 and B_4. Suppose that the sorting program has created three buffers, which we denote as In_1 and In_2 (these buffers will be used for input) and Out (this buffer will be used for output), as illustrated in Figure 7.8. Since the contents of the program's buffers are accessed as an array of records, the strategy of the Merge procedure can be applied as follows to merge the pair of blocks:

```
ReadBlock(B₁, In₁)
ReadBlock(B₂, In₂)
Merge into buffer Out buffers In₁ and In₂ one record at a time, at each step
  comparing the Keyfield of the leading records of the input buffers
When buffer Out fills, WriteBlock(B₃, Out)
Merge into Out remainder of buffers In₁ and In₂
WriteBlock(B₄, Out)
```

Note that, after each merge step, we must check if buffer Out is full. When Out becomes full, we "flush it" by writing its contents to block B_3 and then continue merging as before.

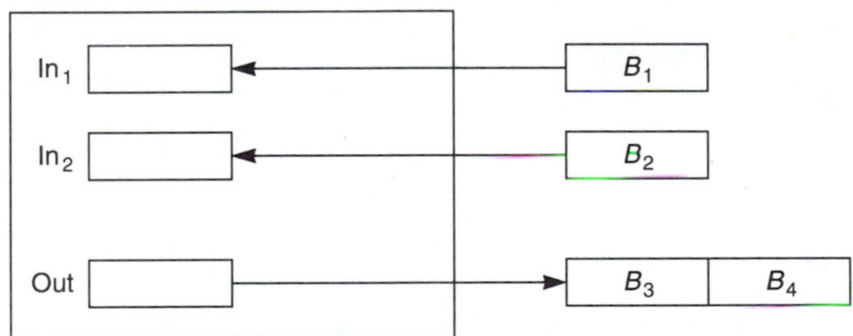

Figure 7.8 In_1, In_2, Out, and blocks to be sorted

We can generalize this technique to obtain an algorithm that merges two large collections of sorted records, each stored over many blocks of external storage. The term **sorted run** refers to a sorted collection of records stored in two or more blocks of storage. In general, these blocks need not be physically contiguous, but for simplicity we shall assume that our sorted runs are over contiguous blocks. (See exercise 7.7 for the generalization.) The following procedure merges a pair of sorted runs of arbitrary size:

```
procedure MergeRuns(s1,n1,s2,n2,b)
  { Merge a pair of sorted runs stored in blocks s1. . .(s1+n1) and s2. . .(s2+n2)
    into a single sorted run stored in blocks b. . .(b+n1+n2+1). In the special
    case that one of the runs is empty, n1 or n2 will be passed in as −1; in this
    case, the resulting sorted run is stored in blocks b. . .(b+n1) if n2 = −1 or
    blocks b. . .(b+n2) if n1 = −1. It is assumed that the program buffers In1, In2,
    and Out have been created and that the destination disk blocks have been
    allocated. }

  { curblock1 and curblock2 indicate the blocks of the runs contained in buffers
    In1 and In2 }
  curblock1 ← s1
  curblock2 ← s2
  ReadBlock(s1, In1)
  ReadBlock(s2, In2)

  { outblock indicates the block to which the current contents of buffer Out is to
    be written }
  outblock ← b
  Initialize buffer Out to empty

  while (curblock1 ≤ (s1+n1)) and (curblock2 ≤ (s2+n2))
    select the smaller leading record of In1 and In2 and append it to Out

    if Out is full
      WriteBlock(outblock, Out)
      outblock ← outblock + 1
      set buffer Out to empty
    endif
    if (In1 is exhausted)
      curblock1 ← curblock1 + 1
      if (curblock1 ≤ (s1+n1) )
        ReadBlock(curblock1, In1)
      endif
    else if (In2 is exhausted)
      curblock2 ← curblock2 + 1
      if (curblock2 ≤ (s2+n2) )
        ReadBlock(curblock2, In2)
      endif
    endif
  end while
  { At this point, exactly one of the runs is exhausted }
  append any remaining records from buffer Out and the remaining run to
  the output blocks, starting with block outblock
end MergeRuns
```

Not yet addressed by our development of the external sorting algorithm is how to create the sorted runs to be merged initially and how to sequence the subsequent merges. In an internal application, Mergesort is often implemented as a recursive algorithm. In an external application, however, it is more natural to implement Mergesort in an iterative, bottom-up fashion. The following describes at a high level an external Mergesort algorithm.

```
procedure Mergesort(F,S,N)
  { Sort the file in blocks F+1,F+2,. . .,F+N. Blocks S+1, S+2, . . . , S+N are
    available for use as a scratch file. It is assumed the three buffers, In1, In2,
    and Out, have been created for use by the the procedure. For simplicity, we
    assume that N is divisible by 3. }
  { PHASE I: Create initial sorted runs.
      Initially we don't distinguish between input and output buffers local to the
      program. }
  { Read in three blocks at a time, use an internal sorting algorithm to sort
    these blocks, and then write out the resulting three-block sorted runs. }
  for i: = 0 to ( (N/3) - 1 )
     ReadBlock(F+(3*i)+1, In1)
     ReadBlock(F+(3*i)+2, In2)
     ReadBlock(F+(3*i)+3, Out)
     Use an internal sorting algorithm to sort the records in the buffers In1, In2,
        and Out
     WriteBlock(F+(3*i)+1, In1)
     WriteBlock(F+(3*i)+2, In2)
     WriteBlock(F+(3*i)+3, Out)
  end for
  { Blocks F+1, . . . , F+N are now partitioned into N sorted runs of size three
    blocks each }
  { PHASE II: Merge runs }
  runsize ← 3
  BaseSou ← F
  BaseDes ← S
  while (runsize < N)
     { Merge pairs of runs of size runsize to create runs of size 2*runsize. The
       last run may be shorter than runsize (it may even be empty), in which
       case the last run created will be shorter than 2*runsize. }
     runstart1 ← BaseSou+1
     runend1 ← (runstart1+runsize-1)
     runstart2 ← (runstart1+runsize)
     runend2 ← min{ N, (runstart2+runsize-1) }
  while ( runstart1 ≤ N )
     MergeBlocks(runstart1, (runsize-1), runstart2, (runend2 - runstart),
                   ((BaseDes+1) + (( BaseSou+1) - runstart1)) )
     runstart1 ← runend2+1
     runend1 ← min{ N, (runstart1+runsize-1) }
     runstart2 ← (runstart1+runsize)
     runend2 ← min{ N, (runstart2+runsize-1) }
  end while
  runsize ← 2*runsize
     { We now have runs of size runsize }
     BaseTmp ← BaseDes
     BaseDes ← BaseSou
     BaseSou ← BaseTmp
  end while
  if (BaseSou=S) then
     copy contents of blocks S+1. . .S+N to F+1. . .F+N
  endif
end Mergesort
```

Analysis of Mergesort

We now analyze the efficiency of the Mergesort algorithm, focusing first on the required number of block accesses.

The Mergesort algorithm consists of two phases: Phase I performs the internal sorts that create the initial runs of size three blocks each, and Phase II performs a series of merges until a single sorted run is created. The number of block accesses required to complete each Phase is as follows:

Phase I: Each of the N blocks must be read and written exactly once.
Total for Phase I: $2N$ block accesses.

Phase II: At each pass (i.e., iteration of the **while** loop), each of the N blocks is read and written exactly once, for a total of $2N$ block accesses. The effect of each pass is to halve the number of sorted runs (approximately, ignoring round off); the algorithm terminates when there is a single sorted run. Since the number of initial sorted runs is $N/3$, the number of passes is approximately $\log_2(N/3)$.
Total for Phase II: approximately $2N * \log_2(N/3)$ block accesses.

Total for Mergesort: approximately $2N + [2N * \log_2(N/3)]$ block accesses.

We now consider whether anything can be done to speed up the algorithm. The problem definition, as presented earlier, severely constrains our options. In particular, the fact that the sorting program has available to it only three I/O buffers restricts us to a *two-way* Mergesort in which each Phase II pass merges *pairs* of sorted runs. Suppose, however, that the number of I/O buffers is somewhat flexible. We consider two different types of variations in the specification of the sorting problem:

1. Additional program buffers can be allocated to the sorting program. This assumption is reasonable if the sorting program has allocated to it a certain fraction of the computer's internal memory. If system administrators determine that it is necessary to enhance the efficiency of the sorting program, this fraction can be increased.
2. The sorting program already has allocated to it the maximum possible amount of internal memory, but it is possible to tailor the block size to enhance the efficiency of the sorting program. This assumption is reasonable if, for example, the sorting program is a "system program" that already uses all available internal memory. (Perhaps in this case, the system buffers and the ADT program buffers are one and the same.) Further, if the sorting program is a critical system program, it is reasonable that we can redefine the block size (which is often a software parameter) to enhance sorting. Note that, if we reduce the block's size, we will be able to increase the number of I/O buffers available to the sorting program while respecting the hardware constraints on the availability of internal memory.

We consider the sorting algorithm under each of these problem modifications in turn.

Additional Program Buffers: Suppose that we can make available to the sorting program $K + 1$ program buffers. Each buffer stills holds a single disk block, which still holds M data records. A K-way Mergesort is defined to merge collections of K sorted runs at each Phase II pass. To implement this strategy, the Merge algorithm must be modified. In particular, the Merge algorithm keeps the currently leading block of each of the K runs to be merged in one of its input buffers. To determine which record from the K runs is to be appended next to the output buffer, the leading record from each of the K input buffers must be compared. This modification is depicted in Figure 7.9.

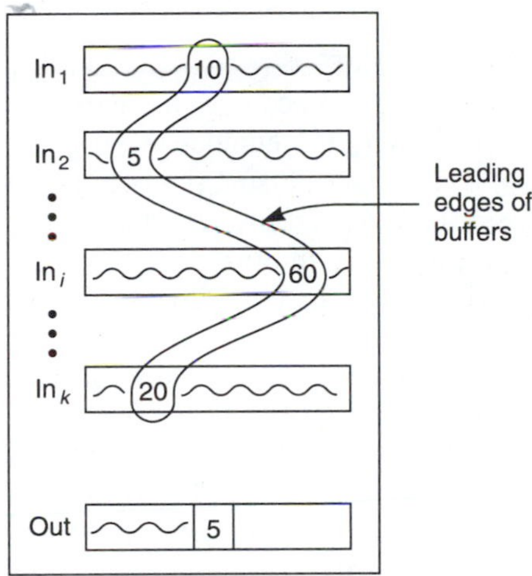

Figure 7.9 *K*-way merge

In addition to enabling K-way merging, the allocation to the sorting program of $K + 1$ buffers permits the Mergesort algorithm to create larger initial sorted runs. In particular, the algorithm creates $N/(K+1)$ initial sorted runs of size $K + 1$ blocks each.

The effect on the efficiency of Mergesort of these modifications is as follows:

Phase I: Each of the N blocks still must be read and written exactly once. Total for Phase I: $2N$ block accesses.

Phase II: Each Phase II pass still reads and writes each block exactly once. The number of passes, however, is reduced, both because the number of initial runs is $N/K + 1$ rather than $N/3$ and because each pass reduces by a factor of K (rather than 2) the number of sorted runs. Consequently, the number of passes is reduced to approximately $\log_K[N/(K + 1)]$.
Total for Phase II: approximately $2N * \log_K[N/(K + 1)]$ block accesses.

Total for K-way Mergesort: approximately $2N + \{2N * \log_K[N/(K + 1)]\}$ block accesses.

We observe that while the number of *block accesses* decreases as K increases, the time required to *merge* a collection of K runs increases with K, even when the total number of records within the collection of runs is held fixed. This is a consequence of the fact that at each step of the merge algorithm, K leading records must be compared. Hence, the time required by the algorithm to merge a collection of r records partitioned (approximately equally) into K sorted runs is $O(K*r)$. While the reduction in block accesses that results from increasing K typically far outweighs the increased time required for the merges, it should be noted that a minor modification to the merge algorithm in fact can decrease the sensitivity to K of the cost of the merge steps. As is described in exercise 7.5, a priority queue can be used to manage the leading records of the input buffers, yielding an $O(\log K*r)$ merge algorithm.

Redefining the Block Size: The preceding discussion illustrates that we can speed up Mergesort by increasing the number of program buffers made available to the program—it is not too surprising that we can speed up a solution by making available more resources. We now consider the scenario in which we have fixed resources (i.e., available internal memory) but flexibility in how to utilize these resources (i.e., we can tailor the block size to the sorting algorithm).

As before, let R be the number of data records in the file F to be sorted. Since the original statement of the problem specifies that we can allocate three I/O buffers of size M records each to the sorting program, $C = 3*M$ is the amount (measured in terms of the number of records of the type stored in file F) of buffer space that can be allocated to the sorting program. Hence, if we wish to perform a K-way Mergesort, we must partition this space into $K + 1$ I/O buffers of size $C/(K + 1)$ records each. Since the block size and the buffer size must coincide, the block size also is $C/(K + 1)$ records, and thus the number of blocks in file F is $R/[C/(K + 1)] = R*(K + 1)/C$. (These numbers are approximate, as we ignore rounding off to simplify the discussion.)

We now analyze the number of block accesses required to perform a K-way Mergesort in terms of these parameters:

Phase I: Each of the $R*(K + 1)/C$ blocks must be read and written exactly once. Note that Phase I produces R/C sorted runs of size $(K+1)$ blocks each.
Total for Phase I: approximately $2*R*(K + 1)/C$ block accesses.

Phase II: Each Phase II pass reads and writes each block exactly once. The number of passes is approximately $\log_K(R/C)$.
Total for Phase II: approximately $[2*R(K + 1)/C]* \log_K(R/C)$ block accesses.

Total for K-way Mergesort: approximately
$[2*R*(K + 1)/C] + [2*R*(K + 1)/C]*\log_K(R/C)$ block accesses.

We thus can write as a function of K the number of block accesses required by a K-way Mergesort, assuming a fixed internal memory capacity of C

records:

$$Accesses\ (K)=(2*R*(K+1)/C)\ +\ (2*R(K+1)/C)*\log_K(R/C)$$

Analysis of the function *Accesses* (K) reveals that the function is *monotonically increasing* in K (for $K \geq 1$). Thus, we can conclude that the number of block accesses required by a K-way Mergesort *increases with* K and, hence, a *two-way Mergesort minimizes the number of required block accesses*.

While choosing $K = 2$ minimizes the number of block accesses required by a K-way Mergesort, we must question—in light of the current problem specification—the appropriateness of *required number of block accesses* as the sole measure of an algorithm's efficiency. As we have stated, it is generally true that block accesses dominate the cost of an algorithm; however, it must be noted that, when comparing K-way Mergesorts for differing values of K, the block accesses performed by the different versions of Mergesort may not have equal cost. In particular, as K increases, the block size decreases, and we therefore must consider whether an access of a small block contributes to cost as much as an access of a large block. To answer this question, we recall the two constituents of the cost of a block access:

- *Access delay:* The time required to move the disk head to the appropriate location on the disk before the block can be read or written.
- *Transmission delay:* The time required to transmit the data from the disk to an I/O buffer or from an I/O buffer to the disk.

Generally speaking, access delay is relatively insensitive to block size, and hence the total access delay incurred by an algorithm can be estimated accurately by a function that is linear in the required number of block accesses, independent of the block size. In contrast, transmission delay is determined primarily by the number of bytes transmitted. We therefore conclude that, when comparing the efficiencies of algorithms that access blocks of differing sizes, the number of block accesses required is a good predictor of access delay but not necessarily of transmission delay. A better predictor of transmission in this context is *total number of bytes transmitted*. Hence, when considering the efficiency of K-way Mergesort, we should consider an expression of the form

$$I/O\_Time(K)=w_1*Accesses(K)\ +\ w_2*Bytes(K)$$

where *Accesses* (K) is as defined previously, *Bytes* (K) is the total number of bytes that must be transmitted by a K-way Mergesort, and w_1 and w_2 are constant weights that scale for the relative contribution to the cost of a block access of access and transmission delays. The appropriate values for these weights depend on the hardware characteristics (e.g., speed of head movement and bandwidth of the data channel) of the computer system of interest.

It is relatively straightforward to derive an expression for *Bytes* (K). Observe that, regardless of the block size, Phase I of a K-way Mergesort requires each byte of file F to be read and written exactly once. Similarly, each pass of Phase II requires each byte of file F to be read and written exactly once.

Hence, if B is the total number of bytes in file F,

$$Bytes(K)=2*B+2*B*(\log_K (R/C))$$

Note that *Bytes* (K) is *monotonically decreasing* in K, and, therefore, the terms *Accesses* (K) and *Bytes* (K) of *I/O_Cost* (K) exert competing effects on total cost. We conclude that the optimal value for K depends ultimately on the value of the weights w_1 and w_2, and, as indicated earlier, these values depend on the hardware characteristics of the computer system of interest. Exercise 7.6 further explores the problem.

SUMMARY AND ANNOTATED BIBLIOGRAPHY

This chapter introduces the basic model we shall use to build external memory implementations for the RDM. The chapter discussed the characteristics of, and interactions between, internal and external memory, described the role of program and system buffers, and illustrated how simple block operations (e.g., ReadBlock, WriteBlock, Allocate, and DeAllocate) can be used to construct and process data files. We presented an external sorting algorithm as a vehicle for illustrating many of the principles arising when interacting with external files. Additionally, as will be seen in later chapters, an efficient external sorting algorithm is of value in the context of many file structures and query optimization algorithms.

Chapters 8 and 9 describe how the primitives introduced in this chapter are used to form the complex external structures that are employed in the implementation of the RDM. Structures including ISAM, B-trees, hashed files, and multifile Join supports all are described and analyzed in terms of the primitives presented here.

Chapter 10 considers the topic of transaction management. Transaction management techniques in large part are necessitated by two of the characteristics required by a database system and provided by external memory: persistent storage that allows concurrent access. Section 1.5 provided a simple scenario illustrating that care must be taken if we are to allow multiple users simultaneous access to the same data. Further, while external memory's persistent nature (it survives most system failures) is one of its most important features, we must take care here too in order to ensure that the data stored in external memory can be made consistent with reality once the system is brought back after failure.

The book's final chapters consider query processing algorithms. These algorithms operate with respect to the file structures and transaction management techniques to be described in Chapters 8, 9, and 10, and their efficiencies are analyzed in terms of the number of block accesses they perform. We shall conclude that, by necessity, the query optimizer is a rather sophisticated collection of algorithms. Collectively, the material in Chapters 8 through 13 describe the central techniques of an RDM implementation, techniques that, to a large extent, determine the quality of the implementation.

EXERCISES

1. Discuss the advantages and disadvantages of external memory (e.g., a disk) relative to internal memory.
2. Identify real applications that require the characteristics of external memory and ones that potentially could be implemented in internal memory.
3. We have assumed the existence of procedures Allocate and DeAllocate. Describe a memory management package to support these operations.
4. Describe how a finite circular queue can be used to manage a paging strategy that is based on the time of last access of the blocks held in internal memory. Describe a more sophisticated paging strategy based on weighted usage; that is, a priority value is associated with each block of storage.
5. Describe how a priority queue can be used by the internal merge procedure of the Mergesort algorithm to mitigate the effects of increasing K.
6. The quantity $I/O\_Time(K)$ is defined at the conclusion of Section 7.4. Suppose that the parameters that define this quantity have the following values: $R = 100{,}000$; $B = 10{,}000{,}000$; $C = 100$; $w_1 = 1$; $w_2 = 10$. Find the value of K that minimizes $I/O\_Time(K)$.
7. Modify the Mergesort algorithm so that we can relax the assumption that blocks of the file to be sorted are contiguous.
8. Modify the Mergesort so that only one scratch file is required, but we overwrite the original file.
9. Modify the Mergesort algorithm so that it can operate on a file stored on a sequential-access tape. You may assume that several tape drives are available to the sorting algorithm.
10. Section 7.2 describes a class of memory devices known as WORM (write once/read many). While such devices are inappropriate for implementing highly dynamic RDMs (i.e., when Insert, Delete, and Modify operations are frequent), these devices may be appropriate when Update operations are rare. Describe how a WORM device could be used to implement an RDM under the assumption that Update operations are rare. *Hint:* Modifications to tuples must be implemented in a manner that does not require the overwriting of existing values.

CHAPTER 8

File Structures for an External Search Table

In this chapter, we consider external memory implementations for the ADT search table. This study leads us to several classic file structures, including ISAM, B-trees, and hashed files.

The primary objective of Chapter 2 was to define the search table and RDM ADTs. Additionally, Chapter 2 peeked behind the wall separating the definitions of these ADTs from their implementations by considering some basic internal memory structures and algorithms. This chapter and the next continue to explore implementations for these two ADTs, focusing on external memory implementations. Paralleling the presentation of Chapter 2, we first develop techniques for implementing a single search table, and then, in Chapter 9, we build on these techniques to develop implementations for the collection of search tables that comprise an RDM. The reader should keep in mind throughout these discussions that we are considering implementations for precisely the same two ADTs that were studied in Parts I and II of the book; what is new in Part III is the requirement that the data be stored in external memory.•

8.1 AN OVERVIEW OF SEARCH TABLE IMPLEMENTATIONS

The search table's definition includes the two relational operators Project ($\Pi_{<L>}$) and Select (σ_F) and the three Update operators Add, Delete, and Modify. Recall that Select is an extremely flexible operator in that its Boolean formula F can reference, in any logical combination, any attributes from the operand table. Further, this Boolean formula can specify range (e.g., $25 \leq \text{Age} < 50$), as well as exact match (e.g., Name = "Smith") conditions. This flexibility drove our development of internal data structures for the search table in Chapter 2. In particular, the need to support retrievals based on arbitrary combinations of attribute values led to the concept of indexing, while the need to support range qualifications was one of the factors leading to schemes that support efficient, ordered retrievals.

Before considering specific external search table implementations, it will be advantageous to review indexing and ordered retrievals and to consider some general consequences for these concepts of an external memory environment.

Indexing

In Chapter 2, we saw that the flexibility of the Select operator requires that a search table's data be organized in multiple ways. An initial, brute force implementation that was considered maintains multiple copies of the data, with each copy organized to efficiently support a particular type of selection, for example, a selection based on the value of a particular attribute. This implementation was rejected for most applications on the grounds that such redundancy introduces severe problems, including excessive memory requirements, excessive overhead when performing certain Update operations, and the potential that the copies of the data will become inconsistent with one another.

Indexing was introduced as a means of providing multiple organizations of a search table's data without maintaining multiple copies of the data. Recall from Chapter 2 that a dense index is a collection of index records such that there is a one-to-one correspondence between these records and the data records. Multiple organizations of the data is provided by maintaining multiple indices, each organized to support efficient retrievals based on the value of one of the search table's attributes. Under this scheme, there is only a single copy of the data records, and these records are maintained as a heap (i.e., no organization is maintained on the data records).

This indexing scheme is quite adequate for an internal memory environment. It provides efficient retrievals when selections are based on an attribute that is indexed, while mitigating many of the problems associated with maintaining multiple copies of the data. We shall discover shortly that indexing in an external environment has many of the same advantages as in an internal environment, as well as some important additional advantages. On the other hand, we shall also discover that the characteristics of an external environment mandate modifications to the indexing schemes as we have described them. For example, while ordered retrievals can be processed efficiently against an ordered index (e.g., a 2–3 tree) in internal memory, such retrievals in external memory may require that the data records be organized in a manner that reflects the required retrieval order. Ordered retrievals are discussed below.

As a final introductory remark regarding indexing, recall that in Chapter 2 we indicated that indexing induces several important optimization problems. Because indexing an attribute has both positive and negative effects on efficiency, an important problem in designing an implementation for a search table or RDM is choosing which attributes to index. A second type of optimization problem arises in query processing since a query optimizer, in general, has many options regarding which indices to utilize and how to utilize them in combination. These and other aspects of database design and query optimization are considered beginning in Chapter 9.

Ordered Retrievals

An ordered retrieval is a retrieval in which qualifying tuples are returned in some prescribed sequence that is based on the values of one or more attributes. The most common ordered retrieval returns tuples sorted on the values of some single attribute. Other ordered retrievals return tuples sorted on a concatenation of attribute values (e.g., Department · Salary), or based on an ordering different from a standard sort (e.g., ordered by a hash value). Unless otherwise specified, we shall take ordered to mean sorted on the value of a single attribute in the following discussions.

Observe that ordered retrievals cannot be specified within relational algebra or tuple calculus since expressions in these languages evaluate to sets of tuples, and sets, by definition, are unordered collections of elements. Ordered retrievals arise primarily in two contexts:

1. Many commercial query languages extend relational algebra and tuple calculus by allowing a Retrieve statement to specify an ordering on the tuples returned. This is a desirable facility since the user often requires that the result of a query be displayed in a manner convenient for human inspection.
2. Certain query processing algorithms require that they be able to efficiently access tuples in some prescribed order. The Merge join algorithm presented in Section 2.5 is an example of such an algorithm, requiring that the tuples of each operand table be accessed in order sorted on the Join attribute. A second example is found in range queries. A range query of the form $\sigma_{v \leq A \leq v'} T$ can be processed most efficiently if the tuples of T are stored physically sorted on attribute A; this organization minimizes the required number of block accesses. Generally speaking, the more efficiently tuples can be accessed in sorted order, the more efficiently a range qualification can be processed. Hence, we shall generally assume that processing algorithms for the range query $\sigma_{v \leq A \leq v'} T$ require an ordered retrieval.

Because of the importance of ordered retrievals, it is necessary to develop external implementations that support them efficiently. In Chapter 2, we considered the basic internal search table implementations with respect to how efficiently they support ordered retrievals and concluded that sorted arrays, sorted linked lists, and search trees provide efficient support for ordered retrievals while unsorted arrays, unsorted linked lists, and hashing schemes do not. More abstractly, we say that an internal memory implementation supports an ordered retrieval efficiently if the implementation provides a means of going directly (i.e., without searching) from the ith tuple in the order to the $(i + 1)$st tuple in the order. Note that the $(i + 1)$st tuple may be physically adjacent to the ith tuple (as in the sorted array), or it may be reachable from the ith tuple by following a pointer (as in the sorted linked list and search tree). In the context of internal memory, the difference in the efficiencies with which the physically ordered and logically ordered implementations support an ordered retrieval is of little significance.

In an external environment, the range of efficiencies with which the standard implementations support ordered retrievals is far wider than in an internal environment. The wide range of efficiencies in an external environment is a consequence of the relatively large expense of a block access. To illustrate, we consider the efficiencies with which several basic types of external implementations support ordered retrievals:

1. *Order is unsupported:* By this we mean that the data file is not physically ordered relative to the required retrieval order nor is there a logical structure (e.g., indices or interrecord pointers) on the data file that supports the ordered retrieval. In this case, an external sort must be performed on the data file as part of the ordered retrieval. Note that, in general, this sort must not alter the original organization of the data file since this organization may be required to support other processing tasks. Hence, the sort must either create a temporary sorted version of the data file or pipe the records to the algorithm requesting the ordered retrieval in sorted order (i.e., feed the records to the algorithm, without actually storing the records in sorted order); in the latter case, the result of the ordered retrieval is said to be an **ordered stream**.

2. *Order is supported logically:* By this we mean either that pointers chain together the data records in the required order or that an ordered index (e.g., a search tree) is imposed on the data file. While these schemes allow the $(i + 1)$st data record to be accessed from the ith data record by following pointers, in many contexts the support for ordered retrievals provided by these schemes is not adequate. This is so because, in general, the $(i + 1)$st data record will reside in a different block than will the ith data record. Therefore, the number of block accesses required for an ordered retrieval can approach the number of data records retrieved. In fact, when many data records are to be retrieved, it may be more efficient to ignore the ordered chain and instead sort the data file physically before processing the ordered retrieval, as described previously.

While a logically ordered data file does not efficiently support ordered retrievals in general, there are several important tasks requiring certain types of ordered retrievals that are supported efficiently by these organizations. One such task is the processing of a range query in which only a small number of tuples satisfy the qualification. In this case, once the first qualifying record is located, either an ordered chain or an ordered index can be used to efficiently locate the remaining qualifying records. Additionally, an ordered index efficiently supports an important variation of an ordered retrieval: an ordered retrieval in which only the values of the attributes on which the order is based need be retrieved. For example, the query "Retrieve, in sorted order, the salaries of all employees" can be processed, without accessing any data records, simply by traversing an ordered index on salary. Further, as we shall see in Chapter 11, one important variation of the Merge join algorithm requires that we visit the values of the Join attribute of each operand table in sorted order.

3. *Order is supported physically:* The organization of choice for supporting ordered retrievals of data records stores the records in a manner that physically reflects the required retrieval order. There is a range of degrees to which the physical organization may reflect the required retrieval order, and the closer

the correlation, the more efficiently is the ordered retrieval supported. The possible physical organizations include:

a. Ordered over contiguous blocks. As is defined in Chapter 7, a pair of blocks is contiguous if the blocks are physically "adjacent" in the sense that the disk head can move directly from one block to the other without passing over any other blocks. Let $B_1, \ldots, B_i, \ldots, B_N$ be a numbering of data file F's blocks such that block B_i is physically adjacent to block B_{i+1}, for $1 \leq i \leq N - 1$. We say that data file F is **ordered over contiguous blocks** (with respect to some specified ordering of the file's records) if all records in block B_i precede in the record ordering all records in block B_{i+1}, for $1 \leq i \leq N - 1$. Such an organization allows ordered retrievals to incur minimal block access time: Each block needs to be accessed only once, and disk head movement is minimized between accesses. Note that we do not require the records to be ordered within a single block of a contiguously ordered file. While having the records ordered within a block would slightly speed an ordered retrieval, this savings, in general, is inconsequential relative to the overall time required for the ordered retrieval (i.e., generally, the time to sort a single block in internal memory is far less than the time to access that block).

b. Ordered over chained blocks. While storing a file ordered over contiguous blocks is the most efficient support for an ordered retrieval, maintaining such an organization in the face of Updates often is infeasible. An attractive alternative is to provide the order by chaining together the blocks using block pointers as described in Section 7.3. In this organization, every record in a block B precedes in the record ordering every record in the block that follows block B on the ordered chain. This structure supports ordered retrievals only slightly less efficiently than does the contiguous structure. Like the contiguous structure, each block is accessed only once. The added cost is incurred because the time to move the disk head from a given block to the next block on the chain generally is slightly greater than the time required to move the head to an adjacent block. This loss in efficiency, however, in most contexts is more than compensated for by the increased ease with which Updates can be handled.

c. Approximately ordered. In some contexts, a relaxation of the ordered chaining scheme may be desirable. Here, groups of k records consecutive in the required order are stored unordered within fixed-size neighborhoods of blocks, where a neighborhood generally is defined to be an interval of blocks on the chain small enough to simultaneously fit in internal memory. Under this scheme, an ordered retrieval is processed by reading into internal memory each neighborhood in turn, and performing an internal sort on the neighborhood's blocks. While each block still is accessed only once, the overhead for the internal sort may be of some significance. The advantages of this scheme over the basic ordered chain (scheme b) stem from the fact that it may reduce the movement of data records across blocks required by insertion algorithms.

d. Clustered on an attribute. A slightly different type of physical ordering is known as **clustered on an attribute**. Data file F is clustered on attribute A if, for each A value v occurring in the data file, the data records with A value v are spread over (approximately) the fewest possible number of blocks. For example, if k data records fit per block of a file clustered on attribute A and M records have an A value of v, all such records would be spread over approximately $CEIL(M/k)$ blocks. By specifying that the number of blocks required be only approximately equal to the theoretical minimum number, we allow some blocks not to have k records (e.g., for when deletions leave empty space) and we allow situations in which the $M < k$ records with some A value are spread over two blocks. Note that if a data file is ordered based on the values of attribute A, the file necessarily is clustered on attribute A. One motivation for clustering a data file on attribute A is to efficiently support a query such as $\sigma_{A=v} T$, when many records qualify. Since in some contexts it is easier to maintain a file clustered on an attribute than ordered on the attribute (see exercise 8.3), if exact match queries, rather than true range queries, are the motivation for the organization, clustering may be an appropriate choice. In the remainder of this chapter, we shall not again consider schemes that cluster, without ordering, a data file on an attribute; however, later chapters will consider clustered files, especially as an efficient structure for supporting certain join operations.

Two remarks are appropriate at this juncture. First, it should be apparent that only one type of ordered retrieval can be supported physically, unless we are willing to duplicate the data file. Second, physically ordering a file on a given attribute does not obviate the need for an index on that attribute. Note, for example, that an index on a physically ordered file is useful in processing exact match retrievals, as well as in locating the first qualifying record in a range query. This supporting index is useful also in maintaining the file's ordering in the face of insertions; that is, it is used to locate where in the data file a new record is to be inserted.

8.2 FILE STRUCTURE DESIGN: FOUR DIMENSIONS OF CHOICE

The physical ordering of a data file, along with the index on the attribute (or concatenation of attributes) on which the physical ordering is based, is called the **primary file structure;** each additional index into the data file, along with the data file, is called a **secondary file structure.** The design of the primary and secondary file structures is a critical task in the implementation of search tables and RDMs. We now begin to address this task.

Suppose that we wish to design a structure, either primary or secondary, to support processing based on the attribute A. There are a vast number of structures from which to choose, including those to be described later in this chapter, countless variations on these structures, and structures substantially different from anything we shall consider in this text. Despite the great diversity of file structures, it is possible (and useful) to classify them along four dimensions:

- Is the data file physically ordered on attribute *A*?
- Is the index on attribute *A* dense?
- Is the index on attribute *A* ordered?
- Are the records in the data file free to move about?

Specifying a decision along each dimension does not completely specify a file structure: There are, after all, far more than 16 possible structures. However, the decisions made along these dimensions go a long way toward determining the behavior and applicability of the structure with respect to a particular set of processing requirements. Therefore, it will be instructive to consider each of the four dimensions of choice, in the abstract, before discussing specific file structures.

Is the Data File Physically Ordered on Attribute *A*?

This dimension of choice determines whether or not the data file's primary structure is to be based on attribute *A*. Section 8.1 discussed some of the motivations for physically ordering a data file on one of the attributes (or on a concatenation of attributes) and described three physical ordering schemes. Those three schemes share the following property, which we use to define the generic term **physically ordered.** The definition is implicit with respect to some particular sequence based on attribute *A* (e.g., sorted on attribute *A*).

> **Definition 8.1** A data file is **physically ordered** on attribute *A* if the records in the data file can be retrieved in a sequence ordered on *A* while accessing each block in the data file only once.

The definition generalizes, in the obvious way, to data files ordered on a concatenation of attributes, such as Department · Salary.

Since a file can be physically ordered on only one attribute (or concatenation of attributes), we must carefully consider the anticipated processing requirements before choosing a primary file structure. Factors that would lead us to choose a primary structure based on attribute *A* include

- Frequent retrievals specifying that tuples are to be returned in a sequence ordered on attribute *A*.
- Frequent retrievals based on a range qualification of the form $V \leq A \leq V'$, such that many tuples qualify.
- Frequent Joins with *A* as the Join attribute, such that many tuples are in the resulting table.

In some situations, it is reasonable not to physically order a data file on any attribute. The motivation for this decision is that an unordered data file is easier to maintain in the face of Updates than is an ordered data file. Hence, if updates are frequent relative to operations such as those listed earlier, it may be desirable to maintain only secondary structures for the data file in question.

Is the Index on Attribute *A* Dense?

In Chapter 2, we defined a **dense index** on attribute A to be a collection of index records that is in one-to-one correspondence with the data records. If data record R has value V for attribute A, then the corresponding index record is (V,p), where p is a pointer to the location at which record R resides. In internal memory, a pointer is typically an array subscript or a value from a programming language's data type that is used to represent a record's address. Later, we discuss various options for implementing in external memory a record pointer.

While a dense index is a very useful and common structure, other types of index structures are important as well. A **sparse index,** for example, is another useful type of structure. Like a dense index, a sparse index on attribute A is a collection of records of the form (V,p). Unlike a dense index, there is a one-to-many correspondence from index records to data records; that is, each index record corresponds to many data records. For example, suppose that the records of a sparse index are

$$(V_1,p_1), \ldots, (V_n,p_n)$$

with $V_1 < V_2 < \cdots < V_n$. A common sparse indexing strategy is for index record (V_i,p_i) to correspond to all data records with a value V for attribute A such that $V_i < V \leq V_{i+1}$. Pointer p, rather than being a pointer to a single data record, is a pointer to the collection of data records with an A value falling within this range. For example, p might be the number of the block that contains the corresponding data records, or it may be the pointer to the first of a list of several blocks containing these records.

Is the Index on Attribute *A* Ordered?

We say that a dense index is an **ordered index** on attribute A if it supports the efficient retrieval, in a specified order, of the A values of the data records. The term *efficient,* in this context, is generally taken to mean that each block of the index is accessed only once and that the data file is not accessed at all. Such an index could be used to process efficiently a query such as "Retrieve, in sorted order, the salaries of all employees" and supports an important version of the Merge join algorithm.

We make two observations regarding this definition of an ordered index:

1. The definition specifies that an ordered index must be dense. Note that if an index is not dense, it could not possibly be used to retrieve all values of the attribute in question without accessing the data file.

2. The requirement that an ordered index be capable of supporting the ordered retrieval of attribute values while accessing each block of the index only once is a bit strict and, in fact, whether a particular index structure meets this requirement may depend on certain characteristics of the computing environment. For example, whether or not the basic B-tree index structure introduced in Section 8.4 meets this requirement depends on the amount of available internal memory; if this amount is not sufficient, some blocks of the index may have to be accessed multiple times. Obviously, it is somewhat arbitrary that the definition of an ordered index requires that index blocks be accessed only once—structures that approximate this behavior are also useful for ordered retrievals of attribute values, and, in many contexts, such index structures can be considered to be ordered.

We reiterate that an ordered index, by itself, does not efficiently support general ordered retrievals of data records, that is, when the entire record is required. Such retrievals require a physically ordered data file.

Are the Records in the Data File Free to Move About?

A data record R is **pinned** if some other record points to record R and if this pointer to R specifies a location at which R is to be found. In this case, R cannot be moved to outside the location indicated by the pointer unless the pointer can be updated to reflect the change in location.

The concept of pinning is closely tied to the implementation of record pointers. We first distinguish between the two types of records that can contain a pointer to a data record R:

1. *Another data record:* In some search table and RDM implementations, a data record R' will point to data record R. R' may be in the same data file as R, or it may be in a different data file from R. For example, the scheme presented in Section 8.1 for logically ordering a data file utilizes pointers between records of the same data file, while some schemes for supporting the joining of two tables of an RDM utilize pointers between records of different data files.

Schemes that permit data records to point into a data file can lead to serious restrictions on the structure of that data file. If data record R should have to be moved (e.g., to maintain a physical ordering on the data file in the face of Updates), generally it is not feasible to locate all the data records that point to R, and, hence, it is not feasible to update all the pointers which point to R.[1] Therefore, when data records point into a data file, we are restricted to file structuring schemes that do not require movement of data records, except for

[1] The reader might consider using backpointers to address this problem. Such a solution is not as satisfactory as it first may appear—see exercise 8.2.

movement that can be tolerated without requiring pointers to be updated. Exactly how much movement of data records can be tolerated without requiring pointers to be updated depends on the nature of the pointers themselves; various options for implementing pointers are discussed later.

2. *A record in an index or other support structure*: Indices and other support structures (e.g., structures that support a Join on a particular attribute) generally contain records that point into the data file(s) on which they are defined. Typically, however, these pointers present far less of a problem than do pointers emanating from data records. Two factors combine to mitigate the problems: (*a*) The database system, as normal practice, keeps track of the support structures that point into each data file (otherwise, the query processor could not know to utilize the structures), and (*b*) given a data record, the record in a support structure that references that data record generally can be found quite efficiently. For example, consider a dense index I on attribute A into data file DF, and suppose that a data record R must be moved from its current location to a new location in DF. The index record in I corresponding to R can be located simply by searching the index for a record (V,p), where V is the value of R's attribute A and p points to R in its current location. This index record can be located quickly since the index is structured to efficiently support retrievals based on values of attribute A. Once R is moved to its new location, the pointer in the index record is updated to reflect the change.

While it is not unreasonable to update records in a support structure each time corresponding data records are moved, this overhead may somewhat negate the advantage of having the structure in the first place. Consequently, it often is desirable to employ, for at least some support structures, a pointer scheme that can tolerate the movement of data records without requiring that pointers be updated.

As the preceding discussion indicates, there are several options for implementing record pointers. Some types of pointers pin records in a very restrictive manner, other types give at least some freedom of movement, while one type of pointer gives complete freedom of movement. Following is a description of three common schemes, along with the advantages and disadvantages of each:

1. *Exact address pointers:* Under this scheme, a pointer p to record R is a pair (*Bn,Pos*), where *Bn* is the number of the block in which record R resides and *Pos* is the record's position within the block (e.g., in terms of bytes from the beginning of the block or the number of records preceding R in the block). If this scheme is used, following a pointer is very fast, but records are pinned to a particular location within a block and cannot be moved without updating all such pointers to them.

2. *Block number plus key:* Under this scheme, a pointer p to record R is a pair (*Bn,Key_val*), where *Bn* is as in scheme 1 and *Key_val* is the value of a set of attributes of R that forms a key (as defined in Section 5.4). Under this scheme, a pointer is followed by retrieving the indicated block and then

searching for the record in this block with the specified key value. Following a pointer under this scheme is almost as fast as under the exact address scheme, and records now are pinned to only a block rather than to a location within a block. However, it should be noted that (*a*) generally, there is little advantage in being able to move a data record within a block (e.g., recall that there is little to be gained from requiring an ordered data file to store records ordered within a block), and (*b*) the value of a key (which may be comprised of several attributes) could require far more storage than does the position indicator used in the exact address method.

3. *Logical key pointer:* Under this scheme, a pointer p to record R is simply *Key_val,* where, as in scheme 2, *Key_val* is the value of a set of attributes of R that forms a key. The pointer scheme assumes that there exists an index I into the data file on the attribute(s) that form the key and that a pointer is followed by using this index to retrieve the data record identified by *Key_val*. As we shall see in the sections to follow, such an index retrieval typically requires three or four block accesses, which makes following this type of pointer somewhat less efficient than following the previous two types of pointers. The advantage of this scheme, of course, is that records are not pinned at all—they can be moved anywhere without updating pointers of this type.

It should be noted that the records in the index I used as stated to follow a pointer cannot themselves employ logical key pointers. That is, this particular index must contain records of the form (*Key_val,p*), and p must be a pointer of one of the first two types described (or some similar pointer type). Thus, when a record in the data file is moved, the corresponding pointer in this index must be updated; however, locating this pointer is not a difficult task.

We now summarize the preceding discussion on pointers and pinning:

1. If a data file contains records that may be pointed to by other data records, we assume that it is not feasible to find and update these pointers. Consequently, records in such a data file can be moved only to a location that does not require pointer updates. If the pointers are implemented using either of the first two schemes, the records must remain within their original blocks; if the third scheme is employed, the records are free to move anywhere.
2. If the records in a data file contain records that may be pointed to only by records in a support structure (e.g., an index), we assume that it is feasible to find and update these pointers. However, the overhead of updating these pointers can be significant, and it therefore may be desirable to utilize logical key pointers in the records of at least some support structures.

In the following presentations of file structures, we shall generally assume that a pointer scheme that allows data records to move about freely is employed. From time to time, however, we shall consider the modifications that are necessitated by the use of more restrictive pointer schemes.

8.3 ISAM FILE STRUCTURES

ISAM stands for **indexed sequential access mechanism.** Variants of the ISAM file structure have been employed since the early days of file processing and remain important today. ISAM structures are relatively easy to implement and are particularly attractive when the dominant processing tasks require ordered retrievals of data records and when Updates are relatively infrequent.

ISAM is a primary file structure with a sparse index. That is, an ISAM file structure for attribute A (or collection of attributes) physically orders the data file sorted on attribute A and imposes on this data file a sparse index. We do *not* assume that the attribute(s) on which the ISAM structure is based form a key; that is, the query $\sigma_{(A=V)}T$ can evaluate to a set containing many tuples. Under the assumption that the attribute(s) on which the ISAM structure is based do form a key, the implementation described here can be simplified considerably (see exercise 8.8).

Figure 8.1 illustrates the general form of an ISAM file structure. The blocks comprising the data file are chained together in the sorted order; to support the chaining, each block contains a Next_Block pointer as depicted in Figure 8.1. It will also be convenient to assume that each block stores its own number in a field called Cur_Block. This allows, for example, the contents of a block to be read into a program buffer, modified, and then written out to the appropriate location on disk.

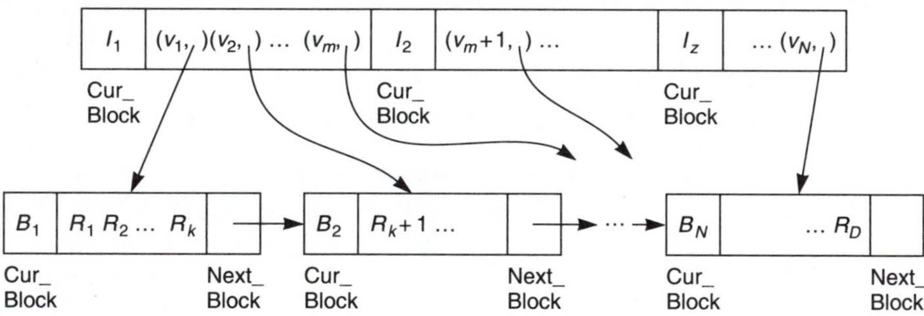

Figure 8.1 General form of an ISAM file structure

Suppose that the blocks which comprise the data file are numbered $B_1, \dots, B_N$, such that block B_{i-1} proceeds on the sorted chain block B_i, $2 \le i \le N$. The sparse index on attribute A will contain N records, each corresponding to one of the blocks of the data file. The index record corresponding to block number $B_i(2 \le i \le N)$ is of the form (V_i, B_i), where V_i is greater than or equal to the value of attribute A in all records in block B_{i-1} and is less than or equal to the value of attribute A in all records in block B_i. To simplify some of the algorithms, we assume further that the first index record (V_1, B_1) is such that V_1 is a value that is interpreted as being smaller than any value that might be compared to it; e.g., a special "null" value might play the role of V_1, which, by convention, is interpreted as being smaller than any value that is compared to it. It is important to observe that, under this definition of the index structure, index records are permitted to contain values V_i that do not appear in the data file. We therefore refer to the values in the index records as **separators** since the function of V_i is to separate for search algorithms the values of attribute A stored in block B_{i-1} of the data file from those stored in block B_i.

We make several additional observations regarding the structure of the sparse index. First, we generally would expect there to be far fewer index records than data records. If there are D data records and if k data records fit per block, the number of index records (which also is the number of blocks in the data file) is approximately D/k. Further, an index record is expected to be far smaller than a data record since it contains only a subset of the data record's attributes (often, a cardinality one subset) plus a block number. If $c * k$ index records can fit per block of external storage (where c is often 10 or more), the number of blocks that would be required to store the index file in external memory is approximately $|I| = (D/k)/(c * k) = D/(c * k^2)$. For small data files, $|I|$ may be only one or two, in which case we actually might decide to store the entire index in internal memory. Typically, however, $|I|$ is sufficiently large that we must store the index externally. Our presentation will assume that this is the case.

The index file is stored physically sorted on the values V_i of the separators. It is convenient to require that the index records be stored sorted within blocks and to require further that, whenever two separator values V_i and V_j are equal, the ordering of index records (V_i,B_i) and (V_j,B_j) reflects the ordering on the data file chain of blocks B_i and B_j. Observe that, under these conventions, the index record that corresponds to the ith data file block is also the ith record in the index file. It is convenient to assume also that, like data file blocks, each index file block stores its own number in a field called Cur_Block.

We initially assume that the index file is stored sorted over contiguous blocks. This assumption allows us to search the index directly by means of a binary search. To illustrate the search procedure, consider how we would use the ISAM structure to process the query $\sigma_{A=V}T$. The first step is to determine the largest integer $i(1 \leq i \leq N)$ with the property that the index record (V_i,B_i) is such that $V_i < V$. Observe that, by the definition of the ISAM structure, if the data file contains any records with A value equal to V, at least some of these records will reside in either block B_i or B_{i+1}, and none of these records will reside in blocks $B_1, B_2, \ldots, B_{i-1}$. In particular, if $V_{i+1} > V$, all qualifying records will reside in B_i, if $V_{i+1} = V$, at least some qualifying records (if there are any) will reside in either B_i, B_{i+1}, or both. If there are so many data records with A value equal to V that they are spread over several blocks of the data file, these records will appear in consecutive blocks of the data file's chain, beginning in either block B_i or B_{i+1}.

Consequently, once the integer i described earlier is determined, block B_i of the data file must always be accessed and searched for qualifying data records. Additional accesses to blocks that follow B_i on the chain also may be required. The search of the chain may stop at block B_j $(i \le j \le N)$ when either

1. B_j is found to contain at least one data record with an A value greater than V, or
2. Index record (V_{j+1}, B_{j+1}) is such that $V_{j+1} > V$.

We employ a binary search to efficiently determinc the largest integer i such that $V_i < V$. Algorithm SearchIdx searches a sparse index stored sorted over contiguous blocks. The algorithm returns the index record (V_i, B_i), where i is as described earlier, and returns in *IdxBl* the contents of the index block in which this index record is found. The algorithm is recursive and should be invoked initially with the numbers of the first and last blocks of the index file. By our conventions, the value V_1, which is in the first block of the index file, is such that $V_1 < V$ and, therefore, the required i exists with respect to the index file segment searched by the initial call, that is, the entire index file. Note, however, that the required i does not necessarily exist with respect to the segments searched by subsequent recursive calls—if a recursive call SearchIdx$(V,F,L,(V_i,B_i),IdxBl)$ is generated such that $V_j \ge V$ for all the index records V_j in blocks $F, \ldots, L$, the algorithm returns as its result the last index record (V_i, B_i) appearing in block $F - 1$. The reader should convince himself or herself that, in such a case, this is the correct outcome of the algorithm.

```
procedure SearchIdx(V,F,L,(Vi,Bi),IdxBl)
  { Search the index file segment stored sorted over blocks F,F+1,. . .,L for the
    largest integer i with the property that the index record (Vi,Bi) is such that
    Vi<V. Return the index record (Vi,Bi) and return in IdxBl the index block
    containing this index record. In the event that all the index records in blocks
    F,. . ., L are such that Vj≥V, return the last index record (Vi,Bi) appearing in
    block F−1 and return in IdxBl this block. Note that, by our conventions for
    the separator value V1, the latter case cannot occur if F is the actual first
    block of an ISAM's sparse index, and hence does not occur when the procedure
    is invoked with F equal to the number of this block. }
  M ← CEIL((F+L)/2)
  ReadBlock(Buff, M)
  if (Buff contains index records (Vr,Br) and (Vr+1,Br+1) such that Vr<V≤Vr+1)
    { Desired index record found }
    (Vi,Bi) ← (Vr,Br)
    IdxBl ← Buff
  elseif (Buff contains only index records (Vr,Br) such that V≤Vr)
    if (M=F)
      { This case cannot occur if F is the first block of the entire sparse index of
        an ISAM structure. }
      ReadBlock(Buff,M−1)
      Let (Vi,Bi) be the last index record in Buff
      IdxBl ← Buff
    else
      SearchIdx(V,F,M−1,(Vi,Bi),IdxBl)
```

```
      endif
    else
      { In this case, Buff contains only index record (V_r,B_r) such that V>V_r }
      if (M=L)
        Let (V_i,B_i) be the last index record in Buff
        IdxBl ← Buff
    else
      SearchIdx(V,M+1,L,(V_i,B_i),IdxBl)
    endif
  endif
end SearchIdx
```

The algorithm ExactMatch, which evaluates the expression $\sigma_{A=V} T$ against an ISAM file structure on attribute A, utilizes SearchIdx. The algorithm is written to create a stream STR of qualifying tuples. The stream can be used by the process that invokes ExactMatch to create a stored table corresponding to the expression's value, or it can be piped to another process (e.g., to a Join algorithm or to an algorithm that sends the result to an output device).

```
procedure ExactMatch(V,F,L,STR)
  { Create stream STR consisting of all tuples satisfying the exact match
    criterion A=V. F and L are the numbers of the first and last blocks of the
    sparse index of the ISAM file. }
  Set STR to empty
  SearchIdx(V,F,L,(V_i,B_i),IdxBl)
  B ← B_i
  DONE ← false
  while (not DONE)
    { Access data file }
    ReadBlock(Buff, B)
    Append to stream STR all records in Buff with A value = V
    B ← Next_Block pointer of Buff
    DONE ← ( (B = NIL)
               or (Buff contains at least one record with an A value greater
               than V))
  end while
end ExactMatch
```

An algorithm for evaluating the range query $\sigma_{V \leq A \leq V'} T$ against an ISAM file structure on attribute A can be written in a similar fashion. Like ExactMatch, Range is written to create a stream STR of qualifying tuples. Note that STR is guaranteed to be ordered on the A values of the qualifying tuples.

```
procedure Range(V,V',F,L,STR)
  { Create ordered stream STR consisting of all tuples satisfying the range
    criterion V≤A≤V'. F and L are the numbers of the first and last blocks of
    the sparse index of the ISAM file. }
  Set STR to empty
  SearchIdx(V,F,L,(V_i,B_i),IdxBl)
  B ← B_i
  DONE ← false
```

```
    while (not DONE)
      { Access data file }
      ReadBlock(Buff, B)
      Append to stream STR all records in Buff with V≤A<V', sorting within
      data blocks if necessary
      B ← Next_Block pointer of Buff
      DONE ← (B = NIL) or (Buff contains at least one record with A
                                      value > V')
    end while
  end ExactMatch
```

Summary of the Efficiencies of the ExactMatch and Range Algorithms: Each algorithm invokes SearchIdx to locate the block B_i of the data file that must be searched first. SearchIdx accesses at most $CEIL(\log_2 M) + 2$ blocks, where M is the total number of blocks in the index file. The number of data blocks then accessed depends on the number of records that qualify and on how these records are spread across blocks. Note, however, that at most two data blocks containing no qualifying data records will be accessed by either algorithm.

The processing against an ISAM file structure of updates is a bit more involved than is the processing of retrievals. First consider the implementation of the search table operation Insert(T,R), where table T is implemented as an ISAM file structure on attribute A and where the A value of R is equal to V. The first phase of the Insert algorithm identifies and retrieves the block of the data file in which the ExactMatch algorithms would first search for a record with an A value of V.

```
{ The sparse index is over blocks F,F+1, . . . , L }
SearchIdx(V,F,L,(V_i,B_i),IdxBl)
{ Note that i is such that V_i<V≤V_i+1 (or is N in case V≥V_N), and index record
  (V_i,B_i) is in IdxBl. }
B ← B_i
ReadBlock(Buff, B)
```

At this point, we attempt to add the new data record R to the block currently in *Buff*. This block might have room for a new data record as a result of previous deletions or as a result of a design decision not to completely fill blocks initially. (Deletions and initial "fill factors" are discussed later.) If there is space in the block in *Buff* for a new record, we simply insert R there and write *Buff* to disk. Observe that, by the way the block B read into *Buff* was chosen, the data file remains physically ordered and the index's separators remain valid.

Complications arise in the Insert algorithm when the block read into *Buff* by the preceding steps is full. When this occurs, we employ one of a host of alternative strategies in an attempt to avoid allocating a new block to the data file. Most implementations of Insert will read at least the next block of the data file into a second buffer and see if it has space for a new data record. That is, the following ReadBlock is attempted:

```
B' ← Next_Block pointer of the block in Buff
if (B' ≠ NIL )
  ReadBlock(B', Buff')
```

Assuming that B' is not NIL, we check the block in $Buff'$ for free space. If this block has space, existing records are redistributed between B and B' so that, after R is added and the buffers are written to disk, the data file remains physically ordered.

Following the redistribution, the index generally must be updated. For example, in Figure 8.2, we see that the value $V_{i+1} = 50$, which previously separated the A values in blocks B_i and B_{i+1}, is not a valid separator after the redistribution. To update the index, index record (V_{i+1}, B_{i+1}) must be located and modified. Note that the call

```
SearchIdx(V,F,L,(Vi,Bi),IdxBl)
```

issued at the beginning of the insertion process retrieved into *IdxBl* the block that contains record (V_i, B_i). Since the index file is sorted physically, record (V_{i+1}, B_{i+1}) will usually be in this same block. When this is not the case, the next block of the index file must be retrieved. Under our current assumption that the index is stored sorted over contiguous blocks, the block we require immediately follows the block contained in *IdxBl*. Thus, the number of the desired block is one greater than the value stored in the Cur_Block field of *IdxBl*. Once obtained, index record (V_{i+1}, B_{i+1}) is modified by replacing V_{i+1} with a value V'_{i+1} greater than or equal to all A values in block B_i and less than or equal to all A values in block B_{i+1}.

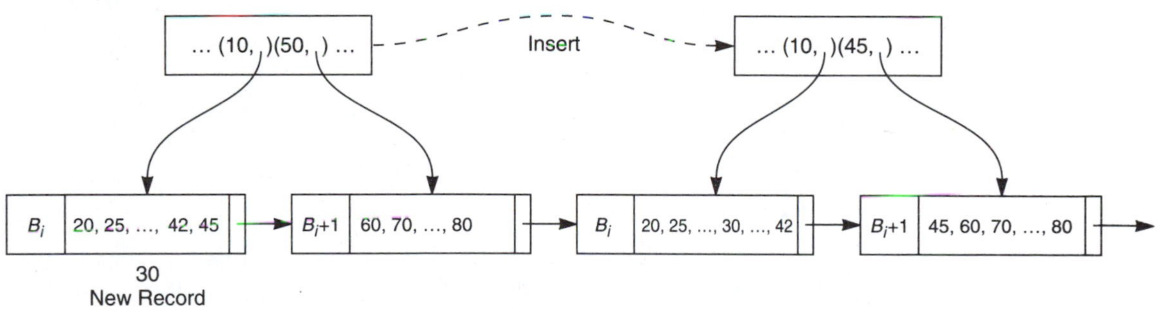

Figure 8.2 Distributing data records between two adjacent blocks

Of course, it is possible that both blocks B_i and B_{i+1} will be full. In this case, we must decide how many more blocks our implementation should check for free space before giving up and adding a new block to the data file. The implementation might check the block B_{i-1} that precedes block B_i in the data file (its identity can be obtained through the index), it might check several blocks following and preceding block B_i, or it might give up immediately after finding that block B_{i+1} is full. Most implementations do not look far beyond blocks B_{i+1} and B_{i-1} because doing so incurs a relatively large amount of work, both in the actual search for free space and in the subsequent redistribution of data records and the updating of the index file.

Whatever decision is made with regard to how many blocks to check for free space, our implementation must be able to handle the case where no free space is found. In this event, a new block B_i' is acquired from the operating system with the call

```
Allocate(B'i, 1)
```

Block B_i' then must be inserted on the data file's ordered chain between blocks B_i and B_{i+1} (see Figure 8.3). The Next_Block pointer of block B_i (which still is in *Buff*) is set to B_i'. A buffer *Buff'* is used to assemble the contents of block B_i'. The Next_Block pointer in *Buff'* is set to B_{i+1}, and records are distributed between *Buff* and *Buff'* so that all A values in *Buff'* are greater than or equal to those in *Buff*. Some implementations additionally distribute records between B_i, B_i', and other nearby blocks (e.g., B_{i+1} and B_{i-1}), especially if these blocks are in program buffers from when they were checked for free space. After the redistribution, the buffers containing the blocks that were modified are written to disk.

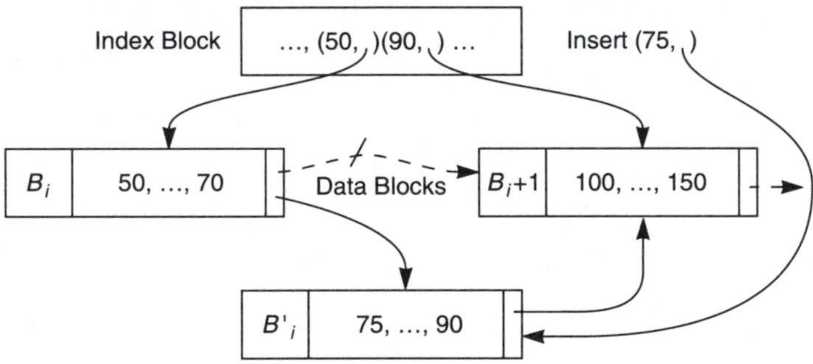

Figure 8.3 Insertion of new block into data file

The insertion of a new block into the data file requires that the index be updated in a manner not yet considered. After the data file is modified to accommodate the new block B_i' as just described, a new index record (V_i', B_i') must be created, where V_i' is greater than or equal to all A values in block B_i and less than or equal to all A values in B_i'. This new index record then must be inserted into the index file in a way that preserves the file's physical ordering. In particular, the new record (V_i', B_i') must be inserted between index records (V_i, B_i) and (V_{i+1}, B_{i+1}). This insertion of a new record into the index file can *almost* be handled by the procedure outlined earlier for the insertion into the data file of a new data record. After all, the index file, like the data file, is a physically ordered file. There is, however, a new twist. We have been assuming that the index file has two properties not applying to the data file: The index records are ordered *within* blocks, and the index file is stored sorted over *contiguous* blocks. The first of these properties can be maintained via minor changes in the insertion algorithm. However, the property that the file is stored sorted over contiguous blocks cannot be easily maintained when we encounter an insertion requiring that a new block be added to the index file. In general, the only way to preserve the property that the index file is stored sorted over contiguous blocks is to rewrite the entire index, including the new block, to a new set of contiguous blocks.

A strategy requiring that the entire index file be rewritten whenever a new block is added to it is feasible only when the index file occupies just a few blocks and only when Updates are rare. Hence, to address the more typical situation, we must rethink the requirement that that the index file be stored over contiguous blocks. The primary motivation for requiring that the index file be stored sorted over contiguous blocks was to support the binary search employed by the algorithm SearchIdx. Clearly, a binary search cannot be performed directly on a file in which the blocks are chained together in the sorted order since, in this case, there is no efficient means of locating the middle block at each recursive step of the algorithm. However, we can impose a secondary structure on a chained index file that allows the binary search to be performed "indirectly."

Figure 8.4 depicts a structure consisting of pointers to the N blocks of the index file. The structure stores only block pointers (i.e., block numbers) and is physically ordered over contiguous blocks (or over contiguous cells of an internal array if the structure is small enough) so that the pointer to the ith block in the index follows immediately the pointer to the $i - 1$st block in the index,

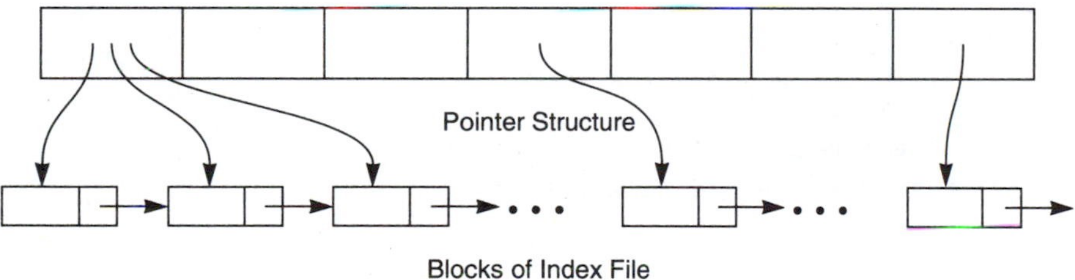

Figure 8.4 Structure supporting a binary search of a chained index file

$2 \leq i \leq N$. Note that block pointers can be allocated a fixed amount of storage (e.g., one or two bytes) and, since they are stored physically ordered, the location of the pointer to the ith index block can be calculated easily. The binary search of a chained index file therefore can be supported, requiring only minor modifications to the algorithm SearchIdx (see exercise 8.7).

Of course, when a new index block is added to the index file, a new block pointer must be added to the pointer structure in a manner that maintains the structure's physical ordering. The key observation is that, typically, the pointer structure is quite small and often can be stored in internal memory. For example, the pointer structure for an index file of 1,000 blocks (which, depending on data record and block sizes, might be sufficient to index millions of data records) requires only a few thousand bytes of storage. Even when the index file is so large that the pointer structure must be kept externally, it is unlikely that it will require more than a few blocks. Consequently, it is reasonable to rewrite the pointer structure whenever the addition of a new block pointer cannot be accommodated by the current structure.

This concludes our discussion of the basic Insert algorithm. We consider now an algorithm for implementing the search table operation Delete(T,($A = V$)), which requires that we remove from the search table T all tuples with an A value of V. As before, we assume that table T is implemented as an ISAM file structure on attribute A. The implementation of Delete is very similar to that of the retrieval operations. A procedure similar to ExactMatch is used to visit every block of the data file that might contain a record with an A value of V. In the case of the Delete operation, however, modifications must be made to the data file and index file to effect the removal of the matching records.

We consider now the required modifications. Suppose that as we inspect block B_i of the data file (which we have read into a program buffer), we encounter a record R with an A value equal to V. One way to remove this record is to overwrite its contents with some special null symbol. A more common method is to maintain a sequence of **deletion bits** at the beginning of each block of the data file, such that each bit encodes the status of one of the block's "record slots" (see Figure 8.5). By convention, the ith deletion bit is set to 0 to indicate that the block's ith record slot is empty—its contents are to be treated

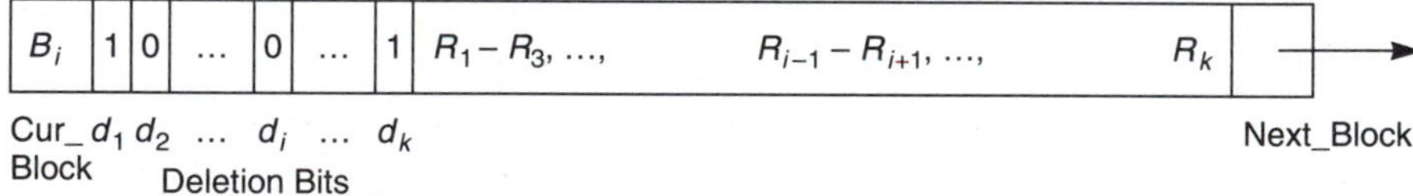

Figure 8.5 Data block with deletion bits

as garbage. Hence, each time the Delete algorithm finds a record it needs to delete, it sets to 0 the corresponding deletion bit. Similarly, the Insert algorithm can detect free space in a block by searching for a deletion bit set to 0. If such a bit is found, the Insert algorithm can insert a new record into the corresponding slot, provided that it then sets the corresponding bit to 1. (Recall that we currently assume the records of the file are not pinned; shortly, we consider the consequences of pinned records.) Search algorithms, of course, must ignore the contents of slots whose corresponding deletion bits are 0.

Observe that when a data record is deleted, the sparse index does not need to be updated, assuming that the block containing the record remains part of the data file. That we can avoid updating the index values in this case is one advantage of treating these values as separators rather than insisting that they be actual data values. When a deletion leaves a data block empty, we normally will want to remove the block from the data file chain and invoke procedure DeAllocate to return the block to the system for future use. In fact, if a deletion leaves a block sparsely populated, we may wish to combine the contents of this block with an adjacent block so that the block can be deleted. (In this case, separator values may need to be adjusted.) A block is removed from the chain as a node would be removed from any linked list. Observe that the Next_Block pointer of the record that precedes the block to be deleted must be adjusted; the identity of this block can be obtained from the index. Once the data block is deleted, the corresponding index record must be deleted as well. This is accomplished in a manner that closely parallels the deletion of the data record. Of course, when an index block is removed, the pointer structure depicted in Figure 8.4 must be updated.

> ***Summary of the Efficiencies of the Insert and Delete Algorithms:*** The Insert and Delete algorithms each calls SearchIdx, which requires at most $CEIL(\log_2 M)+2$ block accesses, where M is the total number of blocks in the index. The number of data blocks that must be read and written depends, in the case of Insert, on how many blocks are checked for free space and, in the case of Delete, on the number of records to be deleted and on how these records are spread across blocks. Additionally, certain insertions and deletions will require that separators in the index and block pointers in the pointer structure be updated, and, occasionally, they will require that the entire pointer structure be rewritten.

As a final comment on the basic ISAM Insert and Delete algorithms, we note that the algorithms, as presented, assume that the ISAM structure is used to initiate the Update. That is, the effected data records or record slots are located via the ISAM index. This is a reasonable assumption for the search table Add operation since this operation is given a record that contains values for all the table's attributes and since ISAM is a primary structure requiring that the data file be physically sorted with respect to the attribute it indexes. For the Delete operation, however, the situation is potentially different. For example, consider the operation Delete(T,($B = Y$)), where B is an attribute different from the attribute A on which the ISAM structure is based. In this case, an index on B, rather than the ISAM index on A, would be used to locate the data records to be deleted. Hence, the procedure for locating records based on values of attribute B must be coordinated with the segments of the ISAM deletion procedure that maintain the integrity of the ISAM index and data file. Similarly, of course, the ISAM insertion and deletion procedures must be coordinated with the segments of the procedures that maintain the integrity of any other indices that may be defined on the data file. In particular, other indices may need to be updated when data records are inserted, deleted, or moved.

ISAM Structures when Data Records Are Pinned

Our discussion of the ISAM structure has assumed that data records are free to move about the data file. For example, records must move across block boundaries as part of the Insert algorithm. We now consider the modifications to the structure that are necessary when pointers in other data records pin records in the ISAM data file to particular blocks.

Suppose that data records are pinned by other data records to their current blocks in an ISAM structure and that we attempt to perform an insertion. Once the Insert algorithm locates and reads into a program buffer the data file block B_i into which the new record should be inserted, we inspect the block for free space. If the block has space for the new record, we simply insert the record as before. However, if the block is full, we can no longer allocate a new block and redistribute the data records. One approach to dealing with this problem is to allocate a new block and, conceptually, hang it off of block B_i as part of an **overflow chain**.

Figure 8.6 depicts the overflow structure. Note that, while we depict the blocks on the overflow chain headed by B_i as being orthogonal to the ordered chain, the Next_Block pointers actually are set as if we had inserted these blocks into the ordered chain between blocks B_i and B_{i+1}. The two tangible differences in structure between the standard ISAM structure on attribute A and the structure with overflow chains are

1. No ordering is maintained on the data records that reside within an overflow chain. In general, the block on an overflow chain into which a new record is placed is determined by where there is room, not by the record's A value. This is in response to the restriction that records not be moved from one block to another.

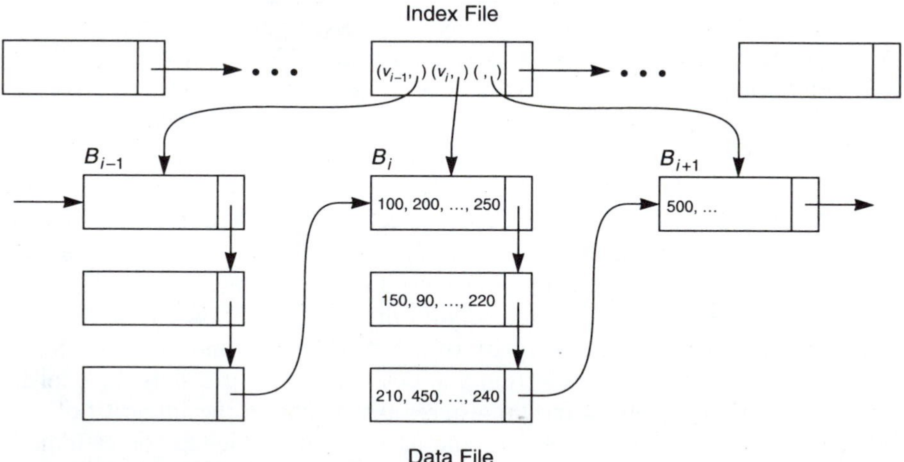

Figure 8.6 ISAM structure with overflow chains

2. The sparse index contains only one record corresponding to the collection of blocks on any one overflow chain. In particular, when a data block is full and a new block is allocated, the index is not updated in any way. In a sense, the block B_i and the overflow chain hung off block B_i form one large "virtual block," and all data records in this virtual block correspond to index record (V_i, B_i) and have A values V such that $V_i \leq V \leq V_{i+1}$, $1 \leq i \leq N - 1$. This implies, of course, that all data records in the virtual block headed by B_i have A values greater than or equal to all A values in the virtual block headed by block B_{i-1} and less than or equal to all A values in the virtual block headed by block B_{i+1}.

What is the effect of this modification on the efficiencies of the search table operations? The Retrieve and Delete operations may suffer considerably since, whenever the standard algorithms would need to search a block B_i, the modified algorithms must search the entire virtual block headed by block B_i. Another consequence for deletions of data records being pinned by other data records is that after record R has been removed from its slot in a block, this slot cannot necessarily be reused because other data records may still point to R. If these pointers are implemented with the exact address method (using a block number plus a position), a record that replaces R at a given position could erroneously be found at the end of such a pointer. To handle this situation, many implementations expand the meaning (and size) of the deletion "bit" so that it has three values: FULL, EMPTY, and REUSE. A value of FULL indicates that the corresponding slot contains a record that currently is present in the file. A value of EMPTY indicates that the corresponding slot contains garbage. Note that if a pointer leads to a slot whose corresponding bit is EMPTY, the pointer is to be interpreted as a NIL pointer. Because of the possibility that pointers may point to EMPTY slots, Insert algorithms may not reuse such slots. A value of REUSE indicates both that the contents of the slot are garbage and that the slot may be reused.

When a new block is allocated to a pinned file, all of its slots are REUSEable. When an insertion (see the following) adds a record to a slot, it changes the corresponding bit to FULL; when a deletion removes a record from a slot, it changes the corresponding bit to EMPTY. An inherent problem with this scheme is the difficulty in detecting when a deletion bit can be set back to REUSE. Before a bit can be set back to REUSE, we must somehow verify that no records point to the corresponding slot. Generally, this is a difficult task, and many schemes simply never attempt to reuse slots unless, of course, all relevant files in the database are rebuilt. One method allowing slots to be reused requires that the database system maintain **pointer counts**. Under this scheme, every slot in a pinned file has a counter associated with it that tells how many records point to it. Whenever a record is deleted, in addition to setting the corresponding deletion bit to EMPTY, the counter for each slot to which that record points must be decremented. Whenever the counter for a slot reaches zero, the deletion bit for that slot can be changed from EMPTY to

REUSE. A second type of scheme performs periodic **garbage collection**, scanning the files for EMPTY slots to which no records point. Both schemes require that information be available specifying where pointer fields reside in each record type.

It may have occurred to the reader that the "block number plus key" pointer method avoids the problems of reusing space. If we follow a pointer (*Bn*,*key_val*) to block *Bn* and there is in this block no record with *key_val*, we can assume that the record has been deleted and treat the pointer as NIL. This is a valid approach provided that keys are unique identifiers *over time*. That is, the way we have defined a key previously, no two records that are simultaneously present in a data file can have the same value on the key fields. However, our definition allows for the possibility that at time T_1 a record with key value K is inserted, at time T_2 this record is deleted, and at time T_3 a different record with key value K is inserted. If it happens that this second record with a key value of K is inserted into the same block as was the first (which is not that unlikely if the file is ordered on the key attribute), a pointer to the first record could be misinterpreted as being non-NIL.

We consider now the modifications required for Insert to operate on a pinned data file. We first attempt to insert a new record into the block B_i into which the Insert algorithm for unpinned ISAM structures would attempt to insert the record. If this block has no reusable space, the algorithm checks to see if an overflow chain off B_i exists. If not, a new block is allocated to start the overflow chain, and the new record is placed in this block. If the overflow chain exists, the first block B_0 on the chain is inspected for reusable space. If there is reusable space, the record is inserted there. If there is no space, the Insert algorithm may simply allocate a new block and insert it at the head of the overflow chain (i.e., between blocks B_i and B_0), placing the new record in the new block. Another option available to the Insert algorithm when B_0 is full is to traverse the overflow chain in search of reusable space. Or, to reduce the expense of this search, a "pool" of reusable space for each overflow block can be maintained. Whether these methods are appropriate or not depends on whether space could become reusable. If there is no scheme for identifying reusable space (e.g., garbage collection or pointer counts), then there is no sense in looking beyond the first block B_0 of the overflow chain—in this case, there can be no reusable space further down the chain.

Finally, consider the effects on ordered retrievals of the overflow chains. The performance of ordered retrievals, such as those used in processing some range queries, in which only a few records qualify will degrade in the same manner as will exact match retrievals: Entire virtual blocks, rather than single blocks, will have to be searched for qualifying records. Consider, however, an ordered retrieval in which a large portion of the data file qualifies, for example, an ordered traversal of the entire data file. If each overflow chain can fit in internal memory in its entirety, then each chain can be viewed as a neighborhood as defined in the context of the third ordering scheme presented in Section 8.1. In this case, the modified ISAM data file still is a physically ordered file in the sense that an ordered traversal can be performed by reading each block only once into internal memory—each overflow chain is read into internal memory, sorted internally (but not written back to external memory; why?), and the records in this chain then are appended in the required order to the result stream. The ability to perform this ordered traversal efficiently depends, of course, on the assumption that the overflow chains do not grow too long. In some applications environments, an overflow chain becoming larger than what internal memory can accommodate signals that the ISAM structure has degraded to a point where it should be reorganized.

The Use of Fill Factors

Various aspects of the previous discussion have alluded to the file design parameter known as the **fill factor**. The fill factor f of a file (either a data file or an index file) indicates that when the file originally is created, each block should be filled to only $f\%$ of its capacity. The motivation for using a fill factor of $f < 100$ is to anticipate growth and thereby lessen the work required on insertions. For example, in the standard (unpinned) ISAM structure, a well-chosen fill factor delays the need for the Insert algorithm to redistribute data records, update the index, and acquire new blocks.

We briefly consider two contexts in which the fill factor is a particularly important design parameter:

1. *Pinned files:* An appropriately chosen fill factor can at least delay the need for overflow chains since this will allow some insertions into the blocks B_i to which the index records point directly.
2. *Maintaining an ordered data file over contiguous blocks:* We have been assuming that the standard (unpinned) ISAM data file is stored ordered over a chain of blocks rather than being ordered over contiguous blocks. In Section 8.1, we indicated that in several contexts there is a small advantage to storing the file ordered over contiguous blocks, although generally this structure is too difficult to maintain in the face of Updates. Note, however, that when the ISAM data file is first built, we may request a collection of contiguous blocks (although we still utilize Next_Block pointers in anticipation of Updates that will necessitate chaining). If a fill factor $f < 100$ is selected, we may be able to maintain this structure for some time. And, of course, a file in which only a few blocks are out of the contiguous order will approximate the behavior of a file ordered over contiguous blocks. Note, however, that since a data file with a fill factor of less than 100 generally occupies more blocks than would a file of the same records with a fill factor of 100, until insertions begin to fill the blocks, some operations may require more block accesses than if we had used a fill factor of 100.

8.4 B-TREES

B-trees are perhaps the most important general-purpose file structures employed today. In this section, we shall present four B-tree variants:

- *The basic B-tree:* A dense index, organized as a search tree, indexing an unordered data file (see Figure 8.7).

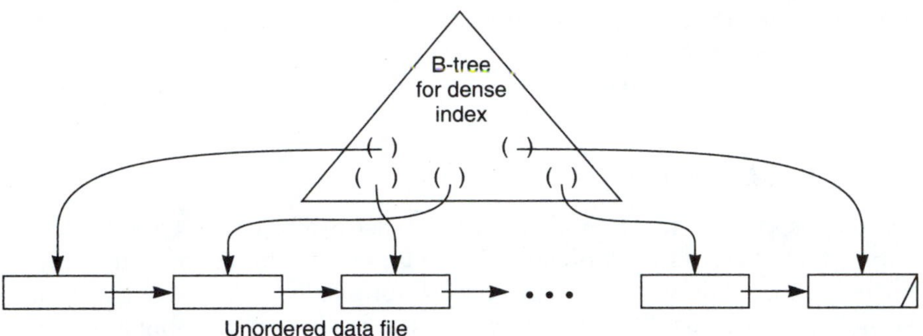

Figure 8.7 Basic B-tree

- *The B^+-tree:* A sparse index of separator values, organized as a search tree, indexing a physically ordered dense index that indexes an unordered data file (see Figure 8.8).

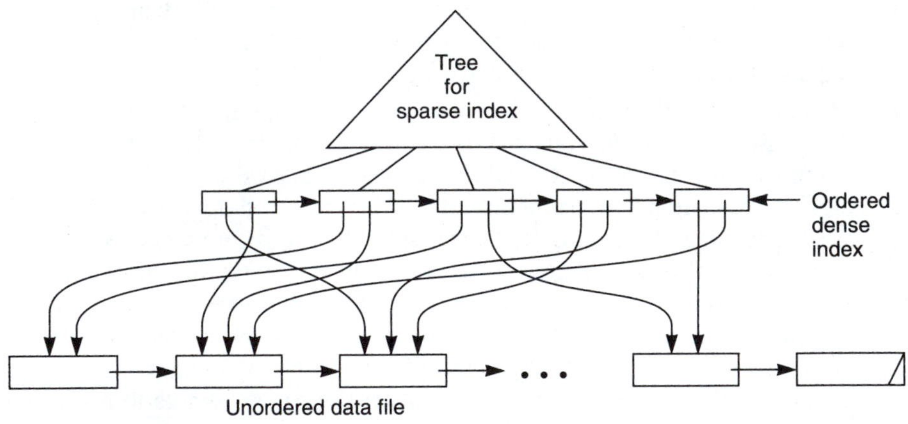

Figure 8.8 B^+-tree

- *B-trees as primary file structures:* Modifications of the basic B-tree and B^+-tree in which the data file is kept ordered. The B^+-tree with an ordered data file is a close relative of the popular **VSAM (virtual sequential access mechanism)** file structure (see Figure 8.9).

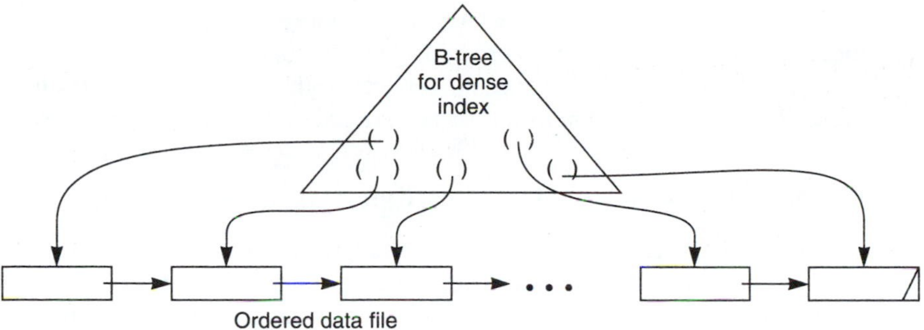

Figure 8.9*a* Primary B-tree

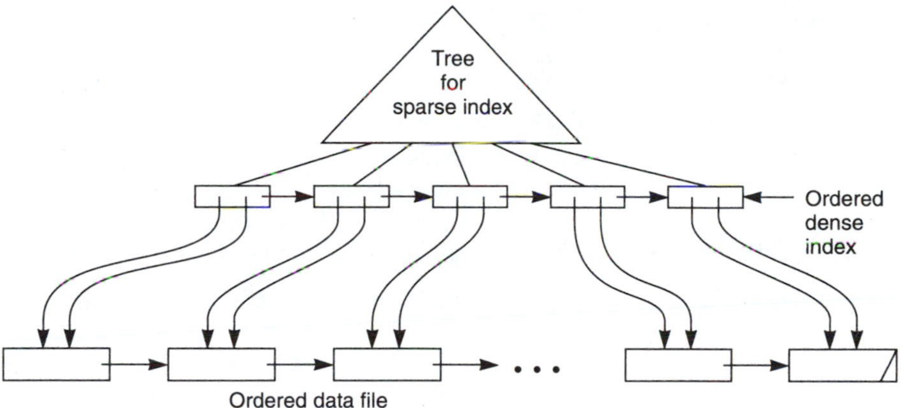

Figure 8.9*b* Primary B$^+$-tree

Our strategy for implementing the B-tree structures will differ in one important regard from the strategy applied to ISAM structures. Recall that we defined an ISAM structure on attribute *A* to permit two or more records in the data file to have the same *A* value. This capability was provided without major modifications to the standard ISAM structure and algorithms. While we wish that our B-tree implementations also be applicable when duplicates can be present in the data file, the properties of a B-tree mandate that we use a special technique to handle duplicate values. In particular, when two or more data records have the same *A* value, the B-tree's dense index will "compress" the corresponding index records so that they are grouped together over the minimal possible number of blocks, in a structure external to the tree. The major motivation for this decision is that if we instead placed index records with duplicate *A* values directly in the B-tree, these records could be scattered over several blocks, thus degrading the performance of several important operations. A second advantage of our scheme is that it allows us to develop the basic algorithms as if duplicate values were not possible, resulting in a significant simplification. Hence, our strategy in the following sections will be first to define the structures assuming no duplicate values and then to introduce compressed index records as a means of accommodating possible duplicates.

An Introduction to Search Trees for External Memory

The B-trees and the related structures we shall study in this chapter are instances of a general structure known as a **search tree.** Chapter 2 reviewed properties of the most common internal memory search trees: the binary search tree and the 2–3 tree. B-trees are adaptations of these structures, designed expressly for the external memory environment. In fact, B-trees will be viewed as a direct generalization of 2–3 trees. The following is a convenient recursive definition of a **tree.**

Definition 8.2 T is a tree if

1. T is empty, in which case T is called an **empty tree,** or
2. T is a nonempty collection of nodes along with a partitioning into a single node n and $k \geq 0$ nonempty trees, called **subtrees** of n. n is the **root** of T, and the root of each nonempty subtree of n is a **child** of n. A node that has only empty subtrees is called a **leaf**.

The **degree** of a tree T is the maximum number of children that any node has. A **path** in T is a sequence $n_1, n_2, \ldots, n_i, \ldots, n_k$ of nodes such that for each i, $2 \leq i \leq k$, n_i is a child of n_{i-1}. The **level** of a node n in T is the length of the (unique) path in T from the root of T to n. (We consider a path containing k nodes to have length k so that the root of T is at level 1.) The **height** of T is the maximum level over all of its nodes.

The nodes of the search trees considered here will contain index records. One variety of external search tree, like the internal 2–3 tree of Chapter 2, will contain the records of a dense index in its nodes. A second variety of external search tree we shall consider contains in its nodes the records of a sparse index, which contain separator values.

A defining characteristic of a search tree is that the values stored in its nodes are organized in such a manner that a particular value, if present, can be located very quickly by following a single path beginning at the root. In particular, as we descend the tree, we can determine, by inspecting the values in any given node n, which subtree of n would contain the desired value, if that value were present. The following is the ordering property inherent in search trees. (Recall that, for the moment, we are assuming that the tree contains no duplicate values.)

Definition 8.3 A tree T is a **search tree** if, whenever a node n in T has k nonempty subtrees $t_0, t_1, \ldots, t_{k-1}$, n has $k-1$ values denoted V_1, $V_2, \ldots, V_{k-1}$ and numbered such that $V_1 < V_2 < \cdots < V_{k-1}$. Further, it must be the case that all the values in t_0 are less than V_1, all the values in t_i are greater than V_i and are less than V_{i+1} $(1 \leq i \leq k - 2)$, and all the values in t_{k-1} are greater than V_{k-1}.

There are two important consequence of this definition:

1. It can be determined if a value is present in a search tree by following a *single* path, starting at the tree's root and terminating at or before a leaf. Hence, searches can be performed in time proportional to the height of a search tree.
2. The values in a search tree can be visited in sorted order by performing a generalized in-order traversal. The traversal begins at the root of the search tree and applies a recursive strategy. When the algorithm arrives at a node n containing values $V_1, V_2, \ldots, V_{k-1}$ and having subtrees t_0, $t_1, \ldots, t_{k-1}$, the algorithm traverses subtree t_0, visits value V_1, traverses subtree t_1, visits value $V_2, \ldots,$ visits value V_{k-1}, and traverses subtree t_{k-1}. If the search tree resides in internal memory, this would imply that ordered retrievals of index values could be performed efficiently. We shall see, however, that if the search tree resides in external memory, such a traversal of the search tree efficiently implements ordered retrievals of index values only if there is an ample amount of internal memory.

Because the time for searches (and also for insertions and deletions) against a search tree of a particular, fixed degree is proportional to the height of the search tree, we wish to keep the height of such a tree as small as possible while performing a reasonable amount of maintenance on insertions and deletions. The problem with the basic binary search tree is that insertions and deletions can skew the tree so that it approaches the structure of a linear linked list with linear time behavior; a 2–3 tree is a search tree that can be kept balanced efficiently in the face of Updates, thereby addressing this problem. We shall generalize a 2–3 tree to a B-tree, a tree of degree greater than three, that is appropriate when the tree is to reside in external memory. Before presenting this generalization, however, it is instructive to consider why a tree of degree greater than three generally is not appropriate when the tree resides in internal memory.

Recall that a 2–3 tree is potentially shorter than a completely balanced binary tree containing the same collection of values since its internal nodes can have up to three children. This potential reduction in height, however, is *not* what gives a 2–3 its advantage over a binary search tree. In fact, in the absence of Updates, we would prefer to search a completely balanced binary search tree than a shorter 2–3 tree containing the same set of values. This is the case because when a node n of a 2–3 tree has three children it also contains two values. Therefore, two comparisons may be required to determine which branch to follow from n. In general, fewer comparisons are required to search a root-to-leaf path in a completely balanced binary search tree than to search a root-to-leaf path in a 2–3 tree in which every internal node has three children and two values.

The reasons we use 2–3 trees in internal memory are that: (1) the number of comparisons required to search a 2–3 tree is not far from the number required to search a completely balanced binary search tree, both being approximately $\log_2$ (number of values in the tree); and (2) insertions and deletions can be implemented in approximately $\log_2$ (number of values in the tree) time against a 2–3 tree (in a manner which preserves the 2–3 tree structure), while there is no known way to accomplish this against a binary search tree in a manner that guarantees that the tree will remain completely balanced.

As a result of these observations, it is clear that, in the context of internal memory, there is little motivation for considering search trees of a degree higher than three. In fact, to do so would increase the expected number of comparisons required and hence could be counter-productive. The characteristics of external memory, however, do motivate the use of much higher degree trees. In external memory, the nodes of a search tree correspond to disk blocks that are linked together using block numbers as pointers to form a tree (see Figure 8.10). Thus, following a pointer from a given node to one of its children requires a block access. Since block accesses are far more expensive than comparisons, in an external environment we desire a tree structure that minimizes the number of block accesses required as we follow a root-to-leaf path, even at the expense of more comparisons per node.

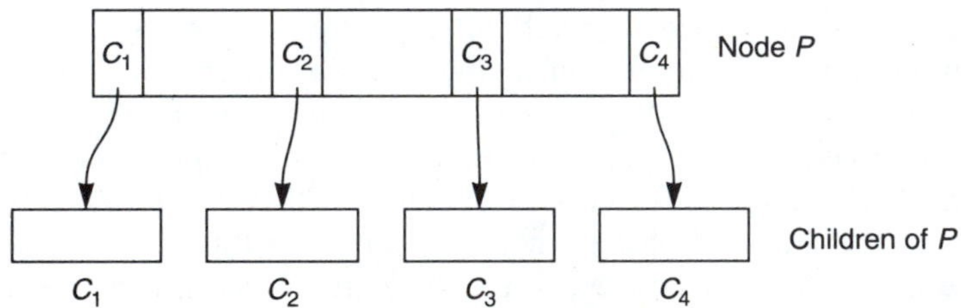

Figure 8.10 Blocks linked together to form a tree

Consequently, in an external environment, we will generally want a balanced search tree of the *maximum possible degree*. This maximum is a function of the block size—in calculating the largest degree tree that a given block size can support, we must account for

1. The information that must be stored in the index records. For example, if we are storing a dense index in the search tree, each index record is a pair (V,p), where V is an attribute value (or the concatenation of a collection of attribute values) and p is a pointer to a data record.
2. The fact that each block of a degree k B-tree must reserve space sufficient to hold k child pointers.

3. The fact that each block needs to contain certain bookkeeping information, such as deletion bits and a Cur_Block field that stores the block's own number.

With these factors accounted for in the calculation, we will generally set the degree of our search tree to be the largest odd integer that the block size can accommodate. The preference for an odd degree is a convenience that simplifies the algorithms.

We are now ready to present the B-tree variants enumerated at the beginning of this section.

The Basic B-Tree

What we call the basic B-tree is a secondary file structure; that is, the data file is not ordered on the attribute(s) indexed by the B-tree. This B-tree organizes the records comprising a dense index into a search tree. As we shall see, whether or not the index can be considered ordered (as defined in Section 8.1) depends on whether or not the B-tree procedures can be allocated a sufficient amount of internal memory to hold h blocks simultaneously, where h is the height of the B-tree. The B^+-tree, introduced in the next subsection, is designed to support efficient, ordered retrievals of index values, even when internal memory is limited.

We begin by defining a B-tree's structure.

Definition 8.4 A k-degree B-tree is a search tree whose leaves all are at the same level, whose nodes each contain between $k - 1$ and $(k \textit{ div } 2)$ records (with one field designated as the **value field**), and whose internal nodes each have one more child than record. An exception to this structural requirement is that the root of a B-tree is permitted to contain as few as one record, in which case it will have two children.

Observe that a 2–3 tree is a B-tree of degree three.

One benefit of a B-tree's structure is captured by the following lemma.

Lemma 8.1 A k-degree B-tree containing N records has height no more than $CEIL\left(\log_{(k \textit{ div } 2)+1}\left(\frac{N}{k \textit{ div } 2}\right)\right) + 1$

Proof Left as exercise 8.9.□

The following is a version of the ExactMatch algorithm for evaluating the expression $\sigma_{A=V}T$ against a B-tree on attribute A. The algorithm is a natural generalization of a binary search tree and 2–3 tree algorithms. As already indicated, at this point we are assuming that there are no duplicate A values in the tree; later, this assumption will be dropped.

```
procedure ExactMatch (T,V,R,found)
  { Search the B-tree whose root is block number T for an index record with
    value V. If such an index record exists, return found equal to true and return in
    R the corresponding data record; otherwise, return found equal to false. }
```

```
ReadBlock (Buff,T)
if (Buff contains an index record (V,p) )
  Follow pointer p to the qualifying record in the data file and return in R this
    record
  found ← true
elseif (node T is a leaf of the tree)
  found ← false
else
  { T is an internal node with values V1 < · · · < Vm (where (k div
    2)≤m≤k−1), and with subtrees t0, . . . ,tm }
  Let i be the smallest integer such that Vi>V, or m+1 if V>Vm
  { We must search subtree ti−1 }
  C ← value of T's child pointer to the root of subtree ti−1
  ExactMatch (C,V,R,found)
endif
end ExactMatch
```

Summary of the Efficiency of the ExactMatch Algorithm: The number of block accesses required to search the tree is no greater than the height of the tree, and a bound on this height is given in Lemma 8.1. If the search locates an index record (V,p), we must follow pointer p into the data file. The number of additional block accesses required to follow p depends on the nature of the pointer—just a single access is required if p includes a block number, but another index will have to be searched if p is only a key. Observe that every search of a B-tree (as well as every insertion and deletion) begins at the root. Some implementations therefore store the root node in internal memory, reducing by one the number of block accesses required by the operations.

It will be convenient to use the ExactMatch procedure in contexts other than the processing of user-generated retrieval requests. For example, we shall employ the procedure as the initial step of our Insert and Delete algorithms. To maximize its utility, we extend ExactMatch so that it returns two additional pieces of information:

1. We wish to return in a parameter *IdxBl* the index block at which the search terminates. If value V is found in the B-tree, this will be the block containing the index record with value V. If the value V is not found, this block will be the leaf at which the search terminates. The modification required is to add the assignment statement

   ```
   IdxBl ← Buff
   ```

   immediately following each of the two assignments to parameter *found*.
2. It will be necessary to also construct an explicit stack, accessible after ExactMatch terminates, representing the path of blocks from T (at the bottom of the stack) to the parent of *IdxBl* (at the top of the stack). Ideally, we would store the blocks appearing on the path on this stack, as this would reduce the number of blocks that must be accessed in the fu-

ture (e.g., by the Insert and Delete operations). However, this luxury requires a stack large enough to hold h blocks, where h is the height of the tree. In some contexts, there will not be enough internal memory available to store this many blocks. In such a case, we must be content to store only the numbers of the blocks along this path on the stack. While this allows us to reconstruct the path, it does require a block access each time we move up the tree from child to parent.

We let S denote a stack that is passed as an argument to ExactMatch. Where possible, S will contain actual blocks, but when this is impossible, S will be a stack of only block numbers. The stack is constructed by adding the statement

```
Push(S,Buff)
```

immediately before the recursive call to ExactMatch or, in the case that S is to contain only block numbers, the statement

```
Push (S,T)
```

Hence, we shall assume that ExactMatch is a procedure

```
ExactMatch (T,V,R,found,IdxBl,S)
{ Search the B-tree whose root is block number T for an index record with
  value V. If such an index record exists, return found equal to true and
  return in R the corresponding data record; otherwise, return found equal
  to false. IdxBl contains the block at which the search (successful or not)
  terminated. S is a stack of either blocks or of block numbers on the path
  from T to the parent of IdxBl. }
```

Before seeing how the Insert and Delete procedures are implemented, we consider an algorithm for evaluating the range query $\sigma_{V \leq A \leq V'} T$ against a B-tree. The algorithm creates a stream STR of qualifying tuples that is guaranteed to be ordered on the A values of the qualifying records. A high-level statement of the algorithm is as follows:

```
procedure Range (T,V,V',STR)
  { Create ordered stream STR consisting of all tuples satisfying the range
    criterion V≤A≤V'. T is the block number of the root of the B-tree. }
  ReadBlock (T,Buff)
  { Let the values in T be V1< · · · <Vm }
  if (T is a leaf)
    for i: = 1 to m
      if (V≤Vi≤V')
        Retrieve from the data file the record R pointed to by index record
          (Vi,pi)
        Append to STR the data record R
      endif
    end for
  else
    { T is an internal node with subtrees t0, . . . ,tm }
    if (V<V1)
```

```
        { We must search subtree t0 }
        C ← value of T's child pointer to the root of subtree t0
        Range (C,V,V',STR)
      endif
      if (V≤V1≤V')
        Retrieve from the data file the record R pointed to by index record (V1,p1)
        Append to STR the data record R
      endif
      for i: = 1 to m−1
        if ( (V<Vi+1) and (V'>Vi) )
          { We must search subtree ti }
          C ← value of T's child pointer to the root of subtree ti
          Range (C,V,V',STR)
        endif
        if (V≤Vi+1≤V')
          Retrieve from the data file the record R pointed to by index record
             (Vi+1,pi+1)
          Append to STR the data record R
        endif
      end for
        if (Vm<V')
          { We must search subtree tm }
          C ← value of T's child pointer to the root of subtree tm
          Range(C,V,V',STR)
        endif
    endif { Test if T is a leaf }
  end Range
```

This statement of algorithm Range is intentionally vague with regard to when ReadBlock statements must be issued to bring blocks into program buffers. The algorithm does specify that a ReadBlock is issued at the beginning of each recursive call to access the root block B of the subtree currently being searched. Note, however, that block B must be inspected after each return from a recursive call that is issued to search a subtree of B. As Range is now written, each ReadBlock reads into the same program buffer *Buff* the root of the subtree currently being searched. Since *Buff* is not local to the recursive procedure, *Buff* is continually overwritten and will not contain block B upon return from the recursive calls that search B's subchildren.

One solution to the problem simply is to insert the statement

```
ReadBlock (T,Buff)
```

following each recursive call to Range (except for the last call that searches the last subtree t_m). Note that the implicit recursive stack of local environments includes block number T so that, upon return from any recursive call, the required block number (the number of the "current" root block) is restored to parameter T.

While the preceding solution is correct, it is potentially expensive—a ReadBlock is now issued up to m times for a node with m children. As was discussed in Chapter 7, a ReadBlock may or may not require an actual disk access, depending on whether the system buffer happens to contain the requested block. Since the ReadBlocks for a node (especially nodes low in the tree) would be issued in close temporal proximity, it is possible that some of these ReadBlocks require only that a system buffer be copied to *Buff*. However, our analysis cannot count on this fact, and we must conclude that each block with m children may incur up to m block accesses.

A more efficient solution than the foregoing follows the approach outlined for the ExactMatch algorithm and maintains a stack of the actual blocks visited. Range could, as does ExactMatch, declare a stack parameter and push onto it the root block before each recursive call. However, in the case of Range, this stack does not need to be accessed outside the scope of the procedure. It therefore is simpler to declare a local variable *CurRoot*, which then automatically becomes part of the stack of local environments generated by recursive calls to Range. Hence, all that is needed is to copy into *CurRoot* the contents of program buffer *Buff* following the ReadBlock at the start of the procedure and to subsequently inspect *CurRoot* whenever information from the current root block is required. While this scheme allows each block of the B-tree to be accessed at most once, it is feasible only when there is enough internal memory to hold h blocks, where h is the height of the B-tree.

With these observations in mind, we analyze the efficiency with which the basic B-tree supports range queries and other ordered retrievals.

Summary of the Efficiencies of Ordered Retrievals: We consider the efficiency with which the B-tree supports several related types of operations:

1. Ordered retrievals requiring data records. Since the basic B-tree scheme does not maintain the data file ordered on the indexed attribute A, a number of data block accesses equal to the number of qualifying records may be required. This is acceptable only when the number of qualifying records is small. The number of required accesses of index records depends on how the qualifying index records are distributed throughout the tree and on whether or not there is sufficient internal memory to maintain a stack of blocks. Generally speaking, if the degree of the B-tree is much larger than the number of qualifying records, most of the qualifying index records would be expected to lie within a single root-to-leaf path (with most in a single leaf), and, hence, the total work required will be dominated by data block accesses.

   The basic B-tree scheme is not a sufficient support for operations that require the ordered retrieval of many data records. Such operations are motivation for the primary B-tree structures considered in a later subsection.

2. Ordered retrievals requiring only values of the indexed attribute. Consider, for example, an operation that requires the ordered retrieval of all the values in the B-tree. As indicated previously, this operation can be performed while accessing each B-tree node only once, provided that enough

internal memory is available to store a quantity of blocks equal to the height of the tree. When this requirement is satisfied, the B-tree has the characteristics of an ordered index and supports this traversal as efficiently as possible. On the other hand, when the memory requirement is not satisfied, an internal node with m children may be accessed m times. Such performance may not be acceptable and is one motivation for the B^+-tree considered in the next subsection. A second, related motivation for the B^+-tree is found in traversals (e.g., to support certain range queries) that require the retrieval of only a subset of the index records currently present. Even if a root-to-leaf path can be stored internally, there remains a concern regarding how the qualifying index records are distributed throughout the tree. Generally speaking, nodes (especially internal nodes) can contain a mixture of qualifying and nonqualifying records, and, in fact, algorithm Range may access some blocks that contain only nonqualifying records. As we shall see, the structure of the B^+-tree is such that a particular collection of qualifying records is often spread across fewer blocks of a B^+-tree than of a conventional B-tree.

We turn now to the implementation against the basic B-tree of the search table operators Add and Delete. It is the B-tree's Insert and Delete algorithms that make the B-tree such a powerful general-purpose file structure; the algorithms are guaranteed to maintain the tree's balance yet do not themselves incur much overhead.

Consider first Insert (T,R), where the A value of R is equal to V and where a secondary index on attribute A of table T is implemented as a B-tree. The first step of the insertion process is to locate where record R should be placed in the data file. Although the data file is unordered with respect to attribute A, it might well be ordered with respect to some other attribute. For example, the primary structure of the data file might be an ISAM file structure on attribute B. If this is the case, the first phase of the insertion process uses the ISAM insertion algorithm to insert R into its proper location in the data file and to update the ISAM index. If, on the other hand, there is no ordering on the data file (i.e., it is a heap with no primary structure), we are free to insert R at any convenient location. For example, we would typically employ a memory management scheme that allows us to efficiently locate a reusable slot in some existing data file block or, if no such slot exists, that allocates a new block to be linked to the data file.

After we complete the process of inserting R into the data file and modifying the primary structure (if one exists), each secondary structure on the data file must be updated. We consider here the steps involved in updating the B-tree on attribute A. The procedure that performed the insertion of R into the data file must return a pointer p to R that can be passed to the B-tree Insert procedure. The nature of p depends on the type of pointers to data records we chose to place in the B-tree's index records (e.g., an exact address pointer or a logical key pointer). Thus, we assume that, sometime after R has been inserted into the data file, the query optimizer invokes the B-tree insertion procedure with the call

Insert $(T,(V,p))$
{ Insert into the B-tree whose root is block number T the index record (V,p). }

At this point, our task is to insert the index record (V,p) into its correct position in the B-tree. We first use procedure ExactMatch to attempt to locate an index record in the B-tree containing value V. For the moment, assume that no index record in the B-tree has an A value of V, and hence ExactMatch will fail, returning in *IdxBl* the leaf L at which the search terminated. Recall that stack S is returned containing the sequence of blocks (or of block numbers, in the case of limited internal memory) corresponding to the path from root T to the parent of leaf L.

To complete the insertion, we must perform one or more of the following steps. The number of steps required depends on the B-tree's state prior to the insertion. The B-tree is of degree k.

Step I: Determine if leaf L (the contents of which reside in *IdxBl*) contains fewer than $k - 1$ index records. If so, R simply is inserted into its proper sorted position in block L, which then is written to disk. No adjustments to the other nodes of the B-tree are necessary.

Step II: If L is full, we check its adjacent siblings for space. Note that to access L's siblings, we require the child pointers contained in L's parent P. If the stack returned by ExactMatch contains actual blocks, P is already in internal memory; however, if only block numbers are on the stack, we must read P into a buffer. Once we have P, we use its child pointers to access L's adjacent siblings. (L will have only one adjacent sibling if it is P's first or last child.) If either adjacent sibling has space, we "rotate" the records contained in block L, the adjacent sibling L', and the parent P. The rotation is depicted in Figure 8.11. The rotation should move a sufficient number of records into L' so that L and L' contain an approximately equal number of records. This completes the Insert operation for the case in which L's sibling has room.

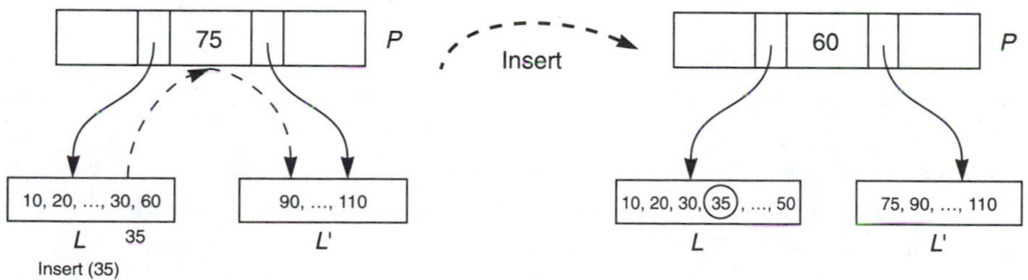

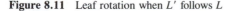

Figure 8.11 Leaf rotation when L' follows L

Step III: If L's siblings are found to be full, we must perform a block splitting operation. The split is depicted in Figure 8.12. Here, a new block L_N is acquired from the system, and index records, including the new index record, are distributed evenly between L and L_N. In addition, the separating index record (i.e., the index record with the median value among those in L) is sent up to the parent P, as is the number L_N of the new block that is used as a pointer to P's new child.

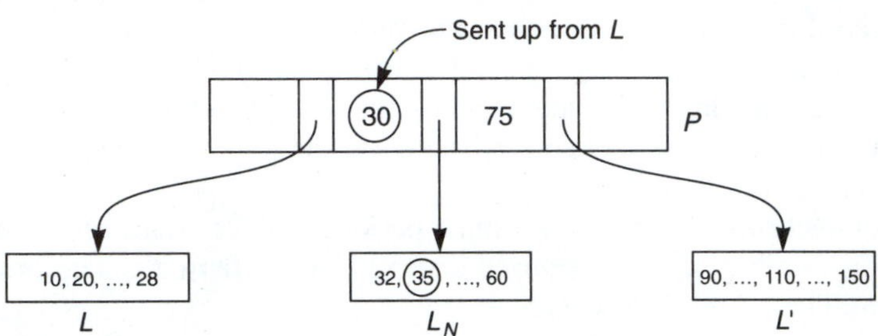

Figure 8.12 Leaf split

Step IV: At this point, we must modify P to accommodate both the index record that was sent up to it and a pointer to the new block, which we would like to make a child of P. Observe that we now are beginning to recursively apply the insertion strategy to each node as we move up the tree. If P has room for a new index record and child pointer, we are done. If not, we check adjacent siblings of P. If a sibling S has room, we rotate index records between P, P's parent M, and S. This operation is depicted in Figure 8.13. The new twist here is that since P is an internal node, it has children. Some of these children must now become children of S instead, and hence child pointers must be moved from P to S. In particular, if S is to the left of P and receives r new records, it must also receive P's r leftmost children. Similarly, if S is to the right of P and receives r new records, it must also receive P's r rightmost children.

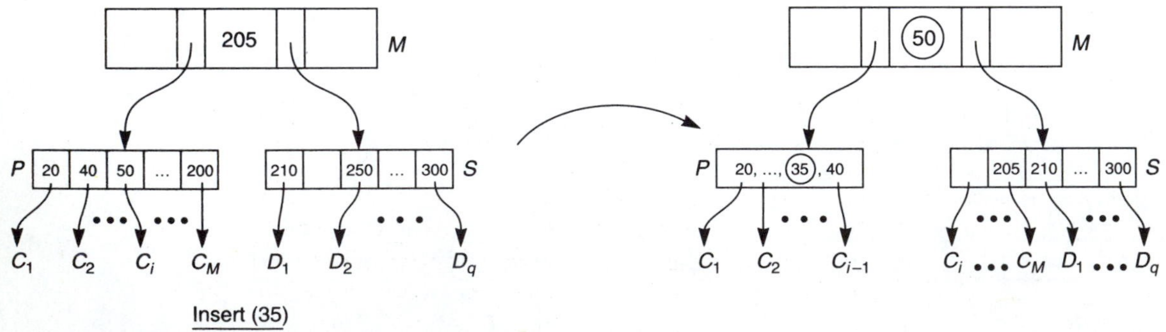

Figure 8.13 Rotation with internal nodes

If P's adjacent siblings have no room for additional index records and children, a new node is created, index records and children are divided evenly between P and the new node, and the index record with the median value, along with a pointer to the new block, are sent up to parent M. This operation is depicted in Figure 8.14.

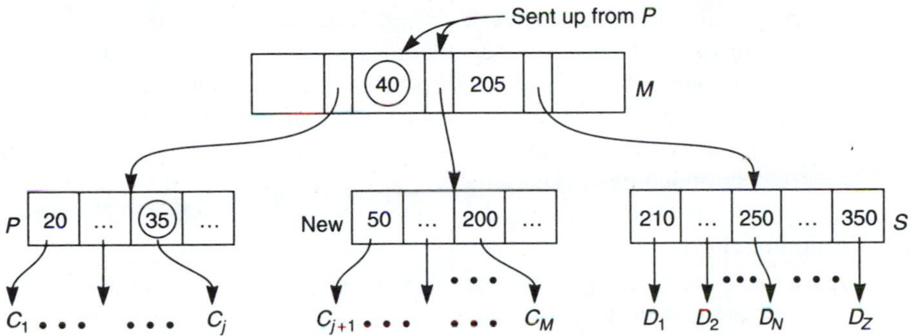

Figure 8.14 Internal node split

Step V: We continue moving up the tree, stopping as soon as a node can accommodate, without the need for a split operation, the index record and child pointer sent up to it. A special case arises when the insertion propagates all the way to the root T and when T itself has to be split. Here, index records and children are divided between T and a new node Q, and the index record with the median value is "sent up." In this case, however, T has no parent to receive this index record and become the parent of T and Q. Hence, we acquire another new node T', insert into it the index record that was sent up, and make T and Q children of T'. Note that T' is now the root of the tree and the height of the tree has increased by one. It is only in this case—when no node along the path from L to T can accommodate a new record without splitting—that the height of the B-tree increases.

We turn now to the implementation of the search table's operator Delete(T,($A = V$)), which requires that we remove from the search table T all tuples with an A value of V. We initially develop the Delete algorithm under the assumption that the table contains no duplicate values in any of the attributes referenced herein, and hence each Delete operation considered herein removes at most one record from the data file.

Because we are assuming that the B-tree on attribute A is a secondary structure, we must more closely consider issues that arose only tangentially in the deletion against the ISAM file, which is a primary structure. In particular, we must consider the contexts in which the operator Delete(T,($A = V$)) might be invoked.

1. The operation is requested directly by the user or a program. In this case, we first use the B-tree ExactMatch algorithm to locate the data record with an A value of V. Once this data record R to be deleted is located (assuming it exists), the next step, at least conceptually, is to perform the actual deletion of R via the data file's primary structure. For example, if the primary structure is on attribute C, the procedure for performing the deletion Delete(T,($C = Z$)) against this primary structure must be invoked, where Z is the value in data record R of attribute C. After data record R is removed, the procedure for updating each index into the data file must be called with R's value of the corresponding attribute. Since some work has already been expended in locating the index record corresponding to data record R in the B-tree on A, a good search table implementation will coordinate the processing to reduce the duplication of effort.
2. A user or a program requests a deletion based on the the value of some attribute other than A; for example, the user or program requests the operation Delete(T,($B = U$)). In this case, we locate the record to be deleted in the data file by means other than the B-tree on attribute A (e.g., we use an index on attribute B). Once the data record R to be deleted is located, the deletion proceeds as described previously. The actual deletion of the data record is effected via the primary structure, and then the procedure for updating each index into the data file is called with R's corresponding value for each attribute. It is at this point that the call Delete(T,($A = V$)) would be generated.

To focus on the problem of removing from the B-tree the index record IR corresponding to the data record R that has been deleted from the data file, we assume that, regardless of how the deletion was invoked initially, we have located the node containing IR in the B-tree. In particular, assume that the block numbered W contains IR, that the contents of this block are in *Buff*, and that the contents of the blocks (or at least their numbers) that form a path from root T to the parent of block W are accessible on a stack.

Our strategy is to always remove an index record from a leaf. If W is a leaf, we simply remove IR from there. If, on the other hand, W is an internal node, we locate the in-order successor (or in-order predecessor) of IR, that is, the index record visited immediately after IR (or immediately before IR) in the ordered traversal of the tree. When IR does reside in an internal node W, its in-order successor is the smallest valued index record in the leftmost leaf L of the subtree of W that the in-order traversal visits immediately following IR. Observe that the search tree ordering property would be preserved if we were to move IR's in-order successor (or in-order predecessor) into the slot in W that IR currently occupies. This observation allows us to reduce the removal of any index record to the removal of an index record residing in a leaf. The strategy is summarized as follows.

Let W be the B-tree node containing the index record IR to be removed

```
if(W is a leaf)
  remove IR from W
else
  find the in-order successor IR' of IR and the leaf L containing it
  { The in-order successor of IR is found by following the path described
    earlier. We assume that the blocks (or their numbers) along this path are
    pushed onto the stack so that, when L is reached, the stack contains the
    path from T to the parent of L. Also, block L is in Buff. }
  copy IR' to the slot in W containing IR (hence overwriting IR)
  remove from L IR'
endif
```

In what follows, we use L to refer to the leaf from which an index record was removed; this is W in the case that W is a leaf, and otherwise is the leaf containing the in-order successor of IR.

The removal of the index record from L would complete the deletion, except for the fact that L might now contain only $((k \ div \ 2) - 1)$ records and hence violate one of the structural requirements of a k-degree B-tree. To maintain the structural properties of a B-tree following a deletion, we require a sequence of steps that is the mirror image of the sequence performed to maintain a B-tree's structure following an insertion:

Step I: Determine if, after the index record is removed from L, L contains at least $(k \ div \ 2)$ index records. If so, the deletion is complete, and L (which is contained in *Buff*) is written to disk. Note that no further adjustments to the other nodes of the tree are necessary.

Step II: If the deletion leaves L with only $((k \ div \ 2) - 1)$ records, we check L's adjacent siblings to see if they have records they can spare. If one of these adjacent siblings L' contains more than the minimum of $(k \ div \ 2)$ records, we perform a rotation of records involving blocks L, the adjacent sibling L', and parent P, as is depicted in Figure 8.15. The rotation should move a sufficient number of records into L so that L and L' contain an approximately equal number of records. This completes the deletion for the case in which L's sibling can spare one or more index records.

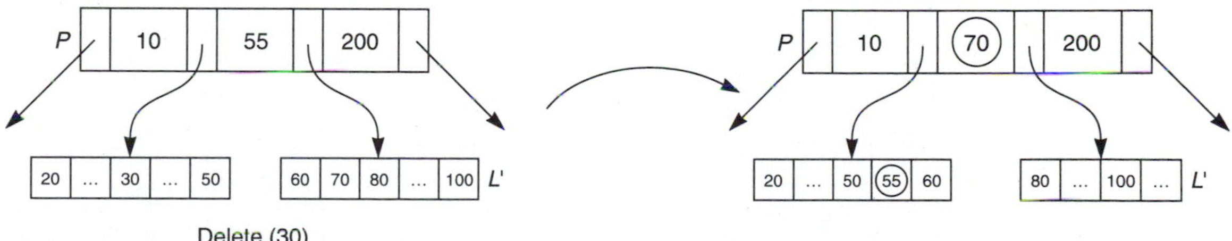

Figure 8.15 Leaf rotation when L' follows L

Step III: If neither of L's siblings can spare an index record, we must perform a block merging operation. The merging of L with the sibling L' that follows L is depicted in Figure 8.16; the merging of L with the sibling that precedes L (as is required when L is the last child of its parent) is completely analogous. Here, the index records that L' contains are moved into L, as is the index record from parent P that separated L and L'. That is, the index record (V_i, p_i) in parent P such that all values in L are less than V_i and all values in L' are greater than V_i is moved into L. Also, the child pointer to L' is removed from P, and block L' is deallocated. Note that L is guaranteed to have room for these new index records since we reach this step only when L has $((k \text{ div } 2) - 1)$ records and L' has $(k \text{ div } 2)$ records—observe that $((k \text{ div } 2) - 1) + (k \text{ div } 2) + 1 = k - 1$ when k is odd.

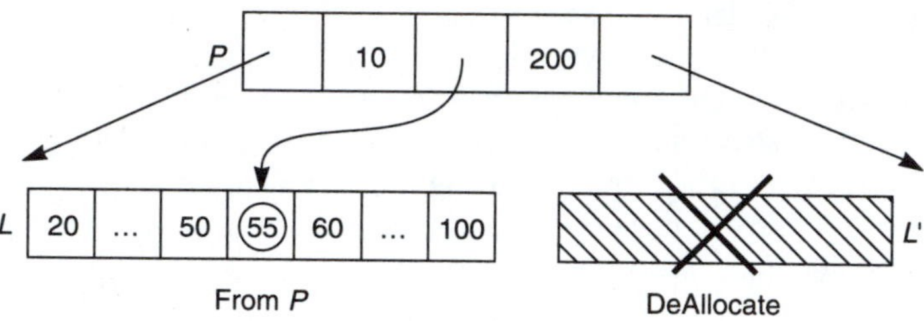

Figure 8.16 Leaf merge

Step IV: As in the Insert procedure, we now apply the strategy recursively as we move up the tree. If parent P now has fewer than $(k \text{ div } 2)$ records [in which case it will have fewer than $((k \text{ div } 2) + 1)$ children], we check to see if an adjacent sibling can spare a record (and a child). If so, we rotate as depicted in Figure 8.17. If neither sibling can spare a record (and child), we merge P and a sibling, as is depicted in Figure 8.18.

Step V: We continue moving up the tree, stopping as soon as a node can tolerate, without requiring a Merge operation, the removal of one of its index records and children. A special case arises when the deletion propagates all the way to the root T. Recall that the definition of a B-tree per-

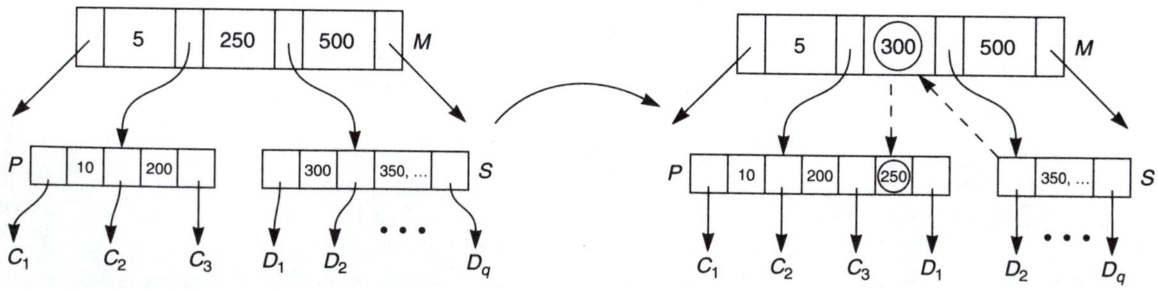

Figure 8.17 Rotation with internal nodes

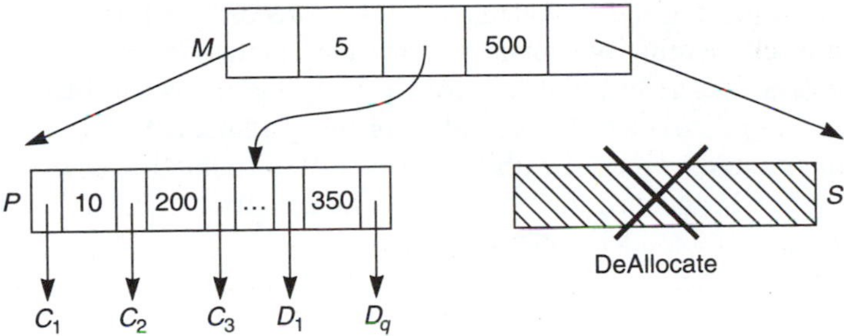

Figure 8.18 Merging internal nodes

mits the root to contain as few as one record, in which case it will have only two children. If this is the case before the deletion, and the deletion propagates to the root (i.e., one of T's children is removed, and T's index record is sent down to the surviving child Q), then block T itself is removed, and child Q becomes the new root of the tree.

Summary of the Efficiencies of the Insert and Delete Algorithms: Each insertion and deletion begins by traversing a root to leaf path, requiring h block accesses. In the worst case, the insertion or deletion propagates all the way up to the root. As we ascend the tree from each node C to its parent P, we may need to read P back into internal memory; this depends on whether or not we store a path of blocks or only block numbers. In either case, as we work at a level of the tree, we may additionally need to access as many as two of P's siblings, and we may need to allocate or deallocate a node. Of course, whenever a change is made to a node, a WriteBlock operation is required also. Hence, in the worst case, an Insert or Delete can require a number of block accesses (Reads, Writes, Allocates, and DeAllocates) that is several times the height of the tree. It can be shown, however, that if insertions and deletions arrive in a random pattern, then, on average, the Insert and Delete algorithms will be able to complete their work at the level immediately above the leaf L at which the modifications are begun.

Modifications to Accommodate Duplicate Values: Our presentation has assumed that the collection of index records contains no duplicate A values; however, we wish for the B-tree structure to be applicable even when the data file contains duplicate A values. We now describe a strategy for handling duplicate values.

Our strategy for handling duplicate A values continues to enforce the restriction that the B-tree contains at most one index record with any particular A value. When more than one data record contains the same A value V, rather than having distinct index records in the B-tree for these data records, we shall have a single record in the B-tree with value V, and this record will point outside the tree structure to a "compressed" collection of index records. The members of this compressed collection of index records will point to the data records with this A value V. To see how we can implement this strategy, consider the form of a B-tree index record that we have been using. An index record is a pair (V,p), where V is a value for the attribute A being indexed, and p is a pointer to a data record with an A value of V. To handle possible duplication of A values in the data file, we modify the definition of an index record to allow p to be a simple block pointer as well.

Figure 8.19 depicts a B-tree record (V,Bn) pointing to a block Bn that itself contains pointers to the data file records with an A value of V. If there are so many data records with a single A value that pointers to all these data records cannot fit in a single block, we simply chain additional blocks of pointers off the block Bn pointed to by the B-tree record. To eliminate unnecessary block accesses, the pointer p in the B-tree index record (V,p) will point directly to a record in the data file as before, unless there is more than one data record with an A value of V. A major benefit of this method for handling duplicate values is that it prevents index records with the same value from being scattered across many nodes of the B-tree. Such scattering would degrade the performance of many of the operations we have been considering. (Consider, for example, the processing of the query $\sigma_{A=V}T$, when many tuples qualify. See exercise 8.13.)

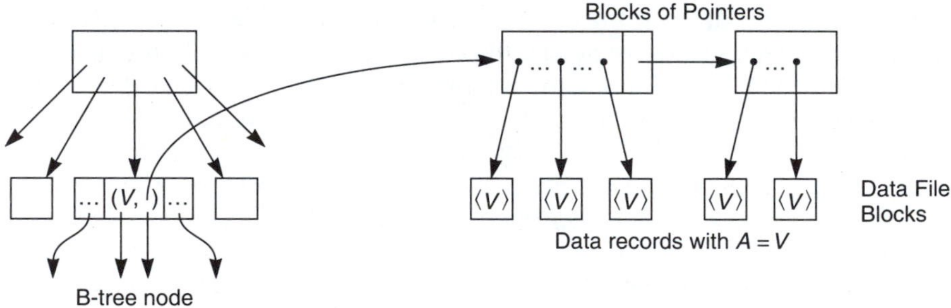

Figure 8.19 B-tree record pointing to block of pointers

The strategy we have described requires that we be able to interpret a pointer p in the appropriate manner. To satisfy this requirement, we add a **duplication bit** to each index record in the B-tree. When the bit in index record $(V,p,0)$ is 0, only one data record has an A value of V and p is a pointer to this data record; when the bit is 1, more than one data record has this A value and p is the number of a block that contains pointers to these data records (or to the head of a chain of such blocks). The retrieval algorithms presented earlier are easily modified to work in conjunction with these conventions.

The modifications required for the Insert and Delete procedures are minor also. When we insert a new record R with an A value of V into the data file, we attempt to add to the B-tree an index record (V, p), where p is a pointer to R. Recall that the first step of this insertion is to call ExactMatch to attempt to locate an index record containing value V. The following describes the required action:

```
if (ExactMatch fails to find index record with value V)
  Insert into the B-tree index record (V,p,0) as before
  { The duplication bit of the index record is 0 }
elseif (ExactMatch locates an index record (V,p',0)
  Allocate a block Bn and initialize it to contain data record pointers p and p'
  Replace in the B-tree index record (V,p,0) with (V,Bn,1)
else
  Let the index record ExactMatch locates be (V,Bn,1)
  if (block Bn is not full)
    Add to block Bn pointer p
  else
    Add new block Bn' to the chain headed by Bn, adding pointer p to the new
      block
  endif
endif
```

The modifications for Delete are analogous. First suppose that we have removed from the data file the single record R, that R has an A value of V [e.g., the user requests Delete(T,($B = W$)), and one of the qualifying records has A value V], and that p is a pointer (of the type employed by the B-tree) to R. As before, ExactMatch first is invoked to locate the index record with an A value of V in the B-tree. The subsequent action is described as follows:

```
if (ExactMatch locates (V,p,0))
  Delete from the B-tree index record (V,p,0) as before
elseif (ExactMatch locates (V,Bn,1))
  remove p from block Bn (or from another block on this chain)
  DeAllocate the block that contained p if it becomes empty
  if (chain now contains only one pointer, p')
    DeAllocate block containing p'
    Replace in the B-tree index record (V,Bn,1) with (V,p',0)
  endif
endif
```

Similarly, suppose the user requests Delete(T,($A = V$)), and hence all data records with an A value of V are to be removed. After we remove from the data file the matching records, we modify the B-tree as follows:

```
if (ExactMatch locates (V,p,0))
  Delete from the B-tree index record (V,p,0) as before
elseif (ExactMatch locates (V,Bn,1))
  DeAllocate all blocks on the chain headed by Bn
  Delete from the B-tree index record (V,Bn,1) as before
endif
```

B^+-Trees

One difficulty with the basic B-tree scheme presented in the previous subsection is that it behaves as an ordered index only in environments that have a sufficient amount of internal memory to store a number of blocks equal to the height of the tree. The B^+-tree is a modification of the B-tree that behaves as an ordered index even when internal memory is limited. Further, a collection of logically consecutive index values will often be spread across fewer blocks of a B^+-tree than of a B-tree, hence increasing the efficiency of certain operations such as range queries.

The structure of a B^+-tree on attribute A is shown in Figures 8.8 and 8.20. Figure 8.8 depicted the tree as consisting of two components: a sparse index of separator values and a dense index into an unordered data file. Figure 8.20 presents an alternative view of a B^+-tree: Here, we view the B^+-tree as a single structure, a B-tree in which the leaves contain a dense index for the data file and are chained together linearly.

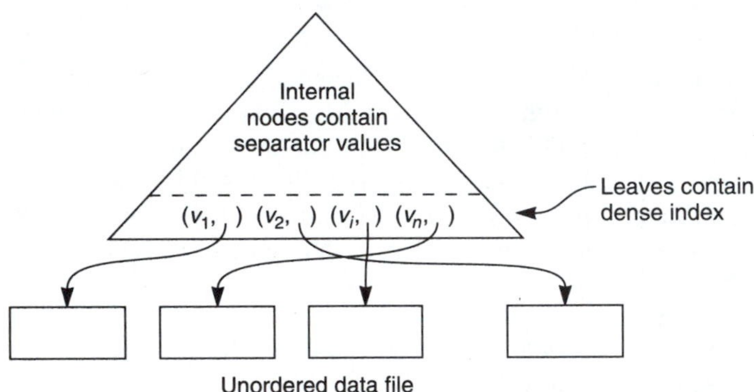

Figure 8.20 B^+-tree viewed as a single structure

We describe the B^+-tree from the perspective of Figure 8.20. The tree's nodes contain two types of index records: The leaves of the B^+-tree contain records (V,p) that constitute a dense index on attribute A, while the internal nodes of the B^+-tree contain records (V) with a single field whose values may or may not be actual A values. The purpose of these values is to separate the dense index records contained in the tree's leaves for the search algorithms.

The definitions presented in an earlier subsection apply directly to a B^+-tree. In particular, a k degree B^+-tree has the search tree ordering property (as slightly relaxed here), its leaves all are at the same level, and its nodes contain numbers of records and children falling into the permissible ranges for a tree of degree k. As in the previous subsection, we shall assume that no two dense index records have the same value V—duplicates are handled by the scheme introduced for the basic B-tree. However, because a separator value appearing in an internal node of a B^+-tree may appear also as an A value in a leaf, we must slightly relax the ordering property to allow equality of values in certain cases.

Definition 8.5 A tree T is a (relaxed) **search tree** if, whenever a node n in T has k nonempty subtrees $t_0, t_1, \ldots, t_{k-1}$, n has $k - 1$ values, denoted $V_i, V_2, \ldots, V_{k-1}$ and numbered such that $V_1 < V_2 < \cdots < V_{k-1}$. Further, it must be the case that all the values in t_0 are less than or equal to V_1, all the values in t_i are greater than V_i and are less than or equal to $V_{i+1} (1 \leq i \leq k - 2)$, and all the values in t_{k-1} are greater than V_{k-1}.

A B$^+$-tree is searched with essentially the same algorithm that searches the B-tree. The main difference is that every search must progress all the way to a leaf since only leaves are guaranteed to contain actual A values and since only leaves contain pointers to data records. The following is the ExactMatch procedure modified for a B$^+$-tree:

```
procedure ExactMatch (T,V,R,found,IdxBl,S)
  { Search the B+-tree whose root is block number T for a dense index record
    with value V. If such an index record exists, return found equal to true and
    return in R the corresponding data record; otherwise, return found equal to
    false. IdxBl contains the leaf at which the search (successful or not)
    terminated. S is a stack of either blocks or block numbers on the path from
    T to the parent of IdxBl. }
  ReadBlock(Buff,T)
  if (Buff contains a leaf node)
    if (Buff contains an index record (V,p))
      Follow pointer p to the qualifying record in the data file
      Return the record in R
      found ← true
      IdxBl ← Buff
    else
      found ← false
      IdxBl ← Buff
    endif
  else
    { T is an internal node with values V1 < · · · < Vm (where (k div
      2)≤m≤k−1), and with subtrees t0, . . . , tm }
    { Add to the stack of blocks or block numbers }
    Push(S,Buff) or Push(S,T)
    Let i be the smallest integer such that Vi≥V, or m+1 if V>Vm
    { We must search subtree ti−1 }
    S ← value of T's child pointer to the root of subtree ti−1
    ExactMatch(S,V,t,found)
  endif
end ExactMatch
```

We now take a closer look at the dense index contained in the leaves of the B$^+$-tree. Note that, in Figure 8.20, the leaves are chained together linearly by Next_Block pointers. Since the search tree ordering property of the B$^+$-tree implies that all the values in any leaf L are less than all the values in any leaf to the right of L, the dense index is a file physically ordered over a chain of blocks. This dense index structure is known as a **sequence set** and gives the B$^+$-tree additional utility over the basic B-tree.

We consider now how the sequence set is used to process ordered retrievals of A values. An ordered retrieval of all the A values is performed simply by traversing the sequence set from left to right. No accesses of internal tree blocks are required (we assume that a pointer to the first block of the sequence set's chain is available), and each block of the dense index is accessed only once. The range query $\Pi_{<A>}(\sigma_{A=V}T)$ is processed by first issuing the call

ExactMatch(*T,V,R,found,IdxBl,S*)

and then traversing the sequence set, beginning at block *IdxBl* and following Next_Block pointers until a block containing an index value greater than V' is encountered. (Of course, if the query omits the projection and hence requires data records, each time a qualifying index record (V_i,p_i) is encountered, the pointer p_i must be followed.) The advantage of the B^+-tree implementation over that of the basic B-tree is that an index block never needs to be accessed more than once, even when the availability of internal memory is limited. Additionally, the number of blocks over which a collection of qualifying index records is spread may be fewer when the index is stored in a B^+-tree's sequence set rather than in the internal nodes of a B-tree.

The modifications required for the Insert and Delete algorithms are minor. For each of these operations, ExactMatch locates the leaf L on which work must begin. For Insert, slight modifications to the B-tree algorithms are required to account for the fact that the internal nodes store only separator values and not index records. For example, suppose that leaf L is full and that adjacent sibling L' is found to have room for an additional index record. As with the B-tree, we distribute records between L and L' so that the new index record can be inserted in its proper position. However, as Figure 8.21 illustrates, parent P does not participate initially in this redistribution since it contains only separator values. After the redistribution, we adjust the value in P

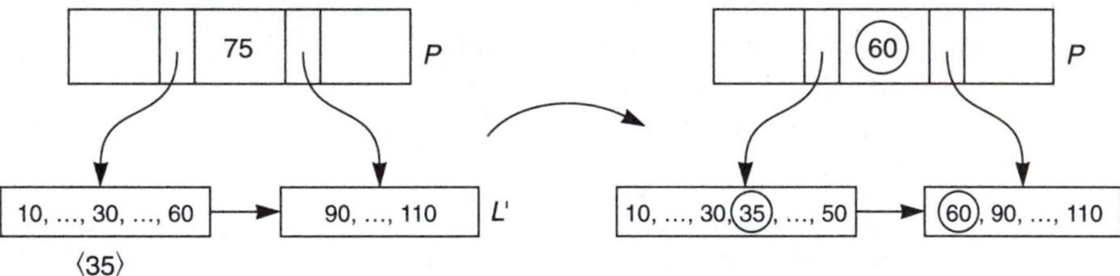

Figure 8.21 Distributing values between L and L'

that separates the values in L from those in L'. Any value greater than all the values in L and less than or equal to all the values in L' can be used. For example, the smallest value now in L' can be used. No other separators in the tree need be adjusted.

The case in which the siblings adjacent to L have no room requires similar modification. First, when we acquire a new node L_N, L_N must be inserted in the

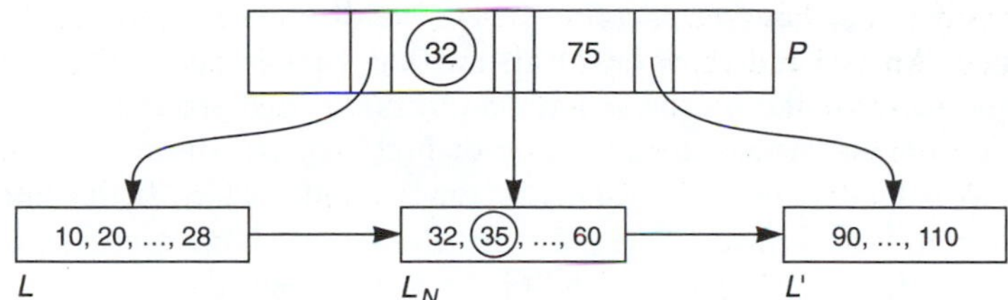

Figure 8.22 Inserting new leaf

sequence set between nodes L and L', as is shown in Figure 8.22. Records, including the new index record, are then distributed evenly between L and L_N. At this point, a value separating L and L_N must be added to parent P, along with a pointer to the new child L_N. If P cannot accommodate these additional pieces of information, the insertion propagates up the tree as in the B-tree's Insert algorithm.

Deletion begins with ExactMatch locating the leaf L containing the record of the dense index to be removed. If, after the removal, L contains only (k *div* 2) $-$ 1 records, we check to see if an adjacent sibling L' has more than (k *div* 2) records. If so, we divide records evenly between L and L' and update the separator in parent P. If L has no sibling with more than (k *div* 2) records, we must merge L with an adjacent sibling. Figure 8.23 depicts the merging of L with the sibling L' that follows it; the merging of L with the sibling that precedes L (as is required when L is the last child of its parent) is completely analogous. Here, the index records which L' contains are moved into L. Node L' is removed from the sequence set by setting the Next_Block pointer in L to point to the block to which L' was pointing and by deallocating L'. Parent P must then be modified by removing its pointer to L' and the value that was separating L and L'. If P cannot tolerate this deletion, the process propagates up the tree as in the B-tree's Delete algorithm.

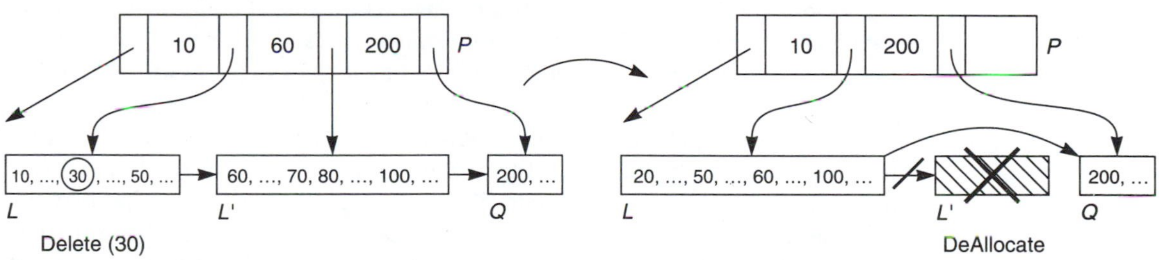

Figure 8.23 Leaf merge

We consider one last point before concluding our discussion of the B$^+$-tree. It may have concerned the reader that a B$^+$-tree might contain more nodes, and have greater height, than does a B-tree, when both are indexing the same data file. After all, a B$^+$-tree contains all the index records contained in the B-tree and, additionally, contains a sparse index. While this observation is true, a mathematical analysis (see exercise 8.11) reveals that only minor differences in size are to be expected. It is easy to show that, in any tree in which each internal node has m children, the proportion of nodes that are leaves is approximately $(m - 1)/m$. Hence, in a B^+-tree of high degree, the number of nodes required to hold the separator values is small compared with the number of nodes required for the entire tree. Also, for sufficiently large files, the height of the B^+-tree will be within one of that of the B-tree, and the heights in fact often will be equal.

Several proposed variations to the scheme presented here add to the competitiveness of the B^+-tree *vis-á-vis* the B-tree. For example, because separators need not be actual A values, schemes can be devised that use very small separators (e.g., truncated A values) in internal nodes, thus allowing more index records and more children per node. This scheme, however, complicates the algorithms since we now require dynamic definitions for the conditions *node is full* and *node is too sparse*. The interested reader is referred to Comer (1979) and Knuth (1973) for more details on this and other search tree variants.

The B-Tree as a Primary File Structure

The B-tree schemes described in the previous two subsections provide very good support for most search table operations. However, since we so far have presented B-trees only as secondary structures, we cannot expect them to efficiently support ordered retrievals of data records. Fortunately, the B-tree schemes can be easily transformed into primary structures. As we did in our presentation of the ISAM structure, we shall begin by assuming that the data records are free to move about the data file and then shall consider the modifications required when the data records are pinned to particular locations.

Generally speaking, any secondary file structure on attribute A can be transformed into a primary structure on A as long as the structure provides a means of quickly identifying where a new record should be placed in the data file to preserve the file's ordering. When this is the case, we can continue to view the data file as a structure distinct from the index file and modify the algorithms that insert records into the data file so that they use the index to find the proper position for new data records. We shall develop the primary B-tree implementations by applying this general technique. We note that some implementations, rather than treating the B-tree and the data file as distinct structures, treat the blocks of an ordered data file as the leaves of a B-tree. The two approaches lead to slightly different algorithms, each having minor advantages over the other in certain regards. We favor the approach of treating the tree and the data file as distinct structures, both because this leads to a somewhat more efficient implementation in the face of pinned records and duplicate values and because the scheme is less *ad hoc* in that it results from the application of a general technique.

Our main task, then, is to demonstrate how a B-tree on attribute A can be used to determine where a new record R is to be inserted in a data file ordered on A. We are interested in turning both the basic B-tree and the B^+-tree into primary structures, and we describe a single method applicable to both structures. The method is conceptually simple and utilizes the following variant of the ExactMatch algorithm:

```
LocatePos(T,V,PosPtr)
  { Return in PosPtr a pointer to a record in the data file that either immediately
    precedes or immediately follows in the sorted order a record with A value
    V. }
```

The implementation of this algorithm is almost identical to that of ExactMatch for either the B-tree or the B^+-tree. The modifications to ExactMatch are described on a case-by-case basis:

Case I: ExactMatch locates a dense index record (V,p). In this case, the new record has the same A value as does the record pointed to by p. Since the new record can be inserted "on either side" of the record pointed to by p, LocatePos simply returns in *PosPtr* the value p. (If the pointer in index record (V,p) actually points to a block of pointers, each pointing to a data record with an A value equal to V, then in the foregoing let p denote any one of these pointers. We employ this convention in Cases II and III as well.)

If the B-tree, or the B^+-tree, does not contain a dense index record with value V, ExactMatch terminates in a leaf L. This leads to Case II or III.

Case II: Leaf L contains at least one index record (V_i,p_i) such that $V_i < V$. Let (V_j,p_j) be the index record in L with the largest value such that $V_j < V$. Then the record to which p_j points immediately precedes the new record in the ordering. Hence, LocatePos returns the value p_j in *PosPtr*.

If neither Case I nor II applies, Case III will.

Case III: Leaf L contains at least one index record (V_i,p_i) such that $V_i > V$. Let (V_j,p_j) be the index record in L with the smallest value such that $V_j > V$. Then the record to which p_j points immediately follows the new record in the ordering. Hence, LocatePos returns the value p_j in *PosPtr*.

After LocatePos returns a value for *PosPtr*, we follow *PosPtr* to the record R' in the data file. The new record R can be inserted into the block B in which R' resides, provided, of course, that B has room for a new data record. If block B is full, we go through much the same process as described for inserting a record into an ISAM data file. First, we check the blocks B_1 and B_2 adjacent to B on the ordered chain. Note that in the structure we are currently describing, we have no easy way of accessing the block that precedes B unless the data file's chain is doubly linked, and, hence, we shall assume that the chain is doubly linked. If either B_1 or B_2 has room, we can distribute records evenly between them, inserting the new record R in its proper location. If neither adjacent block has room, we allocate a new block, insert it in the ordered chain, and distribute records (including the new record) between B and the new block to preserve the ordering.

Note that this redistribution of data records does not require any changes to the structure of, or values in, the B-tree or the B^+-tree. However, when data records move between blocks, we must update all indices that point to these records by means of a block number. Since the primary B-tree and B^+-tree are likely to use such pointers, a good implementation will coordinate the procedure LocatePos with the steps that perform the actual insertion and redistribution of data records in an effort to reduce the number of tree nodes that are accessed more than once. Even with good coordination, it is apparent that Insert and Delete procedures that move many data records across block boundaries in an attempt to keep the file from spreading over a large number of sparsely populated data blocks incur a large penalty. Is a redistribution worth the effort, or should we simply place a minimal number of records in the new block? To begin to answer this question, note that the major motivations for attempting to keep the blocks of the data file uniformly populated are: (1) to efficiently utilize storage space, and (2) to reduce the number of blocks that must be accessed when performing an ordered retrieval of a large number of data records. Note, however, that the efficiency of insertions and of retrievals and deletions that qualify only a small number of data records is fairly insensitive to the distribution of data records over the blocks of the data file since this distribution does not affect in any way the structure of the B-tree or B^+-tree. Consequently, the relative importance of the various search table operations should be weighed carefully before deciding how much effort the Insert and Delete algorithms should expend in an attempt to keep the blocks of the data file uniformly populated rather than allowing new blocks to be sparse, at least in the short term.

Regardless of the strategy adopted for the Insert and Delete algorithms, some records will have to move between blocks to keep the data file ordered; hence, the scheme described here is not directly applicable to pinned data files. To accommodate a pinned data file, we modify the structure in much the same way as we modified the ISAM structure. Suppose that the block B into which a new data record R must be inserted to preserve the ordering is full. As in the ISAM structure, we hang a new block off B into which we insert the new record (see Figure 8.6). Hence, the original blocks of the data file may become the heads of chains of virtual blocks. As with the ISAM data file, the best we can do is keep the virtual blocks ordered; that is, if B_i precedes B_j on the data file's ordered chain, the A values of all data records in the virtual block headed by B_i will be less than or equal to the A values of all the records in the virtual block headed by B_j. We cannot, however, maintain the ordering of the records within a virtual block.

The performance of ordered retrievals of the entire data file (or a large portion of it) against the search trees and the ISAM structure are affected in exactly the same manner. In particular, as long as the sizes of the virtual blocks do not exceed the capacity of internal storage, we have a physically ordered file over ordered neighborhoods, and an ordered retrieval incurs only the penalty of internally sorting each neighborhood. On the other hand, the performance of most other operations against a B-tree or B^+-tree degrades less than against the ISAM structure because the tree schemes utilize dense index records that point to individual data records rather than to the virtual blocks pointed to by ISAM's sparse index records. Hence, a retrieval, after locating in the search tree each qualifying dense index record, follows the pointer directly to the (actual) block containing the qualifying data record. Of course, the performance of some retrievals that qualify many logically consecutive records will degrade somewhat if the use of the overflow technique increases the number of distinct blocks over which the qualifying records are spread. However, even this number of blocks can be expected to be far less than the number over which the qualifying records would be spread in a data file not ordered on the attribute in question.

We conclude this section by considering the choice between the B-tree and the B^+-tree as a primary structure. It at first might appear that, when the data file is ordered on attribute A, there is no motivation for the B^+-tree's sequence set, since an ordered traversal of the A values can be performed by visiting in order the data records and projecting on the desired attribute. Observe, however, that since data records are generally far larger than index records, the dense index file, whether it be structured as a B-tree or as the sequence set of a B^+-tree, will be spread over far fewer blocks than will the data file. Consequently, when we require only A values, we prefer to obtain them by traversing the dense index file rather than the data file. Therefore, the choice between a B-tree and B^+-tree as a primary structure boils down to the same issues as does the choice between them for a secondary structure: whether or not there is sufficient internal memory to hold simultaneously h blocks, where h is the height of the tree, and whether the typical collections of A values that must be retrieved can be expected to be spread across significantly more blocks of a B-tree than of a B^+-tree.

8.5 HASHING

Chapter 2 considered hashing as an internal search table implementation. Since the external hashing schemes presented in this section resemble the internal scheme, the reader is urged to review the discussion appearing in Chapter 2.

External hashing, like internal hashing, is a special-purpose search table implementation, providing excellent support for exact match retrievals, insertions, and deletions. On the other hand, hashing generally is incompatible with many ordered operations, including range queries and retrievals sorted on the indexed attribute, be it retrievals of the entire data record or of just the attribute value. Further, the basic external hashing schemes work best when the size of the data file is fairly static and when we have a good estimate of this size at the time we initialize the implementation. The dynamic hashing schemes presented in a later subsection, however, overcome this static-size limitation to a large extent.

The Basic External Hashing Scheme

As is described in Chapter 2, a hash function maps attribute values into addresses. In an internal environment, these addresses are typically the subscripts of an internal array. In an external environment, because of the large number of addresses required, addresses usually correspond to locations within an external structure known as a **hash table**. A hash table is a collection of locations, typically numbered 0, 1, 2, . . . , $B - 1$, which is stored over a set of contiguous blocks of external memory. The hash table locations are referred to as **buckets**. Because we store the hash table over contiguous blocks, the number of the block containing each bucket i (denoted $HT[i]$) can be calculated quickly.

In the scheme we shall describe first, each hash table bucket contains a pointer to the head of a chain of blocks. These chains partition, based on the bucket into which an index record's value hashes, the records of a dense index (see Figure 8.24). When designing the implementation, we should attempt to choose the number of buckets B so that the average chain length is quite small—generally one or two blocks. Note that, since each block on a chain contains many index records, B is generally far smaller than the expected number of data records. For example, if k index records fit per block and we expect N data records, we would require $CEIL(N/k)$ buckets to achieve an average chain length of one. Further, since the buckets of the hash table store

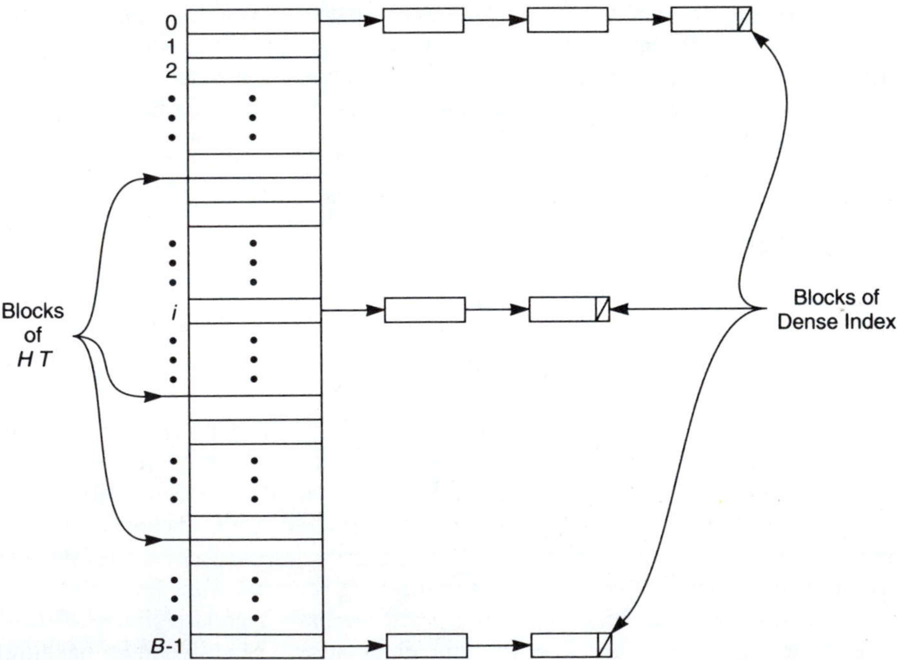

Figure 8.24 External hash table

only block pointers, we would expect many more than k buckets to fit per block. If $c * k$ buckets fit per block (where c might be four or five), the number of blocks required for the hash table would be about $N/(c * k^2)$.

Of course, achieving a small average chain length is not by itself sufficient to ensure that the hashing scheme will efficiently support the search table operations for which it is designed. We also require that the length of each chain be near this average. As discussed in Chapter 2, this requirement mandates the use of a hash function that is uniform with respect to the expected distribution of data values. Unfortunately, this means that we generally must employ a hash function that does not map logically near attribute values to logically near buckets. Consequently, a hashed dense index is not generally an ordered index with respect to the sequence of sorted attribute values.

The implementations against an external hashing scheme of the exact match Retrieval, Insert, and Delete operations closely parallel their implementations against an internal hashing scheme. The exact match Retrieval $\sigma_{V=A} T$ is performed by computing the hash value $i = h(A)$ and then searching for qualifying index records on the chain of blocks off of bucket $HT[i]$. The pointers of the qualifying index records then are followed into the data file. Insertions and deletions are performed in the obvious way, utilizing some memory management technique to keep the chains as condensed as possible. If $h()$ is well chosen and B is sufficiently large, this will be an extremely fast implementation.

We reiterate that hashing schemes generally are inappropriate supports for the processing of retrievals ordered on the hashed attribute. In particular, it generally is the case that

1. A hashed index is not sorted and the sorted retrieval of the dense index (or a large fraction of it) requires an external sort of the index file.
2. A hashed index does not support the processing of range queries, even when only the value of the indexed attribute is required. Consider, for example, processing the query $\Pi_{<Salary>}(\sigma_{20,000 \leq Salary \leq 120,000} EMPLOYEE)$ against a dense index hashed on Salary. Not only are the qualifying index records scattered across different buckets, but the only way to use the hash function to locate the qualifying records is to hash every integer between 20,000 and 120,000. (If salaries include pennies, the situation is far worse!) Generally speaking, if the number of values from the attribute's domain falling into the specified range is near or exceeds the number of index records, we would be better off simply scanning the entire dense index.
3. A hashed index cannot support an ordered data file on the hashed attribute. In the context of B-trees, we argued that any secondary structure on attribute A could be turned into a primary structure on attribute A, as long as the structure provides a means of quickly identifying where in the data file a new record should be placed to preserve the file's ordering. Unfortunately, a hashed index generally fails to satisfy this requirement. Consider, for example, a hashed index on social security number.

If we are to insert a new record *R* with SS# = 123456789, we could apply the hash function to 123456789 and find which bucket of the index should contain an index record for *R*; however, there is no correspondence between the location of the data records referenced by the other index records in this bucket and the location required for the new data record. As an alternative, we might try hashing logically close SS#'s (e.g., 123456788) in hopes of finding a record indexing an existing data record whose location in the data file is near the location required for the new data record; however, this may require that we hash many values before a "hit" is found.

Dynamic Hashing

Under the assumption that ordered retrievals need not be supported, hashing schemes can provide an excellent search table implementation. Even under this assumption, however, there remains a cause for concern: Worst-case performance may degrade as a result of chains becoming too long. There are two factors that can cause this to happen:

1. Our estimate of the number of data records was too low, and hence we designed a hashing scheme with too few buckets. When this occurs, even if the chains all are of roughly the same length, this length will be too long to support the operations efficiently.
2. The values of the hashed attribute *A* are not distributed as was expected, and, as a result, the hash function is not uniform with respect to the attribute values encountered. When this occurs, the average chain length may be sufficiently short, but several of the chains may be quite long.

The design of hash functions which will be uniform with respect to various distributions of data values is not our immediate concern here—the interested reader is referred to Knuth (1973) for a sampling of the enormous amount of literature that exists on this topic. Our concern here, rather, is the design of dynamic hashing schemes that behave gracefully when no good estimate is available on the number of data records and, more generally, when this number fluctuates over the life of the application. We point out, however, that such dynamic hashing schemes do, in fact, tolerate nonuniform hashing of data values far better than does the basic hashing scheme. Consequently, when a dynamic hashing scheme is employed, the use of a hash function uniform with respect to the data values encountered often is not a major concern, although the behavior of such a scheme is enhanced when uniform, or near uniform, hashing is achieved.

Dynamic hashing schemes fall into two categories: **reorganization schemes** and **maintenance schemes**. A reorganization scheme proceeds like the basic hashing scheme of the previous subsection until performance degrades beyond a certain limit of tolerance. When this occurs, a substantial amount of work must be performed to correct the problem. A maintenance scheme, on the other hand, performs a bit of extra work on insertions and deletions to prevent any significant degradation in performance. Thus, reorganization schemes are analogous to search tree implementations in which no effort is made to keep the tree balanced and where the tree is rebuilt once it gets too skewed. Maintenance schemes are analogous to 2–3 tree and B-tree schemes where special techniques are employed at each Update to keep the tree balanced. Reorganization schemes are appropriate when the database system can be brought offline periodically, while maintenance schemes are called for when the system must be online continuously.

A Simple Reorganization Scheme: Suppose that we have implemented a hashing scheme with B buckets and that, after a while, the chains become too long. The obvious, brute force way of reorganizing the structure is to rehash the index records into a larger hash table. In particular, suppose we decide to increase the number of buckets to $B' > B$, using a hash function h' that maps attribute values to locations 0, 1, 2, . . . , $B'-1$ in a new hash table HT'. We might consider performing the reorganization as follows:

```
for (each record (V,p) in the dense index)
  i ← h'(V)
  Let B_HT' be the block of HT' containing bucket i
  ReadBlock (Buff,B_HT')
  Bn ← HT'[i]
  if (Bn not NIL)
    ReadBlock (Buff',Bn)
  endif
  if ((Bn not NIL) and (block Bn in Buff' has room))
    insert into Buff' (V,p)
    WriteBlock (Buff',Bn)
  endif
  else
    { Add a new block to the head of the chain pointed to by HT'[i] }
    Allocate a new block W
    Initialize Buff' to a block containing (V,p)
    Set to Bn the Next_Block pointer of Buff'
    HT'[i]  ← W
    WriteBlock (Buff',N)
    WriteBlock (Buff,B_HT')
  endif
end for
```

This algorithm is hopelessly inefficient, even in the context of an offline application. An index record not requiring a new block to be allocated incurs two ReadBlocks and one WriteBlock; an index record requiring a block to be allocated incurs two additional WriteBlocks. When one considers that a dense index file often contains many millions of records, it becomes clear that this approach is generally infeasible. Not surprisingly, there exist algorithms that more intelligently sequence their block accesses, thereby reducing the number of accesses required. For example, in Chapter 11, we shall consider an algorithm known as **Grace join**. Although Grace join is an implementation of the relational Join operator, the algorithm is useful in other contexts as well since it efficiently constructs a hash structure on the data files to be joined. In particular, the first phase of Grace join could be used as an efficient alternative to the preceding algorithm whenever a new hash structure must be built for an existing data file.

While the first phase of the Grace join algorithm is appropriate when initializing a hash structure from scratch, the problem at hand is somewhat different—in our problem, the index file already is hashed, and we wish to modify how it is hashed. Several schemes have been developed for exploiting an existing hash structure in support of the reorganization. We describe here a simple, yet effective, scheme developed by Aho, Hopcroft, and Ullman (1974) and Ullman (1982). The scheme assumes that the current hash table *HT* has *B* buckets, numbered 0, 1, . . . , $B - 1$, and that the hash function is of the form

```
h(V)=INT(V) mod B
```

where *INT* is an injective function mapping values of the hashed attribute *A* into integers in [0..Φ], where Φ is greater than the number of buckets we possibly could need to accommodate the index file. For example, if *A* is a social security number, *INT* could be the identity map. If *A* is a character string, *INT* could interpret the bytes in the string's internal representation as an integer.

At the heart of the reorganization scheme is the following number theory theorem.

Theorem 8.1 If $k \ mod \ B = i$, then $k \ mod \ 2B = i$ or $B + i$.

This fact allows us to double the number of buckets while keeping to a minimum the number of block accesses required to perform the reorganization. We define a new hash function

```
h'(V)=INT(V) mod B
```

and create a new hash table *HT′* containing 2*B* buckets, allocated over a new collection of contiguous blocks. Theorem 8.1 allows for an efficient reorganization since it implies that each index record hashes under *h′* to either the same bucket *i* to which it hashed under *h* or to bucket $B + i$. The following algorithm exploits this observation to perform the reorganization while accessing each block of the old structure and each block of the new structure only once. The algorithm assumes that six program buffers are available; the task can be performed with fewer buffers, but at the expense of a more complicated algorithm (see exercise 8.14):

```
let B1 be the number of the block of HT containing HT[0]
let B2 be the number of the block of HT' containing HT'[0]
let B3 be the number of the block of HT' containing HT'[B]
ReadBlock (Buff1,B1)
ReadBlock (Buff2,B2)
ReadBlock (Buff3,B3)
```

```
for i: = 0 to B−1
  if (Buff1 does not contain HT[i])
    B1←B1+1
    ReadBlock(Buff1,B1)
  endif
  if (Buff2 does not contain HT'[i])
    B2←B2+1
    ReadBlock(Buff2,B2)
  endif
  if (Buff3 does not contain HT'[i+B])
    B3←B3+1
    ReadBlock(Buff3,B3)
  endif
  Allocate a new block and place it at the head of chain HT'[i]
  { Contents of block will be assembled in Buff4 }
  Allocate a new block and place it at the head of chain HT'[i+B]
  { Contents of block will be assembled in Buff5 }
  for each block Bj on chain HT[i]
    ReadBlock(Buff6,Bj)
    for each index record IR in Buff1
      Let V be the A value of IR
      j←h'(i)
      if (j=i)
        if (Buff4 is full)
          Write contents of Buff4 to end block on HT'[i]
          Set to empty Buff4
          Allocate new block to end of HT'[i]
        endif
        Add IR to Buff4
      else
        { j is i+B }
        if (Buff5 is full)
          Write contents of Buff5 to end block on HT'[i+B]
          Set to empty Buff5
          Allocate new block to end of HT'[i+B]
        endif
        Add IR to Buff5
      endif
    end for { each index record in Buff1 }
    DeAllocate current block Bj of HT[i]
  end for { each Bj on HT[i] }
  Write contents of Buff4 to end block on HT'[i]
  Write contents of Buff5 to end block on HT'[i+B]
end for { each bucket i = 0,1, . . . , B−1 }
```

While the scheme performs the reorganization fairly efficiently, a potential source of concern is that, after the first reorganization, the base of the hash function's modulus will be divisible by two. There are motivations in some hashing contexts for using a prime modulus and additional motivations for avoiding a modulus divisible by two. However, these motivations primarily concern the hashing of data values that are not uniformly distributed and, in particular, protect against data patterns often encountered in internal hashing applications, such as the implementation of symbol tables that store program identifiers. In contrast, for many database contexts, the concern for nonuniform data is small. The database designer nevertheless must be alert to problems that would be posed to this scheme by certain patterns in the data.

Extendible Hashing: A Maintenance Scheme: There exist several hashing schemes that apply sophisticated Insert and Delete algorithms to maintain one or more highly desirable structural characteristics of a hashed file. One of the earliest and most elegant of these maintenance schemes was developed by Fagin et al. (1979). This scheme, known as **extendible hashing**, has many close parallels with balanced search trees.

The key structural characteristic maintained by the extendible hashing scheme is that each chain of the hashed file has a length of only one block. Additionally, the scheme attempts to utilize storage efficiently by reducing the number of chains when deletions shrink the size of the data file. Extendible hashing's strategy for maintaining this structure—paralleling the balancing strategy of B-trees—is based on operations that split chains when they would otherwise require a second block and that merge chains when they become sparsely populated. At the heart of the extendible hashing scheme is a hash function that gracefully supports such transformations to the structure of the hashed file.

We shall develop the scheme under the assumptions that: (1) a dense index on attribute A is to be hashed, and (2) index records with duplicate A values are not present. The first assumption is desirable (at least initially) because more index records than data records can fit per block and because it allows the data file to be ordered on some attribute other than A. However, as will be discussed later, extendible hashing is not completely inappropriate as a primary file structure, and we shall consider modifications in which the data file itself is hashed in the next subsection. The second assumption is of little consequence since we can accommodate the presence in the data file of duplicate A values by adopting the compressed index record technique described in Section 8.4.

To begin, we describe the form of a hash function that supports the extendible hashing scheme. Let h be a function

$$h: dom(A) \rightarrow \text{PAS}$$

where A is the hashed attribute, $dom(A)$ is the domain of A, and PAS is the **potential address space**. We assume at first that PAS is the set of all length M bit strings (for some integer $M > 0$) and that h is constructed by a randomizing technique [e.g., see Markowsky, Carter, and Wegman (1978)] that ensures that the probability that the ith bit $(1 \leq i \leq M)$ of $h(V)$ is 0 with probability near 0.5, independent of the values of other bits in the string $h(V)$ and of the distribution of data values.

How large should M, and hence PAS, be? Suppose for the moment that each bit string in PAS corresponds to a distinct bucket of hash table HT. We wish to ensure that, even if records with every possible value from the (machine representable) domain of attribute A are present in the data file, the probability is near 0 that more than k (the capacity of an index block) of these A values map under h to the same bit string. Assuming that h satisfies the probabilistic condition described earlier, it is a simple matter to calculate, for any desired $\epsilon > 0$, the smallest integer M such that the probability is less than ϵ that more than k A values map under h to the same bit string (see exercise 8.16). The motivation for choosing an M that yields a very small ϵ is that if more than k A values present in the index file map to the same bit string, the hashing scheme will be unable to accommodate the index file with only a single block on the corresponding chain, and an *ad hoc* overflow method will be required. Therefore, M should be selected so that the probability of this occurring is acceptably minute.

The difficulty with the scheme as described so far is that in order for it to satisfy the probabilistic condition for sufficiently small ϵ, PAS generally will have to be huge. Unless most members of *dom*(A) are simultaneously present in the data file, it would be extremely wasteful to have a hash table with $|\text{PAS}|$ buckets and to allocate to each of these buckets a block of storage. The beauty of the extendible hashing scheme is that, while the potential address space must be huge, the size of the hash table at any point in time usually closely reflects the number of index records present. Even if the number of records fluctuates widely, the hash table will grow and shrink, allowing its size to remain in phase with the number of index records.

The extendible hashing scheme realizes this behavior by imposing on PAS a *dynamic partition*. At any point in the life of the extendible hashing scheme, the current hash table HT will induce a partition into cells on PAS; the size of these cells is variable so that different patterns in the data can be accommodated. In particular, at any point in time, HT will consist of 2^d buckets, for some $1 \leq d \leq M$. This integer d is called the current **global depth** of the scheme and, typically, will be such that 2^d is far smaller than $|\text{PAS}|$. The global depth d specifies that up to d bits (usually the leading d bits) of the hash value $h(V)$ may be used to determine into which partition cell bit string $h(V)$ falls. That is, the finest partition of PAS supported by a hash table HT with global depth d consists of 2^d cells, each corresponding to a bucket of HT, and the cell into which any member of PAS falls is determined by the bit string's leading d bits. Figure 8.25 depicts the finest partition of PAS supported by a hash table with global depth $d = 3$. Each bucket of HT points to a distinct block, indicating that there is a one-to-one correspondence between buckets of HT and cells of the current partition. This correspondence implies that the block into which an index record with A value V is placed is determined by the leading three bits of $h(V)$.

While partitions of the form shown in Figure 8.25 are the finest partitions supported by a hash table of a given global depth, coarser partitions, with variable size cells, also may be induced by a hash table of this same global depth. In fact, hash table HT would evolve to a state corresponding to the finest partition consistent with its global depth only if no coarser partition support-

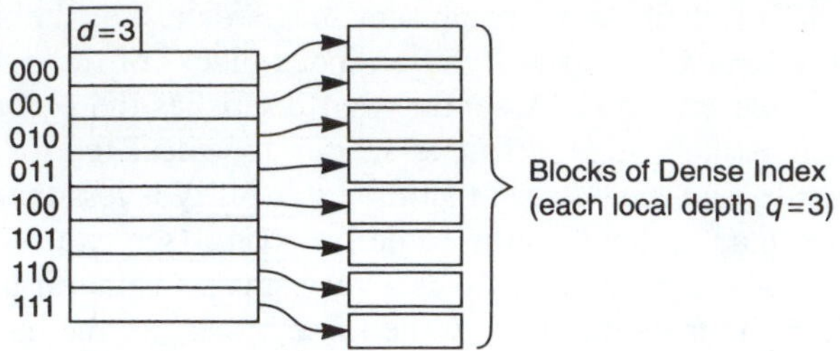

Figure 8.25 Finest partition of PAS supported by *HT* with $d = 3$

able by the scheme can accommodate the collection of *A* values currently appearing in the index file. What coarse partitions are supportable by a hash table of global depth *d*? A hash table with global depth *d* can support any partition in which each cell corresponds to all bit strings in PAS that agree on their leading *q* bits, for some $0 \leq q \leq d$. Note that the individual cells of a given partition may be defined by different *q's*—called the cell's **local depth**—and hence may correspond to differing numbers of bit strings.

The finest partition of PAS for a given global depth is the partition in which each cell has a local depth of *d*. The coarsest partition is the partition consisting of a single cell, whose local depth is 0. Figure 8.26 depicts the partition corresponding to an *HT* with $d = 3$ and a single cell with local depth 0. Note that all buckets of *HT* contain a pointer to the same block; all the cells of the finest partition are collapsed to a single cell, and all buckets of *HT* correspond to this cell. When the extendible hashing scheme is in this state, all index records are placed in the single block.

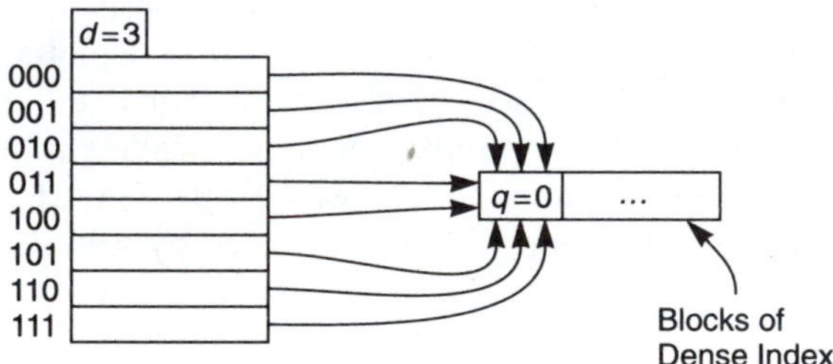

Figure 8.26 Global depth = 3; local depth = 0

Figure 8.27 depicts a partition of PAS corresponding to an *HT* with $d = 3$ and cells with differing local depths. Again, buckets point to the same block to collapse the corresponding cells of the finest partition. In Figure 8.27, for example, the hash table corresponds to the partition

{ {bit string whose leading bit is 0}, {bit strings whose leading two bits are 10}, {bit strings whose leading three bits are 110}, {bit strings whose leading 3 bits are 111} }

The local depths of these cells are 1, 2, and 3, respectively.

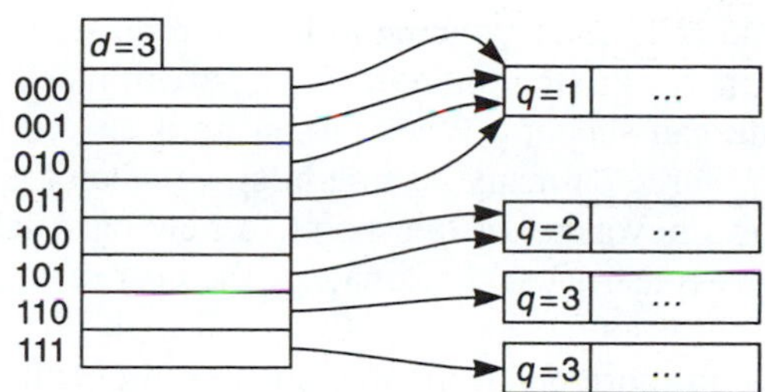

Figure 8.27 Global depth = 3; varying local depths

The ability to support partitions with varying local depths allows clusterings under h of attribute values to be "smoothed." Suppose, for example, that HT is the current hash table, inducing on PAS a particular partition, and that a new index record IR with A value V is to be inserted into the index file. Suppose further that bit string $h(V)$ falls into a cell C of HT's partition already containing k index records (see Figure 8.28). If the local depth of cell C is $q < d$, we can split C, creating two new cells, each with a local depth of $q + 1$, while other cells of the partition are left unchanged. With high probability, this finer partition will distinguish the index records [based on the $(q + 1)$st bit of their hash values] which hashed into C, allowing the index records (including IR) to be distributed between the two blocks implementing the new partition cells (see Figure 8.29).

In this way, when the current population of A values hashes in clusters to bit string prefixes, partition cells corresponding to heavily represented prefixes

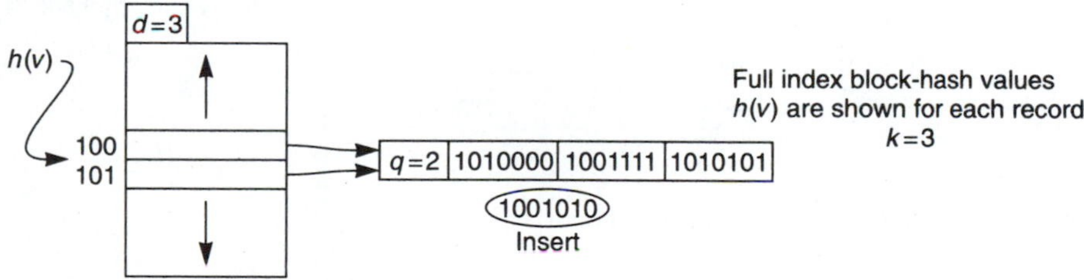

Figure 8.28 Insertion of IR into full block ($k = 3$)

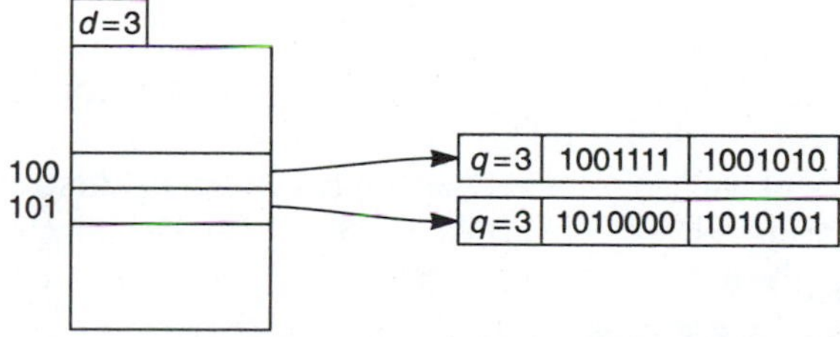

Figure 8.29 Refining the partition and splitting the full block

can be refined, while cells corresponding to lightly represented prefixes remain coarse. Of course, there is a limit on how fine a partition cell a hash table with a given global depth can support. When clustering is severe (in the sense that many hashed values agree on many leading bits), or when the number of index records simply grows beyond a certain point, a new hash table with a larger global depth must be constructed. Fortunately, the cost of this operation is not prohibitive.

We now describe in more detail the implementation of the extendible hashing scheme. Assume that hash table *HT* has global depth d. *HT* is stored externally, over a collection of contiguous blocks according to the binary counting sequence, so that the bucket labeled by the string of d 0's is first and the bucket labeled by the string of d 1's is last. Thus, given a bit string $b = h(V) \in PAS$, we can calculate the number of the block that contains the bucket $HT[b_{|d}]$, where $b_{|d}$ denotes the leading d bits of b.

Each bucket $HT[s]$ (s is a length d bit string) contains a pointer to a block of the index file. This block contains an integer q ($q \leq d$ and represents the local depth) and implements the partition cell corresponding to those strings of PAS whose leading q bits agree with the leading q bits of s. The block thus will be pointed to by the $2^{(d-q)}$ physically contiguous buckets of *HT* which are labeled by bit strings whose leading q bits agree with the leading q bits of s and will contain all index records whose A values hash to such bit strings. Figure 8.30 summarizes this structure for a hash table with global depth $d = 3$.

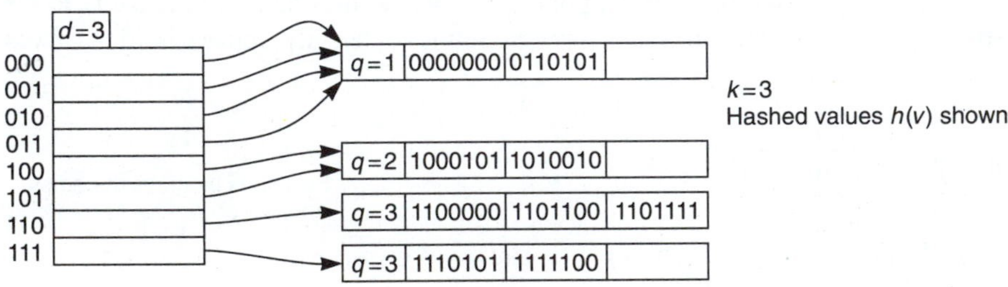

Figure 8.30 More detailed hash table with varying local depths

Now that we have presented the basic structure and strategy of the extendible hashing scheme, we describe how exact match retrievals, insertions, and deletions are implemented against a scheme whose current global depth is d. The exact match query $\sigma_{A=V}T$ is implemented by computing $b = h(V)$, accessing the block containing $HT[b_{|d}]$, and retrieving the index block pointed to by this bucket. If the index block contains an index record (V,p), the data record pointed to by p then is retrieved.

The insertion of an index record is implemented by first using the exact match procedure to retrieve the index block B that should contain an index record with the given A value. There then are three cases to consider:

1. The index block B has room for the index record. In this case, we simply insert into block B the new record. No further action is required.

2. The index block B does not have room for the new record. If the local depth q of block B is less that the global depth d, we split the block. This operation corresponds to refining, within the limits of the current global depth d, the partition of PAS. The split operation requires that we
   a. Acquire a new block B' for the index.
   b. Set to point to B' the $2^{(d-q-1)}$ pointers emanating from the buckets of HT that are labeled with bit strings whose leading $q + 1$ bits agree with the the $q + 1$ leading bits of $h(V)$. Note that these pointers previously pointed to block B.
   c. Set to $q + 1$ the local depths of blocks B and B'.
   d. Divide the index records (including the new index record) between blocks B and B', based on the $q + 1$st bit of the strings to which the records hash. Observe how this step distributes the index records based on the refined partition of PAS.
   e. Unless all the index records hash into bit strings that agree on their leading $q + 1$ bits, the insertion is complete. In the extremely unlikely event that the split did not succeed in making room for the new record, we must recursively apply the split operation to the block that received all the index records. The process continues until either we reach a bit on which at least some of the records differ or until the global depth of HT is reached. In the latter case, we must increase the global depth as is described in case 3.
3. We are unable to insert the new record without increasing the global depth of HT. That is, the finest partition of PAS supportable by a hash table of the current global depth d forces more than k index records into the same partition cell. We therefore increase the global depth of HT to $d + 1$. This operation has the effect of splitting each of the buckets in HT—the bucket labeled with the length d string b is split into two buckets, one labeled with the string $b \cdot 0$ and the other labeled with the string $b \cdot 1$. For simplicity, we shall assume that the new hash table HT', which has twice as many buckets as did HT, is stored over a new collection of contiguous blocks.

The new hash table HT' can support a finer partition of PAS than could HT. However, at least conceptually, we initialize HT' to implement the same partition that HT implemented at the time we were forced to increase the global depth. As is depicted in Figure 8.31, we accomplish this initialization by copying into each pair $HT'[b \cdot 0]$ and $HT'[b \cdot 1]$ of buckets the block pointer from $HT[b]$. It is important to note that no index blocks need to be accessed. Since we have not altered the local depths of the partition cells represented by the index blocks, HT' indeed implements the same partition of PAS as did HT. Of course, our motivation for increasing the global depth was to support a partition that could accommodate the insertion of a new index record. Therefore, we return to step 2, which now will be able to refine the partition cell

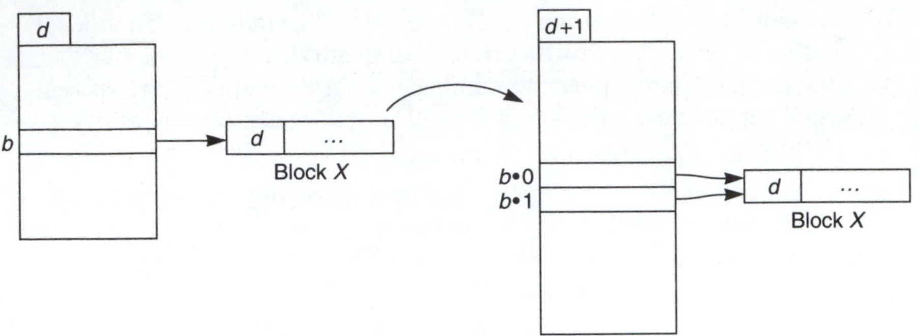

Figure 8.31 Increasing global depth from d to $d + 1$

into which the new index record must be placed. Note that in the extremely unlikely event that the split to be performed in step 2 does not succeed in making room for the new record, the global depth again will have to be increased.

We now illustrate these steps by performing a sequence of insertions, beginning with the hashed file of Figure 8.30. The sequence is depicted in Figure 8.32. To simplify our diagrams, we assume that the capacity k of a block is only three index records; in reality, the number might be several hundred.

1. Insert an index record whose value hashes into the bit string 1000111. Since the global depth of *HT* is 3, we use the first three bits and retrieve the block pointed to by *HT*[100]. Since this block can accommodate the new index record, we simply insert it there, as is shown in Figure 8.32*a*.
2. Insert an index record whose value hashes into the bit string 1010011. We retrieve the block pointed to by *HT*[101], which is the same block pointed to by *HT*[100]. This block now is full, but since it represents a partition cell with local depth 2, we can split the block. As is shown in Figure 8.32*b* the split is successful in making room for the new record.
3. Insert an index record whose value hashes into the bit string 1001000. This record belongs in the block pointed to by *HT*[100], and, since this block has room, we place it there as is shown in Figure 8.32*c*.
4. Insert an index record whose value hashes into the bit string 1001101. This record belongs in the block pointed to by *HT*[100], but this block now is full. Further, the block represents a partition cell with local depth 3, and hence it cannot be split. We therefore increase the global depth of the hash table, creating the new hash table *HT'* shown in Figure 8.32*d*. The block pointed to by *HT'*[1000] and *HT'*[1001] now can be split, allowing the new index record to be inserted. The resulting state of *HT'* is shown in Figure 8.32*e*.

Now consider the implementation against the extendible hashing scheme of deletions. Assume that we wish to delete the index record with value *V* from

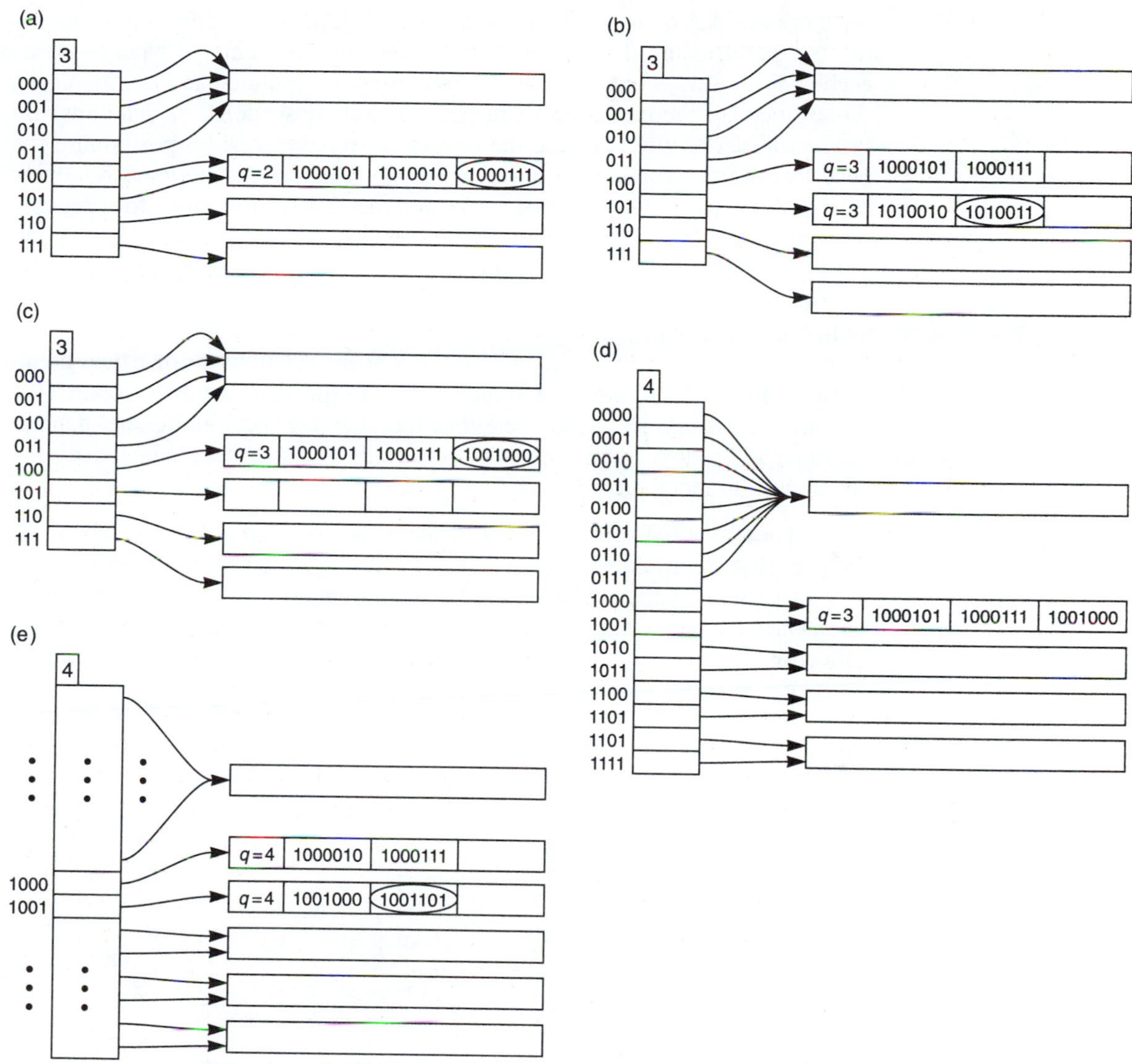

Figure 8.32 Sequence of insertions

the index file. The hash function first is used to locate the index block that would contain the index record if it were present, and, assuming that it is present, the record is removed. Following the removal of the index record, it may or may not be desirable to attempt to shrink the index file and the hash table. In many environments, it is appropriate for the Delete procedure to terminate after the record is removed, without attempting to shrink the structures. This might well be the case, for example, in an environment where external memory is relatively inexpensive compared with processing costs. This contention is based on the observation that high storage consumption is the primary penalty incurred by sparsely populated, or even empty, blocks—since each chain is always only one block long, sparsely populated and empty blocks do not increase the cost of exact match retrievals, insertions, or deletions.[2] In fact, such blocks will decrease the cost of some insertions by postponing the need for split operations. In environments where external memory is relatively expensive, it still might be appropriate for the Delete procedure to terminate without attempting to shrink the structures if it is the case that the file is growing rapidly and insertions can be expected to soon reuse the space created by deletions.

In other environments, especially environments where external memory is a scarce resource, it may be desirable to implement deletions so that they do attempt to shrink the index file and hash table. To this end, we define operations that are the reflections of the operations that increase local and global depths. Consider the following two types of operations that might be enabled by the deletion of an index record:

1. Suppose that index blocks B and B' have the same local depth q. Then it is the case that HT contains $2^{(d-q)}$ pointers to each of B and B' and, further, that each of these collections C and C' of pointers emanate from $2^{(d-q)}$ buckets of HT labeled by bit strings agreeing on their leading q bits. If, additionally, the collection $C \cup C'$ of $2^{(d-q+1)}$ pointers emanate from buckets of HT labeled by bit strings agreeing on their leading $q - 1$ bits, we say that B and B' are **siblings**. In Figure 8.33, for example, blocks B and B' are siblings. Note that the sibling relationships are a function of the current partition and that, in general, not all blocks will have siblings. In Figure 8.33, for example, block X has no sibling.

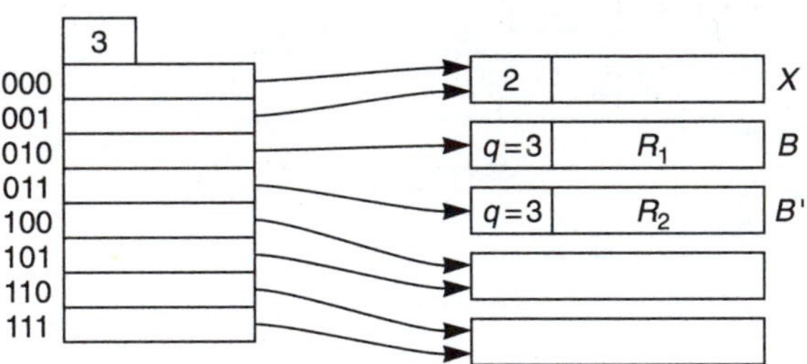

Figure 8.33 Global depth = 3; B and B' are siblings

The significance of sibling index blocks is that they are candidates for merging. If deletions leave the combined number of records in siblings B and B' less than the capacity k, these blocks can be merged. The Merge operation copies into B all the records in B', thus allowing B' to be deallocated. The partition

[2] See, however, the discussion in the next subsection on hashing variants.

implemented by the hash table is updated by decreasing the local depth of B and modifying all buckets in HT that used to point to B' so that they now point to B. Observe that such a Merge operation might enable subsequent merges since B (which has a new local depth) may now be a sibling of another sparsely populated block. Note, for example, that block X, which had no sibling in Figure 8.33, is the sibling of block B in Figure 8.34.

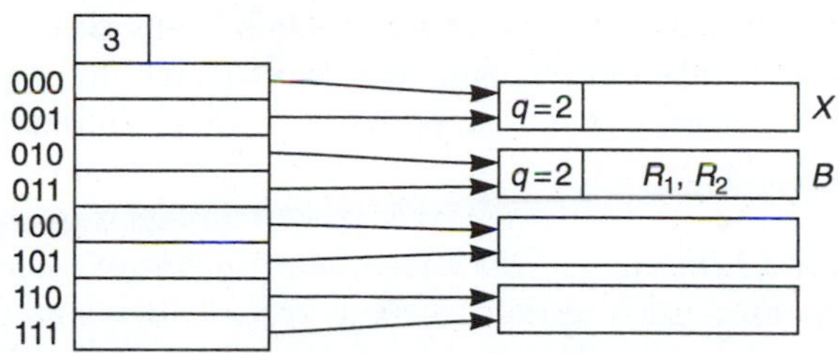

Figure 8.34 Merging of sibling index blocks B and B'

2. If the partition implemented by HT reaches a state in which each local depth is strictly less than the global depth, the global depth can be decreased by 1, resulting in a halving of the size of the hash table. If hash table HT with global depth d satisfies this condition, then, for each pair $b \cdot 0$ and $b \cdot 1$ of length d bit strings, $HT[b \cdot 0]$ and $HT[b \cdot 1]$ point to the same index block. HT', with global depth $d - 1$, is obtained from HT simply by setting each bucket $HT'[b]$ to point to the common index block pointed to by $HT[b \cdot 0]$ and $HT[b \cdot 1]$; no changes to the index blocks are required. Figure 8.35 illustrates the effect of the operation. We note that HT can be transformed in place to HT'. See exercise 8.18 for details.

Extendible hashing schemes that incorporate these operations into their deletion procedures require policies governing when the operations should be performed. For example, it probably is a bad idea to merge sibling blocks when their combined record count is exactly k. This policy would be susceptible to thrashing—sequences of insertions and deletions that require blocks to be split

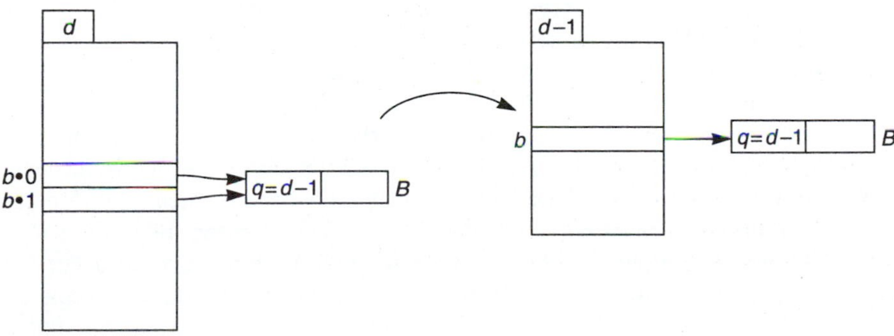

Figure 8.35 Decreasing the global depth

and merged continually. A better policy might be to merge sibling blocks when their combined record count is approximately $0.75 * k$. Whatever policies are chosen, the hashing scheme will require a strategy for detecting when the conditions of the policy are met; it is crucial that the work required to implement the policy not dominate the cost of the scheme. Frequently, an implementation will store extra information in the hash table in order to reduce the number of block accesses required to detect various conditions. One common technique is to store a count of the number of records in each index block in the hash table, thereby obviating the need to access index blocks merely to check whether or not they are sparse enough to be merged. Exercise 8.19 considers such implementation details.

Summary of the Efficiency of the Extendible Hashing Scheme: The processing of an exact match retrieval such as $\sigma_{A=V}T$ always requires only two block accesses (the hash table block containing the required bucket and the index block to which this bucket points) to locate the index record (V,p) with the specified value or to determine that no such index record exists. If an index record (V,p) does exist, additional accesses are required to follow pointer p into the data file.

An Insert or Delete operation that does not require index blocks to be merged or split requires two blocks to be read and the effected index block to be written. An insertion requiring that index block B_1 be split additionally requires that a new block B_2 be allocated and written and that half the pointers in the hash table that pointed to B_1 be changed so that they point to B_2; a deletion requiring that index blocks B_1 (which contained the deleted record) be merged with sibling B_2 additionally requires that B_2 be accessed and deallocated and that all the pointers in the hash table that pointed to B_2 be changed so that they point to B_1. For both the Insert and Delete operations, the number of block accesses required to modify the hash table pointers depends on the number of pointers that previously pointed to B_1 and B_2 and on the number of hash table blocks across which these pointers are spread. Note that, as described earlier, it is possible (although unlikely—see exercise 8.17) that a single insertion or deletion will require more than one split or merge operation. Note also that one or more additional hash table accesses may be required on some deletions to determine whether blocks can be merged with their siblings.

Periodically, an Insert or Delete operation, in addition to requiring that blocks be merged or split, will require that the global depth of the hash table be increased or decreased. Each of these operations is performed by accessing each block of both the old and new hash table exactly once. Both operations can be performed without accessing any blocks of the index file.

The worst-case performance of the extendible hashing scheme occurs in the unlikely event that many bits of the hash values are required to separate just a few index records. In particular, suppose that there are $k + 1$ index records (k is the number of index records a block can hold) and that the hash values of these records agree on their leading L bits. Then, the insertion of the last of these index records will cause repeated block splits and global depth increases until the global depth reaches $L + 1$. This implies that, although only $k + 1$ index records are present, the hash table contains 2^{L+1} buckets. (Note, however, that the scheme can be implemented so that index blocks that would otherwise be empty are not actually allocated.) Fortunately, the probability that a small number of records will push the scheme to a large global depth is extremely small, provided that h is a randomizing function or that the data values are drawn from a uniform distribution. See Fagin et al. (1979) for a more detailed analysis.

We conclude that the extendible hashing scheme provides excellent support for exact match retrievals, insertions, and deletions. In fact, for very large files, the only disadvantages the extendible hashing scheme suffers compared with B-tree schemes is the excessive storage it requires in pathological cases and its inability to support ordered retrievals. We conclude our discussion on hashing by presenting variations of the hashing schemes that, at least in some contexts, do provide support for some important ordered retrieval operations.

Ordered Hashing Variants

Recall that the term *ordered retrieval* is defined with respect to some specified sequence that is based on the values of an attribute or combination of attributes. Up to this point, the sequence of interest has always been *sorted on an attribute's value*. However, other sequences may be of interest as well. In this section, we consider hashing variants that support ordered retrievals, both when the ordered retrieval is with respect to a standard sorted sequence and when the ordered retrieval is with respect to a sequence ordered on the *hash values* $h(A)$. While the latter order at first might appear unnatural, it in fact supports a useful version of the Merge join algorithm presented in Chapter 11.

Extendible Hashing as a Support for Sorted Retrievals: We have been assuming that our hashing schemes employ randomizing hash functions. The motivation for randomizing hash functions is that they help to overcome nonuniformities in the distribution of data values that otherwise would lead to clusterings of hashed values and thus to unacceptably long chains. While the choice of a hash function is important to the success of any hashing scheme, we observe that the extendible hashing scheme's dynamic partition is itself a powerful mechanism for coping with the clustering of hashed values and that this mechanism may lessen our concern for how well the hash function avoids clustering. This observation is not meant to imply that the expected distribution of data values should not influence our choice of a hash function—if the values we encounter are hashed in an extremely skewed fashion, the extendible hashing scheme could require an unacceptably large hash table. The point rather is that the extendible hashing scheme can tolerate a good deal of clustering before performance (in this case, storage requirements) becomes unacceptable.

This observation may tempt us to construct, in some circumstances, an extendible hashing scheme that employs an order-preserving hash function, perhaps even the identity map. For example, we might simply use the binary representation of the values being hashed. Note that if h is any order preserving map to length M bit strings in the sense that $V < V' \rightarrow h(V) \leq h(V')$, then the truncation of h to the leading d bits (for any $d \leq M$) preserves order in this same sense. Hence, if an extendible hashing scheme employs an order-preserving hash function, hash table HT, of any global depth, has the property that all the values stored in the block pointed to by $HT[i]$ are greater than all the values stored in the block pointed to by $HT[i-1]$ $i \geq 2$. Therefore, if we chain together the index blocks as depicted in Figure 8.36, we can retrieve in sorted order all the values in the dense index by traversing the sorted chain; that is, the dense index is now ordered with respect to the sorted order.

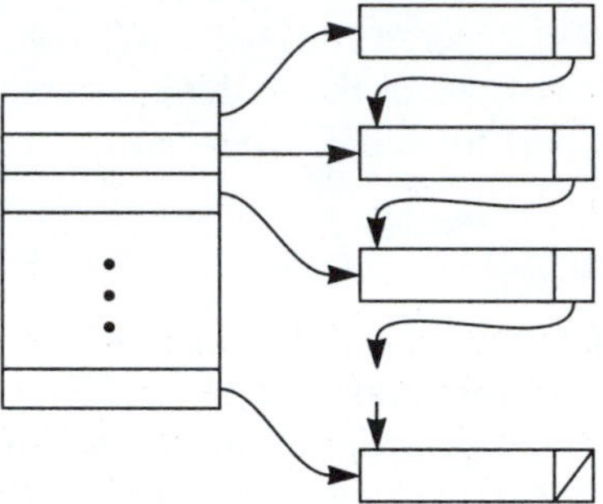

Figure 8.36 Chained hash blocks

The scheme just depicted supports ordered retrievals, such as $\Pi_{<A>} T$, that require only the value of the hashed attribute and also a version of the Merge join algorithm that requires only the values of the Join attributes to be retrieved in sorted order. Range queries, such as $\Pi_{<A>}(\sigma_{V \leq A \leq V'} T)$, requiring only the value of the hashed attribute, are also supported efficiently. We can answer such a range query by searching the index blocks that lie on the chain between (and including) the blocks pointed to by the buckets to which V and V' hash. Observe that of the blocks in this interval, only the first and last can contain index records that do not qualify. Further, if the Delete algorithm is implemented so that it merges sparsely populated blocks, we would generally expect the number blocks searched to closely reflect the numbers of qualifying index records.

When ordered retrievals of the entire data record are required, we might consider hashing the data file rather than the dense index. That is, we define the hash table so that its buckets point to blocks of the data file rather than to index blocks. The algorithms described previously are easily modified to work on this structure. Note that one disadvantage of hashing the data file rather than the index file is that, since data records are generally far larger than index records, a given population of records generally will require a larger hash table when the data file is hashed.

Retrievals Based on the Hash Ordering: Suppose that we use an arbitrary hashing scheme (where the chains may be of any length) and an arbitrary (e.g., randomizing) hash function to organize a dense index on attribute A. If we chain together the blocks as depicted in Figure 8.36, we can easily retrieve the index records in order sorted by the hash values $h(A)$. Similarly, if we hash the data file, we can retrieve the data records in order sorted by the hash values $h(A)$.

While at first there may seem to be little motivation for supporting these types of ordered retrieval, there are in fact some important algorithms—variants of the Merge join, for example—that such retrievals support. To illustrate, recall that a version of the standard Merge join algorithm for a table stored in internal memory was presented in Section 2.5. The essence of this algorithm, as well as of the external memory version of the algorithm, is that if the tables T_1 and T_2 to be joined are each stored sorted on the Join attribute, the Join can be computed in one pass. This is accomplished by simultaneously traversing the tables in sorted order, forming tuples in the result whenever attribute values are found to match.

In Chapter 11, we shall consider in detail several external memory variants of the Merge join algorithm. One variant can be used if the data files (or dense indices into the data files) corresponding to the operand tables T_1 and T_2 are stored hashed on the Join attributes, provided that the same hash function h is used for both files. (For simplicity, assume that the basic hashing scheme is used; the technique can be generalized to apply to the extendible hashing scheme as well.) Let HT_1 and HT_2 be the hash tables for T_1 and T_2, respectively. When T_1 and T_2 are so stored, it is the case that, for any i in the range of h, all the records of T_1 that hash to bucket $HT_1[i]$ can join with only records in T_2 that hash to bucket $HT_2[i]$, and vice versa. This observation will allow us to develop a Merge join algorithm in Chapter 11 that accesses the data records (or index records) of the operand tables in order sorted by their hash values. We postpone the details of this algorithm until Chapter 11 and conclude our discussion by observing that this Merge join algorithm will be able to compute the Join with a single pass of the data files (or index files) provided that either

1. For each i, the chains of buckets $HT_1[i]$ and $HT_2[i]$ can fit in internal memory at the same time, or
2. Within each hash chain, the records are stored sorted on the value of the Join attribute. Such an organization can be supported through trivial modifications to the Insert and Delete algorithms. We note that this organization in which records are stored sorted within each hash chain has a benefit beyond that of supporting the Merge join algorithm: If an operation requires the records to be retrieved in the standard sorted order, the Mergesort algorithm (see Section 7.4) can use the hash chains as initial sorted runs, thus reducing the algorithm's required number of passes.

SUMMARY AND ANNOTATED BIBLIOGRAPHY

In this chapter, we presented the fundamental techniques and structures employed in external storage implementations of the ADT search table. In addition to studying the most important specific external structures—ISAM, B-tree, and hashed files—we studied the general issues and principles arising in the design of the files used in an implementation.

One fundamental issue in the design of an external file is the choice of the file's primary structure. A primary structure has two components: a physical ordering on the file's data records and an index structure that efficiently supports both retrievals and the maintenance, in the face of insertions, of the physical ordering. A file's primary structure typically specifies that its data records are to be stored physically sorted on some attribute A (or on the concatenation of several attributes). Since a file's primary structure determines how the file's records are to be stored physically, a file may have only a single primary structure; therefore, the choice of a file's primary structure is an extremely important design decision. Among the factors that would lead us to choose a primary structure that is physically sorted on attribute A for the file implementing search table T are that we frequently must: (1) support operations that return tuples of T sorted by their A values; (2) support range queries of the form $\sigma_{V \leq A \leq V'} T$ that qualify many tuples; and (3) join table T, based on attribute A, with one or more other tables of an RDM.

The second component of a primary structure on attribute A is an index on A that both supports rapid searches for tuples with specified values of attribute A and allows us to efficiently identify where in the data file new tuples are to be inserted. Of the structures studied in this chapter, the sparse index of an ISAM file and several varieties of B-trees satisfy both criteria, while a hashed index generally does not support the latter criterion.

It sometimes is appropriate to impose no primary structure on a file—that is, to store its data records as a "random" heap of records. This design decision might be appropriate because maintaining a physical organization incurs a large overhead. Hence, if updates are frequent and operations that benefit most from a physical organization (such as the operations described earlier) are rare, it may be best to choose not to impose any primary structure on the file. The existence of pinning pointers into the file—pointers to data records that restrict where on the disk the records may reside—is a factor that greatly increases the difficulty of maintaining a physical organization and, hence, may contribute to the decision not to impose a primary structure.

The flexibility of the Search table's Select operator, which qualifies tuples based on potentially complex logical combinations of the values of arbitrary attributes, often mandates the extensive use of secondary indices. Unlike the index component of a primary file structure, a secondary index points into a data file whose organization is independent of the index. That is, a secondary index on attribute A points into a data file that may be either a heap or organized for a primary structure on some attribute other than A. Consequently, an arbitrary number of different secondary indices may be maintained on the same data file. A secondary index on attribute A of table T supports operations that qualify few tuples (e.g., an exact match query such as $\sigma_{A=V}T$) with essentially the same efficiency as do primary structures but are comparatively poor when entire data records must be retrieved in a specified order (e.g., as is required for the efficient processing of a range query such as $\sigma_{V' \leq A \leq V}T$) since, without a primary structure on attribute A, qualifying data records are likely scattered over many disk blocks. While secondary indices generally are far easier to maintain in the face of updates than are primary structures, their use does incur some overhead, in both storage costs and the effort required to update the index when the underlying table is updated. Consequently, the database designer must use care in deciding which of a table's attributes to index. The index selection problem is considered more fully in Chapter 9.

The chapter studied in detail several specific primary and secondary file structures. The ISAM file structure is a simple primary structure that utilizes a sparse, linearly structured index on a sorted data file. The B-tree, the most important general-purpose file structure, was first proposed in Bayer and McCreight (1972). We studied several B-tree variants and considered their use as both primary and secondary structures. See Comer (1979) for a further tutorial on the use of several of the B-tree variants discussed here. Hashed indices were presented as a specialized index structure, providing excellent support for exact match retrievals and some types of Update operations but failing to support ordered retrievals, in general. In addition to the basic hashed file structures, we described the dynamic hashing schemes of Aho, Hopcroft, and Ullman (1974); Ullman (1982); and Fagin et al. (1979).

The structures described in this chapter for implementing a search table are the primitives out of which we construct external memory implementations for an RDM. Chapter 9 begins our study of external memory RDM implementations by considering how to define the search tables that comprise an RDM, how to map these search tables to data files, and how to structure the data files. The final chapters of the book consider algorithms that operate on the file structures specified for the RDM implementation.

EXERCISES

1. The rows of the following table are labeled with search table processing operations, the columns with file structures. For each row of the table, rank each of the three file structures (1 = best; 2 = middle; 3 = worst) with regard to how efficiently it supports the operation in question.

	ISAM	B^+ Tree (Secondary)	Hashed File
Range query			
Exact match			
Insert/Delete			

2. The chapter argues that when data records may point into a file using pointers that pin records to a particular location, records in the file may not be moved. A possible way around this problem is to have each data record in a pinned file point back to each record that points to it. Describe the details of such a scheme. Your scheme should address the problems of not knowing in advance how many backpointers will be required for each record in the data file and that this number may vary over time and from record to record. Analyze the effort required to update all relevant pointers when a new pinning record is inserted and a pinned record is moved.
3. Describe techniques for maintaining a data file clustered on attribute A. Consider both pinned and unpinned cases. How does the required effort compare with the case when we maintain the file sorted on attribute A?
4. Consider an application in which we are required to perform sorted traversals that require the entire data record. Suppose further that data records are pinned to blocks so that it is not possible to keep the file physically sorted in the face of insertions. Consider two storage schemes:
   a. Maintain a hashed data file.
   b. Maintain an ISAM file in which each index record points to the head of a virtual block rather than to a single block.

   Observe that under either scheme, it is possible to keep the records within each data block sorted (although, of course, the records will not be sorted between data blocks). For each of the two storage schemes mentioned, describe what, if any, advantage with regard to the sorted traversal operation is gained by doing this. You may assume that there is more than enough internal memory to hold an entire hash bucket or virtual block and that ample external storage space is available.
5. Consider linking together the records of a hashed data file in sorted order. The idea is to make a sorted traversal feasible. What effect does this scheme have on the Insert and Delete operations (in terms of expected number of block accesses)? Assuming only one block can be kept in main memory at once, analyze the expected number of block accesses required for a sorted traversal. State your assumptions.
6. Suppose we had an ISAM file modified to accommodate pinned records, as described in this chapter. Describe how the records can be linked together to make sorted traversals more efficient. What effect does this plan have on the Insert and Delete operations (in terms of expected number of block accesses)? Assuming only one block can be kept in main memory at once, analyze the expected number of block accesses required for a sorted traversal. State your assumptions and compare this scheme with the hashing scheme of exercise 5.
7. Modify the SearchIdx algorithm of the ISAM implementation to ac-

count for the fact that the index file is a sorted chain of blocks and that an array of block pointers is maintained to enforce the order.

8. The ISAM implementation presented in the chapter makes no assumptions on the attribute(s) being indexed. Under the assumption that the attribute(s) on which the ISAM structure is based do form a key, the implementation described can be simplified considerably. Identify where the simplifications occur.
9. Prove Lemma 8.1, that a *k*-degree B-tree containing *N* records has height no more than

$$CEIL\left(\log_{(k\ div\ 2)+1}\left(\frac{N}{k\ div\ 2}\right)\right) + 1$$

10. This problem considers worst-case insertions and deletions.
    a. Begin with a degree $m = 5$ B-tree (the basic B-tree in which a dense index is scattered throughout the tree) with a height of at least 3. Give a complete trace of the effects of an insertion that causes the height of the tree to increase.
    b. Begin with a degree $m = 5$ B-tree (the basic B-tree in which a dense index is scattered throughout the tree) with a height of at least 3. Give a complete trace of the effects of a deletion that causes the height of the tree to decrease.
11. The chapter considered four B-tree variants:

    Secondary B-tree—dense index throughout entire tree pointing to heap

    Secondary B^+-tree—dense index in leaves pointing to heap

    Primary B-tree—dense index throughout entire tree pointing to ordered data file

    Primary B^+-tree—dense index in leaves pointing to ordered data file

    For each scheme, compare

    - Space requirements
    - Block accesses (best/worst/expected) for

      Retrieve

      Insert

      Delete

      Traverse sorted (just keys)

      Traverse sorted (data records)

    Base your analysis on the following:

    D = total number of data records

    M = maximum number of data records per block

$2 * C * M$ = maximum number of index records per block (thus, degree of B-tree is $2 * C * M + 1$)

C = number of blocks that main memory can hold

For simplicity, assume that pointers are so small in comparison with key values that they effectively take up no space.

12. A variation of the basic B-tree scheme does not allow nodes to become less than two-thirds full (rather than less than one-half full). Develop algorithms (at a high level) for insertions and deletions under this scheme. Weigh the potential advantages and disadvantages.
13. The chapter assumes a method for handling duplicate values in a B-tree by means of an auxiliary structure. An alternative method places the duplicate values within the tree, using some convention regarding which branch to take in case of ties. Compare the potential efficiencies of the two methods (in terms of possible number of block accesses) to process the query $\sigma_{A=V}T$, when m tuples qualify.
14. Modify the hash table reorganization algorithm of Section 8.5 so that it requires fewer than six program buffers. What is the fewest number of buffers that support the reorganization? What are the effects on efficiency?
15. Suppose we use an extendible hashing scheme to structure a file of records whose keys come from the range $0 \ldots 2^k - 1$ (no two records can have the same key value). For simplicity, assume that the hash function is the identity map. Suppose each index block can hold 2^i index records. What is the smallest maximum global depth needed to *guarantee* that no index chain will contain more than one block? What is the smallest number of records that can force the scheme to its maximum global depth? Describe a minimal cardinality collection of index records that would cause the bucket directory to reach this maximum size.
16. Let hash function h satisfy the probabilistic conditions of Section 8.5. Demonstrate how, given any $\epsilon > 0$, we can calculate the smallest integer M such that the probability is less than ϵ and that more than k A values map under h to the same bit string of length M.
17. Given that hash function h obeys the conditions of the previous problem, derive a bound on the probability that a single insertion or deletion will require more than one split or merge operation.
18. Describe an algorithm that can decrease *in place* the global depth of hash table HT, obtaining HT'.
19. A common technique is to store a count of the number of records in each index block in the hash table, thereby obviating the need to access index blocks merely to check whether or not they are sparse enough to be merged. Describe how such a scheme can be implemented. Be sure to consider how the information is updated when the table is modified. Analyze the expected savings and overhead of such a scheme.

CHAPTER 9

Designing a Relational Data Model's Physical Schema

The two primary factors determining the efficiency of an RDM's implementation are the physical organization of its data and the query optimization algorithms that map high-level queries into implementation-level programs that operate on this data. The basic storage structures for implementing single search tables that were studied in the previous chapter are among the primitives from which RDM implementations are built. One concern of this chapter is the problem of using these primitives to design the files that store an RDM's implementation-level tables. But before we can design an RDM's file structures, there is an even more fundamental problem to tackle: We must design the schemes for the RDM's implementation-level tables and specify how these tables map to data files. Chapters 4, 5, and 6 considered the design of implementation-level table schemes with respect to *semantic integrity* and, in response to this concern, introduced the theory of normalization. This chapter considers the design of implementation-level table schemes with respect to *efficiency*. The problems of designing implementation-level table schemes and of designing files for storing the tuples of these tables are referred to collectively as **physical schema design.•**

Physical schema design is one critical component of an RDM implementation. A second critical component of an RDM implementation—the query optimizer—is considered in Chapters 11, 12, and 13. It soon will become clear, however, that the problems of physical schema design and query optimization are closely intertwined. To decide how to design the RDM's physical schema, one must know how the query optimizer will utilize the structures chosen for the implementation. To design a query optimizer, one must know which structures may be present and the behavior of these structures. The overall optimization problem is enormously difficult. In fact, it should be kept in mind that the term *optimization*—be it applied to the design of a physical schema or to the selection of a query processing strategy—is used rather loosely. Generally speaking, there is little hope of finding the absolute best solution. Rather, we seek to make reasonable decisions that will lead to acceptable performance.

We begin in Section 9.1 with an overview of the physical schema design problem. Section 9.2 then considers the design of implementation-level tables, focusing on how the definition of these tables can affect the efficiency with which queries and updates are processed. Section 9.3 considers the problem of designing files for storing implementation-level tables. This section includes a description of a scheme in which several implementation-level tables are stored in a single file and considers the general problem of index selection. The chapter concludes with an example of a real-world design problem.

9.1 AN OVERVIEW OF PHYSICAL SCHEMA DESIGN

As indicated in the introductory paragraphs to this chapter, physical schema design encompasses the design of implementation-level tables and of file structures for storing these tables. To place the problem of physical schema design in perspective, recall that an RDM implementation consists of several levels of abstraction, including those depicted in Figure 9.1 and summarized in the following:

1. *Interface-level tables:* An RDM's interface-level tables are the tables with which most users interact. The typical user constructs queries and updates against these tables.

Interface-level tables of the RDM
↓
Implementation-level tables of the RDM
↓
Physical files

Figure 9.1 Levels of abstraction

2. *Implementation-level tables:* Tables at the implementation level are characterized by the fact that their tuples are in one-to-one correspondence with data records.[1] In many RDM implementations, the implementation-level and interface-level tables coincide exactly. However, we have seen that the theory of normalization can motivate the design of implementation-level tables that differ from interface-level tables. In this section, we shall see that efficiency considerations also sometimes motivate the design of implementation-level tables that differ from interface-level tables. When interface and implementation-level tables do differ, it is the responsibility of the query optimizer to map queries and updates stated against the interface-level tables into queries and updates stated against implementation-level tables.
3. *Physical files:* Physical files were the object of study in the previous two chapters. In those chapters, we implicitly assumed a one-to-one correspondence between implementation-level tables and physical files. Since each block of external memory "belongs" to at most one data file, this as-

[1] Here, *data record* has its natural meaning of a collection of fields disjoint from the fields of other records. This eliminates the possibility of using "logical records" that share fields to define the one-to-one correspondence, a possibility that would weaken the effect of the one-to-one restriction, possibly allowing tables at higher levels of abstraction to qualify as implementation-level tables.

sumed correspondence implies that all the records contained in any single data block correspond to the tuples of a single implementation-level table. While this one-to-one correspondence between implementation-level tables and physical files is by far the most natural and common way to store the data of an RDM, other mappings of tables to files are also useful in certain contexts. In Section 9.3, for example, we shall consider RDM implementations in which several implementation-level tables map to a single data file, allowing a single data block to contain records corresponding to tuples from more than one implementation-level table. The questions of how implementation-level tables map to physical files and of how to structure these physical files (e.g., using the techniques of the previous chapter) are major decisions in physical schema design.

9.2 DESIGNING AN RDM'S IMPLEMENTATION-LEVEL TABLES

When we studied the theory of normalization in Chapters 5 and 6, our perspective was that we were supplied with one or more interface-level tables and a set of dependencies associated with each of these tables. Our goal was to design, for each interface-level table, a collection of one or more implementation-level tables that organizes the information contained in the interface-level table in a semantically sound manner. We saw that it often is desirable to map a single interface-level table to several implementation-level tables to avoid the problems associated with redundancy.

Because implementation-level tables typically closely reflect the structure of the data files, the normalization process can have a major impact—both positive and negative—on the efficiency of an implementation. In the discussion that follows, we shall use the interface-level table

UNIV_RECORDS(Pname, Dept, Salary, Course#, Sect#, Semester, Sname)

to illustrate some of normalization's potential effects on efficiency. The semantics of table UNIV_RECORDS are as follows. For every distinct course ever offered by our university (where a distinct course is identified by its Course# and Sect# and the Semester in which it was taught), the table contains a tuple for each student who was enrolled in this course, and this tuple also supplies information about the professor who taught the course. For example, the tuple

Smith CS 60000 CS101 001 Fall90 Jones

indicates that Professor Smith taught CS101, Section 001, in the fall semester of 1990. The tuple also indicates that Professor Smith is in the computer science department, that she earns $60,000 a year, and that the student Jones was enrolled in CS101, Section 001, in the fall semester of 1990.

Suppose that the set $\Phi = \{$Pname $\rightarrow$ Dept Salary, Course# Sect# Semester $\rightarrow$ Pname, Sname Course# Semester $\rightarrow$ Sect#$\}$ of dependencies is known to apply to UNIV_RECORDS. Suppose further that, on average, a professor has taught 20 distinct courses and that the average course has an enrollment of 50 students. A scheme that maps tuples of UNIV_RECORDS directly to data records clearly would suffer from massive redundancy. The theory of normalization suggests that instead of a direct implementation, we decompose the table UNIV_RECORDS into several implementation-level tables. For example, we might map the interface-level table UNIV_RECORDS into the three implementation-level tables

PROF(Pname, Dept, Salary)
TEACHING_HISTORY(Pname, Course#, Sect#, Semester)
ENROLL_HISTORY(Sname, Course#, Sect#, Semester)

It can be verified that this is a lossless decomposition with respect to Φ, that the functional dependencies in Φ can be enforced on the decomposition, and that each of the table schemes is in 4NF.

In the following discussion, scheme A refers to the scheme that uses table UNIV_RECORDS as both an interface- and implementation-level table, and scheme B refers to the scheme that normalizes by decomposing UNIV_RECORDS into the three implementation-level tables PROF, TEACHING_HISTORY, and ENROLL_HISTORY. For purposes of illustration, we shall assume that scheme A stores its single data file physically sorted (chronologically) on Semester, while scheme B stores the data file corresponding to its table TEACHING_HISTORY physically sorted (chronologically) on Semester.

We now consider how the decision of whether to normalize or not impacts on various aspects of performance.

Normalization's Impact on Storage Costs and Certain Bulk Retrievals

Normalization generally reduces redundancy and hence the amount of external memory required to store the information embodied by the interface-level tables. Such a reduction has the obvious advantage of reducing storage costs, but it may also have the effect of improving the efficiency of certain retrievals that require traversals of the data files.

To illustrate this last point, consider the preceding university example and the query

$$\Pi_{<Pname, Course\#>}(\sigma_{V \leq Semester \leq V'} UNIV\_RECORDS)$$

stated against the interface-level table UNIV_RECORDS. We would be able to process this query more efficiently against scheme B than against scheme A because in scheme B, we need to access only the file corresponding to table TEACHING_HISTORY, and the qualifying records in this file are spread over far fewer blocks than are the qualifying records in the file corresponding to scheme A's table UNIV_RECORDS. In particular, not only are the tuples in UNIV_RECORDS larger than those in TEACHING_HISTORY (and hence fewer fit per block) but, since the average course has an enrollment of 50 students, on average 50 times more tuples will satisfy the selection ($\sigma_{V \leq Semester \leq V'}$

UNIV_RECORDS) than the selection ($\sigma_{V \leq Semester \leq V'}$ *TEACHING_HISTORY*). Thus, we would expect a major difference in the efficiency with which the two schemes support such a query.

The benefits of scheme B's clustering over relatively few blocks of the qualifying tuples of each of its tables could be so great that we would prefer to process even the query

$$\Pi_{<Pname, Salary, Course\#>}(\sigma_{V \leq Semester \leq V'} UNIV\_RECORDS)$$

against scheme B than against scheme A. This is true despite the fact that the query against scheme B requires a Join between implementation-level tables PROF and TEACHING_HISTORY. Assuming appropriate indices exist, the cost of this particular Join is small in comparison with redundancy's impact on the cost of processing the query against UNIV_RECORDS.

Normalization's Impact on Update Efficiency

Since we focus here on efficiency, we assume updates will be performed correctly against either design. Note, however, that performing updates correctly against scheme A could be extremely time consuming. If, for example, we wish to give Professor Smith a 10 percent raise, we must update the data records corresponding to each of Smith's approximately 1,000 tuples in table UNIV_RECORDS. If, on the other hand, we employ scheme B, only the data record corresponding to Smith's single tuple in table PROF must be updated.

Normalization's Impact on Queries Requiring Joins

Earlier, we considered the query

$$\Pi_{<Pname, Salary, Course\#>}(\sigma_{V \leq Semester \leq V'} UNIV\_RECORDS)$$

and argued that the query could be processed more efficiently against scheme B than against scheme A, despite the fact that a Join is required against scheme B. This circumstance actually is a bit unusual and results from the fact that the Join is specialized and was chosen to illustrate the potential harm of severe redundancy. More typically, a query involving a single interface-level table that requires a Join between tables of a decomposition could be processed faster if the single interface-level table is implemented directly instead of the decomposition. For example, in the university database, queries such as

$$\Pi_{<Pname, Sname>}(UNIV\_RECORDS)$$
$$\Pi_{<Pname, Salary, Sname>}(UNIV\_RECORDS)$$
$$\Pi_{<Course\#, Sect\#, Sname>}(\sigma_{Pname = \text{"Smith"}} UNIV\_RECORDS)$$
$$\Pi_{<Pname, Salary, Sname>}(\sigma_{V \leq Semester \leq V'} UNIV\_RECORDS)$$

would most likely (assuming the tables are implemented in a straightforward manner, with a reasonable choice of index structures) be processed faster against scheme A then against scheme B.

Of normalization's effects on efficiency, only the last is negative. Unfortunately, this type of effect often dominates. Hence, in the context of each particular application, we must weigh carefully, in light of the processing tasks we expect to encounter, the trade-offs between gains in semantic integrity and losses in efficiency. In some cases, we will discover that a heavy penalty is incurred by normalization and, as a consequence, we must consider two courses of action:

1. *Do not decompose:* In certain circumstances, we may decide not to normalize certain interface-level tables but rather to map them to identical implementation-level tables. This is an appropriate decision only in the context of applications in which the importance of queries that would require costly Join operations if we were to decompose clearly outweigh the benefits of normalization. If we decide not to decompose, we must be extremely careful to verify that updates do not violate integrity constraints, as inconsistencies arising in the database are perhaps the most disastrous consequence of implementing unnormalized table schemes. Of course, the cost of verifying the integrity constraints must be factored into the design decisions.
2. *Decompose, but attempt to mitigate the Join penalty:* For most applications, the benefits of normalizing will outweigh the penalties. This is especially so because, with care, we can define storage structures that greatly mitigate the costs of the Join operations necessitated by the decomposition. Suppose, for example, that for the purposes of normalization we have decomposed interface-level table T into implementation-level tables $T_1, T_2, \ldots, T_k$, where $k \geq 2$. Typically, there is a frequently encountered class of queries requiring a specific Join between the k implementation-level tables (or some subset of the k tables) that would require only a Select and Project against interface-level table T. The aspect of physical schema design that defines the map from implementation-level tables to files has the opportunity to introduce storage structures tailored to support efficient processing of such classes of queries. With care, the mapping of the implementation-level tables to file structures can be defined in such a way that the Joins in question can be performed in a highly efficient manner. Later in this chapter we shall consider several such file structuring techniques.

Data Aggregation Decisions

Normalization decisions form one class of issues that must be considered in the design of an RDM's implementation-level tables. Another class of issues involves **data aggregation** decisions. Data aggregation decisions are viewed best in terms of entity/relation (E/R) diagrams. The reader at this time may wish to review the E/R diagram terminology introduced in Section 4.1.

Normalization decisions involve the question of when to split an entity in an attempt to reduce redundancy. Such a split results in two or more entities

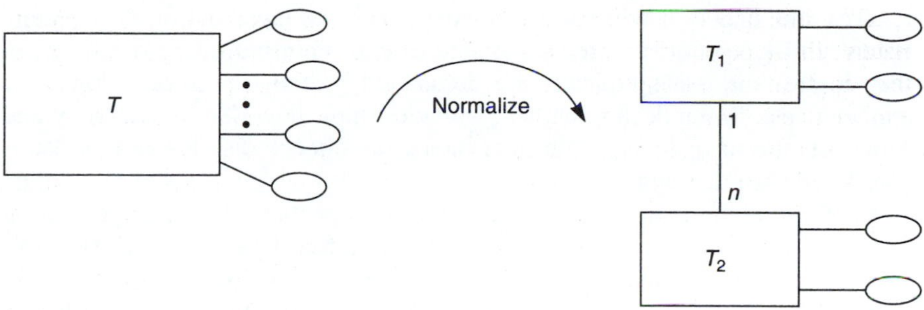

Figure 9.2 Entities connected by $1:n$ relationships

connected by one or more $1:n$ or $n:m$ relationships, as is depicted in Figure 9.2. Aggregation decisions, on the other hand, involve questions of when to split an entity in a manner that will result in $1:1$ relationships connecting the resulting entities and when to merge into a single entity two or more entities connected by $1:1$ relationships. These aggregation decisions are depicted in Figure 9.3.

Whereas the decision factors in normalization are primarily redundancy reduction versus the costs incurred by Joins, the decision factors in data aggregation are primarily how we wish attributes to be partitioned into physical

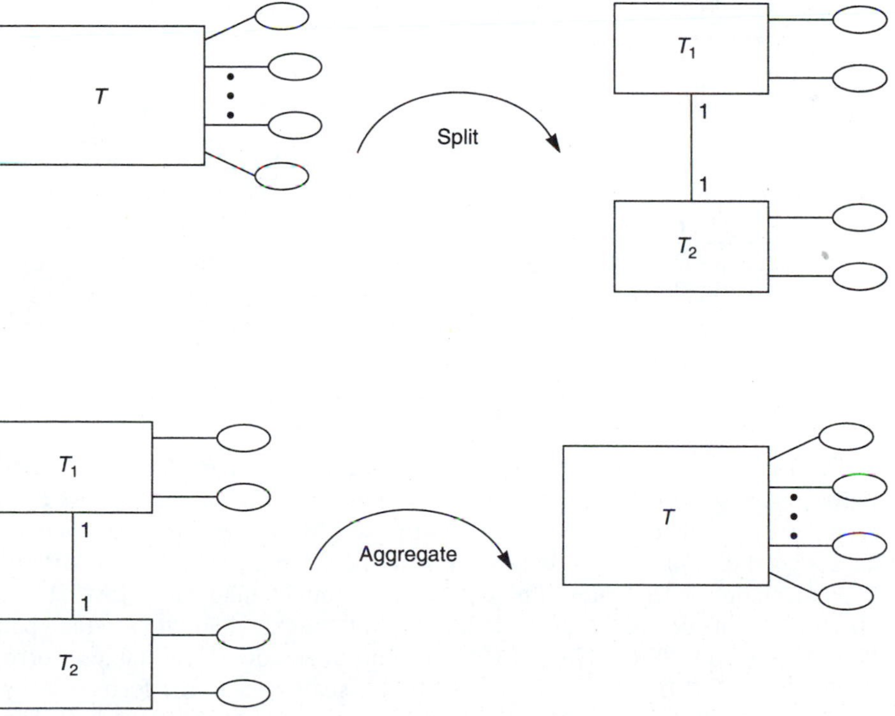

Figure 9.3 Entities connected by $1:1$ relationships

records and, hence, how we wish the attributes to be layed out on disk. While issues of disk layout can arise to a limited extent in normalization decisions, in that context the issues typically are dominated by the factors of redundancy and Join cost. When dealing with 1 : 1 relationships, however, redundancy and Join costs are of relatively little importance, and hence disk layout can dominate the design decision.

We illustrate by example the most important aspects of the data aggregation decision. Suppose that we are given an interface-level table EMP(SS#, A1, . . . , A99) and told that the functional dependency SS# → A1 . . . A99 applies to table EMP. Suppose further that we are told that no functional or multivalued dependencies that are not logical consequences of this dependency, or that are not trivial dependencies, apply to EMP. If we wish to view the information embodied by the table EMP as an E/R diagram, we find that there are many ways to partition the attributes {A1, . . . , A99} into different entities related by the attribute SS#. Figure 9.4 depicts three alternative E/R diagrams for this information. Observe that the functional dependency SS# → A1 . . . A99 for EMP implies that each of the relationships in Figure 9.4 is 1 : 1.

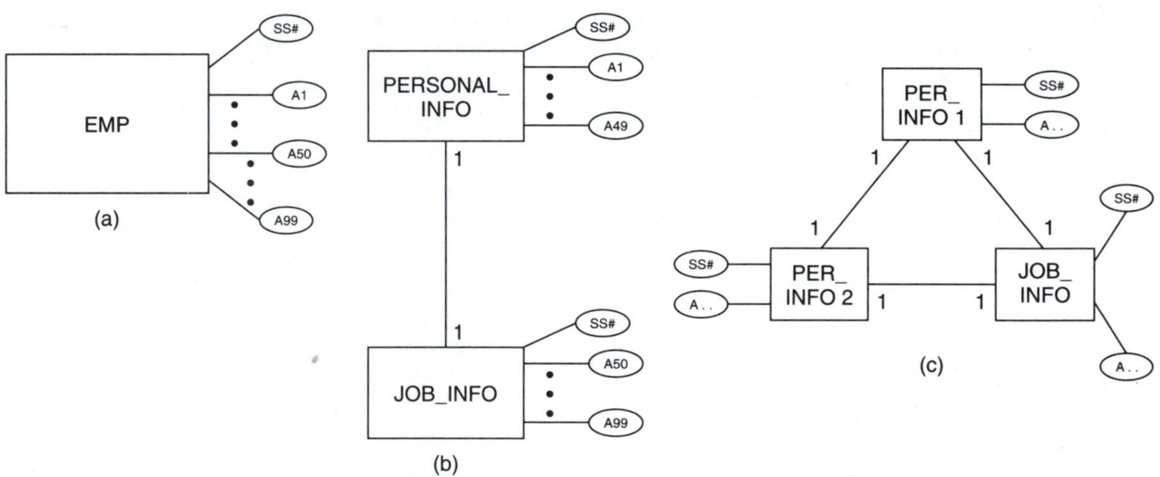

Figure 9.4 E/R diagrams for three different views of the data

The factors that have influenced users to select EMP(SS#, A1, . . . , A99) as their interface-level table are outside the context of this discussion. As database designers, although we must support table EMP at the interface level, we have a good deal of freedom in how we map the interface-level table EMP into implementation-level tables. For example, we might map table EMP to an identical implementation-level table, or we might map it to the pair JOB_INFO and PERSONAL_INFO of implementation-level tables corresponding the E/R diagram of Figure 9.4b. We shall refer to the former design as implementation scheme A and the latter as implementation scheme B. Figure 9.5 depicts these two implementation options.

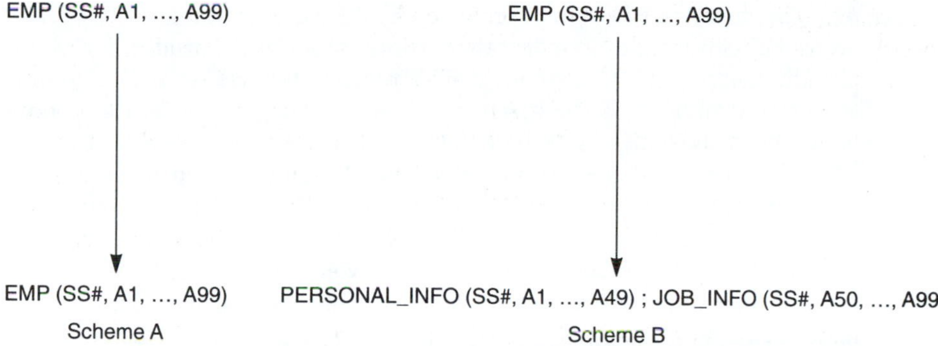

Figure 9.5 Two mappings of EMP to implementation-level tables

In choosing between the two implementation schemes, we observe first that each of the three table schemes EMP, JOB_INFO, and PERSONAL_INFO is in 4NF since the only nontrivial functional or multivalued dependencies involve superkeys on the left side. Further, observe that although SS# is duplicated in scheme B, the storage requirements for the two schemes are very close, and that in either case there are no apparent vulnerabilities to inconsistent updating. Hence, our decision of implementation-level tables is not driven in this situation by normalization or redundancy concerns.

What should drive our decision in this case is our expectation of the types and frequencies of queries that will access particular subsets of the set {SS#, A1, . . . , A99} of attributes. The following are some of the major factors to be considered:

1. *Individual queries whose referenced attributes are contained in either {SS#,A1, . . . , A49} or {SS#,A50, . . . , A99}*: Consider a query that references attributes from exactly one of the sets, for example, the query $\Pi_{<S>}(\sigma_F(EMP))$, where S is a subset of one of the attribute sets and Boolean formula F references attributes in only this same set. There are several subcases to consider:

   a. The selection criteria qualifies a single tuple: Such a query might be $\Pi_{<S>}(\sigma_{SS\#=x}EMP)$, where S is a subset of either {SS#,A1, . . . , A49} or {SS#,A50, . . . , A99}. In this case, provided that an index exists on SS#, it does not much matter whether we use implementation scheme A or B. If the index on SS# is a B-tree or a hashed dense index, we can retrieve the qualifying tuple with a single data block access, regardless of which implementation-level table is used, and the structure and size of the data records do not affect the speed of the search of such an index. (Note, however, that the sizes of the records in the data file can somewhat affect the speed of a search of an ISAM or hashed data file.) On the other hand, if no index on SS# is present, we must scan a data file, and we would prefer to scan a file corresponding to implementation-level table JOB_INFO or PERSONAL_INFO since such a file would be spread over fewer blocks than would the file corresponding to table EMP.

b. The query requires an ordered retrieval, and it is viable to physically order the relevant files to reflect the retrieval ordering. Consider, for example, the range query $\Pi_{<S>}(\sigma_{v \leq A1 \leq v'} EMP)$ which projects on and references attributes contained in {SS#,A1, . . . , A49}. Suppose we are to choose between an implementation in which the data file corresponding to table EMP is maintained physically ordered on A1 and an implementation in which the data file corresponding to the table JOB_INFO is kept physically ordered on A1. In this case, there can be a significant advantage in using scheme B since the records to be retrieved would be expected to be spread over far fewer blocks than under scheme A. This case includes also an exact match retrieval $\Pi_{<S>}(\sigma_{A=v}(EMP))$, where many tuples satisfy the condition $A = v$. Here, if it is reasonable to maintain the files in question so that records with equal *A* values are clustered, we again would prefer to retrieve from scheme B.

c. The query qualifies a collection of nonsequential tuples. We say a collection of tuples is **nonsequential** if it is not viable to keep the data files in question ordered in a manner that will contiguously store the tuples in this collection. Operations requiring the retrieval of a collection of nonsequential tuples include ordered retrievals when it is not viable to physically order the data files to reflect the retrieval ordering (e.g., because other physical orderings are more important or because maintenance costs are too high) and queries with a selection criterion that is the disjunction of many exact match conditions (e.g., $\Pi_{<S>}(\sigma_{A1=v1 \vee \cdots \vee A_k=v_k}(T))$). The behavior of operations in this class are analogous to that of a sequence of operations in class *a*, and the design considerations discussed in the context of that class apply here as well.

2. *Individual queries that reference attributes appearing in both the sets {A1, . . . , A49} and {A50, . . . , A99}*: For example, a query $\Pi_{<S>}(\sigma_F(EMP))$, where *S* has a nonempty intersection with each of {A1, . . . , A49} and {A50, . . . , A99}. Processing such queries against implementation scheme B requires a Natural join between the tables JOB_INFO and PERSONAL_INFO. Observe, however, that because of the 1 : 1 nature of the Join (the Join attribute SS# is a key of each table), the Join is such that for each tuple retrieved from the first table, exactly one tuple needs to be retrieved from the second. At worst, this requires a second index search on SS# followed by an access to a block of the second data file. In fact, we can obviate the need for the second index search by using pinning pointers between tables to connect tuples with matching SS#'s. This pointer scheme actually is a special case of the ring structure to be introduced in Section 11.5.

With these observations in mind, we consider two subclasses of this query class:

a. A single tuple, or a collection of nonsequential tuples, qualifies. In this case, the number of data block accesses required to process the operation against implementation scheme B is approximately twice that which would be required against scheme A since each hit in the first file requires an access into the second file. Additionally, unless tuples are linked between files, scheme B requires a second index search.

b. Many tuples qualify, and it is feasible to order the data files in question so that the qualifying tuples are stored contiguously. In particular, we mean that

For implementation scheme A, the file containing EMP records is stored ordered in such a way that the qualifying EMP records are stored contiguously (e.g., the query is a range query on attribute A_i and the file is stored sorted on A_i).

For implementation scheme B, the records that must be concatenated to form the qualifying tuples of EMP are stored contiguously in each file and in a compatible order (e.g., the query is a range query on A_i, the file implementing PERSONAL_INFO is stored sorted on A_i, and the *j*th record in each file agrees on the SS# attribute).

In this case, the records that must be accessed to process such operations against scheme A and scheme B are spread over approximately the same number of blocks, and each of these blocks need be accessed only once in either case. Hence, the schemata are essentially equivalent as supports for this subclass of query.

With these sample situations in mind, we make some general remarks regarding the data aggregation problem. Given the scheme $T(A_1, \ldots, A_n)$ of an interface-level table, a key $K \subseteq \{A_1, \ldots, A_n\}$, and the fact that no dependency that does not follow from the key dependency applies to scheme T, there are many possible semantically sound aggregations of the set $\{A_1, \ldots, A_n\}$ of attributes into implementation-level table schemes. In particular, each partioning of the set $(\{A_1, \ldots, A_n\} - K)$ corresponds to a semantically sound RDM schema definition, and there are $\Omega(2^m)$ partitionings of an m-element set. In an attempt to solve the aggregation problem, researchers have studied the problem using combinatorial optimization techniques. Although approaches to the problem differ, the following remarks apply in most cases:

1. To model the aggregation problem, we require a specification of the anticipated queries and updates, and this specification must indicate both the structure of the queries and updates (e.g., which attributes each query or update references) and the expected frequency with which each query and update will be performed.

2. Modeling the aggregation problem requires a cost function that evaluates how well a candidate schema will support the anticipated processing. While many different cost functions have been proposed, most correlate cost with the expected number of block accesses required to support the anticipated processing. An abstraction of the preceding examples indicates how we might predict the number of block accesses required to process the anticipated queries and updates against a candidate schema. A query qualifying one tuple from an interface-level table and requiring attributes that are spread across k implementa-

tion-level tables incurs k data block accesses, assuming appropriate indices exist. On the other hand, a query that qualifies many contiguously stored tuples, or that selects based on unindexed attributes, incurs a number of block accesses that is roughly proportional to the number of attributes, required by the query or not, that reside in the tables containing the required attributes. Hence, a cost function can yield a first approximation of the number of block accesses required to process the anticipated queries and updates against a candidate schema by computing some weighted combination of

a. the number of distinct implementation-level tables the operations must access, and

b. the total number of attributes, required or not, appearing in these tables.

3. The preceding remarks make it apparent that one class of operations is most efficiently processed against an implementation schema in which there are few tables, each consisting of many attributes, so that it is unlikely that any particular operation in this class will need to access the blocks of more than a few of the tables. On the other hand, another class of operations is most efficiently processed against a schema in which there are many tables, each with few attributes, so that it is unlikely that any particular operation in this class will need to access blocks containing many unneeded attributes. The optimization problem requires that we find an implementation schema that optimally balances these competing factors. Unfortunately, even extremely simple versions of this optimization problem are NP-hard, all but ruling out any hope of constructing a polynomial time algorithm for solving the problem exactly. On the other hand, researchers have proposed a variety of efficient aggregation heuristics for constructing solutions that, although they cannot guarantee optimality, appear to perform well in practice. The interested reader is referred to Babad (1977), Hammer and Niamir (1979), Helman (1989), and March (1983).

We make a final observation before progressing from the design of implementation-level tables to the design of physical files. The observation is that many of the aggregation decisions we have considered here could also be considered in the context of physical file design. That is, after we have designed the implementation-level tables, we could map these tables to files in a way that aggregates attributes differently than they are aggregated in the implementation-level tables. For example, if the RDM scheme contains two implementation-level tables $T_1(K, A_1, A_2, A_3)$ and $T_2(K, A_4, A_5)$ and if K is a key of each table, a file design decision could be to implement the tables with a single file. This decision would have the same effect as if we had aggregated the attributes of T_1 and T_2 into a single implementation-level table. Although there is little reason in practice to insist that such aggregation decisions be made when designing tables rather than files, for pedagogical reasons we shall generally assume that aggregation decisions are made in the context of table design. On the other hand, in the context of file design, we shall consider schemes that map RDM implementation-level tables connected by $1:n$ relationships into a single file. Such schemes differ fundamentally from the attribute aggregation strategies considered here in that they attempt to efficiently support the Joins necessitated by a normalization process that decomposed an interface-level table into several implementation-level tables. The functionality of the relationships between the tables that result from the normalization process dictates that we consider this strategy in the context of file, rather than table scheme, design since collapsing such table schemes would undo the beneficial effects of the normalization process.

9.3 DESIGNING THE PHYSICAL FILES

Once an RDM's implementation-level tables are specified, the next step in physical schema design is the design of the physical files that are to store the tables' data. We view the design of physical files as a two-phase process:

Phase I: The design of the map from an RDM's implementation-level tables to data files. By definition, there is a $1:1$ correspondence between an implementation-level table's tuples and data records. We nevertheless have some freedom in how we map these tables to data files. For example, we shall consider schemes that map several implementation-level tables to a single data file, allowing the records corresponding to the tuples of these different tables to be interspersed within the same data block.

Phase II: The design of the structures for the data files. In this phase, we structure the data files produced by Phase I, using methods such as those presented in Chapter 8.

We now consider these two phases of file design.

Mapping Implementation-Level Tables to Data Files

Given the collection $T_1, T_2, \ldots, T_k$ of an RDM's implementation-level tables, the most natural mapping to data files is the one-to-one mapping to the collection $F_1, F_2, \ldots, F_k$ of **homogeneous** data files. Each F_i is homogeneous in the sense that all the records in F_i are of a single type, matching the scheme of table T_i. In certain contexts, however, we might consider mapping two or more tables to a single data file F. In this case, F is said to be a **heterogeneous** file since it contains records of more than one type. Our primary motivation for considering heterogeneous data files is that they may efficiently support certain important Joins between implementation-level tables.

Before considering heterogeneous files in the context of our specific application, we consider what is involved in utilizing and maintaining heterogeneous files in general. Recall that we have viewed disk blocks as conceptually consisting of *slots* that hold records. While the blocks of a homogeneous file consist of slots of a uniform size, the blocks of a heterogeneous file consist of slots of differing sizes. When a block is allocated to a heterogeneous file, we think of the block as having no slots yet defined; when the first records are inserted into such blocks, we carve out slots of the appropriate sizes for the records. As with homogeneous files, we associate a deletion "bit" with each slot to encode one of the values FULL, EMPTY, or REUSE. (The value REUSE is required only if the records in the file are pinned to blocks.) Since the number of slots that a block of a heterogeneous file contains may vary over time (since its composition in terms of record types may vary), we reserve at each block's beginning a sufficient amount of space to store k deletion bits, where k is the number of records of the smallest type that can fit per block. In addition to associating a deletion bit with the slots of a block, we must also associate information that allows us to navigate through the records currently in a block. Note that the location (i.e., bytes from the beginning of the block) of the beginning of the ith slot depends on the sizes of slots $1,2, \ldots, i-1$. Hence, we store not only the status (FULL, EMPTY, or REUSE) of each slot at the beginning of each block but also the location of the slot's beginning. Further, we associate with each FULL slot information that tells us the type of record that is stored in that slot.[2] With these conventions, we can traverse any single implementation-level table stored in a heterogeneous file by accessing each block of the file and then using the bookkeeping information stored at the front of the block to direct us to records of the correct type.

Maintaining a heterogeneous file in the face of insertions and deletions presents some new problems. Slots left EMPTY (or REUSEable, in the case of pinned files) should be reused by insertions. With heterogeneous files, however, a record of a particular type can be inserted only into a slot that is of sufficient size. Consequently, if the mix of record types present in the file should change over time, there is the potential that the file will be left with many empty slots that cannot accommodate new records because the new records are too large for these slots. Additionally, if we insert a record into a slot that is smaller than the slot, we may be left with a small piece of the old slot that is unusable in the future. To address such problems, it may be necessary to employ memory management techniques that reconfigure the records within their blocks from time to time, for example, by moving all active records to the beginning of the block so that free space is contiguous at the end of the block. Such a reconfiguration, of course, must account for any pointers into the file pinning records to particular slots.

While heterogeneous files do incur some overhead, in certain situations their benefits are great enough to justify their use. Suppose, for example, that the normalization process has led us to decompose interface-level table T into implementation-level tables $T_1, T_2, \ldots, T_k$. It is likely that the evaluation of many user queries will require the evaluation of the Join $T_1 \bowtie T_2 \bowtie \cdots \bowtie T_k$. One way to support this Join efficiently is to map the tables $T_1, T_2, \ldots, T_k$ to a

[2] This is a conceptual description of the bookkeeping information that must be maintained. In practice, the information described would be condensed.

single, heterogeneous data file. The strategy is particularly appropriate if

1. $k > 2$.
2. For some numbering of the tables in the decomposition, T_i is in $1:n$ relationship with T_{i+1}, for $1 \le i \le k - 1$. That is, the operand tables can be numbered so that the set of attributes common to T_i and T_{i+1} is a superkey of T_i, for $1 \le i \le k - 1$.

We shall illustrate the scheme first under the assumption that each of these two conditions is satisfied. Later, we shall see that the scheme can have some limited benefits even if $k = 2$. The scheme we describe here can also be applied, with some modifications, in cases where the second condition is not satisfied. Exercise 9.1 considers this possibility.

To illustrate the use of heterogeneous files, consider again the three implementation-level tables

```
PROF(Pname, Dept, Salary)
TEACHING_HISTORY(Pname, Course#, Sect#, Semester)
ENROLL_HISTORY(Sname, Course#, Sect#, Semester)
```

As in the earlier discussion, we shall assume that these tables have resulted from normalizing the interface-level table UNIV_RECORDS(Pname, Dept, Salary, Course#, Sect#, Semester, Sname). Additionally, we shall continue to assume that {Pname} is a key of table scheme PROF, that {Course#, Sect#, Semester} is a key of table scheme TEACHING_HISTORY, and that {Sname, Course#, Semester} is a key of table scheme ENROLL_HISTORY. Hence, both of the preceding conditions are satisfied. The following hierarchy depicts the relationships of interest between the tables:

```
PROF
 | 1
 |    --- HAS_TAUGHT
 ↓ n
TEACHING_HISTORY
 | 1
 |    --- WAS_ENROLLED
 ↓ m
ENROLL_HISTORY
```

To simplify the following presentation, we shall assume that none of the three tables PROF, TEACHING_HISTORY, or ENROLL_HISTORY contains dangling tuples with respect to the Natural join. In practice, we might wish to allow dangling tuples; for example, the tuple for a new professor who has not yet taught any classes would dangle. The modifications to allow dangling tuples are straightforward and are explored in exercise 9.2.

Since users will be interacting with the interface-level table UNIV_RECORDS, it is likely that many queries will require the computation of the Join

PROF ⋈ TEACHING_HISTORY ⋈ ENROLL_HISTORY

To support this Join efficiently, we consider a structure in which the three implementation-level tables are mapped to a single data file that is organized to reflect the hierarchical nature of the relationships. With each tuple p of PROF we store those tuples $t_1, \ldots, t_i, \ldots, t_n$ of TEACHING_HISTORY such that p[Pname] = t_i[Pname]. With each tuple t of TEACHING_HISTORY, we store those tuples $e_1, \ldots, e_j, \ldots, e_m$ of ENROLL_HISTORY such that t[Course#, Sect#, Semester] = e_j[Course#, Sect#, Semester]. This structure is illustrated in Figure 9.6.

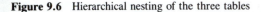

p t_1 s_1
⟨Smith, CS, 50K⟩⟨Smith, 463, 01, F91⟩⟨Tom, 463, 01, F91⟩

s_2 t_2 s_n
⟨Sue, 463, 01, F91⟩, ...⟨Smith, 502, 01, F91⟩⟨Fred, 502, 01, F91⟩ • • •

Figure 9.6 Hierarchical nesting of the three tables

Note how this organization effectively stores the Join PROF ⋈ TEACHING_HISTORY ⋈ ENROLL_HISTORY but avoids the redundancy that would be incurred if we were to directly store the interface-level table UNIV_RECORDS. The organization allows the Join PROF ⋈ TEACHING_HISTORY ⋈ ENROLL_HISTORY to be assembled efficiently, often with a single pass of the data file. Section 11.5 provides the details of the processing algorithm.

We observe that an improvement in both the time and space efficiency of this scheme can be achieved if we collapse common attribute values, as is depicted in Figure 9.7.[3] Since for any tuple p in PROF, all the tuples $t_1, t_2, \ldots, t_i, \ldots, t_n$ of TEACHING_HISTORY that are stored with p agree on the value of attribute Pname, we need to store this common value only once. Further, since for each of these tuples t_i, all the tuples $e_1, e_2, \ldots, e_j, \ldots, e_m$ of ENROLL_HISTORY that are stored with t_i agree on the values of the attributes Course#, Sect#, and Semester, we need to store these common values only once. This collapsing of common attribute values can substantially reduce the number of blocks over which the file is spread, and hence can reduce the cost

p t_1 s_1 s_2
⟨Smith, CS, 50K⟩⟨–, 463, 01, F91⟩⟨Tom, –, –, –⟩⟨Sue, –, –, –⟩

s_2 t_2 s_n
⟨Smith⟩⟨–, 502, 01, F91⟩⟨Fred, –, –, –⟩

Figure 9.7 Hierarchical nesting, collapsing key value

[3] Technically, this collapsing of common attribute values violates our pedagogical restriction that the tuples of an implementation-level table be in 1 : 1 correspondence with *physical* data records.

of the Join PROF ⋈ TEACHING_HISTORY ⋈ ENROLL_HISTORY as well as that of other operations. Note that if there are so many tuples with common attribute values that the tuples are spread over several blocks, we should store this common value once in each of these blocks, so that operations never require an extra block access to find a record's attribute values.

As we shall see in Section 11.5, this heterogeneous file scheme compares favorably with other schemes as a support for the Joins reflecting the hierarchical relationship. For $k > 2$, the scheme supports the k-table Join better than any other method we shall consider. For $k = 2$, a Join algorithm that merges physically sorted data files is a close competitor, although, in some contexts, the heterogeneous scheme has some advantages.

Since the heterogeneous file scheme is a primary file structure (it defines a physical organization on the data file, although there is some freedom in how the tuples are ordered within the hierarchy), we cannot definitively assess its value until we analyze it with respect to two additional criteria:

1. How well does the scheme support other operations? Other operations may be affected adversely by the scheme. In fact, the considerations here are similar to those that arose in the previous section when we considered aggregation decisions—the effect of the heterogeneous scheme, like that of a scheme that defines large aggregates, is to spread the tuples of a single table over many blocks. Consequently, any operation that requires traversals of only one of the implementation-level tables (e.g., a range query whose required attributes are contained in a single table) will suffer simply because the tuples that must be accessed are scattered over many blocks. On the other hand, an operation retrieving a single tuple will not suffer, provided that indices exist that make direct searches on the heterogeneous file unnecessary.
2. How difficult is the scheme to maintain? In general, a physical scheme is more difficult to maintain than is a logical scheme. We have already discussed the complexity of maintaining heterogeneous files in general; we now consider the problem of maintaining the hierarchical nesting structure induced by mapping a collection of implementation-level tables connected by a sequence of $1:n$ relationships to a single data file. The maintenance problem is much like that associated with a physically sorted file. When tuples are inserted in one table, we must find their proper place in the file based on the value of the Join attributes. Assuming that the table is indexed on the Join attributes, the position is located easily. We then must make room for the new record, which may require that we move records between blocks, closely paralleling the steps required to maintain a physically sorted file. If the data records are pinned to blocks, we must modify the structure so that movement of records between blocks can be avoided. The required modifications employ an overflow technique analogous to that employed when we maintain a pinned file physically sorted. See exercise 9.3 for details. In general, the difficulty of maintaining the heterogeneous structure is roughly comparable to the difficulty of maintaining a physically sorted file.

Structuring the Files

Once an RDM's implementation-level tables have been mapped to data files, the task at hand is to select primary and secondary structures for these files. Chapter 8 presented basic techniques for structuring files corresponding to individual, isolated search tables. In this section, we consider additional issues arising in the context of structuring a collection of files that implement the tables of an RDM. These additional issues include indexing a heterogeneous data file, specialized logical structures to support intertable operations, and the general index selection problem.

Indexing a Heterogeneous Data File: One set of issues arises when a heterogeneous file is used to store the tuples of several implementation-level tables. The previous discussion implies that it is extremely important to extensively index such files to efficiently support the most common retrievals and updates. Fortunately, many of the dense indexing techniques considered in Chapter 8 can be applied virtually intact to heterogeneous files.

Consider, for example, a situation in which heterogeneous file F stores the tuples of tables T_1,T_2, and T_3. Suppose that we expect to frequently encounter queries of the form $\sigma_{C=v} T_3$, where C is one of the attributes in table T_3. To support such a query efficiently, we would maintain a dense index on attribute C of table T_3. As does a dense index on a homogeneous file, this dense index on heterogeneous file F consists of a collection of records $<val,ptr>$, where ptr is a pointer to a tuple t in T_3 such that $t[C] = val$ (e.g., ptr specifies both the number of the block in F that contains tuple t and t's value on a key of T_3). Note that it is irrelevant to the structure of the dense index that tuples of the three tables are interleaved in F since we are assuming the presence in the blocks of F of bookkeeping information that allows us to identify the tuples belonging to any one of the tables T_i.

While a dense index that does not impose a physical structure on the data file is completely compatible with a heterogeneous file, such is not the case for an index that does impose a physical structure on the data file. Suppose, for example, that table T_3 is at the "bottom" of the relationship hierarchy and that we consider imposing a primary structure that requires that tuples of T_3 be stored physically sorted on attribute C. It is clear that such a physical ordering generally will not be compatible with the placement with T_2 tuples of T_3 tuples mandated by the heterogeneous file structure. If, on the other hand, table T_3 is the root of the relationship hierarchy, we could structure the heterogeneous data file so that tuples of T_3 are stored in F physically sorted on attribute C. However, since the interleaving in F of tuples from the three tables spreads the tuples of T_3 over a large number of blocks, many of the benefits of storing T_3 physically sorted are lost.

Specialized Logical Structures to Support Intertable Operations: There are a host of logical structures that can be employed to speed intertable operations such as Joins. These structures generally "connect" tuples from tables that are stored as distinct homogeneous data files. Although such logical structures cannot support Joins as efficiently as does the heterogeneous file structure, they have the advantage of not imposing a physical structure on the data files and, hence, are compatible with other organizations and are generally easier to maintain. An example of a logical Join support for tables stored in internal memory is the table of pointers introduced in Section 2.5. Section 11.5 will consider two logical Join supports for tables stored in external memory.

The General Index Selection Problem: Consider the following problem. An RDM consists of implementation-level tables $T_1, \ldots, T_M$ that have been mapped to data files $F_1, \ldots, F_N$. For each data file F_i, we wish to choose a primary structure (or decide not to have a primary structure) and zero or more additional secondary structures. Observe that the choice of a primary structure for F_i includes the selection of the attribute(s) on which the physical ordering is to be based and a selection of the index structure (e.g., B-tree or ISAM) that will support the physical ordering. Choices for secondary structures include the decision of what attributes (or combinations of attributes) to index and the types of indices to be used in each case.

What are the factors that must be weighed when making such design decisions? We begin by observing that the presence of a structure can have both positive and negative effects. The potential positive effects of a structure include

P1: The structure can speed the processing of certain retrievals. For example, an index on attribute A of table T may greatly speed the processing of queries such as $\sigma_{A=v} T$ and $T \underset{A=B}{\bowtie} T'$.

P2: The structure can speed the processing of certain updates. For example, an index on attribute A can speed the processing of Delete $(T, A = v)$.

The potential negative effects of a structure include

N1: The structure incurs storage costs. For example, a dense index contains a record <*val*,*ptr*> for every tuple in the table. Further, in the case of a structure that imposes a physical ordering on the data file, the data records may be spread over more blocks than would otherwise be required since we are restricted in how updates can be accommodated.

N2: The structure incurs an overhead on updates. Whenever records are inserted into and deleted from a data file, every index into the file must be adjusted. Further, when records are moved across blocks, all indices using pinning pointers must be adjusted. Additionally, a primary structure incurs overhead since it is difficult to maintain in the face of updates.

In summary, there are trade-offs associated with the decision to maintain each of its many potential primary and secondary structures for an RDM. To make intelligent design decisions, we require information regarding the anticipated processing requirements of the application. Ideally, we would be given a collection of the application's most important queries and updates, with an indication of the relative frequencies of these transactions and of the importance of fast response time for each. We should also be given an indication of the relative cost of various resources, such as disk storage and processing time.

Unfortunately, perfect information regarding processing requirements is rarely available, and even approximate information is hard to come by. Nevertheless, so that we may explore the nature of the design optimization problem, we shall suppose that we indeed do have reliable information. Consider, under this assumption, how we might select primary and secondary structures for the data files. At first it might appear that we could make a structuring decision for each attribute of each table in isolation of the decisions for each of the other attributes. For example, we might consider a design algorithm of the following form:

```
for (each table Ti)
  for (each attribute Aj in Ti)
    for (each potential structure S on Aj)
      assess the benefits to response time of S
      assess the penalties to response time of S
      consider the storage costs incurred by S
    end for
    decide which, if any, structure to maintain on Aj
  end for
end for
```

This is a rather naive design algorithm that fails to account for many important issues, including the interaction of structuring decisions. A more sophisticated algorithm accounts for the following:

1. The benefit of one structure depends on the presence of other structures. Suppose, for example, that one of the anticipated queries is $\sigma_{(A=v)\wedge(B=v')}(T)$. It is not possible to assess the benefits to this query of indexing attribute A in isolation of the decision of whether attribute B is to be indexed. For example, if attribute B is not to be indexed, the benefit of indexing A may be great, outweighing the penalties of its overhead. On the other hand, if attribute B is to be indexed, it may be the case that the benefit to this query of also indexing A is small (or none), and, as a consequence, the overhead outweighs the gain. In general, indexing decisions must be considered in combination.
2. Primary structures that are mutually exclusive. Only one primary structure is possible for a given data file, and a method is required for making a good, if not optimal, selection. It is important to note that this decision cannot be made in isolation of other structuring decisions. For example, in selecting between a primary structure sorted on attribute A and a primary structure sorted on attribute B, it is necessary to evaluate each choice in the context of the decisions regarding secondary structures that would be made in each case.
3. Intertable considerations. Points 1 and 2 would make the design problem difficult even if there were no interactions between tables; intertable op-

erators only increase the problem's complexity. For example, the benefit to a query such as $T_1 \underset{A=B}{\bowtie} T_2$ of an index structure on $T_1.A$ depends on whether (and how) $T_2.B$ is indexed. Similarly, the benefit to this query of a primary structure on A depends to a large extent on whether there is a primary structure on $T_2.B$.

These observations imply that entire designs, rather than individual decisions, must be evaluated.

Definition 9.1 Let $T_1, \ldots, T_M$ be the implementation-level tables of RDM $\mathcal{R}$, and let $F_1, \ldots, F_N$ be the data files to which these tables map. A (simple[4]) **design configuration** is a specification of

1. The primary structure for each F_i.
2. Whether or not a secondary structure is to be maintained for each attribute A_j of each table T_k. If a structure is to be maintained for an attribute, the design configuration must specify the type of structure. In a simple configuration, we assume that if a file's primary structure is based on A_j, then no secondary structure will be built on A_j.

In general, the number of candidate design configurations can be enormous, even when attention is restricted to simple configurations. Suppose, for example, that each T_i maps to its own homogeneous file, and thus $N = M$. To simplify the combinatorics further, suppose that each table contains the same number a of attributes. Let p denote the number of different primary structures available once we specify the choice for the attribute on which the structure is to be based, and let s denote the number of secondary structures available for any given attribute, including "no structure." Then,

- The number of primary structures for a table is $(a * p)$.
- The number of combinations of secondary structures for a table, if a primary exists, is s^{a-1}.
- The number of combinations of secondary structures for a table, if no primary exists, is s^a.

Hence, the number of possible designs for a single table is

$$(a * p)(s^{a-1}) + s^a = s^{a-1}(ap + s)$$

The total number of design configurations for all N files thus is

$$[s^{a-1}(ap + s)]^N$$

---

[4] We are defining configurations that are *simple* in the sense that (*a*) we do not allow multiple structures on any attribute and (*b*) we do not consider single structures on sets of attributes [e.g., an index on (Dept,Location)]. While nonsimple configurations may be useful, the restriction to simple configurations serves to simplify the discussion.

Consider now a second attempt at a simple algorithm for file structure design:

```
for (each design configuration D)
  Evaluate the cost of D with respect to the anticipated processing
    requirements and resource costs
end for
Select a least cost configuration D*
```

We put aside for the moment the possibility that the algorithm might require an inordinate amount of time simply to generate all design configurations and focus on the fact that we must be able to assess the cost of each candidate configuration. The storage costs of a candidate configuration can be assessed fairly easily, provided that we have an estimate on the number of tuples expected for each table. However, assessing the costs of processing the anticipated queries and updates against a candidate configuration is a more difficult task. Observe that this component of cost evaluation really is asking

> If the structures specified by design configuration D are implemented, how well will *our query optimizer QO* process the anticipated queries and updates?

The key point is that the benefits and drawbacks of the structures specified by a design configuration depend not only on the anticipated queries and updates but also on the query optimizer that will be used to process them. This dependence on the **target optimizer** QO is felt in several regards, including the following:

1. QO's algorithms for utilizing indices when processing Selects and Updates. Consider, for example, a query such as $\sigma_{((A=a)\wedge(B=b)\wedge(C=c))}(T)$. Before we can attempt to compare the merits of design configurations specifying various combinations of indices on attributes A, B, and C, we must know what algorithms are available to QO for utilizing indices when processing such a query. For example, if more than one of these indices is present, does QO possess an algorithm that will use the indices in conjunction? If QO can use only one index for such a query, how will it choose which index to use? Similarly, how will the query optimizer maintain indices following an update? We consider the issue of index utilization in Section 11.1.
2. QO's algorithms for processing Joins. Before we can compare the merits of design configurations specifying various indices and primary structures, we must know what algorithms are available to QO for utilizing these structures when processing a Join. For example, if QO possesses a Merge join algorithm, design configurations that specify primary structures on $T_1.A$ and $T_2.B$ may evaluate very favorably because such designs support the highly efficient Merge join algorithm to process $T_1 \bowtie T_2$. On the other hand, if QO does not possess a Merge join algorithm, these primary structures may be of little value. Similarly, knowledge of the indexed Join algorithms available to QO is necessary before we can evalu-

ate the relative merits of configurations specifying various combinations of secondary structures. We consider Join algorithms in Sections 11.2 through 11.5.

3. QO's method for selecting implementation programs. Even if we know all the algorithms available to QO for implementing the relational operators, we need to know what implementation-level program QO will select for a given query or update, given that a particular design configuration is implemented. Observe that a design configuration that is "good" in the sense that it supports excellent methods for processing the queries may not be good with respect to target optimizer QO if QO will not discover these excellent methods. Chapter 12 considers the process in which the query optimizer selects its implementation-level program.

In addition to this dependence on the query optimizer, there is a dependence on the database system's transaction management techniques. Transaction management issues are considered in Chapter 10.

In summary, two factors combine to make the design optimization problem extremely difficult:

1. There are a huge number of candidate design configurations.
2. Evaluation of each configuration is a formidable task.

The evaluation problem is often solved by invoking a modified version of the target optimizer. This modified optimizer is passed a query or update, a design configuration, and a description of "representative" instances of the RDM tables. The optimizer then reports back the implementation-level program that it would construct for processing the query in the situation described, along with an estimate of the cost (e.g., in number of block accesses) that would be incurred to process the query or update using this program.

Unfortunately, the huge number of candidate design configurations is a more fundamental obstacle than is the evaluation of a single candidate. It can be shown that, even if the target optimizer is available to perform cost evaluation, the problem of finding an optimal design configuration is NP-hard.[5] This result implies that, for some design problems, we should expect to spend time exponential to the number of tables and attributes if we are to find the optimal design configuration.

On a more positive note, there exist many efficient heuristics that in many cases find optimal, or at least good, designs. One simple design heuristic is based on the observation that often an RDM is composed of several independent groups of tables. That is, the tables of the RDM can be partitioned into groups $G_1, \ldots, G_k$ such that none of the anticipated queries or updates references a table from more than one G_i. In this case, we have k essentially inde-

[5] This result assumes that the target optimizer is a reasonably typical optimizer and uses indices in a reasonable way.

pendent design problems. If each of the G_i has a reasonably small number of attributes, it may be feasible to solve exactly the k optimization problems and combine the subconfigurations to form an optimal configuration for the original problem. Other design heuristics work on groups of attributes that appear to be closely coupled in the sense that they are referenced together frequently by the anticipated queries and updates. Since these attribute groups may not be strictly independent of one another, such heuristics are not guaranteed to produce globally optimal design configurations, although they appear to perform well in many real-world applications. The interested reader is referred to Finkelstein, Schkolnick, and Tiberio (1988) for further discussions on such design heuristics.

9.4 A SAMPLE DESIGN PROBLEM: DESIGNING A LIBRARY DATABASE

We have now discussed the many phases of database design, presenting techniques for mapping to a physical schema an initial representation of a database's informational requirements (e.g., as stated in an E/R diagram or an initial RDM scheme). These discussions have focused on design techniques ranging from normalization to the selection of primary and secondary file structures.

In a typical real-world application, the database designer is rarely presented with a neat, well-defined design problem. Rather, he or she is presented with a sometimes nebulous description of the informational and processing requirements of an application and forced to make reasonable decisions given the description available. In this closing section, we present a sample statement of an application's informational requirements and suggest that the reader attempt to obtain a sound database design by applying the techniques we have studied.

Description of the Library Application

A library maintains records of the publications (books and journal articles) that it holds, author biographical information, and library patron information. In particular, the following information is maintained:

For Each Book

Author(s). Maximum 200 bytes.

Title. Maximum 100 bytes.

Publisher. Maximum 50 bytes.

Publisher address. Maximum 100 bytes.

Year of publication. 1 byte.

Abstract. Maximum 500 words, 20 bytes each.

Key words. Maximum 20 words, 20 bytes each.

Library call number. 10 bytes.

Number on shelf. 1 byte.
Number checked out. 1 byte.

For Each Article

Author(s). Maximum 200 bytes.
Title. Maximum 100 bytes.
Journal name. Maximum 100 bytes.
Journal volume number. 1 byte.
Date of publication. 5 bytes.
Abstract. Maximum 500 words, 20 bytes each.
Key words. Maximum 20 words, 20 bytes each.
Library call number. 10 bytes.
Number on shelf. 1 byte.
Number checked out. 1 byte.

Additionally, each book and article includes a bibliography. A bibliography is a collection of entries of the form

Author(s). Maximum 200 bytes.
Title. Maximum 100 bytes.
Journal name. Maximum 100 bytes (if a journal article).
Journal volume number. 1 byte (if a journal article).
Publisher. Maximum 50 bytes (if a book).
Publisher address. Maximum 100 bytes (if a book).
Date of publication. 5 bytes.

There is no limit to the size of each bibliography.

For Each Author

Name. Maximum 20 bytes.
Date of birth. 5 bytes.
Date of death. 5 bytes.
Nationality. 10 bytes.

For Each Patron

Name. Maximum 20 bytes.
Address. Maximum 100 bytes.
Checked out books. A list of call numbers, no maximum.
Due dates. An associated list of dates, no maximum.
Fines owed. 2 bytes.

Assume that in our computer environment, each disk block is of size 1024 bytes.

The following identify the 15 most frequent operations. Listed with each operation is an estimate of the number of times this operation is performed per 100 library operations.

1. Given a call number, print all information for the publication with that call number (7 per 100).
2. Given a title, print all information for the publication with that title (12 per 100).
3. Given a Boolean expression of key words and dates (e.g., *Key words contain "computer" and ["database" or "relational"] and the publication date is between 1990 and 1992*), print all information about publications that meet the criterion of the Boolean expression (9 per 100).
4. Given an author name, print all information for the publications for which the name is listed as an author (6 per 100).
5. Given an author name, print all information stored about that author (3 per 100).
6. Given an author name, print the title and call number of each publication whose bibliography lists at least one publication attributed to that author (3 per 100).
7. Given a call number, determine the number of copies of the publication on shelf and checked out. If all copies are checked out, determine the patrons who have the publication checked out and the corresponding due dates (11 per 100).
8. Given a patron, determine what publications the patron has checked out, identifying those that are overdue, and report any fines currently owed by the patron (12 per 100).
9. Add an entry for a new publication (2 per 100).
10. Given a call number, update the corresponding entry. For example, update the number of on-shelf and checked-out copies (7 per 100).
11. Add a bibliographical entry for a new author (2 per 100).
12. Given an author, update the corresponding bibliographical entry. For example, record an author's date of death (1 per 100).
13. Add or delete a patron entry (4 per 100).
14. Given a patron, update the corresponding entry. For example, update the books checked out by the patron or the fines owed by the patron (12 per 100).
15. Print a report, in some easy to consume format, containing all information currently stored in the database (1 per 100).

Since the frequencies per 100 of these operations sum to less than 100, you are to assume that additional, as yet unspecified, operations are to be performed. Use your judgment to anticipate what other important processing tasks might not be identified here.

Design Goals

Your task is to obtain logical and physical RDM schemata. It is suggested that you begin with an E/R diagram and map to an RDM, asserting functional and multivalued dependencies that reasonably follow from the description. Identify any ambiguities that arise in the application's description, and state the assumptions you wish to make to resolve these ambiguities. (In a real application, you of course would have the opportunity to interact with the user community to identify functional and multivalued dependencies and to resolve ambiguities.) Next, apply normalization techniques to obtain a semantically sound RDM scheme. Finally, develop a physical schema that efficiently supports the anticipated processing. As discussed earlier in this chapter, proper optimization of the physical schema depends on the target optimizer. You might make simple assumptions about the target optimizer, or you might exploit your own knowledge of some target optimizer of your choosing. You might also revisit this design problem after we study query optimizers in Chapters 11 and 12.

SUMMARY AND ANNOTATED BIBLIOGRAPHY

In this chapter, we considered the problem of physical schema design for the RDM. This design problem consists of several, interacting phases:

1. *The design of implementation-level tables:* While we considered the design of implementation-level tables from the perspective of semantic integrity in Chapters 5 and 6, this chapter considered this design problem from the perspective of efficiency. We demonstrated how the database's expected usage patterns should influence the aggregation and decomposition decisions that determine the structure of the implementation-level tables. This design problem has been studied extensively by a good number of researchers; Babad (1977), Hammer and Niamir (1979), Helman (1989), March (1983), Smith and Smith (1977), Teorey and Fry (1982), and Yao and Kunii (1982) form a somewhat representative sample of results in this area.
2. *The mapping to data files of implementation-level tables:* The most straightforward mapping to data files of an RDM's implementation-level tables yields one homogeneous file for each table. The chapter considers also a many-to-one mapping in which a group of tables are mapped to a single heterogeneous data file and argues that such an implementation can be appropriate if queries frequently join these tables to pursue a hierarchical relationship that exists between the tables. ORACLE is one of the commercial relational database systems that supports a many-to-one mapping of groups of tables to a single heterogeneous data file.
3. *The structuring of physical files:* Because an RDM consists of many, interrelated table components, the problem of structuring the files that

implement the tables is far more complex than is the single search table implementation problem considered in Chapter 8. First, we may wish to impose logical structures that efficiently support their joining on certain subsets of the tables. Second, the index selection problem—in which primary and secondary structures are chosen for the tables—is extremely difficult because of both the combinatorial explosion in the number of candidate designs and the difficulty of evaluating a single design. The reader is referred to Finkelstein, Schkolnick, and Tiberio (1988) for discussions of approaches to this problem.

As the chapter emphasizes, there is much interaction between the target query optimizer and the design of the physical schema since the benefits and drawbacks of the structures specified by a candidate schema depend heavily on the query optimizer that will be used to process the queries. Hence, when we consider the query optimization problem in Chapters 11, 12, and 13, we shall revisit and refine many of the issues considered in this chapter.

This chapter concludes Part Three. Part Four considers in detail the algorithms that operate on the implementation structures presented in this and the previous chapter. This study begins in Chapter 10 by considering the fundamental problem of maintaining the database's integrity in the face of concurrent transactions, system failure, and intentional user misuse. Chapter 10 assumes that we have at hand implementation-level programs consisting of file-level Read and Write operations and presents techniques for performing these accesses in a manner that ensures that the database's integrity will not be violated, even if several of these programs attempt to simultaneously access the same data item and even if there should be a software or hardware failure. Chapters 11, 12, and 13 then consider query optimization, the process of mapping high-level queries to efficient implementation-level programs.

EXERCISES

1. Describe a modification to the the heterogeneous file scheme described in Section 9.3 that allows the scheme to be used even when the relationships in the hierarchy are $n:m$ rather than $1:n$.
2. Describe a modification to the the heterogeneous file scheme described in Section 9.3 that allows the scheme to be used even when tables may contain dangling tuples with respect to the Natural join in question.
3. Describe how the heterogeneous file scheme would be maintained in the face of updates. Consider how the functionality of the relations in the hierarchy, and the possible presence of dangling tuples, affect your algorithms. Consider the problem both for pinned and unpinned data records.
4. Let $T_1(A,B,C,D)$ and $T_2(A,E,F)$ be two implementation-level tables that we map to a single heterogeneous data file. Assume that A is a key of table T_1. For each of the following operations, describe the structures

(e.g., secondary indices) you would use to efficiently support the operation. Remember, each scheme you choose here must be compatible with the heterogeneous file structure. In describing your choice of structures for each operation, analyze how the fact that the heterogeneous file structure is being used affects the efficiency with which you can support the operation.

a. Exact match retrieval on A of T_1 records.

b. Exact match retrieval on A of T_2 records.

c. Range retrieval on A of T_1 records.

d. Exact match retrieval on E of T_2 records.

e. Range retrieval on E of T_2 records.

f. $\sigma_{A=V}(T_1 \bowtie T_2)$.

g. $T_1 \bowtie_{B=E} T_2$.

5. Suppose we have a collection of records of the form $R(A1, \ldots, A20)$. Assume these records are so large that very few will fit per block. Assume also that $A1$ is a key for the collection of records. Consider the following operations:

   i. Print all 20 fields of the record with $A1 = V$.

   ii. Print all 20 fields of the records such that $A1$ falls in the range $V1 \ldots V2$. Assume 50 percent of the records qualify.

   iii. Print fields $A1$, $A2$, and $A3$ of the record with $A1 = V$.

   iv. Print fields $A1$, $A2$, and $A3$ of the records such that $A1$ falls in the range $V1 \ldots V2$. Assume 50 percent of the records qualify.

   a. Suppose that each of operations i, ii, and iii is performed 33 percent of the time, while operation iv is performed 1 percent of the time. Describe a file structure scheme that efficiently supports this situation. Briefly describe how each operation is performed under your scheme, and analyze its efficiencies.

   b. Suppose that operation iv is performed 70 percent of the time, while each of operations i, ii, and iii is performed 10 percent of the time. Describe a file structure scheme that efficiently supports this situation. Briefly describe how each operation is performed under your scheme, and analyze its efficiencies.

6. Conjecture simple query optimization algorithms and, with respect to your optimizer, describe how the existence of an index on attribute A of table T affects the benefit of

   a. An index on attribute B of table T for the query $\sigma_{A=V \wedge B=V'} T$.

   b. An index on attribute A of table S for the query $T \bowtie S$.

PART **FOUR**

Implementations of the Relational Data Model Abstract Data Type—The Algorithms

CHAPTER 10

Transaction Management and Database Security

This chapter begins Part Four: The Algorithms. Most of the material in the part's four chapters deals with query optimization, the mapping of high-level queries stated against an RDM (or, as in Chapter 13, an alternative data model) to efficient implementation-level programs. Before embarking on our study of query optimization, however, this chapter considers an even more fundamental algorithmic problem: the problem of *managing the execution* of implementation-level programs. That is, in this chapter we shall assume that we have obtained from the query optimizer a collection of implementation-level programs that access our RDM's data, and we shall explore the problems that arise when we attempt to execute these programs. As we shall illustrate in Section 10.1, the problems of primary concern result from programs attempting to access the same data concurrently, and from the inevitability of occasional program and system failures. The solutions described in the sections that follow are the basic techniques of the component of an RDM implementation know as the **transaction manager.•**

The chapter also includes a discussion of database security and integrity in Section 10.7. While transaction management techniques address problems that can occur because of system design flaws or failure, Section 10.7 considers problems that arise directly from the actions of database users. These are user actions that, by their nature, would compromise the integrity or security of the database. Some of these problems are caused by user carelessness and others by malicious user behavior. We shall survey several different types of user abuse and discuss techniques for reducing their prevalence and containing their impact.

10.1 TRANSACTION MANAGEMENT ISSUES

In Section 1.5, we presented a classic example of the type of problem that can arise in a multiuser environment. In this example, two customers, at approximately the same time, attempt to purchase from different ticket agents the last seat on Flight 888. We can view the actions of each ticket agent as initiating a copy of the following program:

```
read into x seats available on Flight 888
if (x > 0)
  if (customer wishes to purchase seat)
      decrement x
      write x to seats available on Flight 888
  endif
else
  inform customer flight is sold out
endif
```

Two observations are in order:

1. The program presented here is written at an abstraction level somewhere between that of a high-level query language and that of an implementation-level program. Conceptually, we can think of this program as being obtained as an intermediate step in the query optimizer's translation of an embedded SQL program (e.g., the program invoked by the ticket agents) into an implementation-level program written at the level of ReadBlock and WriteBlock operations. Programs at the intermediate level shown in Figure 10.1 access data via operations that read and write individual data items, e.g., individual attribute values. As will soon become apparent, this is the appropriate level of abstraction at which to address the problems of concern to the transaction manager. It should be emphasized, however, that such intermediate-level programs ultimately are translated into implementation-level programs utilizing ReadBlock and WriteBlock operations. That is, if the transaction manager issues the request read(attribute *A* of record *R*), system software translates this request into ReadBlock(*Buff*,*Bn*), where *Bn* is the number of the block containing record *R*. In this chapter, we generally shall work in terms of programs that read and write data items, assuming implicitly that the software system performs translation to block-level operations.

High-level queries
↓
Item-level read/write ← (transaction manager "program")
↓
Block-level read/write ← (file system implementation-level program)

Figure 10.1 The transaction manager operating at an intermediate level of abstraction

2. If two invocations of the program are executed **serially** (i.e., one after the other), the results are correct. For example, if agent 1 invokes a copy of the program first, customer 1 decides to buy the ticket, agent 1's invocation of the program updates the database and terminates, and only then agent 2's copy of the program begins execution, customer 2 will be told that the flight is sold out. This serial execution of the two copies of the program produces correct results.

In contrast to the second observation, problems such as that illustrated in Section 1.5 arise because, in a multiuser environment, programs generally do

Time	Agent 1's Invocation	Agent 2's Invocation
t_1	read into x seats available on flight 888 customer 1 thinks	
t_2		read into x seats available on flight 888
t_3	decrement x write x to seats available on flight 888	
t_4		decrement x write x to seats available on flight 888

Figure 10.2 Execution sequence yielding incorrect results

not execute serially; rather, the operations of several programs are interleaved. For example, Figure 10.2 shows an execution schedule for the two invocations of the program that leads to incorrect results.

This execution schedule produces incorrect results since, at time t_4, when customer 2 purchases a ticket, in reality there are no seats remaining on the flight (the seat-remaining count stored in agent 2's program's variable x is not current). The problem illustrated by this example is an instance of the **lost update** problem. Here, the update performed by agent 1's invocation of the program is lost since agent 2's invocation operates on an out-of-date piece of information (the seat-remaining count stored in program variable x), and when it updates and writes x to disk, agent 1's update is overwritten and hence lost. The net effect of the execution schedule of Figure 10.2 is that the seat-remaining count is decremented only once, although two customers have bought a seat.

If interleaving the execution of programs can result in problems such as this, why does the transaction manager not insist that programs execute serially? The answer is that such a strict scheduling policy would tend to underutilize our computing resources, thereby inflicting unnecessary and, perhaps, intolerable delays. Suppose, for example, that once agent 1's copy of the program is invoked, customer 1 takes a long time deciding whether or not to purchase a ticket on flight 888. While customer 1 is making the decision, customer 3 approaches agent 3 and inquires about flight 222. A scheduling policy that forbids interleaved program execution would force customer 3 to wait until agent 1's invocation of the program completes, which can happen only after customer 1 makes a decision. However, since customers 1 and 3 are interested in different flights, there is no reason why customer 3's request cannot be processed concurrently with customer 1's.

It is apparent from our examples that one of the challenges of the transaction manager is to schedule program execution so that results are correct yet needless delays are not incurred. One technique employed by many transaction managers is **locking.** The idea behind locking is to forbid one program from accessing a *particular* data item while another program is accessing this data item. In our previous examples, when agent 1's invocation of the program accesses the seats available attribute for flight 888, this data item could be locked, preventing agent 2's invocation of the program from accessing the attribute until the first invocation, after writing to disk the updated value of this item, releases its lock. Note that since customer 3's request does not require access to the seats available attribute of flight 888, her request can be processed concurrently with the program servicing customer 1.

Locking is a complex technique that the forthcoming sections study in greater detail. For now, we make several observations regarding locking:

1. Locking alone does not guarantee that interleaved executions produce correct results. Beginning in Section 10.3, we shall explore this fact and seek constraints (called **protocols**) on how programs utilize locks to ensure the correctness of interleaved executions.
2. Locking leads to its own set of problems, most notably **deadlock.** To illustrate the problem of deadlock, consider the following example.

Time	Program 1	Program 2
	lock A	
		lock B
t_i	request B	
t_j	wait	request A
	wait	wait
	⋮	⋮

In this example, program 1 cannot proceed past its request for a lock on B until program 2 releases its lock on B, and program 2 cannot proceed past its request for a lock on A until program 1 releases its lock on A; that is, each program is waiting for an item locked by the other program, a situation known as deadlock. Section 10.5 considers strategies both for avoiding deadlock and for dealing with deadlock when it occurs.
3. It is desirable to grant different types of locks on a data item, depending on how the program requesting the lock is to utilize the data item. For example, if program 1 is to read but not modify item A, it can request a "read lock," which allows other programs to simultaneously read item A but prohibits other programs from modifying the item until program 1 releases its lock on it. On the other hand, if program 1 must modify an item B, it must request a "write lock," prohibiting other programs from either reading or modifying the item until program 1 releases the lock.

Another concern of the transaction manager is what happens when a program terminates "prematurely." Premature program termination might be caused by a system hardware or software failure, be induced by the transaction manager as part of a deadlock resolution scheme, or be a result of a fault in the logic of the program itself (e.g., an infinite loop or division by zero).

Consider first a simple example in which only the following program is executing at the time of a system failure:

```
Program 1
read A into x
x ← x−1000
write x to A
Read B into y
y ← y+1000
write y to B
```

What are the consequences of the system failing sometime after x is written to A, but before y is written to B? If the validity of the database requires that the execution of this particular program not change the sum $A + B$ (as would be the case if the program is transferring funds from bank account A to bank account B), the database is in an invalid state immediately following a failure between the two writes.

The example illustrates clearly that when premature program termination occurs, simply leaving the database in the state that results from partial execution is not acceptable. What, then, are the options? First, we might consider **undoing** (also know as **rolling back**) the partial execution by restoring all database values to what they were before execution began. This approach, of course, may require that the system maintain information (e.g., a **transaction log**), which allows the actions of a program to be undone. Once the database values have been restored to what they were prior to program execution, we could attempt to execute the program again; however, in cases where the program termination was caused by a fault in program logic, it may be that the program cannot or should not be run to completion.

As an alternative to undoing the execution of a prematurely terminated program, we might try to resume the execution of a program that has "almost" completed at the time of failure. For example, perhaps the only action preempted by a system failure was the writing by the program to the database of a few new values. Following failure, we can attempt to write those changes that were preempted to the database, an action known as transaction **redo.** Again, we require a transaction log, this time so that we can know which Write operations were intended and, since we cannot always know exactly what data has been written into the database before the failure, we must have a method that produces correct results even if some program operations are reexecuted.

The work of the transaction manager in this case, although not trivial, is straightforward. Assuming that logs are maintained properly (see Section 10.4), the database can be brought to a consistent state through some combination of Undo and Redo procedures. The preceding example is extremely simplistic, however, in that it assumes only one program is executing at the time of the failure. Suppose, for example, that the following program is executing also

```
Program 2
read A into z
z ← z+100
write z to A
```

```
Time      Program 1            Program 2
------------------------------------------------
          read A into x
          x ← x−1000
          write x to A
                               read A into z
                               z ← z + 100
                               write z to A
t
          read B into y
          y ← y−1000
          write y to B
```

Figure 10.3 Lost update due to rollback

and consider the problems that potentially arise if the programs execute in the sequence shown in Figure 10.3. If program 1 terminates at time t, we cannot simply undo its operations, for if A is restored to its value prior to the execution of program 1, the *update of program 2 is lost*.

As another example of the interaction between abnormal program termination and concurrency, consider the interleaved program execution in Figure 10.4. Suppose $(w - x) = 0$ and hence program 1 terminates in an error state. The logic of program 1 is to blame for its premature termination, and it cannot reexecute after it is undone. Program 2, therefore, took actions (updating the values of C, D, and E) based on a value $(A = 233)$ that never "really" appears in the database. When program 1 is undone, therefore, the actions of program 2 must be undone as well. Further, if other programs acted based on the values of C, D, and E that program 2 wrote to the database, they too must be undone. The root of this problem is that program 2 read **dirty data,** a data value written by a program that must be undone. As observed, not only must programs 1 and 2 be undone but so too must any program that acted on a value written by program 2, or any program that acted on a value written by any program that acted on a value written by program 2, and so forth. This phenomenon, known as **cascading rollback,** must be avoided since it is extremely expensive to rectify.

This section has surveyed many of the problems arising in a multiuser database environment. In Section 10.2, we define the concept of a transaction and

```
Program 1              Program 2
------------------------------------------------
read A into x
x ← 233
write x to A
                       read A into y
                       if (y = 233)
                         read and update C,D,E
                       endif
read B into z
read C into w
v ← B/(w−x)
```

Figure 10.4 Execution leading to cascading rollback

specify what we mean by the *correct behavior* of a collection of transactions. The remainder of the chapter then considers some of the techniques employed by the transaction manager to ensure correct behavior and, hence, address problems such as those surveyed in this section.

10.2 TRANSACTIONS: WHAT THEY ARE AND HOW THEY SHOULD BEHAVE

The first new concept we introduce is that of a **transaction.** In the previous section, we referred to the objects of study as *programs*. The term *program* was sufficient then because the programs we considered coincided naturally with transactions. In general, however, programs often are divided into several transactions, and also, transactions can arise from collections of high-level, standalone queries as well as from programs.

A transaction is a user-defined unit of execution that might be a single, standalone query (e.g., an SQL statement), a user-defined collection of standalone queries, an entire program that accesses a database (e.g., an embedded SQL program), or a user-defined segment of a program that accesses a database. In other words, a transaction is a user-defined unit of execution that contains a collection of one or more database accesses. The user delineates the beginning and end of a transaction, and, as we shall see, the transaction manager has the responsibility of ensuring that certain conditions are met regarding the effects of the transaction's database accesses. We note also that while the user may compose transactions at the level of embedded SQL programs, these transactions are mapped to lower-level accesses of database items, as was illustrated in the previous section. We shall continue to study at this level of abstraction the problems of transaction management.

Figure 10.5 summarizes the relationships between concepts.

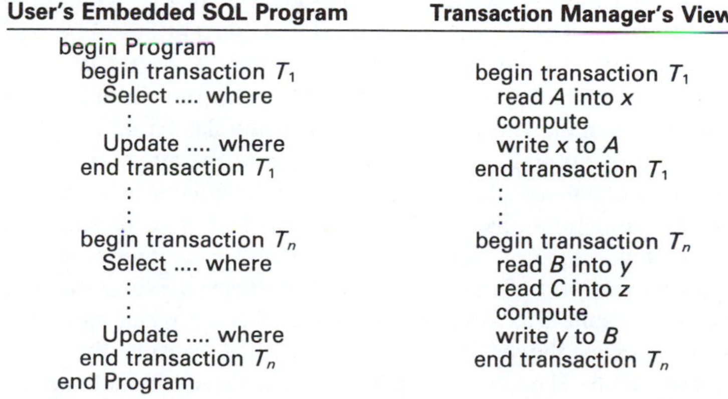

User's Embedded SQL Program
Transaction Manager's View
begin Program
begin transaction T_1
Select .... where
:
Update .... where
end transaction T_1
:
:
begin transaction T_n
Select .... where
:
:
Update .... where
end transaction T_n
end Program
begin transaction T_1
read A into x
compute
write x to A
end transaction T_1
:
:
begin transaction T_n
read B into y
read C into z
compute
write y to B
end transaction T_n

Figure 10.5 User program and transactions produced by query optimizer

Before we can consider when a user should group a given collection of database accesses into a transaction, we must specify the requirements of transaction execution. The two critical requirements a transaction manager is required to enforce are that the execution of any transaction be an **all-or-nothing proposition** and that the execution of any collection of transactions be **serializable.** When a transaction manager satisfies these two requirements, it is said to provide **transaction atomicity.** We now discuss each of the two components of atomicity.

That a transaction is an all-or-nothing proposition means simply that, once a transaction begins executing, either all of its effects on the database will be carried out or none of its effects will be carried out, and hence the database will be as if the transaction never began execution. The funds transfer program is a classic example of why this requirement needs to be enforced—it clearly is not acceptable for the transaction to make only some of its changes to the database. If a transaction must terminate before its last update to the database is applied, the transaction manager must either undo the actions that were executed, or the manager must complete the transaction's execution. Note that the all-or-nothing property permits a transaction simply to be undone and not restarted; different strategies are permissible governing whether undone transactions are reexecuted automatically.

It is clear that a logically indivisible work unit such as the funds transfer procedure should be contained entirely in a single transaction. Should a single transaction contain more than one logically indivisible work unit? While it is permissible to define an entire program to be a single transaction, this is not always desirable. Suppose, for example, that a single program contains both the account transfer routine and an interest calculating routine. If, after the account transfer routine completes execution, the system fails while executing the interest calculation routine, there is no reason why the account transfer routine needs to be undone. However, if both these routines are part of the same transaction, the all-or-nothing property may actually force the transaction manager to undo the effects of the account transfer routine. In this sense, a transaction defines a **unit of rollback**—once some transaction T of a program completes, T never needs to be undone (provided several key conventions to be introduced shortly are obeyed), even if the program containing T should later terminate abnormally. Therefore, for efficiency's sake, transactions should be no larger than what is necessary to ensure the integrity of the database.

While the all-or-nothing requirement pertains to the effect of the execution of a single transaction, serializability pertains to the effect of the execution of a collection of transactions. Serializability is a critical concept and, in fact, is generally adopted as *the criterion of the correctness* of an interleaved execution schedule for a collection of transactions. An interleaved execution schedule is said to be serializable if *its effect is equivalent to some serial (noninterleaved) schedule*. To illustrate the definition of serializability, consider the two transactions in Figure 10.6. The two serial executions of these transactions are T_1 followed by T_2, denoted $(T_1 T_2)$, and T_2 followed by T_1, denoted $(T_2 T_1)$. If the ini-

T_1
read A into x
$x \leftarrow x - 1000$
write x to A
read B into y
$y \leftarrow y - 1000$
write y to B

T_2
read A into u
$u \leftarrow 2*u$
write u to A
read B into v
$v \leftarrow 2*v$
write B to v

Figure 10.6
Two transactions

tial values of A and B are

$$A = 3000;\ B = 5000$$

then the outcomes of the two serial executions are

$$(T_1\,T_2)\ A = 4000;\ B = 8000$$
$$(T_2\,T_1)\ A = 5000;\ B = 9000$$

An execution schedule is serializable (and hence considered correct) if and only if it leaves the database with one of these two sets of values.

The most obvious serializable schedules for T_1 and T_2 simply run T_1 and then T_2 or T_2 and then T_1. However, as discussed earlier, to more fully utilize our computing resources, we wish to allow interleaved executions. Figure 10.7 is a serializable, interleaved schedule. This schedule produces the same results

T_1	T_2
read A into x	
$x \leftarrow x - 1000$	
write x to A	
	read A into u
	$u \leftarrow 2*u$
	write u to A
read B into y	
$y \leftarrow y - 1000$	
write y to B	
	read B into v
	$v \leftarrow 2*v$
	write B to v

Figure 10.7 Serializable, interleaved execution

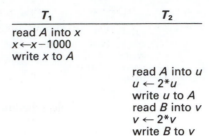

T_1	T_2
read A into x	
$x \leftarrow x - 1000$	
write x to A	
	read A into u
	$u \leftarrow 2^*u$
	write u to A
	read B into v
	$v \leftarrow 2^*v$
	write B to v
read B into y	
$y \leftarrow y - 1000$	
write y to B	

Figure 10.8 Nonserializable execution

as if we were to run T_1 followed by T_2. On the other hand, Figure 10.8 is a nonserializable and, hence, incorrect schedule. Assuming the same initial values as above, the results produced by this schedule are

$$A = 4000;\ B = 9000$$

which is not one of the two permissible outcomes.

The concept of a serializable schedule is central to much of the material in this chapter. Before considering techniques for ensuring that a schedule is serializable, we study further some of the consequences of a schedule being serializable. We first consider why serializability is an appropriate notion of correctness. Intuitively, if a single transaction T is correct, T preserves the correctness of the database, where *correctness of the database* means that its values accurately reflect the state of reality at some point in time. Hence, if the database is in a correct state before T begins execution, a correct transaction T will leave the database in a correct (and presumably more current) state when its execution completes, provided that T encounters no "interference" from other transactions. This should be the case regardless of the specifics of the database's state before the execution of T, provided only that the database state is correct. Note that it may be the case that T and T' both are correct transactions, but an interleaved execution schedule for T and T' in fact creates interference, and, as a result of the interference, the correctness of the database is not preserved. The execution schedule of Figure 10.2 provides a classic example of this phenomenon.

Suppose now that C is a collection of transactions, each of which is correct in the foregoing sense. If we choose any serial execution schedule for the transactions in C (e.g., T_1 followed by T_2, . . . , followed by T_N) and the database is in a correct state before the execution of the first of these transactions, then the database will be in a correct state following completion of the last of these transactions. Consequently, if a (possibly interleaved) schedule for the transactions in C is serializable, since the schedule is equivalent to some serial execution, it also has the property that if the database is in a correct state before execution begins then the database will be in a correct state when the schedule completes execution. Thus, *the correctness of a serializable schedule is founded on the principle that a single transaction is considered to be correct if and only if the execution of any sequence of individually correct transactions is correct*.

It is important to emphasize that a serializable schedule need be equivalent to only *one* serial schedule. Consider, for example, the transactions of Figure 10.6. As we observed, there are two serial schedules, T_1,T_2 and T_2,T_1, each leaving the database in a different state. The theory does not allow us to prefer one result over the other—both schedules and both results are equally correct, and if an interleaved schedule produces either of these results, it is considered correct. Observe that if correctness requires (the effect of) one of the transactions executing before the other, our only recourse, based on the current concepts, is to define a single transaction T that combines in the required order the two transactions.

We now explore the relationship between serializability and transaction **isolation,** another important concept of transaction management. That a transaction manager supports transaction isolation can be described (loosely) as follows:

> The actions of a transaction T, with regard to its effects on the database, can be modeled in terms of a **snapshot implementation.** When T begins execution, it takes a snapshot of those items in the database that it may need to access and stores this snapshot in some local memory $DB(T)$ that only T can access. During its execution, when T needs to read database values, it reads them from $DB(T)$. Further, when T writes values, it writes them to $DB(T)$. Only when T completes execution does it write $DB(T)$ to the database, thereby actually effecting its changes. Further, the writing of snapshot $DB(T)$ to the database is an indivisible action. Note that, conceptually, these requirements imply that any other transaction T' creates its snapshot $DB(T')$ either before T writes any of its changes to the (real) database or after T writes all its changes to the (real) database. In particular, no snapshot $DB(T')$ will reflect only some of the changes made by other transactions.

It turns out that the serializability of transactions actually implies the preceding notion of transaction isolation, although this relationship is somewhat subtle. To begin, we must analyze exactly what the isolation condition asserts. The most important point to observe is that the condition gives only a *functional* description of a transaction's effect on the database, and the actual step-by-step execution of transactions may be quite different from a snapshot implementation; hence, a schedule can provide isolation, without utilizing local snapshots at all. To illustrate this point, consider the interleaved execution schedule shown in Figure 10.9. As before, all reads and writes are with respect to the real, shared, database (i.e., local snapshots are not used).

This schedule clearly does not correspond *operationally* to a snapshot implementation. First, T_2 begins by accessing A after T_1 has incremented its value and written it to the (real) database, yet at the time T_2 reads A, T_1 has not com-

T_1	T_2
read A into x $x \leftarrow x+1$ write x to A	
	Read A into v $v \leftarrow 2*v$ write v to A
Read B into y $y \leftarrow y+1$ write y to B	
	read B into w $w \leftarrow 2*w$ write w to B

Figure 10.9 Transaction isolation without local snapshots

pleted execution; hence, if T_1 were operating on a local snapshot, T_2 would not see the changes T_1 made to A. Further, the value T_2 reads from B differs from the value B had at the time T_2 began execution; hence, T_2 clearly is not reading its values from a local snapshot. Nevertheless, the effect of this schedule on the database is as if T_1 executes first, creates and makes changes to its local snapshot, completes and writes its modified snapshot to the database, and then T_2 executes in the same manner. Hence, provided neither transaction terminates prematurely (e.g., due to system failure), this schedule in fact does provide transaction isolation. (As we shall see in Section 10.4, because of the possibility of premature termination, Figure 10.9 is a poor schedule. In fact, the protocol proposed in Section 10.4 for dealing with premature termination will indeed closely resemble a snapshot implementation.)

In light of the preceding discussion, it is fairly clear that if an execution schedule is serializable, it necessarily provides transaction isolation. To see this relationship, observe that if an execution schedule for a collection of transactions is serializable, then the execution of this schedule is equivalent to the execution of some serial schedule, say $T_1, T_2, \ldots, T_i, \ldots, T_N$. But then this execution is also equivalent to a snapshot implementation in which transaction T_i begins execution and makes its local snapshot $DB(T_i)$ after T_{i-1} has completed execution and written $DB(T_{i-1})$ to the database, for $2 \leq i \leq N$.

While serializability implies transaction isolation, serializability requires more than does isolation. Consider, for example, the lost update problem illustrated by the execution schedule of Figure 10.2. Suppose that before execution, there are 10 seats available on flight 888, and let transaction T_1 be agent 1's invocation of the program and transaction T_2 be agent 2's invocation of the program. The execution schedule of Figure 10.2 provides transaction isolation since it is equivalent to the snapshot implementation in Figure 10.10.

Despite the fact that that the execution schedule of Figure 10.2 is equivalent to the preceding snapshot implementation and hence provides transaction isolation, the schedule is *not* serializable. The schedule of Figure 10.2 decre-

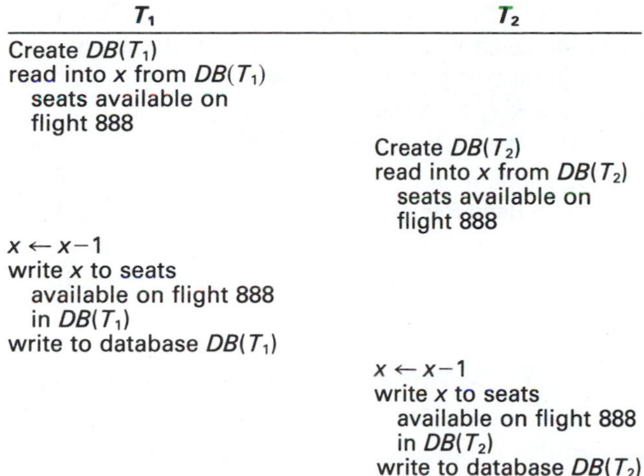

T_1
T_2
Create $DB(T_1)$
read into x from $DB(T_1)$
seats available on
flight 888
Create $DB(T_2)$
read into x from $DB(T_2)$
seats available on
flight 888
$x \leftarrow x-1$
write x to seats
available on flight 888
in $DB(T_1)$
write to database $DB(T_1)$
$x \leftarrow x-1$
write x to seats
available on flight 888
in $DB(T_2)$
write to database $DB(T_2)$

Figure 10.10 Snapshot implementation

ments by one the seats available attribute in the database (resulting in the value 9), while either of the two serial executions decrements by two the seats available attribute in the database (resulting in the value 8). Hence, the serializability condition detects a problem with the schedule of Figure 10.2 not detected by the isolation condition alone. As we shall see in Section 10.6, the problem with the snapshot implementation of Figure 10.10 can be explained and detected in terms of **snapshot conflict:** At the time T_2 writes snapshot $DB(T_2)$ to the database, $DB(T_2)$ is outdated in the sense that it was derived from an instance of the database that conflicts with the instance resulting from T_1's writing of $DB(T_1)$.

Now that we have defined the concept of a transaction and specified how a transaction manager's execution of a collection of transactions must behave, we are ready to begin considering how the transaction manager can provide the required behavior. Section 10.3 focuses on serializability, while Section 10.4 focuses on recovery. Section 10.5 considers the problems of deadlock and livelock, and Section 10.6 augments the basic techniques described in the earlier sections by surveying several alternative techniques that the transaction manager can employ.

10.3 LOCKS, PROTOCOLS, AND SERIALIZABILITY

Locks

One of the basic tools a transaction manager employs to ensure correct behavior is a **lock.** Section 10.1 informally introduced the notion of locking as a method for controlling concurrent access to data items. In our simple model of transaction management, there are two types of locks that a transaction may be granted on a database item:

- **SLocks** (shared, or read, locks): If a transaction holds an SLock on a database item, other transactions may be issued SLocks on that same item, but other transactions may not be issued XLocks (see the following) on the item. Similarly, a transaction will not be granted an SLock on an item if some other transaction already holds an XLock on that item.
- **XLocks** (exclusive, or write, locks): If a transaction holds an XLock on a database item, other transactions may not be issued either SLocks or XLocks on that item. Similarly, a transaction will not be granted an XLock on an item if some other transaction already holds an SLock or XLock on that item.

Before transaction *T* may read from the database an item *A*, it must be granted either an SLock or an XLock on *A*. Similarly, before transaction *T* may write to the database a value for item *A*, it must be granted an XLock on *A*. This convention that a transaction must hold an appropriate lock on an item before it reads or writes that item is a simple example of a transaction **protocol.** A transaction protocol is a rule governing the construction of transactions that the transaction manager enforces and that its scheduling algorithms therefore may assume all transactions obey.

A transaction requests an SLock on item *A* with the statement

```
SLock(A)
```

and requests an XLock with the statement

```
XLock(A)
```

A transaction releases either type of lock on *A* with the statement

```
Release(A)
```

Hence, typical sequences of statements appearing in transactions are

```
Transaction 1
    :
  SLock(A)
  Read A into x
    :
  { perform work }
    :
  Release(A)
Transaction 2
    :
  XLock(A)
  { Typically, a transaction reads an item before modifying it }
  Read A into y
    :
  { perform work }
    :
  modify y
    :
  write y to A
  Release(A)
```

When a transaction executes a lock request, the transaction manager must determine whether or not the request can be granted. Conceptually, the transaction manager maintains a table with an entry for each database item *A* specifying what types of locks are held on *A* and by which transactions. The transaction manager uses this table, in conjunction with the previous definitions of SLocks and XLocks, to determine if a lock request can be granted. If the manager grants its lock request to a transaction, the transaction continues its execution, able to access the data item on which it now holds a lock. If, on the other hand, a transaction manager must deny a lock request, the requesting transaction cannot continue execution. Exactly what happens next depends on the scheduling conventions of the transaction manager. The simplest consequence of a denied lock request is that the requesting transaction waits until the required lock is released. However, as was illustrated in Section 10.1, this wait could be of infinite length if deadlock occurs—the phenomenon of two or more transactions each waiting for locks held by the other. Techniques for avoiding and resolving deadlock and other similar problems are studied in Section 10.5; for now, we shall simply assume that these problems do not occur and that transactions wait for their requested locks, which eventually are granted.

Before concluding this introduction to locking, we observe that locking may be implemented at a level of abstraction different from the level at which transactions request locks. In the locking model just described, locks are requested on individual database items, which we have been equating with individual attribute values. In a large database, the number of attribute values easily could be in the hundreds of millions. Because of the large overhead associated with managing this many locks (recall the description of the transaction manager's lock table), locks often are implemented at a higher level of abstraction. For example, if a transaction requires access to attribute *A* of tuple *t* of table *T*, the actual lock granted may be on the entire tuple *t*, a collection of tuples in table *T*, the entire table *T*, or perhaps defined with respect to a unit of physical storage, such as the disk block in which tuple *t* resides.

Note that while coarse locks incur less overhead than do fine locks, they generally support less concurrency. The implementation parameter governing the level at which locks are implemented—the **locking granularity**—is therefore of considerable importance. Observe, however, that a model that allows transactions to request locks at the finest level of granularity affords the transaction manager maximum flexibility since the manager can always implement coarser locks and map between levels of abstraction. Hence, we shall continue to assume that transactions lock at the item level, keeping in mind that the locks actually may be implemented at a coarser level. In Section 10.6, we shall consider again the issue of locking granularity.

The Two-Phase Locking Protocol and Serializability

Consider now the question, "Do locks, in conjunction with the simple protocol that a transaction acquire the appropriate lock before accessing an item, prevent all the problems considered in Sections 10.1 and 10.2?" The answer to this question, unfortunately, is no. Before demonstrating the validity of this answer, however, we consider a problem that locking and this simplest of protocols do address: The class of lost update illustrated by the execution of Figure 10.2.

The execution of the airline agents' transactions, with locking, might take the form described in Figure 10.11. Here we see that locking prevents an execution sequence in which some transaction T_1 writes an updated value for an item A to the database *between the times that some other transaction* T_2 *reads and writes a value for A,* thereby causing T_1's Update to be lost.

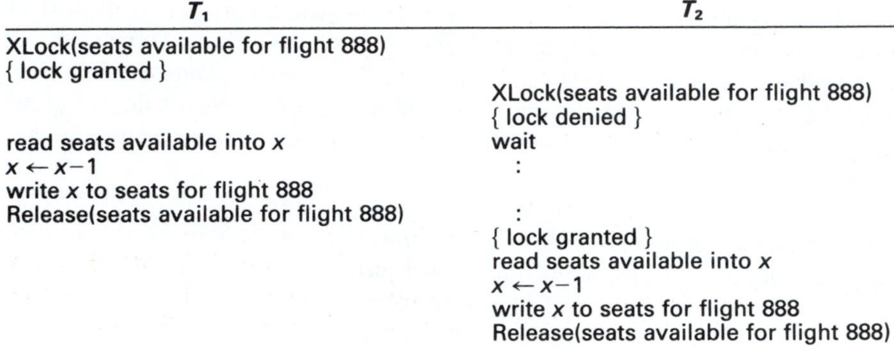
T_1
T_2
XLock(seats available for flight 888)
{ lock granted }
XLock(seats available for flight 888)
{ lock denied }
read seats available into x
wait
$x \leftarrow x-1$
write x to seats for flight 888
Release(seats available for flight 888)
{ lock granted }
read seats available into x
$x \leftarrow x-1$
write x to seats for flight 888
Release(seats available for flight 888)

Figure 10.11 Airline transactions with XLock

We observe also that transactions might well utilize locks in a somewhat different manner from that illustrated by Figure 10.11. For example, in Figure 10.11, each transaction immediately requests an XLock before it is known that the customer wishes to purchase a ticket; it would not be unreasonable for the transactions first to request an SLock so that the number of seats remaining could be determined, and only once the customer decides to purchase a seat would a request for an XLock be issued. Such a strategy could lead to an execution of the form shown in Figure 10.12, which is an example of deadlock: Each transaction is denied an XLock because the other transaction has an SLock on the required item. As we shall discuss in Section 10.5, the transaction manager has the responsibility of detecting and resolving such a situation, most likely by aborting one of the two transactions and hence releasing its SLock so the other transaction can proceed. The important point to observe in the context of the current discussion, however, is that, as in the previous example, *locking prevents the transactions from proceeding in a manner that would result in a lost update.*

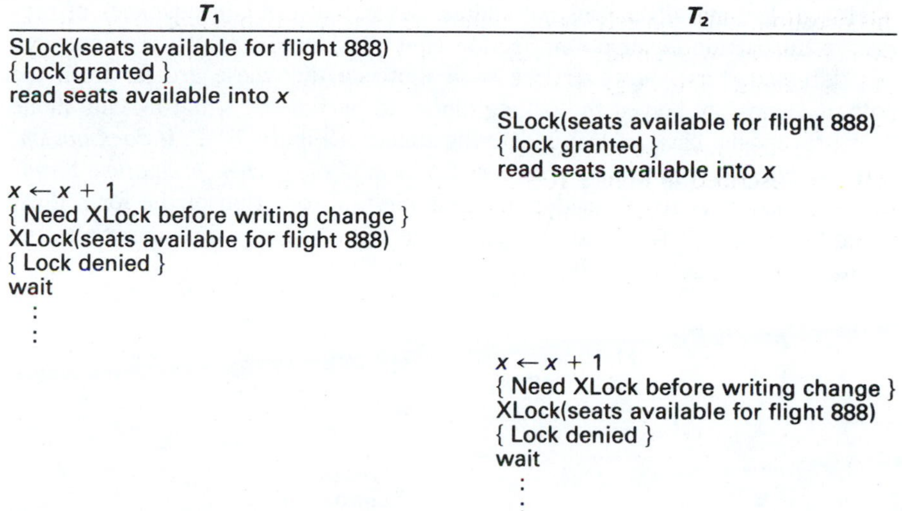
T_1
T_2
SLock(seats available for flight 888)
{ lock granted }
read seats available into x
SLock(seats available for flight 888)
{ lock granted }
read seats available into x
$x \leftarrow x + 1$
{ Need XLock before writing change }
XLock(seats available for flight 888)
{ Lock denied }
wait
$x \leftarrow x + 1$
{ Need XLock before writing change }
XLock(seats available for flight 888)
{ Lock denied }
wait

Figure 10.12 Deadlock

While locking prevents the class of lost update exemplified by the airline reservation example of Figure 10.2, there are many important problems not addressed by locking alone. For example, the class of lost update seen in Figure 10.3 is not addressed simply by locking. That execution, with locking, might take the form of Figure 10.13. Despite the fact that locks are respected, if the system crashes after time t but before T_1 completes and if T_1 is undone as described earlier, the update of T_2 is lost. Hence, while locking does prevent our first class of lost update, it does not prevent the class caused by premature termination and rollback. Further, it is easy to see that the cascading rollback problem illustrated by the execution of Figure 10.4 also is not prevented by locking alone.

Time	T_1	T_2
	XLock(A)	
	read A into x	
	$x \leftarrow x - 1000$	
	write x to A	
	Release(A)	
		XLock(A)
		read A into z
		$z \leftarrow z + 100$
		write z to A
		Release(A)
	XLock(B)	
	read B into y	
	$y \leftarrow y - 1000$	
	write y to B	
	Release(B)	

Figure 10.13 Lost update due to rollback

Hence, locking alone does not address several severe consequences of premature transaction termination; Section 10.4 considers how such problems can be addressed. First, however, we shall illustrate that these are far from the only problems not solved by locking alone. In particular, while locking alone does prevent the class of lost update illustrated in Figure 10.2, *it does not ensure serializability (and hence correct behavior), even when premature termination is not an issue*. Consider, for example, an execution of the form illustrated by Figure 10.14. While this execution respects locks, it is unserializable for the reasons discussed following Figure 10.8.

T_1	T_2
XLock(A)	
read A into x	
$x \leftarrow x-1000$	
write x to A	
Release(A)	
	XLock(A)
	XLock(B)
	read A into u
	$u \leftarrow 2*u$
	write u to A
	read B into v
	$v \leftarrow 2*v$
	write v to B
	Release(A)
	Release(B)
XLock(B)	
read B into y	
$y \leftarrow y-1000$	
write y to B	
Release(B)	

Figure 10.14 Nonserializable execution that respects locks

How, then, can we use locks to ensure transaction serializability? One solution is found in transaction protocols. We have been assuming that transactions obey the protocol that a transaction must hold an appropriate lock on an item before it reads or writes that item. This protocol is as unrestricted as a protocol gets—all a transaction must do is acquire a lock before accessing an item. By enforcing more restrictive protocols on transactions, it is possible to address problems that locking alone does not solve.

The **two-phase locking protocol** is a simple protocol that ensures serializability, provided that no transaction must be terminated prematurely and undone. Informally, the two-phase protocol specifies that each transaction has a **growing phase** followed by a **shrinking phase.** During the growing phase, locks may be requested. The first occurrence in a transaction of a Release statement marks the end of the growing phase and the beginning of the shrinking phase. Once a transaction enters its shrinking phase, it may not request additional locks. Formally, we have the following definition.

Definition 10.1 A transaction T obeys the **two-phase locking protocol** if T executes no lock requests (XLock or SLock) once it executes any Release statement.

It can be shown that the following properties apply to the two-phase locking protocol:

1. If each transaction in a collection of transactions obeys the two-phase protocol, then any execution schedule (which completes normally) for these transactions is serializable. Exercise 10.3 proves this assertion.
2. Given any execution schedule for a collection of transactions obeying the two-phase locking protocol, an equivalent serial schedule can be obtained by ordering the transactions with respect to the time at which each transaction is granted its last lock. That is, if an execution schedule S for a collection $\{T_1, \ldots, T_N\}$ of transactions, each obeying the two-phase locking protocol, results in transaction T_i obtaining its last lock before transaction T_{i+1} obtains its last lock $(1 \leq i < N)$, then S is equivalent to the serial execution schedule $T_1, T_2, \ldots, T_N$. Exercise 10.4 proves this assertion.
3. Let T_1 be any transaction that violates the two-phase locking protocol, such that every value read by T_1 affects in some way at least one value T_1 writes to the database. Then there exist some transaction T_2 and some execution schedule S for T_1 and T_2, such that S is not serializable. Exercise 10.5 proves this assertion.

To illustrate these definitions and concepts, consider the transactions in Figure 10.14. Observe that transaction T_1 is not two phased since in it the statement XLock(B) follows the statement Release(A). Consequently, there are nonserializable schedules for executing T_1 interleaved with certain other transactions—Figure 10.14 is one such execution schedule. Suppose now that T_1 is rewritten so that it obeys the two-phase protocol. For example, rewrite T_1 as

```
T1'
XLock(A)
XLock(B)
read A into x
x ← x−1000
write A to x
Release(A)
read B into y
y ← y−1000
write y to B
Release(B)
```

Since T_2 of Figure 10.14 also obeys the two-phase locking protocol, every execution schedule for T_1' and T_2 is serializable. For example, the schedule for T_1' and T_2 in Figure 10.15 is serializable.

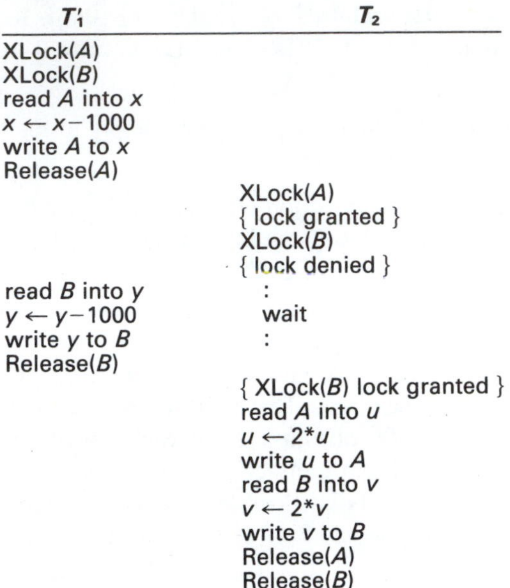

T'_1	T_2
XLock(*A*)	
XLock(*B*)	
read *A* into *x*	
$x \leftarrow x-1000$	
write *A* to *x*	
Release(*A*)	
	XLock(*A*)
	{ lock granted }
	XLock(*B*)
	{ lock denied }
read *B* into *y*	:
$y \leftarrow y-1000$	wait
write *y* to *B*	:
Release(*B*)	
	{ XLock(*B*) lock granted }
	read *A* into *u*
	$u \leftarrow 2*u$
	write *u* to *A*
	read *B* into *v*
	$v \leftarrow 2*v$
	write *v* to *B*
	Release(*A*)
	Release(*B*)

Figure 10.15 Two-phase locking leads to a serializable schedule

It is easy to see that the schedule in Figure 10.15 is serializable and, in particular, is equivalent to the serial execution schedule T'_1 followed by T_2. The conceptual key to why this schedule is serializable while the schedule of Figure 10.14 is not is that in Figure 10.14 transaction T_2 accesses *partial results* of T_1—it accesses the value T_1 writes to *A* but accesses *B* before T_1 has effected its update to *B*. Similarly, T_1 accesses partial results of T_2—it accesses *A* before T_2 has effected its update to *A* but accesses the value T_2 writes to *B*. In contrast, the two-phase locking protocol obeyed by T'_1 forces T_2 to wait for its XLock on *B* until after T'_1 has updated this item, hence T_2 reads both values after T'_1 has updated them, and T'_1 reads both values before T_2 updates them.

It is instructive to consider also the transaction T'_2 that results by rewriting T_2 so that it updates *A* before it requests a lock on *B*. T'_2 still obeys the two-phase locking protocol, and hence the schedule in Figure 10.16 is serializable. In the case of the schedule of Figure 10.16, although T'_2 accesses *A* before T'_1 has updated *B*, T'_2 still may access *B* only after T'_1 has updated it and released its lock. Hence, as is the case in Figure 10.15, the two-phase locking protocol ensures that each of *A* and *B* has been updated by T'_1 at the time T'_2 accesses that item.

The juxtaposition of the schedules of Figures 10.15 and 10.16 with that of Figure 10.14 serves to illustrate why two-phase locking prohibits a transaction from releasing an XLock prior to its acquisition of other locks. Observe that two-phase locking additionally prohibits SLocks from being released prior to the acquisition of other locks. The example in Figure 10.17 illustrates the need

T_1'	T_2'
XLock(A)	
XLock(B)	
read A into x	
$x \leftarrow x-1000$	
write A to x	
Release(A)	
	XLock(A)
	{ lock granted }
	read A into u
	$u \leftarrow 2*u$
	write u to A
	XLock(B)
	{ lock denied }
read B into y	:
$y \leftarrow y-1000$	wait
write y to B	:
Release(B)	
	{ XLock(B) lock granted }
	read B into v
	$v \leftarrow 2*v$
	write v to B
	Release(A)
	Release(B)

Figure 10.16 Two-phase locking again leads to a serializable schedule

T_1	T_2
SLock(A)	
read A into w	
Release(A)	
	XLock(A)
	SLock(B)
	{ locks granted }
XLock(B)	
{ lock denied }	
:	
wait	
:	read A into z
:	read B into y
	$z \leftarrow (y + z)$
wait	write z to A
	Release(A)
:	Release(B)
{ XLock(B) granted }	
read B into x	
$x \leftarrow (x + w)$	
write x to B	
Release (B)	

Figure 10.17 Danger of releasing SLock early

for this requirement by demonstrating the danger of a transaction releasing an SLock before the transaction has acquired all of its required locks.

Suppose that the initial value of each of A and B is 1. There are two possible serial executions of the transactions in Figure 10.17: T_1 followed by T_2, producing $A = 3$ and $B = 2$, and T_2 followed by T_1, producing $A = 2$ and $B = 3$. However, the execution in Figure 10.17 produces $A = B = 2$ and, hence, is not serializable. Conceptually, the problem with the schedule of Figure 10.17 is that T_1 updates B using a value of A ($A = 1$) that is current only before T_2 runs, and T_2 updates A using a value of B ($B = 1$) that is current only before T_1 runs. Clearly, this behavior would not be possible if the transactions were run serially. The problem illustrated by this nonserializable schedule stems from T_1's early release of its SLock on A; if T_1 obeyed the two-phase protocol and, hence, held its SLock on A until after it acquired XLock(B), T_2 would be forced to wait for T_1's update to B.[1]

We make a final observation before concluding this section. While the two-phase locking protocol is sufficient to ensure serializability when transactions

Time	T_1	T_2
	XLock(A)	
	XLock(B)	
	read A into x	
	$x \leftarrow x - 1000$	
	write x to A	
	Release(A)	
		XLock(A)
		XLock(C)
		read A into z
		$z \leftarrow z + 100$
		write z to A
		read C into w
		$w \leftarrow w + 200$
		write w to C
		Release(A)
		Release(C)
t		
	read B into y	
	$y \leftarrow y - 1000$	
	write y to B	
	Release(B)	

Figure 10.18 Two-phase protocol and premature termination

[1] Note that, like the execution schedule of Figure 10.10, the execution schedule of Figure 10.17 illustrates that the snapshot restriction of transaction isolation is not as strong as serializability since the results of this nonserializable execution could be obtained by a snapshot implementation. Again, the problem is snapshot conflict. See Section 10.6 for details.

run to completion, the protocol is not sufficient in the face of premature termination. To illustrate this point, we consider the execution schedule of Figure 10.18, which is a variation on Figure 10.13. It is apparent that both transactions obey the two-phase protocol, and, hence, if they run to completion, the schedule of Figure 10.18 is serializable. Suppose, however, that the system crashes at time *t*. As was indicated earlier, when the system restarts, the transaction manager, as one of its recovery mechanisms, will undo transaction T_1. In this event, the update of T_2 is lost, and hence, the execution of T_1 and T_2 that includes the rollback of T_1 has the effect of executing only partially T_2 and does not produce results equivalent to any serial execution of the transactions. Additionally, it can be shown that cascading rollback is not prevented by the two-phase locking protocol. In the next section, when we study premature termination and recovery mechanisms, we shall see that one way to prevent these problems is to strengthen the two-phase locking protocol so that a transaction does not release its XLocks until just before it completes execution.

10.4 RECOVERY AND A STRONGER TWO-PHASE LOCKING PROTOCOL

Transaction Failure and Recovery Principles

We say that a transaction **fails to complete** (or is **incomplete,** or **fails**) if, for whatever reason, one or more of its planned updates are not written to the database. There are several causes of transaction failure, including,

- *Program error:* The transaction contains a "bug," such as a division by zero, an infinite loop that results in the transaction exceeding an execution time limit, or an attempt to lock an item on which the transaction does not have privileges. Such a program error causes the transaction to abort in the middle of its execution, perhaps at a point before one or more of its planned Write statements are reached. A transaction containing a program error should not be rerun until the error is corrected.
- *Action by the transaction manager:* As a method of resolving deadlocks and other conflicts, the transaction manager may terminate a transaction in the middle of its execution. As in the case of failure due to program error, a transaction so terminated by the transaction manager may have failed to reach one or more of its planned Write statments. In this case, however, the transaction might be able to run to completion if restarted.
- *Self-abort:* A transaction may decide that it should terminate and have its actions undone. For example, it might write to the database and then, based on some computations, decide to "back out," canceling the updates it made to the database. To implement self-aborts, most transaction models supply an explicit statment such as "rollback" or "abort." We simplify the discussion by considering self-aborts to be a special case of transaction

manager–induced failure—when a transaction's abort statement is processed, the transaction manager takes action to terminate the transaction as just described. The only difference from the preceding description is that, following a transaction self-abort, it may be inappropriate to rerun the transaction without modification.

- *System failure:* Shutdowns caused by hardware failure or by bugs in the operating system, database system, or other system software will be referred to as system failure, i.e., a system crash. When the system crashes, all transactions currently executing terminate. Further, the contents of internal memory (which include I/O buffers) are assumed lost. However, we assume that external memory (including the disks on which the database resides) is not affected by system failure.

It is apparent that if, for any of these reasons, a transaction terminates before its natural completion, its effect on the database may be incomplete and, if left uncorrected, could violate atomicity. Further, system failure in particular has several implications for database integrity, beyond the obvious fact that such an event prevents the completion of any transaction that happens to be executing at the time of the crash. To better describe the different types of transaction failure and the corrective measures required by the transaction manager, we introduce into the transaction model two new statements: **end of transaction** (**EOT**) and **commit.**

- *EOT (end of transaction):* EOT is the last statement appearing in a transaction; it simply marks the physical end of the transaction.
- *Commit:* In our model, Commit is an explicit statement that must appear in a transaction before the EOT statement. The only statements that may appear between Commit and EOT are writes to the database and lock releases. The transaction manager, at the time in a transaction's execution that its Commit statement is reached, checks that the transaction already holds the necessary locks to allow execution of any Write statements that follow the Commit. If the transaction does not hold all such locks, the transaction manager treats this as a program error and terminates the transaction; otherwise, the Commit is accepted and, at this point, the transaction is considered to be a **committed transaction.** Once committed, the transaction proceeds to execute any Write and Lock releases that follow the Commit statement.[2]

The significance of a transaction being committed is that the only failure to which it now is vulnerable is that caused by system failure. At first, it might further appear that a committed transaction's only vulnerability to system fail-

[2] This is a bit of a simplification. As will be seen later in this section, when the transaction manager processes a Commit statement, it performs additional actions involving a transaction log file. If there should be system failure before these actions on the log are completed, the Commit statement is not accepted, and the transaction is not committed.

ure is failure occurring between the time when the transaction commits and its EOT is reached. Recall, however, that we assume that when a system failure occurs, the contents of internal memory lost. The significance of this fact to a transaction that has reached its EOT statement is that whether or not the transaction's updates actually have been applied depends on when the system writes its I/O buffers to the database. In particular, it is possible that a transaction's execution of a Write statement has only the effect of changing the contents of a system I/O buffer (see Chapter 7) and that the contents of this buffer are written to the database only at a time deemed appropriate by the operating or file system. If a system failure occurs before the I/O buffer is written, the buffer's contents are lost; in this event, since a transaction that has written to the buffer will not have had all of its planned writes applied to the database, the transaction must be treated as incomplete, despite having reached its EOT statement.

We are in a position now to describe the principles of recovery. It is the responsibility of the transaction manager to take the corrective measures described next as soon as possible following the failure to complete of one or more transactions. When a failure results from a program error or an action initiated by the transaction manager itself, these measures should be taken immediately (really as part of the abort procedure); when transactions fail as a result of system failure, these measures should be taken as part of the computer system's startup procedure.

When transaction T fails to complete, the transaction manager must take one of the following two corrective measures. The appropriate measure depends on whether or not T has committed.

- *T has not committed:* In this case, the transaction manager's responsibility is to erase from the database all effects that this transaction may have had. In particular, the transaction manager *returns the values of all data items that have been written by T to the values that these items had before T began execution.* This measure is referred to as transaction **undo** or **rollback.**
- *T has committed:* In this case, the transaction manager's responsibility is to make sure that all Write statements executed by T and all Write statements that appear between the Commit and EOT statements have been applied to the database. Since this may require reissuing certain Write commands, this measure is referred to as transaction **redo.**

While these recovery principles specify the effects that individual transactions' updates must have on the database, the requirements force us to confront two important questions:

1. How can a transaction be undone or redone following transaction failure? The short answer is that the transaction manager maintains a **transaction log file** that records changes that each transaction makes, or intends to make, to database items. Assuming that proper logging procedures are followed, the log file, even in the face of system crashes, will contain

enough information to allow all uncommitted transactions to be undone and all committed transactions to be redone. A later subsection considers in greater detail the management and use of the transaction log file.

2. What are the potential effects on the behavior of concurrently executing transactions of the Undo and Redo procedures, and what conventions are required to ensure correct behavior? This question is addressed in the following subsection.

Interaction of Transactions: Protocols Revisited

Suppose for the moment that we have a method for maintaining a transaction log file, allowing the transaction manager, following transaction failure, to undo uncommitted transactions and redo committed ones. There remain several serious concerns regarding the behavior of concurrently executing transactions. To illustrate some of the potential problems, we revisit two of our previous examples.

Consider first the execution schedule given in Figure 10.19, derived from that of Figure 10.18. Suppose that at time t transaction T_1 is forced to terminate. If the failure of T_1 results from a program error or from the action of the transaction manager, there is no reason to suspect that T_2 must be redone. If the failure of T_1 results from a system crash at time t, assume that time t is sufficiently far beyond the time of T_2's EOT that all I/O buffers affected by T_2

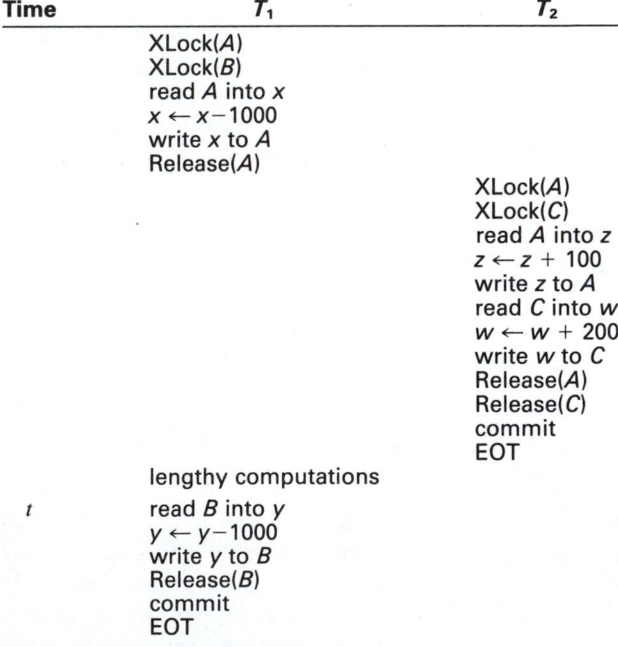

Time	T_1	T_2
	XLock(A)	
	XLock(B)	
	read A into x	
	$x \leftarrow x-1000$	
	write x to A	
	Release(A)	
		XLock(A)
		XLock(C)
		read A into z
		$z \leftarrow z + 100$
		write z to A
		read C into w
		$w \leftarrow w + 200$
		write w to C
		Release(A)
		Release(C)
		commit
		EOT
	lengthy computations	
t	read B into y	
	$y \leftarrow y-1000$	
	write y to B	
	Release(B)	
	commit	
	EOT	

Figure 10.19 A lost update problem revisited

have been written to the database, and, hence, there again is no reason to suspect that T_2 must be redone. On the other hand, since T_1 is an incomplete transaction, the transaction manager will undo T_1 which, by definition, restores A to the value it had before T_1's execution. As a result of this restoration, T_2's update to A is lost—an incorrect behavior that violates atomicity. This update is lost despite the fact that both T_1 and T_2 obey the two-phase locking protocol, and further, for the reasons just cited, it is unreasonable to expect the transaction manager to redo a transaction like T_2, which had not been prevented from having its updates written into the database (and, hence, by our definition is a completed transaction) long before the problem involving T_1 occurred.

To illustrate a second potential problem of the recovery procedure, consider Figure 10.20, a modified version of the execution schedule of Figure 10.4.

Suppose that T_1 terminates after T_2's EOT statement is reached but prior to T_1 reaching its Commit statement. Hence, T_1 must be undone. Unfortunately, restoring A to its value prior to T_1's execution (assuming this value differs from 233) invalidates the action of transaction T_2; however, since T_2 may have com-

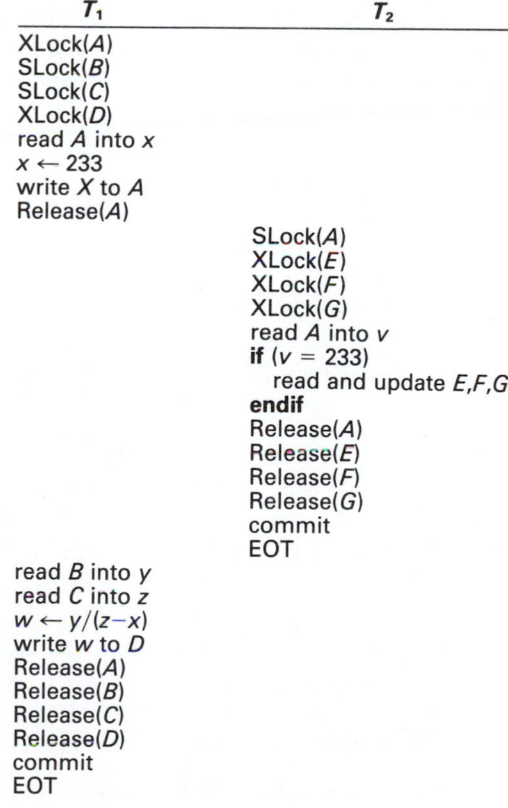

T_1	T_2
XLock(A)	
SLock(B)	
SLock(C)	
XLock(D)	
read A into x	
$x \leftarrow 233$	
write X to A	
Release(A)	
	SLock(A)
	XLock(E)
	XLock(F)
	XLock(G)
	read A into v
	if ($v = 233$)
	read and update E,F,G
	endif
	Release(A)
	Release(E)
	Release(F)
	Release(G)
	commit
	EOT
read B into y	
read C into z	
$w \leftarrow y/(z-x)$	
write w to D	
Release(A)	
Release(B)	
Release(C)	
Release(D)	
commit	
EOT	

Figure 10.20 Dirty data and cascading rollback revisited

pleted (in the sense that all of its updates had been applied to the database) long before T_1's termination, it is unreasonable to expect the transaction manager to rectify the situation. Note also that rectifying the situation would require more than simply redoing the writes executed by T_2 and hence would be beyond the scope of the Redo procedure outlined earlier for committed transactions. Further, as observed earlier, this problem would cascade to any transactions whose actions were based on the values written by T_2 to E, F, and G, and so forth. Observe that, as does the lost update problem of the previous example, these problems arise despite the fact that the transactions obey the two-phase locking protocol.

The problems illustrated by these examples stem from a common source: A transaction T releases an XLock on an item A before T has committed. Hence, if failure occurs, the transaction manager will undo T, restoring A to its value prior to the execution of T. Consequently, any transaction that updates A following the start of T's execution, but prior to the undoing of T, will have its update overwritten by the Undo procedure. Additionally, any transaction that performs an action based on the value written to A by T will have acted based on a dirty data value—a data value written to the database by a transaction that is later undone.

These observations suggest a way to prevent the problems associated with the recovery procedure. We strengthen the two-phase locking protocol to include the provision that XLocks not be released until after a transaction's Commit statement is accepted. This leads to the following **strong two-phase locking protocol.**

Definition 10.2 A transaction T obeys the **strong two-phase locking protocol** if

1. T obeys the two-phase locking protocol, that is, if T executes no lock requests (XLock or SLock) once it executes any Release statement, and
2. T does not release XLocks until after its Commit statement is accepted.

Since the second restriction prevents transactions from accessing database values that may later be undone, it is clear that this restriction eliminates the problems exemplified by the previous two examples. Observe, however, that the second restriction, without the first, is not sufficient. If we enforced only the second restriction, a transaction could acquire locks after releasing an SLock, and a schedule similar to that of Figure 10.17 would be susceptible to serializability problems. Hence, we must enforce both of these restrictions.

We observe also that, in some contexts, a further strengthening of the two-phase locking protocol is useful. The **write-restricted strong two-phase locking protocol** adds the following to the preceding two restrictions:

3. T does not write into the database until its Commit statement is accepted.

The motivation for this added restriction is that when it is respected, transactions never need be undone. That is, since the recovery procedure restores data items written by an uncommitted transaction to their values prior to the transaction's execution and since an uncommitted transaction that obeys the third restriction cannot have written any values to the database, the recovery procedure in this case need take no action.

The next section considers the management of the log file and how it is used in the recovery process, under the assumption that transactions obey either the strict two-phase locking protocol or the write-restricted version of this protocol.

Managing the Log File and Applying the Recovery Procedure

Assuming that one of the two versions of the strong two-phase locking protocol is obeyed, the management of the transaction log file and recovery from failure are accomplished by conceptually simple methods. The implementations of these methods are complicated somewhat by efficiency considerations, in particular, the desire to minimize the frequency with which I/O buffers must be written to disk. In this section, we focus on the conceptual aspects of the methods; for details on the implementation of methods designed to minimize the required number of buffer writes, the reader is referred to the Summary and Annotated Bibliography section appearing at the end of the chapter.

We first describe the actions taken to maintain the log file by the transaction manager as it executes transactions. We assume that the current tail of the log file is assembled in a system I/O buffer called *LogBuf*. When this buffer fills, it automatically is appended to the end of the log file on disk; additionally, we assume that the transaction manager can explicitly **force write** the contents of this buffer even before it fills.

For each transaction T being executed, the transaction manager creates log file entries as follows:

1. *When T is to be granted an XLock on A:* If T obeys the write-restricted version of the strong two-phase locking protocol, no log file entry is created at this time; if T obeys only the strict two-phase locking protocol, the transaction manager creates the entry described here so that the Undo procedure can be applied to T if necessitated by failure. Just prior to granting T the XLock on A, the transaction manager determines the current value V of A and creates a log record $(T,A,initial,V)$.[3] At this time, the transaction manager may simply append this log record to *LogBuf,* but it is critical that *LogBuf* be written to disk before the effects of any writes made by transaction T to A are written to disk. This principle, known as **write-ahead logging,** is necessary because, without

[3] Note that the two-phase locking protocol implies that T will not request more than one XLock on any single item A (T cannot request a lock after it releases the XLock) and hence a transaction T will generate for any single item A at most one log record of the form $(T,A,initial,V)$.

it, the system could crash between the times that T's update to A is written to disk and *LogBuf* [which contains (T,A,*initial*,V)] is written to disk. This eventuality would make the undoing of T at recovery impossible. We observe that the overhead required to support such a write-ahead logging policy is, in some contexts, a motivation for the write-restricted version of the strong two-phase locking protocol.

2. *When T executes a statement to write value V to database item A:* The transaction manager appends to *LogBuf* the record (T,A,*new*,V). In this case, it is not necessary to ensure that this log record is written to disk before the update to A is written to disk. The reason that write-ahead logging is not necessary here is that this log record is never required to undo T, and step 3 ensures that before T's Commit statement is accepted, this log record will have been written to disk, hence allowing T to be redone if necessitated by failure.

3. *When T executes its Commit statement:* The transaction manager determines the value V of each item A to be written by T following the Commit and appends to *LogBuf* a record (T,A,*new*,V) for each such value to be written. Note that it is a simple matter to determine these values since only writes and lock releases may lie between the Commit and EOT statements. The transaction manager then appends the record (T,*commit*) to *LogBuf* and force writes *LogBuf* to the end of the log file on disk. At this point, T's Commit statement is accepted. Note that this force writing of *LogBuf* ensures that a log record for every value that T needs to write to disk—including those described in step 2—is written to disk before T's Commit statement is accepted. (Question: Before accepting the Commit, why not force write to disk all changes made by T, rather than creating and writing the log file entries described here? See exercise 10.9.)

Given that the transaction manager maintains the log file as just described, we have a simple recovery procedure. We describe the procedure for recovery from a system failure; the procedure for undoing a transaction that has failed for other reasons is even simpler (see exercise 10.8). Upon restarting the system after a failure, the following actions are taken:

1. All locks held by transactions that were active at the time of the system failure are released.
2. The log file is searched for records (T,A,*initial*,V) such that there is no corresponding (T,*commit*) record. Such a T must be undone by restoring each data item A to value V, for each record of this form found. Note that such action is required only for transactions that do not obey the write-restricted version of the strong two-phase locking protocol; those that do obey the write-restricted version and have not committed have not written into the database, and the log contains no records of the preceding form corresponding to such transactions.
3. The log file is searched for records of the form (T,*commit*). For each record of this form found, T must be redone. This means that for every

record (T,A,new,V) found in the log file, the value V must be written to item A. Note that if this update had already been written to the database, the action is valid, although unnecessary. (If the log contains multiple values for the same item A, only the most recent entry is applied.)

The recovery procedure suggests a log file management issue not yet discussed: When can entries be deleted from the log file? It is clear that once the log entries corresponding to transaction T are applied to undo or redo T, these entries may be deleted from the log. (This assumes the undo or redo proceeds without further failure. See exercise 10.9.) Note, however, that if post-undo and post-redo are the only times entries are removed from the log file, the number of entries in the log file for committed transactions will accumulate between the times of system failures. This unchecked growth has implications not only for the amount of disk storage required for the log file but also for the amount of work required by step 3 of the recovery procedure since, as described, that step redoes all transactions T for which the log file contains an entry $(T,commit)$, regardless of how long ago T was run.

This observation makes apparent the desirability of removing entries for committed transactions that will not need to be redone from the log file. When can we be sure that committed transaction T will not need to be redone? The answer is that T will not need to be redone if all updates made by T have been written to the database. One way to exploit this observation would be to keep track of the I/O buffers that contain values T has written and signal the transaction manager when all such buffers have been written to the database. A method more commonly employed by actual systems is to periodically **checkpoint** the system. At a checkpoint, normal transaction processing is temporarily halted, and all system buffers are force written to the database. Immediately following a checkpoint, all entries for all committed transactions can be removed from the log file. Since the process of checkpointing can be rather costly, an important system design problem is the optimal scheduling of checkpoints. See Haerder and Reuter (1983) for a discussion of various checkpointing strategies.

10.5 DEADLOCK AND LIVELOCK

The simple schedule of Figure 10.21 illustrates a problem inherent in locking: deadlock. More generally, deadlock occurs when each transaction in some set of transactions is waiting for a lock on an item held by another transaction in this set. In the example of Figure 10.21, $\{T_1,T_2\}$ is the set of transactions involved in deadlock.

There are a wide range of approaches to the deadlock problem. The classes of approaches at the extremes of this range can be described as

- *Avoidance strategies:* In their purest form, these strategies are based on protocols that further restrict the way transactions may request locks. If transactions obey the protocol, deadlock is impossible, and no additional

Time	T_1	T_2
	XLock(A)	XLock(B)
t_i	XLock(B)	
	{ Lock denied }	
t_j	wait	XLock(A)
	wait	{ Lock denied }
	wait	wait
	⋮	⋮

Figure 10.21 Deadlock

mechanisms are required to detect and resolve deadlock. These strategies are considered pessimistic in the sense that they assume a deadlock will occur unless actions are taken in advance that will certainly prevent it from occurring.

- *Detect-resolve strategies:* In their purest form, these strategies do not further restrict the protocols and, hence, allow deadlock to occur. These strategies expend effort looking for deadlock and resolve the deadlock, typically by undoing and reexecuting transactions. That is, the strategies rely on transaction manager–induced failure and recovery procedures to resolve deadlock. These strategies are considered optimistic in the sense that they allow transactions to proceed as usual and confront deadlock only when it certainly has occurred.

The advantage of an avoidance strategy is that transactions are not undone and reexecuted due to deadlock, and hence computing resources are not wasted on these processes. On the other hand, the protocols of avoidance strategies have the disadvantage that they may increase the time it takes a transaction to complete because the protocol forces the transaction to lock more than it needs and to wait simply because giving it access to some item, even if the item is available at the time of the request, could possibly lead in the future to deadlock. Detect-resolve strategies have the advantage that they allow transactions to proceed in a less restrictive manner, often leading to faster completion. On the other hand, the strategies force the transaction manager to devote resources to undoing and re-executing transactions, and also to the task of deadlock detection.

While the classification of strategies into the two classes avoidance and detect-resolve is of some conceptual use, it is not surprising that many strategies that have been proposed and implemented lie on a continuum between the two extremes. Many useful strategies in the middle ground possess properties of both extremes and achieve a good balance. In what follows, we sample a strategy from each extreme, and then sample a few middle-ground strategies.

An Avoidance Strategy

There are several strengthenings of the strict two-phase locking protocols, each of which is guaranteed to prevent deadlock. Perhaps the simplest such strengthening is the following additional requirement:

> **Up-front locking** A transaction, as its first execution steps, must request *all* the locks it will need for its entire execution.

When transactions obey this restriction, the transaction manager treats the lock requests of a transaction T as a single unit. It grants T's lock requests only when *all* the locks requested are available; if even only one of T's requested locks is unavailable, no locks are granted to T, and the transaction must wait until all its requested locks become available.

It is apparent that deadlock is impossible when this protocol is obeyed: If some transaction T is waiting for a lock, it cannot itself hold any locks, and hence no transaction can be waiting on T. While up-front locking eliminates the problem of deadlock, the protocol makes transactions vulnerable to a second type of problem: **livelock.** Livelock is a phenomenon in which a transaction T waits "forever" for its required locks because other transactions keep being granted the locks T requires before T is granted them.

Before illustrating the livelock problem and proposing a remedy, we consider more closely how the transaction manager determines, at the time a lock on item A is released, to which transaction a new lock on A should be granted when more than one transaction is waiting for such a lock. The following discussion assumes that all locks are XLocks; see exercise 10.10 for the generalization to the case where SLocks, as well as XLocks, are present.

Prior to the introduction of the up-front locking protocol, it was reasonable to assume that the transaction manager maintains a simple queue $Q(A)$ of the transactions waiting to be granted a lock on item A; when a transaction issues a lock request for A that cannot be granted, it is placed at the end of the queue. In this way, when a lock on A becomes available, the transaction waiting the longest for the lock can be granted the lock. Note that, as long as no single transaction holds its lock on A for an infinite length of time (e.g., which could be the case if the transaction is involved in deadlock or runs "forever" because of a program bug), a transaction that enters $Q(A)$ can be assured that it eventually will be granted its lock on A.

When the up-front locking protocol is used, however, livelock can result if we implement what might appear to be the logical extension of this lock-granting policy. The phenomenon of livelock is illustrated by the simple example in Figure 10.22. Suppose that each transaction of Figure 10.22 enters the system at the time of its first lock request. When T_2 first issues its lock requests, they are (both) denied because one of the requested items, A, already is locked by T_1. Consider now T_3's request for a lock on B. Although this is one of the locks T_2 already has requested, the temptation is to grant the lock to T_3 since T_2 cannot be granted its locks (T_1 still has A locked). However, this is a dangerous policy. To see the potential consequences of such a policy, suppose that the transaction manager does grant T_3's lock request. Then, when T_1 releases its lock on A, T_2 still can't be granted its locks because T_3 now has B locked. Further, if T_4 is granted its request for a lock on A, T_2 still cannot be granted its

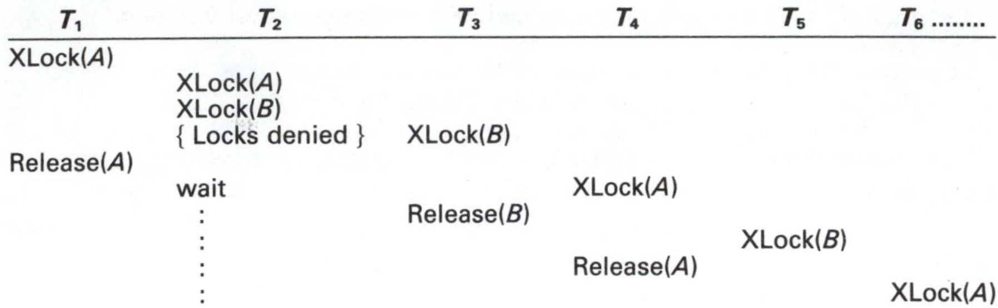

T_1	T_2	T_3	T_4	T_5	T_6 ....
XLock(A)					
	XLock(A)				
	XLock(B)				
	{ Locks denied }	XLock(B)			
Release(A)					
	wait		XLock(A)		
	:	Release(B)			
	:			XLock(B)	
	:		Release(A)		
	:				XLock(A)

Figure 10.22 Livelock of T_2

locks at the time T_3 releases its lock on B. As the example of Figure 10.22 indicates, T_2 will be kept waiting as long as transactions enter the system and request and release locks in the pattern shown. T_2 thus is livelocked.

The lock-granting policy that leads to livelock in Figure 10.22 is to grant a transaction's request for a lock on an item (e.g., grant T_3's lock request on B), despite the fact that T_2 had already requested this lock. A lock-granting policy that avoids livelock is to deny a transaction's lock request on an item A whenever some other waiting transaction has requested that item earlier, even if that longer waiting transaction cannot be granted its locks because other requested items are locked by other transactions. Hence, when the up-front locking protocol is used, the transaction manager grants transaction T's lock requests exactly when (1) every lock requested by T is available and (2) no transaction has been waiting longer than T for any lock T requests.

While the up-front locking protocol in combination with the preceding lock-granting policy avoids the problems of deadlock and livelock, the conventions can have undesirable consequences for performance. One consequence is that a nontrivial amount of computing effort must be diverted from the execution of transactions to the management of locks. A second, often more significant consequence, is that the conventions can lead to inordinate delays in the time between transaction initiation and transaction completion. Such delays may result when a transaction is prevented from progressing past its lock requests when, if not for the transaction manager's policies, the transaction would be able to perform at least some of its required actions. As an example of the delays in completion time that can result from the lock-granting policy, consider the execution depicted in Figure 10.22, and suppose that transaction T_1 is a lengthy process that holds its lock on A for a long period of time. Suppose further that T_3 is a simple process that can complete shortly after its lock request is granted. The lock-granting policy will prevent transaction T_3 from progressing past its lock request until T_2 is granted and releases its locks, despite the fact that B is available while T_1 is executing and, hence, that T_3 could complete its request almost immediately.

The nature of database transactions tends to amplify the type of problem just illustrated, often making the employment of deadlock avoidance techniques im-

```
print("Enter SS# of employee to be given 10% raise; enter 0 to quit.")
read(get_SS)
while (get_SS ≠ 0)
  UPDATE (EMPLOYEE.Salary = EMPLOYEE.Salary*1.1)
    WHERE EMPLOYEE.SS=get_SS
  print("Enter SS# of employee to be given 10% raise; enter 0 to quit.")
  read(get_SS)
end while
```

Figure 10.23 SQL-level transaction

practical. Consider, for example, the transaction in Figure 10.23, stated at the level of an embedded SQL-like program. According to our conceptual processing model, the query optimizer maps this high-level transaction into a lower level transaction that locks and accesses database items. If the resulting transaction is to obey the up-front locking protocol, all lock requests must be issued at the beginning of the transaction. However, since there is no way of knowing at the start of execution which EMPLOYEE tuples are to be modified, compliance with the up-front locking protocol requires that the transaction lock the entire EMPLOYEE table. An even more dramatic illustration of the undesirable consequences of up-front locking is a transaction that accesses exactly one table from among a large collection of tables, with the identity of the accessed table determined by computations and queries performed by the transaction. Unfortunately, such a transaction would need to lock all the tables in this collection if it is to comply with up-front locking.

The conclusion we draw from these examples is that an up-front locking protocol often necessitates the locking of far more items (e.g., many more tuples or even many more tables) than a transaction actually needs to access. This situation only amplifies the transaction delays illustrated earlier since the likelihood is increased that several transactions will be vying for locks on the same items. Consequently, deadlock avoidance strategies rarely are appropriate for realistic database applications, and instead, methods such as those described in the next two subsections are employed.

Detect-Resolve Strategies

Consider now a strategy at the opposite end of the spectrum from the deadlock avoidance strategy. That is, make no attempt to avoid deadlock but rather detect deadlock when it occurs, and then take some action that will resolve the deadlock. Of course, we shall continue to assume that one of the versions of the strict two-phase locking protocol is obeyed so that executions are serializable and the simple recovery algorithms can be applied in the event of transaction failure.

As its name implies, the implementation of a detect-resolve strategy has two components: deadlock detection and deadlock resolution.

- *Deadlock detection:* A directed graph can be used to represent the locking pattern of the collection of executing transactions, and the presence in the graph of a directed cycle will indicate deadlock. Specifically, a **wait-for** graph for the collection of transactions currently executing consists of a vertex v_i for each executing transaction T_i. The edges of the wait-for graph indicate which transactions are waiting for the locks held by other transactions—there is a directed edge from v_i to v_j exactly when T_j holds a lock that T_i has requested. The graph is updated in the obvious way when transactions begin and terminate and when locks are requested and released.

It is fairly easy to see that there is a deadlock situation exactly when the wait-for graph contains a directed cycle (see exercise 10.1); hence, to detect deadlock, the transaction manager need only run a cycle detection algorithm. How often should the cycle detection algorithm be run? Observe that a cycle can be created only when an edge is added to the graph—hence, it certainly is sufficient to check for cycles each time an edge is added. While such a strategy will detect deadlock as soon as it develops, the overhead incurred might be too high. As an alternative, the transaction manager might check for cycles after every kth edge is added (for some $k > 1$) or at regular time intervals. The penalty for infrequent cycle checks is that a deadlock state can go uncorrected for some period of time.

- *Deadlock resolution:* The standard method of deadlock resolution is to terminate one of the transactions involved in the deadlock. Note that such a termination falls into the category of *transaction manager–induced failure,* as considered in the previous section. Hence, if a transaction T is terminated to resolve deadlock, it is undone (if necessary), its locks are released, and it is restarted.

  A question that remains is, "Which transaction involved in deadlock should be terminated?" For simplicity, assume that the transaction manager checks for cycles after each lock request that leads to edge additions and that when a cycle is detected, resolution immediately is undertaken. Hence, for example, when transaction T issues an XLock request on item A that cannot be granted immediately, edges $e_1, \ldots, e_p (p \geq 1)$ from transaction T to the transactions holding locks on A are added to the wait-for graph. Because we are assuming that no cycles existed before transaction T's lock request, we may assume that at most p distinct cycles now exist and that each cycle involves at least one of the newly added edges $e_1, \ldots, e_p$. Further, each of these cycles can be broken by terminating any transaction on the cycle. There are several reasonable methods for choosing the transaction on each cycle to terminate, including terminate the youngest transaction, terminate the transaction whose lock request created the deadlock, and terminate the transaction that has performed the least amount of work or is easiest to undo. We might consider also identifying an "optimal" collection of transactions whose termination will break all the newly created cycles. Note that if the write-restricted version of the strict two-phase locking protocol is employed, no work is required to undo the terminated transaction, thus providing additional motivation for the restriction when detect-resolve strategies are employed.

Middle-Ground Strategies

The middle-ground strategies share the property with detect-resolve strategies that they do not employ protocols to prohibit *a priori* schedules that could lead to deadlock, and rather rely on transaction termination as a key mechanism. They share with the avoidance strategies the property that they don't wait until a deadlock has certainly arisen before taking action. The advantage of these middle-ground strategies over the extremes is that they are far more dynamic, and hence flexible, than avoidance strategies, yet they do not require that resources be diverted to deadlock detection. Several studies suggest that these middle-ground strategies perform well in practice.

Perhaps the simplest way to eliminate the need for deadlock detection is by means of a **transaction time-out.** Simply put, this technique assumes that if a transaction has been waiting for a lock past some prespecified maximum wait period, then the transaction is involved in deadlock. In response to time-out, the transaction manager terminates, undoes, and restarts the waiting transaction. While some transactions that actually are not involved in deadlock will be terminated, if the maximum wait period is set carefully, this occurrence is rare.

An approach similar to transaction time out is **lock time-out.** Here, a prespecified maximum locking period is placed on each lock, and when a transaction has held any single lock for this length of time, the lock becomes **vulnerable.** A transaction continues to hold a vulnerable lock on item A as long as no other transaction is waiting to lock A; however, if one or more transactions are waiting for a lock on A, the transaction holding the vulnerable lock is terminated. In addition to resolving deadlock when it does occur, the lock time-out strategy may be of some benefit to average transaction completion time since it favors the execution of transactions with small-to-average resource needs over the execution of transactions with intense needs, effectively giving low priority to the execution of the latter type of transaction.

Each of the time-out strategies is prone to **starvation**—a phenomenon in which a transaction is restarted and terminated repeatedly—and systems implementing these strategies must employ policies to ensure that every correct transaction will complete after a reasonable number of retries.

Wait-die and **wound-wait** refer to instances of a class of strategies that terminates transactions before deadlock actually develops yet avoids complex detection procedures and overly restrictive protocols and is not prone to starvation. When a transaction begins execution, it is a assigned a unique identifier, referred to as the transaction's **id.** Often, this id is derived from the system clock so that the older the transaction, the smaller the id. However, the id's can be assigned in other ways, such as by a random number generator. Whatever method is employed to assign id's, when transaction T_1's id is smaller than transaction T_2's id, we shall say that T_2 is *younger* that T_1 and that T_1 is *older* than T_2. We assume that a transaction retains its original id until it completes execution, even if the transaction is terminated and restarted one or more times before a successful completion.

Under the wait-die strategy, if T_1 requests a lock held by T_2 and T_1 is older than T_2, T_1 simply waits; if younger transaction T_2 requests a lock held by older T_1, T_2 is terminated. Under wound-wait, if older transaction T_1 requests a lock held by T_2, T_2 is terminated; if younger transaction T_2 requests a lock held by older T_1, T_2 simply waits. As exercise 10.11 demonstrates, deadlock and livelock are both impossible under either wait-die or wound-wait, and a correct transaction will complete after a finite number of restarts.

Since the strategies considered in this subsection all require transactions to be terminated, undone, and restarted, the write-restricted version of the strict two-phase protocol is often a good complement to these methods.

10.6 ADDITIONAL ISSUES AND TECHNIQUES

Transaction management is a major topic, and so far in this chapter, we have described the basic issues and solution techniques. In this section, we sample a few additional issues and techniques, including locking precision, alternative concurrency control mechanisms, and concurrency control in a distributed database environment.

Locking Precision

There are two dimensions along which we can control the precision of locks: locking granularity and locking semantics. Choices are considered along each dimension in an attempt to allow more concurrency, without sacrificing correctness and without introducing more overhead than is justified by the resulting increase in concurrency.

Locking Granularity: In this chapter, we have worked with transactions that reference (i.e., lock and access) items at the level of individual attribute occurrences. We observed that a translation most likely is performed so that, at the implementation level, locking is performed at a much coarser granularity. An important decision in the design of a transaction management system is the level of granularity at which locks are implemented. While fine granularity locking provides high precision in what a transaction locks, and, hence, reduces unnecessary lockout, it also incurs a good deal of overhead for lock management. Many studies [e.g., Reis and Stonebraker (1977, 1979)] suggest that in typical applications, relatively coarse locks, at the level of at least a physical block and perhaps even groups of blocks, are the most cost effective.

When locking at the physical level, that is, the locking unit is defined in terms of a physical object such as a disk block, there is the opportunity to exploit characteristics of the physical structure. For example, if a data file will always be accessed via a B-tree and of the nodes of this B-tree (which are disk blocks) are a locking unit, we can devise protocols that exploit the fact that a path down from the root will always be followed. When all transactions that access the data file are known to acquire and release locks only in a hierarchical pattern corresponding to the the B-tree structure, protocols that do not require two-phase locking, yet guarantee serializability, can be devised. See Silberschatz and Kedem (1980) for details.

Locking Semantics: A second dimension in locking precision is locking semantics—what does a lock "mean"? We have so far utilized XLocks and SLocks, lock types whose semantics can be summarized by the **compatibility matrix** given in Figure 10.24. For example, the value Y in entry M[SLock,SLock] indicates that transaction T_j can be granted an SLock on an item on which transaction T_i already holds an SLock. The other entries indicate situations in which a lock request must be denied.

		T_i Holds	
		SLock	XLock
T_j Requests	SLock	Y	N
	XLock	N	N

Figure 10.24 Locking compatibility matrix

While SLocks and XLocks reflect the semantics of how locks permitting general reading and writing of items should behave, there is no reason we cannot define additional, special-purpose lock types. As an example, consider a scientific application in which two common operations are

1. Read an item A and determine whether $A = 0$.
2. Read an item A and double its value; that is, write back $2 * A$.

If transactions have available only SLocks and XLocks, when a transaction needs to check A for a zero value, it must first acquire an SLock on A, while a transaction that needs to double A must first acquire an XLock on A. Consequently, the semantics of these lock types prevent a transaction from performing one of these tasks on A as long as another transaction holds the lock required to perform the other of these tasks on A.

It is apparent, however, that the preceding tasks don't conflict in the sense that the performance of one does not in any way affect the results of the other. This might motivate the introduction of two new lock types, Z_Check_Lock and Double_Lock, whose semantics are expressed by enlarging the compatibility matrix as shown in Figure 10.25. Note, for example, that if a transaction needs to double the value of item A, it acquires a Double_Lock on A, allowing a second transaction concurrently to acquire Z_Check_Lock on A and determine if A's value is zero.

		T_i Holds			
		SLock	XLock	Z_Check_Lock	Double_Lock
T_j Requests	SLock	Y	N	Y	N
	XLock	N	N	N	N
	Z_Check_Lock	Y	N	Y	Y
	Double_Lock	N	N	Y	N

Figure 10.25 Enlarged locking compatibility matrix

Hence, by supporting richer lock semantics, we allow a transaction to more exactly specify what it is going to do to the items it locks, thereby potentially allowing the transaction manager to admit additional execution schedules as serializable. However, as new lock types are allowed, it becomes increasingly more difficult to characterize exactly what protocols will and will not ensure serializability, mandating the use of more *ad hoc* schedule analysis methods. See exercise 10.2 for details.

Timestamping and Optimistic Concurrency Control

Section 10.5 contrasted optimistic (detect-resolve) and pessimistic (avoidance) methods for addressing the problem of deadlock. In analogy, the locking and protocol schemes we have considered previously are the basis of relatively pessimistic methods for ensuring that the effects on the database of concurrent transaction execution satisfies certain correctness properties, most notably, serializability. In this section, we outline two relatively optimistic methods that do not restrict *a priori* how a transaction may be constructed or executed. The first method, **timestamping,** verifies at the time a transaction attempts to access an item that certain simple conditions are satisfied, terminating and restarting the transaction if the conditions are not satisfied. The second method, even more optimistic than timestamping and deemed by its originators Kung and Robinson (1981) as **optimistic concurrency control,** resembles the snapshot model of execution described in Section 10.2 and illustrated by Figure 10.10. In optimistic concurrency control, a transaction executes until its completion, at which time potential serialization problems are analyzed; if problems may exist, the transaction is undone and restarted. As with the optimistic deadlock methods, the methods considered in this section are most appropriate when the probability is small that transactions will concurrently access the same item.

Timestamping: The basis of the timestamping method is the assignment to a transaction when it begins execution of a unique **timestamp,** which we shall assume is the current time of the system clock. Note that the larger the timestamp, the younger (more recently initiated) is the transaction. The timestamping method controls transaction execution so that whenever a collection of transactions completes execution, the effect of this execution will be equivalent to the *temporal serial execution* of the transactions, that is, the execution that first runs the oldest transaction in the collection, then the next oldest, and so forth.

Conceptually, every database item *A* has associated with it the following pieces of information:

- *Read timestamp:* The timestamp of the youngest transaction that has read item *A*.
- *Write timestamp:* The timestamp of the youngest transaction that has written a value to item *A*.

In practice, implementations of the method use default times so that only some database items are labeled explicitly.

As a transaction executes, there is no explicit locking or unlocking of database items. Rather, when a transaction attempts to read or write an item, the transaction manager decides whether or not to permit the operation by comparing the transaction's timestamp to the appropriate (read or write) timestamp of the item. Specifically, the transaction manager's rules can be expressed as follows, letting t be the timestamp of transaction T and $r(A)$ and $w(A)$ the read timestamp and write timestamp of item A, respectively. Recall that the larger the timestamp, the younger the transaction.

Transaction *T* Attempts to Read Item A

```
if (t≥w(A))
  { T is no older than the youngest transaction that wrote to A }
    allow T to read A
    if (t>r(A))
      { Update A's read timestamp }
      r(A) ← t
    endif
else
  { T is older than the youngest transaction that wrote to A. In the temporal
    serialized schedule it would be impossible for T to read such a value. }
    terminate T
    undo T
    assign to T a new timestamp based on current time, and restart T
endif
```

Transaction *T* Attempts to Write a Value to Item A

```
if ( (t≥w(A)) and (t≥r(A))
  { T is no older than the youngest transaction that read or wrote to A }
    allow T to write to A
    { Update A's timestamps }
    r(A) ← t
    w(A) ← t
elseif (t≥r(A))
  { T is older than the youngest transaction that wrote to A, but is no older
    than the youngest transaction that read A. This implies that in the temporal
    serialized schedule, T's update to A is overwritten before any transaction
    read the value that A wrote, i.e., in this execution, it is as if updates made
    by T never took place. }
    ignore the write request, but allow T to continue execution
else
  { In this case, t<r(A), and hence a transaction T' younger than T has read the
    item A. In the temporal serialized schedule, it would be impossible for T to
    write a value to A after a younger T' has read the value of A. }
    terminate T
    undo T
    assign to T a new timestamp based on current time, and restart T
endif
```

Observe that since the timestamping method does not rely on locks, deadlock is not an issue. However, starvation is an issue with which systems implementing the timestamping method must deal by employing policies to ensure that every correct transaction will complete after a reasonable number of retries. We note also that techniques can be employed so that a transaction does not actually write into the database until it completes, thereby reducing the cost of undoing transactions. See Coulouris and Dollimore (1988) for more details on implementations of the timestamping method.

Optimistic Concurrency Control: The optimistic concurrency control method of Kung and Robinson (1981) utilizes, for each executing transaction, a private work space in which the transaction makes all its changes to database items. For the purposes of this discussion, we simplify the method and view the work space of transaction T as behaving like snapshot $DB(T)$, as defined in Section 10.2. Recall that in our snapshot model, a transaction T, when it begins execution, makes its own local copy $DB(T)$ of the items in the database that it may need to access. As T executes, all accesses to database items are made to $DB(T)$, and only when T completes its execution are the values that T wrote to $DB(T)$ written to the actual database.

To ensure the serializability of executions, it is necessary that the transaction manager check for conflict at the time a transaction T attempts to write $DB(T)$ to the actual database. Recall, for example, that the schedule of Figure 10.10 is not serializable since, in effect, the update of T_1 is lost. We explained the problem in terms of snapshot conflict: At the time T_2 writes snapshot $DB(T_2)$ to the database, $DB(T_2)$ is outdated in the sense that is was derived from an instance of the database that conflicts with the instance resulting from T_1's writing of $DB(T_1)$.

When optimistic concurrency control is employed, a check for snapshot conflict must be made at the time each transaction T attempts to write $DB(T)$ to the actual database. At this time, T is validated against each transaction in the set $\{T_1, \ldots, T_i, \ldots, T_n\}$ of transactions that have already written to the database $DB(T_i)$ and whose execution overlaps the execution of T. For each such T_i, it is determined whether T_i wrote a value to any item read or written by T. If any of these T_i did write to such an item, conflict is present, and T is terminated [before it can write $DB(T)$] and restarted. For example, in Figure 10.10, at the time T_2 attempts to write to the database $DB(T_2)$, it would be determined that there is a conflict with T_1 since T_1 wrote a value to the seats available on flight 888, an item both read and written by T_2. Consequently, T_2 would be terminated and restarted.

As with the timestamping method, policies must be employed to prevent starvation and ensure that every correct transaction will complete within a finite number of tries. Note that, since the optimistic concurrency control technique utilizes local snapshots and does not write changes to the actual database until it is determined that conflicts are not present, no cost is incurred undoing a transaction when termination and restart are required.

Transaction Management in a Distributed Environment

In Section 1.5, we introduced the concept of a distributed database in which data resides, and processing is performed, at several nodes of a computer network. For completeness, we mention here that in such an environment, the complexity of transaction management is increased greatly. Four of the more important transaction management issues introduced by a distributed environment are

- *Locking of logical items:* When portions of the database are replicated, different physical copies of the same logical item (e.g., different copies of seats available attribute of flight 888) reside at different sites. Concurrently executing transactions must produce results on the distributed database that are consistent across all copies, necessitating that a lock on one copy of an item produce the effect of locking all copies.
- *Deadlock and livelock detection:* The detection of deadlock and livelock when many sites are involved in processing becomes more difficult.
- *Commitment of distributed transactions:* A transaction completes successfully only if it completes successfully on all sites. That is, it must be able to effect its changes on data at all sites, and hence before the actions of a Commit can be taken (e.g., writing updated values to the actual database), the transaction manager must ensure that the effects of the transaction can be committed at all sites. Since failure at any single site implies that the entire transaction must be undone at all sites, protocols for distributed committing of transactions are more complex than those for single-site Commits.
- *Increased cost of rollback:* If a transaction makes changes to multiple copies of a data item, the cost of undoing the transaction obviously is increased. This factor must be considered when choosing which of the strategies presented in the previous sections to extend and modify for a distributed database system.

Chapter 13 considers additional aspects of a distributed database environment.

10.7 ENHANCING DATABASE INTEGRITY AND SECURITY

The preceding sections of this chapter considered techniques for preserving the integrity of a database in the face of "system problems," problems that, for example, might arise from the database system's careless scheduling of concurrent database accesses and from system hardware or software failures. As a result of such problems, user actions—perfectly legitimate in their own right—might have unintended consequences, leaving the database in a state inconsistent with reality.

In contrast, the problems surveyed in this section arise directly from the actions of database users. In particular, we are concerned here with protecting the database from user operations that, *by their nature,* would compromise the integrity or security of the database. Some of these problems are caused by user carelessness, for example, a user update leaving the database in a state that violates one of its integrity constraints. Other problems are caused by malicious user behavior, for example, a user accessing information he or she is not authorized to obtain, or even modifying data with malicious intent. This chapter surveys several different types of user abuse and discusses techniques for reducing their prevalence and containing their impact.

Integrity Constraint Checking

In Chapters 4, 5, and 6, we studied integrity constraints (e.g., functional and multivalued dependencies) primarily in the context of database design. In the database design context, integrity constraints are used to characterize database instances that a candidate design must be prepared to handle gracefully—the implicit assumption being that the integrity constraints will be enforced when users attempt to update the database, and hence instances violating these constraints will not arise in practice. There, of course, are many additional motivations, having nothing to do with database design, for integrity constraint enforcement. In general, integrity constraints are used to identify those database states that can arise only from error or from an intentional, malicious act; constraint enforcement should protect the database from transitions into such states.

Chapter 6 considered the problem of enforcing on a lossless decomposition $D = (T_1, \ldots, T_k)$ of table scheme T a set F of functional dependencies for T. As is summarized by the commutativity diagrams of Figures 6.1 through 6.8, it is highly desirable to be able to verify, without joining the T_i to reconstruct T, whether a proposed update is consistent with F. As we discovered in Chapter 6, provided that D is an F-enforceable decomposition, methods exist for verifying F by inspecting only the table(s) T_i in D affected by the update. On the other hand, if D is not F-enforceable, at least part of the Join $\bowtie_{i=1}^{k} T_i$ must be computed to verify that a proposed update is consistent with F.

While F-enforceability is an important concept, it is only a single illustration of a far more general concern: How can arbitrary integrity constraints be enforced efficiently? The question has no simple answer because many different types of integrity constraints are encountered in practice, and each type of constraint requires its own enforcement technique. Current research into constraint enforcement focuses on questions such as the following:

1. How can it be determined which constraints must be verified following an update; that is, which constraints could become violated when a given update is applied to a current database instance?

2. How can constraints best be checked; for example, how can we determine what subset of a table instance requires inspection to verify that a constraint continues to hold following an update?
3. Given a set of constraints, what physical design (e.g., choice of file structures for the RDM tables) would make constraint enforcement most efficient?
4. What is a reasonable constraint checking policy? For example, should constraints be checked following every update, following a given number of updates, or only at the explicit request of the database administrator?

To this point, we have applied integrity constraints to identify and disallow illegal updates. There is an alternative means of applying some types of integrity constraints, a means that attempts to maintain the integrity of the database by "completing" the update that the user has requested explicitly. Consider, for example, multivalued dependencies, as defined in Section 6.3. Multivalued dependencies are referred to as **tuple-generating** dependencies because the presence in a table instance of one collection of tuples implies the presence of certain other tuples, else a multivalued dependency would be violated. Hence, if the user attempts to insert one collection of tuples into a table instance currently obeying a multivalued dependency, the DBMS can attempt to "complete" the update by adding to the instance those additional tuples that the multivalued dependency implies must be present also. Since in many cases there is more than one set of tuples whose addition would complete an update, the DBMS requires rules for selecting the set of tuples to add; often, these rules require user interaction. Exercise 10.15 explores this issue.

This use of tuple-generating dependencies is an instance of the more general concept of a **database trigger.** A trigger has the general form

<P, A>

where *P* is a predicate applied to a database instance (e.g., *P* is the predicate *table EMPLOYEE contains no employee tuples that have value D in the Dept attribute*) and *A* is an action (e.g., *A* is the action *delete from the table DEPARTMENT the tuple for this department D*). The DBMS has the responsibility of checking all trigger predicates when a user transaction (e.g., an update) that could cause the predicate to become true is processed, and to execute the action associated with all predicates that do become true. In the preceding example, the predicate *table EMPLOYEE contains no employee tuples that have value D in its Dept attribute* would be checked each time tuples are deleted from table EMPLOYEE and, if the predicate is ever found to be true for some department *D*, the system would delete from DEPARTMENT the tuple for *D*.

While integrity checking and triggers provide a means of enhancing the integrity of a database, their implementation incurs a significant overhead. Much current research is directed toward minimizing this overhead, but further advances are necessary before their extensive use becomes practical in general-purpose applications.

Traditional Access Restrictions

The remainder of this section considers problems associated with intentional misuse of a database system. It should be noted that most of these problems of misuse, and the techniques employed to address them, are not unique to a database system. Rather, the problems must be addressed in the setting of essentially any computing environment where security is a concern.

Traditional approaches to computer security are based on **access restrictions.** These restrictions include

1. *Physical restrictions:* The physical restriction approach limits system access to only careful guarded ports. For example, a highly secure computing system may place the computer and all terminals connected to it in a closely guarded room; dial-ups and network links are prohibited. Security personnel control access to the room and, hence, to the computer.

2. *User authentication:* Often, it is not practical to physically restrict system access to the extent described in item 1 since such an isolated computing environment is in conflict with modern computing requirements for networks of communicating computing systems. Hence, for all but the most sensitive applications, techniques for user authentication are preferred over physical protection as the means of controlling system access.

   By far the most prevalent authentication technique is a password system—the user identifies himself or herself with a secret word, a string of characters known only to the user. By employing variants of the encryption techniques discussed later, the password system can be made arbitrarily hard to crack. However, even with the password arbitrarily hard to crack, unauthorized access may still be gained from users' carelessness in guarding the password, for example, writing down the password and then carelessly discarding it. State-of-the art authentication techniques attempt to address the problem of the "purloined password" by means that include physical card keys (credit card–like magnetic strips), voice or hand print recognition, and keystroke analysis (analyzing whether the speed and pattern of keystrokes are consistent with past behavior for the user).

3. *Permissions:* A computing system typically restricts the actions of even its legitimate users. For example, an operating system typically provides protections, controlling the files and programs each user may access and the types of access (e.g., read or write) that the user is permitted. Commercial DBMSs typically provide finer granularities of control. For example, a typical relational DBMS supports the granting of permissions at a fine granularity, such as that illustrated by the following command:

```
PERMIT READ on EMPLOYEE.SS#, EMPLOYEE.Name
  WHERE EMPLOYEE.Dept = "Toys"
  TO User=Jones
  AT Terminal=tty1
  ON Monday..Friday, 9am..5pm
```

This command grants to a specific user, using a specific terminal at a specific time, permission to read two of the attributes of the tuples for employees in the toys department. While such access controls are quite useful in theory, they are only as reliable as the operating system is secure. That is, if the operating system has weak points that allow one user to "become" another user or get another user's privileges, the database system's protection mechanisms are of little value.

Because the techniques just described are both vulnerable and incomplete (incomplete in the sense that, as is illustrated next, there are types of misuse not addressed by access controls), more sophisticated security measures may be employed to complement traditional access control techniques. We now survey two such security measures.

Data Encryption

Data encryption is arguably the surest method of limiting data access on a computing system. Because data encryption algorithms can be implemented essentially independently of other system components (e.g, essentially independent of the operating system and DBMS), the security of encrypted data is limited only by the security of the encryption algorithms themselves. And encryption algorithms, such as the public key encryption scheme of Rivest, Shamir, and Adleman (1978) (known as **RAS**), are extremely secure indeed. The primary drawback of encryption as a database security mechanism is that it will degrade the response time of some operations to a degree that, in certain contexts, may not be acceptable.

The basic data encryption concept is as follows: We identify a piece of data D (e.g., D may be a numeric- or string-valued tuple attribute) to which we wish only a certain user (or users) to have access. Rather than store D directly in its conventional form, we employ an **encryption algorithm** E that maps D to some other value $E(D)$, which we store in place of D. $E(D)$ is meaningless to a user unless he or she is able to apply to the stored value $E(D)$ a **decryption algorithm** E^{-1} which maps $E(D)$ back to $D = E^{-1}(E(D))$. Of course, the crux of the technique is that only the authorized user be able to apply to $E(D)$ the decryption algorithm E^{-1} to obtain D.

A second desirable property of an encryption scheme is that only authorized users be able to modify data. There are two components of this goal, both of which are met by the RAS encryption scheme:

1. We wish to deny an unauthorized user the ability to modify existing data values. If the authorized user stores the encrypted version $E(D)$ of data value D, other users should not be able to replace $E(D)$ with some other value X, which the original user would then decode to some meaningful value $D' = E^{-1}(X)$. While the denial to the unauthorized user of the ability to replace one value with another can be no more complete than the operating and database systems are secure, the nature of the en-

cryption algorithm can make such a surreptitious modification apparent to the authorized user. That is, the unauthorized user will be unable to construct a value X that the decryption algorithm E^{-1} maps to a meaningful value—while the original value D may be overwritten, at least the authorized user will realize that the value has been altered illegitimately. In the best case, the valid data value will be recoverable from a modify-protected log file or database backup.

2. We wish to deny an unauthorized user the ability to add and delete data values. As in the case of data modification, the inability of the unauthorized user to construct data values that the decryption algorithm E^{-1} maps to meaningful values effectively denies the unauthorized user the ability to add data values. While the denial to the unauthorized user of the ability to delete a data value can be no more complete than the operating and database systems are secure, such a deletion can be made apparent to the authorized user. For example, an encrypted count of tuples can be maintained, or encryption can be applied in such a way that deletion of any data value makes meaningless the result of applying the decryption algorithm to the remaining data values. Again, once the illegitimate modification is detected, the deleted data values may be recoverable from a log file or database backup.

Since the details of the RAS encryption scheme are not related directly to our discussion, we refer the interested reader to Rivest, Shamir, and Adelman (1978) for a complete description. In closing, however, we do wish to consider the interaction between the database system and the encryption algorithm. In the case where the encrypted attribute is never part of a search criterion, the interaction is essentially nonexistent. On retrievals, for example, a user program employs the DBMS to retrieve tuples as usual and then applies the decryption algorithm where necessary to obtain the actual data values. Similarly, when a tuple is inserted, the encryption algorithm is employed where appropriate to encrypt attribute values, and the database system then stores this tuple as usual. In each case, the only overhead incurred is the time required to apply the encryption or decryption algorithm. If, however, we were to encrypt an attribute that may be used in a search criterion, database operations become more complex since, for example, encrypted values may have to be decrypted as tuples are checked for qualification. See exercise 10.17.

Monitoring and Dynamically Restricting User Actions

The techniques considered so far attempt to prohibit certain prespecified and well-defined actions, such as an unauthorized user gaining access to a system without a proper account and an authorized user accessing or modifying data to which he or she should not have access. We conclude this section by considering briefly a more nebulous type of computer misuse. This type of misuse is characterized by the fact that no single action of the user is specified in advance as being forbidden, but a sequence of such user actions taken together has an effect that is undesirable or malicious. Examples of this type of misuse include

1. Sequences of legitimate actions that have the effect of gaining for a user the privileges of another user.
2. Interactions with a program to which the user does have access privileges but in a manner, unanticipated by the program's designers, that compromises the computing system's integrity.
3. Sequences of database interrogations, each legitimate by itself, but whose net effect is to provide the user with information he or she is not privileged to obtain.

The first two types of misuse are not unique to a database context. A promising new general-purpose technique for addressing these types of computer misuse is based on **audit trail analysis.** Audit trail analysis supports an approach to computer security that attempts to identify suspicious computer activities as they are occurring. The approach is intended to augment the traditional access control mechanisms discussed earlier by scrutinizing the activities of users once they have gained access to the computing system.

An audit trail can be maintained for a variety of user activity types, logging, for example, operating or database system commands. The basic unit of the audit trail is called a **transaction.** A transaction provides a trace of a primitive user action by recording attribute values that characterize the action. For example, a transaction might include the attributes *user_id, command, port, time, elapsed_cpu,* and *status_code*. A sample instance of this transaction is

user_id=Fred, command=execute program x, port=tty8,
time=1992.05.19.09.23.12.119, elapsed_cpu=1.4, status_code=OK

Sequences of such transaction instances are collected and analyzed using techniques that include the following:

1. Look for violations of expert-supplied rules. An example of an expert-supplied rule is

   (command=execute program x) $\Rightarrow$ *elapsed_CPU* < 1

   With this expert rule in place, this transaction template would be flagged as suspect, indicating that further investigation is appropriate.
2. Look for statistically unusual behavior. In contrast (and complementing) expert rules, an analysis system performs statistical analyses. For example, rather than a rule specifying *a priori* that program x not require more than one unit of CPU time, the system can deduce that program x requiring more than one unit of CPU time is a statistically rare event and hence requires investigation.
3. Look for patterns that are statistically more similar to known misuse behaviors than to known normal behaviors. If, for example, we had historical patterns of misuse that indicate program x requiring more than 1 unit

of CPU time is closely correlated with a particular type of computer misuse (e.g., a user assuming superuser privileges), this transaction would be treated as highly suspect.

The audit trail analysis problem is quite difficult because expert rules are difficult to obtain, because statistical analysis is difficult because of the enormous number of potential transaction instances and relatively small sample of transaction instances available, and because there few known misuse patterns. Audit trail analysis is an ongoing research area, and the reader is referred to Helman, Liepins, and Richards (1992); Lunt et al. (1990); and Vaccaro and Liepins (1989) for a discussion of current techniques.

The third category of misuse listed earlier is unique to the database context and can be considered a special case of the more general monitoring problem. To illustrate this type of misuse, suppose we have a database, accessible to the general public, that is meant to provide only statistical information without associating specific data values with specific individuals. For example, our university might maintain a database containing data such as faculty ages, salaries, and ethnic backgrounds. The intent is to support statistical queries of the form "What is the average salary of male faculty members between the ages 50 and 60," which do not associate specific data values with specific individuals.

While the intent of statistical databases is to allow users to obtain only aggregate quantities, **tracker queries** often can be applied to compromise the confidentiality of these databases. A tracker query consists of one or more legitimate user requests for statistical information whose answer(s) allows the user to violate confidentiality by deducing actual information associated with a specific individual. For example, suppose we know a good deal of information about our friend Bill Smith and wish to learn his salary. We can violate the database's confidentiality, first by posing a sequence of queries that narrows down the qualifying set *S* to a single individual that includes Bill Smith and then by asking for the average salary of individuals in the set *S*. Consider, for example, the following sequence of queries:

```
/* We know Bill is male CS professor between the age 40 and 50 */
Query 1: COUNT(*)
      FROM FACULTY
    WHERE (FACULTY.Dept="CS")
        AND (FACULTY.Age >= 40) AND (FACULTY.Age <= 50)
Response: 10
/* We know Bill went to Oxford */
Query 2: COUNT(*)
      FROM FACULTY
    WHERE (FACULTY.Dept="CS")
        AND (FACULTY.Age >= 40) AND (FACULTY.Age <= 50)
        AND (FACULTY.Degree_From = "Oxford")
Response: 2
```

```
/* We know Bill is single */
Query 3: COUNT(*)
      FROM FACULTY
    WHERE (FACULTY.Dept="CS")
       AND (FACULTY.Age >= 40) AND (FACULTY.Age <= 50)
       AND (FACULTY.Degree_From = "Oxford")
       AND (FACULTY.Marital_Status = "Single")
Response: 1
/* We now can deduce Bill's salary */
Query 3: AVG(FACULTY.Salary)
      FROM FACULTY
    WHERE (FACULTY.Dept="CS")
       AND (FACULTY.Age >= 40) AND (FACULTY.Age <= 50)
       AND (FACULTY.Degree_From = "Oxford")
       AND (FACULTY.Marital_Status = "Single")
Response: $50,000
```

The foregoing is a simple example of a tracker query; far more sophisticated scenarios exist as well. See, for example, Denning, Denning, and Schwartz (1979).

Techniques proposed for addressing the problems posed by tracker queries include

1. Imposing a lower bound on the number of tuples that can be in a qualifying set. If a query's qualifying set of tuples fails to achieve this lower bound, the query is disallowed. Because techniques exist for deducing information regarding the complement of any set of tuples, a dual upper bound on the size of qualifying sets must be imposed also.
2. Perturbing aggregate computations (e.g., with random changes to data values or with probabilistic rules that determine whether or not to include in the computation a given tuple) in a manner that affects only minimally the accuracy of results while making difficult the exact tracking of individual data values.
3. Applying audit trail analysis techniques to detect query patterns that appear to be of a tracker nature, preventing the system from responding further when such patterns are detected.

Unfortunately, the goals of supporting a totally confidential database and a maximally useful and statistically accurate database are in conflict. Hence, the objectives of total confidentiality and high functionality must be weighed carefully in the context of given application.

SUMMARY AND ANNOTATED BIBLIOGRAPHY

The primary concern of the transaction manager is to ensure the correct behavior of concurrently executing transactions and to ensure graceful recovery from failure. We introduced transaction atomicity as the basic requirement that the transaction manager must support. Transaction atomicity requires that (*a*) a transaction's execution be an all-or-nothing proposition, even in the face of premature termination, and (*b*) the execution of a collection of transactions be serializable, that is, equivalent to some serial execution of the transactions.

Locking was introduced as the basic mechanism for achieving atomicity. Locking alone does not guarantee atomicity, however, leading to the introduction of protocols. The two-phase locking protocol—a stipulation that a transaction acquire all its locks before any are released—ensures serializability, assuming that there are no premature transaction terminations. The interaction between premature termination, recovery, and serializability leads us to strengthen the two-phase locking protocol. To support atomicity's all-or-nothing requirement, transactions may need to be undone following a premature termination. This, in turn, may lead to unserializable behavior in the form of lost updates, the reading of dirty data values, and cascading rollback. The strong two-phase locking protocol—a strengthening of two-phase locking that requires that Write locks not be released until after a transaction's Commit statement is accepted—was introduced to address these problems.

Given that transactions obey the strong two-phase locking protocol, a simple recovery algorithm is possible. Transactions that have not committed are undone, while transactions that have committed are redone. We discussed the information that must be contained in a transaction log file to support these recovery procedures, and we considered procedures for managing the transaction log file to guard against untimely system failure. An important system-level optimization problem is the design of a strategy for deciding when I/O buffers are written to disk. This decision affects the size of the log file and the efficiency of the recovery algorithm since intended writes of committed transactions must be kept in the log (and redone by the recovery procedure) until we can be sure the updates actually have been written to disk. We discussed the basic strategies for scheduling the writing of I/O buffers to disk; the reader is referred to Haerder and Reuter (1983) for a more in-depth discussion of this topic.

When locking is employed as a transaction management mechanism, the problems of deadlock and livelock must be addressed. We considered several strategies, ranging from avoidance to detect-resolve. Since the protocols required to ensure deadlock avoidance are too restrictive for many database applications, a detect-resolve or middle-ground strategy is often more attractive. Several middle-ground strategies were considered, including the wound-die and wait-wound strategies of Rosenkrantz and Stearns (1978). Also of concern in the design of a locking-based transaction management system is the specification of locking granularity. We discussed the basic trade-offs between coarse and fine locking granularities, indicating that several studies [e.g., Reis and Stonebraker (1977, 1979)] suggest that relatively large granule locks often are best.

There are many additional topics in transaction management that this chapter could only survey. We considered alternatives to locking, including timestamping and the optimistic concurrency control technique of Kung and Robinson (1981) [see also Coulouris and Dollimore (1988)]. Preliminary studies indicate that these techniques are quite competitive with locking-based approaches, especially when the probability of conflict is small, and in distributed database environments. Ceri and Pelagatti (1984) discuss transaction management issues for a distributed database environment.

The chapter also considered issues of integrity constraint enforcement and database security. Data encryption and audit trail analysis are among the more sophisticated database security techniques now employed. We outlined the public key encryption scheme (RSA) of Rivest, Shamir, and Adleman (1978). The theoretical foundations of this scheme are rooted in number theory, and the security of the scheme depends on the conjectured intractability of factoring very large composite numbers. Several experimental audit trail analysis systems have been implemented, including IDES [Lunt et al. (1990)] and Wisdom and Sense [Vaccaro and Liepins (1989)]. Helman, Liepins, and Richards (1992) consider the mathematical foundations of such systems. We also considered problems related to tracker queries in statistical databases, a problem studied extensively in Denning, Denning, and Schwartz (1979).

This chapter opened Part Four. The issues of transaction management considered in this chapter arise after the query optimizer has mapped a high-level query or user program to an implementation-level program. The next two chapters consider just how the query optimizer performs this mapping.

EXERCISES

1. The wait-for graph was introduced in Section 10.5 as a method for detecting deadlock. Prove that a deadlock situation exists if and only if the wait-for graph contains a directed cycle.
2. In analogy to the use of wait-for graphs to detect deadlock, a **serialization graph** can be used to determine whether a schedule S is serializable. The nodes of the graph are the transactions scheduled by S, and a directed edge from T_i to T_j is used to indicate that T_i must precede T_j in any serial schedule equivalent to S. If the graph is constructed properly, the graph not containing a directed cycle is sufficient to ensure that the schedule is serializable.
   a. Describe when an edge should be placed from T_i to T_j if transactions use only XLocks.
   b. Describe when an edge should be placed from T_i to T_j if transactions use both SLocks and XLocks.
   **c.* Describe when an edge should be placed from T_i to T_j if transactions use general lock types defined by a compatibility matrix.
   **d.* Why can't the result be strengthened to say that the schedule is serializable if and only if the graph is cycle free? What assumptions on transaction behavior would support the if and only if condition?

3. Prove that if each transaction in a collection of transactions obeys the two-phase locking protocol, then any execution schedule (which completes normally) for these transactions is serializable.
4. Prove that given any execution schedule for a collection of transactions, each obeying the two-phase locking protocol, an equivalent serial schedule can be obtained by ordering the transactions with respect to the time at which each transaction is granted its last lock.
5. Let T_1 be any transaction that violates the two-phase locking protocol, such that every value read by T_1 affects in some way at least one value T_1 writes to the database. Prove that there exist some transaction T_2 and some execution schedule S for T_1 and T_2, such that S is not serializable.
6. Construct an example illustrating why a transaction should not be permitted to acquire an SLock on some item B after it has released an SLock on some other item A.
7. Consider the third step of the procedure for managing the transaction log file, as presented in Section 10.4. An alternative step is, before accepting the transaction T's Commit statement, force write each I/O buffer that contains an update made by T, and then force write T's Commit to the end of the log file on disk. The advantage of this strategy is that a committed transaction does not have to be redone at recovery. What are the disadvantages of this strategy?
8. Section 10.4 describes a recovery procedure that is applied following system failure. Describe recovery procedures for transactions that fail for reasons of a program bug, transaction manager–induced failure, and self-aborts.
9. It is possible that the system will fail while the transaction manager is performing its recovery procedure. Describe what precautions the transaction manager can take to ensure that it is able to resume the recovery process following such failure.
10. Suppose that some transactions are waiting for SLocks on an item A, while others are waiting for XLocks on A. Describe a policy for determining to which waiting transactions locks should be granted. Your policy should support as much concurrency as possible, but it must not be prone to livelock.
11. Prove that deadlock, livelock, and starvation are impossible under the wait-die and wound-wait schemes of Section 10.5.
12. Propose scheduling policies to address the problem of starvation in the context of transaction and lock time-outs, timestamping, and optimistic concurrency control.
13. Describe how default timestamps can be associated with some database items to avoid the need to explicitly assign to every database item a read and write timestamp.
14. Demonstrate that there exist schedules for transactions that violate the two-phase locking protocol that the timestamping method would permit.

Demonstrate that there exist schedules for transactions that obey the two-phase locking protocol that the timestamping method would prohibit.

15. Construct an example that demonstrates that there can be several sets of tuples that, when added to a table instance following a user insert, would complete the update so that the table's multivalued dependencies are obeyed.
16. Describe how a user deletion can be completed so that a table's multivalued dependencies are obeyed.
17. Suppose that an RDM is implemented in internal memory as is described in Chapter 2. Suppose further that attribute values on which we perform Selects and Joins are encrypted. Demonstrate how the query-processing algorithms presented in Chapter 2 could be modified to account for the encrypted data values.

CHAPTER 11

Query Optimization, Part I: Implementing the Relational Operators

Chapter 9 considered physical schema design, one of the two components of an RDM's implementation that decisively affects efficiency. In this chapter and the next, we consider the second decisive component, the query optimizer.

The query optimization process maps a high-level query or update into an implementation-level program that operates on the file structures storing an RDM's data. In general, this program is composed of a collection of algorithms implementing the relational operators. Hence, just as file structures are the primitives of physical schema design, implementation-level algorithms for the relational operators are the primitives of the query optimization process. This chapter presents an extensive study of algorithms for implementing the relational Select and Join operators, defining, analyzing, and comparing several alternative algorithms for each of the operators. While implementation-level algorithms must be defined for the other relational algebra operators as well, we focus here on algorithms for only Select and Join so that we may give a thorough presentation of those algorithms that are most likely to have the greatest impact on the efficiency of an RDM implementation. Select algorithms are studied in Section 11.1, while Join algorithms are studied in Sections 11.2 through 11.5.•

In addition to our interest in the primitives of query optimization, we are interested as well in the *process* of query optimization, the process by which the query optimizer chooses between candidate strategies for evaluating a query or effecting an update. Section 11.6 considers a problem crucial to the query optimization process, the problem of predicting the efficiency with which a candidate strategy could be executed against a given RDM instance. Chapter 12 then studies the query optimization process as a combinatorial search problem. Chapter 13 considers query processing in data models which extend the RDM.

11.1 SELECT ALGORITHMS

Recall that in Chapter 2 we defined a **partial-match retrieval** to be a selection of the form

$$\sigma_{(A_1 op\ v_1) \wedge \cdots \wedge (A_k op\ v_k)}(T)$$

where $\{A_1, \ldots, A_k\}$ is a subset of the attributes in T and *op* is a comparison operator (e.g., $=$, $<$, $>$). Chapter 2 considered the issues involved in processing such an expression when table T is stored in internal memory. The main issue considered in that context was how to choose an index to drive the processing when more than one of the A_i are indexed. The conclusion reached in Chapter 2 was that we should use the index on the attribute A_i for which the restriction $(A_i \; op \; v_i)$ filters the most tuples.

We now consider approaches to processing the partial-match retrieval $\sigma_{(A_1 \; op \; v_1) \wedge \cdots \wedge (A_k \; op \; v_k)}(T)$ when table T is stored in external memory. To simplify the discussion, we shall assume that each *op* is "=" and that the A_i appearing in the selection are distinct. We shall consider three approaches to the processing of such a query:

1. Use one index to drive the processing.
2. Use two or more indices in conjunction.
3. Use specialized index structures.

Single-Index Algorithms

Suppose that one or more of the attributes A_i are indexed. The following is the basic form of a processing algorithm that uses index I_i on A_i to drive the retrieval of tuples:

```
Use index I_i to identify the blocks B_1, . . . , B_m of
  data file F that contain tuples t satisfying (t[A_i] = v_i)
for j := 1 to m
  Read block B_j
  for (each tuple t in B_j)
    if (t satisfies the remaining qualifications)
      Add to the result tuple t
    endif
  end for
end for
```

The question at hand is, When there is a choice of indices I_i to drive the processing, how is the decision made? Inspection of the preceding algorithm reveals that its efficiency depends primarily on two factors:

1. The number of block accesses required to search I_i.
2. The number m of blocks of data file F over which tuples satisfying $(t[A_i] = v_i)$ are spread.

Assuming that one of the standard techniques (such as those described in Chapter 8) is employed for implementing each of the indices, the number of block accesses required to search any of the I_i will be quite similar. Consequently, the effect on the relative efficiency of the algorithm under different choices for I_i is dominated by the second factor, the number m of blocks of data file F over which tuples satisfying $(t[A_i] = v_i)$ are spread. This number, in turn, is a function of both the number of tuples that satisfy $(t[A_i] = v_i)$ and of how the data file F is structured physically (i.e., F's primary structure). Consequently, when selecting an index I_i to drive the processing, it is not enough to ask which qualification $(A_i = v_i)$ filters the most tuples. We must ask also how these tuples are likely to be distributed across data blocks.The following calculations provide reasonable estimates.

Case I: Data file F is stored physically ordered (or clustered) on attribute A_i. In this case, a reasonable estimate of m is

(the number of tuples t such that $(t[A_i]=v_i)$/(the average number of tuples of T that are stored per block of F)

Case II: Data file F is not stored physically ordered (or clustered) on attribute A_i. In this case, a reasonable estimate of m is

(the number of tuples t such that $(t[A_i]=v_i)$)

If a large percentage of the tuples in T satisfy this qualification, this formula will most likely slightly overstate the value of m since, in this case, several such tuples often may reside in a single block.

The query optimizer can perform this calculation for each of the A_i on which there is an index and drive the processing with the I_i yielding the smallest estimate for m. This approach, of course, assumes that we have a method of estimating the number of tuples t such that $(t[A_i] = v_i)$, and of estimating the average number of tuples stored per block. The estimation problem is considered in Section 11.6.

Pointer Intersection Algorithms

The expense of block access in an external memory implementation makes an alternative processing strategy attractive for many situations. To illustrate this alternative strategy, suppose that we must process the partial match retrieval $\sigma_{(A_1=v_1) \wedge (A_2=v_2) \wedge \cdots \wedge (A_k=v_k)}(T)$ and that there are dense indices I_1 and I_2 on A_1 and A_2, respectively. Assume further that the dense indices use the same method to point to data records, for example, a pointer in each index is a (block_number, key) pair. An alternative to selecting one of the indices to drive the processing is to use the indices in conjunction in the manner described by the following algorithm:

```
Search index I1 for index records (v1,ptr), adding to temp1
  the pointer ptr
Search index I2 for index records (v2,ptr), adding to temp2
  the pointer ptr
intersect ← (temp1 ∩ temp2)
for (each pointer ptr ∈ intersect)
  Retrieve from F the tuple t pointed to by ptr
  { Note that pointers in intersect can be arranged so that no block of F need
    be read more than once. }
```

```
    if (t satisfies the remaining qualifications)
      Add to the result the tuple t
    endif
  end for
```

Note that the algorithm relies on the fact that I_1 and I_2 are dense indices and, hence, that each index record (v, ptr) in either index uniquely identifies a record t of F. Hence, a tuple t satisfies both the qualifications $(A_1 = v_1)$ and $(A_2 = v_2)$ if and only if both indices I_1 and I_2 contain a pointer to t.

We now compare the efficiency of this pointer intersection method to that of the single-index method considered previously. Without loss of generality, suppose that the single-index method uses I_1 to drive the processing. The trade-off then is between the number of block accesses required by the pointer intersection method to search I_2 and the number of data block accesses that are saved as a result of performing the intersection of pointers. (We assume here that the pointers can be accumulated and intersected in internal memory. If this is not the case, the pointer intersection method will incur a few more block accesses than is indicated by the following analysis.)

Assuming that one of the B-tree or hashing schemes presented in Chapter 8 is used, the number of block accesses required to search I_2 for tuples satisfying $(t[A_2] = v_2)$ can be expected to be in the neighborhood of three to five, even if the data file is quite large. Note that the method described in Chapter 8 for "collapsing" index records corresponding to data records with the same attribute value implies that the required number of accesses into I_2 is fairly insensitive to the number of matches.[1]

Consider now the number of data block accesses saved by the pointer intersection method. A data block access is saved exactly when a block of F contains a tuple t with $t[A_1] = v_1$, but no tuple t' with $t'[A_1] = v_1$ and $t'[A_2] = v_2$. Consider two extreme cases:

Case I: Data file F is stored physically ordered (or clustered) on attribute A_1, and only a few blocks (e.g., one or two) are required to store tuples t such that $(t[A_1] = v_1)$. In this case, few, if any, data block accesses can be saved.

Case II: Data file F is not stored physically ordered (or clustered) on attribute A_1, and no block contains more than one tuple t such that $(t[A_1] = v_1)$. In this case, the number of data block accesses saved is equal to

the number of tuples t such that $t[A_1]=v_1$ and $t[A_2]\neq v_2$

In many situations, this number will be quite large.

Again we see that when choosing a method for performing the selection, a query optimizer requires information regarding both the distribution of data

[1] It should be observed that this might not be the case if we were considering range conditions [e.g.,$(v \leq A_2 \leq v')$] rather than simple exact matches.

values and of how tuples with particular data values are spread over blocks of the data file.

Note that if several of the attributes $A_1, \ldots, A_k$ are indexed, it might be desirable to intersect the pointers of three or more of these indices. The trade-off once again is between the number of block accesses required to search additional indices and the number of data block accesses saved, leading to the problem of selecting an optimal subset of indices to intersect. See exercise 11.3 for details.

Specialized Structures

The methods considered so far utilize the general-purpose indexing schemes described in Chapter 8. We conclude this discussion by briefly describing some specialized index structures designed specifically to support partial-match retrievals.

One such specialized structure is the concatenated field index to which we have alluded several times. To illustrate, suppose that we frequently expect to encounter retrievals of the form

$$\sigma_{(A_1=v_1) \wedge (A_2=v_2) \wedge F} T$$

where attributes A_1 and A_2 are referenced in conjunction and where F is a conjunction of exact-match conditions whose attributes vary from query to query. In this case, we can treat $A_1 \cdot A_2$ as a single attribute and build a single index with records of the form $(v_1 \cdot v_2, ptr)$. Here, *ptr* will be a pointer to a record t with $t[A_1] = v_1$ and $t[A_2] = v_2$.

The concatenated field index supports an algorithm with the advantage of the pointer intersection method that only blocks containing tuples satisfying both of the qualifications $(A_1 = v_1)$ and $(A_2 = v_2)$ need be retrieved, yet the algorithm needs to search only a single index. It must be noted, however, that since the index records are larger when the attributes are concatenated, the index structure is spread over more blocks and may be somewhat more expensive to search than an index on either attribute alone. Further, the concatenated field index is less of a general-purpose structure than are independent indices on A_1 and A_2. While the concatenated index can be used (with little penalty) to process qualifications based on A_1 only, it is of little use in processing qualifications based on A_2 only.

Of course, if we expect selections to frequently reference the subset $\{A_1, \ldots, A_s\}$ of the attributes, we can build a concatenated index on these s attributes. The difficulty with such an approach, however, is that it is hard to predict what attributes will be referenced in conjunction and that each such index is of only limited value for other selections. This problem is addressed by various indexing schemes for partial-match retrievals that are somewhat more flexible than the concatenated field scheme. Such schemes are able to utilize values specified for *any* subset of the attributes to limit the search; the more values that are specified, the smaller is the fraction of the data file that needs to be inspected. These partial-match schemes compare favorably with the other schemes we have considered when processing selections in which many attributes are referenced but compare less favorably with selections that reference only a few of the attributes. See exercise 11.4 for more details.

11.2 BASIC JOIN ALGORITHMS

This section presents and analyzes several of the basic Join algorithms from which a query optimizer can choose each time it processes a query containing a Join operator. Sections 11.3, 11.4, and 11.5 then consider more complicated or specialized Join algorithms.

Chapter 2 presented several Join algorithms for an RDM stored in internal memory. Since those algorithms foreshadow much of the material in the current section, the reader may wish to review Section 2.5 at this time.

The selection of a method for performing a Join is driven primarily by (1) the structures that exist on the data files in question since different methods require different structures, and (2) the values of certain parameters (e.g., the number of tuples in the operand tables, the number of blocks over which these tuples are spread) that affect the costs of the methods. In the following paragraphs, we define the parameters on which our analysis of the methods depends; Section 11.6 briefly discusses techniques for estimating the values of some of these parameters.

Let $T_1 \underset{A=B}{\bowtie} T_2$ denote the expression to be computed. We assume for now that T_1 and T_2 are each an implementation-level table that is stored by itself in the homogeneous data files F_1 and F_2, respectively. In Sections 11.4 and 11.5, we shall consider the problem of processing a query containing more than one Join, leading to several additional issues and methods, including pipelining and the use of heterogeneous file structures.

The following parameters are used to characterize the Join problem. For $i = 1, 2$ define

c_i = The number of tuples in operand table T_i. Since T_i is an implementation-level table, c_i also is the number of data records in F_i.

b_i = The size in blocks of F_i. This number is at least c_i divided by the number of records (of the type stored in F_i) that can fit per block of external memory. b_i may be greater than this quotient if, for example, deletions leave empty slots in the data blocks.

c_J = The number of tuples in the join $T_1 \underset{A=B}{\bowtie} T_2$.

$c_{SJ(1,2)}$ = The number of tuples in the **semi-join** $T_1 \underset{A=B}{\triangleright} T_2$, where the Semi-join operator $\triangleright$ is defined by

$$T_1 \underset{A=B}{\triangleright} T_2 = \Pi_{T_1}(T_1 \underset{A=B}{\bowtie} T_2)$$

That is, the Semi-join evaluates to the set of tuples from the first operand that join with at least one tuple from the second operand. Note that the

Semi-join is *not* a commutative operator—we use $c_{SJ(2,1)}$ to denote the number of tuples in the Semi-join $T_2 \underset{A=B}{\triangleright} T_1$. The Semi-join operator is useful in defining and analyzing various aspects of several of our Join algorithms.

Broadly speaking, methods for computing Joins fall into one of four classes:

1. Methods that require no special file structures. The only method in this class we shall consider is the Unindexed loop join.
2. Methods that require the prior existence of appropriate secondary structures. Methods in this class include the Indexed loop join, the Merge join of indices, and methods that exploit specialized logical structures such as rings and tables of pointers.
3. Methods that require the prior existence of appropriate primary structures. Methods in this class include the Merge join of data files and methods that exploit the hierarchical nesting in heterogeneous files of implementation-level tables.
4. Methods that build structures as part of the processing. Methods in this class construct indices or other structures before or during the processing of the Join.

As we move from class 1 to class 3, efficiency of the Join method generally increases. While methods in class 3 generally are the fastest, the structures they require are the hardest to maintain and, of course, preclude other primary structures that might support other operations, including different Joins; that is, only one family of Joins can be supported physically per table. Methods in class 4 can have the characteristics of those in both classes 2 and 3, but the work required to construct the structures often is significant.

In the following subsections, we present several important Join algorithms. For each algorithm, we enumerate the structures required, state the algorithm, and analyze its efficiency. We consider other factors of importance as well, such as special properties of the result relation (e.g., Is it produced sorted on the Join attribute?). Such special properties are of potential importance since the Join may be part of a larger expression or, more generally, used as input to another process. To account for this possibility, we define our Join algorithms so that they create a result stream STR that is piped to the calling routine. We shall not specify how the calling routine controls its access to STR. In some cases, the calling routine may be fed the stream automatically, a block at a time. In other cases, the calling routine may explicitly request to be fed the next tuple, at the time the tuple is required. We shall not concern ourselves with how this interface is controlled and shall assume only that a program buffer (of a size of one block) is allocated to the Join program for the purpose of accumulating and holding tuples of the result stream until they are requested. The reader should keep in mind that, often, the calling routine writes to disk the blocks of the result stream as it receives them. In this case, the calling routine incurs an additional number of block accesses equal to the size of the result relation (or twice its size, if the calling program later reads the result from disk). This cost often is a significant component of the overall Join cost and, in some contexts, overshadows the efficiency differences of the various methods.

Unindexed Loop Join

Compute: $T_1 \underset{A=B}{\bowtie} T_2$, constructing the unordered result stream STR.

Assumptions: $k + 2$ denotes the largest number of buffers the Join program can be allocated. The algorithm reads and stores in buffers k blocks at a time of F_1 and a single block of F_2. The last buffer is used to accumulate tuples of the result stream STR.

Algorithm:

```
for (each group of k blocks of F1)
  Read the k blocks into buffers
  for (each block of F2)
    Read the block
    for (each tuple t in the buffers holding F1)
      for (each tuple u in the buffer holding F2)
        if (t[A]=u[B])
          Append to result stream STR the tuple t · u
        endif
      end for
    end for
  end for
end for
```

Analysis: Each block of F_1 is read once and each block of F_2 is read $CEIL(b_1/k)$ times for a total of

$$b_1+b_2*CEIL\ (b_1/k)$$

block accesses. It thus is apparent that the Unindexed loop join should use as the outer table (playing the role of T_1 in the preceding algorithm) the smaller operand. That is, if $b_2 < b_1$, we should modify the algorithm to use T_2 as the outer table.

Indexed Loop Join

Compute: $T_1 \underset{A=B}{\bowtie} T_2$, constructing the unordered result stream STR.

Assumptions: An index I exists on attribute B of F_2. The Join algorithm can be allocated three buffers, plus whatever memory is required for searches of index I.

Algorithm:

```
for (each block B of F1)
  ReadBlock(Buff, B)
  for (each t of F1 in Buff)
    Retrieve via index I each record u in F2 such that u[B]=t[A],
      placing each u in temp
    Append to STR {t}·temp
  end for
end for
```

The Append statement uses the notation $\{t\} \cdot temp$. In general, if S_1 and S_2 are sets of tuples from tables T_1 and T_2, respectively, $S_1 \cdot S_2$ is defined provided that all tuples in both sets have the same value on the Join attributes A and B. In this case, $S_1 \cdot S_2$ is the set of tuples obtained by concatenating s_1 and s_2 for each $s_1 \in S_1$ and $s_2 \in S_2$. In other words, we take the Join of the two sets of tuples, but we know in advance that all pairs match.

Analysis: Each block of F_1 is read once, contributing b_1 block accesses. For each of the c_1 tuples t in F_1, we must search index I for entries leading us to tuples u of F_2 such that $u[B] = t[A]$. The exact number of block accesses required to search I depends on the type of index that I is and, to a small extent, on the number of matching tuples u. We use I_s to denote the average number of index block accesses incurred while searching for a value $t[A]$. Once we have searched the index, we must retrieve from data file F_2 each matching tuple u. In the worst case, the retrieval of each matching tuple u incurs a block access, and so we estimate the number of F_2 block accesses incurred by each t to be equal to the number of tuples u in F_2 such that $u[B] = t[A]$.[2] Since the total number of matches (over all t in F_1) is the number c_J of tuples in the result of the Join, we estimate the total number of F_2 block accesses to be c_J. Hence, the number of block accesses required by the Indexed loop join is approximately

$$b_1 + c_1 * I_S + c_J$$

It is apparent from this analysis that if both operand tables are indexed on the Join attribute, then the Indexed loop join should use as the outer relation (playing the role of T_1) the smaller table.

How does the efficiency of the Indexed loop join compare with that of the Unindexed loop join? Consider the Indexed loop join with T_1 as the outer table. This implies that T_1 is the smaller table or that T_1 is indexed while T_2 is not. Let us assume for the sake of this analysis that T_1 is the smaller table and, hence, that the Unindexed loop join uses T_1 as the outer table also. In this case, the

[2] We ignore here the possibility that more than one data block access is required to find a particular u, once the index is searched. More than one data block access might be required, for example, in an ISAM structure with pinned records.

Unindexed loop join requires

$$b_1+b_2*CEIL(b_1/k)$$

block accesses. Hence, the Indexed loop join requires fewer block accesses than the Unindexed loop join if and only if

$$c_1*I_S+c_J < b_2*CEIL(b_1/k)$$

It is apparent that realistic parameter values can be chosen to satisfy, or violate, this inequality. See exercise 11.7 for a further analysis.

When comparing the cost of the Indexed and Unindexed loop joins, it should be noted that the amount of internal processing required (finding and assembling the tuples that match) can be dramatically less for the Indexed loop join. In certain contexts, this can be a significant factor.

Other Considerations:

1. If each table has an ordered index on the Join attribute, the Merge join on indices presented later in this section should be considered as a possible alternative.
2. If file F_2 is clustered on the value of attribute B, then the cost of the Indexed loop join may be substantially less than indicated previously. The source of the savings when this is the case is that the c_J term in the preceding cost formula is reduced because the k tuples of F_2 that match a given tuple t may be spread over far fewer than k blocks, especially if k is large and tuples of F_2 are small relative to a block's capacity. Note that this consideration could lead us to use the smaller of the two operands as the inner table in cases where only this table is clustered on the Join attribute. If both F_1 and F_2 are clustered on the value of the Join attribute, however, one of the Merge joins on data files presented later in this section should be considered as a possible alternative.

Standard Merge Join of Data Files

Compute: $T_1 \underset{A=B}{\bowtie} T_2$, constructing the result stream STR sorted on attributes A and B.

Assumptions: F_1 is physically sorted on attribute A, and F_2 is physically sorted on attribute B. We first present the algorithm under the assumption that the physical ordering is either over contiguous blocks or is over a chain of linked blocks. Later, we consider modifications for when the file is organized as sorted neighborhoods, as defined in Section 8.1.

We assume further that the Join algorithm can be allocated three buffers and, additionally, enough internal memory to hold, for any single value v, min $\{|\sigma_{A=v}(T_1)|, |\sigma_{B=v}(T_2)|\}$ tuples. The following statement of the algorithm is simplified by assuming that, for every value v, there is enough internal memory to hold $|\sigma_{A=v}(T_1)|$ tuples; if this is not the case for some values v, the algorithm simply would reverse the roles of T_1 and T_2 when these values are encountered.

Algorithm:

```
Read into Buff_1 the first block of F_1
{ Recall that tuples might not be sorted within the blocks of a physically sorted
  file }
Sort the contents of Buff_1
Read into Buff_2 the first block of F_2
{ Recall that tuples might not be sorted within the blocks of a physically sorted
  file }
Sort the contents of Buff_2
R_1 ← first record in Buff_1
R_2 ← first record in Buff_2
{ By convention, if we read past the last block of either file, the corresponding
  buffer will signal "empty" }
while (neither Buff_1 or Buff_2 is "empty")
  if (R_1.A=R_2.B)
     { Let v be the common value }
     temp ← ∅
     while ((Buff_1 not "empty") and (R_1.A=v))
        temp ← temp ∪ {R_1}
        Let R_1 be the next record in Buff_1 or, if Buff_1 is exhausted,
          read into Buff_1 and sort the next block of F_1 and
          let R_1 be the first record in Buff_1, assuming Buff_1 is not "empty"
     end while
     { R_1 is now the first record in Buff_1 such that R_1.A > v }
     while ((Buff_2 not "empty") and (R_2.B=v))
        Append to STR temp·{R_2}
        Let R_2 be the next record in Buff_2 or, if Buff_2 is exhausted,
          read into Buff_2 and sort the next block of F_2 and
          let R_2 be the first record in Buff_2, assuming Buff_1 is not "empty"
     end while
     { R_2 is now the first record in Buff_2 such that R_2.A > v }
  elseif (R_1.A < R_2.B)
     Let R_1 be the next record in Buff_1 or, if Buff_1 is exhausted,
       read into Buff_1 and sort the next block of F_1 and
       let R_1 be the first record in Buff_1, assuming Buff_1 is not "empty"
  else
     { R_1.A > R_2.B }
     Let R_2 be the next record in Buff_2 or, if Buff_1 is exhausted,
       read into Buff_2 and sort the next block of F_2 and
       let R_2 be the first record in Buff_2, assuming Buff_1 is not "empty"
  endif
end while
```

Analysis: Each block of each of F_1 and F_2 is read exactly once. Hence, the cost is

$$b_1 + b_2$$

block accesses.

We observe that in all cases the number of block accesses required by this Merge join algorithm is no greater than the $b_1 + b_2 * CEIL(b_1/k)$ required by the Unindexed loop join; equality is achieved only when the smaller relation fits entirely in internal memory (i.e., $b_1 \leq k$). In more typical situations, the number of block accesses required by this Merge join is substantially less than the number required by the Unindexed loop join. Further, in all cases, the amount of internal processing required by the preceding Merge join algorithm is less than that required by the Unindexed loop join.

Now compare the $b_1 + b_2$ block accesses required by this Merge join with the $b_1 + c_1 * I_S + c_J$ block accesses required by the Indexed loop join. In most cases, the number of accesses required by the Merge join is substantially less; an exception can occur only when both the number of tuples c_1 in the outer table T_1 is far less than the number b_2 of blocks in the inner table T_2 and the number of tuples c_J in the result of the Join is extremely small (i.e., on average, fewer than one tuple per block of F_2 has a match in T_1).

Other Considerations: If the files are organized as sorted neighborhoods, we still can perform the Merge join with a single pass of each data file, provided that we can simultaneously fit in internal memory one neighborhood from each file. In this case, the preceding algorithm is modified so that instead of reading the next block from file F_i, an entire neighborhood is read. Once read, a neighborhood is sorted internally, after which the Merge step can be applied to the blocks in internal memory. Since a neighborhood may consist of many thousands of records, the time required to internally sort the neighborhoods may be a significant component of the overall cost of the algorithm. If we cannot simultaneously fit pairs of neighborhoods in internal memory, blocks will have to be accessed multiple times, and performance therefore will deteriorate.

Standard Merge Join of Indices

Compute: $T_1 \underset{A=B}{\bowtie} T_2$, constructing the result stream STR sorted on attributes A and B.

Assumptions: Each of F_1 and F_2 has an ordered index, denoted I_1 and I_2, on the Join attribute (A or B). Each record in each of these indices is of the form <*val*,*ptr*>, where *val* is a value of the Join attribute (A or B) and *ptr* is a pointer to a record in the corresponding data file with this value in the attribute. There are no assumptions on the physical structures of the data files.

The traversals of the ordered indices must be coordinated so that index records are returned to the Join algorithm as needed. In particular, we assume that the calls Init_Traverse (I_1,STR_1) and Init_Traverse (I_2,STR_2) initiate the index traversals and that the progression of the traversals is driven by the calls Get_Next(STR_1) and Get_Next(STR_2), which cause each traversal to return the next index record in the traversal sequence. Get_Next returns the NULL record to indicate the traversal has completed. Note that since the traversals are running simultaneously, if the indices are standard B-trees, enough internal memory must exist for two stacks, each the height of the corresponding B-tree, or else index blocks are accessed repeatedly. If the indices are B^+-trees, only one block of each index needs to be in memory at any one time.

As does the Merge join of data files, this Join algorithm additionally requires that enough internal memory be available to hold, for any single value v, $\min\{|\sigma_{A=v}(T_1)|, |\sigma_{B=v}(T_2)|\}$ tuples and still have enough internal memory to read a single data block. The following statement of the algorithm is simplified by assuming that, for every value v, there is enough internal memory to hold $|\sigma_{A=v}(T_1)|$tuples; if this is not the case for some values v, the algorithm simply would reverse the roles of T_1 and T_2 when these values are encountered.

Algorithm:

```
Init_Traverse(I1,STR1)
Init_Traverse(I2,STR2)
IR1 ← Get_Next(STR1)
IR2 ← Get_Next(STR2)
while (neither IR1 or IR2 is NULL)
  if (IR1.val = IR2.val)
    Issue a sequence of calls to Get_Next(STR1)
      to retrieve all index records from I1 with the
      common value IR1.val = IR2.val=v. These records are
      consecutive in the traversal order.
    Retrieve from the data file F1 into temp the collections of data
      records pointed to by these index records
    Issue a sequence of calls to Get_Next(STR2)
      to retrieve (individually) each index record from I2 such that
      IR2.val=v. These records are consecutive in
      the traversal order. As each index record is returned,
      retrieve from the data file F2 each data record t
      pointed to by this index record and append to STR temp·{t}
    { These sequences of calls to Get_Next terminates with IR1
     containing the first index record of I1 with value greater than v
     and IR2 containing the first index record of I2 with value greater
     than v. If the traversal of either file is complete,
     IR1 or IR2 will contain the NULL record. }
  elseif (IR1.val < IR2.val)
    Get_Next(STR1)
  else
    { IR1.val > IR2.val }
    Get_Next(STR2)
  endif
end while
```

Analysis: Each block of each index is read once, contributing $Ib_1 + Ib_2$ block accesses, where Ib_1 and Ib_2 are the number of blocks in I_1 and I_2, respectively. (In the case of a B^+-tree, Ib_i is the number of blocks in the sequence set.) The number of data blocks accessed depends on how tuples match between tables. Each tuple in T_1 that has a match in T_2 is retrieved once, and each tuple in T_2 that has a match in T_1 is retrieved once. Since we make no assumptions on the physical organization of F_2, we must assume that each tuple retrieved incurs a block access. Hence, the total number of data block accesses is

$$c_{SJ(1,2)} + c_{SJ(2,1)}$$

that is, the sum of the sizes $|(T_1 \triangleright T_2)| + |(T_2 \triangleright T_1)|$ of the Semi-joins. Note that this sum never is greater than $c_1 + c_2$ and achieves this value exactly when neither table contains dangling tuples. Note also that the sum is never greater than than $2 * c_J$, and is strictly smaller than this value except when there is a 1 : 1 correspondence between matching tuples of the two tables.

The total cost of the Merge join on indices is thus

$$Ib_1 + Ib_2 + c_{SJ(1,2)} + c_{SJ(2,1)}$$

Comparing this number of block accesses with the $b_1 + b_2$ required by the Merge join of data files, we see that the data file version typically will be significantly more efficient. The index version will have the advantage only when the dense indices are significantly smaller than their data files and the sizes of the Semi-joins are extremely small (i.e., on average, fewer than one tuple per block of each file has a match in the other file). When comparing the Merge join of indices to the Merge join of data files, it should be noted that the Merge join of indices requires only secondary structures (ordered indices), while the Merge join of data files requires primary structures. Hence, the index version of the algorithm may be feasible in situations where the data file version is not.

Since the Merge join of indices, like the Indexed loop join, requires only secondary structures, it is appropriate to compare the efficiencies of these algorithms. Recall that the Indexed loop join requires $b_1 + c_1 * I_S + c_J$ block accesses. Generally speaking, we would expect the sum $(Ib_1 + Ib_2)$ appearing in Merge join's formula to be significantly smaller than the sum $(b_1 + c_1 * I_s)$ appearing in Loop join's formula, the only exception being when T_1 is several orders of magnitude smaller than T_2. In comparing the remaining terms—$(c_{SJ(1,2)} + c_{SJ(2,1)})$ from Merge join and c_J from Loop join—recall that we already have observed that Merge join's term is never more than twice Loop join's term. Further, if, on average, each tuple in each table has more than two matches in the other table, Merge join's term will be smaller. We thus conclude that, in most cases, the Merge join of indices will be significantly faster than the Indexed loop join.

Other Considerations:

1. The analysis assumes that there is enough internal memory to simultaneously store
   a. $\min\{|\sigma_{A=v}(T_1)|, |\sigma_{B=v}(T_2)|\}$ tuples, for each value v, and
   b. If the indices are (regular) B-trees, two stacks of blocks, each of size equal to the height of the corresponding B-tree.

If there is not enough internal memory to store all the tuples from both tables with some value v in the Join attribute, tuples from one of the tables with this value v will have to be accessed more than once. Exercise 11.8 considers how to analyze and optimize the work requirements in this situation. Even with such memory restrictions, however, the algorithm can be implemented so that the number of data block accesses never exceeds $2 * c_J$.

If (regular) B-trees are used and the second requirement is violated, index blocks will be accessed repeatedly (see Chapter 8), and the required number of block accesses can be substantially higher than the preceding analysis indicates. This requirement thus strongly motivates the use of B^+-trees rather than B-trees.

2. If one (or both) data files is clustered on the Join attribute, the number of block accesses may decrease significantly. The source of the savings in this case is that for a value v in the Join attribute JA such that $|\sigma_{JA=v} T_i| = k$, the number of blocks over which the matching records are spread can be far fewer than k, especially if k is large. Note that if both files are clustered on the Join attribute, the cluster Merge join on data files presented later in this section should be considered as an alternative.

Merge Join Variants

Alternative Orderings on the Join Attributes: The previous two versions of the Merge join algorithm assume that either the data files or the index files are physically sorted on the Join attributes. We observe, however, that there is nothing magical about the sorted ordering. That is, the algorithms can be applied, with minor modifications, as long as the data or index files corresponding to the operand relations are physically ordered in some common way. In practice, this common ordering, if not sorted on the Join attributes, is most likely to be ordered according to a common hash function. We consider now data file and index file Merge joins, when the files are hashed by a common function on the Join attributes.

- *Merge join on hashed data files*: Suppose that data files F_1 and F_2 are stored on the chains of hash tables HT_1 and HT_2, respectively, and that the same hash function is employed to hash attribute A of F_1 and attribute B of F_2. Observe that, in this case, if data record R is stored on the chain off of bucket $HT_1[i]$, then all records that join with R are stored on the chain off of bucket $HT_2[i]$, and vice versa.

  There are several methods that can be applied to process the Join while accessing each block of the hashed data files only once. If we are willing to maintain the data records sorted on the Join attribute within each chain of each of the two hash structures, we can apply the standard Merge join algorithm independently to each pair $HT_1[i]$ and $HT_2[i]$ of chains. Alternatively, we can eliminate the need for storing the chains sorted, provided that we we can fit in internal memory simultaneously, for each i, all the blocks on the shorter of the chains $HT_1[i]$ and $HT_2[i]$ plus a single block of the other chain. For example, suppose that all blocks of chain $HT_1[i]$ fit in internal memory. After reading into buffers all the blocks on chain $HT_1[i]$, we read into a buffer B each block of $HT_2[i]$ and, for each tuple t in B, look for joining tuples in the buffers that hold the blocks of $HT_1[i]$.

- *Merge join on hashed indices*: Suppose now that dense indices I_1 and I_2 (on the Join attributes A and B) for data files F_1 and F_2 are stored on the chains of hash tables HT_1 and HT_2, respectively, and that a common hash function is used. The Merge join algorithm for these structures is quite similar to the preceding algorithm for operating on hashed data files. If we are willing to maintain the index records sorted within each chain of each of the two hash structures, we simply apply the standard Merge join on indices technique independently to each pair $HT_1[i]$ and $HT_2[i]$ of the chains. If we wish to avoid maintaining the chains sorted, a little extra care is required to avoid retrieving the same data record more than once. In particular, for each i, it is necessary to store simultaneously in internal memory both chains $HT_1[i]$ and $HT_2[i]$. Once a pair of chains is in internal memory, they can be sorted and the standard Merge join on indices then applied. Note that this second approach is reasonable (both computationally and with respect to the amount of internal memory required) provided that each chain is only a few blocks in length.

  As does the standard Merge join on indices, this variant requires that each block of each index be read once and incurs (at worst) $c_{SJ(1,2)} + c_{SJ(2,1)}$ data block accesses.

We shall see in Section 11.3 that Merge join algorithms based on a common hash function arise also as a component of another type of join algorithm, known as **Grace join**.

Cluster Merge: We already have seen that if the data files corresponding to one of the operand tables are clustered on the Join attribute, both the Indexed loop join and the Merge join of indices may be sped up significantly. If the data files corresponding to both operand tables are clustered on the Join attribute, a variant Merge join of data files can be defined whose efficiency, in some contexts, approaches that of the standard Merge join of data files.

In addition to requiring that the data files be clustered on the Join attributes, this Merge join variant requires that one of the data files be indexed on the Join attribute. The following statement assumes that F_2 is indexed on attribute B:

```
for (each A-value v encountered while traversing data file F1)
  Collect in temp all records of F1 containing this value.
  { These records are stored contiguously in F1. }
  Retrieve via index each record t in F2 with t[B]=v.
  { These records are stored contiguously in F2. }
  As each t is retrieved, append to STR temp · {t}.
end for
```

The efficiency of this algorithm depends heavily on the number of distinct values that are present for attributes A and B. In all cases, the algorithm accesses each block of F_1 once. The best we can hope for is that each block of F_2 contains records with a single B value, in which case each block of F_2 is accessed only once and performance is almost as good as for the standard Merge join. (There is in the Cluster join the extra cost of a look-up into F_2's index for each distinct A value encountered in F_1.) The other extreme is that the number of distinct values in each Join attribute is almost equal to the number of tuples in the corresponding operand relation, in which case the number of index look-ups approaches the number of tuples in T_1 and the number of F_2 block accesses approaches the number of tuples in the result of the Join. In this case, performance approaches that of the Indexed loop join. In most cases, we would expect the performance of the Cluster join to be somewhere between the two extremes.

11.3 JOIN METHODS THAT CREATE ORGANIZATIONS

Consider a situation where we must process the Join $T_1 \underset{A=B}{\bowtie} T_2$ but neither file F_1 nor F_2 has a structure that can be used in the computation. Of all the methods considered so far, only the Unindexed loop join is applicable in this case. In such a situation, a query optimizer has the option of performing the Join using an algorithm, such as the Unindexed loop join, requiring no special structures or, alternatively, of creating on the spot a structure that supports a more efficient Join algorithm.

These same considerations in fact apply even if some useful structures do exist. For example, if a query requires a Join between two very large tables, even if there is an index on the Join attribute of one of these tables, the query optimizer might create sorted copies of the data files so that it can perform a Merge join. Such a decision would be justified if the cost of the sort plus the cost of the Merge join is less than the cost of the Loop join that is supported by the existing index.

Generally speaking, the decision of whether to build a structure to support the processing of the query at the time a query is encountered must be based on a careful comparison of expected costs. In particular, the decision must be based on a comparison between the cost of processing the query using existing structures and the total cost of building one or more structures and then using the structures to process the query. In certain contexts, it may be appropriate to take into consideration the fact that some structures, once built, can be maintained and used for future queries of a similar nature. In this case, the cost of constructing the structure should be amortized over several queries.

We shall consider here two types of structures a query optimizer might construct at the time it is required to process the Join $T_1 \underset{A=B}{\bowtie} T_2$:

1. The query optimizer might create sorted copies of the data files. Note that if we were to sort the original data files rather than creating sorted

copies, all pinning pointers into the data files would have to be adjusted. Even if pinning pointers into the data files emanate from only secondary structures (and not from data records), the updating of these pointers is a substantial task and, in most contexts, could not reasonably be performed while processing an interactive query. By creating a sorted copy of the data file, we avoid these costs, although we probably would not attempt to maintain the copies once the Merge join algorithm has computed the Join in question. Therefore, the sorting costs generally cannot be amortized over future queries.

2. The query optimizer might create new secondary structures. There are many versions of this strategy; we present here a variation of a method known as the **Grace join**. This method creates hashed dense indices for the operand tables, using a common hash function. Once these structures are created, the Merge join on hashed indices is performed. In many contexts, it is reasonable to maintain these secondary structures for use in processing future queries. In this case, it may be appropriate to amortize over several queries the cost of building the structures.

We first consider the strategy of building sorted copies of the data files. Chapter 7 presented and analyzed several versions of an external Merge sort algorithm. The version most applicable in the current context assumes that the sorting program has no control over buffer and block sizes and can be allocated some fixed number $k + 1$ of buffers. In this case, we would perform a k-way merge sort, requiring approximately

$$2b + 2b*CEIL(\log_k(b/(k+1)))$$

block accesses to sort a file consisting of b blocks. Hence, the cost of sorting data files F_1 and F_2 before applying the Merge join algorithm is approximately

$$2b_1 + 2b_1*CEIL(\log_k (b_1/(k+1))) + 2b_2 + 2b_2*CEIL(\log_k(b_2/(k+1)))$$

block accesses. Following the sort of the data files, we perform the Merge join algorithm, requiring $b_1 + b_2$ block accesses. The total number of block accesses required by the sort-and-merge strategy thus is

$$3b_1 + 3b_2 + 2b_1*CEIL\ (\log_k(b_1/(k+1))) + 2b_2*CEIL\ (\log_k(b_2/(k+1)))$$

We illustrate the decision a query optimizer might make by considering a situation in which no structures supporting the required Join exist, and the optimizer is to choose between the Sort-and-merge strategy and the Unindexed loop join algorithm. Recall that the number of block accesses required by the the Unindexed loop join depends on the number of blocks of the outer table that can be kept simultaneously in internal memory. Since we are currently assuming that $k + 1$ is the maximum number of blocks that can be kept in internal memory and since the Unindexed loop join must keep in internal memory, in addition to blocks of F_1, one block of the inner table and at least one block of the result stream, $k - 1$ is the number of blocks of the outer table that can be kept in internal memory. Assuming that $b_1 \leq b_2$ and, hence, that T_1 is used as the outer table, the number of block accesses required by the Unindexed loop join algorithm is

$$b_1+b_2*CEIL(b_1/(k-1))$$

The simplest situation to analyze is when b_1 and b_2 are approximately equal. Let us assume this situation and let b denote this common value. In this case (simplifying ceiling functions by rounding down), the formula for the Sort-and-merge strategy reduces to

$$6b + 4b \log_{k+1}(b/k+1)$$

while the formula for the Unindexed loop join reduces to

$$b + b^2/k$$

Hence, the Sort-and-merge strategy requires fewer block accesses than the Unindexed loop join exactly when

$$5b + 4b \log_{k+1}(b/k+1) < b^2/k$$

We conclude that for any fixed value of k, the Unindexed loop join strategy is preferable for small file sizes b, but, as b grows, the Sort-and-merge strategy eventually will have the advantage, and this advantage becomes arbitrarily great as b grows arbitrarily large.

Exercises 11.9 and 11.10 consider the choice between strategies under various assumptions on the sizes of the files; they also compare the Sort-and-merge strategy with the Indexed loop and Merge join on indices algorithms under the assumptions that the structures required by these latter algorithms exist.

A second class of strategies builds secondary structures on the operand files. We present one of the many instances of this class of strategies, a variation of the Grace join algorithm. Like the Sort-and-merge strategy, the Grace join strategy has two phases: the first builds the required structures, and the second uses these structures to support an efficient Join algorithm. Unlike the Sort-and-merge strategy, the version of Grace join presented here builds a structure that could be reasonably maintained and used in the future.

Grace join builds the hashed dense index structures that support the Merge join on hashed indices presented in Section 11.2. The task at hand is to describe how the required hashed indices can be constructed efficiently. To begin, we determine the number of buckets B that should comprise the hash tables HT_1 and HT_2 of the dense indices being created for the data files F_1 and F_2. We shall create the hash table chains unsorted, and hence the Merge join algorithm requires that, for any $0 \leq i \leq B - 1$, both chains $HT_1[i]$ and $HT_2[i]$ fit simultaneously in internal memory, while leaving enough internal memory for

1. The retrieval and concatenation of matching data records as is described by the standard Merge join of index files algorithm of Section 11.2.

2. The storage of each segment of the result stream awaiting piping to calling routine. We assume that this requires a single block of storage.

Let L denote the maximum combined length that a pair of chains $HT_1[i]$ and $HT_2[i]$ can have, while allowing these chains, plus the data necessitated by items 1 and 2, to reside in internal memory. We select the number of buckets B to be such that the average length of a chain in HT_1 plus the average length of a chain in HT_2 is no greater than L.[3] To determine the required value B, we must estimate the number of blocks that will be in the dense indices that we shall be building. If we know (or have an estimate of) the numbers b_1 and b_2 of blocks in the data files F_1 and F_2, we can estimate the number of blocks in dense index files I_1 and I_2 as (ceiling of) b_1/d_1 and b_2/d_2, respectively, where d_i is the ratio (number of index records that fit per block of I_i)/(number of data records that fit per block of F_i). We see that B must satisfy $(b_1d_1 + b_2d_2)/B \leq L$ or, equivalently, $B \geq (b_1d_1 + b_2d_2)/L$. We therefore take the number of buckets B to be the smallest integer greater than or equal to the quantity $[(b_1d_1 + b_2d_2)/L]$.

To build the hashed dense indices I_1 and I_2, we select a hash function h, such as the modulo-B hash function, which maps from values of the Join attributes to $\{0, 1, \ldots, B - 1\}$. Consider now how to apply to each data file F_i hash function h to build the hashed dense index I. We first consider the situation where internal memory is large enough to hold $B + 1$ disk blocks plus a hash table of B buckets (i.e., B block pointers). As exercise 11.11 illustrates, such an assumption is not unreasonable, even for moderately large data files. Figure 11.1 depicts how internal memory will be utilized in this case.

Assuming there is sufficient internal memory for the configuration depicted in Figure 11.1, the hashing of F_1 proceeds as follows. (The hashing of F_2 is completely analogous.) Each block Bn of F_1 is read into the data block buffer. Hash function h is applied to the value v of the Join attribute A in each record of this data block, obtaining the value $h(v) = i \in \{0, 1, \ldots, B - 1\}$. We then attempt to insert the index record $<v,Bn>$ into the buffer holding the current head block of $HT_1[i]$'s chain. If the buffer is full, we simply write its contents to a disk block, setting $HT_1[i]$ so that it points to this block. We then begin to assemble in $HT_1[i]$'s buffer a new head block for the chain, with $<v,Bn>$ being this block's first index record. The process continues until each data record, in each block of F_1, has been processed.

Before considering the case in which there is insufficient internal memory for the configuration depicted in Figure 11.1, let us consider the efficiency of the Grace join algorithm when there is sufficient internal memory. The phase

[3] Observe that we in fact might desire this average combined chain length to be even shorter than L, to (*a*) decrease the probability that for some i the combined length is greater than L, a condition that would require some of the blocks on chains $HT_1[i]$ and $HT_2[i]$ to be accessed more than once; (*b*) decrease the amount of internal processing required to sort the chains in the course of the Merge join; and (*c*) anticipate the growth of the files, assuming that we intend to maintain the structures for future use.

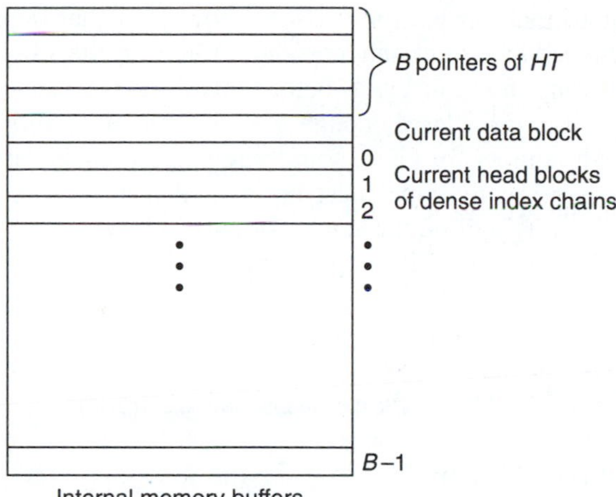

Figure 11.1 Utilization of internal memory, when there is enough

of the algorithm that builds the hashed dense indices requires that each block of each of the data files F_1 and F_2 be read once and, similarly, that each block of each resulting index I_1 and I_2 be written once. Hence, the total number of block accesses required for the building phase is

$$b_1 + b_2 + b_1/d_1 + b_2/d_2$$

Once the indices are built, the Merge join of indices is performed as described previously, requiring

$$b_1/d_1 + b_2/d_2 + c_{SJ(1,2)} + c_{SJ(2,1)}$$

block accesses. (If, due to nonuniformity in the hash function h, for some i the combined length of chains $HT_1[i]$ and $HT_2[i]$ is greater than L, some blocks on these chains will have to be accessed more than once, slightly increasing the preceding count.) Therefore, the total number of block accesses required by the algorithm, assuming sufficient internal memory for the configuration depicted in Figure 11.1, is approximately

$$b_1 + b_2 + 2b_1/d_1 + 2b_2/d_2 + c_{SJ(1,2)} + c_{SJ(2,1)}$$

Recall that the number of block accesses required by the Unindexed loop join is

$$b_1 + b_2 * CEIL(b_1/k)$$

where k is the largest number of blocks of the outer file F_1 that can fit in memory, while leaving room for the other data that the algorithm requires. As the sizes b_1 and b_2 of the operand files increase, the product $b_2 * CEIL(b_1/k)$ will dominate the analysis, and hence the number of block accesses given by the preceding formula for Grace join eventually will be smaller than the number required by the Unindexed loop join. Note, however, that depending on the values of L and k (which are closely correlated) and on the values of the other parameters appearing in the formula, before this crossover occurs, the sizes of F_1 and F_2 may need to grow large enough to violate the assumption that there is sufficient internal memory for Grace join to be performed as described. In this case, the analysis presented next must be applied instead. The conclusion of that analysis, however, will be the same: for sufficiently large values of b_1 and b_2, the Grace join algorithm will outperform the Unindexed loop join.

Now consider the case where there is insufficient internal memory for the configuration depicted in Figure 11.1. In this case, one approach is to begin the building phase of the algorithm with internal memory configured as depicted in Figure 11.2. As the figure suggests, we initially create a pseudo–hash table HT^0 consisting of B^0 buckets, where B^0 is chosen small enough so that there is sufficient internal memory for the foregoing configuration. Each pseudochain corresponds as follows to an aggregation of chains from the hash table HT we shall eventually construct. Let $m^0 = CEIL(B^0/B)$. For each $i = 0, 1, 2, \ldots, B^0 - 1$, the chain off of $HT^0[i]$ corresponds to the aggregation of the chains off of $HT[im^0]$, $HT[im^0 + 1], \ldots, HT[(i + 1)m^0 - 1]$. (The chain off of $HT^0[B^0 - 1]$ may correspond to fewer chains of HT.) The initial pass of the building phase of Grace join (call it pass 0) builds HT^0 exactly as the entire building phase built HT when there was sufficient internal memory. Hence, pass 0 (applied to data file F_i) is completed with

$$b_i + b_i/d_i$$

block accesses.

Once pass 0 has created the pseudo–hash table HT^0, one or more additional passes are required to refine HT^0 into HT. Each of these subsequent passes refines the chains of the current pseudo–hash table into smaller chains that are

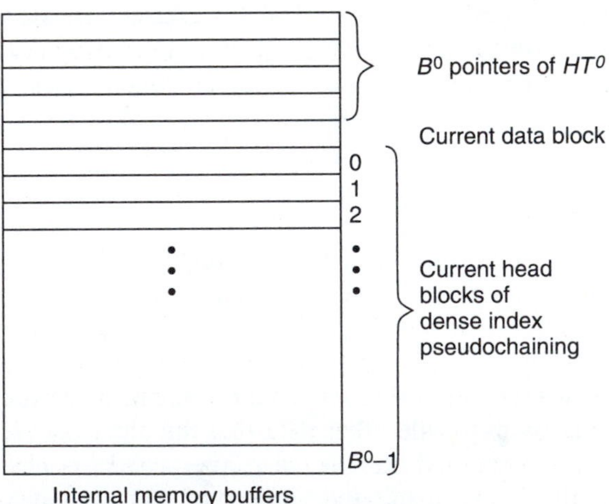

Figure 11.2 Utilization of internal memory

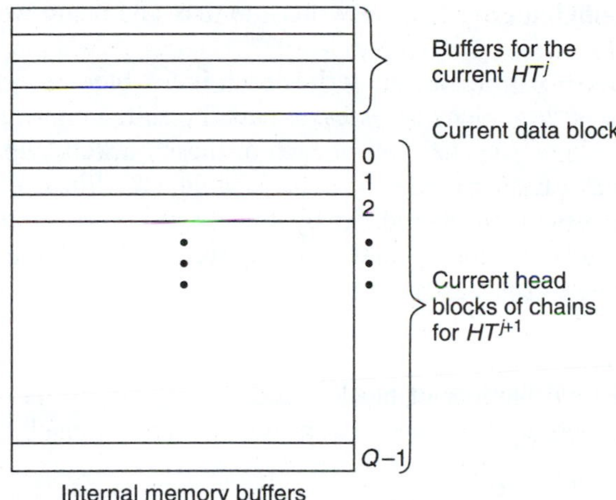

Figure 11.3 Configuration for the refinement passes

stored off of a new hash table which contains more buckets than the old table. After a sufficient number of passes has been performed, the desired hash table HT, with its B buckets, is obtained. To implement these refinement phases, we configure internal memory as shown in Figure 11.3. First, we reserve enough memory so that the current hash table can fit in internal memory. Note that as the number of buckets in the hash table grows, more internal memory will be required for the table. However, for all but the largest of data files, two or three blocks should suffice, even for the final hash table HT. Suppose that, after reserving enough internal memory for the current hash table, there remains enough memory for $Q + 1$ buffers. One of these buffers is used to hold a pseudochain block as it is being refined, and the remaining Q buffers are used to assemble chains for the new hash table being created. To simplify our analysis, we shall assume that the same number Q of buffers is used on each refinement pass. Observe that, unless the hash table is unusually large, Q will be close to B^0.

Consider the effect of the $(j + 1)$st refinement pass. Suppose we begin with hash table HT^j containing B^j buckets; hence, each pseudochain of HT^j corresponds to approximately $m^j = CEIL(B^j/B)$ chains of HT. Pass $j + 1$ has B^j iterations, numbered $0, 1, \ldots, k, \ldots, B - 1$. At the kth iteration, the chain off of $HT^j[k]$ is refined into $m^{j+1} = CEIL(m^j/Q)$ chains of HT that are hung off of buckets $HT^{j+1}[kQ]$, $HT^{j+1}[kQ + 1]$, $\ldots$, $HT^{j+1}[(k + 1)Q - 1]$. Thus, HT^{j+1} will have $B^{j+1} = Q * B^j$ buckets. (On the algorithm's last pass it may be that $m^j < Q$, in which case the refinement will be into fewer than Q buckets.) Buffer p, $0 \le p < Q$, is used to assemble the chain for $HT^{j+1}[kQ + p]$. The refinement is effected by reading each index block on chain $HT^j[k]$ into the designated buffer. Hash function h is applied to each index record in the buffer to determine into which of the Q new chains the index record belongs. If the corresponding buffer is full, we write it to disk and begin work on the next block of this chain.

Each refinement pass reads and writes each index block exactly once, contributing a total of $2b/d$ block accesses. If pass 0 results in hash table HT^0 consisting of B^0 buckets, the chain off of each of these buckets will correspond to $m^0 = CEIL(B/B^0)$ chains of the final hash table HT. Since each refinement pass (except possibly the last) reduces by a factor of Q the number of chains of the final hash table to which chains of the current hash table correspond, the number of refinement passes required is approximately

$$\log_Q(m^0)$$

Therefore, the total number of block accesses incurred by the building phase (pass 0 and the subsequent refinement passes) is approximately

$$b + b/d + 2b/d * \log_Q(m^0)$$

The total number of block accesses incurred by the Grace join algorithm for operand files F_1 and F_2, therefore, is approximately

$$(b_1 + b_1/d_1 + 2b_1/d_1 * \log_Q(m^0)) + (b_2 + b_2/d_2 + 2b_2/d_2 * \log_Q(m^0)) \\ +(b_1/d_1 + b_2/d_2 + c_{SJ(1,2)} + c_{SJ(2,1)})$$

We now compare the number of block accesses required by this version of Grace join with the number required by the Unindexed loop join. Assume that $b_1 \leq b_2$ and $b_1/d_1 \leq b_2/d_2$, and recall that the number of block accesses required by Unindexed loop join is

$$b_1+b_2*CEIL(b_1/k)$$

where k is a constant depending on the amount of available internal memory. Recall also that the number of buckets B in HT is approximately equal to $[(b_1d_1 + b_2d_2)/L]$, where L is a constant depending on the amount of available internal memory. Since d_1 and d_2 are constants also and since $c_{SJ(1,2)}$ and $c_{SJ(2,1)}$ are related by constants to b_1 and b_2, respectively, we see that the number of block accesses required by Grace join is $\Theta(b_2 \log b_1)$, while the number required by the Unindexed loop join is $\Theta(b_1 * b_2)$. We conclude, therefore, that as the sizes of the operand tables grow, performance of Grace join becomes arbitrarily better than that of the Unindexed loop join. Further, the hashed indices created by Grace join can be maintained and used for future queries.

The exercises compare the efficiency of Grace join with that of the Sort-and-merge method and also consider a variation of Grace join in which copies of the data files, rather than dense indices, are hashed.

11.4 *k*-WAY JOINS

We consider now the problem of processing a query of the form $T_1 \bowtie T_2 \bowtie \cdots \bowtie T_k$, where $k > 2$. Note that this expression contains Natural join, rather than Equi-join, operators. We begin with this case because properties of the Natural join operator allow us to simplify the details of various aspects of the discussion. Later in this section, and again in Chapter 12, we shall consider expressions containing the Equi-join operator, at which time we shall point out the additional considerations arising in that context.

Observe first that the expression $T_1 \bowtie T_2 \bowtie \cdots \bowtie T_k$, technically, is not a syntactically complete relational algebra expression since it is not parenthesized to indicate how the Join operators should be associated. For example, the expression $T_1 \bowtie T_2 \bowtie T_3 \bowtie T_4$ could be interpreted in any one of a number of ways, including

$$(((T_1 \bowtie T_2) \bowtie T_3) \bowtie T_4)$$
$$((T_1 \bowtie T_2) \bowtie (T_3 \bowtie T_4))$$
$$(T_1 \bowtie (T_2 \bowtie (T_3 \bowtie T_4)))$$

The reason that we can omit parentheses from high-level queries such as this is that the Natural join operator is **associative**. Thus, all of these expressions, as well as all other associations of the Joins, are logically equivalent in the sense that, for all instances of the operand tables, the expressions evaluate to the same value. As a result of this associativity, the syntax $T_1 \bowtie T_2 \cdots \bowtie T_k$ is logically unambiguous.

Not only is the Natural join operator associative, it is **commutative**, provided that we ignore the order in which the attributes appear in the result table, that is, if we take the perspective that tuples are functions mapping from attribute names to values. This commutativity implies that many additional logically equivalent expressions can be obtained by reordering the operand tables before parenthesizing the expression. For example, each of the following expressions is logically equivalent to the expressions listed earlier:

$$(((T_3 \bowtie T_2) \bowtie T_1) \bowtie T_4)$$
$$((T_4 \bowtie T_2) \bowtie (T_1 \bowtie T_3))$$
$$(T_1 \bowtie (T_4 \bowtie (T_3 \bowtie T_2))$$

The associativity and commutativity of the Natural join operator is of great significance to the query optimization problem. No matter how the user happens to construct the expression, the query optimizer is free to reorder the tables and reassociate the operators. As we shall illustrate, such transformations can have a tremendous impact on processing efficiency. To begin, we introduce

$$\bowtie \{T_1, \ldots, T_k\}$$

as a generic notation for an expression consisting of $k - 1$ Natural joins between the tables $T_1, \ldots, T_k$. This notation is intended to emphasize that, at the logical level, an expression with $k - 1$ Natural joins can be viewed as consisting of a single operator over an unordered collection of k operand tables.

We consider now the query optimizer's task of mapping the expression

$$\bowtie \{T_1, \ldots, T_k\}$$

to an implementation strategy. There are available to a query optimizer two basic classes of strategies for evaluating the expression $\bowtie \{T_1, \ldots, T_k\}$:

1. Map the expression $\bowtie \{T_1, \ldots, T_k\}$ to a sequence of binary Joins (i.e., select a fully parenthesized version of the expression), and choose an implementation algorithm for each Join. This strategy allows us to use, with some modifications, many of the Join algorithms presented earlier in this section. Modifications to these algorithms are required when one or both operands of a particular Join are streams resulting from previous Joins rather than stored relations.
2. Use a special algorithm that treats the $k - 1$ joins as a single operation. Such algorithms apply when the Join attributes interact across the k tables in particular patterns and, in some cases, will be the most efficient way of evaluating the expression.

Implementation as a Sequence of Binary Joins

We begin by considering the first of these approaches. We use a **join tree** to represent each "translation" of the expression $\bowtie \{T_1, \ldots, T_k\}$. Consider, for example, the case where $k = 4$. Figure 11.4 gives the Join trees representing the translations $(((T_3 \bowtie T_2) \bowtie T_1) \bowtie T_4)$, $((T_1 \bowtie T_2) \bowtie (T_3 \bowtie T_4))$, and $(T_1 \bowtie (T_4 \bowtie (T_3 \bowtie T_2)))$ of the high-level expression $\bowtie \{T_1, T_2, T_3, T_4\}$.

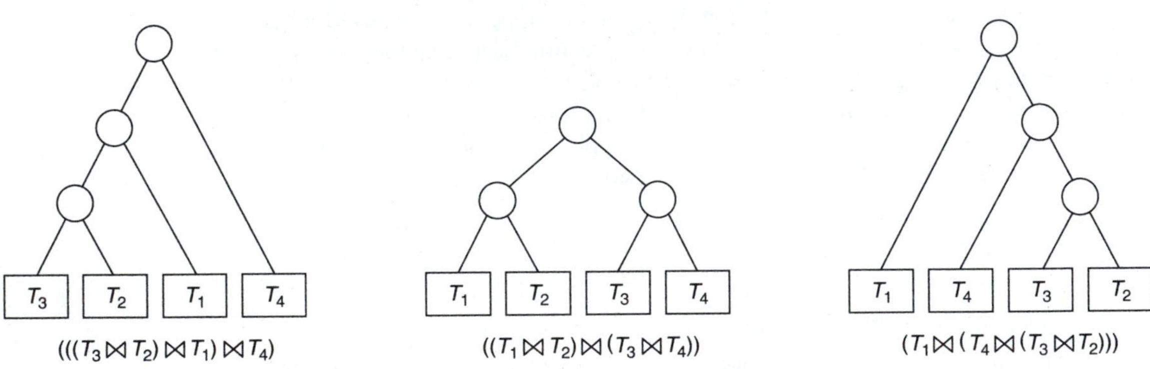

Figure 11.4 Join trees with their corresponding expressions

The selection of a Join tree is a critical task in the processing of the expression $\bowtie \{T_1, \ldots, T_k\}$ since the choice impacts on efficiency in several ways, including

1. The choice of a tree affects the sizes of intermediate results.
2. The choice of tree affects whether or not the sequence of Joins can be computed in a pipeline.
3. The choice of a tree affects the availability of storage structures to support the computation.

We now explore each of these effects.

Sizes of Intermediate Results: Different Join trees can lead to intermediate results of different sizes. To illustrate the dramatic effect the choice of a Join tree can have on the sizes of intermediate results, consider the following example. Suppose that the four operand tables have the following schemes:

$T_1(A,B)$
$T_2(C,D)$
$T_3(A,E,F)$
$T_4(C,F,G)$

Suppose further that the current instance of each table scheme contains 1,000 tuples and that the sizes of the Joins $(T_1 \bowtie T_3)$ and $(T_2 \bowtie T_4)$ are 2,000 tuples each and that attribute F in tables T_3 and T_4 takes on only the value 0 or 1, with equal frequency, and independently of the values in a tuple's other attributes.

Observe that, under these assumptions, the Join tree corresponding to the expression $((T_1 \bowtie T_3) \bowtie (T_2 \bowtie T_4))$ twice joins tables of 1,000 tuples each and then joins a pair of tables of 2,000 tuples each. Every other Join tree JT is inferior to this tree in the sense that JT must, at some point, perform Joins or Cartesian products between very large operand tables. For example, a next-best Join tree (in terms of sizes of intermediate results) corresponds to the expression $(((T_1 \bowtie T_3) \bowtie T_4) \bowtie T_2)$ and first joins a pair of tables of 1,000 tuples each, then joins a pair of tables of 2,000 and 1,000, and then joins a table of approximately 1,000,000 and a table of size 1,000. Other trees are even worse. For example, the tree corresponding to the expression $((T_1 \bowtie T_2) \bowtie (T_3 \bowtie T_4))$ takes the Cartesian product of a pair of tables of size 1,000 each, takes the Join of a pair of tables of size 1,000 each, and then joins a table of size 1,000,000 and a table of size approximately 500,000.

Ability to Pipeline: The choice of tree affects whether or not it is feasible to compute the sequence of Joins in a **pipeline**. To appreciate the desirability of pipelining, note first that, in general, we would expect intermediate results of the form $W_1 \bowtie \cdots \bowtie W_m$ (where $\{W_1, \ldots, W_m\} \subset \{T_1, \ldots, T_k\}$) to be too large to store in internal memory. Consequently, when computing the expression $\bowtie \{T_1, \ldots, T_k\}$, we generally would write intermediate results to temporary disk files as they are computed, and then read back blocks of these disk files into main memory as they are needed for future Joins. For example, suppose we select the Join tree corresponding to the association $((T_1 \bowtie T_2) \bowtie (T_3 \bowtie T_4))$ from Figure 11.4. The standard way of evaluating this expression is as follows:

Compute $T_1 \bowtie T_2$, writing to disk the intermediate result J_1
Compute $T_3 \bowtie T_4$, writing to disk the intermediate result J_2
Compute $J_1 \bowtie J_2$, reading from disk the operands

Since the sizes of the intermediate results can be quite large (often larger than the original operand tables), the block accesses incurred in the course of reading and writing these intermediates can often dominate the costs of evaluating the expression.

These observations lead many query optimizers to look favorably on families of Join trees that define a sequence of Joins amenable to the piping of partial intermediate results to the next Join so that only the final result is written to disk. In particular, left-leaning trees corresponding to associations of the form $(((T_1 \bowtie T_2) \bowtie T_3) \bowtie T_4)$ support such a strategy. The basic idea behind pipelining is that as tuples $t_1 \cdot t_2$ in the result of the Join $T_1 \bowtie T_2$ are generated, these tuples are streamed to a loop that computes $(T_1 \bowtie T_2) \bowtie T_3))$; in essence, the stream of $t_1 \cdot t_2$ tuples is used to probe table T_3 for tuples t_3, which join with each tuple $t_1 \cdot t_2$. When these tuples t_3 are retrieved, they are joined with the probing $t_1 \cdot t_2$ tuples to form $t_1 \cdot t_2 \cdot t_3$, which, in turn, are used to probe T_4.

Several of the Join algorithms presented in the previous sections can be used when one of the operands is a stream. The simplest algorithms to adapt to this context are the Loop joins, with the stream of tuples playing the role of the outer table. To illustrate, suppose that we have selected the tree specifying the Join sequence $(((T_1 \bowtie T_2) \bowtie T_3) \bowtie T_4)$ and that each T_i is indexed on the set of attributes it shares with tables $T_1, \ldots, T_{i-1}$, for $i = 2, 3, 4$. The following collection of nested **for** loops summarizes the pipeline strategy for evaluating $(((T_1 \bowtie T_2) \bowtie T_3) \bowtie T_4)$. We use the notation $S_1 \odot S_2$ to represent the Natural join of the sets S_1 and S_2 of tuples, given that we know each $s_1 \in S_1$ and $s_2 \in S_2$ match on the common attributes.

```
for (each tuple t in T1)
  Retrieve into Temp2 via index tuples in T2 that match
    t on the join attributes
  Join t with each tuple in Temp2, forming J2 ← {t} ⊙ Temp2
  for (each tuple j2 in J2)
    Retrieve into Temp3 via index tuples in T3 that match
      j2 on the join attributes
    Join j2 with each tuple in Temp3, forming J3 ← {j2} ⊙ Temp3
    for (each tuple j3 in J3)
      Retrieve into Temp4 via index tuples in T4 that match
        j3 on the join attributes
      Join j3 with each tuple in Temp4, forming J4 ← {j3} ⊙ Temp4
      Append to result stream STR each tuple in J4
    end for
  end for
end for
```

The total number of tuples retrieved, over all iterations, into $Temp_i(1 < i \leq k)$ is the size of the Join $T_1 \bowtie T_2 \bowtie \cdots \bowtie T_i$. If we make no assumptions regarding the physical structure of F_i, we must charge each of these retrievals a block access. (If F_i is stored clustered on the Join attribute, the number of block accesses can be considerably less.) Additionally, each block of the first table T_1 is read once, the index on each $T_{i+1}(1 < i \leq k - 1)$ is searched once for each tuple in $T_1 \bowtie T_2 \bowtie \cdots \bowtie T_i$; however, the final result is written to disk (and this, by the calling program). Comparing the number of block accesses incurred by the Pipeline strategy with the number incurred by the standard implementation of the sequence of Indexed loop joins, we find that the standard implementation incurs the block accesses described earlier and, additionally, the block access required to write to disk each intermediate result $T_1 \bowtie T_2 \bowtie \cdots \bowtie T_i (1 < i < k)$ and the block accesses required to read back into internal memory each of these results.

We observe that other shaped Join trees, such as those corresponding to the expression $((T_1 \bowtie T_2) \bowtie (T_3 \bowtie T_4))$, do not easily support a Pipeline strategy. One fundamental difficulty is that most Join algorithms require the tuples of one of the two operand tables to be accessed repeatedly, a requirement that cannot be satisfied when both operands are streams. One Join algorithm that does not require tuples in either operand to be accessed repeatedly is the Merge join. In our example, if the algorithms used to compute the Joins $(T_1 \bowtie T_2)$ and $(T_3 \bowtie T_4)$ each produces its result stream sorted on the attribute on which the Join between $(T_1 \bowtie T_2)$ and $(T_3 \bowtie T_4)$ is based, it is theoretically possible to perform the Merge join between the ordered streams. However, the required synchronization is quite complex, and most existing optimizers do not attempt pipelining in this context.

We conclude that pipelining is a strong motivation for selecting left-leaning trees. On the other hand, the ability to pipeline is not always the decisive factor in Join tree selection. For example, in some situations, other shaped trees may induce far more favorably sized intermediate results than will any left-leaning tree, and this factor could dominate.

Availability of Structures to Support the Computation: The selection of a Join tree should take into account the storage structures that exist on the operand tables. For example, suppose the schemes for the four operand tables are as follows, where starred attributes indicate the existence of an index.

T_1(A*,B*)
T_2(B*,C)
T_3(A,E*)
T_4(B,E)

The Join tree corresponding to the expression $(((T_1 \bowtie T_2) \bowtie T_3) \bowtie T_4)$ allows only the first join to exploit the existence of an index, while the Join tree corresponding to the expression $(((T_4 \bowtie T_2) \bowtie T_3) \bowtie T_1)$ allows each of the three joins to exploit the existence of an index.

We observe also that the selection of an appropriate Join tree may allow result streams to be created possessing a useful ordering, such as sorted on the attributes participating in a subsequent join. Consider, for example, the expression

$((T_5(A,B) \bowtie T_6(A,C)) \bowtie T_7(A,D))$

where each of T_5 and T_6 has an ordered index on attribute A and T_7 is stored sorted on attribute A. If the first join is performed by merging indices, the result stream will be ordered on attribute A, allowing the second join to be performed as a Merge join, even if the result stream is piped without being stored.

Similarly, we may wish to construct a secondary structure as an intermediate result is being written to disk. For example, if there is sufficient internal memory, the 0th pass of the building phase of the Grace join algorithm can be performed as the result stream is written to disk, thereby reducing the number of block accesses required to perform a subsequent Join involving this intermediate result.

In summary, different Join trees may support implementation strategies of dramatically different efficiencies. The brute force method of selecting the single best way to evaluate the expression $\bowtie \{T_1, \ldots, T_k\}$ would have to consider each Join tree and, for each tree, consider the different ways to implement the Joins it specifies. In practice, there often are far too many alternatives to consider each explicitly. Consequently, we are confronted with a difficult and important combinatorial search problem. Chapter 12 considers in detail this and other search problems that arise in query optimization.

Special *k*-way Join Algorithms

The second class of methods for evaluating the expression $\bowtie \{T_1, \ldots, T_k\}$, rather than refining the abstract *k*-way Join into a sequence of binary joins, applies a specialized algorithm that operates simultaneously on the *k* operand tables. We consider here two specific methods from this class:

1. A ***k*-way merge join** algorithm, applicable when there is a single set S of attributes such that, for each pair of tables T_i and T_j $(i \neq j)$, the attributes common to T_i and T_j are exactly S.
2. A **semi-join decomposition** algorithm, applicable when one of the operand tables shares one or more attributes with each other table but the remaining tables share no attributes with each other.

We observe that the pipelining strategies considered in the previous section have some of the flavor of a specialized *k*-way algorithm; although pipelining does refine the *k*-way Join operator into a sequence of binary joins, it tightly couples the processing of the $k - 1$ joins. Later in this section, we shall comment further on the relationships between the pipelining strategy and the specialized methods considered here.

We begin by developing the *k*-way Merge Join algorithm. To illustrate, consider the following table schemes:

```
PAYROLL(EMP#, Salary, Taxes)
CURRENT_JOB(EMP#, Dept, Manager)
DUTIES(EMP#, TaskCode, Start, Completion)
PERSONAL(EMP#, Dependent, Relationship, Age)
```

The semantics of these table schemes imply that {EMP#} is a key of PAYROLL and CURRENT_JOB but that it is not a key of DUTIES or PERSONAL. Suppose that the most common queries involve pairs of these tables, so it is reasonable to conjecture that either each table is kept physically sorted on EMP# or at least that ordered indices (e.g., B^+-trees) on EMP# exist for each table.

Suppose that, from time to time, we encounter a query that requires evaluation of the expression $\bowtie$ {*PAYROLL,CURRENT_JOB,DUTIES,PERSONAL*}. One way to evaluate such an expression, given the storage structures described, is to generalize the binary Merge join algorithms to *k*-way Merge join algorithms. These generalizations closely parallel the generalization to a *k*-way Merge sort of the two-way merge sort, as was presented in Chapter 7. Suppose, for example, that each data file is stored physically sorted on EMP#. In this case, we can simultaneously traverse the four data files, accumulating for each EMP# value encountered all tuples of each file matching this value. We assemble tuples in the Join from this collection and move on to the next value in the files. Observe that this algorithm performs the Join while accessing each block of each file only once. The binary Merge join on ordered indices generalizes to a *k*-way Merge join in an analogous fashion.

Note well that this very efficient strategy is applicable only in the special case where a single set of attributes is common to all tables. For example, considering again the tables

```
PROF(Pname, Dept, Salary)
TEACHING_HISTORY(Pname, Course#, Sect#, Semester)
ENROLL_HISTORY(Sname, Course#, Sect#, Semester)
```

from Chapter 9, we see that the expression $\bowtie$ {*PROF,TEACHING_HISTORY, ENROLL_HISTORY*} could not be evaluated by a *k*-way Merge join algorithm since TEACHING_HISTORY (or an ordered index into it) would have to be traversed simultaneously ordered on Pname (to merge with PROF) and on {Course#, Sect#, Semester} (to merge with ENROLL_HISTORY). Since these traversal orders are generally incompatible, the Merge join strategy is not applicable in this case.

It is interesting to observe that the *k*-way Merge join algorithm could be derived by modifying a pipelined sequence of Merge joins so that unnecessary searches are eliminated. We see in the pipelining strategy that once the tuples $t_1 \cdots t_i$ in the Join $T_1 \bowtie \cdots \bowtie T_i$ are created based on $S = v$, this S value is used to retrieve tuples from table T_{i+1}. Extra coordination is required to exploit the fact that tuples $t_1 \cdots t_i$ are generated ordered on S, while table T_{i+1} is stored ordered on S. In particular, our traversal of T_{i+1} must pick up from where it left off each time a new $t_1 \cdots t_i$ is generated. Exercise 11.6 explores this derivation of the algorithm in more detail.

We now consider an algorithm, known as **semi-join decomposition**, which is an integral part of INGRES's query optimizer. We shall derive this algorithm by modifying the pipelined Indexed loop join algorithm so that the number of redundant retrievals is reduced. The algorithm is applicable to the evaluation of the expression $\bowtie \{T_1, \ldots, T_p, \ldots, T_k\}$ when one of the tables T_p shares with each other table T_i some set of attributes S_i, while tables T_i and T_j share no attributes for all i and j different from p and such that $i \neq j$. In this case, table T_p is called the **pivot table**. The efficiency of the Decomposition algorithm depends on each table $T_i (i \neq p)$ being indexed on the set S_i of attributes it shares with the pivot table.

Before deriving the Semi-join decomposition algorithm, we present an example designed to indicate when the conditions necessary for the algorithm's applicability might be satisfied in practice. Consider an RDM containing the following table schemes:

EMP(EMP#, Dept, Manager)
PAYROLL(EMP#, Salary, Taxes)
STOCKS(Dept, Item)
MANAGERS(Manager, YearsExper, Supervisor)

The expression $\bowtie \{EMP,PAYROLL,STOCKS,MANAGERS\}$ can be evaluated by the Semi-join decomposition algorithm since the condition given previously is satisfied, with EMP being the pivot table. Further, it seems likely that each of the tables PAYROLL, STOCKS, and MANAGERS would be indexed on the attribute shared with EMP, which makes the algorithm a viable candidate. Abstracting from this example, we observe that the condition required for the Semi-join decomposition algorithm may be satisfied when there is a single table (the pivot) that defines some entity in terms of a set of attributes and other tables store more detailed information about these attributes.

Motivation for the Semi-join decomposition algorithm's computational strategy is found by analyzing the behavior of the Pipeline algorithm considered earlier in this section. Consider, for example, the Join $\bowtie \{T_1,T_2,T_3,T_4\}$ where the conditions for the applicability of the Semi-join decomposition are satisfied, with T_1 the pivot table. Suppose further that the scheme for T_1 is $T_1(A,B,C))$ with attribute A shared with T_2, attribute B shared with T_3, and attribute C shared with T_4.

Consider the execution of the pipelined Indexed loop join algorithm on the Join tree corresponding to the expression $(((T_1 \bowtie T_2) \bowtie T_3) \bowtie T_4)$. Let $t_1 = <a,b,c>$ be the tuple of T_1 selected at the start of the current iteration of the outer **for** loop, and consider the set J_2 of tuples constructed as $\{<a,b,c>\} \odot Temp_2$. Since all tuples in $Temp_2$ match $<a,b,c>$ on attribute A and since T_2 does not contain attributes B or C, each tuple in J_2 is of the form $<a,b,c> \cdot t_2'$, where t_2' denotes a member of $Temp_2$ with the redundant A value removed. Once J_2 is constructed, the algorithm iterates through its tuples. For each $j_2 \in J_2$, the algorithm searches for and retrieves tuples t_3 of T_3 such that $j_2[B] = t_3[B]$. Observe, however, that each tuple in the set J_2 has the same value b for its attribute B (i.e., the value $t_1[B]$). Therefore, the pipelined Indexed loop join algorithm will search T_3 repeatedly (once for each member of the current J_2) for tuples with a B value of b.

More generally, assume the the tables $T_1, \ldots, T_k$ have the attribute pattern required for the Semi-join decomposition algorithm, with T_1 the pivot table, and consider the evaluation by the pipelined Loop join algorithm of the expression $(\ldots ((T_1 \bowtie T_2) \bowtie T_3) \bowtie \cdots \bowtie T_k)$. Once J_i is constructed for the iteration in which the outer **for** loop selects $t_1 \in T_1$, T_{i+1} is searched, once for each tuple $j_i \in J_i$, for tuples t_{i+1} such that $t_{i+1}[S_{i+1}] = j_i[S_{i+1}]$. The key observation is that all these $j_i \in J_i$ have the same value for the attributes S_{i+1}, that is, the value $t_1[S_{i+1}]$. A more intelligent version of the Pipeline algorithm constructs, for each $t_1 \in T_1$, the set $Temp_{i+1}$ with a *single search* of T_{i+1} for tuples t_{i+1} such that $t_{i+1}[S_{i+1}] = t_1[S_{i+1}]$. Once $Temp_{i+1}$ is constructed, J_{i+1} is computed as

$$J_{i+1} \leftarrow J_i \odot Temp_{i+1}$$

The Semi-join decomposition algorithm essentially implements this "optimized" Pipeline strategy, although the following statement of the algorithm uses a slightly different control structure: For each tuple t_p retrieved from the pivot table T_p, we retrieve joining tuples from all the remaining tables, before any tuples are concatenated.

```
for (each tuple p in T_p)
  for (each table T_i, i≠p)
    Retrieve into Temp_i those tuples t of T_i such that t[S_i]=p[S_i]
  end for
  Append to STR the tuples in Temp_1⊙ · · · Temp_{i−1}⊙{p}⊙Temp_{i+1}⊙ · · · Temp_k
end for
```

It should be noted that if on some iteration of the outer **for** loop, any of the sets $Temp_i$ are determined to be empty, the p selected at this iteration of the outer **for** loop dangles, and there is no need to go further in the inner **for** loop. Note how this short circuiting is implicit in the original pipelined statement of the algorithm.

We observe that the algorithm's name derives from the fact that it can be written in terms of the Semi-join operator. In particular, the Retrieve statement within the inner **for** loop can be replaced by the statement

$$Temp_i \leftarrow T_i \triangleright \{p\}$$

We observe also that the Semi-join decomposition algorithm is valid even if tables T_i and T_j share attributes, where neither table is the pivot, provided that the Append statement is replaced by the statement

```
Append to STR the tuples in
Temp_1 ⋈ · · · ⋈ Temp_{i−1} ⋈ {p} ⋈ Temp_{i+1} ⋈ · · · ⋈ Temp_k
```

That is, rather than simply concatenating the tuples, a Natural join checking the equality of the values of common attributes is required. Unfortunately, when nonpivot tables have intersecting attribute sets, the modified Semi-join decomposition algorithm loses much of its advantage over other methods. See exercise 11.12 for a further discussion of this point.

Other Considerations for k-Way Join Expressions:

1. *Expressions containing the Equi-join operator*. For the most part, expressions containing several Equi-join operators are processed using the same techniques presented here for the Natural join operator. The most significant difference is that, when dealing with the Equi-join operator, care must be taken when applying associativity. For example, consider the expression

$$((T_1(A,B,C) \underset{A=D}{\bowtie} T_2(D,E)) \underset{B=F}{\bowtie} T_3(F,G))$$

If we reassociate the operators, we obtain

$$(T_1(A,B,C) \underset{A=D}{\bowtie} (T_2(D,E) \underset{B=F}{\bowtie} T_3(F,G)))$$

Observe that this new expression is syntactically incorrect since the condition for the inner Equi-join is $B = F$, but attribute B does not appear in the operand T_2 of this Join. The correct application of "associativity" requires that the inner Equi-join be changed to a Cartesian product and that the outer Equi-join be changed to a "compound" Equi-join with two equality conditions. The resulting expression is

$$(T_1(A,B,C) \underset{(A=D)\wedge(B=F)}{\bowtie} (T_2(D,E) \times T_3(F,G)))$$

Replacement of Natural joins by Equi-joins necessitates minor changes in the definitions of the specialized algorithms as well. For example, the condition required for the applicability of the k-way Merge join can be stated as follows for expressions containing Equi-joins:

> For some numbering of the attributes, the expression to be computed is equivalent to
>
> $$((..(T_1 \underset{A_1=A_2}{\bowtie} T_2) \underset{A_2=A_3}{\bowtie} T_3) \cdots T_i) \underset{A_i=A_{i+1}}{\bowtie} T_{i+1}) \cdots T_{k-1}) \underset{A_{k-1}=A_k}{\bowtie} T_k)$$

Similarly, the condition required for the applicability of the Semi-join decomposition algorithm can be stated as follows for expressions containing Equi-joins:

> For some numbering of the operand tables and attributes, the expression to be computed is equivalent to
>
> $$((..(T_1 \underset{A_1=B_1}{\bowtie} T_2) \underset{A_2=B_2}{\bowtie} T_3) \cdots T_i) \underset{A_i=B_i}{\bowtie} T_{i+1}) \cdots T_{k-1}) \underset{A_{k-1}=B_{k-1}}{\bowtie} T_k)$$
>
> where $A_1, A_2, \ldots, A_{k-1}$ appear only in T_1.

2. *Expressions that contain operators in addition to Join operators*. Associated with the relational operators is a collection of algebraic identities, based on which expressions can be transformed to produce logically equivalent, but possibly more efficiently evaluable, expressions. In this section, we have considered some of the issues arising from the associativity and commutativity of the Join operator. When an expression contains additional operators, such as Selects and Projects, the optimization task becomes even more difficult. This general problem of algebraic transformation is discussed in Chapter 12.

11.5 JOIN ALGORITHMS THAT EXPLOIT SPECIALIZED RDM STRUCTURES

The RDM's integration into a single ADT of multiple table components allows the use of implementation structures that combine data from, and information about, several tables. For example, Section 9.3 introduced a heterogeneous file structure that hierarchically stores the tuples of several RDM table components. In this section, we shall analyze the support that this physical structure provides for several classes of queries containing multiple joins and also consider two logical supports for Join operations.

Table of Tuple Pointers

We begin with a simple logical structure that was considered in Chapter 2 as an internal memory implementation. We first describe a support for the binary Join $T_1 \underset{A=B}{\bowtie} T_2$ and then indicate how the structure can be generalized to support other, related, types of queries.

The Join support structure is designed for situations where the number c_J of tuples in the Join $T_1 \underset{A=B}{\bowtie} T_2$ is expected to be considerably smaller than the number of tuples in the operand tables; that is, each operand table has a high percentage of dangling tuples. The structure is particularly attractive if, in addition, updates are relatively infrequent.

The Join support is a table of triples $<v, Tname, ptr>$, where v is a value such that both $\sigma_{A=v} T_1$ and $\sigma_{B=v} T_2$ are nonempty (i.e., the value appears in the Join), *Tname* is a table identifier (1 or 2 in this case), and *ptr* is a pointer to a tuple in the operand table indicated by *Tname* with value v in its Join attribute. There is a 1 : 1 correspondence between triples in the Join support and tuples that participate in the Join, and the Join support is maintained physically clustered on the values v. The Join $T_1 \underset{A=B}{\bowtie} T_2$ is computed as follows while traversing the Join support table: For each value v encountered in the course of the traversal, the collection of triples with value v is used to retrieve all tuples from the operand tables that have value v in the Join attribute, and these tuples are assembled and appended to the result stream. As with other Join algorithms considered, we assume there is enough internal memory to assemble this many tuples. Hence, each block of the Join support and each tuple that participates in the join is retrieved exactly once.

To analyze the efficiency of the method, observe that the support table will contain $c_{SJ(1,2)} + c_{SJ(2,1)}$ tuples. Let b_{PT} denote the number of blocks of memory over which these tuples are spread. Since we make no assumptions about the structure of the data file, we must assume that a block access is required each time we follow a pointer from the Join support to one of the data files. Hence, the total number of block accesses required for the Join is

$$b_{PT} + c_{SJ(1,2)} + c_{SJ(2,1)}$$

and it is apparent that the method performs best when there is a large number of dangling tuples.

Of the Join algorithms considered previously, the Merge join of indices is the best in situations where the operand tables contain a high percentage of dangling tuples. Since that Merge join, like the method described here, requires only logical structures on the data files, it is particularly appropriate to compare the efficiency of the current method with that of the Merge join of indices. Recall that Merge join of indices requires

$$Ib_1+Ib_2 + c_{SJ(1,2)} + c_{SJ(2,1)}$$

block accesses, where Ib_1 and Ib_2 are the numbers of blocks in the dense indices on the two data files. Therefore, the Join algorithm described here is more efficient than the Merge join of indices when

$$b_{PT}<Ib_1+Ib_2$$

Observe that the size of an entry $<v, Tname, ptr>$ in the Join support is roughly the same size as an entry $<v, ptr>$ in a dense index. However, a dense index contains an entry for every tuple in the corresponding table, whereas the Join support contains an entry only for tuples that participate in the Join. We conclude that when the operand tables contain a large percentage of dangling tuples, b_{PT} will be considerably smaller than the sum $(Ib_1 + Ib_2)$, and hence in this case, the Join structure described here will support an algorithm requiring significantly fewer block accesses than any method considered previously.

Other Considerations:

1. *Support for related operations*. Consider a query such as $((\sigma_{A=v} T_1) \underset{A=B}{\bowtie} T_2)$ that composes with the Join a selection on the Join attribute. The Join support can process this query extremely efficiently, provided that it is indexed on the value field, that is, if an index is maintained on the Join support allowing efficient retrievals of those entries $<v, Tname, ptr>$ containing a specified value v. Such an index not only is useful in processing queries containing selections but is essential if we are to efficiently update the structure in the face of updates to the operand tables—we use such an index to find where in the pointer table a new tuple and corresponding triple should be inserted and to locate a triple corresponding to a tuple that must be deleted from the data file.

We note that the strategy of this Join support extends directly to k-way join expressions of the form:

$$T_1 \underset{A_1=A_2}{\bowtie} T_2 \underset{A_2=A_3}{\bowtie} \bowtie T_3 \cdots T_{k-1} \underset{A_{k-1}=A_k}{\bowtie} T_k$$

Since each tuple t in the result of the Join is such that $t[A_1] = t[A_2] = \cdots t[A_k] = v$, for some value v, the Join structure we have described here is applicable to this form of Multiple join expressions; the only modification required is to allow each entry *Tname* to assume one of the k values $1, 2, \ldots, k$.

2. *Storage and maintenance costs*. The storage and maintenance requirements for this Join support are roughly the same as those of a dense index on the data files, although the higher the proportion of dangling tuples, the smaller are the relative storage requirements of the join support. Note that the Join support must use pinning pointers to be worthwhile, and these pointers must be updated whenever data records move between blocks.

When considering the use of this Join support, it must be kept in mind that the structure is extremely specialized in that it is useful for only a limited number of queries. For example, the structure is useless for queries such as $\sigma_{A=v} T_1$ not involving the Join in question. Therefore, the maintenance and storage costs of this structure can be amortized over only a small number of queries as compared with more general-purpose structures, such as ordered indices. Consequently, the use of this Join support is likely to be cost effective only when the queries it supports are frequent, and only when a high percentage of tuples dangle.

Hierarchical Nesting of Implementation-Level Tables

Consider now the heterogeneous file structure introduced in Section 9.3 to support the k-way Natural join $T_1 \bowtie T_2 \bowtie \cdots \bowtie T_k$, which is often necessitated by a normalizing decomposition. As before, we shall assume that

> For some numbering of the tables in the decomposition, T_i is in $1{:}n$ relationship with T_{i+1}, for $1 \leq i \leq k - 1$. That is, the operand tables can be numbered so that the set of attributes common to T_i and T_{i+1} is a key of T_i, for $1 \leq i \leq k - 1$. Additionally, none of the tables T_i contain dangling tuples with respect to the Join $T_1 \bowtie T_2 \bowtie \cdots \bowtie T_k$.

Exercise 11.13 considers generalizations to the case where some of the relationships between tables are $n{:}m$. In the following discussion, we shall assume that the tables have been numbered as described earlier and T_1 will be referred to as the **root** table. To simplify the algorithms, we shall assume also that each table T_i shares attributes only with the tables adjacent to it in the numbering, although only minor modifications to the algorithm are required if this assumption is violated.

We wish to compare the efficiency with which this hierarchical structure supports the Join $T_1 \bowtie T_2 \bowtie \cdots \bowtie T_k$ with the efficiency of other methods for computing this Join. We begin with the case where $k > 2$. Previously, we have considered several methods for computing an expression containing more than one Join. Observe that the specialized methods for computing the k-way Join apply only when the Joins have certain properties. For example, all versions of the Merge join, and the method that employs the logical Join support table, require that each tuple t in the result of the Join be such that $t[A_1] = t[A_2] = \cdots = t[A_k] = v$ for some value v, where $(A_i = A_{i+1})$ is the condition for the Join between tables T_i and T_{i+1}. Further, the Semi-join decomposition method applies to a Natural join only when one of the k tables shares attributes with each of the other $k - 1$ tables and no other pairs of tables share attributes. Since neither of these conditions necessarily is satisfied by the Join under consideration, it is not appropriate to compare any of these methods with the method based on the hierarchical file structure. This leaves only methods that evaluate the expression as a sequence of binary Joins, based on some Join tree.

Generally speaking, the hierarchical structure supports evaluation of the Join expression in question far more efficiently than any method that performs a sequence of binary Joins between tables T_i stored in homogeneous files F_i. To compute the Join against the hierarchical structure, we simply traverse the heterogeneous data file. Assuming that, for any tuple t_1 of the root table T_1, internal memory can hold simultaneously all tuples t_{ij} from the tables T_i $(2 \leq i \leq k)$ such that $t_1 \cdot t_{ij}$ is part of a tuple in the Join, the Join can be constructed while accessing only once each block in the heterogeneous file. (Exercise 11.14 considers modifications for when there is insufficient internal memory for this.) It should be noted further that the number of blocks over which the heterogeneous file is spread can be significantly smaller than $\Sigma_{i=1}^{k} b_i$ (where b_i is the number of blocks over which F_i is spread) due to the fact that matching Join attribute values are collapsed and stored only once in each block.

Other Considerations:

1. *Effect on single table operations*. In most cases, we will want to extensively index each table stored in the heterogeneous file structure. Such indexing will reduce the penalty that results from the heterogeneous file spreading over many blocks the tuples of each of the tables. As noted in Section 9.3, such indexing allows exact-match queries that qualify single tuples of each table to be answered with a single data block access. On the other hand, the performance of the heterogeneous structure will be inferior to that of the homogeneous structure for operations that access large collections of tuples that the homogeneous structure could store over a small number of blocks. The same holds true for operations that qualify tuples based on unindexed attributes.

2. *Queries composing a selection with the joins*. In particular, consider a query of the form

$$\sigma_{K_i=V}(T_1 \bowtie T_2 \bowtie \cdots \bowtie T_i \bowtie \cdots \bowtie T_k)$$

where K_i is the set of attributes common to table schemes T_i and T_{i+1} and V specifies a value for each attribute in K_i. Recall that, by assumption, K_i is a key of T_i. A query of this form can be processed extremely efficiently against the hierarchical data file, assuming the existence of an index on table T_i for the set of attributes K_i. First, this index is used to locate the tuple of T_i satisfying the condition $\sigma_{K_i=V}(T_i)$ in the heterogeneous file. If no tuple satisfies this condition, the result of the Join is empty; otherwise, since K_i is a key of T_i, exactly one tuple t_i satisfies the condition. Assuming that such a t_i exists, observe that

a. As we move up the hierarchy from T_i to T_1, t_i is stored with the unique tuple t_{i-1} of T_{i-1} that matches t_i in the Join, t_{i-1} is stored with the unique tuple t_{i-2} of T_{i-2} that matches t_{i-1} in the Join, . . . , and t_2 is stored with the unique tuple t_1 of T_1 that matches t_2 in the Join. Hence, we can construct the subtuple $t_1 \cdot t_2 \cdots t_{i-1}$ appearing in the Join by moving right to left across contiguous blocks of the heterogeneous file. (See exercise 11.15 for a description of a linking scheme that can speed this construction in certain cases.)

b. To compute the final result, we must concatenate the subtuple $t_1 \cdot t_2 \cdots t_{i-1}$ with the value of the expression

$$\sigma_{K_i=v}(T_i) \bowtie T_{i+1} \bowtie \cdots \bowtie T_k$$

This value is computed efficiently by partially applying the algorithm that computes the full Join. That is, all tuples from $T_{i+1}, \ldots, T_k$ that participate in this Join are stored near t_i in the hierarchical structure. These tuples are accumulated as we move left to right from t_i, the tuples then are assembled in internal memory as in the full Join, and each of the resulting tuples $t_i \cdot t_{i+1} \cdots t_k$ is concatenated with $t_1 \cdot t_2 \cdots t_{i-1}$ to form a tuple in $\sigma_{K_i=v}(T_1 \bowtie T_2 \bowtie \cdots \bowtie T_i \cdots \bowtie T_k)$.

Exercise 11.16 considers extensions of the algorithm to cases in which queries contain several selections of the above form.

3. *Queries joining only a subset of the* k *collapsed tables*. Generally speaking, such queries make semantic sense only if they involve tables consecutive in numbering and, thus, correspond to a path through the hierarchy of tables. These queries are of the form

$$T_i \bowtie T_{i+1} \bowtie \cdots \bowtie T_j$$

for some $1 \leq i \leq j \leq k$. Also common are queries of the form

$$\sigma_{A=v}(T_i) \bowtie T_{i+1} \bowtie \cdots \bowtie T_j$$

that select a particular tuple, or collection of tuples, to serve as the "root" of the path through the hierarchy. Assuming the existence of appropriate indices, both forms of these queries can be processed efficiently with straightforward modifications to the algorithms already described. See exercises 11.17 and 11.18 for details.

4. *Only two tables are collapsed; that is,* k = *2*. Our comparisons between the Join performed on the heterogeneous file storing tables $T_1, T_2, \ldots, T_k$ and other methods for performing the Join between these k tables has assumed $k > 2$. One effect of this assumption was to rule out Merge join variants as competitors since these algorithms cannot be applied unless the k tables share a single common set of Join attributes. We conclude this discussion by considering the special case in which $k = 2$ and hence the Merge join of data files is a viable competitor.

A comparison between the Merge join on a pair of homogeneous data files stored sorted on the Join attributes and the Join performed on the heterogeneous file structure storing the two operand tables reveals the following:

a. Efficiency of the Join. Both the Join on the heterogeneous structure and the Merge join require a single pass of the relevant files, accessing each block once. However, because of the collapsing of attribute values, the number of blocks in the heterogeneous file may be less than the combined number of blocks in the two homogeneous data files on which the Merge join algorithm operates. Hence, the number of block accesses required by the Join on the heterogeneous file structure may be smaller than the number required by the Merge join algorithm.

b. Maintenance of the structures. As is observed in Section 9.3, a comparable effort is required to maintain a heterogeneous file structure and the physically sorted homogeneous files required by the Merge join algorithm.

c. Support for other operations. A physically sorted homogeneous file is a more general purpose structure than is the heterogeneous file structure. We have noted in point 1 that the use of the heterogeneous data file degrades performance of queries retrieving collections of tuples that could be stored contiguously in a homogeneous file. For example, performance of the range query

$$\sigma_{V \le A \le V'} T_1$$

where A is the attribute shared by tables T_1 and T_2, will degrade since interspersed with the qualifying tuples of T_1 will be many tuples of T_2; in contrast, the qualifying tuples are stored contiguously in a homogeneous file sorted on Join attribute A.

Ring Structures

We now present a logical counterpart of the heterogeneous file structure just described. Like the heterogeneous file structure, the ring structure we present here is designed to support the k-way Natural join $T_1 \bowtie T_2 \bowtie \cdots \bowtie T_k$, which is often necessitated by a normalizing decomposition. We continue to assume that

> For some numbering of the tables in the decomposition, T_i is in $1:n$ relationship with T_{i+1}, for $1 \le i \le k - 1$. That is, the operand tables can be numbered so that the set of attributes common to T_i and T_{i+1} is a key of T_i, for $1 \le i \le k - 1$. Additionally, none of the tables T_i contain dangling tuples with respect to the Join $T_1 \bowtie T_2 \bowtie \cdots \bowtie T_k$.

As we did for the heterogeneous file structure, we shall simplify our description of the method by assuming further that each table T_1 shares attributes with only tables adjacent to it in the numbering.

Since the ring structure is a logical organization, it is easier to maintain in the face of updates than is the heterogeneous file structure (see exercise 11.19). Further, unlike the heterogeneous file structure that imposes a physical organization on the data, use of the ring structure is compatible with primary structures for the relevant data files (e.g., physically ordering them) that efficiently support operations unrelated to the k-way Join. It must be noted, however, that the ring structure does require the use of pinning pointers, which complicates the maintenance of most primary structures.

We illustrate the ring structure by way of example. Consider again the three implementation-level tables

PROF(Pname, Dept, Salary)
TEACHING_HISTORY(Pname, Course#, Sect#, Semester)
ENROLL_HISTORY(Sname, Course#, Sect#, Semester)

As before, we assume that {Pname} is a key of table scheme PROF, that {Course#, Sect#, Semester} is a key of table scheme TEACHING_HISTORY, and that {Sname, Course#, Semester} is a key of table scheme ENROLL_HISTORY. Hence, the following E/R diagram continues to depict the relationships of interest between the tables:

```
PROF
 | 1
 |  ___HAS_TAUGHT
 ↓ N
TEACHING_HISTORY
 | 1
 |  ___WAS_ENROLLED
 ↓ M
ENROLL_HISTORY
```

The ring structuring technique is applied to the homogeneous data files that result from mapping each implementation-level table to its own file. Figure 11.5 depicts the ring structure for our university example. Each tuple t in root table T_1 (PROF, in our example) is linked to one of the tuples s in the table T_2 (TEACHING_HISTORY, in our example) directly below T_1 in the hierarchy such that $t[K_1] = s[K_1]$, where K_1 is the set of attributes ({Pname}, in our example) common to the two tables. Tuple s contains a pair of pointers. One pointer is used to place tuple s on a chain consisting of those tuples s, s_1, s_2, . . . , s_m from s's own table T_2 such that $s[K_1] = s_1[K] = s_2[K_1] = \cdots = s_m[K_1]$. The second pointer in tuple s is used to point to a tuple u in the table T_3 (ENROLL_HISTORY, in our example) directly below T_2 in the hierarchy such

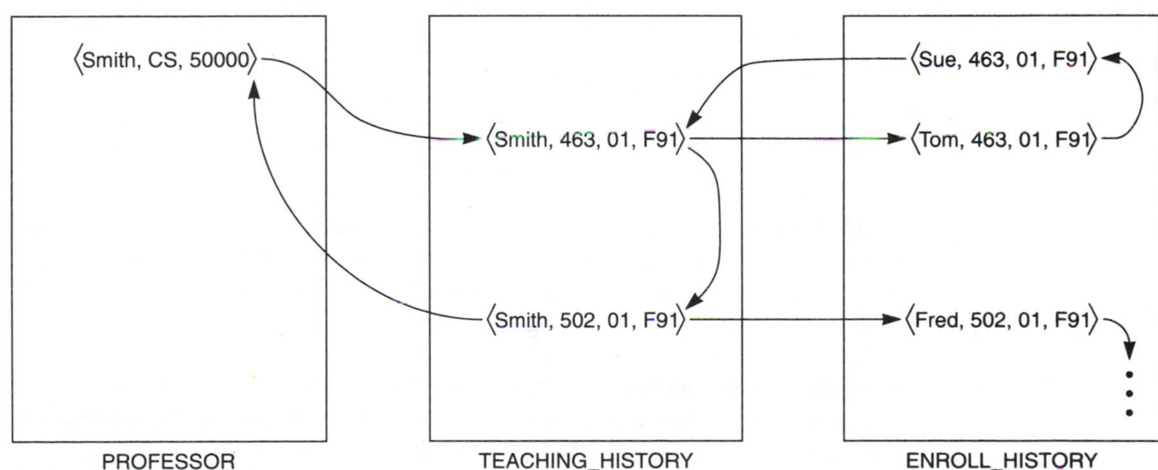

Figure 11.5 Rings linking tuples

that $s[K_2] = u[K_2]$, where K_2 is the set of attributes ({Course#, Sect#, Semester}, in our example) common to the two tables. This linking strategy then is applied to the tuples in table T_3 and to the tuples in the tables further down the hierarchy. As Figure 11.5 illustrates, the last tuple on each intratable chain forms a ring by pointing back to the tuple with which it joins in the previous table. Such backpointers are useful in support of queries that compose Selects with the Joins.

The evaluation of the expression $T_1 \bowtie T_2 \bowtie \cdots \bowtie T_k$ is described by the following recursive algorithm. In the algorithm, for tuple t in table T_i, $LIST(t)$ denotes the collection of tuples in table T_i on t's intratable list, that is, the collection of tuples from T_i that agree with t on the attributes in K_i. Note that $LIST(t)$ includes t. $LINK(t)$ is the tuple in table T_{i+1} to which t's intertable pointer points; that is, t and $LINK(t)$ agree on the attributes in K_{i+1}. If $i = k$ (i.e., T_i is the lowest table in the hierarchy), $LINK(t)$ is NIL.

```
Ring_Join(i,STR)
{ Compute Ti ⋈ Ti+1 ⋈ · · · ⋈ Tk, creating stream STR containing the result. It is
  assumed that i < k. }
  STR ← ∅
  for (each tuple t in Ti)
     Append to STR each tuple in {t}⊙ Eval((LINK(t)))
  end for
end Ring_Join

Eval(s)
{ Compute σKj=s[Kj](Tj ⋈ · · · ⋈ Tk),
  where s ∈ Tj−1. Note that Kj is an attribute in both Tj−1 and Tj and that if j=k,
  Eval returns σKk=s[Kk](Tk). }
    { temp is a set-valued variable local to Eval }
    temp←∅
    for (each tuple s' on LIST(s))
      if(LINK(s')≠NIL)
        temp ← temp ∪ (s'⊙ Eval(LINK(s')))
      else
        temp ← temp ∪ {s'}
      endif
    end for
    return(temp)
end Eval
```

The algorithm computes $\bowtie \{T_1, \ldots, T_k\}$ when it is invoked with the call Ring_Join(1,STR). Observe that the internal memory requirements (e.g., for local copies of the set *temp*) are no greater than that of the Join algorithm on a heterogeneous file.

Analysis: The following analysis reveals that algorithm Ring_Join is not nearly as efficient as the algorithm that operates on the heterogeneous file structure; however, Ring_Join evaluates the expression $\bowtie \{T_1, \ldots, T_k\}$ more efficiently than does any other algorithm considered that requires only logical structures.

Consider the evaluation of the expression $T_1 \bowtie \cdots \bowtie T_k$ by algorithm Ring_Join. The call Ring_Join(1,STR) results in the algorithm accessing each block of F_1 once, contributing b_1 block accesses. For $2 \leq i \leq k$, each tuple in F_i is retrieved once, and we must assume that each of these retrievals incurs a block access. Hence, the total number of block accesses is

$$b_1+\sum_{i=2}^{k} c_i$$

where b_1 is the number of blocks over which F_1 is stored and c_i is the number of tuples in T_i. In most situations, this compares quite favorably with the efficiency of methods that evaluate the expression as a sequence of binary Joins, assuming standard, homogeneous file structures are used.

It is interesting to compare the efficiency of Ring_Join for the special case in which $k = 2$ with that of other methods requiring only logical structures, namely the Indexed loop join and Merge join of indices. The preceding analysis of Ring_Join implies that when $k = 2$, the number of block accesses the algorithm requires is

$$b_1+c_2$$

The number of block accesses required by the Indexed loop join is

$$b_1+c_1*I_S+c_J$$

By observing that the assumed $1:n$ relationship (with no dangling tuples permitted) between tables T_1 and T_2 implies that $c_2 = c_J$, we can conclude that Ring_Join is the more efficient algorithm—the linking strategy eliminates the $c_1 * I_S$ block accesses incurred by Loop join's index searches.

Consider now a comparison with Merge join of indices. The assumption that neither table has dangling tuples implies that the sizes of Semi-joins appearing in the formula describing Merge join's efficiency are equal to the sizes of the operand relations. Hence, in the current context, the Merge join of indices requires

$$Ib_1+Ib_2+c_1+c_2$$

block accesses. This also is considerably more than the number required by Ring_Join.

Other Considerations:

1. *Queries composing a selection with the joins.* This is the class of queries considered in point 2 for the heterogeneous structure. As in the case of the heterogeneous structure, such queries can be processed efficiently against the ring structure, assuming an appropriate index exists. Note how, in this case, the backpointers from tuples in table T_i to tuples in T_{i-1} help us move back up the hierarchy from the point of the selection.
2. *Queries joining only a subset of the* k *collapsed tables.* This is the class of queries considered in point 3 for the heterogeneous structure. We can

process such queries efficiently simply by invoking Ring_Join on the highest table in the hierarchy appearing in the query (i.e., with the call Ring_Join(i, STR), where T_i is the highest table) and modifying the termination condition so that links are not followed from tuples in the lowest table appearing in the query.

11.6 THE PROBLEM OF COST EVALUATION

Chapter 12 considers the problem of how a query optimizer chooses between the many implementation-level strategies available to it for evaluating a query. A prerequisite to solving this optimization problem is that the query optimizer be able to estimate the cost of executing candidate strategies. In this chapter, we have analyzed several Select and Join algorithms, developing formulas predicting the number of block accesses that these algorithms will require. In all cases, these formulas are functions of the sizes of tables. Note that, applying these formulas, in many cases, requires knowledge not only of the sizes of implementation-level tables stored in the database, but also of the sizes of tables that would be computed in the course of a candidate computation. For example, we have seen that when computing an expression of the form $\bowtie \{T_1, \ldots, T_k\}$, the sizes of the tables that are computed as intermediate results significantly influence the cost of a proposed method.

A critical component of cost evaluation thus is the approximation of table sizes. In this overview, we shall focus on the problem of estimating the following quantities:

- Number of tuples in an implementation-level table.
- Number of tuples satisfying a selection criterion.
- Number of tuples in the result of a Join operation.

Additionally, we shall consider the problems of estimating the number of blocks over which a table is stored and of estimating the number of blocks over which tuples satisfying certain conditions (e.g., $\sigma_{A=v} T$) are stored.

It is not difficult to estimate the size of an implementation-level table. With little overhead, we can maintain an accurate count $C(T)$ of the total number of tuples present in table T, as well as the number of blocks $B(F)$ of file F over which these tuples are spread.

While it is not feasible to predict the sizes of all types of computed results exactly, there exist a wide variety of techniques that allow an optimizer to make fairly good estimates. These methods combine bookkeeping information with statistical techniques to arrive at the required estimates. We consider here some basic examples.

In addition to maintaining a count of the number of tuples currently in an implementation-level table, it is fairly easy to maintain a count of the number $V(A)$ of distinct values present in any attribute A for which we have an index—whenever an update is performed on the table, the index must be updated, and little extra work is then required to maintain the count $V(A)$. We can apply to the values of $V(A)$ and $C(T)$ statistical techniques to estimate the size of a computed table such as $\sigma_{A=v}T$. The simplest statistical model assumes that the values of attribute A are *uniformly distributed* in the sense that if tuple t is chosen at random from the current instance of T, the probability is $1/V(A)$ that $t[A]=v$, for any value v of attribute A currently appearing in table T. Under this assumption, the estimate of the number of tuples in $\sigma_{a=v}T$ is $C(T)/V(A)$.

Statistical models are also employed in estimating the sizes of results when attributes interact. For example, we have seen the need to estimate the size of a result such as

$$\sigma_{(A_1=v_1) \wedge \cdots \wedge (A_k=v_k)} T$$

The simplest statistical model for handling this estimation assumes that attributes take on values *independently* of one another. Under this model, if we estimate the fraction of T that satisfies $\sigma_{A_i=v_i}T$ to be f_i [e.g., under a uniform model, $f_i = 1/V(A_i)$], we then would estimate $f = \Pi_{i=1}^{k} f_i$ to be the fraction of T that satisfies $\sigma_{(A_1=v_1) \wedge \ldots \wedge (A_k=v_k)}T$, and, hence, $f * C(T)$ is our estimate of the number of tuples in this result.

The estimation of the size of a Join proceeds along similar lines. Consider, for example, the expression $T_1 \underset{A=B}{\bowtie} T_2$, and suppose that the values of attribute A in T_1 are uniformly distributed in the sense described previously. Suppose further that each value of attribute B appearing currently in table T_2 is a value appearing currently in attribute A of T_1 and that the values of attribute B are uniformly distributed. That is, if tuple t_2 is chosen at random from the current instance of T_2, the probability is $1/V(A)$ that $t_2[B] = v$, for any value v appearing in attribute A, and is 0 for any other value.

Under these assumptions, the size of the Join $T_1 \underset{A=B}{\bowtie} T_2$ can be estimated as follows. Consider an arbitrary tuple $t_2 \in T_2$, and ask, What is the probability that t_2 "matches" some arbitrary tuple $t_1 \in T_1$; that is, what is the probability that $t_2[B] = t_1[A]$? It follows from our assumptions that this probability is $1/V(A)$. Consequently, we would expect, on average, an arbitrary tuple $t_2 \in T_2$ to match $C(T_1)/V(A)$ tuples of T_1. Hence, since there are $C(T_2)$ tuples in T_2, our estimate of the size of $T_1 \underset{A=B}{\bowtie} T_2$ is $(C(T_1) * C(T_2))/V(A)$.

Most existing commercial optimizers employ relatively simple statistical models such as uniformity and independence. Additionally, researchers have proposed the use of more sophisticated distributions, the relaxation of the independence assumptions, and the maintenance of more extensive bookkeeping information. Other researchers have proposed the use of sampling techniques for estimating the sizes of certain tables. For example, the size of a result such as $\sigma_{A=v}T$ could be estimated by inspecting a small fraction of the tuples in table T and extrapolating the size of the result from the frequency with which attribute A assumes the value v in the sample.

Some modeling techniques bring to bear on the estimation problem certain types of semantic information. To illustrate, we consider the use of functional dependencies in estimating the number of tuples in the computed table

$(\sigma_{A=v_1 \wedge B=v_2} T)$. Under the independence and uniformity model we would estimate this size to be $C(T)/(V(A) * V(B))$. Suppose, however, that the functional dependency $A \rightarrow B$ is known to hold for table T. In this case, the assumption that attributes take on values independently is counterindicated since all tuples t in T with $t[A] = v_1$ have the same value in attribute B. Consequently, either $\sigma_{A=v_1 \wedge B=v_2}(T) = \emptyset$ or $\sigma_{A=v_1 \wedge B=v_2}(T) = \sigma_{A=v_1}(T)$. In the former case, the size of the result is 0, while in the latter case, an appropriate estimate of the size, assuming uniformity of A values, is $C(T)/V(A)$. Observe that we need only inspect a single tuple satisfying $\sigma_{A=v_1}(T)$ to determine whether the size of the result is 0 or if it should be estimated to be $V(A)/C(T)$.

Many of the cost formulas we have encountered require that we estimate not only the number of tuples satisfying a given qualification, but also the number of blocks over which these tuples are spread. Estimating such information requires a second level of statistical modeling. For example, suppose that we wish to estimate the number of blocks of file F over which tuples satisfying $\sigma_{A=v} T$ are spread. If F is maintained ordered or clustered on attribute A, we might estimate this number to be $B(F)/V(A)$. If, on the other hand, the primary structure of F is not based on attribute A, we might assume that tuples satisfying $\sigma_{A=v} T$ are spread uniformly over the blocks of F. In this case, we could estimate the probability that any particular block b contains at least one tuple satisfying $\sigma_{A=v} T$ to be $P_A = (1 - ((V(A)-1)/V(A))^k)$, where k is the average number of records stored per block of file F. Hence, the number of blocks of F that contain at least one tuple satisfying $\sigma_{A=v} T$ would be estimated as $B(F) * P_A$.

We note in closing that even if our information regarding table sizes were perfect, our cost formulas would remain imprecise. For example, the formulas assume that every block read actually incurs a disk access, whereas, in reality, some reads do not require a disk access because the required block already happens to be in internal memory. Estimating the actual number of disk accesses is a complex problem as this number is affected by such factors as system load and the operating system's paging algorithms. Additionally, our formulas equate cost exclusively with block accesses, neglecting internal processing costs. While cost estimation procedures based on techniques such as those described in this chapter indeed are imprecise, they nevertheless are employed in most existing database systems, and it is generally acknowledged that they provide a reasonable basis for the selection of an implementation strategy. It is important to realize that devoting large amounts of time to the optimization of an interactive query often would be counterproductive since the time spent selecting a processing strategy for such a query contributes to response time just as much as does the time spent executing a strategy.

SUMMARY AND ANNOTATED BIBLIOGRAPHY

This chapter considered a variety of methods for implementing the relational algebra operators Select and Join. The methods differ with regard to the structures required for their applicability, properties of their result relations (e.g., Is it sorted?), and, of course, the efficiencies with which they are performed. A theme that emerges in the analysis of the methods is that, in general, one method does not dominate another in all situations. There are crossover points defined in terms of such parameters as table size, distributions of attribute values, layout of tuples on disk, and amount of internal memory available that characterize when one method is preferable to another. Hence, if a query optimizer is to make a good selection of a method, it must have available to it accurate estimates of the values of parameters such as these.

Another class of optimizer decisions characterized by crossover points involves the option to construct, at the time of a query's processing, structures to support that processing. As illustrations of such options, we analyzed a Sort-and-merge strategy and a version of the Grace join algorithm. For such an analysis, crossover points are determined by comparing, with respect to estimated parameter values, the cost of performing the query using existing structures and the cost of building new structures and then using them to process the query. To make such a comparison, the query optimizer, in addition to requiring estimates of the parameters described earlier, requires information regarding the expected future frequencies of queries that could utilize the new structures since, in some cases, it is appropriate to amortize the cost of constructing these structures over future queries.

In addition to considering implementations of single Select and Join operators, we considered special algorithms, and special structures, for implementing expressions containing multiple operations. We saw that when processing an expression containing several Join operators, the query optimizer has many Join trees on which it can base its execution, and the best Join tree depends on factors that include sizes of intermediate results and the existence of storage structures. The query optimizer has also the option of employing techniques, such as pipelining {a technique crucial to System R [Selinger et al. (1979)]} and Semi-join decomposition {as implemented in INGRES [Youssefi and Wong (1979)]}, designed specifically for Multi-join queries. Further, certain specialized storage structures, such as heterogeneous file structures, which efficiently support certain classes of multiple join expressions, should be considered when designing the physical schema.

As already indicated, parameter estimation is a critical component of query optimization. In this chapter, we summarized some basic techniques that make simplistic assumptions regarding the distribution of attribute values. More complex methods include the use of more realistic distributions, the relaxation of the independence assumptions, and the use of more detailed statistics (e.g., histograms) [see Christodoulakis (1983); Lynch (1988); Muralikrishna and DeWitt (1988); Piatetsky-Shapiro and Connell (1984); and Vander Zanden, Taylor, and Button (1986)]. Detailed cost estimation depends not only on the parameter values we have considered but also on issues such as memory contention, which is affected by system load and by the computing environment in general. Some sample formulas for performing such estimation appear in Elmasri and Navathe (1989), Korth and Sieberschatz (1986), Selinger et al. (1979), and Vander Zanden, Taylor, and Button (1986). Studies that support the use of these cost estimation techniques have appeared in Mackert and Lohman (1983) and Swami (1989).

The material presented here sets the stage for the next chapter, where we consider how the query optimizer selects from among the methods available for processing a query. Even given perfect information regarding the existence of storage structures and the values of parameters, the query optimization problem is immensely complex. The prime factor contributing to this complexity is the enormity of the space of candidate processing strategies. The next chapter considers techniques by which a query optimizer searches this space.

EXERCISES

1. Suppose we have a table scheme $T(A,B,C)$, where A is a key, uniquely identifying tuples. T is implemented with three secondary indices and a physically unordered data file. There is a (dense) extensible hashing scheme on A and a B^+-tree on each of B and C. [The sequence set of the B^+-tree on B contains records of the form (b,a), where a is the A value of a tuple that has a B value equal to b; similarly for the B^+-tree on C.]
   We wish to process the following query:

   $$\sigma_{((10 \leq B \leq 50) \wedge (60 \leq C \leq 100))} T$$

   Consider three query processing strategies:
   a. Use the B^+-tree on B and then go into the data file.
   b. Use the B^+-tree on C and then go into the data file.
   c. Use both B^+-trees before going into the data file.

   Under what situations would each of these three strategies be the most appropriate to use? Describe the situations as quantitatively as possible.
2. Suppose table T is stored as a disk file, occupying many thousands of blocks. Suppose that the file is unordered with respect to attribute A but that there is a B-tree indexing attribute A. Consider the range query $\sigma_{v \leq A \leq v'}(T)$.
   a. Describe in words or very high level pseudocode how this query could be processed against the structure described. Estimate the number of block accesses required.
   b. The query optimizer always has the option of creating a new structure before it processes a given query. One option in the preceding case is to create a sorted copy of the data file. Why would we create a sorted copy rather than sorting the original file? Estimate the number of block accesses required to perform the query once the file has been sorted.
   c. Of course, the query optimizer, in choosing a processing strategy, would have to take into account the cost of creating the sorted copy of the data file. Describe the information that the query optimizer

must have available to it in making its decision. Characterize when it would be beneficial to create the sorted copy and when it would be best to perform the range query on the unordered data file.

3. In Section 11.1, we considered strategies for processing partial-match retrievals. One strategy considered was to intersect the pointers of the indices on two of the attributes appearing in the query. More generally, suppose that k attributes $A_1, \ldots, A_k$ appear in the query and that each is indexed. In this case, it might be desirable to intersect the pointers of some subset containing more than two of these indices before accessing the data file. Analyze the trade-off between the number of block accesses required to search indices and the number of data block accesses saved. Mathematically formulate the problem of selecting an optimal subset of indices to intersect, and indicate how the query optimizer might approach this optimization problem.

4. One approach to supporting partial-match retrievals on a table with k attributes utilizes what is known as a **partitioned hash function.** The value $h()$ is a bit string of length n, which is interpreted as an integer index into a hash table $HT[0..2^n - 1]$. Partitioned hash function h is formed by concatenating the bit strings mapped to by hash function $h_1, h_2, \ldots, h_k$. The hash value of tuple t is defined as

$$h(t) = h_1(t[A_1]) \cdot h_2(t[A_2]) \cdot \cdots \cdot h_k(t[A_k])$$

Thus each h_i maps a value of attribute A_i into a bit string of length b_i, such that $\sum_{i=1}^{k} b_i = n$.

Describe how this hash function can be used to support Insert, Delete, and partial-match retrieval operations. Analyze the efficiency of partial match retrievals as a function of the attributes specified in the query. When designing the hash function $h()$, how should we determine the number of bits to allocate to each h_i?

5. Consider the relational query $\sigma_{A=x}(T \bowtie S)$, where A is an attribute of the table T. Describe a situation in which it would be advantageous for the query optimizer to apply the Join *before* applying the Select.

6. In Section 11.4, we described a Pipelined join strategy based on Indexed loop joins. Describe a Pipelined join strategy based on Merge joins. Your strategy should eliminate as much redundant work as possible.

7. Specify a set of values for the parameters c_1, I_S, c_J, b_1, and b_2 such that the Indexed loop join requires fewer block accesses than the Unindexed loop join. Specify a second set of values so that the situation is reversed. Characterize in terms of these parameters when one method should be selected over the other.

8. The presentation of several of the Join algorithms in this chapter assumes that there is enough internal memory to store all the tuples from both operand tables with any single value v in the Join attribute. Which

algorithms rely on this assumption? Describe how each of these algorithms is modified when the assumption is not met. Analyze the effect on efficiency of these modifications.

9. Section 11.3 considers the Sort-and-merge join strategy and compares its efficiency with that of the the Unindexed loop join. Suppose that eight buffers can be allocated to the Sort and Join procedures. Assuming that the operand tables are spread over the same number b of blocks, how large does b need to be before the Sort-and-merge algorithm becomes more efficient than the Unindexed loop join? Reformulate the analysis for the case where the tables are spread over differing numbers of blocks.
10. Compare the Sort-and-merge join strategy with the Indexed loop and Merge join on indices algorithms under the assumption that the structures required by these latter algorithms exist. Derive formulas for the comparisons similar to that used in the previous question.
11. Consider the configuration depicted in Figure 11.1 for building the hash structures in support of the Grace join algorithm. Suppose that the data files being joined contain 1,000,000 data records and that 100 index records can fit per block of storage. How much internal memory must be available to accommodate the configuration? On what other factors does your answer depend?
12. Consider the Semi-join decomposition algorithm of Section 11.4, and suppose that distinct tables T_i and T_j share attributes, even though neither of these tables is the pivot. Describe how the algorithm must be modified for this situation, and analyze the modification's effect on efficiency.
13. Consider the Join algorithm presented in Section 11.5 that operates on a heterogeneous data file. How must the storage structure and algorithm be modified when one or more of the relationships in the hierarchy are $n:m$ rather than $1:n$? How must they be modified when dangling tuples may be present?
14. How must the Join algorithm that operates on a heterogeneous data file be modified to accommodate a situation where, for some t_1 in the root table, internal memory cannot hold simultaneously all tuples t_{ij} from the table T_i $(2 \leq i \leq k)$ such that $t_1 \cdot t_{ij}$ is part of a tuple in the Join? What are the effects on efficiency of these modifications?
15. Describe how links between tuples of tables stored in a heterogeneous data file can speed the processing of the query

$$\sigma_{K_i=V}(T_1 \bowtie T_2 \bowtie \cdots \bowtie T_i \bowtie \cdots \bowtie T_k)$$

16. Describe an algorithm for processing a query that composes two or more selections with the Join expression

$$T_1 \bowtie T_2 \bowtie \cdots \bowtie T_i \bowtie \cdots \bowtie T_k$$

against a heterogeneous data file.

17. Suppose tables $T_1, T_2, \ldots, T_i, \ldots, T_j, \ldots T_k$ are stored in a heterogeneous data file. How must the join algorithm be modified to process the query

$$T_i \bowtie T_{i+1} \cdots \bowtie T_j$$

for $1 \leq i \leq j \leq k$?

18. Given the file structure from exercise 17, how must the Join algorithm be modified to process the query

$$\sigma_{A=v}(T_i) \bowtie T_{i+1} \bowtie \cdots \bowtie T_j$$

19. Describe how the ring structure of Section 11.5 can be maintained in the face of Updates to the underlying tables.

*20. Develop and analyze an assortment of algorithms for implementing the relational operators Union, Difference, and Quotient. Your development should parallel that of this chapter, considering algorithms that are applicable under different assumptions regarding the existence of primary and secondary structures on the operand tables and also considering what specialized structures would support highly efficient implementations. As we did in this chapter for the Join operator, identify crossover points at which one method becomes more efficient than another.

CHAPTER 12

Query Optimization, Part II: The Search Problem

Query optimization is a difficult problem that has been the subject of much research. Our primary goals in this chapter are to define various aspects of the query optimization process and to study several commonly employed query optimization techniques.•

To develop a framework in which we can study the query optimization process, we consider side-by-side two abstraction hierarchies that, together, summarize an RDM implementation (see Figure 12.1). The data-abstraction hierarchy depicts the representations of the data supported by the RDM implementation, while the query-processing hierarchy depicts the translation steps a user query passes through as it is processed. We have studied the maps in the data-abstraction hierarchy extensively in earlier chapters, considering the construction of maps from interface-level to implementation-level tables and from implementation-level tables to file structures. To a lesser extent, we have studied the maps in the query-processing hierarchy. We have considered in Chapter 6 the problem of mapping queries and updates stated against interface-level tables to queries and updates against implementation-level tables, and, in the previous chapter, we have considered mappings from algebraic expressions to implementation-level programs, emphasizing maps from the Join operator to Join

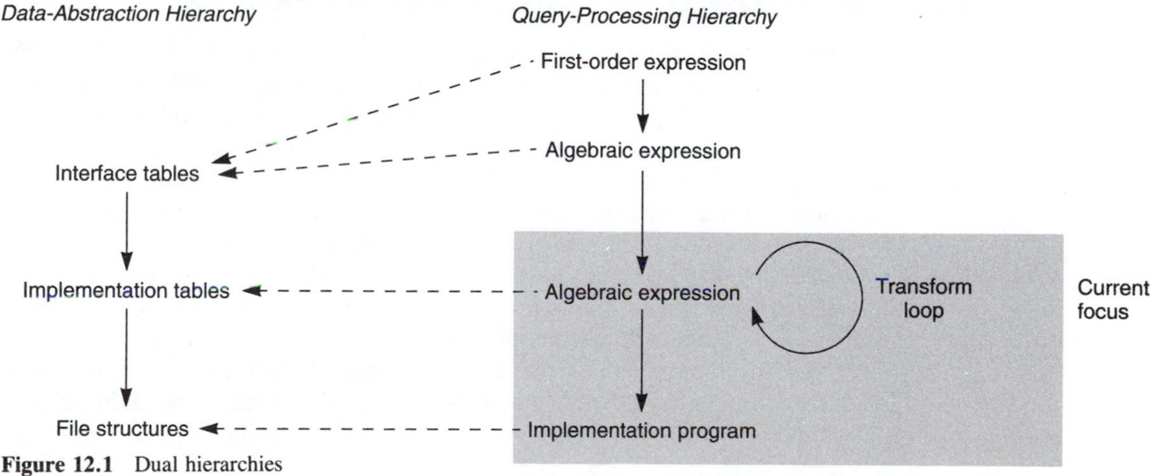

Figure 12.1 Dual hierarchies

implementation algorithms. Additionally, we have briefly considered the transform loop in which one algebraic expression is mapped to another, for example, by applying Join associativity and commutativity.

This chapter focuses primarily on the lower portion of the query-processing hierarchy of Figure 12.1. Here we shall discover algebraic identities that provide the transform loop with many options for mapping one expression to another, and we shall encounter issues that arise when mapping complex expressions containing mixes of Join, Select, and Project operators to implementation-level programs. However, the focus of the chapter is not specific algebraic identities nor specific implementation-level algorithms. Rather, the chapter's focus is *the mapping process itself:* how the maps at various levels of the hierarchy interact, how the collection of maps available to an optimizer defines its search space, how the exploration of the search space is controlled by criteria for selecting which maps to apply, and how candidate processing strategies are evaluated and compared, leading ultimately to the selection of a single mapping of a query to an implementation-level program.

In Section 12.1, we preview the query optimization process by considering abstractly what is involved in optimizing the k-way Natural join query $\bowtie \{T_1, \ldots, T_k\}$. Then, in Section 12.2, we introduce a representation for query-processing strategies at various levels of abstraction and discuss how transformations are used to create alternative processing strategies and to refine high-level processing strategies into implementation-level programs. Section 12.3 considers general techniques for guiding the optimization process by controlling the application of transformations and pruning alternative strategies, and Sections 12.4 and 12.5 focus on specific instances of these techniques. Section 12.6 looks briefly at update processing, while Chapter 13 considers view updating and query processing in the context of "leading-edge" data models.

12.1 AN OVERVIEW OF THE QUERY OPTIMIZATION PROCESS

To preview some of the issues arising in the query optimization process, consider the problem encountered in Section 11.4 of mapping the k-way Natural join expression $\bowtie \{T_1, \ldots, T_k\}$ to an implementation-level program. Our first step was to represent the expression as a graph G containing a node corresponding to each table T_i and a node corresponding to the abstract k-way Join operator. We then selected a map, or sequence of maps, that results in an implementation-level program for evaluating the expression. One possibility—provided that the operand tables obey certain structural assumptions—is to map G directly to an implementation-level program employing the k-way Merge join or Semi-join decomposition algorithm. Alternatively, we can consider the family of maps that refine G into candidate Join trees, each of which specifies a sequence of binary Joins. The collection of candidate Join trees is determined by the laws of algebraic equivalence for the Join operator but may be limited by restrictions on the shapes of the trees the optimizer in question is willing to consider.

Once the candidate Join trees are generated, the next step might be to consider all the implementation-level programs to which each candidate tree can be mapped. That is, for each candidate tree, we might refine its Join operators into Join algorithms, in every possible combination of ways. Then, for each implementation-level program obtained in this manner (and also for the k-way Merge or Semi-join algorithms, if applicable) we would approximate, based on estimates for the relevant parameters (e.g., table sizes), the cost of executing the program. Finally, we could select the implementation-level program with the smallest estimated cost.

Obviously, optimizing the expression $\bowtie \{T_1, \ldots, T_k\}$ as just described requires an enormous effort. Even when k is only moderately large, there is a huge number of trees, a huge number of implementation-level programs for each tree, and the cost evaluating each of these programs is considerable. For these reasons, all practical query optimizers perform some form of heuristic pruning at abstraction levels above implementation-level programs. One type of implicit pruning is to restrict the available maps, thereby reducing the search space *a priori*. For example, System R [Selinger et al. (1979)] will map the graph G to only left-leaning trees, a heuristic based on the preference for executing the Joins in a pipeline. Other optimizers will have available more potential mappings to Join trees but will use heuristic criteria to control the application of these maps. For example, a reasonable heuristic is to avoid, whenever possible, mapping G to a Join tree requiring that a Cartesian product be computed between any pair of tables.

It should be emphasized that the aforementioned pruning rules are heuristics in the sense that they eliminate Join trees, and hence the implementation-level programs to which these trees can map, without performing a detailed cost evaluation. For many typical parameter values (e.g., table sizes) and combinations of storage structures on the tables, the heuristics will eliminate only suboptimal implementation-level programs. In such cases, the optimizer may be able to find an optimal implementation-level program while avoiding a significant fraction of the work required by an exhaustive search. On the other hand, we can specify parameter values and combinations of storage structures that "fool" each of the heuristics mentioned—because the heuristics make their choices without considering these and other implementation-level details, they cannot guarantee that only suboptimal implementation-level programs will be pruned.

Another means of speeding the search is via the application of *exact* optimization techniques that can efficiently solve specific pieces of the query optimization problem. As an example of such a technique, we shall consider in Section 12.5 the dynamic programming algorithm applied by System R to speed its selection of a left-leaning tree and corresponding implementation-level program. This algorithm is of value because even System R's reduced search space, which consists only of programs implementing left-leaning trees, may be too large to search by exhaustive methods. A dynamic programming technique is applied to the search, allowing many left-leaning trees and their implementation-level programs to be eliminated implicitly, while guaranteeing that the optimal program in the search space will be found.

12.2 STRATEGIES GRAPHS: A DYNAMIC REPRESENTATION OF THE SEARCH SPACE

As the next step in studying the query optimization process, we describe a representation for the search space. The literature contains many alternative graph-based representations of queries and their candidate processing strategies; see, for example, Graefe and DeWitt (1987), Jarke and Koch (1984), and Youssefi and Wong (1979). We present here a representation, known as **strategies graphs**, first proposed in Reiner and Rosenthal (1982) and Rosenthal and Charkravarthy (1988), and aspects of our presentation generally follow the perspective espoused in Rosenthal and Charkravarthy (1988). Strategies graphs are particularly compatible with the perspective that the query optimization process consists of a sequence of maps from high-level queries to implementation-level programs. The strategies graph representation also provides an excellent framework for the study of the search techniques employed in the query optimization process. We emphasize at the outset that a query optimizer does not explicitly construct and store strategies graphs; rather, strategies graphs are a convenient tool with which we describe and study an optimizer's behavior.

A strategies graph is a connected, acyclic directed graph $G = (V,E)$. The vertex set V consists of two types of nodes: square nodes representing tables and circular nodes representing operators. Edges in E represent data flow: If table n_1 is an input of operator n_2, then E contains a directed edge emanating from table node n_1 and terminating at operator node n_2. Similarly, if table n_3 results from applying operator n_2 to its inputs, E contains a directed edge emanating from operator node n_2 and terminating at table node n_3. The strategies graphs considered here will always have a single node with no outgoing edges; this **result node** must be a table node and represents the result of the query Q being processed. Further, since all operators have at least one input, only table nodes can have no incoming edges; table nodes without incoming edges are called **base nodes.** Table nodes that are neither base nodes nor the result node are called **intermediate nodes** and represent intermediate results that may be computed in the process of evaluating the query.

Strategies graphs are used to represent, at various levels of abstraction, a query and its alternative processing options. The initial strategies graph of the query optimization process is simply a parsing of the query. For example, Figure 12.2 gives an initial strategies graph for the query $\Pi_{<B,C>}(\sigma_{A=v}(R_1) \bowtie R_2)$. At this level of abstraction, the graph's base nodes are the tables referenced by the query and can be either interface- or implementation-level tables. The operator nodes appearing in graphs at this level of abstraction represent relational

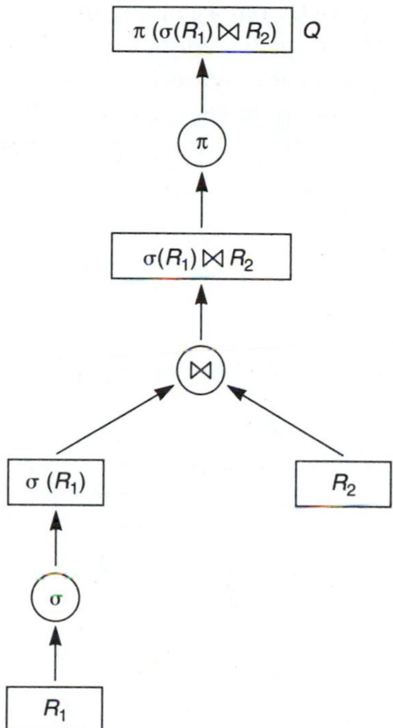

Figure 12.2 Initial strategies graph

operators[1] that, for the sake of this discussion, include *k*-way Join operators, for $k \geq 2$.

The initial strategies graph for a query represents a *single*, high-level strategy. As the query optimization process proceeds, roughly following the path through the query-processing hierarchy shown in Figure 12.1, strategies are added to the graph and, if necessary, are mapped to lower levels of abstraction. In this way, the query optimizer's search space of candidate implementation-level processing strategies eventually is obtained.

We consider now the following questions:

- How are strategies added to a strategies graph?
- How are high-level strategies refined into implementation-level strategies?
- How are alternative strategies evaluated and pruned; that is, how does the search process arrive at its choice for a processing strategy?

As a first step in answering these questions, we describe how a query *Q*'s strategies graph is used to represent alternative strategies for processing *Q*.

[1] Note that, since we assume the initial strategies graph is based on relational operators, we are ignoring here the task of mapping a first-order query (e.g., an SQL query) into a relational expression.

Strategies graph G can compactly represent a multiplicity of candidate processing strategies for its query when we allow some of G's table nodes to have more than one input. For example, Figure 12.3 shows a strategies graph representing two strategies, namely, a strategy that joins R_1 and R_2, applying a selection to the result, and a strategy that applies a selection to R_1 before performing the Join with R_2.

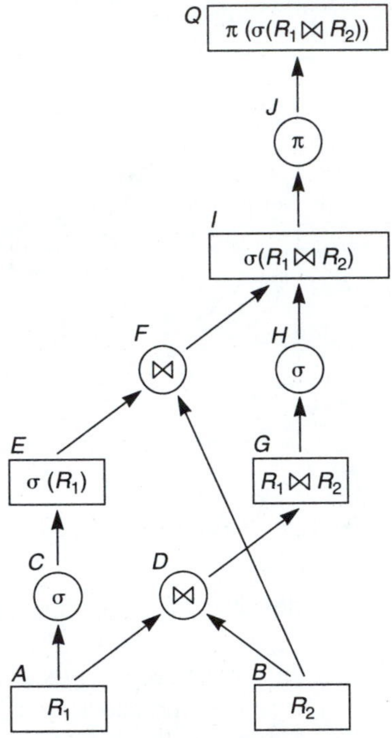

Figure 12.3 Table node with more than one strategy

In general, if any table node of G—be it an intermediate table node or the result node—has more than one input, G represents more than one strategy for obtaining the result node Q. The alternative strategies in G correspond to subgraphs of G with the following structure.

Definition 12.1 A single strategy **embedded** in strategies graph G is any connected subgraph G' of G such that

1. G and G' have the same result node.
2. The base nodes of G' form a subset of the base nodes of G.
3. Each operator node m appearing in G' has in G' all the inputs that it has in G.
4. Each table node of G' has at most one input.

For example, the subgraph of Figure 12.3 induced by the nodes A,B,C,E,F,I,J, and Q is an embedded strategy.

We shall apply the term *embedded strategy* to a subgraph of G that computes an intermediate result, as well as to one that computes the final result Q. When we wish to emphasize that a subgraph computes an intermediate result, we shall use the term **substrategy**; similarly, when we wish to emphasize that a subgraph computes the final result Q, we shall use the term **complete strategy.** For example, the subgraph of Figure 12.3 induced by the nodes A,B,C,E,F, and I is an embedded substrategy for computing the intermediate result $\sigma(R_1 \bowtie R_2)$.

To illustrate these concepts further, consider the partial strategies graph in Figure 12.4, where table nodes n_1 and n_2 are input to operator node m_1 and where table nodes n_3 and n_4 are input to operator node m_2. Each of m_1 and m_2 is the last operation of collections of alternative substrategies for producing the intermediate result n. Observe that if, for each table node $n_i(i = 1,2,3,4)$, the graph contains N_i strategies for obtaining n_i, the graph then contains $(N_1 * N_2) + (N_3 * N_4)$ substrategies for obtaining n. Observe further that each of these substrategies is part of a potentially large number of complete strategies for computing Q. Hence, we see that the number of strategies represented by a strategies graph can grow combinatorially in the size of the graph, where the **size** of a graph is its number of nodes and edges.

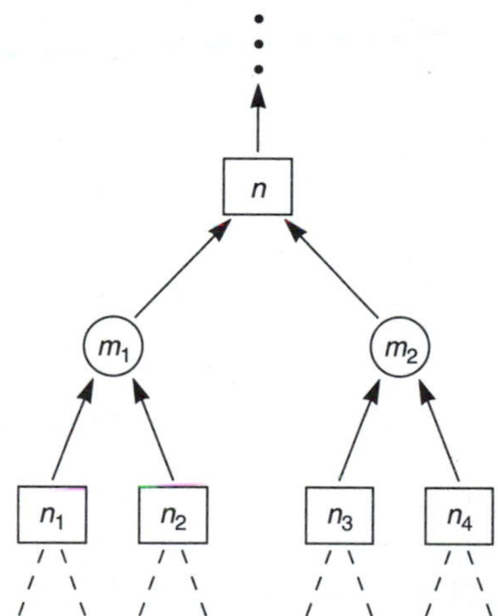

Figure 12.4 Combinatorial explosion in the number of strategies

The result of the query optimization process is the selection of a single strategy from a strategies graph representing the alternative implementation-level strategies available to the optimizer. It is appropriate, however, to view the query optimization process, not as searching a single, static strategies graph, but rather as generating and searching a sequence of strategies graphs. Each member of this sequence of strategies graphs contains at least those implementation-level strategies that were present in previous graphs plus, possibly, newly generated ones. Hence, the final strategies graph in the sequence represents all implementation-level strategies that have been generated throughout the entire process.

The query optimization process generates its sequence of strategies graphs by applying to the graph currently under consideration one of two basic transformation types: **refinement** and **equivalence** transformations. A refinement transformation is applied to a subgraph H of G, replacing H by a subgraph representing computations that are specified at a lower level of abstraction than are the computations represented by H. For example, a refinement might be applied to a subgraph representing a relational operator and its inputs to obtain one or more alternative algorithms for implementing the operator. Figure 12.5*a* depicts a subgraph representing a Join node with inputs T_1 and T_2, while Figure 12.5*b* depicts the refinement of this subgraph into a subgraph representing two alternative Join algorithms.

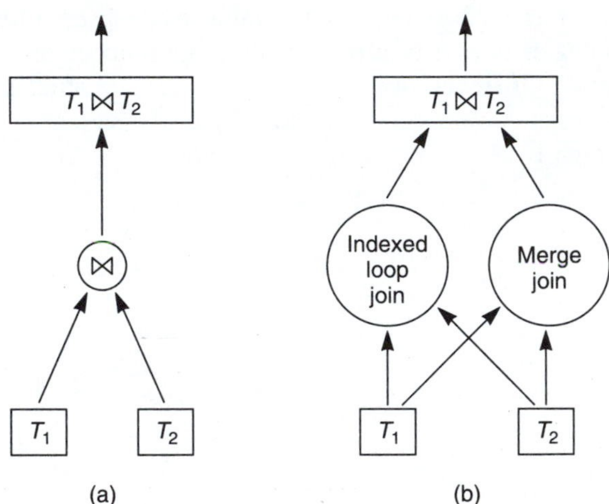

Figure 12.5 (*a*) Algebraic-level Join; (*b*) refined Join

An equivalence transformation can be applied to a (nonbase) table node n of G, provided that G contains at least one strategy S at the level of relational operators for computing the result represented by n. An equivalence transformation is used to create one or more additional strategies for computing n, each of which also is at the level of relational operators. For example, Figure 12.6*a* depicts a strategies graph for the query $\bowtie \{T_1,T_2,T_3,T_4\}$ that represents the single high-level strategy corresponding to the Join association $((T_1 \bowtie T_2) \bowtie (T_3 \bowtie T_4))$. By applying an equivalence transformation to the root of this strategies graph, we can obtain the strategies graph of Figure 12.6*b*, which represents the three strategies corresponding to the associations $((T_1 \bowtie T_2) \bowtie (T_3 \bowtie T_4))$, $(((T_1 \bowtie T_2) \bowtie T_3) \bowtie T_4)$, and $((T_1 \bowtie (T_2 \bowtie T_3)) \bowtie T_4)$. In general, the

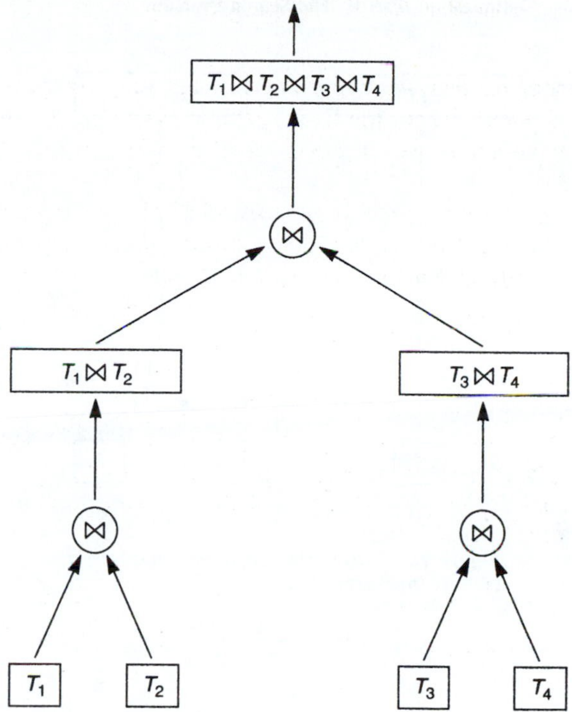

Figure 12.6a Single Join strategy

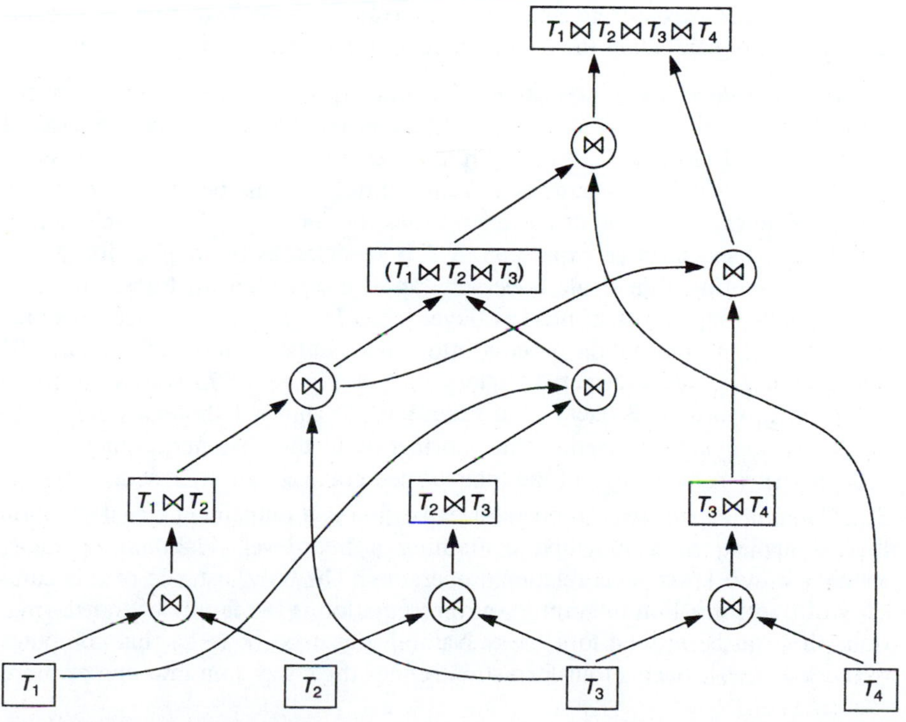

Figure 12.6b Multiple strategies

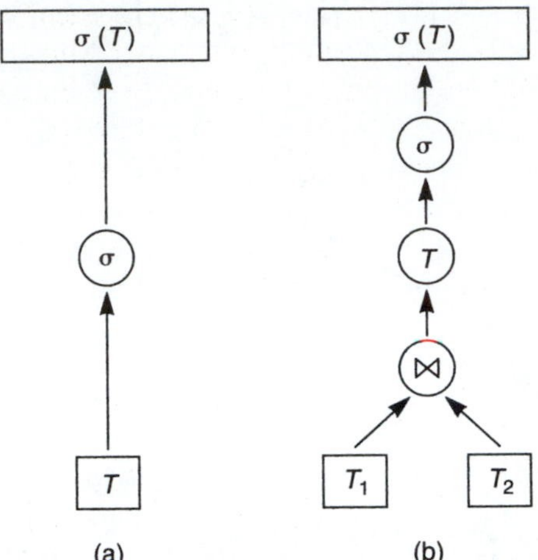

Figure 12.7 (*a*) Initial graph with interface-level table *T*; (*b*) *T* expanded

validity of equivalence transformations follows from equivalences in the relational algebra, such as those discussed in Section 12.4.

It is useful to group refinement and equivalence transformations into categories roughly paralleling the query processing hierarchy of Figure 12.1.

1. *Interface-level table expansion* (also known as *view expansion*): As described earlier, the base nodes of query *Q*'s initial strategies graph correspond to the tables *Q* references. When *Q* references a table *T* that exists only as an interface-level table, *G*'s base node representing *T* must be expanded into a subgraph representing one or more strategies for deriving *T* from implementation-level tables. Such an expansion of *T* is modeled as the application to the node representing *T* (a single node subgraph) of a refinement transformation. For example, suppose that interface-level table $T(A,B,C,D)$ has been decomposed by the normalization process into implementation-level tables $T_1(A,B)$ and $T_2(A,C,D)$, and consider the query $\sigma_{A=v} T$. Figure 12.7*a* shows an initial strategies graph for this query, and Figure 12.7*b* shows a strategies graph obtained by applying a refinement transformation to the base node representing *T*. Note that *T* remains part of the transformed graph, as an intermediate result.

2. *Operator expansion:* An operator expansion is a refinement transformation that is applied to a subgraph containing a high-level relational operator, refining it into lower level relational operators. The only instance of this category of transformation relevant to our presentation is the family of transformations that can be applied to a *k*-way Natural join node ($k > 2$) that computes $\bowtie \{T_1, \ldots, T_k\}$. Such a transformation refines the *k*-way Join into one or more

strategies for computing $\bowtie \{T_1, \ldots, T_k\}$, where each strategy consists of a sequence of binary Joins plus, possibly, a smaller Multi-way join. In particular, each of these strategies consists of a sequence of binary Joins producing an intermediate result $W_1 \bowtie \cdots \bowtie W_s$, for some subset $\{W_1, \ldots, W_s\} \subseteq \{T_1, \ldots, T_k\}$ of the k tables. If $s < k$, this intermediate result is an operand, along with the remaining $(k - s)$ tables, of a $k - (s - 1)$-way Join that produces the result $\bowtie \{T_1, \ldots, T_k\}$. For example, a refinement transformation applied to the strategies graph of Figure 12.8*a* might produce the strategies graph of Figure 12.8*b*, which gives two alternative strategies for computing $T_1 \bowtie T_2 \bowtie T_3 \bowtie T_4 \bowtie T_5$: One strategy joins T_1 and T_2, then joins the result $T_1 \bowtie T_2$ with T_3, and then performs the three-way Join $\bowtie \{(T_1 \bowtie T_2 \bowtie T_3), T_4, T_5\}$; the other strategy joins T_4 and T_5, then joins the result $T_4 \bowtie T_5$ with T_3, and then performs the three-way Join $\bowtie \{(T_3 \bowtie T_4 \bowtie T_5), T_1, T_2\}$. Of course, the three-way Join in each strategy may itself later be refined.

3. *Strategy augmentation:* A strategy augmentation is an equivalence transformation applied to a (nonbase) table node T of G to create one or more alter-

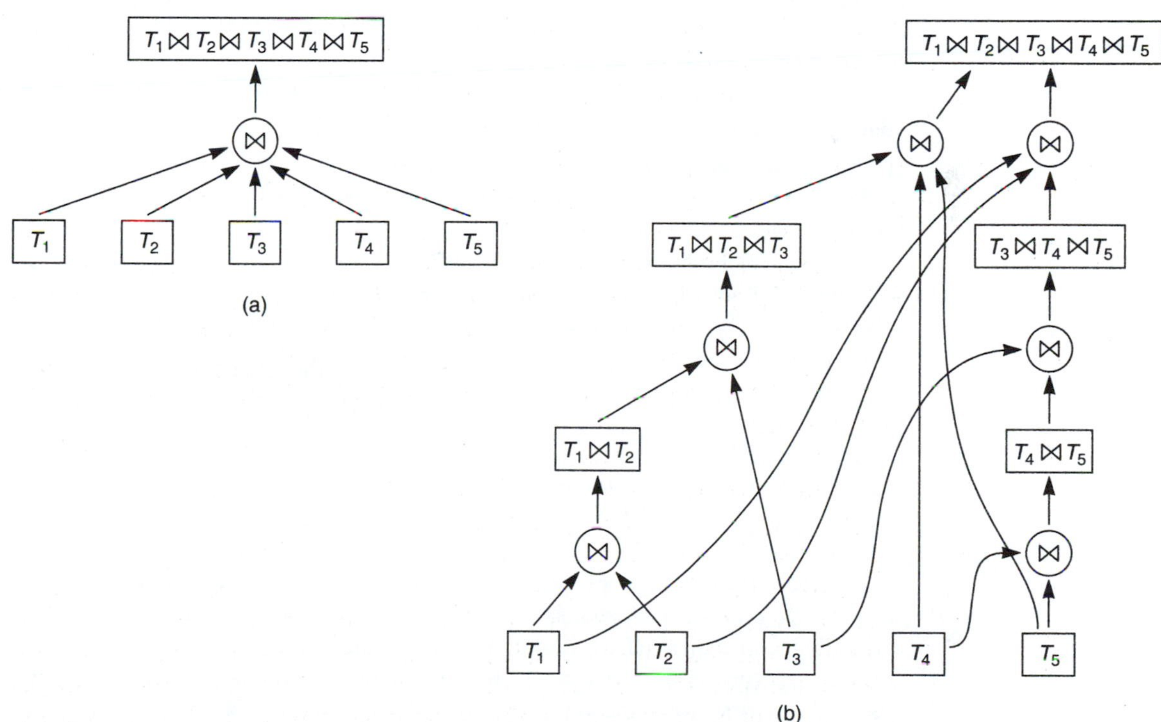

Figure 12.8 (*a*) Five-way node; (*b*) sequences of three-way and binary Joins

native subgraphs that compute T. In the context of our presentation, we shall assume that the strategies represented by the additional subgraphs are obtained by applying laws of algebraic equivalences to one of G's existing strategies S. Hence, this original strategy S, and the strategies added by the transformation, are at the level of relational operators. Figure 12.6 gave an example of such a transformation. Algebraic equivalences that support this category of transformation are discussed in Section 12.4.

4. *Subgraph implementation:* A subgraph implementation is a refinement transformation that is applied to a subgraph H of G to obtain one or more strategies for implementing the algebraic-level strategies represented by H. Figure 12.5 gave an example of such a transformation. Note that, since many of the implementation algorithms we have considered are applicable only when certain conditions are met (e.g., certain structures exist on the files implementing the operand tables), an optimizer can apply such a transformation only after verifying that its applicability conditions are satisfied.

While these broad categories of transformations can be used to describe the process of query optimization in general, particular query optimizers differ with respect to the specific transformations they support. For example, all the transformations that the System R optimizer can apply to refine a k-way Join operator produce left-leaning Join trees; further, this optimizer includes no equivalence transformations that will generate Join trees that are not left-leaning. In contrast, the optimizer of INGRES [Youssefi and Wong (1979)] includes transformations that map a k-way Join operator into Join trees of various shapes, as well as into the Semi-join decomposition algorithm. Generally speaking, optimizers differ both with regard to the sets of algebraic expressions they will consider for a given query and the algorithms they provide for implementing the algebraic operators.

We have been using informally the term *search space* to refer to the set of candidate implementation-level strategies from which an optimizer makes its selection. The following is a more precise definition.

Definition 12.2 Let Q be a query stated against the interface-level RDM $\mathcal{R}$. The (implementation-level) **search space** $QO(Q)$ of optimizer QO for query Q is the set

$$QO(Q)=\{S \mid S \text{ is an implementation-level program for computing } Q \text{ that } QO \text{ will select in the context of at least one implementation and instance of RDM } \mathcal{R}\}$$

This definition of an optimizer's search space highlights the fact that the strategy the optimizer ultimately selects to process a particular query is generally influenced by the RDM's implementation and current instance (e.g., what storage structures exist, how many tuples are present in each table). Not only can such factors affect the optimizer's evaluation of the candidate strategies, but these factors may partially determine which candidate implementation-level strategies an optimizer considers at all. In particular, it may be the case that, in the context of a given implementation and instance of the RDM, optimizer *QO does not even consider* some of the implementation-level processing strategies that it considers in the context of other implementations and instances. For example, in the presence of certain storage structures and table sizes, the heuristic search strategy of an optimizer may suppress the application of certain equivalence transformations, thereby making unreachable one or more candidate implementation strategies. We thus see that the strategies an optimizer *QO* will consider for processing a query *Q* depend on *QO*'s "innate" search space *QO*(*Q*), *QO*'s search strategy, and the interaction between *QO*'s search strategy and the RDM's implementation and current instance.

We again contrast System R and INGRES to illustrate some of these points. Figure 12.9 depicts the relationship between the search spaces SysR(*Q*) and INGRES(*Q*) for a query *Q* of the form $\bowtie \{T_1, \ldots, T_k\}$. The figure illustrates that each of the search spaces has strategies not in the other search space and that there are strategies common to both search spaces. In addition to differing on the definitions of their innate search spaces for many queries, the optimizers differ with regard to how they search their search spaces. The search strategy of System R is based, in part, on the dynamic programming algorithm that we consider in Section 12.5 and is able to guarantee[2] that, for any query *Q*, it will

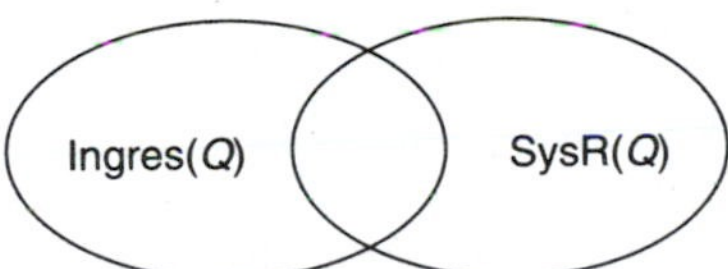

Figure 12.9 Venn diagram

find an optimal strategy from among the strategies in SysR(*Q*). The dynamic programming algorithm is able to find an optimal strategy without performing an exhaustive search of SysR(*Q*)—the algorithm safely prunes many strategies without considering them explicitly; that is, the algorithm infers that many strategies are suboptimal while considering them only **implicitly.** From the perspective of the discussion following Definition 12.2, when *Q* is of the form $\bowtie \{T_1, \ldots, T_k\}$, System R always considers all members of SysR(*Q*)—although some members may be considered only implicitly—and hence is able to produce an optimal member of SysR(*Q*).

In contrast to System R, INGRES employs a search strategy that is not guaranteed, for an arbitrary *Q*, to find an optimal strategy from among INGRES(*Q*). INGRES employs a sophisticated version of a greedy search heuristic that, at each point in the query optimization process, applies only the most attractive transformation to a strategies graph. INGRES's measure of at-

[2] The optimality guarantee is with respect to estimated cost; that is, if cost estimates are inaccurate, the strategy selected may not be the most efficient to execute.

tractiveness generally depends on features of the RDM's implementation and current instance. Hence, in the context of a given RDM implementation and instance, INGRES may not consider—either implicitly or explicitly—certain members of INGRES(Q) and, consequently, may miss the optimal strategy in INGRES(Q).

It must be emphasized that the guarantee of optimality provided by System R does not translate to a guarantee that System R will find a strategy for processing a given query Q that is at least as good as the strategy INGRES finds for processing Q. It is clear from Figure 12.9 that even if INGRES fails to find an optimal strategy from among the strategies in INGRES(Q), it nevertheless may find a strategy better than all strategies in SysR(Q). Another point to consider when comparing query-processing search strategies is that the search for a strategy generally is performed "online," that is, at the time a user query is encountered. Hence, if the goal is to minimize overall **response time**, that is, the time elapsed from when the query is encountered to when the result is obtained, the time required to perform the search for a processing strategy must be considered along with the cost of executing the strategy selected. Of course, if the same queries are likely to be encountered many times in the course of an application, it may be worthwhile to spend a relatively large amount of time finding a processing strategy that can be stored for repeated use.

12.3 SEARCHING AND PRUNING

We now expand some of the points raised by the previous discussion. In this section, we shall describe four critical components of a query optimizer: the transformations available to the optimizer, the optimizer's methods for determining which transformations to apply, the optimizer's methods for pruning high-level processing strategies, and the optimizer's methods for pruning suboptimal implementation-level programs. These optimizer components combine to determine the optimizer's search space, the portion of the search space that is considered in a given situation, and the efficiency with which the search is performed.

Available Transformations

An optimizer cannot and should not include in its repertoire every possible equivalence and refinement transformation. One reason is that, when processing a query, there is time to consider only a fraction of the transformations that are applicable theoretically. Further, in the case of operator refinement transformations, each algorithm to which an operator can map requires implementation software (e.g., if an optimizer can refine a Join operator to a Merge join algorithm, the Merge join routine must be part of the optimizer's software), and a practical limit must be placed on the size and complexity of the query optimizer.

The equivalence transformations made available to the optimizer determine the algebraic-level strategies that can be considered for processing a query Q, and the refinement transformations made available determine the programs that can be considered for implementing these strategies. Hence, when we construct an optimizer, we hardwire into it heuristic decisions regarding which transformations are likely to be the most beneficial—the search space $QO(Q)$ is restricted *a priori* based on these heuristics. An example of such *a priori* heuristics is System R's insistence on left-leaning Join trees: Every k-way Join will be refined to a left-leaning Join tree, and every implementation-level program computes the Join in a pipeline.

Which Transformations to Apply

When searching for a strategy for processing query Q, an optimizer QO typically will not consider every strategy in $QO(Q)$. One way to control the members of $QO(Q)$ that are considered in a given context is by controlling which of the available transformations are applied to the strategies graph in this context.

Often, rules for controlling the application of transformations take the form of precedence lists. The following are some simple examples of such control rules:

```
{ Rule for expanding a k-way join operator to a sequence of k − 1 joins.
  Note that the rule depends only on the structure of the query and hence
  influences the definition of QO(Q). }
if (there exist join trees not requiring any Cartesian products)
  apply all available transformations which refine the operator to such trees
elseif (there exist join trees requiring one Cartesian product)
  apply all available transformations that refine the operator to such trees
elseif (there exist join trees requiring two Cartesian products)
  apply all available transformations which refine the operator to such trees
...
elseif ...
...
endif
{ Rule for expanding the three-way join operator. Note that the rule depends on
  the existence of certain implementation-level structures. }
if (any pair of the tables is stored physically sorted on their join attributes)
  apply available transformations that refine the operator to a sequence of joins
    that associate together such a pair
elseif (any pair of the tables is clustered on their join attributes)
  apply available transformations that refine the operator to a sequence of joins
    that associate together such a pair
...
elseif ...
...
endif
{ Rule for implementing the join T1 ⋈ T2. Note that the rule depends
  on the existence of certain implementation-level structures. }
if (T1 and T2 are stored physically sorted on their join attributes)
  map the join operator to merge join
```

```
elseif (T1 and T2 are stored clustered on their join attributes)
  map the join operator to cluster join
elseif (T1 and T2 have ordered index on their join attributes)
  map the join operator to merge join on indices
...
elseif ...
...
endif
```

In most cases, such rules affect the subset of $QO(Q)$ that is searched in a given context but, by themselves, do not affect the composition of $QO(Q)$. An exception are rules (such as the first rule) that depend only on the structure of the query. Such rules do influence the composition of $QO(Q)$ since they influence the transformations that are to be applied to a particular query, independent of the RDM's implementation and instance.

Other types of rules for controlling the application of transformations take the form of nonmutually exclusive prioritizations of transformations. For example, such a rule might be to apply equivalence transformation A before equivalence transformation B, but once the strategies obtained from transformation A are pursued (e.g., mapped to programs and evaluated), the rule, under certain conditions, directs the optimizer to apply transformation B. Depending on other aspects of the search strategy (e.g., the optimizer's conditions for terminating the search), such prioritization can affect both the speed of the search and the portion of $QO(Q)$ that is searched.

Algebraic-Level Heuristic Pruning

Once we apply equivalence transformations to obtain a collection of algebraic-level strategies for computing an intermediate table n, we must decide how fully to pursue each of these candidate strategies. Fully pursuing a candidate algebraic-level strategy requires that we use refinement transformations to map in all possible ways supported by the optimizer the strategy to implementation-level programs and that we evaluate each of these programs. Control rules discussed earlier may restrict the programs considered, but often we wish additional types of restrictions. We discuss here restrictions that take the form of algebraic-level pruning rules.

Based on heuristic criteria, an optimizer may decide to prune candidate algebraic-level strategies without even considering any programs that implement the strategies. To see how pruning at the algebraic level is modeled by a strategies graph, consider the subgraph given in Figure 12.10, which represents several strategies for computing the intermediate n. Suppose that, after performing some analysis (e.g., analysis based on table sizes and the existence of structures), the optimizer concludes that it is unlikely that an optimal strategy for computing Q will compute the intermediate n using a program implementing a high-level strategy that applies operator m_1 or m_2 as its last step. In this case, the optimizer may **prune** all such strategies by cutting the edges (m_1,n) and (m_2,n).

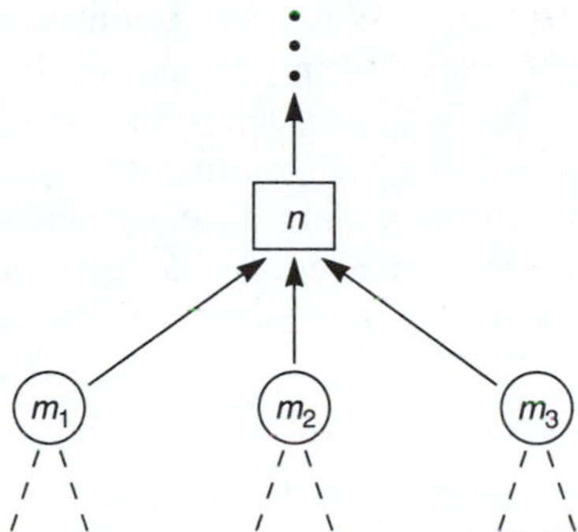

Figure 12.10 Table node n produced by operators m_1 m_2, and m_3

The pruning of algebraic-level strategies can significantly affect the portion of $QO(Q)$ that the optimizer considers. The effect of such pruning is potentially great because of a compounding of combinatorial effects:

1. Combinatorial pruning of algebraic-level strategies: The intermediate result n may be used in many different strategies for computing Q. Suppose, for example, that before pruning, G contains N algebraic-level strategies that use intermediate result n in their computations of Q. If we prune p out of the w high-level strategies G contains for computing n, the effect is to eliminate a total of $(p/w) * N$ high-level strategies for computing Q.
2. Combinatorial pruning of implementation-level programs: Each strategy pruned potentially could have been refined to many implementation-level programs. Note that this number is large also because of combinatorial effects—each algebraic operator can be implemented with several different algorithms, and, therefore, there is a large number of ways to combine these algorithms to form implementation-level programs. Consequently, pruning algebraic-level strategies may preempt the consideration of many of the strategies in $QO(Q)$.

Rules for pruning at the algebraic-level are generally heuristic in nature in that they cannot guarantee that a pruned strategy would not lead to an optimal member of $QO(Q)$. Certainly, the more information a pruning rule utilizes regarding such factors as table sizes and storage structures, the "safer" the rule will be; however, only in extreme cases (e.g., the expected size of intermediate results are orders of magnitude larger using one algebraic-level strategy than another) can a pruning rule, without considering alternative implementations and evaluating costs, make an optimality guarantee.

We note as a modeling issue that pruning high-level strategies and controlling the application of transformations are closely related. In many cases, a particular action of an optimizer could be modeled either as the pruning of an algebraic-level strategy or as a decision not to apply an equivalence transformation that generates this strategy. While an optimizer might implement many algebraic-level pruning heuristics simply by not applying certain equivalence transformations, it nevertheless is instructive to consider the perspective that the transformation is applied and the resulting strategies pruned. The pruning perspective is often illuminating because it clearly models the effect on the portion of $QO(Q)$ that is searched as a result of a decision not to pursue an algebraic-level strategy. In short, it is convenient to have both modeling tools available.

Searching at the Implementation Level

A strategy at the implementation-level is composed of a collection of algorithms that implement algebraic operators. In the previous chapter, we considered the problem of estimating the cost that would be incurred by applying an implementation-level algorithm to its inputs. In the following discussion, we shall proceed under the assumptions that good cost estimates can be obtained, and we define as follows the cost of an implementation-level strategy that is embedded in a strategies graph.

> **Definition 12.3** The **cost of an operator node** (at the implementation level) is the cost of applying to its inputs the operator's specified implementation-level algorithm. The **cost of a strategy** (at the implementation level) is the sum of the costs of its operator nodes.

For example, Figure 12.11 depicts a strategies graph at the implementation level, where we have included in each operator node a cost estimate in terms of some standard unit (e.g., block accesses). From these estimates, we calculate the cost of each strategy embedded in G: The strategy that performs the Join before the Select has cost 120, while the strategy that performs the Select before the Join has cost 50.

The straightforward way to search an implementation-level strategies graph is to individually evaluate each embedded strategy and compare the costs. Unfortunately, this can be quite a time-consuming process, and the approach often is infeasible. The source of the infeasibility is the combinatorial explosion in the number of implementation-level strategies that may be present. Observe that while prior steps in the query optimization process (e.g., prior applications of equivalence and refinement transformations) may have created an implementation-level strategies graph with a reasonably small number of nodes and edges, the combinatorial effect of combining different programs for computing the intermediate results in many possible ways potentially creates a huge number of implementation-level programs. In general, a strategies graph can contain a number of strategies that is *exponential* in its number of nodes and edges. Consequently, even if a strategies graph is obtained by applying a relatively small number of transformations, it may contain an enormous number of embedded implementation-level programs, making it infeasible to explicitly evaluate each one individually.

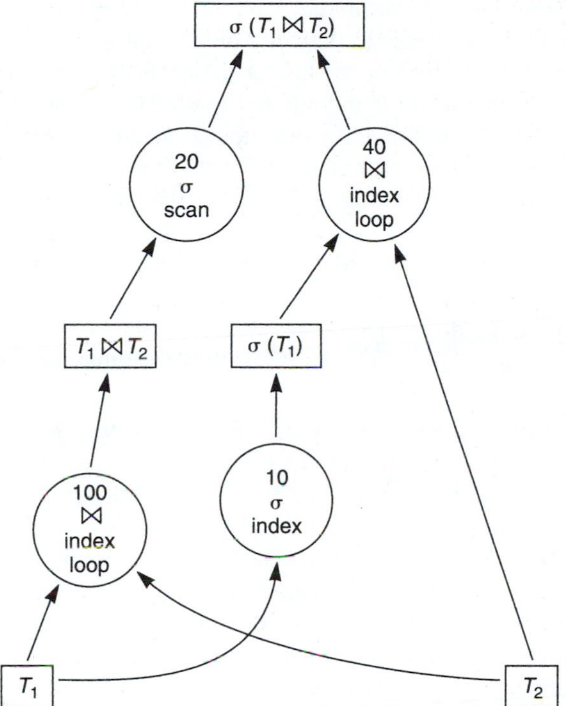

Figure 12.11 Implementation-level graph with operator costs

In an attempt to avoid the explicit consideration of every embedded strategy, optimizers employ a variety of techniques for searching an implementation-level strategies graph. These techniques include

1. *Bounding techniques:* Suppose that we have evaluated a complete strategy *S*, calculating its total cost to be Cost(*S*). As we evaluate the cost of other strategies, we may find that the cost of every substrategy that computes some intermediate result *n* exceeds Cost(*S*). In this case, it is clear that an optimal strategy cannot compute *n*, and hence all strategies that do compute *n* can be pruned safely. This pruning is modeled by cutting all edges emanating from each operator node that takes *n* as input. While such pruning is **safe** (it will not eliminate an optimal strategy) and potentially eliminates many strategies, the required cost condition is likely to be satisfied by only a few intermediate results. The question arises also of how to obtain a good complete strategy to play the role of *S*; the following discussion suggests the use of heuristics to obtain quickly a reasonably good strategy that can then be used in bounding comparisons. Of course, any time the search generates a complete strategy that is better than the current best strategy, this new strategy can be used in future bounding comparisons.

2. *Dynamic programming techniques:* While bounding techniques compare the costs of complete strategies to the costs of substrategies, dynamic programming algorithms compare with one another the costs of substrategies that compute some intermediate result n and attempt to conclude that all but the cheapest can be pruned. As with bounding techniques, when a substrategy is pruned, a large number of complete strategies for Q are often pruned also. The limitation of the dynamic programming technique is that the pruning it employs is safe only when strategies are restricted to a certain form; otherwise, a pruned strategy actually might be part of the optimal strategy, and pruning it will cause the optimizer to select a suboptimal strategy. Despite this limitation in its applicability, dynamic programming remains one of the most powerful search techniques available. Section 12.5 studies dynamic programming in more detail.

3. *Heuristic search techniques:* Like algebraic-level pruning heuristics, implementation-level pruning heuristics can speed the search but are not guaranteed to allow the optimizer to find an optimal strategy. For example, we might relax the bounding rule so that it applies whenever we find that the cost of the best strategy for computing intermediate table node n is 90 percent or more of the best complete strategy found to date. While this approach has intuitive appeal, it is easy to see that it could prune an optimal strategy. Other types of heuristics are employed to determine in what order strategies should be evaluated. There are several motivations for evaluating promising strategies early in the search process, including

a. Obtaining a good strategy S may allow bounding rules to prune many strategies.

b. Often, an optimizer will spend only a fixed amount of time on the search before it terminates, selecting the best strategy it has found so far. For example, INGRES employs a heuristic that correlates the time it will spend searching for a strategy with its estimate of the query's complexity. The rationale for this approach is that a simple query will be processed with acceptable efficiency by any reasonable strategy, and, hence, in this case, relatively little time should be devoted to the search for a strategy.

We note that in an attempt to simplify our discussion, we may have given the impression that an optimizer applies a sequence of transformations to a strategies graph strictly following the hierarchy depicted in Figure 12.1. One consequence of this simplification is that we tend to view each graph as consisting of strategies at a single level of abstraction. For example, we have described the problem of searching an implementation-level strategies graph after all algebraic-level strategies have been refined into implementation-level strategies. The overall optimization process, however, is somewhat more complex than this since, generally, there is an interleaving of equivalence transformations, refinement transformations, and the evaluation of implementation-level programs. For example, an equivalence transformation might be applied to obtain a new algebraic-level strategy S for computing the intermediate result T. A refinement transformation might next be applied to obtain from S one or more implementation-level strategies. These new implementation-level programs might be evaluated immediately, and these evaluations might in turn affect the application of future equivalence transformations if, for example, the evaluations allow for the implicit pruning of certain members of the search space. That is, in some cases, it is possible, based on pruning at the implementation level, to suppress the future generation, refinement, and evaluation of certain algebraic-level strategies.

We now have presented an overview of how general-purpose combinatorial optimization techniques can be applied to the query optimization problem; in the next two sections, we consider specific instances of these techniques. Section 12.4 considers specific algebraic equivalences that support equivalence transformations and considers heuristics for controlling the application of such transformations and for pruning algebraic-level strategies. Section 12.5 then considers specific methods for choosing between implementation-level strategies. In particular, the section illustrates the dynamic programming search technique.

12.4 EQUIVALENCE TRANSFORMATIONS AND ALGEBRAIC-LEVEL PRUNING HEURISTICS

As defined previously, an equivalence transformation is applied to a table node T of strategies graph G and creates one or more alternative strategies for computing T. We assume that the new strategies $S_1, \ldots, S_i, \ldots, S_k$ are at the level of relational expressions and are obtained by applying laws of algebraic equivalence to an existing algebraic-level strategy S. The motivation for adding to a strategies graph those strategies logically equivalent to existing strategies is the possibility that at least one of the new strategies will be more efficiently implementable than any existing strategy. For example, we have seen that the expression $(((T_1 \bowtie T_2) \bowtie T_3) \bowtie T_4)$ might be more efficiently implementable than the logically equivalent expression $((T_1 \bowtie T_2) \bowtie (T_3 \bowtie T_4))$ because of factors such as the ability to compute the expression in a pipeline, favorably sized intermediate results and the availability of structures to support the Joins. It is important to emphasize that, in general, we cannot determine positively that one algebraic-level strategy is more efficiently implementable than another without mapping to and evaluating the programs that can implement the algebraic-level strategies.

The most common class of equivalence transformations is based on **logical equivalences** between relational expressions.

Definition 12.4 Expressions E and E' are **logically equivalent** (denoted $E \equiv_L E'$) if, for every instance of the underlying RDM, the expressions have the same value.

For example, the commutativity and associativity of the Natural join operator allow us to write for all tables T_1, T_2, and T_3,

$$T_1 \bowtie T_2 \equiv_L T_2 \bowtie T_1$$
$$((T_1 \bowtie T_2) \bowtie T_3) \equiv_L (T_1 \bowtie (T_2 \bowtie T_3))$$

Note that the first equivalence holds under the tuple-as-function definition of a table, where column order is immaterial.

A second useful class of equivalence transformation is based on a weaker type of equivalence, known as **semantic equivalence.** Semantic equivalence is defined with respect to a collection of integrity constraints (e.g., functional dependencies, multivalued dependencies, and constraints on the values an attribute can assume) associated with the RDM's table schemes.

> **Definition 12.5** Expressions E and E' are **semantically equivalent** with respect to integrity constraints *IC* (denoted $E \equiv_{S(IC)} E'$) if, for every instance of the underlying RDM *that obeys IC*, the expressions have the same value.

Suppose, for example, that the restriction

$$(\text{Dept} = \text{Toys}) \Rightarrow (\text{Salary} < 30{,}000)$$

is among the integrity constraints *IC* known to apply to table scheme EMPLOYEE(Emp#, Dept, Salary). Then

$$\sigma_{(Salary<50{,}000) \wedge (Dept=\text{"}Toys\text{"})}(EMPLOYEE) \equiv_{S(IC)} \sigma_{(Salary<30{,}000) \wedge (Dept=\text{"}Toys\text{"})}(EMPLOYEE)$$

is a valid semantic equivalence.

Transformations that add new strategies based on semantic equivalences are more difficult to implement than are logical equivalence-based transformations, but they often provide powerful optimization opportunities. In the following, we explore transformations based on both types of equivalences. As we consider the equivalence transformations themselves, we also consider heuristics for controlling their application and for pruning alternatives at the algebraic level.

For brevity, we consider only Joins, Cartesian products, Selects, and Projects. Similar equivalences exists for the other relational operators, but in this brief introduction to the topic, we can only hope to present the reader with the flavor of the optimization opportunities and issues that exist at the algebraic level.

Join and Product Manipulations

We already have discussed the commutativity and associativity properties of the Natural join operator. Under certain conditions, these properties apply as well to the Equi-join and Cartesian product operators and also to expressions containing mixes of these operators.

In the following, $\bigcirc$ denotes either the Natural join, Equi-join, or Cartesian product operator. When more than one $\bigcirc$ appears in the same expression, each occurrence may denote a different operator.

Commutativity: For any tables T_1, T_2, T_3 we have that

$$T_1 \bigcirc T_2 \equiv_L T_2 \bigcirc T_1$$

Two comments are required:

1. As noted earlier for the Natural join, the equivalence is valid under the tuple-as-function definition of a table.
2. When $\bigcirc$ denotes an Equi-join operator, there is an associated condition of the form $A = B$, where A is an attribute of T_1 and B is an attribute of T_2. When we apply commutativity, the expression must be flipped to $B = A$; that is, in the case of Equi-join, the commutativity equivalence is

$$T_1 \underset{A=B}{\bowtie} T_2 \equiv_L T_2 \underset{B=A}{\bowtie} T_1$$

Associativity: If an expression contains only Natural join and Cartesian product operators, the following is a valid logical equivalence:

$$((T_1 \bigcirc T_2) \bigcirc T_3) \equiv_L (T_1 \bigcirc (T_2 \bigcirc T_3))$$

It is important to observe that some Natural joins can become, in effect, Cartesian products. For example, suppose that the preceding $\bigcirc$ operators are Natural joins and that T_1 shares attributes with T_2 and T_3, but that T_2 and T_3 share no attributes. In this case, the expression on the left avoids Cartesian products (both Natural joins involve tables that share attributes), while the Join $T_2 \bowtie T_3$ in the expression on the right in effect is a Cartesian product since no attributes are common to T_2 and T_3. Many heuristics eliminate from consideration (either by suppressing transformation or by pruning) an expression in which Natural joins are performed between tables sharing no attributes whenever alternatives not requiring such Joins are available.

When the Equi-join operator is present, the logical equivalences are a bit more complex. In Section 11.4, we illustrated that blindly applying associativity could lead to syntactically incorrect expressions. For example, the expression

$$((T_1 \underset{A=B}{\bowtie} T_2) \underset{C=D}{\bowtie} T_3)$$

is syntactically correct if T_1 contains attributes A and C, T_2 contains attribute B but not attribute C, and T_3 contains attribute D. Observe, however, that, in this case, the expression

$$(T_1 \underset{A=B}{\bowtie} (T_2 \underset{C=D}{\bowtie} T_3))$$

is syntactically incorrect since C is not in T_2. Hence, we can apply associativity only when the attribute referenced by the second Equi-join is in T_2.

Similar considerations apply when an expression contains combinations of the Equi-join and Natural join (or Cartesian product) operators. For example, the expression

$$((T_1 \bowtie T_2) \underset{C=D}{\bowtie} T_3)$$

is equivalent to the expression

$$(T_1 \bowtie (T_2 \underset{C=D}{\bowtie} T_3))$$

provided that C is contained in T_2. Similarly, consider a transformation from the expression

$$((T_1 \underset{A=B}{\bowtie} T_2) \bowtie T_3)$$

to the expression

$$(T_1 \underset{A=B}{\bowtie} (T_2 \bowtie T_3))$$

In this case, there is no problem with the Equi-join operator; if attribute B is contained in T_2, it certainly is contained in $(T_2 \bowtie T_3)$. Observe, however, that tables T_1 and T_3 may share an attribute C. If this is the case, the equivalence is not valid because the Equi-join operator does not restrict tuples in the result based on the condition $t_1[C] = t_3[C]$, for $t_1 \in T_1$, $t_3 \in T_3$.

Section 11.4 considered criteria for choosing good candidate algebraic strategies for an expression containing many Join operators. We have seen, for example, that each of the following is an important consideration:

- The expected sizes of intermediate results.
- The avoidance, when possible, of Cartesian products.
- The availability of structures to support the Joins.
- The ability to compute in a pipeline the sequence of Joins.

Most optimizers use criteria such as these to prune the candidate strategies to a reasonable number of promising alternatives. However, these are only heuristic criteria based on limited information and their application, in some cases, can cause the optimizer to miss an optimal implementation-level strategy.

Rules for Selection

Since a selection is of the form $\sigma_F T$, where F is a Boolean expression, the laws of Boolean algebra present us with a host of logical equivalences. Many optimizers are geared towards processing selections whose Boolean expressions are in either **disjunctive normal form (DNF)** or **conjunctive normal form (CNF)**. In this context, we say that an expression is in DNF if it is of one of the two forms

$$(C_1 \vee C_2 \vee \cdots \vee C_i \vee \cdots \vee C_n)$$

or

$$\text{NOT } (C_1 \vee C_2 \vee \cdots \vee C_i \vee \cdots \vee C_n)$$

and if each C_i is of the form

$$((A_1 \ op\ v_1) \wedge \cdots \wedge (A_k \ op\ v_k))$$

where the A_i are attributes and each op is a logical comparison operator (e.g.,

=, !=, <, >). Thus, the following is a DNF expression:

(((Dept="Toys") $\wedge$ (Age > 25)) $\vee$ (Salary > 40,000) $\vee$ ((Location = "NYC") $\wedge$ (Salary > 60,000)))

We say that an expression is in CNF if it is of one of the two forms

$(C_1 \wedge C_2 \wedge \cdots \wedge C_i \wedge \cdots \wedge C_n)$

or

NOT $(C_1 \wedge C_2 \wedge \cdots \wedge C_i \wedge \cdots \wedge C_n)$

and if each C_i is of the form

$((A_1\ op\ v_1) \vee \cdots \vee (A_k\ op\ v_k))$

where the A_i are attributes and each *op* is a logical comparison operator. Thus, the following is a CNF expression:

(((Dept="Toys") $\vee$ (Age > 25)) $\wedge$ (Salary > 40,000) $\wedge$ ((Location = "NYC") $\vee$ (Location = "LA")))

A well-known result of Boolean algebra is that any Boolean expression can be transformed into both DNF and CNF. Hence, an optimizer always has the option of transforming the Boolean expression of a Select operator to either of the normal forms. We consider the motivation for transforming to each of the normal forms:

1. *DNF:* The select operation $\sigma_F T$, where F is in DNF, can be processed as a collection of independent partial-match retrievals against table T. For example, if F is $C_1 \vee C_2 \vee \cdots \vee C_i \vee \cdots \vee C_n$, where each C_i is of the form $((A_1 = v_1) \wedge \cdots \wedge (A_k = v_k))$, it is possible to process each selection $\sigma_{C_i} T$ with one of the standard partial-match retrieval algorithms (see Section 11.1) and then to compute the Union of the results.
2. *CNF:* The Select operation $\sigma_F T$, where F is in CNF, can be processed as a collection of independent queries against table T whose results are intersected. For example, if F is $C_1 \wedge C_2 \wedge \cdots \wedge C_i \wedge \cdots \wedge C_n$, where each C_i is of the form $((A_1 = v_1) \vee \cdots \vee (A_k = v_k))$, it is possible to independently process the queries $\sigma_{C_i} T$ and then to compute the intersection of these results. When implementing such a strategy, we can process first the most selective query $\sigma_{C_i} T$, storing in internal memory the qualifying tuples (or pointers to the qualifying tuples if internal memory is limited). We then process the next most selective query $\sigma_{C_j} T$, immediately intersecting each tuple retrieved with the result of $\sigma_{C_i} T$. We continue processing in this manner so that intersections are performed in internal memory while consuming only a modest amount of this scarce resource.

Both classes of methods are used in practice, and the comparison of their efficiencies is highly dependent on the form of the query and on the instance and implementation of the table. The advent of multi-processor computers also makes available a host of simple parallel algorithms for processing DNF and CNF queries. Such options are explored in exercise 12.14.

Another type of equivalence transformation is based on combining sequences of selections into a single Select operator. For example

$$\sigma_F(\Pi_{<L_1>}T) \equiv_L \Pi_{<L_1>}(\sigma_F T)$$

Note that the expression on the left suggests a two-pass implementation in which the outer Select is applied to the result of the inner. In contrast, the expression on the right offers more optimization options, including the application to the expression $F \wedge F'$ of the transformations described previously.

Rules for Projection

A projection is of the form $\Pi_{<L>} T$, where L is a list of attributes. In contexts where the ordering of the columns is important (e.g., the result is to be displayed), L cannot be altered. In other contexts (e.g., where tuples can be treated as functions mapping from attribute names to values), L can be permuted any way we wish.

Another class of equivalences is based on the collapsing of composed projections. Consider, for example, the expression

$$\Pi_{<L_1>}(\Pi_{<L_2>} \cdots (\Pi_{<L_n>}(T)))$$

In order for this to be a syntactically correct expression, the lists L_i must be nested as sets; that is, all the tables appearing in L_1 must appear also in L_2, all the tables appearing in L_2 must appear also in L_3, and so forth. Hence, it is clear that the expression is equivalent to

$$\Pi_{<L_1>}(T)$$

We prefer the second expression as it is simpler than the first and suggests a processing strategy that is performed with a single pass over table T.

Rules Governing the Interaction of Join, Select, and Project Operators

There are many rules of logical equivalence that allow us to manipulate expressions containing combinations of operators. We consider here some of the important rules for manipulating expressions containing combinations of Natural join, Select, and Project operators. The behavior of Equi-join in such combinations is similar to that of Natural join, though considerations such as those seen earlier must be taken into account.

Projection and Selection: Let F be a Boolean expression referencing only the attributes contained in list L. We have that

$$\sigma_F(\sigma_{F'} T) \equiv_L \sigma_{F \wedge F'} T$$

This simple equivalence leads us to two important observations. The first observation is that if we had to choose between a sequence of operations in which the projection is applied before the selection (as suggested by the expression on the left) and a sequence in which the selection is performed before the projection (as suggested by the expression on the right), we would most likely choose the latter sequence. The basis for this choice is that the selection might be aided by indices that already exist on table T, while performing the projection first requires the retrieval of all tuples in T and then the creation of an intermediate table or stream that, in general, will not be indexed.

The second observation is a reiteration of a point first raised in Chapter 2. This is that, when implementing a relational expression, we have more options than simply performing the operators in sequence. In particular, the best implementation of the expression $\sigma_F(\Pi_{<L_1>}T)$ or $\Pi_{<L_1>}(\sigma_F T)$ would be a single-pass algorithm that uses an index to retrieve tuples satisfying the Selects and projects on the attributes in L as the tuples are retrieved. More generally, observe that refinement transformations have been defined to map *subgraphs*, not only single operator nodes, into implementation programs. This definition allows the implementation process to rearrange and combine the relational operators appearing in algebraic-level strategies.

Selection and Natural Join: Among the most important equivalences are those that allow a selection to be performed before a Join. We have that

$$\sigma_F(T_1 \bowtie T_2) \equiv_L (\sigma_F T_1) \bowtie T_2$$

provided that F references only attributes from T_1 and, similarly, that

$$\sigma_F(T_1 \bowtie T_2) \equiv_L T_1 \bowtie (\sigma_F T_2)$$

provided that F references only attributes from T_2. Similar transformations exist also for cases where F references attributes contained in both tables. See exercise 12.5 for details.

The importance of transformations such as these is that they generate expressions that apply Joins to smaller operand tables than do expressions that apply selections to the results of Joins.

Projection and Natural Join: Projections, in some cases, also can be moved inside of Joins. For example,

$$\Pi_{<J>}(T_1 \bowtie T_2) \equiv_L (\Pi_{<J_1>} T_1) \bowtie (\Pi_{<J_2>} T_2)$$

provided that list J contains all attributes common to T_1 and T_2 and where J_i contains those attributes from J that are contained in T_i, $i = 1, 2$.

Heuristics for Choosing between Alternative Expressions: Generally, an optimizer will apply equivalence transformations to obtain candidate strategies that apply Select and Project operators before Join operators. The motivation for this heuristic is that Selects and Projects reduce table sizes, and hence their early application results in Joins between smaller tables. There are several well-known algorithms [see, e.g., Yao (1979)] that take an expression containing Joins, Selects, and Projects as input and "push" the Select and Project operators as far forward as possible.

To illustrate this heuristic, consider the expression

$$\sigma_{A=c}(T \bowtie S)$$

where A is an attribute of table T. It follows from one of our previous equivalences that this expression is equivalent to the expression

$$((\sigma_{A=c} T) \bowtie S)$$

In the strategies graph model, application of an equivalence transformation based on an algebraic identity such as this generates additional strategies. Suppose, for example, that $\sigma_{A=c}(T \bowtie S)$ is an intermediate result in a larger query and is represented by the table node n as depicted in Figure 12.12*a*. When we apply the equivalence transformation to push forward the selection, we obtain the strategies graph in Figure 12.12*b*, which contains two strategies for producing n.

Observe that the strategies graph resulting from the application of this equivalence transformation still includes the original strategy corresponding to the

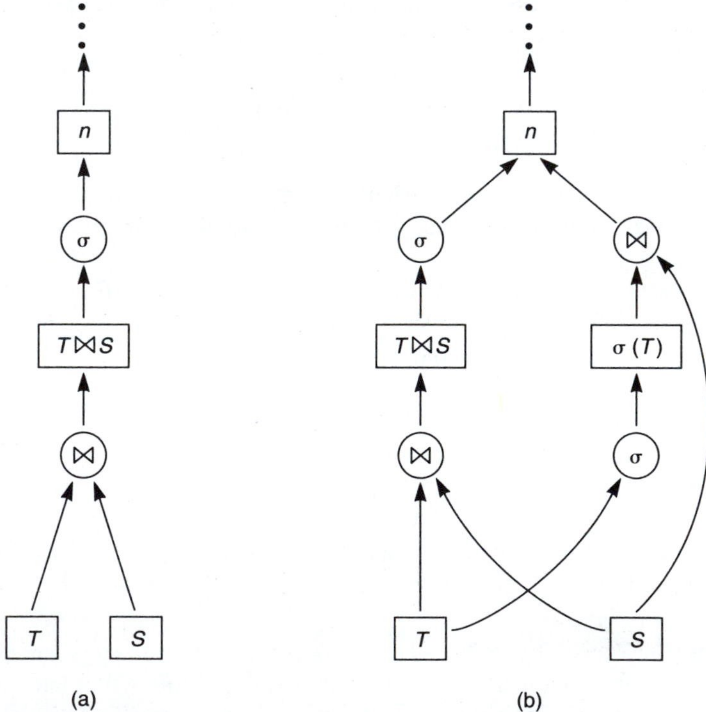

Figure 12.12 (*a*) Single strategy; (*b*) multiple strategies

expression $\sigma_{A=c}(T \bowtie S)$. That is, the heuristic we are describing is to *consider* expressions in which Selects and Projects are performed before Joins. In considering such an expression, it must be noted that there is a potential drawback of applying Projects and Selects early. While this strategy does reduce the sizes of the operands of the Joins, in most cases it forces the Joins to operate on intermediate, rather than base, tables; for example, these intermediate tables may fail to possess certain useful structures possessed by the base tables. That is, while the base tables may have indices and physical orderings to support the Join, the intermediate results generally will fail to be so structured. Considering again the two preceding expressions, we see that it would be disadvantageous to perform the Select before the Join if the selection does not significantly reduce the size of its operand and if the tables T and S are structured in a manner that efficiently supports the $T \bowtie S$ Join.

Hence, while it is very reasonable to generate for consideration strategies that perform projections and selections as early as possible, it is somewhat unsafe to automatically prune the other alternatives. A safer pruning heuristic takes into account the instance and implementation of the underlying RDM. A general principle is that pruning at the algebraic-level cannot guarantee optimality. Further, the more information about the RDM that is considered, the safer is the pruning likely to be.

Semantic Equivalence Transformations

Semantic equivalences based on integrity constraints only recently have begun receiving serious attention as a practical optimization tool, and few, if any, commercial query optimizers at this time employ transformations based on semantic equivalences.

Earlier, we considered the following semantic equivalence:

Assuming

$$(\text{Dept} = \text{Toys}) \Rightarrow (\text{Salary} < 30{,}000)$$

is among the integrity constraints *IC* known to apply to table scheme EMPLOYEE(Emp#, Dept, Salary), then

$$\sigma_{(Salary<50{,}000)\wedge(Dept=\text{"}Toys\text{"})}\, EMPLOYEE \equiv_{S(IC)} \sigma_{(Salary<30{,}000)\wedge(Dept=\text{"}Toys\text{"})}\, EMPLOYEE$$

The expression on the right potentially can be implemented more efficiently than the expression on the left. Suppose, for example, that a dense index on salary is maintained as a B-tree and that a dense index on Dept is maintained as a hashed structure. The expression on the right can be implemented by an algorithm that searches the B-tree for index records with a salary less than 30,000 and intersects these records with the index records for employees in the toys department. The analogous implementation for the expression on the left would have to retrieve more index records from the B-tree and perform the intersection using this larger set.

As a more extreme example, observe that the following equivalence holds:

$$\sigma_{(Salary>50{,}000)\wedge(Dept=\text{"Toys"})} EMPLOYEE \equiv_{S(IC)} \emptyset$$

The expression on the right can be evaluated without accessing the data or index files for table EMPLOYEE.

Other semantic equivalences may allow the elimination of certain Joins. Suppose, for example, that Age is an attribute in table PERSONAL and that it is company policy to allow only people over 25 years of age to work in the liquor department. Then the integrity constraints *IC* for our department store RDM would include

$$(\exists e \in EMPLOYEE)[(e[Dept]=\text{"Liquor"}) \Rightarrow (\exists p \in PERSONAL) \\ (e[Emp\#]=p[Emp\#]) \wedge (p[Age]>25)]$$

In this case, the following is a valid semantic equivalence:

$$\Pi_{<Name,Salary>}(\sigma_{((Dept=\text{"Liquor"})\wedge(Age>21))}(EMPLOYEE \bowtie PERSONAL) \\ \equiv_{S(C)} \Pi_{<Name,Salary>}(\sigma_{(Dept=\text{"Liquor"})} EMPLOYEE)$$

In this section, we have attempted to present the flavor of logical and semantic equivalence transformations and of heuristic criteria for generating and pruning alternatives at the algebraic level. It now is time to move on to the problem of search at the implementation level. We emphasize that often only a fuzzy line divides search at the algebraic and implementation levels and that the processes may be interleaved and even merged.

12.5 SEARCH AT THE IMPLEMENTATION LEVEL

In this section, we consider dynamic programming algorithms for searching the collection of implementation-level strategies appearing in an optimizer's strategies graph. In what follows, we assume that the strategies graph under consideration consists of implementation-level strategies for a query Q and that we can estimate the cost of such strategies using techniques such as those described in Chapter 11.

We previously observed that the number of strategies represented by a strategies graph can be far larger than the size of the graph (i.e., as measured by its numbers of nodes and edges). In many cases, a strategies graph contains a number of strategies that is exponential in its size. Consequently, a search algorithm that can find an optimal strategy among all strategies represented by G, while expending an amount of time polynomial in the size of G, would be of considerable practical value. We now demonstrate that a dynamic programming algorithm, when applicable, has these desirable performance characteristics.

We begin by describing the pruning that is the basis of the dynamic programming algorithm. Consider a strategies graph in which intermediate table node n can be computed by any of the strategies $S_1, \ldots, S_i, \ldots, S_k$. Suppose that, by summing the costs of the operators in each strategy, we determine that $\text{Cost}(S_i) \leq \text{Cost}(S_j)$, $j = 1, 2, \ldots, k$. Under what conditions can we safely prune the S_j, for $i \neq j$? At first it may appear that such pruning is always safe. After all, if a complete strategy S for Q computes intermediate result n using strategy S_j $(i \neq j)$, it would seem that we could replace S_j with S_i and be left with a strategy S' at least as good as S. Hence, the argument goes, pruning S_j could not prevent us from obtaining an optimal strategy for Q.

This reasoning is valid, with the exception of one situation. Suppose that strategies graph G contains an intermediate result m that a single strategy embedded in G can use in more than one way. Consider, for example, the situation depicted in Figure 12.13. Let strategy S denote the strategy consisting of the operators x, y, p, k. Observe that strategy S has the property that table node m is input to two of S's operators, operator y and operator p. We say that such a table node is *used in more than one way* in strategy S. Suppose that the numbers labeling the operator nodes represent our estimate of the cost of applying the implementations specified for that operator to its inputs. Then the cost of computing Q using strategy S is 90, and this is the optimal strategy for computing Q since the only other alternative S' consisting of the operators x, y, z, k has cost 115. Note, however, that if we compare the cost of substrategy S_p (consisting of the operators x and p) with that of substrategy S_z (consisting of

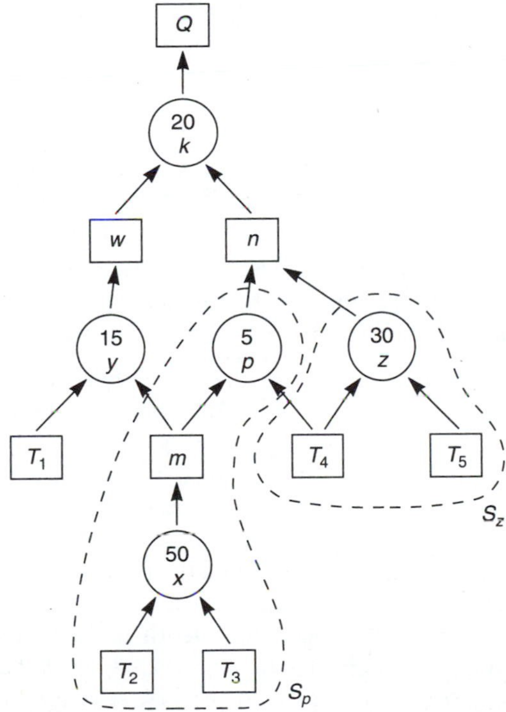

Figure 12.13 Example where dynamic programming's pruning strategy is not valid

the operator z) for computing the intermediate result n, we find that $\text{Cost}(S_z) < \text{Cost}(S_p)$. If, based on this comparison, we were to prune strategy S_p, the optimal strategy S no longer would be available since S requires S_p as a substrategy.

This example reveals the flaw in the argument given earlier in support of the dynamic program's pruning rule. If we attempt to apply the argument by starting with S and replacing its method S_p of computing n with S_z, we find that the resulting strategy S' costs more than S, despite the fact that $\text{Cost}(S_z) < \text{Cost}(S_p)$. The argument fails because some of the work expended anyway to compute table node w (i.e., the work to compute table node m that is an input to operator y) will contribute to the computation of n if we use S_p but not if we use S_z. Put another way, part of substrategy S_p contributes to the computation of w, a factor that cannot be considered when S_p and S_z are compared in isolation of the rest of G. We conclude that, in general, choices between alternative strategies for computing a result n cannot be based solely on the strategies' costs—the choice may be affected also by the potential for using intermediate results elsewhere in a complete strategy.

The preceding discussion motivates the following definition of a family of strategies graphs.

> **Definition 12.6** A strategy S is a **single-use strategy** if, in subgraph S, each table node has at most one output and thus is used by strategy S in only one way. A strategies graph obeys the **single-use restriction** if each of its embedded strategies is single use.

We observe that:

1. Strategies graph G obeys the single-use restriction if and only if, for all distinct table nodes T_1 and T_2 that are input to a common operator node in G, the subgraphs of G rooted at T_1 and T_2 share no table nodes.
2. Strategies graph G may contain a table node with many outputs and still be single use—the requirement is that no *single strategy* embedded in G contain a table node with more than one output.

Next we present a dynamic programming algorithm that efficiently finds the optimal strategy in any single-use graph. We point out that these graphs often arise in practice. For one thing, many natural queries do not to give rise to the opportunity for multiple use. Further, since multiple-use strategies require some extra coordination of the computations, many optimizers do not consider these strategies even when they might be applicable. Hence, the dynamic programming algorithm has a good deal of practical importance.

The dynamic programming algorithm uses a bottom-up traversal to search a single-use strategies graph. The algorithm identifies the best strategy for computing each table node at the time the node is visited. Thus, before a table node n is visited, the algorithm has identified the best strategy for computing each table node "below" n and has computed the cost of this strategy. The following recurrence relation is used to determine the identity and cost of the best strategy for computing n at the time n is visited.

Case I: Table node n is a base node:

Cost (n) = 0
Strat (n) = subgraph consisting of only n

Case II: Table node n is not a base node: Then n is the output of one or more operator nodes $m_1, \ldots, m_i, \ldots, m_t$. Let the table nodes that are the inputs of each m_i be denoted $w_{i1}, \ldots, w_{ik_i}$. As a first step in the computations of *Cost*(n) and *Strat*(n), we compute

$$Cost(m_i) = \left(\sum_{j=1}^{k_i} Cost(w_{ij})\right) + \text{(cost of applying operator } m_i \text{ to its inputs)}$$

$$Strat(m_i) = \{m_i\} \cup \left(\bigcup_{j=1}^{k_i} (Strat(w_{ij}) \cup \{(w_{ij}, m_i)\})\right)$$

The first recurrence sums the costs of the best strategies for computing m_i's input tables and then adds in the cost of applying the implementation specified for operator m_i to these tables. Observe that, for each m_i, *Cost*(m_i) yields the cost of the best strategy *using* m_i *as its last operation* to compute n, while *Strat* (m_i) records the identity of this strategy as a set of nodes and edges.

Once *Cost* and *Strat* have been computed for each operator node m_i that produces table node n as output, we compute the cost and identity of the best strategy for n as follows:

$$Cost(n) = \min_{1 \le i \le t} \{Cost(m_i)\}$$

$Strat(n) = Strat(m_i) \cup \{n\} \cup \{(m_i, n)\}$, where i is a subscript value for which the preceding cost formula is minimized.

The dynamic programming algorithm can be stated as follows:

```
for each table node n in G, visited in some bottom-up order
  if (n is a base table node)
    Cost(n)←0
    Strat(n)←subgraph consisting of only n
  else
    { n is a nonbase table node that is the output of one or more operator
      nodes m1, . . . , mi, . . . , mt. Let the table nodes that are the inputs of
      each mi be denoted wi1, . . . , wiki. }
      compute for each mi:

      Cost(mi)←( Σ_{j=1}^{ki} Cost(wij) ) + (cost of applying operator mi to its inputs)

      Strat(mi)←{mi} ∪ ( ∪_{j=1}^{ki} (Strat(wij) ∪ {(wij, mi)}) )

    Cost(n)←min_{1≤i≤t} {Cost(mi)}
    Strat(n)←Strat(mi) ∪ {n} ∪ {(mi,n)}
      where i is a subscript value for which the preceding cost formula is
      minimized
  endif
end for
```

Analysis: For each nonbase node v in the graph, a sum or minimum is taken over k elements, where k is the number of edges entering v. Such a sum or minimum requires $O(k)$ time. Hence, the total time for all such sums and minimums is O(number of edges in G). Assuming that only constant time is required to estimate the cost of applying an operator to its inputs [as is required for the last term in the formula of $Cost(m_i)$], the dynamic programming algorithm runs in O(number of edges in G) time. The key to the algorithm's efficiency is that it avoids the combinatorial explosion in the number of strategies considered explicitly by pruning all but a single strategy for n at the time table node n is visited.

As indicated previously, the dynamic programming algorithm is valid only on single-use strategies graphs. Unfortunately, the problem of finding an optimal strategy in a general strategies graph is NP-hard, indicating strongly that there exists no algorithm valid for all strategies graphs with a running time polynomial in the size of the graph.

While the preceding discussion gives a concise summary of the action of the dynamic programming algorithm, its perspective is a bit simplistic in that it views the algorithm as searching a preexisting implementation-level strategies graph. In reality, an optimizer probably would not apply refinement transformations to obtain every implementation-level strategy before commencing the dynamic programming search; rather, it would prune as it generates strategies for intermediate results. We shall more accurately illustrate the nature of the search process by considering a specific instance of the general dynamic programming algorithm, the dynamic programming algorithm used by System R to find an optimal left-leaning Join tree.

Let each of $T_1, T_2, \ldots, T_k$ be an implemention-level table, and suppose we wish to find the best pipeline program for processing the k-way Natural join query $\bowtie \{T_1, \ldots, T_k\}$. To simplify our presentation, we introduce an assumption that allows us to establish a one-to-one correspondence between left-leaning Join trees and candidate implementation-level pipeline programs. The assumption is that a binary Join node with W_i as left input and W_j as right input (the W may be base tables or intermediate results) is refined to an implementation algorithm by the following rule:

- If W_i and W_j share attributes and these attributes are indexed in table W_j, perform an Indexed loop join with W_j as the inner table.
- If W_i and W_j share attributes but these attributes are not indexed in table W_j, perform an Unindexed loop join with W_j as the inner table.
- If W_i and W_j share no attributes, compute the Cartesian product with W_j as the inner table.

In all cases, the resulting sequence of Joins is performed in a pipeline. Exercise 12.10 considers the modifications required when the map from algebraic-level to implementation-level strategies becomes one-to-many because, for example, additional Join algorithms such as Merge join are available for use in the pipeline.

The dynamic programming algorithm will find the best implementation-level program embedded in a strategies graph representing all programs that implement, in the manner described earlier, left-leaning Join trees for the query $\bowtie \{T_1, \ldots, T_k\}$. We first describe the form of this strategies graph G. The description of the graph's structure applies to both the algebraic and implementation levels. The base nodes of G represent the k tables $T_1, \ldots, T_k$, and the result node Q represents the value of the expression $\bowtie \{T_1, \ldots, T_k\}$. Since each permutation of the k tables corresponds to a left-leaning Join tree, G will represent a total of $k!$ strategies for computing Q. Result node Q has k incoming edges, where the ith edge $(1 \leq i \leq k)$ connects Join node m_i with Q. The input tables for operator node m_i are the intermediate result $\bowtie \{T_1, \ldots, T_{i-1}, T_{i+1}, \ldots, T_k\}$ and base table T_i. More generally, for every size s $(1 < s < k)$ subset $(W_1, \ldots, W_s\} \subseteq (T_1, \ldots, T_k\}$, G contains a node n representing the intermediate result $\bowtie \{W_1, \ldots, W_s\}$. Then n has s incoming edges; the ith $(1 \leq i \leq s)$ of these edges connects Join node m_i with n. The input tables for Join node m_i are the intermediate result $\bowtie \{W_1, \ldots, W_{i-1}, W_{i+1}, \ldots, W_s\}$ and W_i. Additionally, n, when it is not the result node, has $s - k$ outgoing edges. The jth $(1 \leq j \leq s - k)$ of these edges connects n with a Join node whose other input is some base table node $V_j \in (\{T_1, \ldots, T_k\} - \{W_1, \ldots, W_s\})$; the output of this operator is the intermediate result node $\bowtie \{W_1, \ldots, W_s, V_j\}$. Observe that the graph contains, for every subset $\{W_1, \ldots, W_s\} \subseteq \{T_1, \ldots, T_k\}$, each of the $s!$ left-leaning Join trees that computes the intermediate result $\bowtie \{W_1, \ldots, W_s\}$. Figure 12.14*a* summarizes the generic structure of the graph, while Figure 12.14*b* shows the entire strategies graph for $k = 4$.

The strategies graph for $\bowtie \{T_1, \ldots, T_k\}$ contains $2^k - 1$ table nodes, $k(2^{k-1} - 1)$ operator nodes, and $3k(2^{k-1} - 1)$ edges (see exercise 12.9). While the size of the strategies graph is large, the number $k!$ of strategies represented is far larger, when k is moderately large. Further, a search algorithm that computes explicitly the cost each of the $k!$ strategies visits repeatedly every operator node. Therefore, a search algorithm that visits the nodes and edges only once and runs in time proportional to the number of edges, rather than in time proportional to the number of strategies represented, is highly desirable. Fortunately, the strategies graph for this problem is single use, implying that the dynamic programming pruning rule previously described is applicable. That is, for each table node n, we can compare the incoming strategies and prune all but the best.

The task at hand is to describe an efficient search procedure for applying dynamic programming's pruning rule. In particular, we shall illustrate how strategies are "grown" bottom up at the algebraic level and mapped to the implementation level where they are evaluated and pruned. This discussion will demonstrate that while an algorithm's search space can be modeled by a static strategies graph, an efficient implementation of the algorithm often interleaves the generation of algebraic-level strategies for intermediate results with the refinement, evaluation, and pruning of these strategies.

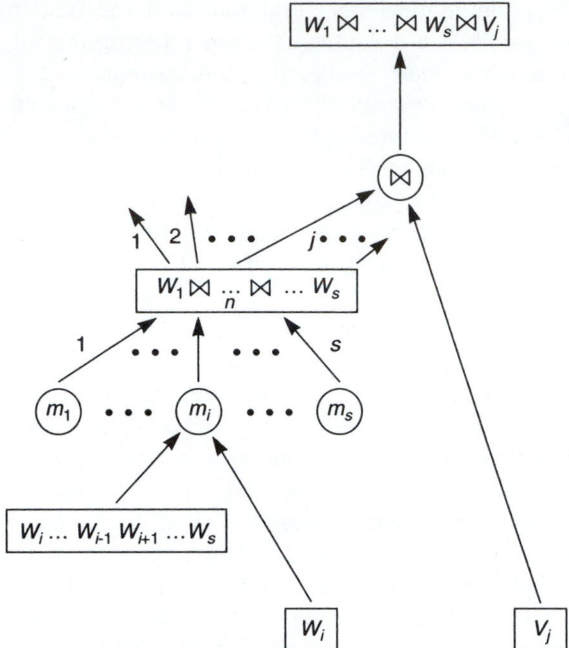

Figure 12.14a Generic structure

We first present a concise statement of the algorithm and then correlate the algorithm's execution with an optimization process that searches a dynamically generated sequence of strategies graphs. The algorithm uses the following definitions and recurrence relations.

For each nonempty subset $Z \subseteq \{T_1, \ldots, T_k\}$, define

Cost(Z) = cost of the best implementation-level strategy for computing $\bowtie Z$
Strat(Z) = identity of an implementation-level strategy for computing $\bowtie Z$ that achieves Cost(Z)

In these definitions and in what follows, when we speak of the best implementation-level strategy, attention implicitly is restricted to pipeline strategies obtained by application of the refinement rules given earlier.

Since we currently are assuming a one-to-one correspondence between left-leaning Join trees and implementation-level programs and since there is a one-to-one correspondence between left-leaning Join trees for the expression $\bowtie Z$ and permutations of the tables in Z, we can represent the value of Strat(Z) as a string over the tables in Z; for example if $Z = \{T_1, T_2, T_3, T_4\}$, the left-leaning tree of Figure 12.15 can be represented by the string $T_2 \cdot T_1 \cdot T_4 \cdot T_3$.

The dynamic programming algorithm computes Cost(Z) and Strat(Z) on sets Z containing successively more tables. The algorithm first computes Cost(Z)

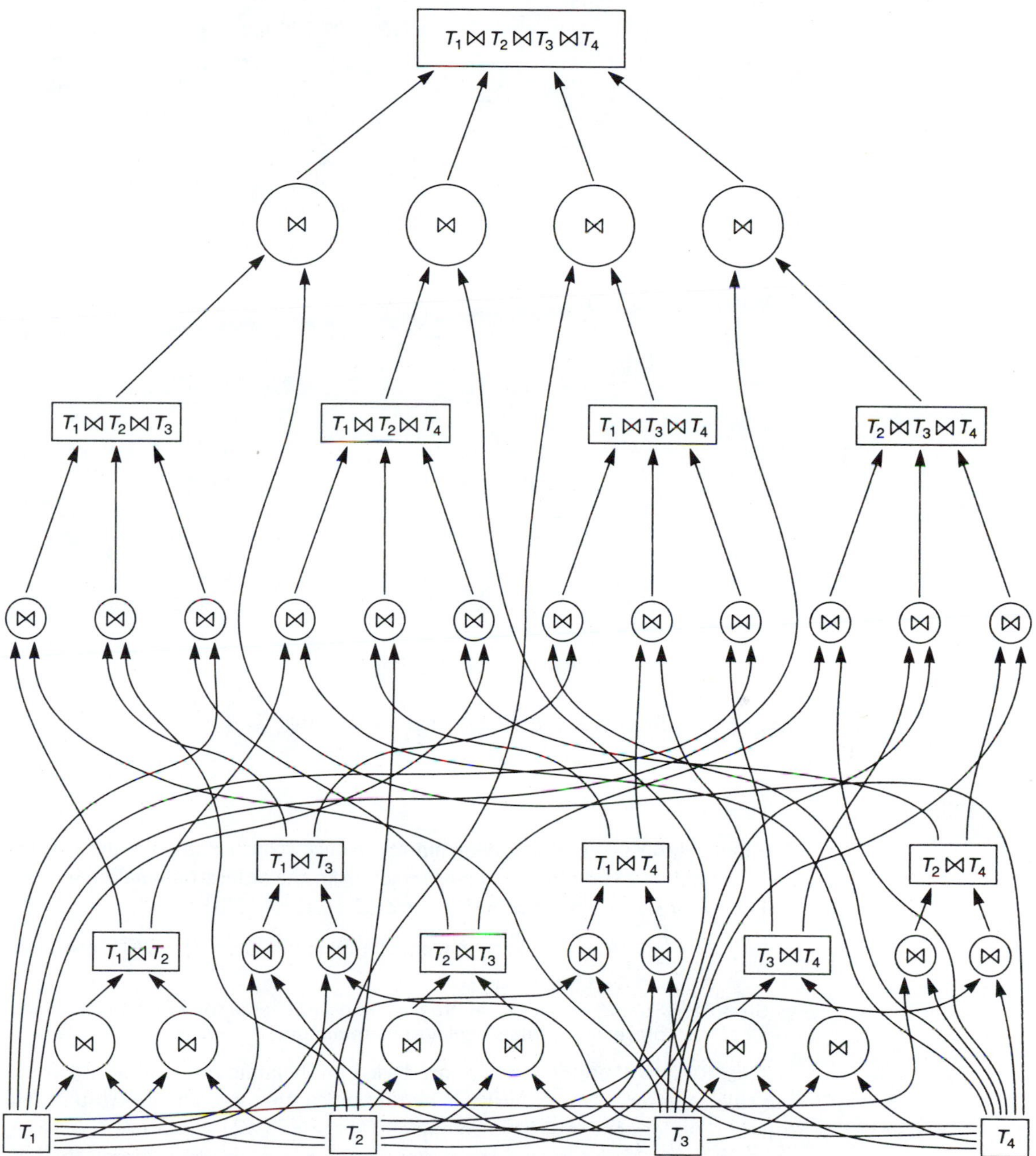

Figure 12.14b Entire graph for $k = 4$

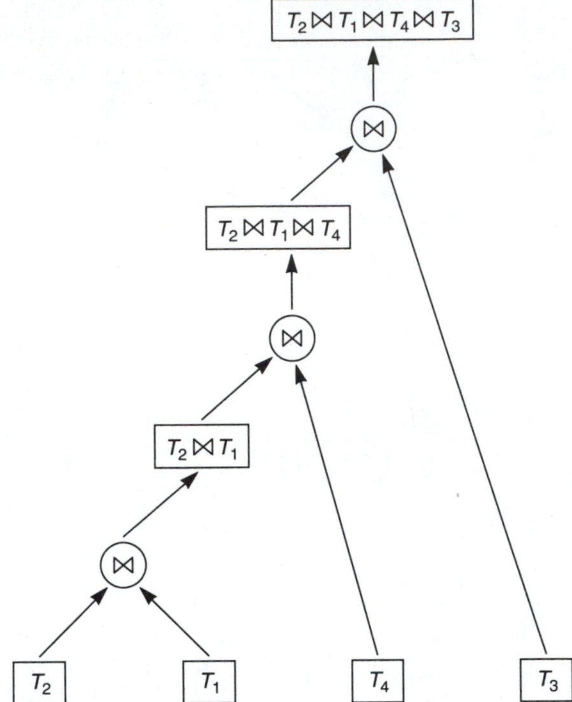

Figure 12.15 A left-leaning Join tree

and Strat(Z) for sets Z containing single tables; that is,

For $1 \le i \le k$
$Cost(\{T_i\}) = 0$
$Strat(\{T_i\}) = T_i$

The algorithm then uses the following recurrence relations to compute Cost(Z) and Strat(Z) values on larger sets of tables from the values on smaller sets:

For every size s ($1 \le s \le k$) subset $Z \subseteq \{T_1, \ldots, T_k\}$,

$$\text{Cost}(Z) = \min_{W_j \in Z} \{\text{Cost}(Z - \{W_j\}) + (\text{cost of joining the result of} \bowtie (Z - \{W_j\}) \text{ with } W_j)\}$$

Strat(Z) = Strat($Z - \{W_j\}$) $\cdot$ W_j, where j is a subscript value for which the preceding formula achieves its minimum

Observe how these recurrences are based on dynamic programming's pruning rule as described previously. When it comes time to compute Cost(Z) and Strat(Z), we already will have computed Cost(Z $-$ $\{W_j\}$) and Strat(Z $-$ $\{W_j\}$), for each $W_j \in Z$. In terms of the strategies graph, we are determining the best strategy for the table node n representing $\bowtie Z$, having already determined the best strategy for the table node n_j representing $Z - \{W_j\}$, for each $W_j \in Z$. Thus, by the time we consider table node n, we have pruned all but a single strategy Strat(Z $-$ $\{W_j\}$) for obtaining each n_j. Consequently, there remain only $s = |Z|$ strategies for obtaining n—each of the Strat($Z - \{W_j\}$) augmented with the one additional Join required to obtain n. We could calculate the cost of each of these strategies for n by summing the operators it contains, but we can save time because we have recorded in Cost($Z - \{W_j\}$) the cost of Strat($Z-\{W_j\}$) and hence need only add in the cost of the last Join. Note that this cost calculation really is done at the *implementation level,* although the refinement of a Join tree to the implementation level is simplified by our assumption that the method for any particular Join is predetermined. Exercise 12.10 considers the modifications necessary when other Join methods are available.

The complete algorithm is stated as follows:

```
for i := 1 to k
  Cost({T_i}) ← 0
  Strat({T_i}) ← T_i
end for
for s := 2 to k
  for (each size s subset Z ⊆ {T_1, . . . , T_k})
    Cost(Z) = min   {Cost(Z−{W_j}) + (cost of joining the result of ⋈ (Z−{W_j})
              W_j ∈ Z
                        with W_j)}
    Strat(Z) = Strat(Z−{W_j}) · W_j,
               where j is a subscript value for which the preceding formula
               achieves its minimum
  end for
end for
```

Analysis: The algorithm runs in $\Theta(k * 2^k)$ time. This can be established by observing that, for each size s $(2 \leq s \leq k)$ subset Z of $\{T_1, \ldots, T_k\}$, the algorithm requires time proportional to s to find the min as it computes Cost(Z). Hence, the total time required by the algorithm is $\sum_{s=2}^{k} s * Choose(k,s)$, and this quantity is $\Theta(k * 2^k)$.

We now correlate the execution of this algorithm with an optimization process that searches a dynamically generated sequence of strategies graphs. The initial strategies graph represents a single high-level strategy and contains a k-ary Join operator and k base tables. See Figure 12.16*a*. The initial step in the search applies an operator expansion transformation to this strategies graph, resulting in the graph shown in Figure 12.16*b*. This graph contains a strategy corresponding to each ordered pair (T_i,T_j) $(1 \leq i \neq j \leq k)$ of tables, for a total of $(k)(k-1)$ strategies for computing Q. The strategy corresponding to the ordered pair (T_i,T_j) contains a single binary Join node with T_i as its left input and T_j as its right input; the result $\bowtie \{T_i,T_j\}$ of this Join is input to a $(k-1)$-way Join operator node whose other inputs are the table nodes in $(\{T_1, \ldots, T_k\} - \{T_i,T_j\})$ and that creates the query result Q. Note that the Join node corresponding to the ordered pair (T_i,T_j), as well as the Join node corresponding to the ordered pair (T_j,T_i), create as their result the intermediate table node $\bowtie \{T_i,T_j\}$; that is, there are two algebraic-level strategies for creating each inter-

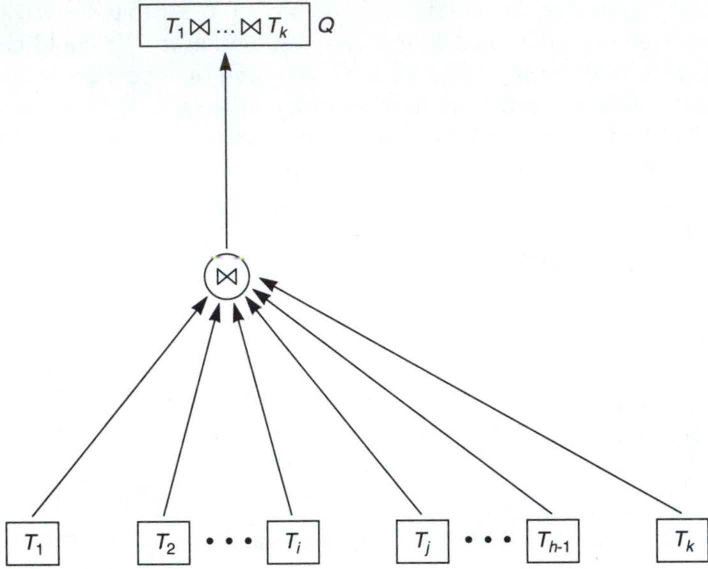

Figure 12.16a Initial strategies graph

mediate result $\bowtie \{T_i, T_j\}$, corresponding to the choice of an inner and outer table.

The next step in the search is to select, for each intermediate node $\bowtie \{T_i, T_j\}$ of the graph just described, the better of the two strategies for computing the result. The selection requires the application of a subgraph implementation transformation to obtain candidate implementation-level programs. We are assuming here a predetermined Join algorithm for each Join, and, hence, the only decision is the choice for the inner and outer tables. The costs of the competing methods for computing $\bowtie \{T_i, T_j\}$ are estimated and the loser is pruned. This step in the search corresponds to the dynamic programming algorithm's computation of Cost($\{T_i, T_j\}$) and Strat($\{T_i, T_j\}$).

After this evaluation and pruning are applied to each intermediate table node $\bowtie \{T_i, T_j\}$, the search progresses to its next phase by applying to the current graph's $k - 1$-way Join operator an operator expansion transformation. More generally, phase s ($1 \leq s \leq k$) of the algorithm (corresponding to iteration s of the outer **for** loop of the dynamic programming algorithm) begins with a strategies graph that contains all strategies for each intermediate result $\bowtie \{W_i, \ldots, W_{s-1}\}$ and the identification of the best of these strategies and its cost. Each such intermediate table node is input to a $(k - (s - 2))$-way Join operator whose other inputs are the tables in $(\{T_1, \ldots, T_k\} - \{W_1, \ldots, W_{s-1}\})$. The first step of phase s is to expand in all ways the $(k - (s - 2))$-way Join operator into one more binary Join and a $(k - (s - 1))$-way Join. The search then proceeds to find the best computation for each size s intermediate result, pruning the other substrategies. The search terminates with a single nonpruned strategy for Q.

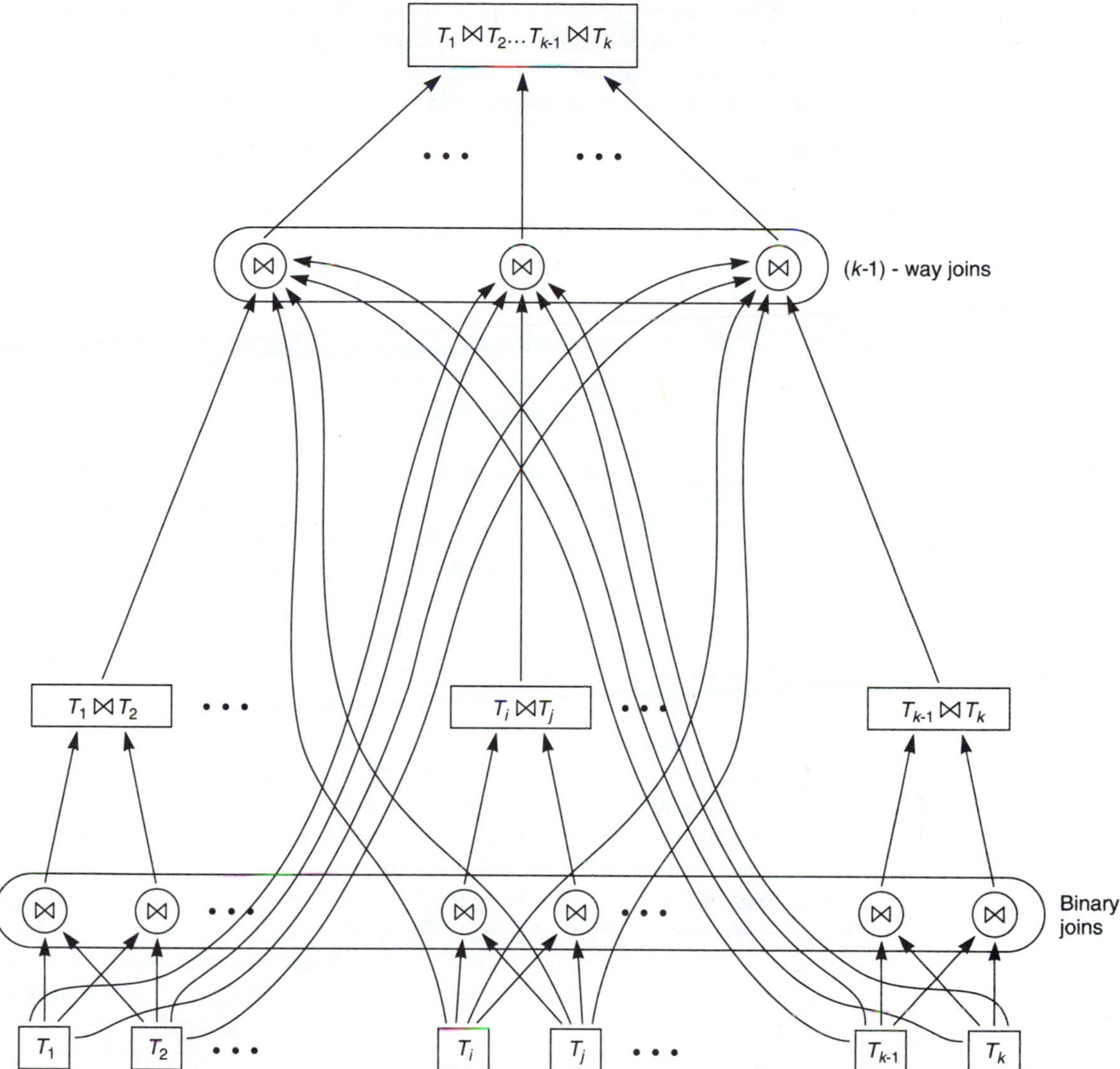

Figure 12.16b First refinement

12.6 UPDATE PROCESSING

We conclude this chapter by briefly considering the problem of Update processing. In this section, attention is restricted to Updates that are stated against implementation-level tables. Chapter 13 considers query processing in the context of leading-edge data models and includes consideration of the problem of processing Updates that are stated against interface-level tables and user-defined views.

There are many important issues related to Updates. The most obvious practical issue is how to efficiently perform Updates that are stated directly against the implementation-level tables. When we have considered Updates in previous chapters, we have assumed simple operators such as

Insert(T,t)
{ Insert into table T tuple t. }

Delete(T,A=v)
{ Remove from table T all tuples t such that $t[A]=v$. }

The primary issues arising in the context of updating an implementation-level table T by means of these operators are how to utilize optimally indices to aid the processing (e.g., how to use indices to find the location for a tuple to be inserted and to find the tuples to be deleted) and how to maintain the indices (e.g., how to maintain the correspondence between index record pointers and data records).

The languages of most relational database systems, however, support Updates that can be as complex as any query. For example, if we have implementation-level tables PROF(Name, Dept, Salary) and TEACHES(Pname, Course, Sect, Semester), the SQL-like statement

```
DELETE TEACHES
WHERE TEACHES.Semester = "Fall 1996"
   AND TEACHES.Pname = PROF.Pname
   AND PROF.Dept = "CS"
```

could be used to delete the tuples for all courses scheduled for fall 1996 taught by computer science professors. Hence, not only are problems such as index utilization and maintenance present in Update processing, but so too is the general problem encountered in query optimization of optimally mapping high-level statements to implementation-level programs.

A second important issue arising in Update processing is integrity checking. Often, we need to verify that a requested Update would not map the RDM to an instance that violates an integrity constraint such as a functional or multivalued dependency. In the context of an Update applied directly to an implementation-level table T, verifying a functional or multivalued dependency for T is not terribly difficult (especially assuming the existence of appropriate indices) since such a constraint involves no intertable relationships. However, we may wish to enforce other types of integrity constraints that do span two or more tables. For example, in Section 12.4, we considered the integrity constraint

$$(\exists e \in EMPLOYEE)[(e[Dept]=\text{"Liquor"}) \Rightarrow ((\exists p \in PERSONAL)$$
$$(e[Name]=p[Name]) \wedge (p[Age]) > 25)]$$

which spans tables EMPLOYEE and PERSONAL. Additionally, a constraint may be stated by the user against a single interface-level table that is decomposed into several implementation-level tables. Verifying integrity constraints that span two or more implementation-level tables can require a significant computational effort (recall our motivation in Chapter 6 for functional dependency–preserving decompositions) and, in the limiting case, may require the joining of the relevant tables.

SUMMARY AND ANNOTATED BIBLIOGRAPHY

In this chapter, we considered the query optimization process from the perspective of combinatorial search. We presented a transformation-based treatment, describing query optimization in terms of a sequence of transformations applied to graphs representing, at various levels of abstraction, the space of candidate query-processing strategies. The strategies graph representation, and aspects of our search model, are due to Reiner and Rosenthal (1982) and Rosenthal and Chakravarthy (1988). Several similar graph-based representations and transformation-based search models have been proposed as well, for example Graefe and DeWitt (1987), Jarke and Koch (1984), and Youssefi and Wong (1979).

Two important components of the query optimizer are its heuristics for algebraic manipulation and for searching at the implementation level. We demonstrated how algebraic equivalences can be used to generate alternatives and discussed techniques for evaluating and pruning the alternatives. Certain subproblems involving algebraic optimization have been well solved; for example, Chandra and Merlin (1977) presents an algorithm for minimizing the number of Joins required in a Project-Select-Join query. In addition to manipulations based on absolute logical equivalences, manipulations based on semantic knowledge (as embodied in integrity constraints) are a technique of potential importance [King (1981)]. As for search at the implementation level, we illustrated how traditional optimization techniques such as dynamic programming, branch and bound, and greedy can be applied to direct the search and prune alternatives. General discussions of combinatorial optimization techniques such as these can be found in Papadimitriou and Steiglitz (1982), Horowitz and Sahni (1978), and Moret and Shapiro (1991).

In several instances, we used the query optimization strategies of System R and INGRES to illustrate specific concepts. Our presentations of these optimizers are based on the descriptions of the prototypes appearing in the literature [Selinger et al. (1979) and Youssefi and Wong (1979)]. These references provide more details on the optimization algorithms and also different perspectives from ours on the process. Current commercial implementations of System R (IBM's DB/2) and INGRES (Relational Techology Incorporated's INGRES) implement extended and improved versions of the strategies described here.

In the next chapter, we study query processing for leading-edge data models. In that context, the advantages of the transformation-based perpective of query optimization will become even more apparent. As we shall see, these data models provide the user with the ability to extend the RDM with new types and operators. To support such extensibility in the data model, it is necessary that the query optimizer itself be easily extended. We shall see that this is the case for optimizers whose architectures reflect the transformation view presented here.

EXERCISES

1. Demonstrate the significance to a query optimizer that operators may obey certain algebraic rules such as commutativity, associativity, and distributivity.
2. Construct simple examples demonstrating that index structures and data distributions of current table instances dramatically affect the quality of candidate processing strategies.
3. Prove that the Select and Project operators commute; that is, prove that for all instances of any table T,

   $$\sigma_F(\Pi_{<L>} T) = \Pi_{<L>}(\sigma_F T)$$

   provided that all attributes referenced by Boolean formula F appear in list L.
4. Prove that the Select operator distributes over the Join operator; that is, prove that for all instances of any tables T_1 and T_2,

   $$\sigma_F(T_1 \bowtie T_2) = (\sigma_F T_1) \bowtie T_2$$

   provided that F references only attributes from T_1.
5. Formulate and prove an identity similar to that of the previous exercise for the case when F references attributes contained in both operands of the Join.
6. What is the maximum number of distinct strategies that a strategies graph consisting of N table nodes, M operator nodes, and P edges can represent?
7. Hand run the general dynamic programming search algorithm on the strategies graph of Figure 12.11.
8. Suppose we wish to process the four-way Natural join query

   $$\bowtie \{T_1, T_2, T_3, T_4\}$$

   Suppose further that T_1 contains 10,000 tuples and is spread over 1,000 blocks; T_2 contains 20,000 tuples and is spread over 1,500 blocks; T_3 contains 5,000 tuples and is spread over 500 blocks; and T_4 contains 50,000 tuples and is spread over 10,000 blocks. Under what conditions (e.g., existence of storage structures, sizes of intermediate results) will the pipeline implementation of the best left-leaning join tree beat a processing strategy based on the best balanced tree, like that of Figure 12.6*a*? Under what conditions is the situation reversed?
9. In Section 12.5, we claimed that the strategies graph for the query $\bowtie \{T_1, \ldots, T_k\}$ contains $2^k - 1$ table nodes, $k(2^{k-1} - 1)$ operator nodes, and $3k(2^{k-1} - 1)$ edges. Prove this claim.

10. What modifications are required to the dynamic programming algorithm that selects the best pipeline program for the query $\bowtie \{T_1, \ldots, T_k\}$ to accommodate a second Join algorithm at the implementation level? How large is the new strategies graph, and what is the running time of the algorithm?

*11. Implement the dynamic programming algorithm for finding the best way to perform a Join in a pipeline. To run your program on sample data, the program will need to access "cost oracles," routines that return information such as the sizes of base tables and intermediates results and the existence of storage structures.

*12. Formulate and implement a best-first branch-and-bound search of an implementation-level strategies graph. Assume the same cost oracles as in the previous exercise. What are good heuristic evaluation functions for controlling the order of the search? How might a good initial bounding processing strategy (for purposes of pruning) be obtained?

*13. Modify your algorithm of the previous exercise so that pruning is permitted, even when it cannot be guaranteed that the pruned strategies are suboptimal. Experimentally analyze the trade-off between running time and quality of solution as more liberal pruning is permitted. If a fixed maximum running time is imposed, does the quality of solution actually increase as more liberal pruning is permitted? Is there a crossover point? How are your results affected by the characteristics of the queries being optimized?

*14. Suppose that we have available n processors that can independently and concurrently access the database tables and their supporting structures. Describe distributed algorithms for processing Select queries in which the Boolean formula is in either DNF or CNF. Under what conditions is one of the normal forms preferable to the other?

*15. Assuming the same multiprocessor environment of the previous exercise, describe how a k-way Join expression can be processed efficiently.

CHAPTER 13

Query Optimization, Part III: Query Processing in the Leading-Edge Data Models

In this, our final chapter, we consider some of the query-processing issues that arise in what might be called "leading-edge" data models. These are data models that are just beginning to be implemented in experimental and commercial systems and for which many research problems remain.

The data models considered in this chapter include those that support queries and updates through **arbitrarily defined user views** and those that support the **universal relation** as the user interface. We also consider extensions to the RDM, including the **deductive database model,** that support complex data definitions such as recursive views and indefinite data. We shall see that these capabilities require not only extensions to the RDM's definitional capabilities but also the development of new classes of query optimization algorithms. We return to the **object-oriented database model,** originally introduced in Chapter 4, and explore how the need to support user-defined types motivates the research area known as **extensible query optimization.** Finally, we consider query optimization in a **distributed database** environment.•

13.1 USER-DEFINED VIEWS

We use the term **view** to refer to a user interface at a higher level of abstraction than implementation-level tables. Hence, the interface-level tables that we have studied extensively form one class of views. As we shall see, however, many other classes of views are of interest also. These include views that, like interface-level tables, stay within the confines of the RDM but have different motivations and properties than our interface-level tables, as well as views that are grounded in data models more complex than the RDM.

In this section, we consider views that lie within the confines of the RDM. To begin, we review the relationship between the interface-level and implementation-level tables that are components of an RDM $\mathcal{R}$'s implementation. The scenario we have considered is that the users present us with a collection $\mathcal{R}_{INT}$ of interface-level tables that we implement as a collection $\mathcal{R}_{IMP}$ of possibly different implementation-level tables. Our motivation for mapping interface-level tables to different implementation-level tables includes normalization and efficiency concerns. Normalization concerns may cause us to decompose interface-level tables, while efficiency concerns may cause us to either decompose or aggregate interface-level tables along 1 : 1 relationships. We always have assumed—explicitly in the case of decomposition and implicitly in the case of aggregation—that $\mathcal{R}_{IMP}$ is an **adequate representation** of $\mathcal{R}_{INT}$ in the sense that all user queries and updates against $\mathcal{R}_{INT}$ can be translated into equivalent queries and updates against $\mathcal{R}_{IMP}$.

Chapters 5 and 6 formally developed results regarding adequate representations in the context of decompositions. Similar notions apply to the 1 : 1 aggregations of tables that we have considered, but, for the sake of brevity, we assume in this summary that the implementation-level tables of $\mathcal{R}_{IMP}$ are obtained by decomposing the interface-level tables of $\mathcal{R}_{INT}$. In this context, the central concept is that of *lossless decomposition*. Recall that if a collection $D = \{T_1, \ldots, T_k\}$ of implementation-level tables is a lossless decomposition (with respect to dependencies Φ) of interface-level table T, then D adequately represents T in the sense that

1. If I_T is an instance of table T obeying Φ and we store the projections I_{T_i} of I_T onto the tables of D, we can process any query stated against T by transforming it into a query against one or more of the T_i. The query against the T_i yields the "correct" result in the sense formalized in Chapter 5.
2. An update against T legal with respect to Φ can be realized by updating the T_i. The original update is realized in the sense that a future query stated against T, when processed against the T_i, yields the "correct" result in the sense formalized in Chapter 6.

While queries and updates stated against interface-level tables always can be translated into operations against implementation-level tables, the translation task can be quite difficult and leads to the aspect of query optimization we have called interface-level table expansion. The important point for the present discussion, however, is that in the context of our interface-level and implementation-level tables, a translation of *every* legal user query and update stated against interface-level tables exists, and further, a legal update stated against an interface-level table has a well-defined effect on the implementation-level tables (i.e., such an update induces a *unique* new instance of the implementation-level tables).[1] As we now shall see, such is not the case for arbitrarily defined user views.

Definition 13.1 A **user-defined relational view** on a collection $\mathcal{R}_{INT}$ of interface-level tables is a table T defined by the expression

$$T \leftarrow E_A$$

where E_A is *any* relational algebra expression over the tables in $\mathcal{R}_{INT}$.

[1] Recall that this uniqueness result as derived in Chapter 5 holds in the restricted context of decomposition instances that are projections of legal instances of the interface-level table.

While for the purposes of this discussion we choose to define a user-defined relational view to be a relational algebra expression, we could allow it also to be, for example, any tuple calculus expression or SQL query.

User-defined views are useful for reasons of convenience, privacy, and security. For example, suppose that

EMP(Emp#, Name, Dept, Salary)
DEPT(Dept, Manager, Location)

are interface-level tables, and, to simplify the discussion, suppose that EMP and DEPT are implementation-level tables as well. For this example, suppose also that the Manager attribute assumes values that are names of managers and that no two managers have the same name. We can define the user view ASSIGNMENT as follows:

$$\text{ASSIGNMENT} \leftarrow \Pi_{<Emp\#,Name,Dept,Manager>} (\text{EMP} \bowtie \text{DEPT})$$

Since a relational expression evaluates to a table instance, this equation defines a table called ASSIGNMENT by specifying how to derive its current instance from the current instances of tables EMP and DEPT. As Figure 13.1 illus-

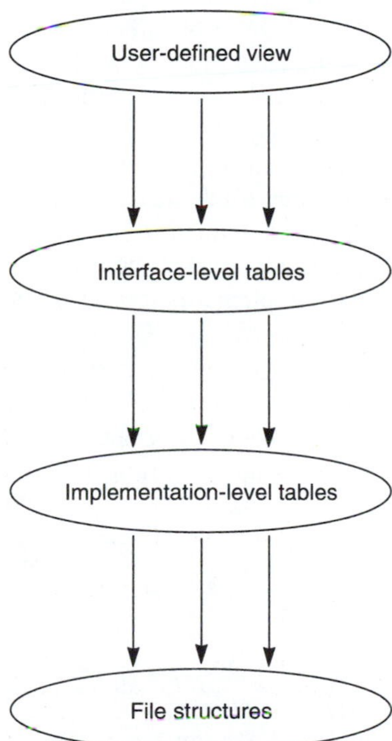

Figure 13.1 View-interface-implementation-files hierarchy

trates, we can think of the view ASSIGNMENT as appearing in the RDM's implementation hierarchy at a level of abstraction above the interface-level tables.

User queries can reference views such as ASSIGNMENT just as if the views were interface-level tables. Of course, whenever a query references a view, the reference must be translated first into references to interface-level tables and then into references to implementation-level tables. This translation problem is an aspect of query optimization known as **view expansion.** Observe that one candidate translation of every view is given by the view's definition. However, an optimizer may wish to search for a more efficiently processable translation. That is, since a view definition is a relational expression, the query optimizer may search for equivalent expressions just as if it were optimizing a user query. Note that, since the view presumably will be referenced repeatedly, the query optimizer may choose to save the translation it constructs for repeated use. However, in some contexts, the quality of a view's translation may depend on such factors as the current instance of the tables from which the view is derived and how the view interacts with the other parts of the query that reference the view. This observation implies that sometimes it may be advantageous to perform view expansion at the time a query referencing the view is encountered.

Hence, we see that a user-defined view shares with an interface-level table the property that, although the tuples of either may exist only abstractly, the query optimizer can always translate queries against either into operations on the stored data. While user-defined views and interface-level tables are similar in this regard, they differ with regard to their behavior under updates. As we have seen, updates stated against interface-level tables always can be realized by updating in a well-defined way implementation-level tables. Such is not the case, however, for arbitrary user-defined views. To illustrate, consider again the view ASSIGNMENT, and suppose that the current instances of tables EMP and DEPT (which, recall, are implementation-level, as well as interface-level, tables) are as follows:

EMP

Emp#	Name	Dept	Salary
111	Sam	Toys	20,000
200	Mark	Toys	25,000
222	Sue	Books	30,000
333	Fred	Books	25,000

DEPT

Dept	Manager	Location
Toys	Jones	10-D
Books	Harris	9-C
Books	Jackson	4-F

Note that, by definition, the current instance of the view ASSIGNMENT is

ASSIGNMENT

Emp#	Name	Dept	Manager
111	Sam	Toys	Jones
200	Mark	Toys	Jones
222	Sue	Books	Harris
222	Sue	Books	Jackson
333	Fred	Books	Harris
333	Fred	Books	Jackson

Observe that employees Sue and Fred are each assigned to both Books department managers Harris and Jackson. This fact is not for us to question—if a user defines the view ASSIGNMENT as given here, we must assume that its semantics are correct.

Consider now the implications of the following updates that a user might specify against the view ASSIGNMENT:

1. Delete from view ASSIGNMENT the tuple <111, Sam, Toys, Jones>. This update can be realized simply by deleting from the table EMP the tuple <111, Sam, Toys, 20,000>. This operation realizes the user's request in the sense that the new instance of ASSIGNMENT (i.e., the instance derived from the new instance of EMP and the instance of DEPT) is exactly the original instance of ASSIGNMENT minus the tuple that the user wished to delete. In the following, we shall assume that this deletion has been implemented as described.
2. Add to the view ASSIGNMENT the tuple <555, Hank, Toys, Jones>. Realizing this update requires that we add to table EMP a tuple t such that t[Emp#] = 555, t[Name] = Hank, and t[Dept] = Toys. However, we do not know what the value of t[Salary] should be. One solution is to assign to t[Salary] a null value $\perp$, but, as we have discussed previously, null values lead to many difficult problems. In the following, we shall assume that this update was disallowed.
3. Delete from the view ASSIGNMENT the tuple <200, Mark, Toys, Jones>. Assuming that we start with the instances of EMP, DEPT, and ASSIGNMENT that result from the deletion described in example 1, this update can be realized in any one of three ways: delete from table EMP the tuple <200, Mark, Toys, 25,000>; delete from the table DEPT the tuple <Toys, Jones, 10-D>; or delete both tuples. Each of these operations realizes the user's request in the sense that the new instance of ASSIGNMENT (i.e., the instance derived from each of the possible new instances of EMP and DEPT) is exactly the original instance of ASSIGNMENT minus the tuple that the user wished to delete. Hence, an update such as this is *ambiguous* in the sense that it does not have a well-defined

effect on the database. In the following, we shall assume that this update was disallowed.

4. Delete from the view ASSIGNMENT the tuple <222, Sue, Books, Harris>. This update *cannot be realized*. To see this, observe that to effect the deletion from ASSIGNMENT of the tuple <222, Sue, Books, Harris>, it is necessary either to delete tuple <222, Sue, Books, 30,000> from EMP or to delete tuple <Books, Harris, 9-C> from DEPT. However, the former deletion has the unintended effect of deleting the tuple <222, Sue, Books, Jackson> from ASSIGNMENT, while the latter deletion has the unintended effect of deleting the tuple <333, Fred, Books, Harris> from ASSIGNMENT. In the following, we shall assume that this update was disallowed.
5. Add to the view ASSIGNMENT the tuple <777, Tom, Books, Harris>. As in the second example, we encounter null value problems since the salary of the new employee is unknown. But, in the current example, even if we agreed to use null values, the update *cannot be realized*. The difficulty is that, by adding to table EMP a tuple of the form <777, Tom, Books, $\perp$ > , we add to ASSIGNMENT not only the desired tuple <777, Tom, Books, Harris> but also the tuple <777, Tom, Books, Jackson>, an effect that was not intended.

As a result of problems such as those illustrated by examples 2 through 5, most commercial relational database systems severely restrict the operations permitted on user-defined views. While most relational database systems allow the user to define and query arbitrary relational views, most systems disallow updates to views in all but a few special cases. While such restrictions certainly eliminate the problems we have described, they eliminate also the possibility of updating through views, even when the updates are realizable and well defined. One consequence of the restrictions placed on views by existing commercial relational database systems is that the database designer is unable to construct an RDM implementation in which interface-level tables map to different implementation-level tables, i.e., a relational database system would place the same restrictions it places on an arbitrary user-defined view on an interface-level table that becomes a view when we map it to different implementation-level tables. This restriction is unfortunate since the design methodology we have described produces implementation-level tables that are not prone to the problems that can arise in general when updating user-defined views. Consequently, if we wish to decompose a user-supplied table T into tables T_1 and T_2 for purposes of normalization, we must force users to state their updates against tables T_1 and T_2 rather than against the original table T.

Current research and prototype systems attempt to extend the utility of views by identifying when updates stated against views are realizable and well defined. That is, rather than disallowing all updates to views, the goal is for the query optimizer to identify and permit those updates whose effects can be realized in a unique way. Such capabilities would allow a database system to support the levels of abstraction in an RDM implementation as we have described it. Additionally, various methods have been proposed for handling unrealizable or ambiguous updates. One approach is to interact with the user to establish the true intent of an update. Other methods define, somewhat arbitrarily, how the query optimizer should select a realization of an update stated against a view when more than one realization exists. As we shall see in the next section, these techniques are also used when similar problems arise in the context of the universal relation mode.

13.2 THE UNIVERSAL RELATION MODEL

Recall that in Section 1.4 we considered the notion of a user interface based on a single, **universal relation** *U*. The scenario leading to the definition of such a table *U* might be as follows:

1. An information analyst consults with the user community, defines the schemes for interface-level tables, and identifies dependencies that apply to these tables.
2. A database designer uses normalization and optimization techniques to map the interface-level tables into implementation-level tables and eventually to file structures.
3. While semisophisticated users can interact easily with the interface-level tables, we wish an even more convenient interface for naive users. Hence, we define a view *U*, called the universal relation, containing all the attributes of all the interface-level tables. Users can now query the database without concern for in which interface-level tables the required attributes appear and without the need for intertable operators such as the Join.

To simplify the discussion that follows, we suppose that the interface-level and implementation-level tables defined in steps 1 and 2 coincide; we refer to these as **base tables.** Consider now the meaning of the following phrase that appears in step 3: *We define a view U, called the universal relation, containing all the attributes*. What, exactly, does this mean? Our first instinct might be to define *U* to be the Natural join of the base tables. Recall, for example, that in Section 1.4 we had base tables

```
EMPLOYEE(SS#,Name,Salary,Dept),
PERSONAL(SS#, Age, Highest_Degree),
DEPARTMENT(Dept,Manager,Location,D_Descript)
STOCKS(Dept, Prod#)
PRODUCT(Prod#, P_Descript)
```

(As in Section 1.4, define the Manager attribute so that its values are social security numbers, and assume that {Dept} is a key of table scheme DEPARTMENT.) We then defined U to be the Natural join

$$\text{EMPLOYEE} \bowtie \text{PERSONAL} \bowtie \text{DEPARTMENT} \bowtie \text{STOCKS} \bowtie \text{PRODUCT}$$

of the five tables.

While it may be intuitive to define U as the Natural join of the base tables, this definition is somewhat arbitrary. For example, in Section 1.4, we considered the request "Retrieve the salary of the manager of the toys department." As a first attempt at a solution, we considered the query

```
SELECT Salary
  WHERE Dept = "Toys"
```

The query does not satisfy the request since, when processed against the table U defined previously, it yields the salaries of all the employees who work in the toys department. The difficulty lies in the fact that the requested information is based on a relationship other than that assumed by the system. In particular, the query is based on a relationship that connects the relevant attributes in the manner embodied by the expression

$$\Pi_{<Salary, Dept(2)>}(\text{EMPLOYEE} \underset{SS\# = Manager}{\bowtie} \text{DEPARTMENT})$$

(In this expression, *Dept*(2) refers to the Dept attribute that comes from the second operand of the Join.) Note that the query

```
SELECT Salary
  WHERE Dept = "Toys"
```

in fact does yield the intended result when processed against the table defined by this Equi-join expression.

The preceding example indicates that the universal relation model's appeal—that the universal relation's definition in terms of base tables is invisible to the user—unfortunately is also a source of inherent ambiguity. In particular, since any *single definition* of a universal relation U is somewhat arbitrary, there always is the danger that a query stated against U, without knowledge of how U is defined, may be interpreted by the database system in a manner unintended by the user. Consequently, the ideal of an interface based on a single, universal relation is somewhat simplistic.

A perspective more practically viable than that of a single universal relation acknowledges that there are generally several ways of "connecting" sets of attributes that might be referenced by user queries. Consider the following definition.

Definition 13.2 Let H be a set of attributes contained in the base tables. A **window function** $[H]$ on H is a function mapping the current instance of the base tables into an instance of a table whose scheme consists of exactly those attributes in H.

Note that there are generally many reasonable window functions for a given collection H of attributes. For example, referring to the preceding five base tables, let H be {Salary, Dept}. Two of the possible window functions for H are

$[H]_1 = \Pi_{<Salary,\ Dept>}$ (EMPLOYEE)
$[H]_2 = \Pi_{<Salary,\ Dept(2)>}$ (EMPLOYEE $\underset{SS\#=Manager}{\bowtie}$ DEPARTMENT)

When the query optimizer encounters a query Q, it determines the set H of attributes referenced and computes the query against the table instance obtained by applying to the current instances of the base tables some window function $[H]$. In the preceding example, if the optimizer uses window function $[H]_1$, the query

```
SELECT Salary
  WHERE Dept = "Toys"
```

will evaluate to the salaries of all employees in the toys department, whereas if the optimizer uses $[H]_2$, this same query will evaluate to the salary of the manager of the toys department.

The fundamental problem, of course, is how to determine the window functions that the query optimizer should use. The simplest window function specification defines, for every subset H of attributes, $[H]$ to be the projection onto H of the Natural join of all the base tables. However, this specification is equivalent to the single universal relation perspective that, as we already have argued, is inappropriate in many situations.

Specifying $[H]$ to be, for every subset H of attributes, the projection onto H of the Natural join of the base tables is one extreme solution. A solution on the opposite extreme has the database designer supply the optimizer with a possibly different window function $[H]$ for each set H of attributes, allowing $[H]$ to be any relational expression of the designer's choosing. In our example, such a specification might be given as

if (H={Dept,Salary})
  $[H] = \Pi_{<Salary,Dept\ (2)>}$(EMPLOYEE $\underset{SS\#=Manager}{\bowtie}$ DEPARTMENT)
elseif (H is contained in any of the base tables T)
  $\Pi_{<H>}T$
elseif (H is contained in EMPLOYEE $\bowtie$ PERSONAL)
  $\Pi_{<H>}$(EMPLOYEE $\bowtie$ PERSONAL)
elseif (H is contained in EMPLOYEE $\bowtie$ DEPARTMENT)
$\Pi_{<H>}$(EMPLOYEE $\bowtie$ DEPARTMENT)
  .
  .
  .

Note that under this specification of window functions, the query

```
SELECT Salary
  WHERE Dept = "Toys"
```

would evaluate to the salary of the manager of the toys department. Of course, it might be the case that the user intends the query to evaluate to the salaries of all employees in the toys department. Clearly, there is no window function specification that can simultaneously satisfy both intentions—we can only guess the intent that will be most common and force users with other intents to write more complex queries. In some cases, user queries may need to explicitly reference base tables to override the window functions. For such queries, the interface would behave like a standard relational query language.

Other approaches to the problem of window function specification fall between the two extremes just discussed. These approaches do not require the designer to specify window functions, yet utilize window functions that are apparently appropriate more often than functions that always project from the Natural join of all the base tables. To illustrate two such approaches, we consider the four base tables

TAUGHT(Prof, Student, Course, Grade)
STUDENTS(Student, Major, GPA)
FACULTY(Prof, Dept, Salary)
ATHLETES(Student, Sport, Status)

and the four queries

*Q*1: SELECT Student, Course, Grade
WHERE Prof="Smith"
{ Intended meaning: Retrieve all students taught by Smith, along with the courses these students took from Smith and the grades they received in these courses. }

*Q*2: SELECT Course
WHERE Dept="CS"
{ Intended meaning: Retrieve the courses taught by professors in the CS department. }

*Q*3: SELECT Major
WHERE Dept = "CS"
{ Intended meaning: Retrieve the majors of students who have taken courses taught by professors in the CS department. }

*Q*4: SELECT Major
WHERE Prof="Smith"
{ Intended meaning: Retrieve the majors of students who have taken courses taught by Smith. }

We begin by observing that, for this example, defining a window function $[H]$ to be the projection onto H of the four-way Natural join of the base tables is a poor choice. Since only some students are athletes, evaluating each of the preceding queries based on such a window function will give incomplete answers. In particular, the four-way Natural join contains a tuple

Prof	Student	Course	Grade	Major	GPA	Dept	Salary	Sport	Status
p	*s*	*c*	*g*	*m*	*gp*	*d*	*sa*	*sp*	*st*

only if student s is an athlete. Hence, even the simple query $Q1$ will yield an incomplete answer when processed against the table instance induced by this window function: The projection onto {Prof, Student, Course, Grade} of the four-way Natural join consists of $<p\ s\ c\ g>$ tuples only for athletes s, and hence processing $Q1$ against this instance yields information about only athletes taught by Smith.

One approach to specifying a window function, rather than beginning by taking the Natural join of all base tables, takes the Natural join of a *minimal* set of tables needed to cover the referenced attributes H and then projects the resulting instance onto H. The following gives the window functions induced by this approach for the sets of attributes referenced by each of $Q1$, $Q2$, and $Q3$:

[Prof, Student, Course, Grade] = TAUGHT
[Dept, Course] = $\Pi_{<Dept,Course>}$ (TAUGHT $\bowtie$ FACULTY)
[Dept, Major] = $\Pi_{<Dept,Major>}$ (STUDENTS $\bowtie$ FACULTY)

Observe that $Q1$ and $Q2$, if processed against the table instances computed from the windows [Prof, Student, Course, Grade] and [Dept, Course], yield the intended answers. Processing $Q3$ against the window [Dept, Major], however, does not yield the intended answer since (STUDENTS $\bowtie$ FACULTY) is really a Cartesian product yielding tuples

Prof	Student	Course	Grade	Major	GPA	Dept	Salary	Sport	Status
p	*s*	*c*	*g*	*m*	*gp*	*d*	*sa*	*sp*	*st*

even when professor p has not taught student s; hence, the projection onto {Dept, Major} of the computed table instance may contain tuples $<m,CS>$, even if no CS professor has taught a student with major m.

Another difficulty with the minimal table approach is that there may be more than one minimal set of tables covering the referenced attributes. For example, the set of attributes {Prof, Major} referenced by $Q4$ is covered by each of {STUDENTS, FACULTY} and {STUDENTS, TAUGHT}. The first of these minimal sets yields the window function specification

[Prof,Major]$_1$ = $\Pi_{<Prof,Major>}$(STUDENTS $\bowtie$ FACULTY)

while the second minimal set yields the specification

[Prof,Major]$_2$ = $\Pi_{<Prof,Major>}$(STUDENTS $\bowtie$ TAUGHT)

Only if we are lucky enough to choose the window function [Prof, Major]$_2$ will query $Q4$ yield the intended answer.

Another approach to the problem utilizes semantic information about the base tables. We describe a simple instance of such an approach by means of example. Suppose that associated with base table FACULTY is the functional dependency Prof $\rightarrow$ Dept Salary and that associated with the base table STUDENTS is the functional dependency Student $\rightarrow$ Major GPA. The approach builds an instance I of a universal relation U over all the attributes that is consistent with the instances of the base tables and also is consistent with the functional dependencies. As a first step, we place in instance I all the tuples from each of the current instances of the base tables, padding each such tuple t

with null values in attribute positions not assigned a value by t. For example, suppose that the current instances of the base tables are as follows:

FACULTY

Prof	Dept	Salary
Smith	CS	50K
Jones	CS	40K

TAUGHT

Prof	Student	Course	Grade
Smith	Sue	463	B
Smith	Tom	463	C
Jones	Tom	500	A

STUDENT

Student	Major	GPA
Sue	Math	3.5
Tom	CS	3.2

ATHLETES

Student	Sport	Status
Sue	BB	Vars

Instance I of U would be initialized as follows:

Prof	Student	Course	Grade	Major	GPA	Dept	Salary	Sport	Status
Smith	⊥	⊥	⊥	⊥	⊥	CS	50K	⊥	⊥
Jones	⊥	⊥	⊥	⊥	⊥	CS	40K	⊥	⊥
Smith	Sue	463	B	⊥	⊥	⊥	⊥	⊥	⊥
Smith	Tom	463	C	⊥	⊥	⊥	⊥	⊥	⊥
Jones	Tom	500	A	⊥	⊥	⊥	⊥	⊥	⊥
⊥	Sue	⊥	⊥	Math	3.5	⊥	⊥	⊥	⊥
⊥	Tom	⊥	⊥	CS	3.2	⊥	⊥	⊥	⊥
⊥	Sue	⊥	⊥	⊥	⊥	⊥	⊥	BB	Vars

The next step in the construction of I uses the dependencies that are known to apply to the base tables to replace some of the null values with constants. For example, the initial version of instance I contains the tuples

Prof	Student	Course	Grade	Major	GPA	Dept	Salary	Sport	Status
Smith	⊥	⊥	⊥	⊥	⊥	CS	50K	⊥	⊥
Smith	Sue	463	B	⊥	⊥	⊥	⊥	⊥	⊥
⊥	Sue	⊥	⊥	Math	3.5	⊥	⊥	⊥	⊥

and the functional dependencies Prof → Dept Salary and Student → Major GPA are known to hold. By applying the dependency Prof → Dept Salary to the first and second of these tuples, we can modify the second tuple to

<Smith Sue 463 B ⊥ ⊥ CS 50K ⊥ ⊥>

Similarly, by applying the functional dependency Student → Major GPA to the second and third tuples, we can modify the second tuple to

<Smith Sue 463 B Math 3.5 CS 50K ⊥ ⊥>

The result of completely applying the functional dependencies to the tuples in the initial instance I is as follows:

Prof	Student	Course	Grade	Major	GPA	Dept	Salary	Sport	Status
Smith	⊥	⊥	⊥	⊥	⊥	CS	50K	⊥	⊥
Jones	⊥	⊥	⊥	⊥	⊥	CS	40K	⊥	⊥
Smith	Sue	463	B	Math	3.5	CS	50K	⊥	⊥
Smith	Tom	463	C	CS	3.2	CS	50K	⊥	⊥
Jones	Tom	500	A	CS	3.2	CS	40K	⊥	⊥
⊥	Sue	⊥	⊥	Math	3.5	⊥	⊥	⊥	⊥
⊥	Tom	⊥	⊥	CS	3.2	⊥	⊥	⊥	⊥
⊥	Sue	⊥	⊥	Math	3.5	⊥	⊥	BB	Vars

It is instructive to observe that, since there are no nontrivial dependencies of the form $W \rightarrow$ Student or $W \rightarrow$ Prof, where W is any set of attributes, a tuple in the resulting instance of U will combine information about professor P and student S if and only if table TAUGHT contains a tuple of the form $<P, S, x, y>$.

This construction of an instance I of universal relation U is the basis of a procedure for specifying window functions. Given any set H of attributes, the window function computes the projection onto H of instance I constructed earlier, where tuples from I having any null values in the attributes of H are eliminated. For example, the window functions for the sets of attributes referenced by queries $Q1$ through $Q4$ compute the following table instances:

[Prof,	Student,	Course,	Grade]
Smith	Sue	463	B
Smith	Tom	463	C
Jones	Tom	500	A

[Dept,	Course]
CS	463
CS	500

[Dept,	Major]
CS	Math
CS	CS

[Prof,	Major]
Smith	Math
Smith	CS
Jones	CS

Observe that each of the four queries, when processed against the corresponding table instance, produces the intended result.

While this last approach to specifying window functions performs well in our examples, it is not foolproof (see exercise 13.10). In fact, the instance *I* of the universal relation that we have described here is a simplified version of what is called a **representative instance.** The full construction of a representative instance is a bit more sophisticated, but even it cannot guarantee that queries will be processed to produce the intended results. Other approaches that utilize different types of semantic information are the object of current research as well. While the various approaches may work well in many situations, it is apparent that no approach can possibly behave correctly in all situations.

In closing, the reader should observe that we have not considered at all the problem of *updating* the base tables through a universal relation. It should be immediately apparent that many of the problems discussed in the last section associated with view updating arise in this context as well. Hence, research into the universal data model must address difficult problems associated with view updating as well as those of window function specification for queries.

13.3 RECURSIVE VIEWS AND THE DEDUCTIVE DATABASE MODEL

Recursive Views

In Section 3.4, we hypothesized the interface-level table PARENT(Child, Par) and attempted to define a table ANCESTOR(Desc,Anc) consisting of exactly those tuples $<d, a>$ such that *d* is a descendant of *a*. We argued that such an ANCESTOR table could not be expressed as a relational expression over the PARENT table; that is, we cannot define a view ANCESTOR within the relational model. We did see, however, that the following recurrence relation could be used to express ANCESTOR in terms of the PARENT table:

$$ANCESTOR_1 = PARENT$$
$$ANCESTOR_i = ANCESTOR_{i-1} \cup (\Pi_{<Child,Anc>}(PARENT \underset{Par=Desc}{\bowtie} ANCESTOR_{i-1})$$

Observe that while specifying such a recursive view requires that we extend the definitional capabilities of the RDM, the object of the definition (ANCESTOR) is nevertheless a table, and thus, the required semantic modifications to the RDM are minimal.

While supporting recursive definitions does not require major semantic extensions to the RDM model, recursively defined views give rise to a new aspect of query optimization. Observe that, unlike other views, a recursive definition cannot be "compiled" into a relational expression over the interface-level tables. How, then, do we process a query referencing a recursive view such as

ANCESTOR? The recursive definition must be translated into an algorithm for evaluating the view.

The most straightforward algorithm for computing the value of ANCESTOR is given by the following loop:

```
ANCESTOR ← PARENT
while (the value of ANCESTOR continues to change)
  ANCESTOR ← ANCESTOR ∪ (Π<Child,Anc>(PARENT ⋈Par=Desc ANCESTOR))
end while
```

This algorithm performs a simple **bottom-up computation.** The algorithm starts with the base table PARENT and builds up the ANCESTOR table one generation at a time. In particular, at the beginning of the ith iteration of the loop, ANCESTOR contains all $<d,a>$ tuples such that a is an ancestor up to i generations removed from d, where a person's parents are defined to be one generation removed, the grandparents two generations removed, and so forth. The ith iteration adds to ANCESTOR all tuples $<d,a>$ such that a is an ancestor $i + 1$ generations removed from d. The algorithm terminates when an iteration fails to change the value of ANCESTOR.

A more efficient bottom-up computation is based on the observation that, at iteration i, only tuples added to ANCESTOR at iteration $i - 1$ can participate in the derivation of new tuples for ANCESTOR. This observation leads to the following refined bottom-up computation:

```
ANCESTOR ← PARENT
{ The attributes of table new are Desc and Anc. }
NEW ← PARENT
while (NEW ≠ ∅)
  NEW ← (Π<Child,Anc>(PARENT ⋈Par=Desc NEW))
  ANCESTOR ← ANCESTOR ∪ NEW
end while
```

The advantage of this computation over the original is that, at each iteration, the Join is taken between PARENT and a table, NEW, that can be expected to contain considerably fewer tuples than the current instance of ANCESTOR.

Bottom-up computations are most appropriate when a query requires the entire view to be materialized. In contrast, consider the query $\sigma_{Desc=\text{"Tom"}}$ (*ANCESTOR*), which evaluates to the set of tuples $<$Tom,$a>$ such that a is an ancestor of Tom. We could use the bottom-up computation to build the entire ANCESTOR table and then select the ancestors of Tom, but this approach is doing a good deal of unnecessary work. An alternative approach is a goal-directed, **top-down computation.** We begin with ANCESTOR(Tom, a) as our *goal;* that is, find all tuples $<$Tom,$a>$, where a represents any value, such that tuple $<$Tom,$a>$ is in table ANCESTOR. We then use the recursive definition of ANCESTOR to generate two *subgoals*:

```
SG1: PARENT(Tom, a) → <Tom, a>
SG2: PARENT(Tom,x) AND ANCESTOR(x,a) → <Tom,a>
```

Subgoal SG1 should be interpreted as saying, "Attempt to find tuples <Tom, *a*>, where *a* represents any value and <Tom,*a*> is in table parent." Observe that all tuples <Tom,*a*> satisfying this subgoal satisfy the goal. Subgoal SG2 should be interpreted as saying, "Attempt to find pairs of tuples <Tom,*a*> and <*a*,*x*>, where *a* and *x* represent any values, <Tom,*a*> is in table PARENT, and <*x*,*a*> can be determined to be in ANCESTOR." Observe that all tuples <Tom,*a*>, such that the pair <Tom,*a*> and <*a*,*x*> satisfy this subgoal, satisfy the goal.

The first subgoal can be solved directly by performing a selection on table PARENT. Suppose, for example, that $\sigma_{Par=\text{"Tom"}}$ (*PARENT*) is equal to {<Tom, Sue>, <Tom,Fred>}. This solution to SG1 allows us to

1. Append to the (previously empty) current value of ANCESTOR the tuples <Tom, Sue> and <Tom, Fred>.
2. Instantiate subgoal SG2, obtaining the new subgoals

    SG2.1: PARENT(Tom,Sue) AND ANCESTOR(Sue,*a*) → <Tom, *a*>
    SG2.2: PARENT(Tom,Fred) AND ANCESTOR(Fred,*a*) → <Tom, *a*>

The recursive definition of ANCESTOR then is applied to these subgoals, obtaining

SG3: PARENT(Tom,Sue) AND PARENT(Sue,*a*) →<Tom, *a*>
SG4: PARENT(Tom,Fred) AND PARENT(Fred,*a*) →<Tom, *a*>
SG5: PARENT(Tom,Sue) AND PARENT(Sue,*a*) AND ANCESTOR(*a*,*e*) → <Tom, *e*>
SG6: PARENT(Tom,Fred) AND PARENT(Fred,*a*) AND ANCESTOR(*a*,*e*) → <Tom, *e*>

Subgoals SG3 and SG4 are solved directly by performing a selection on table PARENT. Suppose, for example, that one of Sue's parents is Jim. Jim then can instantiate *a* in SG3, yielding <Tom, Jim> as a new tuple in ANCESTOR. The tuple <Sue, Jim> of parent is used also to instantiate SG5, obtaining

SG5.1: PARENT(Tom,Sue) AND PARENT(Sue,Jim) AND ANCESTOR(Jim,*e*) → <Tom, *e*>

We continue to solve subgoals containing only PARENT by direct look-up. These solutions generate new tuples for ANCESTOR and allow us also to instantiate subgoals containing ANCESTOR. After all possible instantiations are made, subgoals containing ANCESTOR are expanded by applying the recursive definition of ANCESTOR, and the look-up–instantiate loop begins anew. The process continues until no new tuples for ANCESTOR can be generated.

Observe that, while the bottom-up computation generates the entire ANCESTOR table, the top-down computation generates for ANCESTOR only tuples of the form <*d*,*a*>, where *a* is an ancestor of Tom. In many cases, the top-down computation offers a significant savings.

Generalized Transitive Closures

A view defined in terms of a table T in the manner in which ANCESTOR is defined in terms of PARENT is referred to as the **transitive closure** of T and is denoted T^+. The transitive closure of a table has a natural graph-based interpretation. Recall that the transitive closure G^+ of any directed graph G contains the nodes of G and contains an edge from node x to node y if and only if there is a directed *path* in G from x to y. Figure 13.2 gives a graph G and its transitive closure G^+.

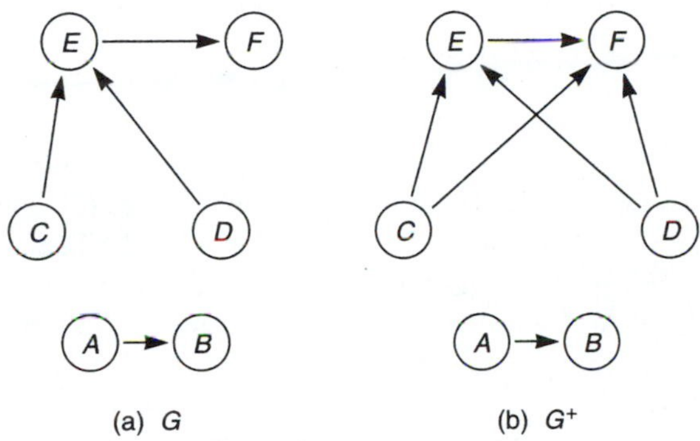

Figure 13.2 (*a*) G; (*b*) G^+

We can represent the ANCESTOR table as the transitive closure of a graph G, where G represents as follows the current instance of the PARENT table. The nodes of G are values that appear in table PARENT, either as Child or Par entries. There is a directed edge from node c to node p if and only if $<c,p>$ is a tuple in PARENT. Figure 13.3 gives an instance of PARENT with its graph representation.

Consider now the transitive closure of G, shown in Figure 13.4. Note that in G^+, an edge connects x and y if and only if there is a directed path in G from

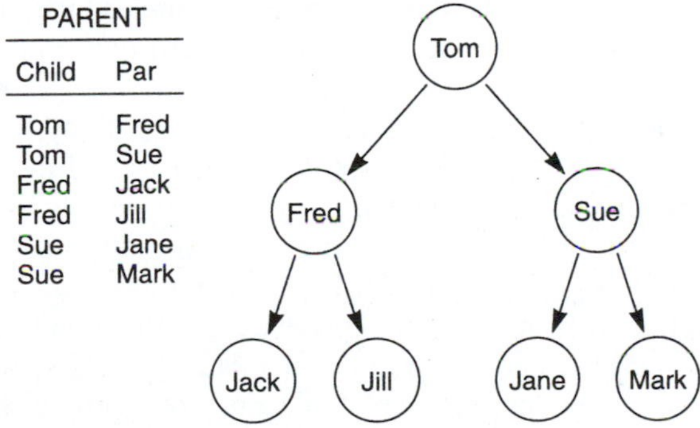

PARENT

Child	Par
Tom	Fred
Tom	Sue
Fred	Jack
Fred	Jill
Sue	Jane
Sue	Mark

Figure 13.3 (*a*) PARENT; (*b*) G representation

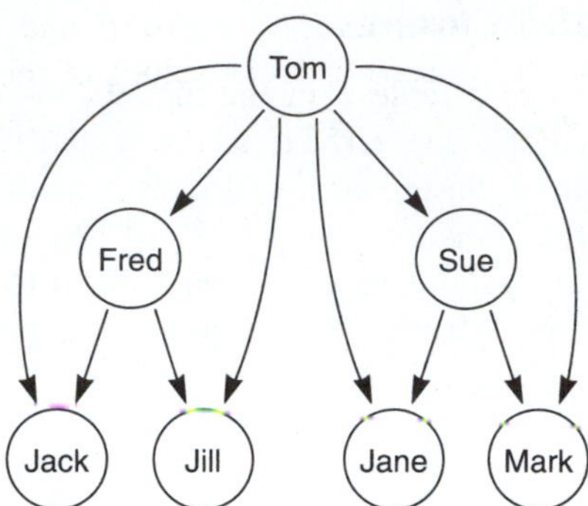

Figure 13.4 Transitive closure G^+

x to y, that is, if and only if y is an ancestor of x. Hence, G^+ contains an edge from x to y exactly when $<x,y>$ is a tuple in the ANCESTOR table.

This graph-based model is useful, not only because it suggests that graph traversal algorithms can be used to compute the transitive closure of a table but also because it is at the foundation of several data models that allow users to conveniently request information based on recursive relationships. Such interfaces are useful in specifying simple transitive closures such as those already considered, as well as in specifying what are known as **generalized transitive closures.** The need to compute generalized transitive closures may arise when "secondary" information is associated with the tuples in the table over which the transitive closure is to be computed.

To illustrate the generalized transitive closure problem, consider the table scheme FLIGHTS(Origin, Dest, Cost, Airline) giving, for each flight in our database, the flight's city of origin, its destination, its cost, and the airline operating the flight. We will want to ask questions about sequences of flights that connect various pairs of cities. Note that if we were interested only in questions such as "Between which pairs of cities are there sequences of flights?" we would ignore the attributes Cost and Airline and compute the transitive closures of the table $\Pi_{<Origin,Dest>}$(FLIGHTS). Since attributes Origin and Dest are the basis of the transitive closure relationship, we shall refer to them as **distinguished attributes.**

In addition to asking about the existence of sequences of flights, we also may have questions regarding the cities in the sequences and the costs of these sequences and questions that involve the airlines operating flights used in a sequence. Such questions require that we utilize the **nondistinguished attributes** Cost and Airline. To begin, we consider how to extend the graph-based representation to capture the information conveyed by the nondistinguished attributes. To represent the current instance of table FLIGHTS, we construct a graph G in which the nodes represent the values of distinguished attributes Origin and Dest. The graph contains an edge from x to y if and only if

FLIGHTS contains a tuple $<x,y,c,a>$, where c and a are values of the nondistinguished attributes. To represent the values of the nondistinguished attributes, we introduce **edge labels.** If FLIGHTS contains a tuple $<x,y,c,a>$, then the edge from x to y is labeled by the pair (c,a). Note that G will contain multiple edges from x to y if FLIGHTS contains distinct tuples $<x,y,c,a>$ and $<x,y,c',a'>$. Figure 13.5 depicts an instance of table FLIGHTs along with its representation as a graph.

Now consider queries we might want to pose against table FLIGHTS and how these queries can be interpreted as "path problems" in the graph G.

Q1: Report on every sequence of flights between Eugene and Green Bay, listing the cities on each sequence and the cost of each sequence. In terms of the graph, we must find every path from Eugene to Green Bay and, as we traverse each such path, sum the costs that label the edges.

Q2: For each ordered pair (x,y) of cities, find the identity and cost of the *cheapest* sequence of flights from x to y. In terms of the graph, we must find the least cost path connecting each pair of nodes.

Q3: For each pair of cities, find the cost of the cheapest sequence of flights that uses only airline X. This query requires that we perform the same work as for Q2 but that we discard any sequence that includes an edge labeled by an airline other than X.

To abstract these queries, we introduce a pair of operators defined on the domains of the values that label the edges. Let S denote the domain of the nondistinguished attribute of interest. The operator $*$ (called **concatenation**) combines the values of edge labels as we compute the closure. In particular, if (x,y) is an edge labeled v_1 and if (y,z) is an edge labeled v_2, the closure contains an edge (x,z) labeled with the value $v_1 * v_2$, which is a member of the domain S. More generally, if $(x_1,x_2), \ldots ,(x_{n-1},x_n)$ is a path in G with labels $v_1,v_2, \ldots ,v_{n-1}$, then the transitive closure contains an edge (x_1,x_n) labeled with the value $((\ldots ((v_1 * v_2) * v_3) * \cdots * v_{n-2})*v_{n-1})$. Note that if G contains more than one path from x to y, the transitive closure will contain more than one edge from x to y, and these edges, in general, will have different labels.

Query Q1 now can be given the following formulation. Let the set of reals be the domain of nondistinguished attribute Cost, and define the $*$ operator to be ordinary addition. Then each edge in the transitive closure from Eugene to Green Bay represents a sequence of flights, and the label of that edge represents the cost of the sequence. Of course, reporting the sequence itself requires that we somehow record the cities visited on the path represented by each edge, a problem we shall address next.

To capture queries Q2 and Q3, we must introduce a second operator $\oplus$ (called **aggregation**). The $\oplus$ operator computes an aggregate value over a set of values from domain S, and this aggregate value also is a member of S. Common aggregate operators include summation, minimization, and maximization.

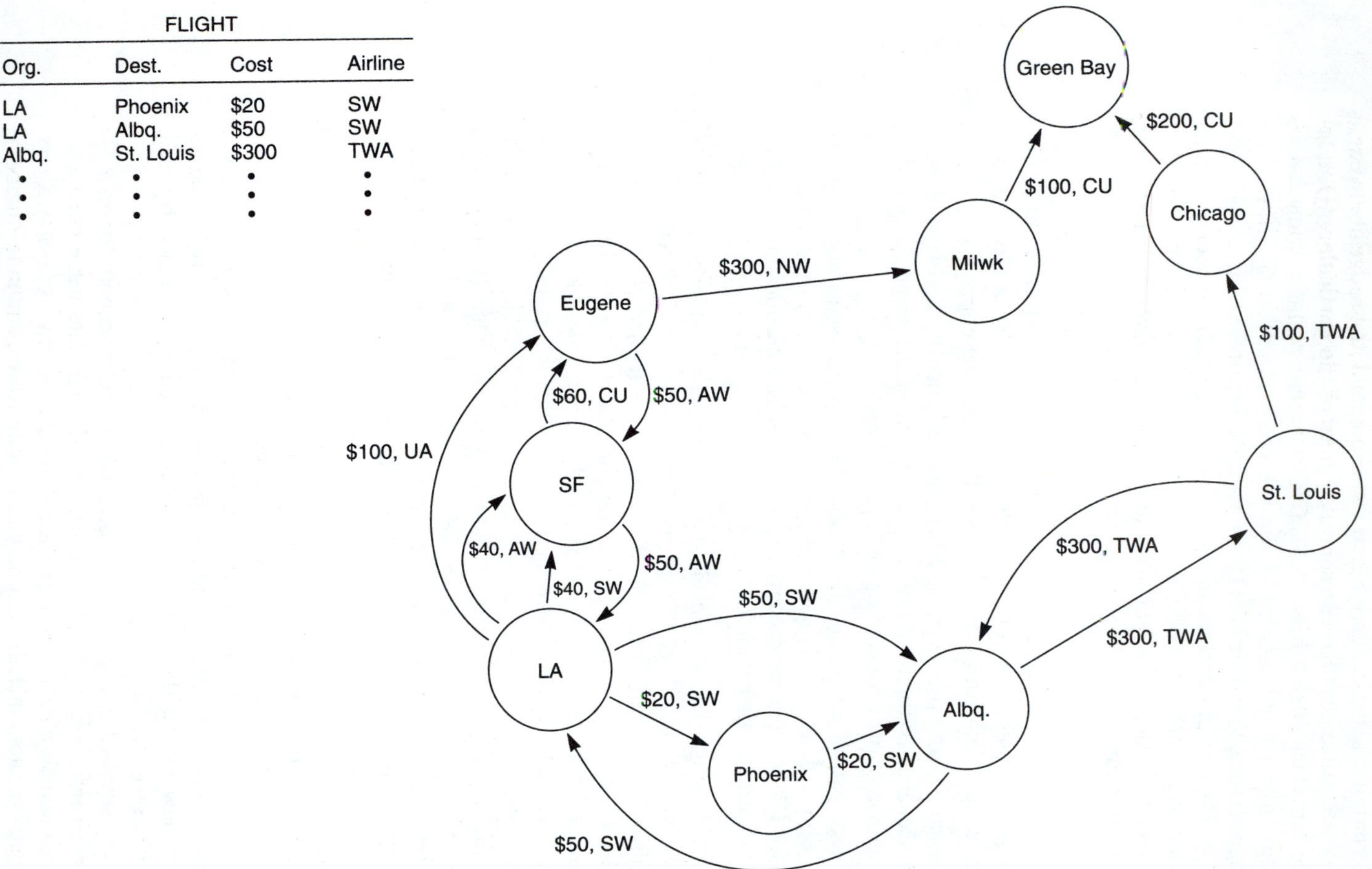

FLIGHT

Org.	Dest.	Cost	Airline
LA	Phoenix	$20	SW
LA	Albq.	$50	SW
Albq.	St. Louis	$300	TWA
⋮	⋮	⋮	⋮

Figure 13.5 Instance of flight along with graph representation

The $\oplus$ operator is used to collapse into a single edge multiple edges between a pair (x,y) of nodes in the transitive closure of a graph. In particular, $\oplus$ is applied to the set of values that label the edges from x to y and the value that results label the single edge.

Query Q2 now can be given the following formulation. Again let the set of reals be the domain of nondistinguished attribute Cost and the $*$ operator be ordinary addition. Define $\oplus$ to be minimization. Then, after $\oplus$ is applied to the transitive closure G^+ of graph G, each pair (x,y) between which there exists a sequence of flights is connected by an edge labeled with the cost of the cheapest such sequence. Q3 is formulated like Q2, except that the operations are applied to the graph G_X consisting of only those edges of G whose Airline label is X.

While we may indeed wish to support a graph-based interface to ease the burden of constructing recursive queries such as Q1, Q2, and Q3, there are several potential benefits of mapping such an interface to an extended RDM model since such an approach allows us to exploit existing design, storage, and query optimization techniques. Consequently, we now consider how generalized transitive closure queries can be stated and processed within an extended RDM framework.

If the table FLIGHT consisted only of the distinguished attributes Dest and Org, its standard transitive closure FLIGHT$^+$ would contain a tuple $<x, y>$ exactly when there is a sequence of tuples $<x,x_1>, \ldots ,<x_n,y>$ in table FLIGHT. To pose and answer queries such as those we have been considering, it is necessary to extend the standard notion of the transitive closure of a table in two directions: the extended closure must record tuple sequences, and it must allow us to perform computations (e.g., using $*$ and $\oplus$) on these sequences. A new relational operator α has been proposed as one means of providing these capabilities. We introduce the α operator by describing how the result α(FLIGHT) of applying the operator to table FLIGHT extends the standard notion of transitive closure.

1. Table α(FLIGHT) records the "derivation histories" of the tuples appearing in the transitive closure of $\Pi_{<Org,Dest>}$ (FLIGHT). To capture this information, α(FLIGHT) is given a new type of attribute, denoted Δ. For each tuple $<x,y>$ in the standard transitive closure ($\Pi_{<Org,Dest>}$ (FLIGHT))$^+$, α(FLIGHT) contains one or more tuples t such that $t[Org] = x$ and $t[Dest] = y$; the value of $t[\Delta]$ is a sequence $<x,x_1>$, $<x_1,x_2>, \ldots , <x_n,y>$ of tuples from FLIGHT that form a path from x to y. More precisely, for every $<x,y>$ in ($\Pi_{<Org,Dest>}$(FLIGHT))$^+$ and every cycle-free derivation $<x,x_1>,<x_1,x_2>, \ldots ,<x_n,y>$ of $<x,y>$ from FLIGHT, α(FLIGHT) contains a tuple t with $t[Org] = x$, $t[Dest] = y$ and $t[\Delta] = <x,x_1>,<x_1,x_2>, \ldots ,<x_n,y>$. Observe that we have defined α(FLIGHT) so that attribute Δ does not record derivations containing cycles, that is, paths that visit the same city more than once. Without this restriction, there could exist an infinite number

of distinct derivations of certain tuples $<x,y>$, for example,

$$<x,x_1>,<x_1,x_2>,<x_2,x_3>,<x_3,y>$$
$$<x,x_1>,<x_1,x_2>,<x_2,x_3>,<x_3,x_1>,<x_1,x_2>,<x_2,x_3>,<x_3,y>$$
$$<x,x_1>,<x_1,x_2>,<x_2,x_3>,<x_3,x_1>,<x_1,x_2>,<x_2,x_3>,<x_3,x_1>,$$
$$<x_1,x_2>,<x_2,x_3>,<x_3,y>$$

.
.
.

In most applications, derivations containing cycles are of no interest (e.g., the shortest flight sequence never contains a cycle), and hence restricting attention to cycle-free derivations is semantically valid.

It should be noted that, since Δ takes on nonscalar values, the tables resulting from the application of the α operator are *not in first normal form*.

2. The α operator performs computations on the derivation histories. In general, the table to which we apply the α operator will contain nondistinguished, as well as distinguished, attributes, and we will wish for at least some of these nondistinguished attributes to appear in the result α(FLIGHT) with meaningful values. For example, our sample queries require that α(FLIGHT) contain the attribute Cost and that for any $t \in \alpha$(FLIGHT), $t[Cost]$ be the cost of the flight sequence $t[\Delta]$. As a first step in addressing this problem, we must introduce a notation that parameterizes α to allow us to specify the desired computation for one or more nondistinguished attributes. Let * be a concatenation operator on the nondistinguished attribute A of table T. Then $\alpha_{(A(*))}T$ specifies that attribute A should appear in table $\alpha(T)$ and that for each $t \in \alpha_{(A(*))}T$, if $t[\Delta] = <x_1,x_2>, \ldots, <x_i,x_{i+1}>, \ldots, <x_{n-1},x_n>$, then $t[A]$ should be computed as $((\ldots ((v_1 * v_2) * v_3) * \cdots * v_{n-2}) * v_{n-1})$, where v_i is the A value in T of the tuple with distinguished attribute values x_i and x_{i+1}. Thus, for example, $\alpha_{(Cost(+))}$FLIGHT specifies that *Cost* should appear in the result and have value equal to the cost of the path of the corresponding derivation. In general, more than one nondistinguished attribute can appear as parameters to α, provided that we supply a concatenation operator for each.

Query Q1 can be stated as $\sigma_{(Org=Eugene \wedge Dest=GreenBay)}(\alpha_{(Cost(+))}\text{FLIGHT})$. To state query Q2, we introduce a $\oplus$ (aggregation) operator that, conceptually, is applied to the result of the α operator. Query Q2 requires the aggregation operator min. We use the notation $\min_{Cost}(\alpha_{(Cost(+))}\text{FLIGHT})$ to specify that when $\alpha_{(Cost(+))}$FLIGHT contains more than one tuple with distinguished attribute values $<x,y>$, the min aggregate should be applied to the Cost values associated with this set of tuples, effectively selecting the tuple with the minimum Cost value. Similarly, Q3 can be stated as $\min_{Cost}(\alpha_{(Cost(+))}(\sigma_{Airline=X}\text{FLIGHT}))$. These queries illustrate one of the virtues of an approach that extends the RDM model—the new α operator can be composed naturally with existing operators, and optimization heuristics for manipulating these expressions can be implemented within the framework of an existing relational query optimizer. The problem of extending a relational query optimizer so that it can handle new operators is considered in Section 13.4.

How does the query optimizer compute $\alpha(T)$, where α may be parameterized with concatenation and aggregation operators? The straightforward implementation has three steps.

Step 1: Compute the transitive closure augmented by the Δ attribute. This can be accomplished via minor modifications to the simple bottom-up transitive closure algorithm. We illustrate with an algorithm for computing α(FLIGHT); we ignore the nondistinguished attributes Cost and Airline and the application of the concatenation and aggregation operators until steps 2 and 3.

```
for (each t ∈ FLIGHT)
  add to α(FLIGHT) the tuple t' defined by t'[Org,Dest]=t[Org,Dest]
    and set t'[Δ] equal to the list (<t[Org],t[Dest]>) containing a single tuple
endfor
while (the value of α(FLIGHT) continues to change)
  for (each pair t ∈ FLIGHT, t' ∈ α(FLIGHT) such that t'[Dest]=t[Org])
    { The following test prevents the introduction of cycles. }
    if (t[dest] does not appear as a value in the list t'[Δ])
      add to α(FLIGHT) the tuple n defined by n[Org]=t'[Org],
        n[Dest]=t[Dest] and set n[Δ] equal to list t'[ Δ]
        extended by <t[Org],t[Dest]>)
    endif
  endfor
end while
```

Step 2: Compute the values for any specified nondistinguished attributes. For the FLIGHT example, if tuple t is in the table resulting from step 1, we compute $t[Cost]$ by

a. Looking up in table FLIGHT the Cost value v_i of each $<x_i, x_{i+1}>$ in the list $t[\Delta]$.

b. Computing $((\ \ldots\ ((v_1 * v_2) * v_3) * \cdots * v_{n-2}) * v_{n-1})$.

Step 3: If aggregation operators are specified, they are applied by searching the table resulting from step 2 for tuples with identical pairs of distinguished attribute values and collapsing these tuples as specified by the aggregation operators.

While this method of implementation is conceptually simple, it can be grossly inefficient. Note, for example, that there may be a huge number of cycle-free paths between any pair $<x,y>$ of cities. Since the first step of the method described computes a table containing a distinct tuple for each distinct path, the method often will be infeasible. Fortunately, if $*$ and $\oplus$ have certain properties (e.g, commutativity, associativity, $*$ distributes over $\oplus$), substantial optimizations may be possible. In this case, a query optimizer may be able to apply the concatenation and aggregation operators "as we go" so that it is not necessary to carry along more than a single tuple for any pair $<x,y>$ of distinguished attribute values. The general idea behind such optimizations is that we can order the computation in such a way that, at any iteration, dynamic programming–like dominance relations allow us to replace the set of $<x,y>$ paths so far considered by an aggregate value for this set. See exercise 13.13 for details.

Deductive Databases

The deductive database (DDB) model is an extension of the RDM that includes some of the capabilities discussed earlier, as well as many additional capabilities. The DDB model extends the RDM while preserving the table as the basic interface object. This is an advantageous characteristic of the DDB model as the semantics of the table and RDM are fairly well understood (e.g., as captured by the theory of normalization) and efficient storage structures and query optimization algorithms exist for these data models.

There is no universally accepted definition of *the* DDB model. Different researchers attribute to the model somewhat differing capabilities. In this overview, we shall present what most researchers consider to be the core concepts and capabilities of the DDB model. A primary tenant of its developers is that the DDB model should provide a framework in which data (in the traditional sense), and facts about the data, are treated uniformly. In particular, a DDB integrates in a single model collections of tables, integrity constraints and other information describing the tables, and axioms specifying how a query processor may reason about the data.

The basic definitional construct of a DDB is the **clause.** Examples of clauses are

```
PROFESSOR(Smith, CS, 50K)
STUD(Tom, CS, 4.0)
PROFESSOR(pname,dept,sal) AND STUD(sname,dept,gpa) ⇒
  PALS(pname,sname)
```

For our purposes, a clause consists of a collection of table names (also referred to as predicates in some presentations of the DDB model), along with arguments for the tables and logical connectives (e.g., $\wedge$, $\vee$, and $\Rightarrow$). Strings consisting of only lowercase letters denote variables—we often give descriptive names to variables so that they resemble attribute names in the RDM. All other strings denote constants. Each of the first two clauses is an example of a **ground atom,** a clause consisting of a single table name whose arguments are all constants. Each ground atom asserts the fact that its arguments form a tuple in the current instance of the corresponding table. Thus, the first clause asserts that <Smith, CS, 50K> is a tuple in the current instance of table PROFESSOR.

The third clause asserts the fact that if PROFESSOR and STUD contain tuples p and s, respectively, such that p and s agree on their second arguments, then table PALS contains a tuple whose first argument is the first argument of PROFESSOR and whose second argument is the first argument of STUD. Note that variables are interpreted as being *universally quantified;* that is, the assertion states that *for all p* and *s* satisfying the preceding conditions, a tuple in PALS is generated. Observe how this clause has the same effect as a relational view defining PALS in terms of a projection from the Join of tables PROFESSOR and STUD.

When a query is processed against a DDB, the query processor must make deductions from the database's facts. As we shall illustrate later, certain aspects of the deduction system are specified by clauses in other parts of the database. For now, we describe some standard deductions that are always applicable. Suppose the user wishes to know what department Professor Smith is in. The user would construct the **query clause**

```
PROFESSOR(Smith, dept, sal) ⇒ Q(dept)
```

The query processor would then attempt to find all values of the variable *dept* for which the fact *Q(dept)* is deducible from the facts contained in the database and the clause

```
PROFESSOR(Smith, dept, sal) ⇒ Q(dept)
```

defining *Q*. If the database contains only the foregoing three facts, the answer to the query is the table *Q* consisting of the single tuple <CS>. Similarly, the query

```
PALS(Smith,sname) ⇒ Q(sname)
```

asks for all of Smith's pals. Again assuming the foregoing three facts, we can deduce the fact PALS(Smith, Tom), and hence the answer to the query is the table *Q* consisting of the single tuple <Tom>.

The clauses of a DDB are partitioned into two sets: The **extensional database (EDB)** consists of all ground atoms and is essentially an instance of an RDM at the interface-table level. These ground atoms are typically stored in a traditional relational database as tuples of tables (or are possibly mapped first to implementation-level tables). The **intensional database (IDB)** consists of all the other clauses and serves to define and describe other elements of the database. We now illustrate various types of IDB clauses and describe their roles.

Complex Data Definitions: The IDB can include a collection of clauses that allow us to deduce that certain tuples belong to certain tables. As previously illustrated by the clause defining table PALS, traditional relational views can be defined by IDB clauses. Additionally, the recursive view ANCESTOR can be defined in the IDB by the clauses

```
PARENT(child,par) ⇒ ANCESTOR(child,par)
PARENT(child,par) AND ANCESTOR(par,anc) ⇒ ANCESTOR(child,anc)
```

Note how this definition of ANCESTOR is equivalent to that given by the recurrence relation considered earlier. It should be read as

> If, for any values of variables *child* and *par*, it can be deduced that <*child,par*> is a tuple in table PARENT [we say that it can be deduced that PARENT(*child,par*) is true], then deduce that <*child,par*> is in ANCESTOR [we say that we can deduce that ANCESTOR(*child,par*) is true]. Further, if, for any values of *child*, *par*, *anc*, it can be deduced that PARENT(*child,par*) is true and if, additionally, it can be deduced that ANCESTOR(*par,anc*) is true, then deduce that ANCESTOR(*child,anc*) is true.

Thus, each of the two clauses gives a way of generating tuples in ANCESTOR, and the set of tuples that can be generated starting with the current instance of table PARENT is, by definition, the current instance of ANCESTOR. Given that these two clauses appear in the IDB, the user can ask for the ancestors of Tom by writing the query clause

```
ANCESTOR(Tom,anc) ⇒ Q(anc)
```

The query processor will then deduce the appropriate set of tuples from the current instance of the EDB table PARENT and the IDB clauses.

An IDB may contain clauses defining data of many variates. For example, clauses can define **indefinite data.** Consider the following indefinite clause:

```
PROFESSOR(Smith, CS, 50K) OR PROFESSOR(Smith, Math, 50K)
```

If the user writes a query clause such as

```
PROFESSOR(Smith,x,y) ⇒ Q(dept, sal)
```

the query processor must deduce as an indefinite answer the table *Q* containing the tuple <CS/Math,50K>, which represents the fact that either PROFESSOR(Smith, CS, 50K) is true or PROFESSOR(Smith, Math, 50K) is true (or that both are true).

Observe that null values in some contexts can be interpreted as indefinite data. For example, the clause

```
PROFESSOR(Smith, ⊥, 50K)
```

can be interpreted as shorthand for the clause

```
PROFESSOR(Smith, CS, 50K) OR PROFESSOR(Smith, Math, 50K) OR . . .
OR PROFESSOR(Smith, English, 50K)
```

where every member of the domain of the second argument is represented. Using this convention, the query clause

```
PROFESSOR(Smith, dept, sal) ⇒ Q(dept, sal)
```

evaluates to a table *Q* consisting of the tuple <⊥,50K>, which can be interpreted as shorthand for the table consisting of the tuple <CS/Math . . . /English,50K>. As we have discussed in earlier chapters, a difficulty with null values is that we must specify exactly how they behave under different database operations. One benefit of the DDB model is that it allows us to specify directly in the database this and other behaviors.

IDB clauses can be used to compactly represent facts about an EDB table that would have to be stored explicitly in the RDM as a large number of tuples. To illustrate, suppose that a computer system needs to maintain a catalogue of user privileges, specifying the programs that each user of the system is permitted to execute. We can model this information as a table

```
PRIV(user, program)
```

Assume also that we have the table PROGRAM(pname, p-info) that lists the names of all the system's programs along with information about each program and the table USER(uname, u-info) that lists the names of all the system's users along with information about each user.

Suppose that there are a total of 10,000 different programs, 1,000 users, and that the typical user has privileges to execute about 10 programs. There are two special cases: A user called "Root" (a superuser) is permitted to execute all the programs in the system, and a handful of "open" programs can be executed by all users. Using the RDM, table PRIV would have to contain one tuple <Root, *P*> for each of the 10,000 programs. Further, for each open program *OP* executable by all users, PRIV would have to contain a tuple <*U*, *OP*> for each of the 1,000 users *U*. Not only does this method of recording information about user Root and open programs require much storage, but determining whether user Root is permitted to execute a particular program and determining whether some user *U* is permitted to execute a particular open program require nontrivial searches.

A DDB offers the following alternative. We can include in the EDB clauses

PRIV(*U*, *P*)

for each nonroot user *U* and each nonopen program *P* that *U* may execute. We include in the IDB the clause

```
PROGRAM(pname, p-info) ⇒ PRIV(Root,pname)
```

which asserts the fact that Root may execute all programs listed in PROGRAM, that is, that <Root, pname> is a tuple in PRIV if pname appears as a program name in PRIV. Similarly, we include in the IDB the clauses

USER(uname, u-info) ⇒ PRIV(uname, OP_1)
USER(uname, u-info) ⇒ PRIV(uname, OP_2)
. . .
USER(uname, u-info) ⇒ PRIV(uname, OP_k)

where OP_i are the open programs. In this manner, some of the tuples of PRIV are listed explicitly in the EDB, while others are defined implicitly by clauses in the IDB. Note, for example, that the query optimizer can deduce, without searching the EDB, the answer to a query asking whether Root may execute some particular program *P*.

***Integrity Constraints*:** IDB clauses can serve also as integrity constraints. Suppose, for example, that an RDM would model some information as a table EMPLOYEE(SS# Name, Dept, Salary) and that we wish to enforce the functional dependency SS# → Name Dept Salary. In a DDB, the EDB would contain a ground atom for every employee tuple, and the IDB would contain the clause

$$\text{EMPLOYEE}(ss, name_1, dept_1, sal_1) \text{ AND } \text{EMPLOYEE}(ss, name_2, dept_2, sal_2) \Rightarrow (name_1{=}name_2) \text{ AND } (dept_1{=}dept_2) \text{ AND } (sal_1{=}sal_2)$$

Whenever the user attempts to add a tuple to EMPLOYEE (i.e., attempts to add to the EDB a ground EMPLOYEE atom), the query processor checks whether the database that would result from the addition is *consistent*. Suppose, for example, that the EDB contains the clause

EMPLOYEE(111, Jones, CS, 30,000)

and the user attempts to add the clause

EMPLOYEE(111, Jones, CS, 40,000)

It follows from the two EDB clauses EMPLOYEE(111, Jones, CS, 30,000) and EMPLOYEE(111, Jones, CS, 40,000) and the IDB clause

$$\text{EMPLOYEE}(ss, name_1, dept_1, sal_1) \text{ AND } \text{EMPLOYEE}(ss, name_2, dept_2, sal_2) \Rightarrow (name_1{=}name_2) \text{ AND } (dept_1{=}dept_2) \text{ AND } (sal_1{=}sal_2)$$

that (30,000 = 40,000), a contradiction.[2] A database from which a contradiction can be deduced is inconsistent and any update that would cause the database to become inconsistent must be disallowed.

The IDB can be used to express many different types of integrity constraints. Suppose, for example, that $T(A_1,A_2,A_3)$ is a table scheme and that we wish to capture the multivalued dependency $A_1 \twoheadrightarrow A_2$. We could place the clause

$$T(x,y,z) \text{ AND } T(x,y',z') \Rightarrow T(x,y',z)$$

in the IDB. This example raises an important point. The scenario for enforcing an integrity constraint such as this multivalued dependency is that when the user attempts to update the database, the query processor must check whether the update would cause the database to become inconsistent. If, for example, the EDB contains the clause $T(A,B,C)$ and the user attempts to add the clause $T(A,B',C)$, a contradiction would exist if the clause $T(A,B',C)$ is not present in the EDB (and cannot be deduced).[3] However, from another perspective, the

[2] As is discussed shortly, the contradiction relies on an axiom, known as the *unique name axiom,* that asserts that distinct constant symbols are not equal.

[3] As is discussed shortly, the contradiction relies on an axiom, known as the *closed world assumption,* that asserts that if $T(x_1, \ldots, x_n)$ cannot be deduced then NOT $T(x_1, \ldots, x_n)$ is true.

clause

$T(x,y,z)$ AND $T(x,y',z') \Rightarrow T(x,y',z)$

could be treated as an implicit definition of some of the tuples in T. That is, just as we previously defined a portion of the table PRIV implicitly with the clause

PROGRAM(pname, p-info) $\Rightarrow$ PRIV(Root,pname)

a query processor might treat the clause

$T(x,y,z)$ AND $T(x,y',z') \Rightarrow T(x,y',z)$

as an implicit definition and, rather than reaching the conclusion that a contradiction exists, reach the conclusion that $T(A,B',C)$ can be deduced.

In general, data generating IDB clauses and IDB clauses that are intended as integrity constraints may not be distinguishable from their syntax alone. Consequently, a convention must be adopted allowing the query processor to distinguish between the two types of clauses and use them as intended. For example, a clause such as

$T(x,y,z)$ AND $T(x,y',z') \Rightarrow T(x,y',z)$

could be marked as an integrity constraint and would not be used by the query processor to deduce tuples in T. Similarly, the clause

PROGRAM(pname, p-info) $\Rightarrow$ PRIV(Root,pname)

could be marked as data generative and would be used to generate tuples in PRIV, but not to enforce integrity constraints. Of course, the user might wish to assert the integrity constraint

PROGRAM(pname, p-info) $\Rightarrow$ PRIV(Root,pname)

and require PRIV to explicitly list the privileges of user Root. This intention can be conveyed by appropriate use of the marking conventions.

Axioms that Define the Logic System: As we have mentioned, some IDB clauses serve to define certain aspects of the logic system with respect to which deductions are made. One motivation for including some of the logic system's properties in the IDB is that the facility makes the database system a self-contained theory. A second motivation is that we may desire slightly differing logic systems for different applications. In principle, we can have a single query optimizer that, depending on the details of the logic system specified, produces different answers to the same queries. For example, we may wish for null values to be treated differently in different applications—this can be accomplished by altering the axioms that govern the behavior of null values.

As an example of the kinds of clauses that are typically present in any DDB, consider the following two types of axioms:

- *Domain closure axioms:* For each argument position of each table T, a **domain closure axiom** is used to specify the permissible values that the argument can take on. For example,

$$T(x_1, x_2, \ldots, x_k) \Rightarrow ((x_1 = V_1) \vee \cdots \vee (x_1 = V_m))$$

has the effect of restricting to the domain $\{V_1, \ldots, V_k\}$ the values tuples in T can assume in their first attribute position.

- *Unique name axiom:* The **unique name axiom** states that distinct constant symbols denote distinct values. The form of the unique name axiom is

$$(V_1 \neq V_2) \wedge \cdots \wedge (V_1 \neq V_M) \wedge (V_2 \neq V_3) \wedge \cdots \wedge (V_2 \neq V_M) \wedge \cdots \wedge (V_{M-1} \neq V_M)$$

where $V_1, \ldots, V_M$ are the distinct constants that may appear in the database (i.e., the constants listed in the domain closure axioms). As we shall see, the unique name axiom is required to support some of the deductions that are normally appropriate.

Of course, a DDB would not store the domain closure and unique name axioms exhaustively. Rather, the DDB would utilize a compact representation for such axioms that the query processor is programmed to interpret in the intended manner.

To see how a query optimizer would use such axioms, consider a DDB in which the EDB contains ground atoms specifying the current instance of table EMPLOYEE and the IDB contains the clause

$$\text{EMPLOYEE(ss, name}_1\text{, dept}_1\text{, sal}_1\text{) AND EMPLOYEE(ss, name}_2\text{, dept}_2\text{, sal}_2\text{)}$$
$$\Rightarrow \text{(name}_1\text{=name}_2\text{) AND (dept}_1\text{=dept}_2\text{) AND (sal}_1\text{=sal}_2\text{)}$$

asserting a functional dependency on EMPLOYEE. If the user attempts to add the ground atom

EMPLOYEE(12MW5, Smith, Toys, 25000)

to the EDB, the query optimizer would disallow the update on the grounds that the new atom and the domain closure axiom

$$\text{EMPLOYEE(ss, name dept, sal)} \Rightarrow \text{(ss=000000001)} \vee \cdots \vee \text{(ss=999999999)}$$

are inconsistent. Similarly, if the EDB contains the ground atom

EMPLOYEE(123456789, Smith, Toys, 25000)

and the user attempts to add the ground atom

EMPLOYEE(123456789, Jones, Books, 30000)

to the EDB, the query optimizer would disallow the update on the grounds that the atoms

EMPLOYEE(123456789, Smith, Toys, 25000) and EMPLOYEE(123456789, Jones, Books, 30000)

and the clause

$$\text{EMPLOYEE(ss, name}_1\text{, dept}_1\text{, sal}_1\text{) AND EMPLOYEE(ss, name}_2\text{, dept}_2\text{, sal}_2\text{)}$$
$$\Rightarrow \text{(name}_1\text{=name}_2\text{) AND (dept}_1\text{=dept}_2\text{) AND (sal}_1\text{=sal}_2\text{)}$$

are inconsistent. Observe that, without the unique name axiom, there is in either case no inconsistency, and the updates would be allowed.

Another aspect of the logic system specified explicitly in a DDB determines under what conditions the query optimizer can deduce that an assertion is false. Observe that in a traditional RDM, a query optimizer would deduce that t is not in EMP if t does not appear in EMP. Similarly, it is natural to deduce for an EDB table EMP that t is not in EMP if there is no ground atom EMP(t). But what of a table for which some or all tuples are defined by IDB clauses? The most natural rule is that if a fact cannot be deduced, the fact may be deduced to be false. This convention is known as the **closed world assumption (CWA)**. The effect of the CWA can be captured by a collection of axioms known as **completion axioms,** but, as with the domain closure and unique name axioms, instead we would typically employ a compact method of conveying to the query optimizer the fact that we wish it to process queries in the context of the CWA.

The CWA allows the query optimizer to behave appropriately in many situations. We consider a few examples:

1. Suppose that the EDB contains ground atoms for EMPLOYEE and FACULTY and that the IDB contains no clauses that generate tuples for these tables. The following query can be used to retrieve the names and social security numbers of employees who are not faculty.

   EMPLOYEE(ss#,name,sal) & NOT FACULTY(ss#) ⇒ Q(ss#,name)

   Suppose that tuple $t = <S,N,SAL>$ in EMPLOYEE. If tuple $<S>$ is not present in FACULTY, because the CWA is operative, the query optimizer can deduce NOT FACULTY(S), and therefore can place in Q the tuple $<S,N>$.
2. Similarly, suppose that the IDB contains the clause

   EMPLOYEE(ss#,name,sal) & NOT FACULTY(ss#) ⇒ STAFF(ss#)

   defining the table STAFF. The CWA is necessary to be able to deduce that any tuples are in STAFF since it is necessary to deduce that NOT FACULTY(t) is true for any tuples t.
3. Previously, we considered the integrity constraint

   $T(x,y,z)$ AND $T(x,y',z') \Rightarrow T(x,y',z)$

   Observe that the CWA is required if the query optimizer is ever to deduce a violation. For example, if we can deduce $T(A,B,C)$ and $T(A,B',C')$ but we cannot deduce $T(A,B',C)$, we have an inconsistency with the constraint $T(x,y,z)$ AND $T(x,y',z') \Rightarrow T(x,y',z)$ only if we can deduce NOT $T(A,B',C)$.

While the CWA is appropriate in the context of the preceding examples, it is not appropriate when a DDB contains *indefinite data*. Consider, for example, the indefinite IDB clause

PROFESSOR(Smith, CS, 50K) OR PROFESSOR(Smith, Math, 50K)

Suppose we cannot deduce the fact PROFESSOR(Smith, CS, 50K). The CWA in this case would allow us to deduce NOT PROFESSOR(Smith, CS, 50K). Similarly, if we cannot deduce PROFESSOR(Smith, Math, 50K), the CWA allows us to deduce NOT PROFESSOR(Smith, Math, 50K). Observe, however, that the clauses

NOT PROFESSOR(Smith, CS, 50K)
NOT PROFESSOR(Smith, Math, 50K)
PROFESSOR(Smith, CS, 50K) OR PROFESSOR(Smith, Math, 50K)

are inconsistent. Thus, it is inappropriate when $T(t)$ is part of a disjunct to deduce NOT $T(t)$ simply because T cannot be deduced.

These observations motivate what is known as the **generalized closed world assumption (GCWA)**. The GCWA allows us to deduce

NOT $T(t)$

if we cannot deduce any clause

$T(t)$ OR C

where C represents some way to complete this disjunction. Note that the GCWA does *not* allow us to deduce NOT $T(t)$ if we cannot deduce $T(t)$ but can deduce $T(t)$ OR C. In the preceding example, since we can deduce

PROFESSOR(Smith, CS, 50K) OR PROFESSOR(Smith, Math, 50K)

the GCWA does not allow us to deduce either

NOT PROFESSOR(Smith, CS, 50K)

or

NOT PROFESSOR(Smith, Math, 50K)

which is appropriate behavior.

We conclude by considering the interaction between the treatment of null values and the GCWA. Suppose that we have an application in which a null value $\perp$ corresponds to an unknown value in a tuple t for an attribute. While the user may not perceive such a null value as being indefinite data, we can allow the query optimizer to reason appropriately about null values by placing in the IDB the clause

$$T(x_1, \ldots, x_{i-1}, \perp, x_{i+1}, \ldots, x_n)$$
$$\Longleftrightarrow$$
$$T(x_1, \ldots, x_{i-1}, V_1, x_{i+1}, \ldots, x_n) \text{ OR } T(x_1, \ldots, x_{i-1}, V_2, x_{i+1}, \ldots, x_n)$$
$$\text{OR} \cdots \text{OR } T(x_1, \ldots, x_{i-1}, V_k, x_{i+1}, \ldots, x_n)$$

where V_1, V_2, . . . , V_k are the permissible values of the ith attribute. (Of course, we would have a shorthand convention that obviates the need for such a lengthy clause.) Note, for example, that if $T(A,B, \ldots, \bot, \ldots, Z)$ appears in the EDB, the preceding clause effectively specifies the "expansion" of this atom to

$T(A, B, \ldots, V_1, \ldots, Z)$ OR $T(A, B, \ldots, V_2, \ldots, Z)$ OR . . .
OR $T(A, B, \ldots, V_k, \ldots, Z)$

Consequently, we have an indefinite clause involving T, and it is appropriate to make the GCWA operative rather than the CWA. Note that, under the GCWA, failure to deduce any of the $T(A,B, \ldots, V_i, \ldots, Z)$ would not, by itself, establish NOT $T(A,B, \ldots, V_i, \ldots, Z)$, which is appropriate behavior in this situation. Note also that if, without invoking the CWA, NOT $T(A, B, \ldots, V_i, \ldots, Z)$ could be deduced for all but one value V_j, we could deduce $T(A,B, \ldots, V_j, \ldots, Z)$. This also reflects the way that null values should behave in the situation described.

We have seen that the DDB model significantly extends the power of the RDM while remaining essentially within the confines of the table-based data model. Such an extension to the RDM induces an architecture in which the new capabilities are provided by software running on top of a relational database system. In particular, a typical implementation architecture for the DDB stores the EDB atoms in a traditional relational database system, utilizing existing storage and design techniques. An automated theorem prover (a system capable of making the deductions required by the DDB model) translates all queries and updates into algorithms referencing EDB tables. This translation then is "passed" to a traditional relational optimizer, allowing existing relational techniques to be brought to bear on the problem.

13.4 EXTENSIBLE QUERY OPTIMIZATION FOR THE OBJECT-ORIENTED DATABASE MODEL

Chapter 4 introduced the object-oriented database model. The reader at this time may wish to review that discussion, particularly the sections relating to extensibility and encapsulation. This section considers how traditional database implementation techniques must be extended to support such a model, focusing on the impact of extensibility on the query optimization problem.

Of all the concepts that arise in the object-oriented model, extensibility has perhaps the greatest impact on the architecture of the query optimizer. What's more, even systems that would not otherwise be classified as being object oriented might support at least some limited forms of extensibility. Hence, the development of techniques that allow a query optimizer to function efficiently in an extensible environment is a research problem of considerable importance.

A high-level, extensible data model such as the object-oriented model may or may not be implemented on top of an RDM-like model. However, the extensible data model will be implemented on top of some base data model that provides a collection of predefined types, operators, storage structures, and a query optimizer. In the following discussion, for the sake of concreteness, we shall illustrate the notion of extensible query optimization by assuming that the base model is the RDM. We make this choice simply because the RDM, its implementation structures, and its query optimization techniques now are familiar to us. There is no claim that the RDM provides the best implementation of an object-oriented model, but whatever base model is chosen for the implementation, the issues and techniques likely will resemble those presented here.

Our earlier discussion of encapsulation and extensible data models indicated that a query optimizer must be able to adjust to the addition of new types and methods. Consider, for example, the following problems arising from the extensibility of a data model:

1. Suppose that when a new type is defined, several alternative methods are supplied for implementing one of the type's operators. When the user poses a query containing the operator, the optimizer must choose one of the methods of implementation. The best choice might depend on such factors as the structures that store the object(s) to which the operator is applied and the number of objects involved.
2. A user-supplied method might include in its code a call to a primitive base model operator, such as a Join. How does the query optimizer choose the Join implementation that should be used in a particular situation? The best choice might depend on details of the user-supplied method and on how the objects involved are stored.
3. A user query might be composed of several base model operators and user-defined operators. The optimizer must choose from among logically equivalent expressions one that is efficiently implementable, and the optimizer must then choose a good combination of implementation algorithms for the operators. The best implementation depends on many factors, including semantic properties of the new and base operators, how the operators interact, properties of the new and existing storage structures, and properties of the new and existing implementation algorithms and how they interact.

Before considering how a query optimizer might be designed to deal effectively with such problems, we review three items critical to the success of a standard relational optimizer's search for a good processing strategy:

1. *Knowledge of the implementation algorithm's properties:* To compare implementations of the relational operators, the optimizer must be able to estimate the cost of using each available algorithm. To this end, the optimizer accesses a **cost function** that takes as parameters such information as table sizes and number of blocks over which tuples are distributed and provides an estimate of the cost of applying the implementation algorithm. The optimizer also requires knowledge of when an algorithm is applicable (e.g., What structures are required?) and properties possessed by the result (e.g., Is it sorted?).
2. *Rules of algebraic equivalences:* As we have seen, optimizers transform expressions to obtain equivalent, but hopefully more efficiently imple-

mentable, expressions. Traditional relational optimizers are able to perform such transformations because they are supplied with identities for the algebraic operators.

3. *A search strategy:* An optimizer does not have time to consider all possible implementations for a query. We have viewed the optimization process as applying a sequence of refinement and equivalence transformations and have argued that a critical component of an optimizer is its heuristics for controlling the application of the transformations.

If these are the components critical to the success of a traditional relational query optimizer, how must an optimizer's architecture be modified to accommodate an extensible data model? We must develop a means of conveying to the optimizer the information it requires to make decisions, and we must give the optimizer a facility for learning about the behavior of user-defined types and methods:

1. *Properties of methods:* When a new method is added to the system, whether it be for a new or existing operator, the optimizer must be supplied with its properties, such as the requirements for its applicability and the properties of its result. A somewhat more difficult task is to supply the optimizer with a cost function that allows the optimizer to approximate the cost of applying the method. Most researchers agree that it is reasonable for the database implementor (DBI) to supply this information when a method is defined. The mechanism for communicating such information is fairly simple.
2. *Algebraic equivalences for the operators:* If the optimizer is to transform expressions into logically equivalent expressions, it must be supplied with rules for logical equivalence. For example, the optimizer must be told:

   - If a new operator is commutative; for example, is it the case that $T_1 \square T_2 \equiv_L T_2 \square T_1$?
   - How a pair of new operators interact with each other; for example, is it the case that $\Delta(T_1 \square T_2) \equiv_L \Delta(T_1) \square \Delta(T_2)$?
   - How new and existing operators interact; for example, is it the case that $\sigma(T_1 \square T_2) \equiv_L (\sigma(T_1) \square \sigma(T_2))$?

   Most researchers agree that the DBI can supply this sort of information also; the form of such information is somewhat complex, with most approaches employing rewrite rules that require the optimizer to apply pattern-matching algorithms when searching for applicable transformations.
3. *Adaptive search strategy:* This is perhaps the most difficult aspect of the problem. Since an online query optimizer generally does not have the time to attempt all transformations and consider all possible implementations for a query, the optimizer must prioritize transformations heuristically. As we have seen, designers of standard relational optimizers hardwire into the optimizer the priorities to be attached to the transformations.

For example, transformations with each of the following effects are often given high priority: push a Select ahead of a Join, associate and commute Joins to avoid Cartesian products, create left-leaning Join trees, and refine a Join operator to a Merge join if the appropriate structures exist. In the case of an extensible data model, however, it does not appear reasonable to expect the DBI to assign priorities to transformations that involve newly defined operators and methods. After all, the search heuristics employed by relational optimizers are the results of many years of research and experimentation.

One promising approach to this problem [see, e.g., Graefe amd Dewitt (1987)] is to design an optimizer that performs a directed search with learning. Simply put, this means that at any point in the optimization process, there exists the current strategies graph G and a collection of transformations that could be applied to various subgraphs of G. The optimizer learns (see the following) a **figure of merit (FOM)** for each transformation that reflects the expected benefit of applying the transformation. The optimizer then applies to G the transformation with the highest FOM, obtaining a new strategies graph G', and the process then continues from G'. After a sufficient number of transformations, a graph representing an implementation strategy will be obtained. Generally, the optimizer will not terminate with the first implementation strategy obtained but rather will backtrack to some previously considered strategies graph and apply to it the transformation with the highest FOM from among those transformations that have not yet been applied to this graph.

Many details must be filled in before this becomes a well-specified search strategy. The most important of these details include:

Learning the figure of merit: Let G be a strategies graph and T a transformation that produces $T(G)$ when applied to G. The figure of merit of T ($FOM(T)$) in this case can be defined as ((Estimated cost of G)/(Estimated cost of $T(G)$)). Observe that the higher the FOM, the greater is the reduction in estimated cost. When a new transformation is added to the optimizer's collection (e.g., as new operators or methods are added to the data model), we must choose an initial FOM, for example 1 or some other value that reflects the DBI's intuition. Over time, the query optimizer observes the values ((Estimated cost of G)/(Estimated cost of $T(G)$)) each time it applies transformation T. It then adjusts FOM(T) to reflect some sort of averaging over the observed experiences. The basic approach described assumes that a single average of the ratios obtained over *all* applications of T is a good predictor of the improvement to be gained by applying T to any particular strategies graph. More sophisticated methods might compute different FOMs for various classes of situations.

Cost evaluation: We have assumed that the DBI supplies a cost function with each method that allows the optimizer to estimate the cost of applying the method to its inputs. Hence, the optimizer can estimate the cost of any implementation-level strategy. It also may be necessary (e.g., to learn a transformation's FOM) for the optimizer to estimate the cost of a higher level strategy that does not specify methods for all its operators. There are several approaches to this estimation problem, ranging from selecting some reasonable method for each operator for purposes of evaluation, to continuing the search down to the implementation-level and using the cost of the best program it finds for implementing it as an evaluation for the high-level strategy.

Hill climbing methods: Suppose that the search has backtracked to a strategies graph G such that all untried transformations applicable to G have an FOM < 1. At first it might appear that no further transformations should be applied to G since each remaining candidate transformation is expected to lead to disimprovement. However, it may be the case that the search should accept a temporary disimprovement in the hopes of enabling a future transformation that will lead to improvement. For example, even though $G' = T(G)$ has a higher estimated cost than G, there may be transformations applicable to G' but not to G that usually obtain a large reduction in estimated cost. The technique of accepting disimprovement is known as **hill climbing,** and there are numerous techniques for governing exactly how much disimprovement should be accepted and in what situations.

An issue closely related to hill climbing is the learning of sequences of transformations. It may be the case that some transformation T has a low FOM but that once T is applied, a second transformation T', with a high FOM, often is enabled. In this case, the optimizer can add to its repertoire the composite transformation $T' \cdot T$ that can be applied in a single step, thereby speeding the search process.

Termination conditions: The optimizer must have criteria for terminating its search. In the context of traditional optimizers, we considered rules based on the amount of time spent on the search, possibly correlated with an estimate of the query's complexity. Other termination conditions include lower bounds on the FOMs of the transformations that we are willing to apply (e.g., terminate if all untried transformations have FOM < 0.5) and conditions based on the slope of the improvements in the implementation strategies that have been generated (e.g., terminate if the last s CPU seconds spent in the search result in less than a 5 percent improvement in the estimated cost of the best implementation strategy found so far).

While the field of extensible query optimization is young, there have been several experimental successes. However, one must have reasonable expectations regarding the quality and efficiency of the search ultimately obtainable by an extensible optimizer. It is not reasonable to expect an extensible optimizer to evolve search strategies by itself that are competitive with those developed for the RDM by researchers over the years. Therefore, if we wish to use an extensible data model, we must be willing to sacrifice some processing efficiency.

On the other hand, early results with experimental systems are encouraging to the point that we can expect in the near future to have feasibly efficient implementations of extensible data models.

13.5 QUERY OPTIMIZATION IN A DISTRIBUTED DATABASE

In Section 1.5, we briefly described a distributed database environment. The reader at this time may wish to review that discussion. A distributed database consists of a collection of physical sites, each containing some type of processor, connected by communication links. The sites may contain, for example, the processors of a single multiprocessor computer, workstations connected by a local area network (LAN), or large computer systems that are spread throughout the world.

We model the topology of a distributed database system as a graph G, with nodes representing the physical sites and the edges representing the communication links that connect the sites. Given such a topology graph G, the data necessary for the application must be allocated to the nodes. There are many different allocation strategies. For example, we might allocate all of the data to a single node, we might partition the data and allocate different pieces of the data to different nodes, or we might replicate some or all the data and store copies of the same data at several nodes. Storing multiple copies of the same data increases reliability and reduces the amount of data that must be transmitted to process queries, but increases storage costs and the cost of maintaining the database in the face of updates. While the problem of data allocation is important, in the current discussion we shall assume that the data has been allocated and shall focus on the consequences for query processing of the distributed database environment.

We view the distribution of data as adding levels of abstraction to the low end of our continuum as shown in Figure 13.6. These levels of abstraction can be summarized as follows:

Interface- and implementation-level tables: These are exactly as before. Of course, we can consider distributed database systems in which another data model (e.g., an object-oriented model) is employed. The data distribution and query-processing issues are essentially independent of the choice of data model, but, for concreteness, we shall assume that the RDM is employed.

Interface-level tables (or other interface objects)
↓
Implementation-level tables
↓
Logical fragmentation of implementation-level tables
↓
Assignment to nodes and structuring of fragments

Figure 13.6 Levels of abstraction in a distributed implementation

Fragmentation of implementation-level tables: Typically, each implementation-level table is partitioned into a collection of logical fragments. Often, a logical fragment is a horizontal subset of the table (e.g., the expression $\sigma_{A=v} T$ defines a horizontal fragment), a vertical subset of the table (e.g., the expression $\Pi_{<L>} T$ defines a vertical fragment), or a mixed fragment [e.g., the expression $\Pi_{<L>}(\sigma_{A=v} T)$ defines a mixed fragment].

Assignment of fragments to nodes and structuring of fragments: The logical fragments are the units of allocation to the nodes of the topology graph. That is, each fragment must be allocated to at least one node and may be allocated to several nodes. How logical fragments are defined and allocated is beyond the scope of the current discussion—we shall assume that logical fragments have been defined and allocated in advance. Once the fragments have been allocated to nodes, we must map the fragments at each node to physical files and structure these files by applying techniques such as those we have studied in the previous chapters.

Since the users interact with interface-level tables (or other interface objects), the fragmentation and distribution of the implementation-level tables must be transparent. That is, the users compose queries and updates as if they were operating in a conventional, centralized environment, placing on the query optimizer the additional burden of determining how to locate the required data and coordinate the processing.

We now take a closer look at what is involved in processing a query Q stated against interface-level tables. Q may be initiated from any node n in the graph; we call node n the **initiation node** of query Q and assume that the result of Q must be made available at the initiation node. The problems involved in processing Q include

Determining the nodes from which to obtain the required data: If some of the data fragments required by Q do not reside at initiation node n, the query optimizer must determine which nodes contain these fragments. Note that if some required fragment *Frag* is replicated, the optimizer must choose from among the nodes containing *Frag*.

Where to perform the required processing: If several nodes have processors available, the query optimizer may choose to perform some of the processing at nodes other than the initiation node. For example, some processing may be done at a node m containing required fragment *Frag* to reduce the amount of data that must be transmitted from m to n. Additionally, the query optimizer may choose to perform processing at several nodes to distribute the computing tasks.

How to route the communications: Once the preceding questions are resolved (or as part of the decision process), the query optimizer must determine how to route the transmission of data through the graph. Routing considerations include path length, speed of the communication links, and queuing delays.

In constructing its query-processing strategy, the query optimizer must balance two primary objectives, which often conflict.

Reduction of transmission time: Transporting data can be time consuming, and the more geographically dispersed the nodes, the more time is required to transmit a fixed amount of data. One approach to the distributed query-processing problem makes the minimization of data transmission time the highest priority. A query optimizer adopting such an approach might always choose to transmit the required data from the nodes closest to the initiation node and do most, if not all, the processing at the initiation node. Remote processing might be performed when it can reduce the amount of data that must be transmitted.

Reduction of processing time: If all processing is done at one location, processing time is determined by the factors discussed in previous chapters. In a distributed environment, however, there is the opportunity to reduce processing time by distributing the required tasks and performing them in parallel. A query optimizer might choose to transport different subcollections of the required fragments to various nodes throughout the graph, perform processing at these nodes, and then transmit the results of this processing to the initiation node for final assemblage. Often, such a strategy increases the amount of data transmitted, but in an LAN or integrated multiprocessor system, transmission costs are small and hence maximizing parallelism may be the dominant consideration.

The distributed query optimization problem therefore presents more options, and requires more decisions, than does the centralized query optimization problem. We conclude this overview by illustrating two specific algorithms applicable to distributed query processing. We demonstrate how the Semi-join operator introduced in Chapter 11 can be used to reduce data transmission and we describe how a Multiway join can be performed in parallel. These methods should be viewed as sample primitives from which a distributed query optimizer constructs its processing strategies.

Application of the Semi-Join Operator

Suppose that the query $T_1 \bowtie T_2$ is initiated at node n and that table $T_1(A, A_1, \ldots, A_{100})$ resides in its entirety at node n (and no part of T_1 resides at any other node) and that $T_2\ (A, B_1, \ldots, B_k)$ resides in its entirety at node m (and no part of T_2 resides at any other node). If our prime objective is to reduce data transmission, how should the Join $T_1 \bowtie T_2$ be performed?

The most obvious strategy transmits T_2 to node n, where the Join is performed. Another strategy—which appears somewhat unreasonable—is to transmit T_1 to node m, perform the Join at node m, and transmit to node n the result $T_1 \bowtie T_2$. The only situation where the second strategy requires less data transmission than the first is when the combined sizes of T_1 and the result of the Join are less than that of T_2.

While the second strategy would seem to be reasonable in only a few, atypical cases, it suggests another option based on the Semi-join operator. Consider the following algorithm:

Transmit from n to m $Proj = \Pi_{<A>} T_1$
Compute at m the semi-join $SJ \leftarrow T_2 \triangleright Proj$
Transmit from m to n SJ
Compute at n the join $T_1 \bowtie SJ$

Observe first that the result of the Join $T_1 \bowtie SJ$ is equivalent to the desired result $T_1 \bowtie T_2$ since SJ is simply T_2 minus the tuples that dangle with respect to the Join. The potential benefit of this strategy is that SJ will be considerably smaller than T_2 if there are many dangling tuples. Further, observe that the data transmission required before the Semi-join can be performed is typically small since only the projection of T_1 onto the Join attributes needs to be transmitted.

A Distributed Join Algorithm

Suppose that the query $T_1 \bowtie \cdots \bowtie T_i \bowtie \cdots \bowtie T_k$ is initiated at node n. To begin, assume that table T_1 has been fragmented horizontally into disjoint subsets of tuples $T_{11}, T_{12}, \ldots, T_{1q}$; that is, $\bigcup_{j=1}^{q} T_{1j} = T_1$, and the T_{1j} are pairwise disjoint. Assume further that, for each $1 \leq j \leq q$, fragment T_{1j} is allocated to node m_j and that each of $T_2, \ldots, T_k$ resides in its entirety at each of these nodes m_j. If our prime objective is to reduce processing time, how should the Join $T_1 \bowtie \cdots \bowtie T_i \bowtie \cdots \bowtie T_k$ be performed?

The most straightforward solution to the problem is to transmit from appropriately chosen nodes to n each of $T_2, \ldots, T_k$, transmit to n the fragments T_{1j}, assemble at n the fragments T_{1j} into T_1, and finally evaluate at n the Join $T_1 \bowtie \cdots \bowtie T_i \bowtie \cdots \bowtie T_k$. An alternative strategy is based on the observation that the Join can be *decomposed* into a collection of subjoins. For example, for $1 \leq j \leq q$, let W_j denote $T_{1j} \bowtie T_2 \cdots \bowtie T_i \bowtie \cdots \bowtie T_k$. Then it is easy to see that

$$\bigcup_{j=1}^{q} W_j = T_1 \bowtie \cdots \bowtie T_i \bowtie \cdots \bowtie T_k$$

This identity suggests the following distributed strategy for computing $T_1 \bowtie \cdots \bowtie T_i \bowtie \cdots \bowtie T_k$:

Compute, in parallel, at each $m_j (1 \leq j \leq q)$
  $W_j \leftarrow T_{1j} \bowtie T_2 \cdots \bowtie T_i \bowtie \cdots \bowtie T_k$
Transmit from each m_j to n the result W_j
At node n, assemble the final result $\bigcup_{j=1}^{q} W_j$

Observe that this distributed strategy might require more data transmission than the straightforward strategy considered earlier since the combined sizes of the partial results $T_{1j} \bowtie T_2 \cdots \bowtie T_k$ may well be larger than the sum of the sizes of the T_i. However, the ability to perform much of the processing in parallel, in many environments, will outweigh the penalty of increased data transmission. In more typical cases, the decision of whether and how to distribute the processing of a Join is more difficult since, typically, the tables and fragments will not be allocated to nodes in the convenient manner described. In such cases, the query optimizer must select the processing nodes, the table T to be distributed to these nodes (playing the role of T_1 in the preceding algorithm), and determine how to fragment and distribute T. Since the transmission needed to distribute the tables as required by the algorithm often incurs a significant cost, the optimizer must carefully consider these decisions and compare the possible implementations of this method with those of other methods available for performing the Join.

SUMMARY AND ANNOTATED BIBLIOGRAPHY

Our concluding chapter has surveyed data models that are the focus of much current research activity. We have attempted to demonstrate that these models are natural extensions of the data abstraction hierarchy with which we have been working throughout the book. In particular, the new data models add layers of abstraction to the top of the hierarchy in support of new user capabilities. In addition to studying the capabilities of the data models, we studied additional query optimization techniques that these capabilities necessitate. We argued that transformation-based relational query optimizers extend naturally to these new models, allowing relational technologies (e.g., optimization algorithms, storage structures, and semantic design theories) to serve as a foundation for systems implementing the models.

The specific data models we considered were updatable views and the universal relation model, recursion and the DDB model, the object-oriented data model, and the distributed database model. Research into the problem of view updating attempts to characterize when an update stated against a view is unambiguous and realizable and has proposed methods for resolving ambiguity when it arises [Dayal and Bernstein (1978) and Todd (1977)]. The universal data model presents to the user a view consisting of a single table. In addition to the problems associated with updating views, the universal model has inherent ambiguity regarding how the underlying tables are combined (e.g., how they are joined) to derive an instance of the universal relation. Window functions are used to derive different universal instances for different queries. Techniques for specifying window functions include those discussed in Maier, Ullman, and Vardi (1984) and Ullman (1989).

The deductive database model was first discussed in Reiter (1984), and a good survey of the central concepts is found in Gallier, Minker, and Nicolas (1984). Techniques for processing recursive queries have been well studied [see Bancilhon and Ramakrishnan (1986) and Ullman (1989) for surveys], but this research area is considered quite open. The α operator was proposed in Agrawal (1988) as a means of extending relational algebra to include transitive closures and generalized transitive closures. Analogies between generalized transitive closures and graph problems, as well as descriptions of graphical interfaces, appear in Cruz, Mendelzon, and Wood (1988) and Rosenthal et al. (1986).

One of the prime research problems that designers and implementors of object-oriented database systems face is how to make a query optimizer extensible so that it can efficiently execute queries containing user-defined data types and operators. Transformation-based approaches to extensible optimization are discussed, for example, in Graefe and Dewitt (1987) and Lohman (1988).

Distributed database environments are of increasing importance and should be viewed as a technology independent of the underlying data model. An overview of many of the important issues in distributed databases can be found in Ceri and Pelagatti (1984). The design of a distributed database system has several important components. One component is the design of the system's topology, a problem studied in Ahuja and Murty (1987), Dionne and Florian (1979), Gerla and Kleinrock (1977), and Hu (1974). Once the topology is specified, the database must be distributed to the nodes of the network [Apers, (1988); Ceri, Navathe, and Wiederhold (1983); and Mahmound and Riordon (1976)]. Finally, a query stated against a unified logical schema must be processed efficiently, requiring algorithms for balancing data transmission and processing costs [Bern et al. (1981), Wong (1983), and Yu and Charp (1984)].

We hope that this book has given the reader a strong foundation for research and development in database management. While past research has resulted in great achievement, many interesting, challenging, and important problems await solution. The science of database management remains a fertile research area.

EXERCISES

1. Define the terms *user view, unrealizable update, ambiguous update, view expansion, universal relation,* and *window function.*
2. Construct a normalized RDM schema and application of interest to you, and define on it a collection of views. Give examples of updates stated against your views that are unrealizable and ones that are ambiguous.
3. Show how your RDM schema of the previous exercise could be modeled with the universal relation model. What window functions are reasonable for this application?
4. Construct a natural example of a recursive view.
5. Define the terms *bottom-up* and *top-down evaluation, generalized transitive closure, EDB, IDB, closed world assumption,* and *generalized closed world assumption.*
6. Give examples of applications for which the distributed database model is attractive and applications for which it is not appropriate.
7. Consider table schemes EMP and DEPT from Section 13.1, and define

the view ALL_INFO as the Natural join EMP ⋈ DEPT. Give examples of

a. An instance of ALL_INFO and an insertion into this instance of ALL_INFO that has no realization as an update to the base tables.

b. An instance of ALL_INFO and an insertion into this instance of ALL_INFO that has more than one realization as an update to the base tables.

8. Explore methods for resolving ambiguities when updates to views can be realized in more than one way. In what situations should user interaction be initiated?

9. Specify a window function, based on the "minimal table approach" of Section 13.2, that yields the intended meaning of the queries Q1 through Q4.

10. Formulate a query such that the representative instance window function of Section 13.2 does not yield the intended meaning.

11. Formulate unrealizable updates and ambiguous updates to the representative instance of Section 13.2.

12. Use the universal relation to model the E/R diagram of Figure 1.14. Specify a window function that gives each query preceding exercise 1.3 its intended meaning.

*13. Let the concatenation operator be addition and the aggregate operator be summation. Formulate and prove algebraic identities governing how these operators interact with each other and with the relational operators. Based on these identities, specify the details of the dynamic programming algorithm cited at the conclusion of Section 13.3.

14. In Section 13.3, we described how to specify deductive database axioms so that null values behave as some unknown value from the appropriate domains. How should null values behave with respect to the match conditions of Join operations? Specify the desired behavior in terms of IDB axioms.

*15. In some applications, it is appropriate for a null value to be interpreted as "attribute not applicable" rather than as "value unknown." Give an example of such an application. Specify the desired behavior in terms of IDB axioms, including how these null values should behave with respect to the match conditions of Select and Join operators.

16. Propose simple implementations and cost functions for the user-defined operators considered in Section 4.3.

17. Propose algebraic equivalences applying to expressions containing the standard relational operators and the user-defined operators considered in Section 4.3.

18. Propose external implementations for a table that contains set-valued attributes. Analyze the time and space efficiency of each of your implementations.

19. Prove the following distributed query-processing problem to be NP-hard. A query initiated at node n requires b_i bytes of relation fragment f_i, $1 \leq i \leq k$. All of the relation fragments are stored in all of the nodes $n_1, n_2, \ldots, n_q$, but none are stored at initiation node n. The time required to transmit one byte of data from any node n_j $(1 \leq j \leq q)$ to node n is one millisecond, and data may be transmitted in parallel from any pair n_j, n_k to n. The query optimizer must determine, for each required fragment f_i, from which node f_i should be transmitted to n. The objective is to minimize the time between the invocation of the query at node n and the time at which all required fragments have been received by n.
20. Prove the validity of the Semi-join algorithm of Section 13.5.
21. Prove the validity of the Distributed join algorithm of Section 13.5.

*22. A strategy for performing a Distributed join consists of a specification of what fragments are to be transmitted to what nodes and of what processing is to be performed at the nodes. Formulate a cost function to model the cost of a Distributed join strategy. Is the problem of finding an optimal Distributed join strategy NP-hard under your formulation? Propose heuristics for constructing good Distributed join strategies.

BIBLIOGRAPHY

Agrawal, R. "Alpha: An Extension of Relational Algebra to Express a Class of Recursive Queries." *Institute of Electrical and Electronics Engineers Transactions on Software Engineering* 14, no. 7 (1988), pp. 879–85.

Aho, A.; C. Beeri; and J. Ullman. "The Theory of Joins in Relational Databases." *Association for Computing Machinery TODS* 4, no. 3 (1979), pp. 297–314.

Aho, A.; J. Hopcroft; and J. Ullman. *The Design and Analysis of Computer Algorithms*. Reading, Mass.: Addison-Wesley Publishing, 1974.

______. *Data Structures and Algorithms*. Reading, Mass.: Addison-Wesley Publishing, 1983.

Ahuja, R., and V. Murty. "New Lower Planes for the Network Design Problem." *Networks* 17 (1987), pp. 113–27.

Apers, P. "Data Allocation in Distributed Database Systems." *Association for Computing Machinery Transactions on Database Systems* 13, no. 3 (1988), pp. 263–304.

Babad, J. "A Record and File Partitioning Model." *Communications of the Association for Computing Machinery* 20 (1977), pp. 22–31.

Bancilhon, F. "Object Oriented Database Systems." *Proceedings of the Association for Computing Machinery SIGMOD*.

Bancilhon, F., and Ramakrishnan, "An Amateur's Introduction to Recursive Query-Processing Strategies." *Proceedings of the Association for Computing Machinery SIGMOD*, 1986, pp. 16–52.

Bayer, R., and E. McCreight. "Organization and Maintenance of Large Ordered Indices." *Acta Informatica* 1 (1972), pp. 173–89.

Beeri, C.; R. Fagin; and J. Howard. "A Complete Axiomatization of Functional and Multivalued Dependencies in Database Relations." *Proceedings of the Association for Computing Machinery SIGMOD*, 1977, pp. 47–61.

Beeri, C., and P. Honeyman. "Preserving Functional Dependencies." *Society for Industrial and Applied Mathematics Journal on Computing* 10, no. 3 (1981), pp. 647–56.

Bernstein, P. "Synthesizing Third Normal Form Relations from Functional Dependencies." *Association for Computing Machinery TODS* 1, no. 4 (1976), pp. 277–98.

Bernstein, P.; N. Goodman; E. Wong; C. Reeve; and J. Rothnie. "Query Processing in a System for Distributed Databases (SDD-1)." *Association for Computing Machinery Transactions on Database Systems* 6, no. 4 (1981), pp. 602–25.

Bradley, J. *File and Data Base Techniques*. New York: Holt, Rinehart & Winston, 1982.

Bridge, J. *Beginning Model Theory*. Oxford: Oxford University Press, 1977.

Ceri, S; S. Navathe; and G. Wiederhold. "Distributed Design of Logical Database Schemas." *Institute of Electrical and Electronics Engineers Transactions on Software Engineering* 9, no. 4 (1983), pp. 487–503.

Ceri, S., and G. Pelagatti. *Distributed Databases Principles and Systems*. New York: McGraw-Hill, 1984.

Chandra, A., and P. Merlin. "Optimal Implementation of Conjunctive Queries in Relational Databases." *Proceedings of the Ninth Association for Computing Machinery Symposium on the Theory of Computing*, pp. 77–90.

Chang, C., and R. Lee. *Symbolic Logic and Mechanical Theorem Proving*. New York: Academic Press, 1979.

Chen, P. "The Entity-Relationship Model: Toward a Unified View of Data."

Association for Computing Machinery TODS 1 (1976), pp. 9–36.

Chen, P. *Entity-Relationship Approach to Systems Analysis and Design*. Amsterdam: North-Holland, 1980.

Childs, D. "Feasibility of a Set-Theoretical Data Structure—A General Structure Based on Reconstituted Definition of Relation." *Proceedings of the 1968 International Federation for Information Processing Congress,* 1968.

Christodoulakis, S. "Estimating Record Selectivities." *Information Systems* 8, no. 2 (1983), pp. 105–15.

Codd, E. "A Relational Model of Data for Large Shared Data Banks." *Communications of the Association for Computing Machinery* 13, no. 6 (1970), pp. 377–87.

______. "Relational Completeness of Database Sublanguages." In *Data Base Systems,* ed. R. Rustin. Englewood Cliffs, N.J.: Prentice Hall, 1972.

______. "Recent Investigations in Relational Database Systems." *Proceedings of the 1974 International Federation for Information Processing Conference,* 1974, pp. 1017–21.

______. "Extending the Database Relational Model to Capture More Meaning." *Association for Computing Machinery TODS* 4, no. 4 (1979).

Comer, D. "The Ubiquitous B-Tree." *Association for Computing Machinery Computing Surveys* 11, no. 2 (1979), pp. 121–38.

Coulouris, G., and J. Dollimore. *Distributed Systems: Concepts and Design*. Reading, Mass.: Addison-Wesley Publishing, 1988.

Cruz, I.; A. Mendelzon; and P. Wood. "G^+: Recursive Queries without Recursion." *Proceedings of the 2nd International Conference on Expert Database Systems,* 1988.

Date, C. *An Introduction to Database Systems, Volume I*. Reading, Mass.: Addison-Wesley Publishing, 1982.

Dayal, U., and P. Bernstein. "On the Updatability of Relational Views." *Proceedings of the International Conference on Very Large Data Bases,* 1978, pp. 368–77.

Denning, D.; P. Denning; and M. Schwartz. "The Tracker: A Threat to Statistical Database Security." *Association for Computing Machinery TODS* 4, no. 1 (1979).

Dionne, R., and M. Florian. "Exact and Approximate Algorithms for Optimal Network Design." *Networks* 9 (1979), pp. 37–59.

Elmasri, R., and S. Navathe. *Fundamentals of Database Systems*. Redwood City, Calif.: Benjamin Cummings, 1989.

Fagin, R. "The Decomposition versus the Synthetic Approach to Relational Database Design." *Very Large Data Bases III,* 1977.

Fagin, R.; J. Nievergelt; N. Pippenger; and H. Strong. "Exendible Hashing—A Fast Access Method for Dynamic Files." *Association for Computing Machinery TODS* 4, no. 3 (1979), pp. 315–44.

Finkelstein, S.; M. Schkolnick; and P. Tiberio. "Physical Design for Relational Databases." *Association for Computing Machinery TODS* 13 (1988), pp. 91–128.

Gallaire, H., and J. Minker. *Logic and Databases*. New York: Plenum Press, 1978.

Gallier, H.; J. Minker; and J. Nicolas. "Logic and Databases: A Deductive Approach." *Association for Computing Machinery Computing Surveys* 16, no. 2 (1984), pp. 153–85.

Gerla, M., and L. Kleinrock. "On the Topological Design of Distributed Computer Networks." *Institute of Electrical and Electronics Engineers Transactions on Communications* 25, no. 1 (1977), pp. 48–59.

Goguen, J. A.; J. W. Thatcher; and E. G. Wagner. "An Initial Algebra Approach to the Specification, Correctness, and Implementation of Abstract Data Types." In *Current Trends in Programming Methodology, Vol. 4: Data Structuring,* ed. R. T. Yeh. Englewood Cliffs, N.J.: Prentice Hall, 1977.

Graefe, G., and D. DeWitt. "The EXODUS Optimizer Generator." *Proceedings of the Association for Computing Machinery SIGMOD,* 1987, pp. 160–71.

Guttag, J. "Abstract Data Types in the Development of Data Structures." *Communications of the Association for Computing Machinery* 20, no. 6 (1977), pp. 396–404.

Haerder, T., and A. Reuter, "Principles of Transaction-Oriented Database Recovery." *Association for Computing Machinery Computing Surveys* 15, no. 4 (1983), pp. 287–317.

Hammer, M., and B. Niamir. "A Heuristic Approach to Attribute Partitioning." *Proceedings of the Association for Computing Machinery SIGMOD International Conference on Managerial Data,* 1979, pp. 93–100.

Helman, P. "A Family of NP-Complete Data Aggregation Problems." *Acta Informatica* 26 (1989), pp. 485–99.

Helman, P.; G. Liepins; and W. Richards. "Foundations of Intrusion Detection." *Proceedings of the Institute of Electrical and Electronics Engineers Computer Security Foundations Workshop V,* 1992, pp. 114–20.

Helman, P., and R. Veroff. *Intermediate Problem Solving and Data Structures: Walls and Mirrors.* Menlo Park, Calif.: Benjamin-Cummings, 1986.

Henschen, L., and S. Naqvi. "On Compiling Queries in Recursive First-Order Databases." *Journal of the Association for Computing Machinery* 31 (1984), pp. 47–85.

Horowitz, E., and S. Sahni. *Fundamentals of Data Structures.* Rockville, Md.: Computer Science Press, 1976.

———. *Fundamentals of Computer Algorithms.* Rockville, Md.: Computer Science Press, 1978.

Hu, T. "Optimum Communication Spanning Trees." *Society for Industrial and Applied Mathematics Journal on Computing* 3, no. 3 (1974), pp. 188–95.

Jarke, M., and J. Koch. "Query Optimization in Database Systems." *ACM Computing Surveys* 16, no. 2 (1984), pp. 111–52.

Kim, W., and F. Lochovsky. *Object-Oriented Concepts, Databases, and Applications.* Reading, Mass.: Addison-Wesley Publishing, 1989.

King, J. "QUIST: A System for Semantic Query Optimization in Relational Databases." *Proceedings of the International Conference on Very Large Data Bases,* 1981, pp. 510–17.

Knuth, D. *The Art of Computer Programming, Volume 3: Sorting and Searching.* Reading, Mass.: Addison-Wesley Publishing, 1973.

Korth, H., and A. Silberschatz. *Database System Concepts.* New York: McGraw-Hill, 1986.

Kung, H., and J. Robinson. "On Optimistic Methods for Concurrency Control." *Association for Computing Machinery TODS* 6, no. 2 (1981), pp. 213–26.

Lewis, H., and L. Denenberg. *Data Structures and Their Algorithms.* New York: Harper-Collins, 1991.

Lohman, G. "Grammar-Like Functional Rules for Representing Query Optimization Alternatives." *Proceedings of the Association for Computing Machinery SIGMOD,* 1988, pp. 18–27.

Lunt, T.; A. Tamaru; F. Gilham; R. Jagannathan; C. Jalali; H. Jarvitz; A. Valdes; and P. Neumann. "A Real Time Intrusion Detection Expert System." *Proceedings of the Institute of Electrical and Electronics Engineers Symposium on Research in Security and Privacy,* 1990.

Lynch, C. "Selectivity Estimation and Query Optimization in Large Databases with Highly Skewed Distributions of Common Values." *Proceedings of the International Conference on Very Large Data Bases,* 1988, pp. 240–51.

Mackert, L., and G. Lohman. "*R** Optimizer Validation and Performance Evaluation for Local Queries." *Proceedings of the Association for Computing Machinery SIGMOD Conference,* 1984, pp. 256–76.

Mahmound, S., and J. Riordon. "Optimal Allocation of Resources in Distributed Information Networks." *Association for Computing Machinery Transactions on Database Systems* 1, no. 1 (1976), pp. 66–78.

Maier, D.; J. Ullman; and M. Vardi. "On the Foundations of the Universal Relation Model." *Association for Computing Machinery TODS* 9, no. 2 (1984), pp. 283–303.

March, S. "Techniques for Structuring Database Records." *Association for Computing Machinery Computer Surveys* 15 (1983), pp. 45–79.

Markowsky, G.; J. Carter; and M. Wegman. "Analysis of a Universal Class of Hash Functions." *Lecture Notes in Computer Science 64*. Springer-Verlag, 1978, pp. 345–54.

Martin, J. *Principles of Data-Base Management*. Englewood Cliffs, N.J.: Prentice Hall, 1976.

Moret, B. "The Algebraic Approach to Data Abstraction: A Tutorial and Survey." Computer Science Department Technical Report CS 83–3, University of New Mexico, 1983.

Moret, B., and H. Shapiro. *Algorithms from P to NP*. Menlo Park, Calif.: Benjamin Cummings, 1991.

Muralikrishna, M., and D. DeWitt. "Equi-Depth Histograms for Estimating Selectivity Factors for Multi-Dimensional Queries." *Proceedings of the Association for Computing Machinery SIGMOD Conference,* 1988, pp. 28–36.

Papadimitriou, C., and K. Steiglitz. *Combinatorial Optimization*. Englewood Cliffs, N.J.: Prentice Hall, 1982.

Piatetsky-Shapiro, G., and C. Connell. "Accurate Estimation of the Number of Tuples Satisfying a Condition." *Proceedings of the Association for Computing Machinery SIGMOD Conference,* 1984, pp. 256–76.

Reiner, G., and A. Rosenthal. "An Abstract Target Machine and Strategy Spaces for Query Optimization." *Database Engineering* 5 (1982).

Reis, D., and M. Stonebraker. "Effects of Locking Granularity in a Database Management System." *Association for Computing Machinery TODS* 2, no. 3 (1977), pp. 233–46.

______. "Locking Granularity Revisited." *Association for Computing Machinery TODS* 4, no. 2 (1979), pp. 210–27.

Reiter, R. "Towards a Logical Reconstruction of Relational Database Theory." In *On Conceptual Modeling,* ed. Brodie; Myopoulos; Schmidt. Springer-Verlag, 1984.

Riengold, E., and W. Hanson. *Data Structures*. Boston: Little, Brown, 1983.

Rissanen, J. "Independent Components of Relations." *Association for Computing Machinery TODS* 2, no. 4 (1977), pp. 317–25.

Rivest, R.; A. Shamir; and L. Adleman. "A Method for Obtaining Digital Signatures and Public-Key Cryptosystems." *Communications of the Association for Computing Machinery* 21, no. 2 (1978), pp. 120–26.

Rosenkrantz, D., and P. Stearns. "System Level Concurrency Control for Distributed Data Base Systems." *Association for Computing Machinery TODS* 3, no. 2 (1978), pp. 178–98.

Rosenthal, A., and U. Charkravarthy. "Anatomy of a Modular Multiple Query Optimizer." *Proceedings of the International Conference on Very Large Data Bases,* 1988.

Rosenthal, A.; S. Heiler; U. Dayal; and F. Manola. "Traversal Recursion: A Practical Approach to Supporting Recursive Applications." *Proceedings of the Association for Computing Machinery SIGMOD,* 1986, pp. 166–76.

Rowe, L., and M. Stonebraker. "The POSTGRESS Data Model." *Proceedings of the Conference on Very Large Data Bases.*

Sadri, F., and J. Ullman. "A Complete Axiomatization for a Large Class of Dependencies in Relational Databases." *Proceedings of the 12th Annual Association for Computing Machinery Symposium on the Theory of Computing,* 1980, pp. 117–22.

Selinger, P., et al. "Access Path Selection in a Relational Data Base System." *Proceedings of the Association for Computing Machinery SIGMOD Conference,* 1979, pp. 23–34.

Sibley, E. *Special Issue of Association for Computing Machinery Computing Surveys* 8, no. 1 (1976).

Silberschatz, A., and Z. Kedem. "Consistency in Hierarchical Database Systems." *Journal of the Association for Computing Machinery* 27, no. 1 (1980), pp. 72–80.

Smith, J., and D. Smith. "Data Abstraction: Aggregation and Generalization." *Communications of the Association for Computing Machinery* 20 (1977), pp. 405–13.

Swami, A. "A Validated Cost Model for Main Memory Databases." *Association for Computing Machinery SIGMETRICS* 17 (1989).

Teorey, T., and J. Fry. *Design of Database Structures.* Englewood Cliffs, N.J.: Prentice Hall, 1982.

Todd, S. "Automatic Constraint Maintenance and Updating Defined Relations." *Proceedings of the International Federation for Information Processing,* 1977, pp. 145–48.

Tsichritzis, D., and F. Lockovsky. *Data Models.* Englewood Cliffs, N.J.: Prentice-Hall, 1982.

Ullman, J. *Principles of Database Knowledge-Base Systems,* 2nd ed. Rockville, Md.: Computer Science Press, 1982.

———. *Principles of Database Knowledge-Base Systems, Vol. 1.* Rockville, Md.: Computer Science Press, 1988.

———. *Principles of Database Knowledge-Base Systems, Vol. 2.* Rockville, Md.: Computer Science Press, 1989.

Vaccaro, H., and G. Liepins. "Detection of Anomalous Computer Session Activity." *Proceedings of the Institute of Electrical and Electronics Engineers Symposium on Research in Security and Privacy,* 1989, pp. 280–89.

Vander Zanden, B.; H. Taylor; and D. Bitton. "Estimating Block Accesses when Attributes Are Correlated." *Proceedings of the International Conference on Very Large Data Bases,* 1986, pp. 119–27.

Wong, E. "Dynamic Rematerialization—Processing Distributed Queries Using Redundant Data." *Trans. Software Eng.* 9, no. 3 (1983).

Yao, S. "Optimization of Query Evaluation Algorithms." *Association for Computing Machinery TODS* 4, no. 2 (1979), pp. 133–55.

Yao, S., and T. Kunii. *Data Base Design Techniques.* New York: Springer, 1982.

Youssefi, K., and E. Wong. "Query Processing in a Relational Database Management System." *Proceedings of the International Conference on Very Large Data Bases,* 1979, pp. 409–17.

Yu, C., and C. Chang. "Distributed Query Processing." *Association for Computing Machinery Computing Surveys* 16, no. 4 (1984), pp. 399–433.

INDEX